North Africa
The Roman Coast

the Bradt Travel Guide

Ethel Davies

edition

www.bradtguides.com

Bradt Travel Guides Ltd, UK
The Globe Pequot Press Inc, USA

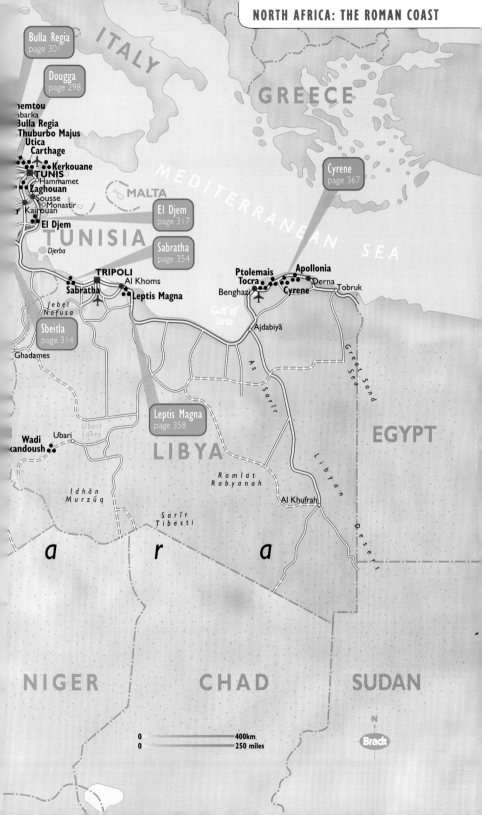

NORTH AFRICA: THE ROMAN COAST

North Africa
The Roman Coast
Don't miss…

Roman ruins
Caracalla Arch, Djemila,
Algeria page 208

The Sahara
Merzouga dunes, Morocco
page 156

Uncrowded Mediterranean coastline
Cyrene, Libya
page 367

Inspiring architecture
Hassan II Mosque,
Casablanca, Morocco
page 97

World-class museums
Ulysses and sirens
mosaic at Bardo,
Tunis, Tunisia
page 290

Morocco

right Take a day trip to Fes to see the famous tanneries page 138

below Goats climb endemic argane trees to get the last of their berries. Once the fruit has passed through their digestive systems, locals harvest the berries and grind them into a highly prized cooking oil page 56

bottom The Hassan II Tower, in Rabat, is all that remains of the Great Mosque; sultan El Mansour had hoped it would be the biggest in the Islamic world page 151

Morocco: Roman ruins

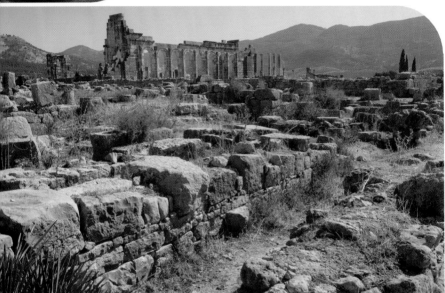

AUTHOR

Ethel Davies was born in California but moved to the UK 30 years ago. Her work as a freelance writer and photographer has appeared in the media in many guises and she has written books on Marrakech and Reykjavik. Her repeated visits to North Africa have given her an appreciation of both the past and the present of the region.

AUTHOR'S STORY

Like most children, I was fascinated by stories about the antics of the Roman gods and goddesses. As I got older and learned about real events, the stories became no less revelatory: discovering that it was the Roman army who first built roads and bridges and constructed aqueducts that pumped water into towns was fascinating – especially when I was told it happened more than 2,000 years ago. This interest has never faded and I pursued my obsession by studying Latin and continuing to read more tales and histories, such as Julius Caesar's *De Bello Gallico*, which chronicles his campaign against the Gauls.

Well and truly hooked, I spent my early travels exploring obvious Roman sites such as Nîmes and Arles in France, and later Rome itself, but it wasn't long before North Africa called. When I first started studying the area, it came as an enormous surprise to discover that the region – known as the Maghreb – boasted so many wonderful Roman remains. Sites I previously thought existed only in the pages of history, such as El Djem and Leptis Magna, were still standing and it was actually possible to visit them!

Naturally, each of the modern-day countries containing these sites has varying histories, cultures and politics. This guide takes advantage of the ancient region's position as a Roman colony to unify the area and present the best sites left over from that period, so travellers can make the most of their own pilgrimage trails.

FEEDBACK REQUEST

Every effort has been made to ensure that the details contained within this book are as accurate and up to date as possible. Inevitably, however, things move on. Any information regarding such changes, or relating to your experiences in North Africa – good or bad – would be very gratefully received. Such feedback is invaluable when compiling further editions. Send your comments to Ethel Davies at ethel@etheldavies.com or to Bradt Travel Guides Ltd, 23 High Street, Chalfont St Peter, Bucks SL9 9QE, England; e info@bradtguides.com.

PUBLISHER'S FOREWORD
Adrian Phillips

The first Bradt travel guide was written in 1974 by George and Hilary Bradt on a river barge floating down a tributary of the Amazon. In the 1980s and '90s the focus shifted away from hiking to broader-based guides covering new destinations – usually the first to be published about these places. In the 21st century Bradt continues to publish such ground-breaking guides, as well as others to established holiday destinations, incorporating in-depth information on culture and natural history alongside the nuts and bolts of where to stay and what to see.

Bradt authors support responsible travel, and provide advice not only on minimum impact but also on how to give something back through local charities. In this way a true synergy is achieved between the traveller and local communities.

* * *

Holidays to North Africa are usually associated with beaches, souks and camels; however, this region is also littered with Roman archaeology – it is, after all, but a short poke away from Italy's boot. You'll find no keener fan of things Roman than Ethel Davies; when we met a couple of years ago to discuss her proposal for this book, I was struck by the fact that – despite her deep knowledge of the period – she had clearly lost nothing of her sense of wonder and excitement. We're proud to further develop our coverage of Africa with such an original, intriguing and passion-filled book.

First published July 2009

Bradt Travel Guides Ltd, 23 High Street, Chalfont St Peter, Bucks SL9 9QE, England
www.bradtguides.com
Published in the USA by The Globe Pequot Press Inc, 246 Goose Lane,
PO Box 480, Guilford, Connecticut 06475-0480

Text copyright © 2009 Ethel Davies
Maps copyright © 2009 Bradt Travel Guides Ltd
Photographs © 2009 Individual photographers

British Library Cataloguing in Publication Data
A catalogue record for this book is available from the British Library
ISBN-13: 978 1 84162 287 3

Photographs All taken by the author except cover
Front cover Leptis Magna, Al Khums, Libya (Wolfgang Kaehler/Alamy)
Back cover North gate at Tiddis; Detail from a mosaic of Silenus, god of the wine press, riding a camel, El Djem
Title page Theatre at Sabratha, Libya; Tunisian man; Dates stall, Tunisia
Maps Maria Randell, Malcolm Barnes (colour map)

Typeset from the author's disk by Wakewing, High Wycombe
Printed and bound in India by Nutech Photolithographers

Acknowledgements

Immeasurable thanks to the people who helped facilitate these wonderful journeys and allowed me to see some of the most magnificent Roman sites still in existence, as well as the beauty and excitement of the North African countries in which they are located today.

MOROCCO To the staff of Explore Worldwide for taking me along; to Ali, a great guide, and his company Ame d'Aventure; to the Rif Hotel in Tangiers.

ALGERIA To The Traveller, especially Irenie Ekkeshis, for enabling me to experience Christmas in Constantine and to Timgad Voyages, a very hospitable local company that managed to come up with a Christmas tree in a Muslim North African country.

TUNISIA To Peter Kirk of Tunisia First for helping me fill the gaps in my must-see list; to the classics department of the Royal Grammar School, Guildford, who let me tag along; to Sammy, our amiable and knowledgeable guide, and his company Eden Tours.

LIBYA To Lauren Szymanoski of the Smithsonian Institution who was my first point of contact; to the staff of High Country Passage, particularly Susannah Dameron and Marya McGinn; to the staff on board Le Levant, and especially to the tour leader, Elisabeth Geismar and the superb lecturers, Dr John Swanson of the American University in Cairo, and Dr Ian Tattersall of the American Museum of Natural History.

AT HOME To Bex, for knowing where to place a comma, synonyms for wedge and how to spell 'peek'; thanks too to everyone who offered their support and encouragement, particularly at the beginning when the enormity of the task seemed insurmountable and towards the end, when it seemed I still had so far to go.

DEDICATION

To my dad, who said I had the skill, but all I needed was the experience.

Contents

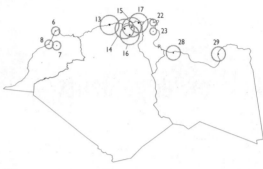

A NOTE ON SPELLINGS

Throughout the guide you will notice an inconsistency between spellings; this is a deliberate result of variation between countries and in each case I have used the local spelling. As a result, Mohamed is spelt with one 'm' in Morocco only, but with a double 'm' (Mohammed) throughout the other North African countries. Similarly, in Algiers Casbah is spelt with a 'c', but everywhere else it carries a 'k'.

LIST OF MAPS

Introduction

The Maghreb – as Morocco, Algeria, Tunisia and Libya are collectively known – is something of a cultural puzzle: it's part of the African continent, yet home to a huge proportion of Arab settlers who came across during the AD633 invasion. However, linking them all is a common history carved – literally – by the Romans. Culturally speaking, there's no trace of their occupation left, but their physical presence is bountiful. Subsequent conquerors each left magnificent mosques and fortresses as their legacy, but none of them compare to the amphitheatres, monuments and temples built by the Romans. Carthage – located in present-day Tunisia – was among the top five cities of the age.

Happily, many of the areas where settlements are located have never been developed, or even re-occupied, so the ruins in several places remain in impeccable condition. What is more, archaeologists are uncovering more and more preserved sites that have been buried by sandstorms and earthquakes over the years. Travellers now have the chance to visit these sites and enjoy the finds while tourist numbers are still low.

I should also note that the reasons for coming to this region are not all buried in the past; today's North African countries have their own delights: the Mediterranean coastline is cleaner and less developed than its counterpart on the northern shore; the souks, smelling of spices and leather, make for an incomparable shopping experience; and the friendly hospitality of the people unforgettable. The rich Islamic culture permeates everything, from quotations carved into the walls of mosques to the evocative calls to prayer that echo out from the minarets five times a day. Sadly, nowadays, any mention of Islam often also raises questions of safety. Those concerned about political disquiet or threat from religious fundamentalism in countries like Algeria or Libya need not worry. These reports are mostly grossly exaggerated and don't take into account the majority of North Africans who are genuinely interested in open-minded foreigners coming to visit. They are eager for foreigners to sample the best of what their country has to offer, whether that means sharing a cup of mint tea, or exploring the remnants of their ancient past.

Part One

GENERAL INFORMATION

Background Information: The Romans

GEOGRAPHY

From AD1–300 the Roman Empire in Africa stretched from ancient Egypt all the way to the province of Mauretania. Even though Egypt was part of Rome's territory and located in North Africa, its importance and history were such that it was its own province. Therefore, for the sake of this guide, the countries that comprise Roman Africa are today's Libya, Tunisia, Algeria and Morocco. The region is now commonly known as the Maghreb (Arabic for 'where the sun sets'). These four countries cover an area of approximately 4,750,000km². They share a Mediterranean coastline of 5,800km, which stretches from Libya's border with Egypt to Tangier in Morocco. Although Morocco has a long Atlantic coast, the Phoenicians (and probably the Romans) are known to have gone only as far as 750km south, to today's city of Essaouira. The last bastion of the Roman Empire on the Atlantic was Sala Colonia, or Chellah, in today's Moroccan capital, Rabat, 278km from the mouth of the Mediterranean, but even that was handed over to Berber locals by AD250.

Rome took on these lands from their Phoenician and Greek predecessors, who established their settlements as stopovers for seafarers. Hugging the coast, trading posts were set up every 20km or so to facilitate smooth plying of the seas. The Phoenicians, with their origins in Lebanon, preferred the wider ports and sandier shores of the region around Tripoli to the west. The Greeks liked the rockier coasts of Cyrene, located further east, that reminded them of their homeland. Eventually, the Romans absorbed both legacies into their own territories, although Cyrenaica continued to speak Greek throughout its occupation.

In Mauretania and Numidia, today's Morocco, Algeria and Tunisia, the Atlas Mountains provided an awesome barrier rising up to 4,167m. To the south of these uplands lay not only distant deserts, but also the local tribes that traversed them. Despite occasional exploratory forays by the Roman expeditionary forces into this dodgy territory, the occupying nation never got very far beyond these mountains. Continual skirmishes on Roman outposts by endemic peoples initially irritated the Romans, and finally led to some of these disputed areas being abandoned, particularly in the case of Mauretania. It also prevented the Romans expanding southwards in countries like Libya and, as a result, the Romans' African lands remained a relatively narrow coastal strip at the north of the continent.

HISTORY

PREHISTORY The first species that began to resemble humans were found in the south of the continent and were labelled *Australopithecus*. Indications of their existence have been found in Morocco. Named 'The Pebble People', their traces, such as rudimentary chopping tools, begin appearing approximately 2.5 million years ago. Over the Palaeolithic (literally 'old stone') era, evolution continued and the genus *Homo*, as in our modern-day species name of *Homo sapiens*, began to be attributed to the newer varieties of increasingly recognisable humans. The different ages continued, but by the Aterian, approximately 40,000 years ago, mankind had evolved into *Homo sapiens sapiens*, the same classification we now give ourselves.

Over the millennia, the climate of the Maghreb had changed from sea to desert to fertile land. By the time of the most extreme modern ice age, circa 20,000 years ago, North Africa boasted a lush landscape and temperate climate. This favourable environment drew people here from further afield, from southeast Asia, and encouraged habitation. About 12,000 years ago, a group emerged in present-day western Algeria and became known as the Oranians, from the modern-day town of Oran. They gradually expanded their territory into neighbouring lands, going as far as Morocco and eastern Algeria. A few thousand years later, the Capsians, named after a region in present-day Tunisia, also began to stand out. Both these tribes were hunter-gatherers. Over further millennia, however, the ice of the north began to retreat, and the south began to warm up. Dryer conditions encouraged settlement, and these groups began to blend with each other as well as with the local populace. Out of this merger came the Neolithic ('new stone') age, together with some of the trademarks of 'civilisation', ie: farming and the raising of cattle, as well as production of ceramics and arrowheads.

From this period came some of the most extraordinary evidence of contemporary life, the examples of beautiful rock art from the now desert regions in Algeria and Libya. At the time of their creation, the region was green and fertile, and the variety of wildlife showed animals that have long since disappeared from the area and, in some cases, altogether. The climate continued changing and drying. By 3000BC the Sahara had regained its Palaeolithic climate and turned once again into a desert, creating the Maghreb by forming a barrier that separated the African lands of the Mediterranean from those in the south. Now the lands of North Africa became recognisable in modern terms, distinct from the rest of the continent. The melange of indigenous people eventually became one group known to the outside world as the Berbers, although the term didn't come to refer to the entire local population of the area until AD700 after the Arab invasion. In contrast, the locals named themselves Amazigh, the 'free people'.

Until about 1000BC, the residents of the region remained relatively undisturbed, leaving their own remains, such as the extraordinary Stonehenge-like Cromlech de M'Zora, close to Tangiers in Morocco, and burial dolmens scattered throughout the area. However, by about the end of this time a new foreign power, the Phoenicians, arrived.

THE PHOENICIANS Stemming from the eastern Mediterranean, around today's countries of Syria, Lebanon and Israel, the Phoenician nation was a major trading power that plied the sea, setting up small settlements all around the Mediterranean to facilitate their transactions. They opened up the central seaway, founding many of the cities that lie along the coast on both the north and south shores. Not bothering with the interior, due to its inhospitality and occupation by other groups, the furthest known outpost of the Phoenicians was in Mogador (Essaouira) on the Atlantic coast of Morocco. Here, as well as in the Gulf of Gabes in Tunisia, they found the murex shells that, ground up, provided the raw ingredients for their legendary purple dye. They were also noted for the establishment of a simplified written language aided by the need to keep accurate records. This script became the precursor to the Greek then Latin alphabets and was literally set in stone. Inscriptions still remain and can be read today

THE BERBERS (PART ONE)

Referring to the indigenous people of the region, the word 'berber' is said to have come from the ancient Greek *barbaros*, meaning foreign. The expression was adapted by the Roman colonists to become *barbarus*, adding strange, rough and uncultivated to its meaning. The Berbers were here long before the Phoenicians arrived and faced every subsequent invading army. Their exact origins are unknown: they're believed to have come out of a merger of two major Neolithic tribes. Calling themselves Imazighen in the plural form, Amazigh in the single – the free people – they were often nomads, primarily in the desert, and some still choose to live as such today. Others worked as farmers. Berbers are ethnically distinct from Arabs, although the two races have mixed over time. The reason for some experts calling them Arab-Berbers is that the Arab invasion of the 7th century AD was so overwhelming that racial integration was inevitable. However, there are still occasional traces of the original features of the race – bright, pale blue eyes, in a dark-haired, dark-skinned face – popping up.

See box *The Berbers (Part Two)* in *Chapter 3*, page 79.

Around 814BC, a date which is conventionally offered but not universally agreed, the Phoenicians established the city of Carthage, the remains of which still exist just outside Tunis, in Tunisia. It was founded by Queen Elissa, better known as Dido, Although flanked by other cities set up by the same traders, it eventually proved to be the centre as well as the namesake for one of the most important historical people of the period, the Carthaginians.

Gradually becoming less and less reliant on the Phoenician city of Tyre, the offshoots turned into a powerful force in their own right. Although still described as Punic, this breakaway nation became known as the people from their new capital, the Carthaginians. The settlements they established grew, turning into more permanent cities.

Less than two centuries after the founding of Carthage, Greeks on the island of Thera were ordered by the Delphic oracle to leave their homes and found a colony on the shores of North Africa. Finding a miraculous spring in the hills overlooking the sea, they set up their new residence in Cyrene, now in Libya. Gradually they spread their influence, and with their initial city, established the four other major cities of the region, Tocra, Ptolemais, Eusperides and Apollonia, known as the Pentapolis.

However, the relationship between the Carthaginians and Greeks, both acquisitive sea traders, was uncomfortable and erupted every so often into belligerence. A period of sporadic war broke out between the two nationalities, and lasted around hundred years. Control of the sea and the booty from the countries on its shores, as well as occupation of nearby Sicily, were usually the reasons for the outbreaks. Towards the end of this period, the Carthaginians joined up with the rising nation of Etruscans from Italy, and ousted the Greeks from Corsica. A Greek colony that had set itself up in Tripolitania was sent back to its own territory. Ultimately the enemies of Carthage proved to be stronger in foreign lands, and the North Africans backed down, giving up Sicily on the way. The island was to change nationalities several times, as its strategic position was extremely important to the navigation of the eastern Mediterranean.

As if to further stake their claim to the area, Alexander the Great's forces marched into Egypt from their national port of Cyrene in 331BC declaring that the ancient homeland of the Pharaohs was now Greek. After his death in 323BC, the conqueror's dominion was divided among his loyal generals, with the lands of

A disinherited aspirant to the throne of Tyre, the capital of the Phoenicians, the recently widowed Elissa fled to escape her brother's kingly wrath. Taking followers with her, she stopped in Cyprus, essentially to pick up more women, and then landed in North Africa. By now nicknamed Dido, possibly meaning 'wanderer', the label was added to her royal status and she became known as Queen Dido.

Arriving in North Africa, she asked for refuge from the locals of only the amount of land that could be covered by a bull's hide. When granted it, she sliced the skin finely, and used the strips to map out the perimeter of a large area, later given the name Byrsa (the Greek for cowhide) Hill. Today, this ruse is the inspiration for a problem in calculus. Byrsa Hill still exists at the ruins of Carthage, overlooking the modern city of Tunis.

Other legends are attached to Queen Dido, including Virgil's version in the *Aeneid*. The goddesses Juno and Venus make Dido and a Trojan, Aeneas, fall in love. A local king, Iarbas, who turns out to be descended from Jupiter, threatens to declare war on the Carthaginians unless Dido marries him. Jealous of the love affair, Iarbas calls upon his father to break up the relationship and the king of the deities duly sends his messenger, Mercury, to tell Aeneas to sail off to the distant wealthy lands of Italy. Sadly, but dutifully, he departs, leaving Dido broken-hearted, furious and suicidal. Watching Aeneas and his ships disappear, she proclaims endless enmity between the Carthaginians and the Trojans, and duly kills herself. Virgil poetically attributes the three later Punic (the Latin adjectival form of Phoenician, the original settlers of Carthage) Wars to this tale.

DIDO'S PROBLEM Dido's problem is based on a passage from Virgil's *Aeneid* and challenges the reader to find the figure bounded by a line that has the maximum area for a given perimeter.

> The Kingdom you see is Carthage, the Tyrians, the town of Agenor;
> But the country around is Libya, no folk to meet in war.
> Dido, who left the city of Tyre to escape her brother,
> Rules here – a long labyrinthine tale of wrong
> Is hers, but I will touch on its salient points in order ... Dido, in great disquiet, organised
>   her friends for escape.
> They met together, all those who harshly hated the tyrant
> Or keenly feared him: they seized some ships which chanced to be ready ...
> They came to this spot, where today you can behold the mighty
> Battlements and the rising citadel of New Carthage,
> And purchased a site, which was named 'Bull's Hide' after the bargain
> By which they should get as much land as they could enclose with a bull's hide.

The solution to Dido's problem is the figure of a semicircle.

North Africa (including Egypt and Cyrenaica, the area around the Pentapolis) going to Ptolemy. This new attribution led to the rise of the Ptolemaic dynasty and some of its more notable characters in history, including Cleopatra VII (69–30BC), which explained why such prominent Egyptians were actually of Grecian origin. Throughout the period of the Romans, the inhabitants of Cyrenaica and Egypt continued to speak Greek.

By now, the Roman republic had already been established and although not involved in Carthage's affairs (yet), a powerful force was rising to the north. In other parts of North Africa, local tribes were banding together and setting up new confederations. By 400BC, far to the west, the Moors joined up to form Mauretania in an area that approximates modern Morocco. The neighbouring lands to the east, along the north of Algeria, were jointly occupied by the Masaesyli and the Massyli. This area became Numidia, another kingdom that bordered the sea. The desert people to the southwest were the Gaetules and to the southeast, the Garamantes, but they existed far beyond the breezes of the sea and were not of immediate concern to the Carthaginians. The later North African invaders, however, would find them a great source of aggravation.

THE PUNIC WARS Expansion attempts on both sides of the Mediterranean by different nations inevitably led to conflict and by 264BC hostilities exploded into the **First Punic War**. Ostensibly an issue over control of Sicily, the battles showed the superiority of an older power, Carthage, versus a younger but rising force, the Romans, and lasted more than 20 years. The North African fleet was finally destroyed in 242BC and the land handed over to the newcomers. Not long after, the Carthaginians had to relinquish the other strategic islands of Corsica and Sardinia.

Carthage survived and began expanding its empire once more. The Barcid dynasty came to power, first with Hamilcar, a successful general and, then, more famously, his son Hannibal. Due to uneasy relations with Rome, aggravated by a hefty war indemnity to the winners, Hannibal remained an avowed enemy. When he attacked the Spanish city of Saguntum, the Romans, under whose auspices the city existed, demanded Hannibal's capture. The Carthaginians refused, leading not only to the **Second Punic War**, 218–202BC, but also the emergence of Hannibal as a gallant legendary figure. His famous battles with Rome involved the crossing of the Alps accompanied by elephants, and included his phenomenal success at the Battle of Cannae, in which he defeated Scipio and his army killing over 35,000 Romans while sustaining a loss of only 6,000 Carthaginians. However, war continued and Scipio, after having seized Carthaginian Spain for Rome, and invading Africa itself, met and defeated Hannibal at Zama in 202BC.

Carthage was devastated though not destroyed, but still forced to give up all foreign territories. Scipio dug a trench, from Thabraca (Tabarka) to Thenae (Sfax), a northwest to southeast line in Tunisia as a border, beyond which the defeated nation no longer had jurisdiction. On the other side was Massinissa, heir to the throne of the Massylians, one of the two tribes of Numidia. Born in 241BC and educated in Carthage, he was always friendly to the Romans, arguably already recognising the stronger force. In appreciation, he was granted the land west of the new Carthaginian line. As King Massinissa, both his power and the Romans allowed his ambition to grow. Imagining a Hellenistic-style African kingdom, he envisaged a land of united tribes, with a regular fleet. Based in Cirta (Constantine, in Algeria), he encouraged farming by example, giving each of his 50 sons large plots of land. Empowered by his success and vision, he began annexing Carthaginian lands. Despite the local protests, Rome ignored the incursions. In 174BC, Massinissa took the area around the Gulf of Sirte in Libya and when he continued, seizing the fertile land to the east, this act of aggression was too much for Carthage. Calling upon neighbours to the east and far west, a war began between the nations, which Massinissa eventually won.

Rome now had proof that Carthage could be defeated by its African ally, but was annoyed that it was able to wage wars against Roman sympathisers. At the same time, the Romans began to have doubts about Massinissa and his visions of a great empire including Carthage. As a way of absorbing the lands of their ancient foes, as well as dampening Massinissa's plans, the Romans launched the **Third – and final – Punic War** in 149BC. Legend has it that on discussing the prospect of war,

1

7

When Hannibal was born, in 247BC, into the Carthaginian 'Royal Family' of the Barcids, his father Hamilcar was already a famous military hero, noted as the victor of the Mercenary War of 241BC. Hannibal travelled with his family to watch the re-establishment of the national empire (after the First Punic War with Rome) by the Carthaginian conquest of the whole of southern Spain. Made to swear that as soon as he was old enough, he would become an enemy of the Roman people, he remained a thorn in the empire's side for his entire life. Upon Rome's unsuccessful demands for Hannibal's capture, after his seizing of Saguntum in Spain, he launched his famous attack on the Roman Empire. In 218BC, at the age of 23, Hannibal assessed that the enemy would never expect an attack from the mountains and worked out a plan to cross the Alps. Knowing also that the Romans feared elephants, the young general incorporated the native animals, a local species now extinct, into the attack force. He lost half his manpower and most of his horses and elephants, yet managed to complete the journey. On the verge of defeating Rome, he was deprived of his victory by lack of reinforcements from Carthage. Two years later, however, at Cannae in southeast Italy, the Carthaginian forces defeated Rome's army under the leadership of Scipio. Carthage lost 6,000 men, while the Romans sustained losses of over 35,000. For a brief period, the warriors from Carthage were truly feared, and for centuries, the expression 'Hannibal ad portas' (Hannibal at the gates), was used to terrify children. The battle might have been over, but the war wasn't lost as far as Rome was concerned, and after seizing Spain from the Carthaginians and invading Africa, Scipio (now given the additional name Africanus, in honour of his successes) and his Romans finally defeated Hannibal and his forces at Zama in 202BC. Hannibal gave up his military aspiration in the hope of going into politics, but this change of occupation proved unsuccessful. Going into exile, he worked as an adviser to the adversaries of Rome. His sworn enemies, however, were determined to hunt him down, and finally, to avoid capture, he took his own life. If contemporary dates and accounts were accurate, he died in 183BC, the same year as Scipio Africanus, the Roman general with whom he waged his career-long war.

someone in the senate stated: 'Carthago delenda est' (Carthage must be destroyed), an expression used today to incite total warfare.

This final campaign, lasting three years, was notoriously cruel. The Romans made impossible demands in their suit for peace insisting the Carthaginians relinquish all arms and ships, surrender 300 noble children as hostages and, if they were to rebuild, only do so 12 miles from the coast. Despite initial agreement, the besieged people found these requirements too much to bear, and dug in their heels. Starving behind their barricades, the Carthaginians were finally defeated when Scipio Aemilianus (grandson of the general from the Second Punic War), broke through their defences. The carnage was appalling and when the dust cleared, only 50,000 people remained, who were sold into slavery. As if to make sure Carthage would never rise again, the land was scattered with salt, rendering the soil infertile. Whether it was actually or merely ceremonially coated was never verified in documented history, but the days of Carthage as an independent nation were over.

THE FIRST COLONIES The Romans absorbed the land that had previously been Carthaginian into a new colony, their first on the continent, called Africa Proconsularis. It was to be governed by an eponymous proconsul.

The province took in the most fertile parts of the area and established a new capital at Utica, north of the salted ruins of Carthage. What was outside its borders went to Numidia, now ruled by the three sons of Massinissa. With such rich land under their dominion, the Romans began to develop agricultural projects. They set up the huge wheat fields that were to feed Rome and lead to North Africa eventually becoming known as the breadbasket of the empire.

THE JUGURTHINE WAR Peace was interrupted when Jugurtha, an illegitimate son of the brother of Micapsa (Massinissa's heir when the other two died) had aspirations for rulership of Numidia. Killing the legitimate heirs, he ascended the throne but ruffled quite a few Roman feathers *en route*. In 112BC Jugurtha attacked the city of Cirta (Constantine in Algeria). In addition, he arranged the slaughter of all adult males. As some of these inhabitants came recently from Italy, the homeland could not let this insult go. The Jugurthine war broke out, ending six years later when Jugurtha's own father-in-law, King Bocchus of Mauretania, was compelled by the Romans to betray him. Handed over to General Sulla, Jugurtha was dragged back to Rome, paraded in chains as an enemy and finally died in prison.

THE END OF THE REPUBLIC King Bocchus and his heirs remained rulers of the western part of Numidia and Mauretania, while the eastern half was left to Hiempsal, a nephew of Jugurtha. Things were happening in the mother country, however, which were to affect not only Rome, but also North Africa.

Rival and powerful factions were growing in Rome and in 60BC, in order to avoid civil war, Julius Caesar, a successful general, suggested the establishment of a governmental triumvirate. Roman lands were divided between three rulers: Marcus Licinius Crassus (Crassus) would get Syria and the East; Gnaius Pompeius Magnus (Pompey) received Spain and Africa; and Gaius Julius Caesar (Caesar) held power over Gaul and its neighbours. The relationship was further cemented by the marriage of Caesar's daughter, Julia, to Pompey. However, in 54BC Julia died, and in 53BC, Crassus was killed in battle. Caesar was becoming ever more popular and began to take legal liberties with his position. Eventually, aided by the qualms of the Senate, Pompey declared (civil) war on Caesar but was defeated at the Battle of Pharsalus in Greece, in 48BC. Appropriately, but unfortunately, the Numidian king, Hiempsal, and his son Juba I sided with Pompey. Caesar's defeated enemy fled to Egypt, but was hunted down and killed there. Nevertheless, his faction remained, and the battle continued. Finally at Thapsus, Tunisia (near Mahdia) in 46BC, Caesar and his loyal Mauretanian forces overwhelmingly defeated the Pompeians. Juba I, whose hope had remained with the remains of Pompey's forces, recognised his defeat and took the honourable way out by 'falling on his sword'. After this suicide, Caesar returned to Rome with Juba's young son Juba II. Rather than parade him through the streets in chains, as had been done with Juba's distant relative Jugurtha, Caesar chose to raise him in the household of Octavia Augusta, the sister of his great nephew and heir, Octavian (later Caesar Augustus). Although seeming at first a merciful gesture, this decision was politically astute: Caesar's family would be raising an heir to a once troublesome province, whose loyalty to Rome would be guaranteed. Caesar also extended the area of Rome's African colony beyond Scipio's line to absorb most of Numidia. The old province was renamed Africa Vetus, while the extension took on the name of Africa Nova. A Roman governor was appointed to oversee this newest of outposts. Not forgetting his backbone of support, Caesar also established colonies for veteran soldiers, granting plots of the most fertile African lands to his loyal army retirees.

Caesar was now sole ruler of Rome and enacted many policy changes including reductions in the power of the Senate. Appointed dictator for life, he was offered the kingship, even though Rome was supposed to be a republic. Despite his refusal, many believed his rejection was insincere. Fearing his usurping of power, on 15

9

March 44BC the senators banded together in a joint assassination of their leader. The story goes that 60 senators each stabbed him. A power vacuum ensued but his adopted son (and actual great nephew) Augustus was handed the mantle of power. A year later, Augustus formed another triumvirate, with two of Julius Caesar's most loyal supporters, Marcus Aemilius Lepidus (Lepidus) and Marcus Antonius (Mark Anthony). Initially successful, there were increasingly frequent arguments between Augustus and Mark Anthony. In 36BC, Lepidus was accused of treason by attempting to take over power in Sicily and was banished to a small island in Italy where he died in 13BC. Outright civil war erupted between Augustus and Mark Anthony and the latter was finally defeated at the Battle of Actium in Greece in 31BC. Although married to Augustus's sister Octavia, Mark Anthony's more famous liaison was with Egypt's queen, Cleopatra VII. Taking refuge in Egypt, Mark Anthony finally took his own life in the Roman way, by falling on his sword. As the sole remaining member of the triumvirate as well as being Julius Caesar's heir, Augustus adopted the name – and imperial rights – of the newly coined expression, Caesar. He became the new emperor, to be known as Augustus Caesar. The republic now became the Roman Empire. However, Augustus and subsequent emperors encouraged the public to believe it remained a republic, as evidenced by later inscriptions.

GOLDEN DAYS Although Julius Caesar had wanted to resurrect Carthage as a Roman city, his assassination prevented it. Augustus, as his heir, reinstated his plans. Once again, the city was on its way to becoming a major centre and eventually the most important one in North Africa. The new emperor created many more colonies, imprinting the Roman stamp on much of this extremely fertile region, and found suitable retirement homes for the country's loyal veterans. He even created a few in distant Mauretania, although at the time it was still an autonomous kingdom.

In 27BC, Augustus granted Roman senators significant power, when he decided to share the government of the empire with them. To protect the lands still under his control, and the settlers within them, Augustus established the Third Augustan Legion, his army in North Africa. The detachment continued in force, more or less, for the next 400 years. Ostensibly military, its initial function was to safeguard Roman territory, especially from the marauding tribes to the south. However, the unit's most important duties shifted to civil ones, as Roman soldiers were some of the best engineers in history. Roads, bridges, aqueducts and even cities were constructed primarily by the military wing of the Romans. In AD14, the headquarters for the legion were at Ammaedara (on the Tunisian–Algerian border), but they were moved to Lambaesis (Algeria) by AD200.

The period of the next two centuries, from just after Augustus's accession to the highest office in Rome to the death of Marcus Aurelius in AD180, was considered the golden age of Rome, or the Pax Romana (Roman peace). It's argued that in North Africa it lasted much longer, possibly even until AD400. Certainly not without the occasional skirmish or uprising, these days were relatively peaceful. During this time the empire flourished and produced some of its greatest achievements. Government became consistent, firmly under the grip of Roman law, even in the furthest colonies. The army engineers worked to facilitate transport via their extraordinarily comprehensive road network. The military brought water to the towns through their many kilometres-long aqueduct systems, and even managed to plumb it in, creating an efficient sewage system with flush toilets. Latin became the standard language throughout the empire, although to the east Greek remained, and the Roman alphabet was made standard. Literature and the arts flourished.

In some of the regions of the empire, Augustus set up client kingships. These gifted kingdoms were headed by locals who had guaranteed their loyalty to

JUBA II AND CLEOPATRA SELENE

One of the most illustrious pairings in Roman history – that of Juba II and Cleopatra Selene – is little known. Both were of North African royal birth, although from the different regions of Numidia and Egypt, respectively. They came together to form one of the Roman Empire's securest provinces.

The first of the Jubas proved his loyalty to Rome, but unfortunately picked the wrong side during the Republican civil wars. Having backed the loser, Pompey, at Thapsus in 46BC, Juba I chose the hero's way out and committed suicide. His young son, Juba II, was taken back to the capital by Julius Caesar. The little boy was given to Caesar's great niece to be raised in her household along with other children. It was not uncommon for such orphans to be taken into Roman families. Royal blood is royal blood, regardless of its origin and the ever-pragmatic Romans recognised the possibilities of future allies. A few years later, in 31BC, after Mark Anthony and his lover Cleopatra's defeat at the Battle of Actium, more children were absorbed into the Octavian home. One of these new arrivals was Cleopatra Selene, their daughter.

Juba was an intelligent child and educated well. When he was in his mid-20s, Augustus granted him the client kingship of Mauretania. Although heir to the no-longer extant country of Numidia, its neighbour was still autonomous and required a loyal leader. Going with him was his new bride, Cleopatra Selene. As one of the last of the Ptolemys, the ancient line that began with Alexander the Great's general Ptolemy, she was the closest thing to an heiress of that ancient land.

As an intellectual, Juba II was interested in the arts as well as sciences and exploration. Throughout his life he wrote serious works on various subjects, including archaeology, language and accounts of voyages. He settled in the capital Iol (Cherchell in Algeria), which he renamed Caesarea. He then built his dream city, Volubilis, in Morocco. The former has been continuously inhabited since ancient days and today there is very little of the period left to see. The latter was deserted after the Arab invasion in the 7th century AD, and, although not the most impressive of Roman ruins, is still visible as a Roman city. Some of its mosaics, left *in situ*, are delightful.

For 20 years, Juba and Cleopatra ruled the country, although very little is known about the queen. When she died in 6BC, Juba continued on the throne for the next 30 years. A second marriage was very short-lived. Towards the end of his life, he shared rulership with the declared heir Ptolemy, his son with Cleopatra, who assumed the leadership when Juba II died in AD23. Legend has it that Juba II and Cleopatra Selene were buried in the enormous Mauretanian Tomb, a large conical mausoleum that remains to this day, overlooking the Roman and modern town of Tipasa in Algeria. Although nothing of their remains has been found inside in recent times, it's possible that grave robbers visited not long after its construction. Alternatively, it could be that the Greco-Egypto-styled mound could have simply been a memorial. It has been dated to be of the correct period.

The story ends unhappily. On a visit to Rome to visit his cousin Caligula, in AD40, Ptolemy, as a king in his own right, deigned to wear the purple produced from the murex shells from his own land, to which he felt entitled. The emperor, feeling that no-one had the right to wear those colours but the supreme ruler, arranged to have Ptolemy killed. As there was no heir, Caligula took away Mauretania's autonomous status and absorbed the client kingdom into the empire. Apocryphal the story may be, but border issues with rebellious Moors might also have hastened the emperor's decision to tighten control on the region.

Rome, in exchange for some of the services the empire could provide (such as military protection etc). In 25BC, Augustus had decided to give the Mauretanian client kingship to Juba II, the son of the previous Numidian king, Juba I. He married Cleopatra Selene, the daughter of Cleopatra VII and Mark Anthony, and in total ruled for 50 years. Upon Juba's death, their son Ptolemy ascended the throne, but was killed in Rome in AD40 after a misunderstanding with the emperor Caligula.

Despite the occasional attacks on the empire from both without (local tribes continued to launch border assaults) and within (a Jewish revolt in AD115 spread from Palestine to Cyrenaica and caused serious damage, although it was quashed in AD118), North Africa boomed. Grain, timber and fish were exploited extremely successfully. Cultivation of olives spread and oil, a source of light as well as an ingredient, grew increasingly important. Garum, a fish paste that featured on the gastronomic palate of the Romans, was also exported. African-born Romans began to have influence in Rome, first as soldiers then as senators.

The first emperor from outside Italy was Trajan from Spain, who came to power in AD98. He and his successor Hadrian, also from Spain, journeyed to North Africa and left impressive traces of their visits that can still be seen today, especially in the Triumphal Arches. Hadrian also set the fashion that turned the classic image of a Roman emperor from clean-shaven to bearded, as evidenced by subsequent statues. Allegedly this change was due to Hadrian's skin blemishes.

The first emperor native to North Africa was Septimius Severus, in power from AD193–211. Born in Leptis Magna, in Libya, he founded the controversial Severan dynasty.

SEPTIMIUS SEVERUS Coming from one of the more elite families of North Africa, Lucius Septimius Severus was born AD145 in the Tripolitanian town of Leptis Magna. Although claiming Latin descent from his mother's side, his father was native, and Septimius's first language was Punic. Throughout the life he spent mostly away from his country of birth, it was said, he never lost his accent. Made senator and then consul by the emperors of the time, in AD191 Septimius was given command of several legions in central Europe. After the death of Commodus and subsequent murder of his successor Pertinax, the army elected Septimius as their new leader and aspirant to the empire's most important position. Never popular with the senate, Septimius attempted to validate his claim to the throne by stating that he was the son of Marcus Aurelius (a blatant lie). One of the members replied by congratulating the new emperor on finding his father. The vociferous joker ended up becoming one of the 29 senators whom Septimius had assassinated. Among those killed were several who had vested interests in North Africa, and whatever local protests might have been brewing among the local elite were crushed there and then.

Septimius Severus was a traveller who didn't forget his origins. To befit a place that bred a Roman emperor, he poured major amounts of money into his home town, leaving a magnificent memorial in his honour that remains to this day. He didn't settle in his enhanced city, however, but continued to mount military campaigns throughout his empire. After three years of fighting in the wild and untamed province of Britannia, Septimius died in York in AD211.

Unfortunately, much of the legacy left by the first North African emperor was his sons and their successors. Caracalla the elder murdered his brother Geta. He was subsequently assassinated by a prefect in the Praetorian Guard, Macrinus, who was then deposed by relatives of Septimius. They substituted an appallingly depraved candidate, Elagabalus, who, needless to say, did not last long. Another cousin, Alexander, appeared, managing to stay in power for 13 years. However, he too was murdered by the army, thereby ending the 42-year Severan dynasty.

On some of the inscriptions found in the Roman Empire, words have been deliberately scratched out from the stone, effectively deleting a name of some dignitary to whom the dedication was once made. Known as *damnatio memoriae*, or damning the memory, this defacement was the Roman way of erasing someone from existence. Historically this sabotage was done to disgrace someone who had caused harm to the empire. In North Africa, this damage was not uncommon. Monuments glorifying members of the Severan dynasty often had the name of Geta scraped off by Caracalla, the brother who murdered him. Subsequently, Caracalla's name was also removed and, in some cases, traces of the entire dynasty.

THE CRISIS OF THE THIRD CENTURY AND DIOCLETIAN The end of the Severan dynasty, and the mostly violent removals from office of its members, encouraged the ambitious to believe the only way to power was either by seizing it, or killing its current representatives. From AD235 to AD284, there were 50 recorded emperors, some with reigns as short as three weeks. The Roman Empire was crumbling at the edges with old enemies to the north and east constantly attacking its borders. The provinces of North Africa closest to Rome remained relatively peaceful, although inhabitants at the edge of the frontier were being seriously hassled by local tribes. In fact, by AD300 Rome had stopped supporting the far west, allowing most of Mauretania to revert to non-Roman inhabitants. Only Mauretania Tingitana, the region around Tangiers and the gates of the Mediterranean, remained in the Empire.

This time of continually changing leaders, lack of support and inconsistent central policy as well as general disillusionment led to a period known as the Crisis of the Third Century. Beginning with the assassination of Severus Alexander, the last of the Severans, and ending with the powerful Diocletian who reorganised much of the Roman political and even geographical infrastructure, Rome narrowly escaped disintegration.

Diocletian, who was emperor from AD284 until his appointed successors took office in AD305, rose from the ranks of the army. He recognised that the empire was getting too unwieldy for one central government and enacted several major reforms that changed its appearance and its nature. Most significantly, he divided it initially into two parts, the west and the east. Within each of these two regions he designated an Augustus, the senior ruler, and a Caesar, the secondary regent. The empire was now a tetrarchy (government ruled by four people). Diocletian acted as Augustus in the eastern half, supported by his Caesar Galerius, while the west, ruled by the co-emperor Maximian, had Constantius as second in command. Further subdivisions continued, effectively delegating power quite a long way down. Within these foreign provinces, the original emperor removed the civilly appointed governors, replacing them with his own favourites, the military equestrians.

Changes were also made in what was left of North Africa. African Proconsularis was split into three sections: Zeugitana to the north, known as Proconsularis, remained governed by a proconsul and retained Carthage as its capital; the newly created Byzacena covered the south of the region and had Hadrumetum (Sousse) as its main city; while Tripolitania, in the west of Libya, continued with Septimius Severus's home town, Leptis Magna, for its seat of government. Cyrenaica, eastern Libya and a Greek-speaking side of the Roman world affiliated with Egypt, became part of the eastern empire.

Other drastic measures were put into place. Diocletian deliberately reduced the effectiveness of the Senate, granting it power only over the city of Rome. Despite his preferences, he couldn't eliminate senators altogether and as a concession set up a branch of them in the capital of his eastern empire, Byzantium (later renamed Constantinople by Constantine the Great and known today as Istanbul). Diocletian also attempted price fixing to control rampant inflation racking the city and brought in a new system of taxation. Neither proved very successful, but at least the concept of wresting back control took hold.

Many other reforms were also enacted, including those increasing the role of the army and decreasing the civil government's. Several of these modifications were enhanced by Diocletian's successor, Constantine, when he took the control of the part of the empire inherited from his father Constantius in AD306. However, there were still too many leaders, and in AD324, after a long period of civil wars, Constantine, now, the Great, defeated the corresponding emperor of the east to become the sole leader of the Roman Empire. A ruthless and forceful man, Constantine continued the reforms despite his newly acquired Christian beliefs. He adopted them in AD312, supposedly after experiencing a vision of a cross in the sky heralding a victory against his rival Maxentius at the Battle of Milvian Bridge in Rome. Whether this conversion was sincere or pragmatic was irrelevant to the Christians, who were now no longer being persecuted. Once the concept of this new religion was accepted, various factions split off, some resulting in violent clashes of belief. Ultimately, all conflicts in North African Christianity were resolved by dissolution, when the Arabs, with their fervent Islamic beliefs, began their invasion from AD642.

THE VANDALS AND THE END OF THE EMPIRE … FOR A WHILE From AD311 to 429, religion seems to have dominated politics. The Donatists, a sect who broke away from mainstream Christianity (see page 24) practised militant enforcement of their beliefs, often causing violent clashes. Some North African-born luminaries from the early history of the Church appeared, such as Synesius of Cyrene, (cAD370– 414), a pagan-turned-Christian bishop who left significant written pieces behind, and St Augustine of Hippo (AD354–430), the legendary Catholic philosopher who greatly affected both religious and secular thought.

There were constant incursions by Berbers, some of whom successfully invaded Roman territory. An earthquake, a tsunami and an attack on Tripolitania by the Austuriani tribe in the mid 4th century AD devastated the cities of Sabratha, Oea (Tripoli) and Leptis Magna. Not long after, a rebellion by the Donatist-supported and Romanised member of the Jubaleni tribe, Firmus, almost succeeded in taking over parts of Mauretania. He was stopped by Roman forces and rival Catholics at Tipasa.

However, there were serious disturbances in the rest of the empire that were soon to affect North Africa. In AD410 the Visigoths, a Germanic tribe, were led by their king Alaric to successfully attack and pillage Rome. At virtually the same time, the Vandals, another tribe from the east of present-day Germany, were on the move. No longer satisfied with the land along the banks of the Danube that Constantine the Great had granted in order to appease them, they began their conquering march south, reaching Spain just before Rome fell. Both tribes cast their eyes on the riches of North Africa, but it was the Vandals who braved the Straits and arrived in large numbers on the shores of Mauretania Tingitana. With the idea of controlling the Mediterranean they moved east, quickly reaching Hippo (eastern Algeria). Religious ideology fuelled the attack, with the Arian Vandals assailing the Catholic city. St Augustine was among those who died during the siege. After 14 months, the Vandals agreed to a truce, making Hippo a Vandal city, and leaving Carthage, the jewel of the Mediterranean, to the Romans. An uneasy peace was established in AD435. However, the chief port of the seas was too tempting to the Vandal leader, Gaiseric, and he broke the accord by attacking

WHAT HAVE THE ROMANS EVER DONE FOR US?

One of the most popular, if controversial, adaptations of the Christ story in its contemporary Roman context, is *Monty Python's Life of Brian*. Although ostensibly a take on an alternative Messiah, it has given rise to some wonderful quotations that provide an insight into how we view ancient Rome today. While the breakout religion of Christianity might have caused difficulties with the Roman authorities (see *Religion*, page 24), the importance of the achievements of the government had to be acknowledged.

The following extract is from the 1979 film, directed by Terry Jones, and written by Graham Chapman, John Cleese, Terry Gilliam, Eric Idle, Terry Jones and Michael Palin.

It's a time of spiritual revolution and consequent discontent, with prophecies of saviours abounding. Many false messiahs appear, with some of their followers being more militant than others.

The interior of Matthias's House. A darkened room with a very conspiratorial atmosphere. Reg and Stan are seated at a table at one end of the room. Francis, dressed in Activist gear – black robes and a red sash around his head – is standing by a plan on the wall. He is addressing an audience of about eight masked activists. Their faces are partially hidden.

Reg: They've bled us white, the bastards. They've taken everything we had, not just from us, from our fathers and from our fathers' fathers.

Stan: And from our fathers' fathers' fathers.

Reg: Yes.

Stan: And from our fathers' fathers' fathers' fathers.

Reg: All right, Stan. Don't labour the point. And what have they ever given us *in return*?

Xerxes: The aqueduct.

Reg: Oh yeah, yeah they gave us that. Yeah. That's true.

Masked activist: And the sanitation!

Stan: Oh yes ... sanitation, Reg, you remember what the city used to be like.

Reg: All right, I'll grant you that the aqueduct and the sanitation are two things that the Romans *have* done ...

Matthias: And the roads ...

Reg (*sharply*): Well yes *obviously* the roads ... the roads go without saying. But apart from the aqueduct, the sanitation and the roads ...

Another masked activist: Irrigation ...

Other masked voices: Medicine ... Education ... Health ...

Reg: Yes ... all right, fair enough ...

Activist near front: And the wine ...

Omnes: Oh yes! True!

Francis: Yeah. That's something we'd really miss if the Romans left, Reg.

Masked activist at back: Public baths!

Stan: And it's safe to walk in the streets at night now.

Francis: Yes, they certainly know how to keep order ... (*general nodding*) ... let's face it, they're the only ones who could in a place like this.

(*more general murmurs of agreement*)

Reg: All right ... all right ... but apart from better sanitation and medicine and education and irrigation and public health and roads and a freshwater system and baths and public order ... what *have* the Romans done for *us*?

Xerxes: Brought peace!

Reg (*very angry, he's not having a good meeting at all*): What!? Oh ... (*scornfully*) Peace, yes ... shut up!

Recorded history begins with the Phoenicians around 1000BC. Although details at this point are still sparse, trading ports and even routes begin to become known. Over in Egypt, the names of individual pharaohs appear. Soon after, wars start to be chronicled with heroes and generals singled out. As time progresses, the accounts become very precise, led mostly by battles, victors and their great deeds. Later, historic personages are described, together with their achievements or follies, and their entourages. Events made important by their consequences are recounted, often in terms of alternative versions or from unusual points of view.

HISTORIANS Homer, who might have lived around 800BC, described the Trojan Wars of 400 years before in his epic, *The Illiad*. The first major verified chronicler of events in the ancient world was Herodotus, 484–425BC. As well as writing about the Persian Wars, Herodotus described his journeys throughout the known lands, including North Africa. Thucydides, writing about the same time, had been an army commander and described the Peloponnesian Wars. Due to cross-referencing of the same information, Herodotus's accounts were more interesting though less accurate. Thucydides didn't concern himself with background but simply told the stories of the conflicts.

Historians became fashionable and prolific, describing both ancient and contemporary happenings. Some of these writers were probably more appropriately called chroniclers. It's only in looking back at their descriptions of current events that they turn into historians. Writers who were there at the time are most likely more accurate than those looking back. However, everyone writes with a bias, and many of the court reporters were trying to get in with the powerful men of the period, whether the emperor or members of the Senate.

Some writers were the rulers themselves, such as Julius and Augustus Caesar, and Juba II, King of Mauretania. Julius Caesar wrote of his wars and battles, including perhaps a *De Bello Africo*, an account of the African Wars. Augustus wrote a description of his own works and deeds, while Juba II was interested in the natural history and geography of his world.

Later writers included the Greek Polybius who in c200BC described the second and third Punic Wars, while Sallust (86–35BC) told the tale of the Numidian rebel, Jugurtha. The best-known and arguably the greatest Roman historian was Tacitus, whose *Histories* written about AD109 included comprehensive accounts of the rise and fall of several emperors.

Historians continued to tell about their contemporaries and comment on the past. Sometimes these accounts conflicted, which made the stories more credible (in that there wasn't one official line to follow) and indicated the individuals' biases clearly. Later on, religious influences began to show, such as with the works of St Augustine of Hippo (Algeria). Almost nothing is documented of the period of the Vandal occupation, with the exception of a comprehensive dowry list dating from AD493, the *Tablettes Albertini*, found in 1928. Simply an inventory, there isn't much detail regarding daily life. No famous people or battles were involved, but this strictly factual register of goods and chattels belonging to a clearly affluent family tells a great deal about what things were like in those days. Soon after, when the Vandals departed and the later Romans returned, the Byzantines had reporters of the period. When the Arabs arrived, they clearly had their own version of events.

It seems there is a clear, logical line to follow about what things happened when, but there are considerable flaws. It's difficult to separate bias from fact, when only one version

Carthage in AD439. Continuing his conquest, the Vandal king moved north, reaching Rome and sacking it once more in AD455. From around AD460, Gaiseric destroyed two imperial fleets, undaunted by the relatively poor attempts to defeat him.

of events was found. If the writer wanted to get in with the emperor, it's not possible to know whether the characteristics attributed to the ruler were accurate, or flattering. Another problem is that many of the documents referred to are either missing or copies from later periods. How many 'Chinese whispers' (or perhaps 'Roman whispers'?) could there be of an AD1600 copy of an AD900 manuscript based on one of the few remaining books of a writer's mostly missing works? Ultimately there is the pragmatic argument of how important is it that we know the complete truth, if such a thing were possible. We have an approximate idea of what happened when and with whom, and that, perhaps, is as good as history gets.

A CHRONOLOGICAL LIST OF SOME OF THE HISTORIANS OF THE PERIOD

Herodotus (480–425BC) 'Father of History', wrote about Persian Wars and travelled extensively throughout the ancient world

Thucydides (c460–400BC) Exiled army commander, knew about and fought in Peloponnesian Wars

Xenophon (450?–355?BC) Continued Thucydides's work, alternative view to Plato's account of Socrates

Polybius (c200BC) Gave Greek perspective to the Second and Third Punic wars

Julius Caesar (100–46BC) Wrote accounts of his campaigns, possibly including *De Bello Africo*, on the North African wars

Salust (86–35BC) Included accounts of the Jugurthine War (112–105BC)

Augustus (63BC–AD14) Autobiography

Livy (59–17BC) Around 29BC wrote history of Rome in 142 books; all but 35 were lost

Juba II (50BC–AD23) Wrote many books, including natural history and geography

Pliny the Elder (AD23–79) Soldier and historian: works include the *Natural History of the Continent of Africa*

Dio Chrysostum (AD40–120?) Philosopher, historian

Plutarch (AD45–125) Wrote biographies on famous Romans, including Pompey and Mark Anthony

Tacitus (AD56–120) Arguably the greatest Roman historian. The *Histories* (*Historiae*) of c100 includes AD69, *The Year of the Four Emperors* (Galba, Otho, Vitellius and Vespasian)

Josephus (AD37–c95) Described the Jewish War of AD75–79. In his *Antiquities of the Jews* around 93 he refers to a man named Jesus.

Suetonius (AD73?–135) Born in Hippo Regius, wrote lives of *Twelve Caesars*, from Julius Caesar to Domitian

Cassius Dio (AD165–229) Retold the history of the Civil Wars AD193–197

St Augustine (AD354–430) Christian writer and philosopher

Tablettes Albertini (AD493) Dowry list of Gemina Januarilla, written on 56 pieces of wood, included information on minutiae of everyday life)

Priscus (cAD500) Writer known mostly for his work on Atilla the Hun in central Europe and western Asia, now mostly lost

Procopius (AD500?–562) Author of the unofficial, secret history of the Byzantine emperor Justinian and his wife Theodora

Corippus (cAD600) Epic poet, born in Africa, describes the events of around AD600 Arab historians (from 640)

For the next 70 years, the Vandals settled into their territory, following much of the Roman style of living. Agriculture continued to thrive, especially olive trees and vineyards. The Vandals adopted the Latin language and the lifestyle choices of the land they had conquered. They didn't seem to be creators, and very little evidence of their occupation survived. Over time, the luxuries of this extravagant lifestyle depleted their military edge and a series of questionable takeovers of command weakened this once powerful force. Meanwhile the Roman Empire continued, although in a somewhat reduced form. While some historians refer to this period as Late Roman, it is also known as the Byzantine era, taking its name from the city, Byzantium. The Emperor Justinian had his eye on the southern Vandal kingdom. He felt his leadership had two major goals: perpetuating the successful domination of the true Christian religion and reconstituting the Roman Empire. In AD533, looking towards the heretical North Africans who followed the Arian sect and maintained control of the Straits of Sicily, he sent a large fleet and an attendant army to attack the Vandals. Under the command of Count Belisarius the Roman force caught the enemy by surprise, successfully defeating them on Tunisian soil. King Gelimer, in the town of Bulla Regia, raced back towards Carthage with his army to refuse surrender terms, but was overwhelmed just outside the city. Despite the occasional vestige of resistance, the Vandal kingdom, after a century of being in control of coastal North Africa, was finally conquered.

THE ARAB INVASION AND THE REAL END OF ROMAN RULE IN NORTH AFRICA The Roman Empire was now back in control of a much smaller province than in its imperial heyday. Berber tribes were constantly biting at its heels, and domination from distant Constantinople was always under threat. The later Romans, or Byzantines, reinforced their cities, often reusing materials to build massive walls and fortresses. The locals were heavily taxed to pay for reconstruction, the military and in some cases the Church. The renewed leadership was not popular. There were constant struggles against the foreigners at the gates as well as civil factions vying for power. The reduced empire became progressively weakened.

Towards the north and east, a religious faith was gathering momentum, stemming from the beliefs of the Arabian-born visionary Mohammad. After his death in AD632, the new religion, Islam (see *Chapter 2*, page 63) began to take serious hold. Under the leadership of the successor of Mohammad, known as the caliph, the Muslim army advanced through the Middle East, first taking control of Jerusalem in AD637, then Palestine and Syria by AD641. Soon after, the forces entered North Africa with Egypt the first to fall. Heading west, the Muslim army found little resistance and Cyrenaica came under their rule. Tripolitania was next, with the conquerors attacking Tripoli and destroying Sabratha. They also went south into the desert area of the Fezzan in attempts to convert the Berber locals. Gregory, the exarch (the Byzantine version of a viceroy, or local representative of the emperor), claimed the leadership of the remnants of the empire for himself in AD646, and retreated to his new capital, Sufetula in Tunisia. The Arabs continued their march, barely impeded by their enemy's army, defeating and killing Gregory *en route* a year later.

The raids continued but domination of North Africa remained out of reach. The Byzantines still cruised the Mediterranean, and internally, rival factions were struggling for control. Okba ibn Nafi, was selected as the new Islamic army leader and by AD670 had seized much of the province to the west. He founded the city of Kairouan. However, the locals wouldn't let this area go without a struggle. Okba attempted to take his religious cause all the way to the Atlantic, but failed. On his return, Chief Koseila of the Berbers, ambushed and killed Okba and most of his men, setting back the Arab invasion for several years. In AD695, the Arab leader Hassan returned to attack Carthage, but was defeated by the fierce Berber queen Kahena, and the losers fell back to Cyrenaica. The nearby Byzantine navy took advantage of this lull and briefly took back the city, but the following year Hassan returned. Subduing Carthage, but believing its position was defensively weak, he founded the modern capital Tunis instead, turning it into a port by constructing a channel that gave it access to the Mediterranean.

The Arabs were very close to achieving their goal. In AD700, Queen Kahena and her troublesome followers were defeated. Finally in AD708, Septem (Ceuta on the Mediterranean coast in today's Morocco), the final outpost of the Roman Empire in North Africa, was taken by the Islamic army.

POLITICS

In the early years after Rome was founded in 753BC, kings were the head of government. The monarchy lasted just over 150 years, when the concept of a republic took over, probably stemming from the idolisation of ancient Greek culture. The original idea included separation of official roles, with executive, judicial and legislative branches of government. The Senate, the last of these sectors, held most of the power. Members were appointed by consuls (the top Roman magistrates), and senators were in for life unless expelled by the moral police, the censors. There was a complicated system of lower elected government officials, most striving to become part of the senatorial elite. The famous motto of SPQR, *Senatus Populusque Romanus,* began here, meaning a government run 'by the Senate and the people'. The main body of lawmakers was authorised to appoint a dictator in case of emergency. This right was exercised in an attempt to calm the situation during the Civil Wars of the late Republic when Julius Caesar was designated to fill the chief executive role. There were objections to his ascension, leading to his famous assassination in the Senate, but by then, the post had been established. His successor, Augustus, reluctantly took on the role, scrupulously maintaining the illusion that the Senate shared his power. The legislative body remained pretty much throughout the empire, but its control varied according to the whims of the man at the top. Subsequent emperors expanded and contracted the role and the territory over which they ruled, and their glories and excesses are well chronicled.

This system applied in its own way to North Africa and the outlying regions of the empire, as most of the inhabitants were far from the politics of Rome. Being granted the designation of *colonia* afforded them certain rights, and when citizenship was offered, their status and privileges were considerably improved. Later, as the provinces thrived, some senators came from these areas, but were probably either very wealthy villa owners or celebrated army veterans, possibly both. The military was an excellent way of rising through the ranks, and it was via this method that the Africans made their mark. The emperor Septimius Severus, for example, was born in Leptis Magna, Libya, and was appointed to the supreme role by his army followers (see page 12). Women were not allowed to be members of the government, although some of the empresses and no doubt many of the businesswomen were quite powerful in their roundabout way.

ECONOMY

The Roman provinces of North Africa were extremely important to the empire not least because of their economic possibilities. Their position gave Rome control of the southern shore of the Mediterranean that allowed not only the domination of trade and power of the region, but also justified their nickname of the sea as the 'Roman Lake'. In addition, the thin coastal strip that remained under Roman jurisdiction afforded a significant amount of agricultural income. The land was very fertile with warm sunshine in the spring and summer and plentiful rainfall in the autumn and winter. With the additional help of the Roman irrigation systems, the soil proved to be extremely productive. A Mediterranean climate is defined as one in which olive trees grow, and olives, as well as cereals, fruit and vegetables, were commercially grown. Up to 40% of all of Rome's granary needs were produced in the region. Large, wealthy estates that were usually the property of veteran military personnel provided excellent incomes for their owners and much food for the people across the sea. In addition, some of the more exotic building and decorative materials, such as the marble quarried at Chemtou in Tunisia, became fashionable, and were exported throughout the Roman world.

CULTURE

ARTWORK The Romans in North Africa left a very large legacy of artwork of the time, much of it depicting everyday occurrences. Mosaics often show ordinary things, such as ploughing the fields or harvesting grain. A few of the floors of dining rooms have been found that illustrate in great detail the extraordinary bounty of what could be, or perhaps even was, served on the table. Occasionally, more spectacular events were immortalised, for example gladiator fights and even an unarmed man, a Christian, for example, being devoured by a lion in the ring. Even mythological subjects, the gods and goddesses, were represented in terms of the era, showing clothing, hairstyles, etc. Certainly, much of what we know about the more typical life of Roman North Africans can be seen in these tiles.

Statues must have been produced in profusion as even now so many remain. Although they are usually stylised, consistency among items of dress gives a feel for what fashions must have been like. Being an officer in the army was something to be proud of and many recently promoted men commissioned commemorative reminders of themselves in uniform. Great men and women, or at least the wealthy ones, also had their features immortalised in stone. From these figures we get an idea of how people looked and frequently acted.

Busts and other depictions of real people also existed, although the accuracy of these effigies is suspect, as anyone who commissions a portrait wants to be seen at their best. Roman sculpture also had a stylistic purpose. Leaders and rulers had to inspire confidence, especially in their subjects in a far-off colony. For example, in North Africa, where locals were most unlikely ever to see their emperor, it was essential that the inhabitants felt they were being governed by just, fair, powerful, competent and, ideally, good-looking people. Certain distinctive traits had to remain in order for identification (such as Hadrian sporting a beard) so long as he could be represented as strong and virile. Sculpture businesses sprang up, with idealised, but headless bodies. The specific portrait heads, specially commissioned, could be added later.

Occasionally, a relatively realistic portrait was smuggled through, identifiable by its somewhat rougher style and less flattering depiction. There has been only one portrait found of Cleopatra Selene, the Queen of Mauretania from around 25BC, currently at the Cherchell Museum in Algeria. She's been recognised due to her 'heavy chin', an inherited trait from her father, Mark Anthony.

GRAVE MARKERS AND INSCRIPTIONS Much of what we know about life in Roman North Africa has come from cemeteries, or necropolises ('cities of the dead'). The dedications and reliefs on the graves give an incredible amount of information. Even after the names have worn away, the carved figures have provided a visual description of who was inside. Frequently couples are shown, in period dress, standing next to each other. Over them is often a protective god, usually Saturn,

MOSAICS

The Crisis of the Third Century actually encouraged one of the most delightful and telling art forms of the Roman Empire. As government broke down, the wealthy Romans no longer felt compelled to donate to philanthropic causes, such as public buildings, fountains (nymphaea) or temples. Instead, they decided to go inwards, showing off their wealth by domestic conspicuous consumption instead. One of the most obvious ways to declare how much money they had was to decorate their homes. These residences were often the sumptuous villas to which Romans had retired, typically long-term army veterans who were frequently granted large estates outside the towns. Whether as part of a working agriculture concern, or simply a place to lay back and relax, these enormous houses were usually lavishly embellished. Mosaics were not only an excellent way to enhance the appearance of a dining room or bathroom, but were also loud declarations of how much the owner could afford. There are examples of more accessible forms of the art in places like some of the public baths or even later religious buildings (although several Christian baptisteries were recycled from previous purposes) but the best stem from private villas.

Typically, mosaics were constructed of small coloured tiles, or tessera (the Greek word for four, as in 'four-sided'). Laid out on floors or walls, these artworks depict a huge variety of subjects. Some are mythological, telling the tales of the various trials, travails and exploits of the deities. Bathing areas could have stories of the birth of Venus, as she rises naked from the waves. Fountains and baths often had the face of Oceanus, the god of the river, or Neptune, god of the sea (especially prevalent in seaside areas).

Some of the most beautiful and elaborate mosaics have been found in dining rooms. Samples of the food that was going to be served were often depicted, in many cases in great detail. Much of what is known about Roman diets was discovered here. For example, in Timgad in Algeria, a huge mosaic shows oysters and prawns proving that even though the villa was some distance from the sea, the hosts could still afford to import seafood for the dinner table. Frequently, tributes to Bacchus, the god of wine and subsequent pleasure and intoxication, are placed here, perhaps as encouragement for the guests to enjoy themselves.

Other examples include daily life, showing the agriculture products and labourers on the estate. Special events are also celebrated, such as gladiatorial battles or the dispensing of justice at the Civil Basilica. Later, Christian themes appeared. In fact, most aspects of daily life, as well as subjects that concerned the Romans, are shown in scenes rendered in these little stones. Although mosaic art began long before this period and continues to this day, the best examples of this form of Roman illustration generally came from the 2nd to the 4th century AD and particularly so in the 3rd.

reclining in his powerful but relaxed stance, half naked and stylised. Other markers present offerings to the gods, showing in stone what was offered in life. There are many such memorials, charming, amusing and very informative.

Inscriptions are essential to our formal knowledge of Roman history. On the North African sites, remains of carved dedications, whether on memorials, sides of buildings or bases of arches, give us information on specific people and when they actually lived. For example, it might be possible to work out the duration of an important governor or consul by the description of what was done in his tenth year of office. In places such as Leptis Magna, a few inscriptions have been found that are bilingual, in both Latin and Punic, which work as a sort of Rosetta Stone, providing translations between the two languages. Although many of the dedications found consisted of flowery language to ingratiate the donor to higher powers, much of this flattery can be sifted through to distil some real information. As with the Egyptians, those people who found a good engraver or were lucky enough for their carvings to remain intact, have a good chance of remaining immortal – even if we don't know anything about them besides their names.

RELIGION

PAGANISM Christianity became the official religion of Roman North Africa when the emperor Constantine the Great converted in AD312. Before that, religious belief was pagan, with a tradition of polytheism going back to the original inhabitants of the area. The Phoenicians brought their gods with them, while the Egyptians, coming in from the east, also carried along a few cults. The Greeks, when they founded Cyrenaica, also brought their religious figures with them. As many of the later settlers were from Italy, their gods followed. Deities were often very personal, and people didn't want to go unprotected. Rather than accepting one god to cover all eventualities, the pagans had several, each with a specific purpose; it suited the needs of individuals in an unscientific age when strange things happened that were totally incomprehensible. As Dr John Swanson, Assistant Provost for Special Academic Programs at the American University in Cairo, argues, 'Religion was the most important way to assert some control in a world that was full of both physical and spiritual danger.' Therefore:

- It was important to get the attention of the forces that had influence (water, rivers, illness, etc); then they had to be named, as knowing what they were called was necessary to get their notice.
- It was essential to domesticate the natural forces: a way had to be found to get them to a place on earth (eg: temples), and then incarnated into an image (eg: a statue, figurine).
- These forces had to be bribed to do what was asked of them. These requests could be accompanied by sacrifice, beautiful gifts (eg: of food or clothing), or the best of what was available or willing to be relinquished.

There were many physical depictions of these forces. They eventually became personified into individual gods and goddesses. Over time, these deities developed personalities, many endowed with traits with which humans could better identify (eg: nobility and loyalty but also jealousy and greed, etc). It was easier to believe that the being that determined one's life was someone to whom the believer could relate. It was also then possible to offer something the god or goddess might like. The Egyptians were the first to leave traces of all powerful beings that had names, but their influence faded, so that by the time of the Romans in North Africa, only a few cult figures remained (eg: Isis and Serapis). The Phoenicians, and especially the Carthaginians, had a coterie of immortals that, to some degree, remained powerful. When the Greeks and then Romans came, many of these important names became absorbed into the concurrent echelon of deities.

By the time of the full occupation, approximately AD40, when Mauretania became absorbed into the empire, Roman gods were the ones most worshipped. A North African variation, however, is that Saturn, rather than Jupiter, tended to be the chief figure. In Greek mythology Cronus, the ruling Titan, was overthrown by his son Zeus. In Rome, the names were changed so that Cronus became Saturn, and Zeus became Jupiter. The cult of Saturn continued, often confused with Jupiter as the main god, and his primary role was in aiding fertility and agriculture. In many Roman cities, whether in Italy or in the provinces, including North Africa, the

There were many, many gods, and each household, like each believer, had favourites. The most common ones in North Africa are listed below, as well as their non-Roman counterparts. Note how many deities are associated with agriculture and fertility, critical in an area in which grain is so important. This list is not definitive.

Roman	Greek	Other	God/dess of
Saturn	Cronus	Baal, Baal Hammon (Punic)	Father of the gods; supreme god; fertility
Jupiter	Zeus	Baal, Baal Hammon (Punic)	Supreme god; sky, thunder, etc
Juno	Hera	Calestis (Carthaginian) Tanit (Punic) Astarte (Carthaginian)	Marriage, wife of supreme god
Minerva	Athena		Wisdom
Bacchus and/ or Liber Pater	Dionysus	Shadrapa (Punic)	Wine, intoxication (also mysteries)
Neptune	Poseidon		Sea
Pluto	Hades		Underworld, also fertility (rebirth)
Oceanus	Okeanus		World's fresh water
Ceres, Cereses	Demeter	Cereses, North African	Grain
Proserpine	Persephone, Kore		Spring Daughter of Ceres
Cupid	Eros		Love
Diana	Artemis		Hunting
Mercury	Hermes		Messenger
Venus	Aphrodite	Anath (Carthaginian)	Love
Apollo	Apollo		Sun, truth, beauty
Aescalapius	Askelapios	Eshmun (Punic)	Medicine
Cybele and/or Magna Mater	Gaia, Rhea	Originated in Asia	Fertility, Mother Earth Mother of the gods
Frugiter		North African only	Crops
Mithras		Originated in Asia	Sun
Isis		Egyptian	Magic, resurrection
Serapis		Egyptian	Another name for Osiris, the Egyptian god of the dead
Hercules	Heracles	Melkart (Punic)	Not a god, but a mythic hero (son of Jupiter)

Capitolium, or capitol, was a prominently placed temple built to honour the three most important deities: Saturn/Jupiter, Lord of the gods; Juno, his wife and protector of marriage; and Minerva, Jupiter's daughter and goddess of wisdom.

Two other eastern deities developed cults that had significant followings. Mithras was an ancient figure, dating back to the 15th century BC in India, although more commonly associated with Persia. Mithraism was embraced mostly by officers in the Roman army, probably due to the virtues of respect and obedience demanded by a religion that mirrored those of the military. One of the versions of his birth has him born in a cave, and the association of the hardships of his life and his concern with the good of mankind have caused some believers to make comparisons with the Christian story. Temples to Mithras have been discovered mostly in towns that began as army camps. Setif in Algeria was founded as a Mithraic city.

The cult of Isis began in ancient Egypt. Originally part of the divine triumvirate with Osiris (later renamed Serapis) her husband and brother and god of the dead, and Horus, her son, Isis's importance increased as the Egyptians began to grant her powers of magic and resurrection. She was later absorbed into the Greek belief system as a way of incorporating eastern loyalty into the Hellenic world, becoming associated with more conventional fertility goddesses. The cult was tailored so that Isis would not be restricted to a particular region. In a way, she was also a precursor to Christianity, advocating a universal, rather than specific belief. Alternatively reviled and accepted by the Romans, there were some later notable North African-born advocates, including the writer Apuleius and the emperor Septimius Severus. To this day there remains a flickering of interest in this religion.

THE IMPERIAL CULT When Julius Caesar defeated the forces of Pompey at Thapsus in 46BC, he returned as sole leader of the previous triumvirate. Effectively offered the emperorship, Caesar helped to sway the populace in his favour by declaring he had divine lineage, that is, he was descended from Aeneas (the Trojan hero of the *Aeneid*), who was allegedly Venus's progeny. Here began the cult of the emperor, in which each subsequent ruler claimed he was god, and demanded the reverence due to a deity. Some rulers took this role very much to heart; for example, the Temple of Septimius Severus in Djemila, Algeria, is one of the most impressive buildings on the site. The assigning of divinity to an emperor was among the conflicts between the state and embryonic Christianity (see below) and one of the reasons for the latter's persecution. However, when Constantine embraced the new faith, the Imperial Cult came to an end.

CHRISTIANITY Despite the persecutions of Christian followers, in force by AD200, and lasting, more or less, till the adoption of the faith by Constantine in AD312, the religion took a firm hold in North Africa. Although Jews were already settled in the area, as the first ones came from Egypt (via Cyrenaica), Christianity seems to have come to the province independently, possibly brought in by sailors, or even settlers from Rome. Tunisia and especially Carthage became the centre of the western empire's most devout Christian believers.

One of the main reasons for the success of the Roman Empire was its acceptance and even absorption of differing faiths. The difficulties with the Christians was that they did they not adhere to the tenets of polytheism. This differing conviction wouldn't necessarily be a problem, but the Christians, in their denial, refused to accept the deification of the emperor (a significant religious and powerful figure in Roman times). This conflict could be circumvented, as it was with the Jews whose belief in one god didn't cause ripples, but many of the new converts felt that they shouldn't pay tribute to an imperial deity. The Christians didn't want to pay taxes or honour the emperor as a god. When they did contribute to the imperial purse, even without paying the attendant reverence, there didn't seem to be a problem. Persecutions increased and decreased as did corresponding rebellion.

Once Constantine became a Christian representative, such singling out should have stopped. However, various factions developed that split the Church and caused a great deal of controversy and in some cases destruction. The Bishop of Carthage, Donatus, around the period of Constantine's conversion in AD312, became the eponymous founder of the Donatists. This sect, born in North Africa and particularly powerful there, claimed that those Christians who relinquished their faith during the time of Roman persecutions should not be allowed back into the Church. This tenet violated one of the more mainstream beliefs of forgiveness.

These returnees were called 'traditors': 'someone who had handed over' (and in some Latin dictionaries, defined as traitor). Not only did the Donatists believe that these betrayers should not be Christian, but also that any religious duty performed by them was invalid. The faction took serious hold, with centres springing up throughout North Africa. Verbal and sometimes physical battles ensued. Periodically, for example at the Council Arles in AD314, the movement was banned, with adherents being threatened with excommunication. However, official sanctions did not deter the believers. Throughout the rest of the Roman occupation followers of Donatism continued supporting their style of Christianity, the practice stopping only with the Islamic invasion of the 7th century AD.

Another group of alleged heretics, the followers of Arius, a spokesman in Alexandria, questioned the divinity of Christ. Although this sect never flourished in Roman North Africa, it made an appearance when the Arian-believing Vandals invaded in AD429.

A TYPICAL ROMAN TOWN

Towns built during the period of the Roman occupation remained remarkably consistent throughout the empire, changing mostly due to the locations chosen for sites, rather than style. There were standard things that appeared in all settlements. Certain buildings were a function of the size and importance of a town and found in all similar urban centres.

Initially built for military use and constructed by the army, especially in the colonies, the Roman town plan was based on a square grid. The town of Thamugadi (Timgad, Algeria) is such a good example that from the air an idealised ground plan is still visible. Remains of a very typical town can be seen there. By having similar layouts and virtually the same facilities in any settlement, no matter where it was located, soldiers and even settlers could feel at home regardless of which colony in which they might find themselves. This repetition was extremely useful to the professional Roman army man, who might be stationed anywhere in the empire. In the early days, the fighting forces came from distant regions, possibly to guarantee Roman rather than local loyalty. At the very least, they could be familiar with their surroundings. These towns were like the Holiday Inns of their day, with facilities and their position hardly varying from colony to colony, so that the professionals could get on with their business.

Many of these municipalities originated from barracks for the Roman soldiers. Development followed, with either the billets themselves being transformed into permanent cities, or nearby residential areas springing up around them. The town of Lambaesis in Algeria is an excellent example of an original location for the soldiers, with a civilian enclave just outside. The amphitheatre, a place of entertainment for both, lies between the two.

All towns had two main roads, coming together at some point in the centre. The boulevard that went north–south was called the *cardo* (Latin for 'a cardinal point'), while the one that went east–west was named the *decumanus* ('belonging to the tenth legion'), sometimes with an arch or marker where they crossed. At Leptis Magna in Libya the dramatic Arch of Septimius Severus is placed right at the intersection. These routes were often covered or lined with columns and ran right through the town.

The **forum** was the main square (known as the *agora* in Greece, and the Greek-flavoured Cyrenaica). Here was where most of the administrative and legal offices were located, and sometimes the markets, if there were no specific areas for them elsewhere. The **civil basilica** was a public building for the hearing of law cases (as compared with the later ecclesiastical basilica, which referred to Church uses). There

MODEL OF A ROMAN TOWN

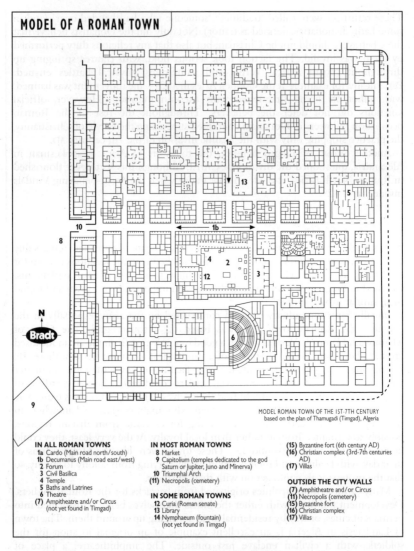

MODEL ROMAN TOWN OF THE 1ST-7TH CENTURY
based on the plan of Thamugadi (Timgad), Algeria

IN ALL ROMAN TOWNS
1a Cardo (Main road north/south)
1b Decumanus (Main road east/west)
2 Forum
3 Civil Basilica
4 Temple
5 Baths and Latrines
6 Theatre
(7) Ampitheatre and/or Circus
(not yet found in Timgad)

IN SOME ROMAN TOWNS
12 Curia (Roman senate)
13 Library
14 Nymphaeum (fountain)
(not yet found in Timgad)

IN MOST ROMAN TOWNS
8 Market
9 Capitolium (temples dedicated to the god Saturn or Jupiter, Juno and Minerva)
10 Triumphal Arch
(11) Necropolis (cemetery)

(15) Byzantine fort (6th century AD)
(16) Christian complex (3rd-7th centuries AD)
(17) Villas

OUTSIDE THE CITY WALLS
(7) Amphitheatre and/or Circus
(11) Necropolis (cemetery)
(15) Byzantine fort
(16) Christian complex
(17) Villas

was also a **temple**, usually dedicated to a specific deity. In some cases, this god could be the emperor, as part of the imperial cult (see *Religion*, page 24). In Djemila in Algeria, the east side of the forum is dominated by the Temple of Septimius Severus (emperor AD193–211). By virtue of its central position, as well as where the official buildings were, this square also became the central meeting place for the people.

Found everywhere in the city were **public baths**. The bathing facilities throughout the ancient Roman Empire were spectacular, often proving the most impressive buildings in a town, and certainly leaving some of the best remains to be seen today. Constructed of tile and often with huge arches for the larger halls, the baths were frequently decked with marble and decorated with mosaics. Some of the most beautiful art works discovered were found on the floors of these complexes. The effort put into their construction reflected the time people spent here. Not only did users clean themselves (although a few of the wealthier homes had private baths, most of their inhabitants visited the public versions), they also came to chat, gossip and linger. These complexes were social, as well as hygienic. Comprising several main areas, the baths could be enormous. Typically, there were three main areas for cleaning: the tepidarium, with luke-warm water; the caldarium, with hot; and the frigidarium, with cold. The last frequently included a pool. Visitors went from room to room. Water was piped in, running throughout the rooms. Heat came from below, via a series of fires under a floor that was propped up by stacks of tiles (hypocausts). Gymnasiums and palestrae (exercise grounds) were often alongside the baths, for those who needed a bit of exertion before they washed.

The **latrines** were an essential part of the baths, as this area was where the entire populace went to relieve itself. Although some of the wealthier houses might have had private washing facilities, their toilets only went as far as chamber pots, which the servants emptied into the streets. The public latrines had water flushing through them, recycling the wastewater from the baths, and were very social affairs. Rows of adjoining seats have been found on the ruins, without dividers between them.

The **theatre** was semicircular with lines of seats rising up, usually built into an existing incline. These venues were often positioned so that a spectacular view, such as a stretch of coastline, or hills rising behind, could be seen, incorporating the natural landscape into part of the scenery. The theatre was an important part of Roman life, providing culture and entertainment to the people. Lifting many of the principles and concepts from the Greek stage, including plot lines, performers acted in masks that represented stock and recognisable characters. Although tragedy was occasionally performed, comedy was more popular. Some of the leading playwrights were Seneca, Terence, Plautus and Apuleius, the last of whom came from North Africa. Although the tradition of the Greek theatre is more prevalent than Roman today, with the tragedies of Aeschylus, Euripides and Sophocles and the comedies of Aristophanes, some Roman plays are still performed as part of the repertoire of many classical theatre companies around the world; the *Golden Ass* by Apuleius was recently revived at the Globe Theatre in London. In more contemporary terms but still very much in the tradition, Stephen Sondheim's *A Funny Thing Happened on the Way to the Forum*, a musical inspired by the works of Plautus, upholds the ancient Roman spirit.

The **amphitheatre**, located outside the city walls, played host to a completely different sort of entertainment. This enormous circular building with seating rising up all the way around held gladiatorial events. Open to the air, the more expensive seats could have large awnings rolled out over them on hot days. A typical programme of entertainment was presented to show how the government looked after its people, for example:

- *1st The state provided protection against beasts*
  The morning show would consist of hunting animals, wild creatures, such as lions or tigers, imported specially for these events.
- *2nd Justice was seen to be done against criminals*
  The midday performance would kill criminals, including, at times during the 2nd–4th centuries, Christians. These executions could be done very creatively, sometimes even combining the morning events with animals pitted against their human opponents.
- *3rd The government could be relied upon to defend its people from foreign enemies*
  The afternoon was reserved for the best-liked event, the battle of the gladiators. Not always a fight between slaves or foreigners, it was possible for a competent, successful free man to make an excellent living. Gladiators themselves were very popular, with fans following their teams similar to

today's football enthusiasts. There have been mosaics found that depict the programmes, as well as the different colours of the rival factions.

Frequently part of the entertainment complex was the **circus**, a large lozenge-shaped 450m long by 100m wide *spina* (track) on which chariots were raced. Very few traces of these venues still exist, and where they do, as in Leptis Magna in Libya, not much can be seen beside some marks in the dirt.

Many Roman towns had specially built **markets**. Some of these sites still have marble tables for their wares (marble stays colder than room temperature, making it a good medium for holding fresh goods, eg: fish). In some cases, sculptures and carvings on the table legs still show some of the items, or the proprietors.

The **capitolium** was a temple complex, often away from the city centre, that revered the main triumvirate of deities: Saturn/Jupiter, the king and sky god; Juno, his wife and protector of marriage; and Minerva, the goddess of wisdom (see *Religion*, page 23). Very important and impressive, even today the remains have large columns rising up and are visible from far way.

The **triumphal arch**, dedicated to a visiting emperor, is often the most visible part of today's ruins, and was probably equally obvious in its day. The large arch rising above the city was meant either to immortalise, or ingratiate, the donors to whatever emperor was to be flattered. Trajan and Hadrian appear frequently, while some of the ones to Septimius Severus may have been constructed by the ruler himself.

Outside the city walls was the **necropolis**, or cemetery. Some of these burial places are very impressive, such as those in Cyrene in Libya, where the tombs are cut into the canyon walls. Found on these sites are the grave markers and tombstones which give an idea as to not only who these people were, but also how they lived. Some of these death memorials give excellent glimpses into their lives, showing their names, faces, clothing, goods and even likes and dislikes. The museums adjoining the sites show off a large collection.

The more important cities where the Roman Senate would sit had a **curia** or Senate house, usually in the forum. Not every town had such important representation, but the few that did housed this government body in fine style.

Probably in most cities, but so far found only in Timgad, is the **library**, where parchments were stored. Probably a smaller version of the one in Alexandria, this storehouse did not hold books but documents. Scholars would come to study and discourse, rather than to borrow material.

Although not yet found in Timgad, in many other urban centres in the Roman Empire the **nymphaeum** (or fountain) would bring fresh water flowing into the city. Often dedicated to some wealthy donor, very impressive examples can be found in many of the North African towns. They were flanked by sculptures, perhaps of Oceanus, god of fresh water, or water nymphs.

After the Vandals came and went, the Byzantines or later Romans returned in the 6th century. Although back on their turf, control was tenuous, and the inhabitants felt they needed to reinforce their position. Using stone that was already cut into usable pieces from the previous buildings, the new tenants built large **forts and walls** to protect themselves. The one in Timgad is very visible, but others, such as in Dougga in Tunisia, are also very prominent.

When Christianity arrived, **churches** began springing up to house the faithful. Although there were periodic persecutions of the new religion, the believers were usually tolerated, as were their sacred buildings. Sometimes the smaller baths were converted to baptismals (as in Djemila in Algeria). In Timgad, the Christian complex was where the rebel faction that split from the main church, the Donatists, worshipped (see *Religion*, page 24). However, all the sites that remained inhabited beyond the 3rd century had churches. The ones in Apollonia in Libya are particularly striking.

Outside the towns were the **villas, or huge estates**. Wealthy residences were usually on nearby acres of the extremely fertile agricultural land that made North Africa such a lucrative part of the empire. Grain, particularly wheat, olives and their oil, vines, grapes and wine, *garum* (fish paste from the harvest of the sea) and many other products fed not only North Africa but also Rome and much of the empire. The owners became very rich and to show off their position, invested heavily in their homes. Some of the most beautiful mosaics and artwork come from these private houses. These large complexes were often two storeys high, with central courtyards that provided cool in the summer's heat, and warmth in the winter. Slaves and workers also lived on the premises. The masters were usually loyal veterans who had served in the army and were rewarded with wealthy spoils. Although seemingly a magnanimous gesture by the government, having ex-soldiers in place in foreign colonies was another way to protect the area for Rome. These villas were functioning establishments, more like working plantations than retirement homes.

2

Practical Information

Even though the Romans saw their provinces of North Africa as one region, the area today represents four different countries. Morocco, Algeria, Tunisia and Libya each have their own geography, climate, pre- and post-Roman history and political system, not to mention all the other features that make their nations and nationalities unique. There are some things common, or at least very alike, to all these regions beside their ancestry. Both the similarities and differences should be taken into account before planning a visit to any of these countries.

WHEN TO VISIT

The best time to visit the Roman coast of North Africa is in the spring. Situated in a fertile belt that enjoys breezes coming off the sea, the region is green and overladen with wildflowers. There can be quite a bit of rain, particularly in the early part of the season, but it freshens the dustier sites and keeps away the likes of snakes and scorpions, that prefer drier weather. Autumn is also a good period to visit, with comfortable temperatures and harvesting taking place. Nights can be cool in both these seasons, so take something warm to wear in the evening, as well as your raincoat.

It might seem obvious not to visit these predominantly desert countries in summer, but this truism applies mainly to the south. For the Roman coast, June through September is a fine time to visit, especially if planning to enjoy the beaches. Temperatures can get fairly high, especially away from the sea and on the sites, but the weather will be sunny and reliable. This period is high season for the seaside resorts and some of them can get very crowded in July and August. Then again, facilities are open and geared up for visitors.

Winter is fine for the same areas to be avoided in the summer, when daytime temperatures are bearable. It can get cold at night, so be prepared with proper clothing. In the north, days may be cool, grey and wet, with sunshine something of a rarity. From October to May cruise ships generally stop running in the Mediterranean, as the seas can get very rough. Even the Phoenicians, Greeks and Romans knew that.

Try to avoid visiting these Muslim countries during the month of **Ramadan** (a floating, lunar-calendar based religious holiday occurring sometime during September and October) when normal timetables are disrupted. See *Sawm*, page 64.

HIGHLIGHTS

For many people, it's a surprise to find such incredible Roman cities on the opposite side of the Mediterranean. As these sites are the emphasis of this book, they get top priority in the highlights. Below are my favourites, in order:

- Leptis Magna (Libya)
- Sabratha (Libya)
- Timgad (Algeria)
- Dougga (Tunisia)
- El Djem (Tunisia)
- Cyrene (Libya)
- Sbeitla (Tunisia)
- Volubilis (Morocco)
- Djemila (Algeria)
- Bulla Regia (Tunisia)

Other highlights worth sampling are:

- The coastline: the whole range, from the developed resorts of Agadir, Morocco and Monastir, Tunisia, to the deserted beaches close to Cyrene in Libya
- The cities: some of the continent's most interesting, from Marrakech, Morocco, with its spectacular souks, to the intense atmosphere of Algiers, Algeria, to the friendliness of Tripoli, Libya
- The architecture: particularly the mosques, from the enormous ones of Hassan II in Casablanca, Morocco, and Emir Abdelkader in Constantine, Algeria, to the tiny iconic ones on the island of Djerba, Tunisia
- The desert: not strictly within the scope of this book, some of the dramatic scenery of the Sahara, including the Merzouga dunes, Morocco, and the rock art and landscape of both the Tasili N'Ajer, Algeria, and the Jebel Acacus, Libya
- The museums, particularly the Bardo in Tunis, Tunisia, which quite possibly has the world's greatest collections of Roman mosaics, and the Jamahiriya in Libya, with its stunning assembly of pieces from its ancient sites.

Generally, suggested excursions to the Roman sites depart from their closest modern cities. It's probably easiest to go from place to place using the main locations as a base, and radiating out from there. If you have extra time, take advantage of the other recommended things to see in the area, as even though the ancient remains are the highlight, the other attractions certainly warrant a view, and they do provide a break from temple overload!

TOUR OPERATORS

Listed below are companies that provide travel to more than one of the countries described in this book. Nearly all the agencies that offer tours including Algeria and/or Libya specialise in historical or archaeological site-based trips. In some cases it is possible to add additional locations and resorts. For specific-region specialists, see the relevant listing in the chapter/section on the individual country. Please check with the companies directly before planning your journey as these destinations are subject to change.

UK

Ace Study Tours 48 Sawston Rd, Babraham, Cambridge CB22 3AP; ☎ 01223 835055; e enquiries@acestudytours.co.uk; www.acestudytours.co.uk. Cultural travel to Morocco & Libya.

Andante Travels The Old Barn, Old Rd, Alderbury, Salisbury SP5 3AR; ☎ 01722 713800;

e tours@andantetravels.co.uk; www.andantetravels.co.uk. Specialists in archaeological tours to Morocco, Tunisia & Libya.

Cox & Kings Sixth Floor, 30 Millbank, London SW1P 4EE; ☎ 020 7873 5000; e sales@coxandkings.co.uk; www.coxandkings.co.uk. Upmarket specialist tours to Morocco, Tunisia & Libya.

Explore Worldwide Ltd Nelson Hse, 55 Victoria Rd, Farnborough GU14 7PA; ↘ 0845 013 1537; ℮ Hello@explore.col.uk; www.explore.co.uk. General adventure company supplying various levels of travel to countries including Morocco, Tunisia & Libya.
Fulani Travel 14 Fron Wnion, Dolgellau, Gwynedd LL40 1SL; ↘/f 01341 421969; ℮ info@ fulanitravel.co.uk; www.fulanitravel.co.uk
Simoon Travel 22 Thorparch Rd, London SW8 4RU; ↘ 0207 622 6263; www.simoontravel.com. Primarily

Libya specialists, Algeria has recently been introduced on the itinerary.
Steppes Travel Travel Hse, 51 Castle St, Cirencester, Glos GL7 1QD; ↘ 01285 880980; www.steppestravel.co.uk
The Traveller & Palinquin 92–93 Great Russell St, London WC1B 3PS; ↘ 020 7436 9343; www.the-traveller.co.uk. Specialists in historical & cultural travel, offering both tours & tailor-made holidays to Algeria, Tunisia & Libya.

IRISH REPUBLIC
Sunway Holidays Marina Hse, Clarence St, Dun Laoghaire, Co. Dublin; ↘ 1 288 6828; www.sunway.ie. Sun holidays to Morocco & Tunisia.

AUSTRALIA & NEW ZEALAND
Intrepid 360 Bourke St, Melbourne, Victoria 3000; ↘ 3 9473 2626; ℮ bourke@intrepidtravel.com; www.intrepidtravel.com. Also branches throughout Australia & in the UK. Adventure travel with a 39-day Cairo to Casablanca overland tour that includes Libya, Tunisia, Algeria & Morocco.

Middle East Tours ↘ 2 9605 3981; ℮ info@ middleeasttours.com.au; www.middleeasttours.com.au. Tours to Morocco, Algeria, Tunisia & Libya including visits to the archaeological sites.

USA
Adventure Center 1311 63rd St, Suite 200, Emeryville, CA 94608; ↘ 800 228 8747; www.adventurecenter.com. Adventure-based tours that cover Morocco, Tunisia & Libya.
Archaeological Tours 271 Madison Av, Suite 904, New York, NY 10016; ↘ 866 740 5130; ℮ ArcTours@ aol.com; www.archaeologicaltrs.com. Tours to archaeological sites in Morocco, Algeria Tunisia & Libya, led by specialists.

High Country Passage 500 Third St, Suite 455, San Francisco, CA 94107; ↘ 800 395 3288; ℮ info@ hcptravel.com; www.hcptravel.com. An upmarket company that also represents the Smithsonian & the American Museum of Natural History; tours to Morocco, as well as a history-based cruise to the region.

MALTA
Mifsud Brothers Ltd 26 South St, Valletta, VLT 1102; ↘ +356 21 232157; ℮ info@mbl.com.mt; www.mbl.com.mt

RED TAPE

Each of the countries of the Roman coast of North Africa has a different system of government, requiring varying prerequisites for visitors. These regulations can change at any time, especially in Algeria and Libya. Travellers should check with the relevant embassy or consulate for the latest information before planning their trip. The details below were correct at the time of going to press.

MOROCCO Citizens of the UK, EU (including Ireland), Australia, New Zealand, Canada and the US require a passport, valid for at least six months from the date of entry into the country, for the duration of their visit. It is essential that visitors make sure that their passports are stamped on arrival into the country. Return tickets are not mandatory.

Visas No visas are needed for a period of up to three months. British nationals (overseas) or British subjects, *without* the right of abode in the UK require a visa.

Customs Visitors can bring in 200 cigarettes or 50 cigars or 400 grams of tobacco; one litre of wine and one litre of spirits; 5 grams perfume. Cameras are permitted.

ALGERIA Citizens of the UK, EU (including Ireland), Australia, New Zealand, Canada and the US, require a passport, valid for at least six months from the date of entry into the country.

Visas Visas are needed by all visitors except those people who will be in transit for less than 24 hours with sufficient funds and documentation and who will not leave the airport (otherwise, a transit visa must be issued). Single-entry tourist visas are issued for 30 days; multiple-entry ones are valid for coming and going for up to 90 days. Business visas can be issued for up to 90 days. Costs vary depending on nationality, and can be obtained at the consulate, or consular section of the embassy. Time required to obtain a visa is dependent upon nationality, but three days is the minimum for British nationals, ten if submitted by post or at peak times. Although there is no longer a requisite amount of funds for each day's stay, foreign currency must be declared on arrival and receipts must be kept (but are not always checked). Return tickets are mandatory.

Customs Visitors can bring in up to 200 cigarettes, 50 cigars or 400 grams of tobacco as well as one bottle of spirits and two bottles of wine. All valuable personal items including electrical goods, jewellery, cameras, video cameras, etc should be recorded on the Currency Declaration Form on entry as there have been instances where visitors who have neglected to do so have had their personal effects confiscated upon departure, although this reprimand is not often put into effect.

TUNISIA Citizens of the UK, EU (including Ireland, but with the exception of those listed below) and Canada, require a passport, valid for at least the duration of their stay from the date of entry into the country. No visas are needed for a period of up to three months. Return tickets are mandatory.

Citizens of the Czech Republic, Estonia, Latvia, Lithuania, Poland and the Slovak Republic require a passport, valid for at least the duration of their stay from the date of entry into the country. They must travel on a recognised package holiday.

Citizens of Cyprus require a passport, valid for at least the duration of their stay from the date of entry into the country. A visa is also needed that allows a stay of up to three months and can be obtained on arrival. Return tickets are mandatory.

Citizens of the US require a passport, valid for at least the duration of their stay from the date of entry into the country. No visas are needed for a stay of up to four months. Return tickets are mandatory.

Citizens of Australia and New Zealand require a passport, valid for at least the duration of their stay from the date of entry into the country. A visa is also needed that allows a stay of up to four months and can be obtained on arrival at immigration. Return tickets are mandatory.

Customs Visitors can bring in 200 cigarettes, one bottle of alcoholic beverage and a reasonable amount (whatever that means!) of perfume.

LIBYA Israeli passport holders, or those people whose documents contain Israeli stamps (whether valid or expired), will be refused entry into the country. It is also difficult for women travelling alone to get a visa and it is therefore recommended they join a group, at least in order to enter Libya. There has been a recent change in policy and it is now required that visitors have the relevant identification details in their passports translated into Arabic. This service can be provided by the tour operator, for which they will charge an additional fee. Otherwise, the transcription must be made by an official translator.

Allowing for the above provisos, citizens of the UK, EU (including Ireland), Australia, New Zealand and Canada require a passport valid for at least six months from the start of their stay in Libya.

Visas Visas are required for all citizens except nationals of Arab countries and Malta. Visas must be obtained before departure, normally costing around L50 (US$100). At present, tourist visas are not being issued to US citizens (although business visas are available to travellers who have Libyan sponsors). However, this situation is very likely to change in the near future. Check with the tour operator or embassy far enough ahead either to allow time for bureaucracy in the processing of a visa (sometimes up to several months), or to change plans.

Recent legislation now requires that tourists have a minimum amount of US$1,000 (or approximately L500) in cash on entering the country and will be checked on arrival. Sometimes documentation that the tour has been pre-paid, or the assurances of the tour operators themselves, will satisfy this demand.

With some exceptions, tourists must travel either with a tour group, or hire a local guide on their arrival.

Customs Visitors can bring in tobacco and alcohol permitted for personal use.

Ⓔ EMBASSIES AND CONSULATES

MOROCCO
Abroad
UK 49 Queen's Gate Gdns, London SW7 5NE; ✆ 020 7581 5001; e mail@sifamaldn.org. Visa section: Diamond Hse, 97 Praed St, London W2 INT; ✆ 020 7724 0719; e moroccanconsulate.uk@pop3.hiway.co.uk
Irish Republic 39 Raglan Rd, Ballsbridge, Dublin 4; ✆ 1 660 9449; e sifamdub@indigo.ie

Australia & New Zealand There is no embassy, but the Consul-General is at 11 West St, North Sydney, NSW; ✆ 2 99576717; f 2 99231053
Canada 38 Range Rd, Ottawa, Ontario K1N 8J4; ✆ 613 236 7391; e ifamaot@bellnet.ca; www.ambassade-maroc.ottawa.on.ca
USA 1601 21st St NW, Washington, DC 20009; ✆ 202 4627979; e fmheld@embassyofmorocco.us

In Morocco
UK 28 Av SAR Sidi Mohamed Souissi, 10105 (BP 45), Rabat; ✆ 537 63 33 33; f +212 (0)537 75 87 09; http://ukinmorocco.fco.gov.uk/en
Irish Republic Handled by the embassy in Portugal: Rua da Imprensa, Estrela 1-4, 1200684 Lisbon; ✆ 21 392 9440; f 21 397 7363

Australia & New Zealand Handled by the Canadian Embassy
Canada (consulate) 13 Bis rue Jaâfa-as-Sadik, Agdal, Rabat; ✆ 537 68 74 00; e rabat@dfait-maeci.gc.ca
USA 2 Av de Mohamed, El Fassi, Rabat; ✆ 537 76 22 65; e rabat.usembassy.gov/contact.html

ALGERIA
Abroad
UK & Irish Republic 1 Holland Pk, London W11 3RS; ✆ 020 7221 7800; f 0207 221 04 48
Australia & New Zealand 9 Terrigal Cres, O'Malley, ACT 2606; ✆ 2 6286 7355; e info@algeriaemb.org.au

Canada 500 Wilbrod St, Ottawa, Ontario K1N 6N2; ✆ 613 789 8505; e info@embassyalgeria.ca
USA 2118 Kalorama Rd NW, Washington, DC 20008; ✆ 202 265 2800; e ambassadoroffice@yahoo.com

In Algeria

UK 12 Rue Slimane Amirat (Ex Lucien Reynaud), Hydra, Algiers; ☎ 21 23 00 68; www.britishembassy.gov.uk/algeria
Irish Republic Embassy of Ireland 'in Algeria' is apparently based in Switzerland, at Kirchenfeldstrasse 68, CH-3005 Berne; ☎ 41 31 352 1442; e berneembassy@dfa.ie
Australia & New Zealand Handled by the embassy in France: 4 Rue Jean Rey, Paris 75724, Cedex 15; ☎ 33 1 4059 3300; e Info.Paris@dfat.gov.au

Canada 18 Mustapha Khalef St, Ben Aknoun 16035, Algiers (postal address: PO Box 464, Ben Aknoun 16306, Algiers); ☎ 770 08 30 00; e alger@international.gc.ca
USA 05 Chemin Cheikh Bachir Ibrahimi, El-Biar 16030, Algiers; ☎ 770 08 2000; e Algiers_webmaster@state.gov; http://Algiers.usembassy.gov

TUNISIA
Abroad

UK & Irish Republic 29 Prince's Gate, London SW7 1QG; ☎ 020 7584 8117; f 020 7225 2884
Australia & New Zealand (consulate-general) Suite 211, Edgecliff Centre, 203–33 Head Rd, Edgecliff, NSW 2027; ☎ 2 9327 1258; e constunsyd@bigpond.com

Canada 515 O'Connor St, Ottawa, Ontario K1S 3P8; ☎ 613 237 0330; f 613 237 7939
USA 515 Massachusetts Av NW, Washington, DC 20005; ☎ 202 862 1850; f 202 862 1858

In Tunisia

UK Rue du Lac Windermere, Les Berges du Lac, Tunis 1053; ☎ 71 108 700; e TVI.tunis@fco.gov.uk
Irish Republic Dalmas SARL, 1 Rue Laroussi Haddad, Zi Sidi Rezig 2033; ☎ 98 307 364; f 71 893 182
Australia & New Zealand Handled by the Canadian Embassy

Canada 3 Senegal St, PO Box 31, 1002 Tunis-Belvedere; ☎ 71 104 190; e tunis@international.gc.ca
USA Les Berges du Lac 1053, Tunis; ☎ 71 107 000; tunisia.usembassy.gov/contact.html

LIBYA
Abroad

UK & Irish Republic 5 Knightsbridge, London SW1X 7LY; ☎ 020 7201 8280; f 020 7245 0588
Australia & New Zealand 50 Culgoa Circuit, O'Malley, ACT 2606; ☎ 2 6290 7900; f 02 6286 4522

Canada 81 Metcalfe St, Suite 1000, Ottawa, Ontario K1P 6K7; ☎ 613 230 0919; e info@libya-canada.org
USA (Libyan Representative Office) 2600 Virginia Av, NW, Suite 705, Washington, DC 20037; ☎ 202 944 9601; f 202 944 9606

In Libya

UK PO Box 4206, Tripoli; ☎ 21 340 3644; www.britishembassy.gov.uk/libya
Irish Republic Handled by the embassy in Italy: Piazza di Campitelli, 300186 Rome; ☎ +3906 697 9121; f +39 06 679 2354
Australia & New Zealand Office 203, Level 20, Alfateh Tower 1, Tripoli; ☎ 021 335 1468; e eric.cantwell@austrade.gov.au

Canada Great Al Fateh Tower 1, 7th Floor, Tripoli; ☎ 021 335 1633; e trpli@dfait-maeci.gc.ca
USA Corinthia Bab Africa Hotel, Souq At-Tlat Al-Qadim, Tripoli; ☎ 021 335 1846; e paotripoli@state.gov

GETTING THERE AND AWAY

With four countries and, more importantly, four political systems, there are not only different routes to enter these lands, but also varying rules for doing so. All have international airports and going by air is the easiest and sometimes even the cheapest way to get there.

All land journeys require sailing across the Mediterranean Sea at some point, whether by taking the short route over the Straits of Gibraltar, or opting for a longer voyage from points further east. Travelling independently by car is possible, but differing border-crossing regulations can sometimes necessitate entering the country by roundabout means. Passengers on trains, buses and shared taxis are subject to the same restrictions, but are usually able to leave one country's transport at the frontier and join the next one's on the other side.

✈ BY AIR

Morocco There are three major international airports and three minor ones, all taking in traffic from foreign parts. Mohamed V in Casablanca is the main arrival point for the country, usually the hub from which further destinations in Morocco are reached. Boukhalef in Tangier and Al Massira in Agadir are the other two. Flights in Europe frequently go directly to Menara Airport in Marrakech, while some land in Fes and Oujda. Flying time from London to Marrakech is approximately three hours and 30 minutes.

From the UK The popularity of Morocco as a short-distance sun holiday destination means that not only do national carriers fly to the country, but also several holiday companies and cheaper bargain airlines. Among them are:

Atlas Blue ☏ 020 7307 5803; www.atlas-blue.com/en. Flies London Heathrow to Tangiers, & London Gatwick to Marrakech. **easyJet** www.easyjet.com. Goes from London Gatwick to Marrakech.

Ryanair ☏ 0871 246 0000; www.ryanair.com. Flights from London Luton to Marrakech. **Thomsonfly** ☏ 0871 231 4691; www.thomsonfly.com. Bargain deals from Manchester to Marrakech.

Due to the frequency and economy of flights to and from London it is always worth considering flying first to the UK, then taking a direct flight from there. However, there are a few airlines that do go directly to Morocco from other destinations.

From Ireland
Aerlingus ☏ 0818 365000; www.aerlingus.com. Flights from Dublin to Agadir.

From Canada
Royal Air Maroc www.royalairmaroc.com. Travels from Montreal to Casablanca. The flight takes around 7 hrs.

Algeria Although the country does have several international airports, Constantine, Batna and Setif among them, most flights go directly to the capital's Houari Boumediene, in Algiers. Connections are excellent from here, and it's very easy to jump on another plane to get to the next domestic destination. Algeria is not a well-frequented tourist destination and relatively few airlines go there. Average journey time from London to Algiers is approximately two hours and 45 minutes.

From the UK
Air Algerie ☏ 020 7486 8068; www.air-algerie.co.uk. Flies London Heathrow to Algiers. **British Airways** ☏ 0844 493 0787; www.britishairways.com. Goes from London Heathrow to Algiers.

Alternatively, it might be worth landing in Paris, from where Air France (*www.airfrance.com*) as well as other airlines originate. There are a couple of companies that go directly to Algeria from North America.

From Canada
Air Algerie ✎ 888 905 0148; e pmalacort@
aviajet.ca; www.airalgerie.dz. Flights from Montreal to
Algiers are available & take around 8hrs & 40mins.

Royal Air Maroc www.royalairmaroc.com. Travels from
Montreal to Casablanca then on to Algiers.

Tunisia There are three international airports, Tunis-Carthage, Habib Bourgibba in Monastir and Djerbna-Zarzis that take the brunt of foreign visitors. Three smaller ones, Tabarka, Sfax and Tozeur, usually absorb the domestic traffic. At present, a new airport is being built at Enfidha to be ready in 2010. It will be located 40km equidistant from both Sousse and Hammamet, both major tourist destinations, and should ease the traffic at the country's main arrival points. Flying time from London to Tunis, for example, is approximately three hours and 30 minutes.

From the UK Tunisia is also a very popular short-distance sun location, which means that national carriers fly to the country, as well as several holiday companies and cheaper bargain airlines.

British Airways ✎ 0844 493 0787;
www.britishairways.com. Flies from London Heathrow
to Tunis.
Thomsonfly ✎ 0871 231 4691; www.thomsonfly.com.
Flies to Monastir from various points in the UK,
including London Gatwick.

Tunisair ✎ 020 7437 6236; e Tunisair.london@
aol.com; www.tunisair.com. Goes from London
Heathrow to various points in the country via its
main hub of Tunis.

Again, if coming from further afield it might be worth considering flying initially to London or Paris, and then continuing the journey from there. From **Canada**, Royal Air Maroc flies to Tunis via Casablanca.

Libya Tripoli International airport is Libya's main air hub, with flights taking about three hours and 45 minutes from London. The country's second airport, Benghazi, accepts both international and domestic flights. Other air options are relatively limited as the country is not yet geared up for tourists.

From the UK
British Airways ✎ 0844 493 0787;
www.britishairways.com. Flies to Tripoli from London
Heathrow.

At present, British Airways is the only airline going directly from London to Tripoli. There are no airlines that go directly from North America to Libya. However, there are several companies that offer flights via other European and North African cities. For example:

Air Malta www.airmalta.com; via Valletta
Alitalia www.alitalia.com; via Rome
Austrian www.aua.com; via Vienna
Egyptair www.egyptair.com; via Cairo

KLM www.klm.com; via Amsterdam
Lufthansa www.lufthansa.com; via Frankfurt
Swiss www.swiss.com; via Zurich
Tunisair www.tunisair.com; via Tunis

⋙ BY RAIL
Morocco Travelling by train to Morocco is a reasonably straightforward and certainly romantic idea, if a little time-consuming (the fastest direct route takes about 48 hours). It's probably most economical to buy the ticket in sections for

each leg of the journey. This method also has the advantage of allowing the traveller to stop *en route*, visiting places like Paris or Madrid. The website 'How to travel by train from London to Morocco' (*www.seat61.com /Morocco.htm*) is extremely helpful and provides all sorts of relevant information. Go via train through Spain to Algeciras and then take the ferry crossing to Tangiers (see *By sea*, page 40). Once in Morocco, the ONCF train network (*www.oncf.ma*) is inexpensive and reliable, but goes no further south than Marrakech. However, the efficient bus service takes over to transport passengers to other destinations. The border with Algeria is not open.

Algeria As with Morocco, it's easy enough to get to Algeria by train by taking to the rails to get to Marseille in France, the closest crossing from the UK. From there, sail across the sea by ferry (see *By sea*, page 40) to any of the five ports within the country. From these points of entry, there is a train service of sorts, which allows the visitor to continue the journey, with bus and taxis to fill the gaps. Although there is no rail network across the border with Tunisia it's possible to take a shared taxi (*louage*) across the frontier at el Kala.

Tunisia As with Algeria, arriving in Tunisia by train is a matter of getting to one of the ferry ports in Europe (Marseille or Genoa in Italy would be the quickest choices) and crossing from there. The website 'How to travel by train and ferry from London to Tunisia' (*www.seat61.com/Tunisia.htm*) gives details. Tunis and Sousse, the ferry ports, both have good bus and train connections.

Libya Getting here by train is very tricky, and should be attempted only if trying deliberately to see if it can be done. The best way to manage it would be to get to Tunisia, then find domestic transport to Ras al-Jedir, the one border post that is open, about 170km west of Tripoli. Once you are in the country, the Libyan authorities require that if not meeting a pre-arranged, each visitor is accompanied by a local representative of a tour operator, including pre-arranged transport (by hire car if travelling independently).

BY BUS Most of the above also applies to travelling by bus. Eurolines (*www.eurolines.com*) provides transport to the European mainland ports on the Mediterranean, from where it's possible to book ferry crossings to North Africa.

BY CAR Borders, especially in Algeria and Libya, are subject to change at a moment's notice. Checking what the current situation is ahead of travelling is mandatory.

Morocco Drive across Spain to Algeciras and take the ferry across the Straits of Gibraltar to Tangier or Ceuta (see *By sea*, page 40). Once in Morocco, driving is easy, with some very good roads as well as a series of fast, but relatively expensive toll motorways.

Algeria Marseille is the closest crossing from the UK, or any of the other embarkation ports from which the Algerian ferries depart (see *By sea*, page 40) and sail over by ferry to one of the five ports within Algeria. Alternatively, the border with Tunisia is open at el Kala so driving from one land to the next is possible, although traffic can cause delays. The closest Algerian town to the Tunisian border is Annaba, and petrol stations can be found here.

Tunisia The recommendations for the journey to Tunisia are similar to Algeria's with the addition of continuing to Italy as an alternative ferry crossing to Marseille (see *By sea*, below). There are six Italian ports from which to depart, Genoa being the closest to drivers from the UK and central Europe, and Trapani in Sicily being the closest to Tunisia. Once you are in the country, both Tunis and Sousse, the disembarkation points, have decent road networks that link easily with the rest of the country.

🚢 BY SEA

Morocco At present, eight operators cross the Mediterranean to Morocco. Most go from Algeciras in Spain to Tangier, Morocco, or Ceuta and Melilla (officially Spain, but actually in Morocco), and take as little as 35 minutes for the crossing. There are also longer scheduled voyages from various points in Spain, France and Italy. Check 'Ferries Guide: Morocco' (*www.cemar.it/dest/ferries_morocco.htm*) for more information.

Algeria In 2008, four lines crossed to destinations including Oran, Algiers, Bejaia, Skikda and Annaba along the coast of Algeria, from ports in Spain and France. Most of the ferries left from Marseille, the trip to Algiers taking around 23 hours. Search 'Ferries Guide: Algeria' (*www.cemar.it/dest/ferries_algeria.htm*) for further details.

Tunisia There are four companies currently plying the Mediterranean to Tunisia, departing mostly from Italy (with the exception of one route from Marseille) and arriving in Tunis. The quickest crossing is from Palermo, Sicily, to Tunis and takes about ten hours, although the 24-hour voyage from Genoa might be more convenient. For further information look at the ferries website (*www.cemar.it/dest/ferries_tunisia.htm*).

Libya There are no commercial passenger-carrying vessels across the sea to Libya. The only way to drive to Libya is via the international border at Ras al-Jedir, Tunisia, about 170km west of Tripoli or the crossing to the east with Egypt at Amsaad that is open – at the moment. Right now, the government requires visitors to be accompanied by a Libyan tour guide for the duration of the stay so incoming tourists should arrange to be met by their local representative.

Cruise ships Cruises traverse the Mediterranean Sea, frequently with special interests including visiting the Roman sites of North Africa. Although few, if any, make stops at all the countries of Morocco, Algeria, Tunisia and Libya on one voyage, any number of combinations are possible. Some of the companies that ply this area of the Mediterranean are:

Adventure Life Voyages 1655 S 3rd St W, Suite 1, Missoula, MT 59801 USA; ☎ 800 344 6118; www.alvoyages.com/ships/clipper-adventurer/14/449/
Archaeological Institute of America AIA Tours PO Box 938, 47 Main St, Suite 1 Walpole, NH 03608-0938; ☎ 800 748 6262; www.archaeological.org/ webinfo.php?page=10004&s_area=Cruise
High Country Passage Representing the Smithsonian Institution & the American Museum of Natural History; ☎ 800 395 3288; www.hcptravel.com. As of 2009, due to the difficulties with getting American visas for Libya, HCP is not running trips to North Africa. However, the instant that the restrictions are lifted, the company will start cruising these regions again.
Only Cruises Travel ☎ 800 644-6659; www.onlycruisestravel.com/north_africa.htm
Swan Hellenic The Cruise Line Ltd, Softech Hse, London Rd, Albourne, W Sussex BN6 9BN; ☎ 0800 008 6677; www.swanhellenic-uk.com/

For more general cruises that go to the region, it's also worth trying www.cruisecompete.com/search.php, typing in 'Mediterranean' in the box for 'region', and the specific country in 'keyword', and seeing who goes where.

Despite the apparent modernity of the countries of North Africa, especially along the northern coast, it's wise to remember that these places are still developing nations. Due to the legacy of their European colonists, facilities sometimes seem as sophisticated as their counterparts in the home country. However, when it's a matter of health issues, things can be quite different. Problems come up that have to do with travelling, or even a change in environment or climate. North Africa does not have reciprocal health care arrangements with Europe.

BEFORE YOU GO Prevention is the best protection of all, and it's important to keep up with immunisations before departure. Check with your doctor as to what injections you might need, as well as how far ahead they need to be done (give yourself plenty of time to allow for the fact that some prophylactics need to be given earlier than others). Algeria, Libya and Tunisia all require yellow fever certificates for those of one year of age or older if you are coming from a yellow fever endemic area. Morocco, however, has no official requirements. Vaccines may be recommended for all these countries depending on how long you are staying and what you are doing. The basics include diphtheria, tetanus and polio (given as an all-in-one vaccine, Revaxis) and hepatitis A. If you are likely to be in more rural areas then vaccination against typhoid may also be recommended. For those working with animals or travelling for a month or more then rabies vaccine will be recommended. The course comprises three doses of vaccine which ideally should be given over 28 days but can be given over 21 days if time is short. Hepatitis B vaccine would also be recommended for those travellers working in medical settings, with children, or who are travelling for a month or more. Again this vaccine is composed of three doses and if time is short may be given over 21 days for those aged 16 or over, otherwise the course is a minimum of eight weeks.

Please note that immunisation recommendations can change, especially in the case of an outbreak of a disease. Keep informed of medical updates before leaving.

TRAVEL CLINICS AND HEALTH INFORMATION A full list of current travel clinic websites worldwide is available from the International Society of Travel Medicine on www.istm.org. For other journey preparation information, consult www.tripprep.com. Information about various medications may be found on www.emedicine.com. For information on malaria prevention, see www.preventingmalaria.info.

UK

Berkeley Travel Clinic 32 Berkeley St, London W1J 8EL (near Green Park tube station); ☎ 020 7629 6233
Cambridge Travel Clinic 48a Mill Rd, Cambridge CB1 2AS; ☎ 01223 367362; e enquiries@ travelcliniccambridge.co.uk; www.travelcliniccambridge.co.uk; ⏲ 12.00–19.00 Tue–Fri, 10.00–16.00 Sat.
Edinburgh Travel Clinic Regional Infectious Diseases Unit, Ward 41 OPD, Western General Hospital, Crewe Rd South, Edinburgh EH4 2UX; ☎ 0131 537 2822; www.mvm.ed.ac.uk. Travel helpline ☎ 0906 589 0380; ⏲ 09.00–12.00 weekdays. Provides inoculations & antimalarial prophylaxis, & advises on travel-related health risks.

Fleet Street Travel Clinic 29 Fleet St, London EC4Y 1AA; ☎ 020 7353 5678; www.fleetstreetclinic.com. Vaccinations, travel products & latest advice.
Hospital for Tropical Diseases Travel Clinic Mortimer Market Bldg, Capper St (off Tottenham Ct Rd), London WC1E 6AU; ☎ 020 7388 9600; www.thehtd.org. Offers consultations & advice, & is able to provide all necessary drugs & vaccines for travellers. Runs a healthline (☎ 0906 133 7733) for country-specific information & health hazards. Also stocks nets, water purification equipment & personal protection measures.
Interhealth Worldwide Partnership Hse, 157 Waterloo Rd, London SE1 8US; ☎ 020 7902 9000;

www.interhealth.org.uk. Competitively priced, one-stop travel health service. All profits go to their affiliated company, InterHealth, which provides health care for overseas workers on Christian projects.

Liverpool School of Medicine Pembroke Pl, Liverpool L3 5QA; ☏ 0151 708 9393; f 0151 705 3370; www.liv.ac.uk/lstm

MASTA (Medical Advisory Service for Travellers Abroad) Moorfield Rd, Yeadon, Leeds, W Yorks LS19 7BN; ☏ 0113 238 7500; www.masta-travel-health.com. Provides travel health advice, anti-malarials & vaccinations. There are over 25 MASTA pre-travel clinics in Britain; call or check online for the nearest. Clinics also sell mosquito nets, medical kits, insect protection & travel hygiene products.

NHS travel website www.fitfortravel.scot.nhs.uk. Provides country-by-country advice on immunisation & malaria, plus details of recent developments, & a list of relevant health organisations.

Nomad Travel Store/Clinic 3–4 Wellington Terr, Turnpike La, London N8 0PX; ☏ 020 8889 7014; travel-health line (office hours only) ☏ 0906 863 3414; e sales@nomadtravel.co.uk; www.nomadtravel.co.uk. Also at 40 Bernard St, London WC1N 1LJ; ☏ 020 7833 4114; 52 Grosvenor Gdns, London SW1W 0AG; ☏ 020 7823 5823; & 43 Queens Rd, Bristol BS8 1QH; ☏ 0117 922 6567. For health advice, equipment such as mosquito nets & other anti-bug devices, & an excellent range of adventure travel gear. Clinics also in Bristol & Southampton.

Trailfinders Travel Clinic 194 Kensington High St, London W8 7RG; ☏ 020 7938 3999; www.trailfinders.com/travelessentials/travelclinic.htm

Travelpharm The Travelpharm website, www.travelpharm.com, offers up-to-date guidance on travel-related health & has a range of medications available through their online mini-pharmacy.

Irish Republic

Tropical Medical Bureau Grafton Street Medical Centre, Grafton Bldgs, 34 Grafton St, Dublin 2; ☏ 1 671 9200; www.tmb.ie. A useful website specific to tropical destinations. Also check website for other bureaux locations throughout Ireland.

USA

Centers for Disease Control 1600 Clifton Rd, Atlanta, GA 30333; ☏ 800 311 3435; travellers' health hotline (f service) 888 232 3299; www.cdc.gov/travel. The central source of travel information in the USA. The invaluable *Health Information for International Travel*, published annually, is available from the Division of Quarantine at this address.

Connaught Laboratories Pasteur Merieux Connaught, Route 611, PO Box 187, Swiftwater, PA 18370; ☏ 800 822 2463. They will send a free list of specialist tropical-medicine physicians in your state.

IAMAT (International Association for Medical Assistance to Travelers) 1623 Military Rd, 279, Niagara Falls, NY14304-1745; ☏ 716 754 4883; e info@iamat.org; www.iamat.org. A non-profit organisation that provides lists of English-speaking doctors abroad.

International Medicine Center 915 Gessner Rd, Suite 525, Houston, TX 77024; ☏ 713 550 2000; www.traveldoc.com

Canada

IAMAT Suite 1, 1287 St Clair Av W, Toronto, Ontario M6E 1B8; ☏ 416 652 0137; www.iamat.org

TMVC Suite 314, 1030 W Georgia St, Vancouver, BC, V6E 2Y3; ☏ 1 888 288 8682; www.tmvc.com. Private clinic with several outlets in Canada.

Australia, New Zealand & Singapore

IAMAT PO Box 5049, Christchurch 5, New Zealand; www.iamat.org

TMVC ☏ 1300 65 88 44; www.tmvc.com.au. Clinics in Australia, New Zealand & Singapore, including: *Auckland* Canterbury Arcade, 170 Queen St, Auckland; ☏ 9 373 3531

Brisbane 75a, Astor Terr, Spring Hill, QLD 4000; ☏ 7 3815 6900
Melbourne 393 Little Bourke St, 2nd Floor, Melbourne, VIC 3000; ☏ 3 9602 5788
Sydney Dymocks Bldg, 7th Floor, 428 George St, Sydney, NSW 2000; ☏ 2 9221 7133

South Africa & Namibia

SAA-Netcare Travel Clinics Sanlam Bldg, 19 Fredman Dr, Sandton, P Bag X34, Benmore, JHB, Gauteng, 2010; www.travelclinic.co.za. Clinics throughout South Africa.

TMVC NHC Health Centre, cnr Beyers Naude & Waugh, Northcliff, P.O.Box 48499, Roosevelt Pk, 2129 (postal address); ℡ 011 888 7488; www.tmvc.com.au.

Consult website for details of other clinics in South Africa & Namibia.

Switzerland
IAMAT 57 Chemin des Voirets, 1212 Grand Lancy, Geneva; www.iamat.org

PERSONAL FIRST AID It's worth taking a basic personal first-aid kit with you. A minimal kit should contain the following:

- A good drying antiseptic, eg: iodine or potassium permanganate (don't take antiseptic cream)
- A few small dressings and plasters
- High factor suncream
- Insect repellent; anti-malarial tablets; impregnated bed-net or permethrin spray for clothing
- Aspirin or paracetamol
- Antifungal cream (eg: Canesten)
- Oral rehydration sachets
- Anti-diarrhoea tablets
- Ciprofloxacin or norfloxacin, for severe diarrhoea
- Tinidazole for giardia or amoebic dysentery
- Motion sickness tablets
- Antibiotic eye drops, for sore, 'gritty', stuck-together eyes (conjunctivitis)
- A pair of fine pointed tweezers (to remove hairy caterpillar hairs, thorns, splinters, coral, etc)
- Alcohol-based hand rub or bar of soap in plastic box
- Condoms or femidoms
- A travel thermometer (digital)
- Needle and syringe kit – and carry a doctor's letter to explain why carrying
- Any regular medication that you take including generic names and doses
- Sore throat lozenges

MALARIA The malaria risk varies from country to country. Libya and Tunisia have no risk of malaria, but Algeria has a small focus of malaria in the Illizi Province in the southeast of the country and Morocco has a small risk from May to October in the eastern part of the country in the rural valleys. In both of these cases tablets are not recommended but it is wise to have an insect repellent to hand containing around 50–55% of the chemical DEET and use it both day and night about every six hours. Insect repellents are also useful to ward off ticks, sandflies and even ordinary flies in all countries.

WATER In the larger cities in Algeria and Tunisia, the water supplies are treated with chlorine, rendering them safe to drink, if a bit harsh on the tummy, which is also from the high mineral content. It is easier therefore to drink bottled water and this applies to all areas of Morocco and Libya too. Although fruit and vegetables might be washed in treated water, it is far better to be cautious. Make sure the former are peeled and the latter are cooked. In some places, milk is untreated, so that it might be safer to use only powdered or tinned products.

DODGY TUMMIES In general, the food of North Africa is healthy, and problems unusual. However, upset stomachs can happen almost anywhere at any time. A change in diet can have adverse effects, even if the food is perfectly safe. Sometimes the problem springs from totally unexpected sources. Watch out for hotel buffets where the food can be recycled too many times. A slight case of the runs, or constipation, is not uncommon, and if things get too uncomfortable, Imodium or similar products can ease the discomfort. Be sure to drink plenty of fluids. If the situation gets more serious, seek medical attention.

HEAT It is extremely important to remember that too much sun can be dangerous in an area as hot and dry as North Africa. It's very easy to burn especially when wandering around Roman sites that have no shade. Wear a hat and sunglasses and make sure to use sunblock, the factor depending on the sensitivity of your skin as well as how much exposure you've already had. Always carry a bottle of water and make sure you keep drinking. It is possible to get too much sun, with resulting heat exhaustion, symptoms of which include headache and dizziness. If prolonged, heatstroke can occur, which is extremely serious and can necessitate hospitalisation.

SNAKE AND SCORPION BITES Most of the time these creatures are invisible, trying to stay out of people's way. However, every so often they emerge, particularly in the summer, and especially at some of the hot, dry Roman sites (for example, Thuburbo Majus in Tunisia). The best solution is simply not to get bitten, avoiding lifting rocks or exploring in holes or cracks. If a bite does happen, don't panic, as most of these reptiles aren't poisonous. To be on the safe side, splint the wound to prevent any movement and get to medical assistance as quickly as possible. If necessary, an anti-venom serum can be applied. Chances are that the local clinic will be familiar with the problem and have the correct solution to hand.

HIV/AIDS Although the official statistics for the diseases' incidence is low, HIV and AIDS are serious issues no matter how rare cases might be. It's best to exercise extreme caution, and if abstinence from sex or injections – the best preventative – is not an option, adhere to the following: always practise safe sex (keep and use a supply of in-date and properly packed condoms); avoid multiple sexual partners; never share personal toiletry items; do not use any blood/blood products (in the incidence of a medical emergency, make sure you go to a reliable doctor, hospital or clinic); never share needles and take a supply of your own to self-administer medication (you will need to carry a note from your doctor detailing your medical need).

RABIES Rabies is carried by all mammals and is passed on to man through a bite, scratch or a lick of an open wound. You must always assume any animal is rabid, and seek medical help as soon as possible. Meanwhile scrub the wound with soap under a running tap or while pouring water from a jug. Find a reasonably clear-looking source of water (but at this stage the quality of the water is not important), then pour on a strong iodine or alcohol solution of gin, whisky or rum. This helps stop the rabies virus entering the body and will guard against wound infections, including tetanus.

Pre-exposure vaccinations for rabies are ideally advised for everyone, but are particularly important if you intend to have contact with animals and/or are likely to be more than 24 hours away from medical help. Ideally three doses should be taken over a minimum of 21 days, though even taking one or two doses of vaccine is better than none at all. Contrary to popular belief these vaccinations are relatively painless.

If you are bitten, scratched or licked over an open wound by a sick animal, then post-exposure prophylaxis should be given as soon as possible, though it is never too late to seek help, as the incubation period for rabies can be very long. Those who have not been immunised will need a full course of injections. The vast majority of travel health advisers including WHO recommend rabies immunoglobulin (RIG), but this product is expensive (around US$800) and may be hard to come by – another reason why pre-exposure vaccination should be encouraged.

Tell the doctor if you have had pre-exposure vaccine, as this should change the treatment you receive. And remember that, if you do contract rabies, mortality is 100% and death from rabies is probably one of the worst ways to go.

FACILITIES In the larger cities, Morocco, Algeria, Tunisia and Libya all have hospitals, some better than others. In Morocco, there are clinics in some of the major hotels and also government hospitals, which provide free or cheap emergency care. In the north of Algeria, there is a reasonable standard of health care but in some places in the south, it's almost non-existent. Private care can meet international standards but is more expensive and demands immediate payment. In Tunisia, there is a developed, but limited, public health system and polyclinics in some of the bigger towns act as hospitals. Again, for private care, money is requested up front. In Libya, the major cities have doctors, clinics and hospitals, but there are few services elsewhere. Uniquely, in Tunisia, at the naval base in Bizerte, along the coast in the northeast, there's a decompression chamber available.

TRAVEL INSURANCE It is *essential* that everyone who travels, let alone to North Africa, has comprehensive travel insurance that includes full medical coverage. No matter how well equipped a country might be to handle any emergency, it's impossible to know ahead of time where a visitor will be when an accident might occur. Cost for evacuation can be extremely high, and it might be that local clinics aren't capable of handling the situation. It's far better to be covered for the worst.

That said, for anything less than a serious situation, most regional services can deal with smaller problems.

SAFETY

North Africa is sometimes considered a Middle East region and, as such, is tarred with the same difficulties as further northeast. Much of the population follows the predominant religion, Islam. Militants do exist in North Africa and sadly, terrorism does occur, although rarely. At the same time, the tradition of Arab hospitality is alive and well, and visitors are generally welcomed heartily. The normal concerns that apply to any tourist region still hold here and it's wise to be aware of local laws.

A FEW BASIC SAFETY RULES
- If you need to take a passport with you, make sure it's in a place that's very difficult for someone else to reach; always carry a photocopy and leave a second copy with someone at home.
- Watch out for your money and take it in several different forms, such as credit cards, debit cards, cash, foreign currency, etc; make sure it's not all stored in one place.
- Always tell someone where you are travelling.
- Act as if you know what you are doing and where you are going; confidence can be a big deterrent.
- Be extremely careful in crowded places, especially markets, making sure items that are worth stealing are hard to reach, or locked away in a hotel safe; serious crime is rare, but pickpockets take advantage of every opportunity.
- If travelling by vehicle, keep valuables locked away and out of sight.
- Stay away from dark, lonely places, particularly at night.

TERRORISM

Morocco Morocco is a very popular tourist destination and does not receive much publicity regarding terrorism. It is an Islamic country and has a significant interface with non-Muslims and can sometimes be the target of potential terrorist threats. Although there have been relatively few extremist events, it would still be wise to be on guard, particularly in the larger cities that have less to offer the tourist, such as Casablanca. Avoid and report suspicious activity.

Algeria Terrorism is clearly the big concern when visiting Algeria. Much of the current fear stems from the 1990s, the 'dark decade' when the military cancelled elections, due to the apparent evidence that an Islamic party would win. Although relative stability returned, there is still a rare occurrence of disruption. The targets of the bombings, in the few instances when they occur, tend to be political. Tourists are rarely, if ever, attacked. There are also militant Islamic strongholds, such as in the northeast, specifically the high Kabylie Mountains. Visitors are advised not to go near these areas. If longer drives are necessary tourist vehicles can be accompanied by security guards, sometimes traveling on motorcycles or cars alongside. In the case of guided walks in the city, particularly in the kasbah in Algiers, a small group of plain-clothes policemen might follow along. Though sometimes intimidating, the idea of such visible protection is merely to assure the visitors that all will be well. After a while, the security presence becomes routine. In addition, there are some basic rules to follow which tours, the most likely and safest method of visiting the country, have put in place. These basic safety precautions include:

- Use air travel as much as possible to avoid any land incidents.
- If going by road, make sure the journey takes place in the daylight – avoid travelling at night.
- Act like a tourist only in the tourist areas, such as the Roman sites in the north.
- Be careful about talking politics and religion – forego the temptation to discuss the situation with the locals. In all cases, do not participate in any local protests, as these events can turn violent.

In addition, if not travelling on a tour or with a group, try to stay at a recognised international hotel that can provide adequate security, if necessary.

Tunisia In general, Tunisia is the most European of the countries and tends to have fewer issues with terrorists. Tourism is also its second-biggest source of income, so the government watches carefully over its foreign visitors. However, in February 2008, two travellers who were on their own were kidnapped very close to the Algerian border. It's therefore recommended to stay within the more popular areas and be careful when approaching Algeria. There are Roman sites close by, some certainly worth the visit, and it's wise to ask the locals for advice. The military exists to protect the country as well as tourists.

Libya Libya is extremely safe, with very few, if any, incidents of terrorism – at least domestically!

CRIME

Morocco The country is dependent on tourism and looks at visitors as being wealthy. Some locals might see this 'affluence' as an opportunity, and crime is sadly not as rare as it should be. Muggings have occurred on empty beaches and dark streets at night. Be careful about buying goods from less than reliable sources, especially with credit cards or when requiring items to be shipped. In some cases, the items are not what they were sold as, and in others the goods never arrive.

On a more serious note, in March 2008 there was a series of robberies at knifepoint in Tangier, a city in which one is always advised to be extremely cautious. In the Rif Mountains, there have been reports of bandits operating. The nearby area of Ketama is where *kif* (marijuana) is grown and the region can be pretty lawless. If in the area, it's best to go straight through without stopping. Even in the nearby tourist town of Chefhchaouen, *kif* may be offered for sale to the passing tourists. Remember that if discovered, penalties for drug offences are severe, and can include significant prison sentences.

Algeria Thanks to its fossil fuel revenues, Algeria isn't poor. It is a hospitable nation and crime is more of an exception than a rule. However, incidents that happen in any large town, such as theft from cars and pickpocketing, are inevitable. Stay away from deserted beaches, as these areas have become target areas for crimes. Nevertheless, criminal activity still occurs less frequently in Islamic countries than in the rest of the world.

Tunisia Again, pick-pocketing and the occasional muggings are reported, but are less frequent than in many other places.

Libya Crime rates are very low, and Libyans are extremely friendly and welcoming. Still, the basic travel caveats should not be ignored.

LAND MINES Certain areas of Libya should be avoided as there may still be potentially active land mines left over from the World War II Africa campaigns. Stay away from parts of Tobruk and the southern border with Egypt. Areas close to Chad, near Tibesti, are closed due to leftovers from that border conflict, as well as other fringe locations. Check with local guides before making plans.

LOCAL LAWS Be aware that there are local laws to which everyone is subject, even foreigners. As the governments are not necessarily as interested in tourists as in citizens, there might be more leniency shown to visitors.

Morocco
- Penalties for drug offences are severe and include long prison sentences, even for possession of so called 'soft drugs'.
- Sentences for serious offences, such as high treason, terrorism, multiple murder and rape, include the death penalty.
- Homosexual acts are illegal and penalties include imprisonment.
- Heterosexual relations outside marriage are also illegal.
- Non-Muslims who attempt to enter mosques may be detained and deported unless the mosque is open to the general public.
- Taking photographs of official buildings and government and military installations or in the vicinity of these places can lead to detention.
- It is illegal to preach religions other than Islam and to import religious materials other than those relating to Islam.
- Possessing pornographic material is illegal.
- Acts or statements criticising or denigrating the monarchy are illegal and can result in prosecution and detention.
- Travellers should not consume alcohol in public places, particularly in traditional and rural areas.

Algeria

- Penalties for possession of illegal drugs, including 'soft drugs', include imprisonment.
- Homosexual acts are illegal and penalties include imprisonment.
- Photography of military or sensitive sites, including military or security personnel, may lead to arrest and detention.
- Serious crime, such as murder or treason, may attract the death penalty.
- It is against the law to attempt to convert Muslims to another faith or to distribute material that may be seen by local authorities as an attempt to do so.

Tunisia

- Penalties for possession, use or trafficking of illegal drugs, including 'soft drugs', include mandatory imprisonment.
- Penalties for some offences, such as murder and rape, include the death penalty.
- Homosexual acts are illegal and punishable by three years' imprisonment.
- Only married couples are permitted to cohabit.
- It is illegal to attempt to convert Muslims to another religion.
- Photography of, or near, government buildings, military establishments or other infrastructure is prohibited.
- It is illegal to import and export Tunisian dinars.

Libya

- Penalties for drug offences are severe and include the death penalty or life imprisonment.
- Other serious crimes, such as murder, may attract the death penalty.
- Sexual relations outside of marriage are illegal and punishments include imprisonment.
- Homosexual acts are illegal and punishments include a minimum three years' imprisonment.
- There are severe penalties for importing and using alcohol.
- Photography around military zones, assets and personnel and police assets and police personnel is illegal and may result in arrest and detention.
- Foreigners involved in business disputes may have their passports confiscated and/or may not be permitted to depart Libya until the dispute has been settled.

WOMEN TRAVELLERS As long as the basic rules that apply to all visitors are adhered to, travelling in North Africa is not dangerous for women on their own. However, it can be oppressive. Local men are interested in foreign females and are constantly looking to chat with them. It is culturally unusual to find women away from male partners or a group. The media encourages the idea that Western women are 'easy' and it's not surprising that local men will want to find out if the rumours are true. The following advice might help to ease some of the difficulties:

- Pay attention to the environment and respect the people and their culture, adhering to the local customs.
- Make sure you dress appropriately for the area. Shorts, bikinis, skimpy skirts and shirts are suitable *only* for tourist resorts and beaches. When in towns, wear trousers and loose-fitting tops that cover the shoulders.
- Ignore the hellos, calls, jeers and whistles unless intending to take the callers up on them. Avoid direct eye contact.
- To discourage unwelcome advances, answer 'Yes' when asked if you are married, even if it's not true. It might be an idea to wear, or at least carry, a wedding ring.

- Don't go out alone at night. If necessary, hire a reliable local guide or taxi driver for company.
- Ask a family or another woman (rather than a man) for directions. An exception to this suggestion is to talk to the local tourist police who are usually marked. It's also possible to tell them if you are being hassled, or have a problem.
- Shout or talk loudly if physically accosted; someone will usually come and help.
- Find accommodation where it's possible to lock the door. Larger international hotels that have good security arrangements, or smaller family places where they look after their guests, are probably the best options.

There are usually quite a few local women in headscarves and it might be wise to carry one along at all times. Wearing one is required when entering a mosque. When the attention gets to be too much, putting on head coverings allows the wearers to blend into the crowd, rendering them virtually invisible.

Male enclaves are not always at first obvious, such as some street-side cafés. After a brief glance, which ones they are will be clear by the absence of females present. A foreign woman, especially if going solo, might be tolerated, but will certainly be the focus of attention. Sometimes, when travelling in the countryside, there is no alternative to stopping in such a place for a well-needed snack or cup of coffee. In this case, smile, be polite and just grin and bear it.

Note that in Libya, at the time of going to press, it is very difficult for women travelling alone to get visas. It might be best to travel in a group. If going solo is essential, a way round it is to join an organised tour to enter and leave the country, but then to go off alone once within the borders. However, this method of travel is *not* recommended as there are too many difficulties *en route*, both logistically and legally.

DISABLED TRAVELLERS Disabled tourists should be able to travel as well as able-bodied ones, as long as certain precautions are taken. Before the trip:

- Contact the airports and airlines to check what specific facilities are available, including access to flights, wheelchair provision, shuttles and special meals.
- Tell all travel services, airlines, hotels, car hire firms, etc, well ahead of time about the disability and its requirements.
- Try to limit the number of connecting flights and arrange extra time for getting from one place to another.
- Ask the tour operator or contact the local tourist office regarding public transport facilities for the disabled. Ask about regulations regarding aids, such as importing medication or travelling with a guide dog. While there, it might be possible to find out about local wheelchair and equipment suppliers.
- If possible, try to contact the hotel or someone who has been there to ask if the rooms are on the ground floor, or have lifts or ramps.
- Be sure to speak to your doctor, detailing your plans and asking advice as to whether it's safe to go and what medication and immunisations you might need. It's wise to take along a letter explaining your medical condition as well as any drugs you need to take, described generically, as brand names vary across the world.
- Make sure all the equipment taken along is in excellent order, perhaps putting in a maintenance check before departure.
- Always carry your itinerary, including hotel addresses, with you so that you can show this list to someone in case you get lost. A phrase guide and reasonable map might also be good to take along.

Although at present there don't seem to be any organised land trips to these countries specifically for the disabled, it should be possible to arrange something tailor-made. Check out the tour operators who specialise in individual bookings.

Alternatively, visiting the area by cruise ship is an excellent way to see the region. More expensive and often theme-specific trips cater for older travellers and are probably better equipped to help less-abled visitors.

GAY AND LESBIAN As homosexual acts are officially illegal in these countries, gay and lesbian relationships have to be conducted with considerable discretion and very few signs of public affection. Although there are instances of same-sex physical liaisons, they are not necessarily considered evidence of homosexuality, and usually stop when one of the partners gets married. There might be a covert gay scene, but it may also be fraught with problems and subject to locals taking advantage of tourists. Despite the legends of those days in the past when people went to Morocco for sex, things have changed. It should be remembered that some of the gays and lesbians in Morocco, Algeria and Tunisia who wanted to live a more open lifestyle have subsequently moved to France, where they feel more welcome.

RACIAL MINORITIES North Africa is a melting pot with almost every colour wandering through the streets. Even the minorities that might not appear local, such as the Chinese or Japanese, are visible, as they are heavily involved with construction and finance. Prejudice is not a part of mainstream Islamic teaching and in general, all races are tolerated.

SENIOR TRAVELLERS Older tourists are welcomed in North Africa and there are tours specifically designed for older visitors. For example, check out Elderhostel (*www.elderhostel.org*) for a trip to Morocco and Tunisia. Otherwise, the basic rules listed in the *Safety* section and some of the medical advice in *Disabled Travellers* should be followed.

FAMILIES The resorts of Agadir in Morocco and Hammamet and Monastir in Tunisia are probably the best places to go for all-round family holidays. There are hotels that offer specialist activities for kids. For older children, visiting Roman sites might be an ideal trip abroad. Museums and ruins are frequently presented in such a way as to be accessible to all age groups and may be of special interest to the enthusiast or student who is passionate about ancient Rome. In addition to the Roman remains, the markets and medinas of the old cities are fascinating, and children might be particularly intrigued by some of the other exotic sights, such as the snake charmers in the Djemaa el Fna Square in Marrakech, Morocco, and the ruins of the *Star Wars* film set near Tozeur, Tunisia.

WHAT TO TAKE

One of the legacies of having been occupied by France is that shopping facilities in its former colonies are very good. There are even French hypermarkets popping up. In Morocco it's possible to find a Marjane in many of the larger towns, while near to Tunis, the capital of Tunisia, there's a shopping complex that includes the giant Carrefour. Algeria is well equipped for items and even Italian-influenced Libya, with its limited and usually state-run supermarkets, can supply most basic needs. Most of what anyone is likely to require when going to these countries can be bought inland, saving a lot of luggage weight and space and in some cases money.

Nevertheless, there are always things that are hard to find locally. Bring along any prescription drugs that are required for the duration and it might be a good idea to take a copy of the prescription itself, in case it needs to be refilled on location. A second pair of eyeglasses is a sensible thing to pack. If intravenous medication is required, carry a clean supply of needles, together with a note from the doctor to explain why they're there. Take a basic first-aid kit that includes Imodium, aspirin/paracetamol/ibruprofen and bug repellent. These items are probably available to buy within the country, but it's best to have them on hand. Despite the low HIV/AIDS statistics, it might be difficult to find condoms when they're needed, especially in Libya. If required, make sure you pack an adequate supply. Tampons and sanitary towels are readily available although the brands might be unfamiliar.

Surprisingly for North Africa, it's a good idea to include some warm clothes. These items are important if travelling in the winter, or going into the desert, where nights all year round can get cold. Light waterproofs are essential if heading north in the winter and especially the spring, as it rains a great deal here. Solid shoes or preferably light hiking boots are important to have along as the Roman sites can be rough to walk on. Make sure you have at least one pair of long trousers and a long-sleeved shirt (for both sexes) when visiting religious sites. It might also be worth bringing along one set of dressy clothes that don't wrinkle for that spontaneous night out. A sunhat, sunscreen and pair of sunglasses are essential, as the sun is deceptively hot and bright; all these are available at the beach resorts in Morocco and Tunisia. Don't forget to have a swimming costume in case that hotel pool or perfect sea is just too tempting to resist.

Take along a camera, even if a cheap one is available in most places. At almost every tourist site there are boxes of film, batteries, compact flashes and throwaways. The larger department stores have quality goods, but some of the smaller shops might be selling items that are well past their sell-by date, or not quite what they seem. It's probably best to take along whatever is necessary, especially if the journey is a relatively short one. Remember, though, that X-ray machines at airports can still be pretty fierce on films, particularly high ISO rated ones, so that it might just be worth seeking out a reliable source on the arrival end, to avoid fogging problems. Books help pass the time during long journeys or gaps in activities and English ones are hard to find locally, so it's worth packing a few. They can always left for other travellers. An iPod or MP3 player/music system or game player uses up idle time well, but make sure chargers and adapters (see below) are included. A pen knife, or even better a combo of tools, such as a Swiss army knife or Handyman, is extremely useful not only for dealing with minor repairs, but also for opening up that spontaneous bottle of wine. Ensure that it's not packed in hand baggage, for if it's found, it will be confiscated at the airport.

The electrical system throughout Morocco, Algeria, Tunisia and Libya is 220v, and takes the familiar European two-pin plug. Make sure that the electrical appliances to be taken along are able to run on this power, and that enough adapters are brought along to deal with all the items that need to be charged at the same time.

$ MONEY

CREDIT CARDS AND TRAVELLERS' CHEQUES Credit cards are not universally accepted, despite the advertisements. In the capital and bigger cities they are more useable, although smaller traders still prefer to deal in cash. Large hotels, restaurants and expensive stores will take them and their use is more widespread in Morocco and Tunisia.

Travellers' cheques are getting more difficult to use, with many traders not knowing what to do with them, let alone accepting them. Banks will exchange them, but usually with a commission. Ask them to be issued in a mixture of large and small denominations of US dollars or euros.

ATMS Hole-in-the-wall money dispensers are becoming the standard method of issuing local currency, although they're still going through a teething process in some of these countries. They are generally reliable in the big cities, but not all accept foreign cards. In Morocco, watch out for daily limits; in Algeria machines often go out of order; in Libya ATMs are not always well serviced and can do nasty things to cards; in Tunisia, ATMs are everywhere and a proven method to obtain dinars.

CURRENCY EXCHANGE Moroccan currency is called the dirham (MAD) and is broken down into 100 centimes. Notes are available in units of 200, 100, 50, 20 and 10 MAD; coins: 10, 5 and 1 MAD; 50, 20, 10 and 5 centimes. The exchange rate is: £1 = MAD12, US$1 = MAD8, €1 = MAD11.

Algerian currency is the dinar (DA) and is broken down into 100 centimes. Notes are available in units of 1,000, 500, 200, 100 and 50 DA; coins: 100, 50, 20, 10, 5, 2 and 1 DA; 50, 20, 10, 5 and 1 centimes. The exchange rate is: £1 = DA107, US$1 = DA73, €1 = DA97.

Tunisian currency is also called the dinar (TND) and is broken down into 1,000 millimes. Notes are available in units of 30, 20, 10 and 5 TND; coins: 1 TND and 500, 100, 50, 20, 10 and 5 millimes. The exchange rate is: £1 = TND2, US$1 = TND1.4, €1 = TND1.8.

Libyan currency is also called the dinar (LYD) and is broken down into 1,000 dirhams. Notes are available in units of 20, 10, 5, 1, ½ and ¼ LYD; coins: ½ and ¼ LYD and 100, 50, 20, 10, 5 and 1 dirhams. The exchange rate is: £1 = LYD1.9, US$1 = LYD1.2, €1 = LYD1.7.

The currency information above was accurate in April 2009.

Airports The bureaux here are usually the first places where it's possible to exchange into local currency. Rates here are standard, about the same as banks in towns, and usually better than hotels. It's always advisable to change at least a little money, especially if local services, such as buses or taxis, will be required immediately. Sometimes these exchange bureaux are closed, especially if you arrive very early or late, and often if they are open there is a large queue of people waiting with the same idea. If travelling independently and you're not in a hurry, do the first exchange here. Otherwise, if in a rush, or with a group, see if it's possible to get away with foreign currency until you arrive at the hotel, or town.

Hotels Most of the larger hotels will offer exchange services, although the rates are rarely as good as banks. In some of the smaller places that are particularly keen to please, it might be necessary to wait until their cash supplies are up, usually at the end of the day, but the advantage is that they might give better rates. When contemplating changing money at the reception desk, it's always worth assessing if the convenience is worth the difference in rate.

Banks These places are always the best to change money, even if the rates they offer don't match those on the street. In addition, the banks give receipts that need to be shown if you want to convert back into Western currencies on departure (although at poor rates – it's best to spend local money locally, leaving just about enough for a cup of coffee at the airport by the end of the trip). Banks are generally open during the following hours but vary according to company, branch and location:

Morocco ⊕ 08.30–12.30 & 15.00–18.30 Mon–Thu, 08.30–12.00 & 15.00–18.30 Fri
Algeria ⊕ 09.00–17.00 Sun–Thu

Tunisia Winter ⊕ 08.00–11.00 & 1400–1615 Mon–Thu, 08.00–11.00 & 13.00–16.15 Fri; summer 07.30–11.30 Mon–Fri
Libya ⊕ 07.00–14.00 & 16.00–18.00 Sat–Thu

Black market Avoid changing money surreptitiously on the street, even if the exchange looks very good. This method is fraught with problems, mostly because there is a very good chance the dealer will rip you off, either with counterfeit notes or fast counting. It might be possible to find an 'honest' trader, but remember that this way of dealing is illegal and always risky.

For tips on bargaining, see page 69.

BUDGETING

Travelling through North Africa is not as expensive as in the UK, the USA, Europe and Australia, but it's not as cheap as it once was. In the legendary hippy days of the 1960s, when anyone who was anyone flocked to Morocco, costs were very low. Now it's not so easy to sleep on the beach (unless properly camping) as the police come and chase dozers away. Basic hotels are still basic, but charge more to stay in them. Morocco remains reasonable and offers the full gamut of facilities, from hostels to world-famous hotels like the Mamounia. General expenses in Algeria are fairly reasonable but accommodation is relatively expensive. Tunisia has excellent facilities and price/quality offers the best value for money. Libya, due to its socialist government, has the lowest costs but has tacked on a couple of extremely expensive provisos: tourists have to travel either with a tour, or with a hired private guide; every visitor who enters the country must have with them a minimum of US$1,000 in cash to show at immigration. The second proviso might be waived if you are vouched for by a reliable tour operator. In other words, bread might be cheap, but travellers have to have a lot of money with them.

It's also worth remembering that Morocco and Tunisia are places that rely heavily on tourist income and cater to it accordingly. Algeria and Libya are fossil-fuel rich and not dependent on tourism. Their visitor infrastructure is not well developed, although both countries are beginning to think a bit more about the additional finance that such an industry could generate.

Please note that these figures are rough approximations based on average prices and have generally been rounded up or down.

MOROCCO Although hanging out for extended periods here is not as much of a bargain as it once was, it's still possible to live fairly inexpensively as a tourist. By spending the night in hostels and some of the cheaper backpacker places, raiding the supermarkets for most meals and taking public transport it's possible to scrape by on MAD165 and still have enough left over for the occasional beer. For middle-of-the-range comfort and a stay in a charming hotel allow MAD850. If you want to splash out and treat yourself with a stay in the more luxurious modern complexes or the fabulous Arabian Nights fantasy resort, give yourself a budget of MAD2,500 a day.

MOROCCO (MAD)

1 litre Coke – from shop	8	Beer, in a cheap bar	32
1 litre water – from shop	5	Bottle of wine – from shop	85

Local bread – from shop	8	Hotel meal	288
Basic meal	43	Taxi/km	2
Better meal	250	Long-distance train	180

ALGERIA Travelling here is not cheap, and accommodation can be relatively pricey and difficult to find. Remember, too, that security is tight and it's still recommended to visit the country via a tour or with a group; individuals might encounter difficulties obtaining tourist visas. However, if you *are* travelling independently, allow a sum of DA2,200 a day as the bare minimum. If you decide to go for a budget that gives more comfort, work with DA5,500 a day. For a stay that allows real luxury and the best sense of safety, splash out with DA22,000 a day.

ALGERIA (DA)

1 litre Coke – from shop	40	Basic meal	500
1 litre water – from shop	30	Better meal	1,250
Beer, in a cheap bar	200	Hotel meal	4,500
Bottle of wine – from shop	250	Taxi/km	100
Local bread – from shop	150	Long-distance train	900

TUNISIA Tunisia offers all levels of accommodation. Frugal travellers can occasionally find cheaper places to stay than in Morocco, and can get by on TND22 a day. If you'd prefer a better level, and would like to stay in a mid-range hotel, bank on spending TND66 a day. For a chance to wallow in superb resorts, including the speciality spa locations, budget on TND440 a day.

TUNISIA (TND)

1 litre Coke – from shop	1.00	Basic meal	5.00
1 litre water – from shop	0.35	Better meal	25.00
Beer, in a cheap bar	4.00	Hotel meal	50.00
Bottle of wine – from shop	10.00	Taxi/km	0.36
Local bread – from shop	2.00	Long-distance train	6.00

LIBYA The opportunities to travel independently in Libya are rare and those joining a tour will have their accommodation and meals decided for them, so to some degree, the daily budget figures given here aren't really relevant. However, there's always a need for a litre of water, or perhaps a taxi ride somewhere, so I've included a short price list as a guide. NB Alcohol is illegal in Libya, so there are no allowances for beer or wine. Averages for train journeys aren't included either as there isn't really an organised network, and travel will be pre-arranged anyway. Please note that as part of your entrance into the country you are required to bring US$1,000 in cash (unless your tour company vouches for this amount), which, with luck, you won't need to spend. Incidentally, as far as souvenirs are concerned, there is almost nothing to buy. Most visitors change money for the duration and find themselves with the majority of their dinars left at the end of the trip. If independent travel were allowed, budget travellers could live on LYD22 a day; a higher level of accommodation and a few extra treats would bring this up to LYD100; and total indulgence would come in at LYD220 a day.

LIBYA (LYD)

1 litre Coke – from shop	1.00	Better meal	12.00
1 litre water – from shop	0.50	Hotel meal	20.00
Local bread – from shop	0.63	Taxi/km	0.50
Basic meal	4.00		

GETTING AROUND

See individual countries.

ACCOMMODATION

It's hardly surprising that the more tourist-oriented countries of Morocco and Tunisia have the widest variety and greatest number of places to stay. Algeria has its French tradition, and retains a few hotels from the colonial past, but its development as a travel destination keeps being halted by political problems. Libya suffers to some degree with the same issues but is just beginning to expand its potential even though the number of its visitor rooms remains relatively small.

Please note that with the current travel restrictions in place in Libya, it's necessary to travel in a group, or with a private guide. Accommodation will already be arranged or provision has to be made for the escort.

All the countries allow **camping**, more or less. Morocco has the best facilities, with some sites catering specifically for motorhomes. It's worth checking the listings to see which ones are the most expensive, or offer extras such as a swimming pool. Tunisia has fewer and more basic ones, with some exceptions, and although Algeria has a small network, many have closed down, and others may not be safe. Libya at present has no organised sites and even though they might allow visitors to sleep on the beach, it's not really a good idea. If venturing into the desert of any of these countries, sleeping in tents, or under the stars is the only way to go. These camps are organised as part of a tour, and although a wonderful experience, are not inexpensive. Staying in **hostels** is a cheap option and there are several located in many of the big cities as well as some smaller towns. Places certified by the Youth Hostel Association (YHA) are the most reliable.

Small, unclassified **hotels** exist everywhere but their facilities and cleanliness are as varied as their owners. Options range from wonderful family-run guesthouses to shabby ones that take advantage of tourists, particularly in Morocco and Tunisia. In Libya, a new crop of mid-range hotels is opening, but the rooms are pricey and the building overrun with business or politically oriented guests. The accommodation ratings in the box below act as a quality guide; each country does have its own accounting system but it's often bewildering. Certainly a one dollar sign rating is going to be as simple as the classified small hotels are going to get, with prices to match. Be prepared for the bare basics. Two/ three dollar-sign places can be very charming, especially if managed by someone who takes pride in their establishment. This level is probably the best compromise if comfort and budget are in competition with each other. Overall, but particularly in Algeria, it's worth investing a little more money to stay somewhere decent, and safer. On that note, family-run places offer a real insight into local life and a secure place to sleep – although they may seem more intrusive at first. Indeed, in some remote places, there is no alternative. It's worth

Practical Information ACCOMMODATION

2

ACCOMMODATION PRICE CODES

Based on price of double room

	Morocco	Algeria	Tunisia	Libya
$$$$$	MAD1,150+	DA10,000+	TND229+	LYD235+
$$$$	MAD865–1,150	DA7,710–10,000	TND135–200	LYD142–235
$$$	MAD575–865	DA5,000–7,710	TND90–135	LYD95–142
$$	MAD288–575	DA2,500–5,000	TND45–90	LYD45 –95
$	MAD72–288	DA1,000–2,500	TND10–45	LYD10–45

noting that rooms in the medina, or old part of town, may be much worse than in the new, but as a compensation, much more authentic and convenient.

International chain hotels such as Ibis, Mercure, Sheraton and Sofitel have their representatives in Morocco, Algeria (though only in Algiers) and Tunisia. As for Libya, at the moment there is only one top-class hotel, in Tripoli, and occupancy is hard to come by due to its popularity with businessmen and diplomats, although more luxury acccommodation venues are scheduled to open soon.

In some of the more tourist-oriented cities, ***dars*** and ***riads***, individuals houses, have been done up to various standards to accommodate visitors. Some of these places are fantastic – often with prices to match – and frequently refurbished to the owner's taste. If it's possible, try to stay at one of these for a more genuine experience.

EATING AND DRINKING

Accusations fly that North African cooking doesn't vary a great deal and after a longer stay eating the same dishes day after day, the complaints might seem justified. The local restaurants try to prepare food that they think foreign visitors will like, but unfortunately it's a little bland and repetitious. However, there is a greater variety than what appears on the standard three-course tourist menu. Take a look at what the locals eat and ask for the same thing from your waiter via the finger-pointing method. Be daring, put in a lot more *harissa* (see box opposite), or order something different from your usual main dish. North African cooking is not the most diverse of cuisines, but with the spirit of adventure, the eating experience can prove to be exciting. If the food does get boring, there are lots of good pasta places springing up to break up any monotony.

The descriptions below are representative of the food available but by no means exhaustive.

BEFORE STARTING To begin a discussion on the food of North Africa, one should be aware of three things that are an integral part of the local cuisine. Perhaps the most prominent is the olive (and its offshoot, olive oil). The main source of income for Tunisia, and important to the economy of all the countries of the Roman coast of North Africa, the olive and its products are not only essential ingredients in most of the prepared dishes but have been since before the Romans.

ARGANE

The scrubby argane tree found only in the southwest of Morocco mostly between Essaouira and Agadir, and in some places in Mexico, grows a fruit the seeds of which have been attributed with all sorts of wonderful properties. Similar to olive oil, argane is an ingredient in cooking, but allegedly without the bitter aftertaste, and can also be used in beauty treatments. What makes the argane so unusual is its harvesting method. Local goats love to eat the fruit and after the easily accessible items are gone, they will climb up into the trees to get to the last tempting morsels. It's very amusing to see a tree full of goats, especially when one reaches too far and falls out. Passed through the digestive system of the goat, the fermented seeds are filtered out from the wastage and ground into oil. Usually produced by co-operatives run and operated by women it's possible to find these small-scale processing plants on the road between Marrakech and Essaouira. Shops throughout Morocco sell the oil.

HARISSA

This very hot, dark red sauce, made predominantly with chilli peppers, and a little garlic, coriander, caraway, cumin and olive oil, is a mainstay of Moroccan, Algerian and Tunisian cooking. It's particularly good for spicing up a bland couscous or tagine. Use – sparingly! – as a starter with bread. It can also be served mixed with carrots or yoghurts, to render it a little more gentle.

The olive itself is hardly ever on show, except as a starter or an accompaniment to alcoholic drinks and on display in the markets, but most of the region's savoury dishes are cooked with the oil.

The second thing to consider when thinking of the local cuisine is spice. Locally grown as well as imported, spices are used liberally in cooking, often giving the dishes their character. Sometimes flavours associated with sweet things in the West are added to savoury dishes, such as cinnamon in *tagines* (the ubiquitous stews) and other times, the opposite is true, like putting fennel into *halvah* (a rich sesame seed-paste dessert). Among other ingredients, the following are commonly used in local recipes: basil, cardamom, chilli, cinnamon, coriander, cumin, fennel, fenugreek, laurel, mint, paprika, parsley, pepper, saffron and sesame.

The final item on the list is bread; it's ubiquitous in North Africa and served with most meals. The main ingredient is wheat, the growing of which was the prime motivation for the Romans colonising the region. In fact, Tunisia, Algeria and sometimes even Morocco and Libya were known as the breadbasket of Rome, due to their prolific production, and importance in supplying grain to the capital. Today, the region remains incredibly fertile, still producing large quantities of wheat and barley. The bread can be delicious in its own right, especially when fresh. Residents in some of the smaller places in the countryside still make their bread by hand. In some traditional villages (eg: Moulay Idris in Morocco), there is a communal oven, and people knead the dough at home and come to the premises to bake it. In the inhabited troglodyte (cave) homes in the mountainous desert region of Matmata in Tunisia, bread is roasted on a flat metal surface over an open fire. Dipped in the locally produced olive oil and honey, it's hard to find anything that tastes better.

STARTERS Vegetable appetisers are common throughout the countries of the Mediterranean and North Africans certainly have their share. Houmous made from ground-up chickpeas (garbanzo beans), and *bab gnoush*, with aubergine (eggplant), are made smooth with the liberal addition of olive oil. In Morocco, the *salade Marocaine*, and in Tunisia, the *salade Tunisienne*, consist of chopped tomatoes, cucumbers and other raw vegetables. Moroccans are very fond of their soups, not only to start a meal, but also sometimes, to replace it. Found on the menu as a first course, but also in the markets at breakfast time, *bissara* is a very thick *potage* that's a common dish in the mornings (as compared with the more usual croissant). Made of split peas and oil, it definitely fills hungry tummies. Another one is *harira*, made from lentils, chickpeas, tomatoes and other vegetables, wallowing in a lamb stock. In the rest of the region, a similar dish is called *chorba*, and although it is restricted to lunch and dinner, it's a hearty soup with meat that can have anything thrown in. The portions can be so generous that it often works as a meal in its own right, especially at midday. Through most of the rest of North Africa, a favourite beginning to a lunch or dinner is *brik* (or *briq*, *brique* or *bureek*, depending on the country and the transliteration). This delicious savoury pastry is made from a fine flaky dough, folded into triangles and stuffed with potatoes, vegetables, chicken, fish, meat or eggs, before

Much of the visual evidence for how the Romans ate applies to the wealthiest citizens, as they were the people who commissioned the mosaics and tombstones that show their meals. Fortunately, there is also quite a bit of written information that refers to everyday eating.

The fertility of the region, both on land and in the sea, provided the local residents with plenty of provisions. Bread came from wheat, which was cultivated in profusion, and like today, was a staple in the diet. It was, and still is, delicious dipped in olive oil. There are ruins of olive presses on many of the Roman sites, and the producers had a system of different-sized vats to distil first, second, third and subsequent pressings and qualities. Olive oil was used in most cooking and remains, even now, one of the most important edible imports from the region. Barley, another of the grain crops, was often made into beer, a drink that, according to legend, Julius Caesar preferred to wine. The local brew was famous, although not always for good reason. In the *Corpus Medicorum Graecorum*, a medical encyclopaedia dating from around AD400, there's a reference made by the author, Orisabius, Emperor Julian's personal physician. He claimed that all beer caused 'flatulence, but especially that made in Cyrene, in North Africa'.

Grapes grew well in North Africa, and wine was liberally produced. Drunk by all classes, in all qualities, it was also exported to other parts of the empire. Remains of the potteries at which the vessels in which the liquid was transported were made, the amphora, can still be seen in places like Tiddis, in Algeria. Of course the effects of fermented grape were revered, personified in the gods of Bacchus and Silenus. Their antics under the influence are the subject of some of the most humourous mosaics of the empire. The richness of the soil allowed other fruit and vegetables to grow and these were harvested and used in various ways, although probably more by the less affluent, who couldn't afford the high price of meat. It is believed that from the time of Augustus, 27BC–AD14, it became so expensive that only the nobles and the very affluent could afford to consume it. It is also said that Augustus preferred the simplicity of peasant meals to the elaborateness of an emperor's table. Figs, pomegranates, truffles and artichokes also added to the diet.

Cattle were bred and eaten, although the upkeep was costly and goats and sheep were also kept, not only for eating, but also for providing milk products, including yoghurt and cheese. The Romans liked fish and seafood, not only on their own, but also as fish paste. *Garum*, an important ingredient throughout the Roman Empire and regularly imported by Rome, was manufactured throughout the Roman provinces of North Africa. Remains of the 'factories' are still visible in seaside locations like Lixus in Morocco and Tipasa in Algeria. Roman North Africans also had a sweet tooth, with generous applications of honey – there was no sugar – adorning yoghurt and fruit to create desserts.

A typical eating routine usually included three meals a day, beginning with *lentaculum*, or breakfast, consisting of bread in diluted wine, as well as fruit and olives. The midday

frying into a crispy hors d'oeuvre. Variations are acceptable: by the sea in Hammamet in Tunisia, the *brik* can be filled with freshly cooked prawn pieces, enhanced with potato and fried egg. Another version of this meat pie is the Moroccan *pastilla*, although the eater would be hard pressed to follow it with another course. It's usually filled with lamb, chicken and as a special treat, pigeon and has a surprising difference – it's sweet! Although treated as a savoury course, the meat is interspersed with almond paste and wrapped up in pastry that's sprinkled with sugar.

MAIN COURSES Couscous is the most famous and typical North African food. Essentially a semolina grain, it's the base for many of the local sauce-based dishes, such as *tagine*. This ubiquitous dish is a spicy stew of meat and vegetables that has meal, *prandium*, would be a small affair, comprising bread and cheese, and perhaps what remained from last night's main course. The meal was often finished with a piece of fruit. The evening was the time for the *cena*, the main eating event for the Romans, and while the wealthy had their multi-course banquets, the average dinner had only three: the *gustus*, a starter, most often of salads or fresh vegetables; the *lena*, which consisted of meat or fish; and the *secunda mensae*, where a 'second table' literally replaced the first one, for the provision of cakes, nuts, fruit and of course, wine, for dessert.

So, what evidence is there for the elaborate meals that the Romans are said to have eaten? Interestingly enough, a recipe book has been handed down from the period, and although its origins are somewhat suspect, it was written, more or less, at the time. *De Re Coquinaria* ('On the Subject of Cooking') was supposedly authored by Marcus Gavius Apicius, a man famous for his descriptions of lavish eating in the 1st century AD. The creation of the book has been dated to 300 years later – but it's still Roman. Several recipes attributed to Apicus were named after him by other chefs, rather than being his own creations. Some of these recipes could well have been served in North Africa, including:

Isicia omentata A kind of Roman burger, consisted of mincemeat with wine, pine kernels and green peppercorns.
Aliter baedinam sive agininam excaldatam Steamed lamb, made use of coriander and cumin to flavour the meat.
Pullum Numidicum Numidian chicken, included the spices of pepper, cumin and coriander, as well as wine, nuts and honey.
Patina de pisciculis Little fish soufflee, featured raisins.
Minutal marinum Seafood fricassee, made from fish fillet and white wine was liberally added.
Sarda ita fit Tuna mashed with wine and spices.
Scillas Prawns plied with vinegar instead of wine, for a change.
Dulcia domestica Homemade dessert concocted from local dates, pine kernels and honey.

It's also worth mentioning *silphium*, a mystery plant from Cyrene in Libya, that's now extinct. The Romans revered this fennel-like plant, making it an essential ingredient in their cooking, but also granting it medical and possibly even aphrodisiac properties. Used to treat all sorts of diseases, it was alleged to act also as a herbal contraceptive. It was so valuable at the time that its effigy was minted on a local silver coin. Able to be grown wild, but not cultivated, over-harvesting eventually rendered it extinct, although not before the last example was supposedly fed to Emperor Nero.

been cooking over low heat for many hours, in a conical clay tagine pot (from which the dish derives its name). There are many different varieties, including chicken with lemon and olives, or prunes, lamb with apricot and prawn in a spicy tomato sauce. Brochettes are pieces of meat on a skewer, then grilled over a fire, or braised. Served almost everywhere, this main course, or fast-food snack is a good alternative when you don't know what to order, or if you just want something simple. Another version of a basic meat dish is *merguez*. Available quickly on the streets, although also served in restaurants, these thin rolls of finely chopped beef or lamb are made spicy by the liberal addition of spicy chilli paste, *harissa,* and then fried. Although more common in Algeria and Tunisia, a milder version is served in Libya, without the hot sauce, called *kufta* (or *kefta*, in Tunisia). To complete the

Based on price of a main meal

	Morocco	Algeria	Tunisia	Libya
$$$$$	MAD285+	DA2,570+	TND45+	LYD50+
$$$$	MAD175–285	DA1,540–2,570	TND25–45	LYD25–50
$$$	MAD100–175	DA900–1,540	TND16–25	LYD15–25
$$	MAD30–100	DA250–900	TND5–16	LYD5–15
$	MAD15–30	DA125–250	TND2–5	LYD2–5

meal, and far too often, restaurants serve French fries alongside whatever else has been ordered. If the food proves too rich, too filling or simply too much, omelettes are on offer almost everywhere, with the advantage of being able to be served plain or stuffed with anything, on request. They're also a good option for vegetarians, or those eaters who've had their fill of stodgy meat.

Surprisingly, fish is not a large part of the traditional menu, perhaps a legacy from the Berbers, who lived in the southern deserts. In general, fresh fish and seafood are available only in or near towns where the catch comes in. Agadir in Morocco was the first sardine port in the world, and remains one of the largest. Further north up the coast, the town of Essaouira displays some of its fresh wares at the port-side local cafés, on a cook-to-eat basis. Otherwise fish and seafood can be consumed at restaurants alongside the sea.

A speciality of Cyrenaica, the eastern and Greek-influenced side of Libya, is *rishda*, a pasta dish, using either very thin noodles or macaroni, topped with beef or lamb and cooked with lentils, chickpeas and tomatoes, and seasoned with garlic and fenugreek.

Vegetarian dishes Vegetables are grown prolifically, particularly in the north of the region. Legumes, pulses, beans and grains are also available, and some places have specialist dishes for them. In Algeria and Tunisia, *chakchouka* (spellings vary) is a vegetable dish served hot that takes advantage of whatever is seasonal, often comprising capsicum (bell pepper), courgettes, tomatoes, fava beans and potatoes, sautéed in olive oil. An Algerian speciality is *mechouia*, although it's also known in Morocco and Tunisia, which is another capsicum dish, this time served as a salad – of sorts. It's made from hot grilled peppers, mixed with onions, tomatoes and garlic. Sadly, vegetarian is a word with which North African cooks are only just beginning to come to terms. Except for places that are very used to Western tourists, there are very few, if any, specially made meals. Some chefs will prepare dishes that don't have meat in them but be careful – sometimes they simply take the chicken, beef or lamb out of a serving that has already been cooked. It might be easier to go with salads, omelettes or specific options, such as a vegetable tagine.

LAGHMI

In Tunisia, the date palm is an extremely important agricultural feature. Even when the fruit is no longer fit for human consumption, due to pollution, as in the palm oasis around the country's industrial capital, Sfax, the trees are tapped. The sap that emerges is left to ferment for about 24 hours, and then produces an extremely potent palm wine known as *laghmi*. It's apparently best appreciated for the rapid high it can create, and the little time it takes to produce the wine. Drinking it is not generally advisable, unless you are looking simply for a taste, or to get drunk very quickly!

Since the Arabic invasion in the 7th century AD and later occupation by the Muslim Ottomans, North Africa has been predominantly Islamic. One of the tenets of Islam is that alcohol (and drug use) is expressly forbidden as 'intoxication makes one forgetful of God and prayer, which is harmful'. However, not only are visitors allowed to bring in imports of the stuff and drinking tolerated, but there is actually a thriving viniculture in Morocco, Algeria and Tunisia. How do these two conflicting philosophies come together?

There is no need for justification whenever tourists are involved. Tourism brings in a great deal of money and in the cases of Morocco and Tunisia provides one of their top sources of income. Drinking is accepted for the infidels, and special bars or areas in higher-class hotels are allocated for foreigners. However, even the locals themselves are partial to a glass of wine or a bottle or beer, discreetly consumed. Before the Arab invasion wine production dated back to Phoenician times. Roman mosaics found in the remains of the North African sites often depicted the gods of wine enjoying their wares. Certainly the climate is excellent for the grape. When the French arrived in the 19th century, they encouraged the wine industry, which still continues, although perhaps in a slightly less enthusiastic fashion. Finding a local beer isn't difficult. It might not be easy to find places to drink in the Medinas (old towns) in these countries, but in the newer or more upmarket areas there are usually bars and restaurants where alcohol is served.

However, Libya is an exception. Alcohol consumption is forbidden, even to the degree that when a recent French cruise ship came through the port of Tripoli, all the alcohol on board had to be locked up while in Libyan waters (and security men came on board to check). However, such beverages can be obtained on the black market, but penalties for its discovery can be severe. Libyans who feel they need a drink can drive over the border into Tunisia, where drinking attitudes are much more liberal. Rumours are flying that the coming of tourism might relax these regulations for visitors, but as of yet, this change has not been confirmed.

DESSERTS In general, North Africans are not very creative with their last courses, at least in restaurants, usually opting for fresh fruit (most often oranges) and dates. However, there is *makhroud*, the Algerian and Tunisian pastry for which all the countries have their own version. A thick, semolina-based cake, cut in various shapes (in Tunisia, and especially in the city of Kairouan, it's a lozenge), it's filled with any of the local dessert specialities. Appearing in various guises, it's stuffed with almonds, hazelnuts and particularly dates, and often stacked on display. In Libya, they're known as *magrood*.

SNACKS AND FAST FOOD North Africa is a haven for snackers, with the native almonds, hazelnuts, and dried versions of apricots, figs and dates, on sale everywhere at relatively low prices. Other nuts and fruits imported from nearby African nations are also around, mostly on market stalls or in small local shops. In addition, the standard less healthy fare such as crisps, chocolate bars and ice cream are generally available. As for fast food, although some big Western chains have touched North Africa, most of the (good) quick eats on offer are still local. For example, rotisserie chickens are constantly roasting on the streets, especially in Morocco and Algeria, and it's easy to stop off and grab a leg or a wing to take away. Ready-to-eat *merguez* as well as other ingredients are for sale, often placed within a baguette, acting as an impromptu meal. Some of the larger petrol stations have adjacent quick-stop cafés that serve fresh and surprisingly inexpensive salads, sandwiches, snacks, coffee and cold drinks.

NON-ALCOHOLIC DRINKS Mint tea is a staple of North Africa, and one of its trademarks. It's omnipresent throughout Morocco, Algeria, Tunisia and Libya. The basic method of preparation is to take tea, usually green, then add almost as many fresh mint leaves as it's possible to stick into a teapot or glass, pour in liberal quantities of sugar, then add hot water. In Tunisia, sometimes almonds or pine nuts are added, while in Libya, the tea can be garnished with peanuts. Even when you are not drinking it, its presence is always around. Bunches of mint are delivered from the back of bicycles or sold in what looks like a green forest on the back of a cart. Mint leaves can be seen being peddled all over town. The drink isn't merely a beverage, it's also a social event. Even more interesting is how the tea is used as part of the sales process. Often, it's served in small glasses while people are viewing carpets or other pricey items for purchase, and then more is presented when the transaction is successfully completed.

As in France or Italy, coffee is available almost everywhere, from the poshest hotels in the big cities to the tiniest cafés in local villages. Small, dark and black, what's known as *café*, or *caffe* in Libya, is recognised as an espresso in English-speaking countries. Very cheap and ubiquitous, it's a staple drink in North Africa. In alcohol-illegal Libya, drinking coffee replaces having a beer. Cappuccinos are hard to find, unless you're at one of the hotels or specialist Western-style coffee houses, as frothy milk doesn't seem to be part of the tradition. Instant coffee, known internationally as 'Nescafé' is generally on offer. The thick, sweet variety, or 'Turkish coffee' as its often called, can also be found.

The southern Mediterranean has the perfect climate for citrus fruits, and the orange juice served from one of the many vendors in the Djemaa el Fna Square in the centre of Marrakech is arguably the best in the world. In Tunisia you can find fresh strawberry juice (when in season) too. Be careful in the hotels, however, as sometimes there's an extra charge for the drink at breakfast even if the fruit might be growing right outside the front door!

ALCOHOLIC DRINKS Despite the Islamic ruling against alcohol (see *Drinking alcohol in Muslim North Africa*, page 61), local and imported beers, and places to drink them, are available in three of the four countries. In Morocco, it can be harder to find a bar or a shop that sells alcohol in the traditional centres of town, but in the newer areas, there's no problem. Algeria is the most secular of the Maghreb nations and Tunisia is the most tourist amenable, so it's easy enough to find bottles of beer and drinking establishments. In these three nations, beer can also be purchased in the large French hypermarkets, as well as some smaller local shops. In Libya, it's still illegal to consume alcohol, although if the tourist industry develops further, concessions may be made for visitors. Not only is wine available in Morocco, Algeria and Tunisia but each also has its own thriving viniculture. The production of these vintages has a history dating back to the Phoenicians, and Roman mosaics extol the virtues of such drinking. Roman villas were full of artwork depicting the patron gods of the grape, Bacchus and Silenus, enjoying the effects of their fermented product. The industry revived with the French occupation in the 19th century and although Muslim religious law frowns upon consumption, secular practice accepts it. Once again, Libya is the exception, as it adheres more closely to Islamic values.

PUBLIC HOLIDAYS

See individual countries for listings.

On average, 98% of the population of the countries of the Roman coast of North Africa is Muslim. Islam often suffers from misinformation in Europe and North America. Below is a very brief explanation of some of the most basic beliefs, as well as how they affect tourists.

The term Islam is an Arabic word meaning 'to accept, surrender or submit'. This definition is applied in religious terms, ie: to God, and the true believer must demonstrate this acceptance by worship and adherence to God's edicts. Muslims believe that God's final message to humanity came through the Prophet Mohammad in the 7th century AD. Prophets are human, not divine, although as perfect as humans can be, and selected by God. Islam does not refute previous monotheistic religions and acknowledges that the Judaeo-Christian sects had their prophets too, eg: Abraham, Moses and Jesus. However, they were not divine. In fact, Islamic religious belief says that it was Abraham who coined the name 'Muslim'. Islam believes that the word of God is given either directly, or via his angels, and Mohammad received his first revelation at the age of 40, in 610, delivered by the angel Gabriel. Over a period of more than 20 years, the angel revealed the tenets and texts of the religion of Islam, that when finished became the book of the Qur'an. In 621 Mohammad reached full spiritual enlightenment. There will be no more true prophets, as God has already given his final words, although some believe that a false one will appear right before the Day of Judgement.

Mohammad began to preach his faith in Mecca, but was driven out by non-believers, so he moved to Medina in 622. From there, Islam gathered so many supporters that it started threatening the rival powers in Mecca. An opposing army was raised to stop the encroachment and a campaign was fought that ultimately failed. Mohammad guaranteed that anyone who remained in the mosque or at home would not be harmed, and, meeting no opposition, entered Mecca as leader of both the conquering army and the new religion. By the time of his death, in 632, Islam had spread throughout the Arab world, becoming the unifying force of Arabia.

Although there are various sects, the two main branches of Islam are Sunni and Shi'a. The former is followed in Morocco, Algeria, Tunisia and Libya, while the largest populations of the latter are in Iran, Iraq and Lebanon. The Sunni concept of predestination is called divine decree while the Shi'a version is called divine justice. There are differences between these two versions of Islam, but the prime one is that in the Shi'a belief, the religious leader or imam must be a descendant of Mohammad and therefore appointed by God, while in the Sunni tradition, the leader can be elected, and 'imam' can also refer to a teacher of Islam. There are also differing laws and interpretations.

The essence of the religion is to follow the Five Pillars of Islam:

1 **Shahadah** (profession of faith) Belief in one God (Allah) with Mohammad as his prophet, and that there will be a judgement day. This is the essence of Islam, and has already been discussed above.

2 **Salah** (ritual prayer) Prayer five times a day, especially on the holy day, Friday. This is the most visible aspect of the religion when visiting any nation where there are active followers, including all the four countries of modern-day Roman North Africa. As there is no intermediary between a believer and God, it is not required to go to a mosque to pray for these five times. However, adherents will take five-minute breaks wherever they are, lay down their prayer rugs and repeat the ritual. In order to reconcile belief and practicality, it's possible to save up devotion time for the end of the day when it's more feasible to perform one's duties, praying less often, but for a longer period.

3 **Sawm** (fasting) During the month of Ramadan with no eating, smoking, drinking or sex, from sunrise till sunset. The event normally takes place sometime during the month of September or October, the exact dates determined by the lunar calendar, the system upon which Muslim religious holidays are decided. Alleged to be the time of the year when the Qur'an started to be divulged, there is a strict regime to be followed during this month. Allowed to have a meal at the first prayer, the pre-dawn one that starts the day, believers must not eat, smoke or have sex until the fourth, or sunset one. Children, the elderly, pregnant women and the sick are exempt. This routine is enacted in order for the faithful to be able to concentrate on their prayers and their faith and read through the entire Qur'an. In practice, it has the result that people are grumpy and not easy to deal with, during the day. If possible, it's best to avoid travelling in these countries during this time. However, if you're looking for a party, come at the end of Ramadan, for the two-day holiday of Eid. The priority is to be with the family, but the family gathers with relatives and friends and goes out, dressing up in new clothes, visiting the local sites, feasting and generally having a good time. It might not be the quietest or easiest period to see the attractions, but the general atmosphere is great fun. Prayer times are also reduced to twice a day, instead of the usual five.

4 **Zakah** (alms tax) Helping poor people, ie: giving alms to the needy, to about 5% of one's income. Giving to those people in need is an extremely important part of Muslim belief and for this reason official charities are hard to find in these countries. It is considered a duty to help others less fortunate. Five per cent is quoted as a handy figure but allocating more to helping the needy would be even better – it all depends on what you can afford.

5 **Haj** (pilgrimage) Journey to Mecca. This must be done by every devout believer who can afford the journey – and it's not cheap. The 3–6-day celebration (the duration dependent on the number of events that the follower feels are important) takes places around December, with dates that are fixed in the lunar calendar, but vary according to the solar. This enormous Islamic gathering draws members of the same faith together in a celebration of oneness in the centre of the world (where the religion originated). The large numbers of participants necessitate the streamlining of rituals. For example, pilgrims can now point at the sacred Black Stone that Abraham and his son were said to have used as a cornerstone of the building, instead of kissing it as they once did. Another adaptation is that the slaughter of an animal can now be delegated to someone else. Some of these rites can be performed in Mecca at other times of the year, the lesser journey called the *umrah*, but this visit doesn't eliminate the necessity to go to the main event at least once. In Morocco, the city of Moulay Idris (see page 139), is said to be holy enough to act in place of Mecca as a pilgrimage destination. However, followers must visit here at least seven times to replace the one Mecca visit. Non-Muslims are not allowed to visit any of the haj locations.

The reward for strict adherence to the Five Pillars of Islam is that all sins will be erased and that after the Day of Judgement, entrance to heaven will be guaranteed.

Morocco, Algeria and Tunisia all include a five-pointed star on their flags as an indication of their adherence to the faith.

MOSQUES, MINARETS AND MUEZZIN Mosques are large halls where people gather to pray and learn. The architectural style varies from country to country, but in general, there is a main building and an adjacent tower, the minaret, from where the *muezzin*, the chosen person, calls the faithful to prayer. In ancient times the man with the strongest voice was asked to do the job, but now the message is broadcast over a loudspeaker. This cry is heard five times a day. The prayer times change daily by about a minute, depending on the position of the sun at the time of year. They are approximately as follows:

At dawn, or first light; midday, or when there is no shadow; around 14.00, when the shadow is as tall as a man/woman; around 18.30, or sunset; and about one hour later, when the horizon is a red line. These calls are very audible, and wake the non-believer as well as the faithful. There is almost no way to avoid hearing the muezzin, especially at around 05.00 or 06.00. However, it doesn't take long to get used to the sound and it's almost pleasant to hear these early 'songs', partly to be reminded that you still have time for a couple more hours of sleep. The words don't vary:

Allah Akbar
(Allah is the Greatest)
Ash-hadu an l il ha illall h
(I bear witness that there is no lord except Allah)
Ash-hadu anna Muhammadan ras lull h
(I bear witness that Muhammad is the Messenger of Allah)
Hayya 'alas-sal t
(Make haste towards prayer)
Hayya 'alal-fal h
(Make haste towards welfare [success])
Allah u akbar
(Allah is greatest)

It is also said that somewhere in there is a phrase that translates as 'prayer is better than sleep', but non-Muslim tourists have been known to argue with that assertion.

In general, the mosques are open only during prayer times and only for Muslims. There are a few exceptions where visitors are allowed to see the interior, including the enormous Hassan II Mosque in Casablanca, Morocco (see page 97), the huge Emir Abdelkader Mosque in Constantine, Algeria (page 215), and the Great Mosque of Okba in Kairouan, Tunisia (page 310). Respect is required when entering, including the wearing of conservative clothing for both sexes and sometimes headscarves for women.

THE MUSLIM CALENDAR Religious dates might seem to have strange dates, compared with the Western, or Gregorian calendar. At the same time, it's a bit confusing when planning a visit to work out when the Islamic holidays are, as they seem to change from year to year. These anomalies are due to the fact that the Muslim calendar's year zero was when Mohammad moved from Mecca to Medina, which coincided with the Western calendar's AD622. Therefore, when it's 2009 in the West, it's 1430 in the Muslim calendar. This figure still seems odd because the Islamic system is also lunar, with each month lasting 29 or 30 days. This numeration is only for religious holidays, while the rest of the country uses the usual Gregorian for secular events.

OTHER RELIGIONS Islam totally dominates the belief front in all the North African countries. There remains a tiny percentage of other faiths. In Morocco, 1.1% is Christian, perhaps retained from France's occupation, while 0.2% is Jewish. The country once had a substantial Jewish population, followers being in the sultan's favour for money-lending and other services. They lived in ghettos, for example in

Ariadne Van Zandbergen

EQUIPMENT Although with some thought and an eye for composition you can take reasonable photos with a 'point and shoot' camera, you need an SLR camera with one or more lenses if you are at all serious about photography. The most important component in a digital SLR is the sensor. There are two types of sensor: DX and FX. The FX is a full size sensor identical to the old film size (36mm). The DX sensor is half size and produces less quality. Your choice of lenses will be determined whether you have a DX or FX sensor in your camera as the DX sensor introduces a 0.5x multiplication to the focal length. So a 300mm lens becomes in effect a 450mm lens. FX ('full frame') sensors are the future, so I will further refer to focal lengths appropriate to the FX sensor.

Always buy the best lens you can afford. Fixed fast lenses are ideal, but very costly. Zoom lenses are easier to change composition without changing lenses the whole time. If you carry only one lens a 24–70mm or similar zoom should be ideal. For a second lens, a lightweight 80–200mm or 70–300mm or similar will be excellent for candid shots and varying your composition. Wildlife photography will be very frustrating if you don't have at least a 300mm lens. For a small loss of quality, teleconverters are a cheap and compact way to increase magnification: a 300 lens with a 1.4x converter becomes 420mm, and with a 2x it becomes 600mm. NB 1.4x and 2x teleconverters reduce the speed of your lens by 1.4 and 2 stops respectively.

The resolution of digital cameras is improving the whole time. For ordinary prints a 6-megapixel camera is fine. For better results and the possibility to enlarge images and for professional reproduction, higher resolution is available up to 21 megapixels.

It is important to have enough memory space when photographing on your holiday. The number of pictures you can fit on a card depends on the quality you choose. You should calculate how many pictures you can fit on a card and either take enough cards or take a storage drive onto which you can download the cards' content. You can obviously take a laptop which gives the advantage that you can see your pictures properly at the end of each day and edit and delete rejects. If you don't want the extra bulk and weight you can buy a storage device which can read memory cards. These drives come in different capacities.

Keep in mind that digital camera batteries, computers and other storage devices need charging. Make sure you have all the chargers, cables, converters with you. Most hotels/lodges have charging points, but it will be best to enquire about this in advance. When camping you might have to rely on charging from the car battery.

Fes, Marrakech and Casablanca, where the largest community remains. In the 1950s and '60s, most moved to Israel, and only about 5,000 are still in Morocco. There is a very small Baha'i community of about 300–500 members. In Algeria, the non-Muslims constitute an even smaller percentage, with a total of only 1% for Christians, including Methodists, Roman Catholics and Evangelicals, and Jews. There was a much greater number of the latter till 1962, when the government forced most of them to emigrate to France, due to financial harassment. A second wave emigrated to Israel. In Tunisia, Christians hold a 1% stake in the religious community, while Jews 'and others', comprise the last whole percentage. Jews once formed a substantial settlement, but were driven out by anti-Semitic propaganda and legislation. The first wave of emigration in 1958 led to 40,000 departing for Israel, while the rest left for France, leaving a group of 1,300. Libya is officially listed as having 3% 'other', with no breakdown of groups. Most of this tiny amount is probably Roman Catholic, perhaps remnants of the Italian presence there. The Jewish community once existed in the country, but despite their formidable presence in ancient Greek and Roman days, in the city of Cyrene, there are now none left.

DUST AND HEAT Dust and heat are often a problem. Keep your equipment in a sealed bag, and avoid exposing equipment to the sun when possible. Digital cameras are prone to collecting dust particles on the sensor which results in spots on the image. The dirt mostly enters the camera when changing lenses, so you should be careful when doing this. To some extent photos can be 'cleaned' up afterwards in Photoshop, but this is time-consuming. You can have your camera sensor professionally cleaned, or you can do this yourself with special brushes and swabs made for this purpose, but note that touching the sensor might cause damage and should only be done with the greatest care.

LIGHT The most striking outdoor photographs are often taken during the hour or two of 'golden light' after dawn and before sunset. Shooting in low light may enforce the use of very low shutter speeds, in which case a tripod/beanbag will be required to avoid camera shake. The most advanced digital SLRs have very little loss of quality on higher ISO settings, which allows you to shoot at lower light conditions. It is still recommended not to increase the ISO unless necessary.

With careful handling, side lighting and back lighting can produce stunning effects, especially in soft light and at sunrise or sunset. Generally, however, it is best to shoot with the sun behind you. When photographing animals or people in the harsh midday sun, images taken in light but even shade are likely to look nicer than those taken in direct sunlight or patchy shade, since the latter conditions create too much contrast.

PROTOCOL In some countries, it is unacceptable to photograph local people without permission, and many people will refuse to pose or will ask for a donation. In such circumstances, don't try to sneak photographs as you might get yourself into trouble. Even the most willing subject will often pose stiffly when a camera is pointed at them; relax them by making a joke, and take a few shots in quick succession to improve the odds of capturing a natural pose.

Ariadne Van Zandbergen is a professional travel and wildlife photographer specialised in Africa. She runs 'The Africa Image Library'. For photo requests, visit the website www.africaimagelibrary.co.za or contact her direct ariadne@hixnet.co.za

CULTURAL ETIQUETTE

PUBLIC AFFECTION It's ironic in a region where public displays of affection between couples is so frowned upon – and virtually forbidden between gay and lesbian ones – that kissing on the cheek between friends is so common. It's not unusual for people of the same sex to do it twice, once on each side, if they haven't seen each other for a while. In more formal situations, shaking hands is still a suitable action when meeting someone. The approach between sexes is more wary, with the man taking the lead from the woman. If there's no physical initiation taken, then the man bows his head in acknowledgement.

PERSONAL SPACE In general, personal space is a lot smaller in these countries. Locals tend to touch, in a friendly fashion, holding hands, patting on the back. Jostling in crowds and in markets, for example, is common, especially if someone is in a hurry. Direct looks, even stares, aren't unusual. Whether this is custom, or simply because tourists are different, is a moot point – get used to it. If you do stare back, especially as a woman you might get quite a bit of unwanted attention. Learn to ignore these looks, unless you want to follow them up.

HOME VISITS If you're lucky enough to be invited into someone's home, dress properly for the occasion. Hosts, especially in Tunisia, see smart attire as a mark of respect. Come armed with small gifts. In all the countries, suitable presents are pastries, sweets or flowers; don't bring wine unless you know the hosts drink alcohol. The Libyans like souvenirs brought from their guests' native land. If travelling there, take a small selection of things with you from home for potential distribution. Conversation at dinner almost always includes discussions about family. It's politeness, not intrusiveness, if you're asked about yours. Try to avoid discussing politics, both privately and in the streets. When leaving, make sure to thank the host, but also say goodbye to each guest individually.

BUSINESS People of the region take great pride in their professional roles and status. Everyone is out to impress; business cards are handed out liberally. Be sure to call someone by his or her title. If you have some qualification that entitles you to be more than a Mr, Ms or Mrs, slip that fact into the conversation and join in the one-upmanship game. Do not cast aspersions on their reputations, even if only joking.

Where once you were asked for a telephone number, now it's for email addresses. This contact is in most cases neither offensive nor designed to to sell anything. North Africans are interested in foreigners and telling their friends they 'know' people in other countries. If you give an email address, in some cases you might well receive a message from your new friend. Be aware that it's possible that if these advances are made to a Western woman, the prospect of obtaining an American, Australian, British or Canadian visa through marriage might tempt a young male Algerian enough to stay in touch.

PHOTOGRAPHS It's impolite and offensive to take photographs of people without asking. If your or their French is non-existent, try to establish eye contact, point to your camera, and then smile. If they smile back, they might be amenable. If shooting with digital, show them what you've done. You each might get a good laugh out of it. If they frown or wave their finger, simply smile again, and walk away. Do not take the pictures if they say no. In some of the rural areas, you might get more refusals than in the big cities or the tourist destinations. Generally in Libya, you'll get an enthusiastic yes and a big smile. Libyans are very friendly and seem to like having their pictures taken.

CLOTHING Especially in the big cities, or the religious sites, it's important to respect the locals by wearing appropriate clothing – long trousers, or knee-length skirts, and T-shirts or conservative upper wear. Shorts and tank tops are reserved for resorts or big hotels only, and bathing suits at the beach or swimming pool. Running around in skimpy attire, especially for females, can be dangerous, as local men might think the girl is 'easy' (see *Safety,* page 48). In most countries, non-Muslims are not allowed to visit mosques. However, when the doors are open to visitors of other religions, women will probably be required to to wear a headscarf. Quite often these are provided at the door. Do not be offended if the guard also hands you a loose-fitting smock. This garment is meant to cover up your shape, so that, according to Islamic belief, praying men will not be 'distracted'.

DRIVING Driving can be a good experience, and generally pretty easy, once you accept different rules. In some places, horns are used liberally. Leave your road rage behind and go with the flow, picking up tips from how others deal with the traffic. You may get stopped periodically by police, particularly in Algeria and Tunisia, as there are frequent border checks. Usually, the policeman smiles and lets you go, but sometimes you will be asked to show your authority papers (eg: car registration or rental agreement). Make sure you have these to hand before you set off.

BARGAINING In Morocco and Tunisia, bargaining for the purchase of goods in the market (except food) is the way to negotiate a deal, not only to bring down the price but also to create a social relationship. Usually the vendor will ask for a price between two and five times what he will eventually settle for. He'll give an amount, you offer a smaller figure than what you're willing to pay. He'll counter with less, you'll offer more than your first suggestion, but less than his price. Eventually, you'll reach mid-ground. Be willing to walk away if necessary. However, if the seller simply refuses to budge, and isn't happy, then you know you've reached his limit. It's then up to you to decide if what you want to buy is worth what he's asking. In Algeria and Libya, bargaining is not the way to go, with prices generally fixed.

GIVING SOMETHING BACK

See individual countries for listings, pages 88, 176, 251 and 338).

Part Two

MOROCCO

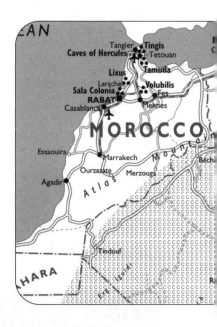

Location North Africa, 32°00'N, 5°00'W. The Atlantic Ocean is to the west, while the Mediterranean Sea is to the north. Algeria lies to the east and the undetermined territory of Western Sahara is to the south. If the latter ever became part of Morocco, then Mauritania would become its southern neighbour.

Size 446,550km²; 23rd-largest country in Africa, 59th largest in the world (not including Western Sahara)

Climate Temperate Mediterranean on the coast, cooler with snow in winter in the mountains, hot and dry in the desert to the south

Status Kingdom

Population 34,343,220 (2008)

Life Expectancy 71.52 years: male 69.16, female 74 (2008)

Capital Rabat, population 1,700,000 (2007)

Other main towns Tangier, Tetouan, Chefchaouen, Casablanca, Meknes, Fez, Marrakech, Essaouira, Agadir

Economy Primarily based on agriculture and phosphate rock mining and processing although tourism is an extremely important source of income. Leather goods, textiles, food processing and construction also add to the financial well-being of the country.

GDP US$3,800 per capita (2007)

Languages Arabic is the official language, with Berber (Tamazight) and its dialects spoken throughout the country; French is still commonly used for business and government.

Religion Muslim 98.7%, Christian 1.1%, Jewish 0.2%

Currency Moroccan dirham (MAD)

Rate of Exchange £1 = MAD12, US$1 = MAD8, €1 = MAD11 (Apr 2009)

National airline/airport Royal Air Maroc; Casablanca: Mohamed V Airport

International telephone code +212

Time GMT all year round

Electricity 220 volts AC, 50Hz; European two-pin plug

Weights and measures Metric

Flag Solid red flag with green pentagram in the centre

National anthem *Hymne Cherifien* (Sharafian Hymn)

National sport Football (soccer)

Public holidays 1 January, New Year's Day; 11 January, Manifesto of Independence; *9 March, Aïd al-Mawlid, Prophet's Birthday; 1 May, Labour Day; 30 July, Feast of the Throne; 14 August, Fête Oued Eddahab, Oued Eddahab Allegiance Day; 20 August, Révolution du Roi et du Peuple, Anniversary of the King and the People's Revolution; 21 August, King Mohamed's Birthday; *21 September, Aïd al-Fitr, End of Ramadan; 6 November, Marche Verte, Anniversary of the Green March; 18 November, Fête de l'Indépendance, Independence Day; *28 November, Aïd al-Adha, Feast of the Sacrifice.

(for 2009: starred dates change according to the Muslim calendar)

3

Background Information

GEOGRAPHY

Morocco sits at the northwest tip of Africa at exactly 32°N latitude and 5°W longitude. The country is relatively narrow, but a generous portion of its coast straddles both the Atlantic Ocean and the Mediterranean Sea. It shares borders with Algeria to the east and the territory of Western Sahara to the south. The limit of this last frontier is under dispute, with the future nationality of the territory still being discussed. If this land were to become Moroccan, then the new international boundary would be with Mauritania to the south. At its present size, it's the 23rd-largest country in Africa, the 59th biggest in the world, covering about the same area as California, in the USA.

The chain of the Atlas Mountains, stretching east through Algeria and eventually ending up in the sea in Tunisia, has three parts in Morocco. The middle (*moyenne*) begins in the centre of the country and heads northeast; the high (*haute*) starts at the same point, rising to great heights before heading west to Agadir; and the Anti-Atlas works its way southwest. The spine of the entire country reaches its peak at Jbel Toubkal, the highest point in North Africa at 4,167m. The snow-covered view in winter is a spectacular backdrop to Marrakech, the city closest to the uplands. The northeast of Morocco has another much shorter and lower range, the Rif Mountains, starting close to Tangier and running north to south. In contrast with the Atlas, the slopes of this range are lush, in keeping with the general arability of the neighbouring land. Agriculture is one of the country's most valuable sources of income, and the majority of it is done in the plains in the shadow of the mountains. Rain in the north, especially along the coast, can be generous in all seasons except summer. The two biggest rivers of the country are the Moulouya, which runs into the Mediterranean, and the Sebou, which opens out into the Atlantic.

South of the Atlas is the desert which at one time was far more effectively cultivated than it is now, though agriculture remains important in the shape of the date harvest. Springs crop up now and then between the cracks in the mountains, or from the underground water table, and create an environment that allows for huge date palms to thrive. Called *palmeraie*, these dark green swathes are an amazing contrast to the red and gold sandy soil. Often, these fields of palms lie in a valley, sneaking up on passing travellers accustomed to barren vistas. Beyond, is the beginning of the Sahara. On the border with Algeria are the dunes of Merzouga, large hills of red sand rising to peaks that look so much like what one imagines the desert to be that they are repeatedly used as film locations. Spectacular, although only covering a small area, they are merely a part of the Saharan landscape.

NATURAL HISTORY

Morocco is an important staging post on the migratory path of birds leaving cold northern Europe for warm southern Africa in the winter, and vice versa during the summer. Some of the flying visitors include ruddy shelducks, crested coots,

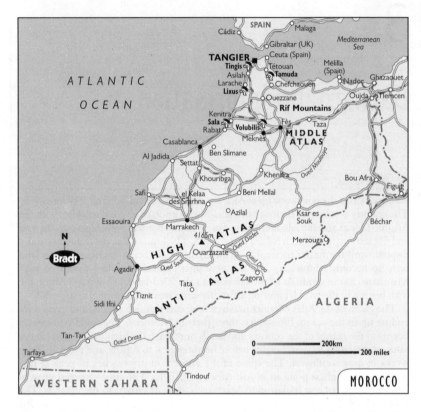

MOROCCO

Eleonara's falcons, Caspian terns, great-ringed plovers, marbled teals, Eurasian spoonbills, purple herons, red-crested pochards, water rails and pied avocets, as well as many others. Wetlands like those where the Moulaya River empties into the Mediterranean Sea, are a nice pit stop for them. In the mountains are the hardier species, such as eagles.

The bays, tidal lagoons and islands are a refuge for some larger sea creatures, including Atlantic hump-backed dolphins, monk seals, loggerhead turtles and fin

THE NATIONAL PARKS OF MOROCCO

Ayachi In the High Atlas Mountains
Bou Arfa Between the middle and high Atlas Mountains
Hoceima On the northeastern (Mediterranean) coast
Ifrane In the Anti-Atlas Mountains
Lake Sidi Boughaba On the northwestern (Atlantic) coast
Merdja Zerka On the northwestern (Atlantic) coast
Tazekka In the middle Atlas Mountains
Talassemtane In the Rif Mountains
Toubkal In the high Atlas Mountains
Souss-Massa On the southwestern (Atlantic) coast
Coast of Dakhla On the southwestern (Atlantic) coast of Western Sahara
Gulf of Khnifiss On the southwestern (Atlantic) coast of Western Sahara
Iles of Essaouira On the western (Atlantic) coast

whales, as well as smaller endangered fish. There are also mammals, like the Barbary apes, a branch of the Gibraltar family, who seem quite happy in the forests of the Ifrane National Park in the Atlas Mountains. Other animals that can be seen in some of the preserved areas are the North African striped weasel, African wildcat, common genet and common otter.

In Roman times, large mammals were more common. Barbary lions – captured locally for the games – are now extinct in the wild, although examples still exist in zoos. There is talk of attempting to reintroduce these animals into their original location, but modern-day demands on the area make this unlikely. There was also a species of North African elephant that thrived locally. Smaller than the modern-day ones found in the south of the continent, this family was believed to have roamed the entire area. Hannibal (see page 8) was said to have used these elephants when crossing the Alps. Sadly, no specimens of the species survive.

The desert is home to the desert fox (fennec) and larger animals, such as the elusive gazelle. The terrain is harsh, but the increase in tourists looking for a Sahara adventure is changing the environment and probably having a detrimental affect on the wildlife.

National parks have been set up in order to preserve the fragile environments, such as lakes and oases that are havens for exotic plans and flowers.

POST-ROMAN HISTORY

By AD710, the Islamic religion and Arabic culture of the invaders had begun to take hold. Less than eight decades later, the holy man Moulay Idris – alleged to be a direct descendant of the Prophet Mohamed – set down the foundation for an Arab state and the first dynasty, the Idrisites. He used the Roman site of Volubilis as his base, although he later moved his capital up the hill to a town still named after him. His son, Moulay Idris II inherited his power, extending his area of influence and moving his capital to Fes.

The Berbers took over in 1062, uniting the country and establishing a new dynasty, the Almoravids. In power for another 80 years, they expanded their territory as far as Spain to the northwest, and Libya to the east. Weakened by overextension and accusations of moral laxity they fell prey to a new stricter Islamic dynasty, the Almohads. A little over 50 years later, the sultan took southeastern Spain. By 1212, his successor was defeated, and Morocco once again was broken down into separate areas, each under different local tribal control.

Although the Merenids stood above the rest, for 300 years the country continued to fall apart. By about 1550 a new tribe, the Saadians, successfully battled the incumbent power to make themselves rulers. The next in line, Sultan Ahmad, took control and proved to be one of the most successful rulers of the country, his reign lasting more than 20 years. Towards 1600, the age of plunder on the seas, Morocco took its share, gaining infamy as pirates of the Barbary Coast (the name came from Berber, the local adaptation of Barbarian, the label the Europeans put on the local tribes of North Africa). By 1660 the country succumbed to the advances of the next dynasty hungry for rulership, the Sharifian, or Alaouite. The current king's lineage stems from here.

The country alternating between good and bad rulers, by just about 1800, Moulay Slimane, an orthodox Muslim, advocated a policy of isolationism. Although relations with Europe were severed. the weakened Morocco fell prey to invaders, including the Spanish, to whom they had to cede various towns along the coasts.

By 1904, the European powers were eyeing countries of North Africa. They agreed Britain's 'sphere of influence' would include Cyprus and Egypt; Italy would look after Libya; and France would add Tunisia and Morocco to the countries under its care. Within a decade, rebellions began, initially in the Rif Mountains against the occupying Spanish. Not long after, the Moroccan nationalist movement instigated demands for independence. After World War II, Sultan Mohamed V continued the calls, and was exiled by the French in 1953. In 1955 he returned, eventually to lead the country as king when France finally let go and granted Morocco its freedom in March 1956. In April of that year, Spain gave back the land it held, while in October Tangier was finally returned.

In 1961, the first king of independent Morocco, Mohamed V, died, leaving the kingdom to his son, Hassan II. In 1975, 350,000 Moroccans marched into the Western Sahara, calling for it to be 'returned' to Morocco. Named the Green March, the nationals claimed that the land was theirs on historic grounds. In 1979 all of the Western Sahara was absorbed into the country, when Mauritania gave up the final third. The independence organisation of this disputed land is continuing its struggle, although it seems to have lost its way for the present, despite support from Algeria and Libya.

In February 2004, King Hassan II died, leaving his son Mohamed VI to continue his reforms. A much more dynamic and high-profile ruler, the new king has instigated several modernisations, including major construction to develop the tourist potential of the country. More significantly, especially to his people, is the Mudawana, legislation passed in 2005 by parliament. Meaning family code, this law changes the nature of marriage and the family within the country. Polygamy can still exist, but it now requires that the first or additional wife approves; divorces have to be civil as well as religious with resolution in a court of law; the house remains with whichever parent retains the children; marriage at 15 is no longer allowed; and sexual harassment has become an offence with legal consequences.

POLITICS

Morocco has always had a single leader in power, outside of its period as a French colony, and the sultan of the past has translated into the modern king. Today, the country is a constitutional monarchy. Although the king's position is hereditary, handed down from his father and grandfather (since independence in 1956), the rest of the government comprises a mixture of appointed and elected members. As Chief of State, the king takes an active role, especially in the executive or leadership branch of government. He appoints the head of government Prime Minister after elections but chooses his own council of ministers. Despite these leading positions being appointed by the king, the country has functioned with a multi-party system since its first days as an independent nation. There are at least 20 political parties representing the different factions, left, right and centre, and more are being formed - and dissolved - all the time. Each has its own leaders, acting in both government and pressure groups and taking up seats in parliament.

The legislative, or law-making, branch is made up of a two-house, or chamber, parliament. The upper house consists of participants in the 270-seat Chamber of Councillors who serve nine-year terms. The elections for these seats are staggered, so that there is an election for one-third of the members every three years. These councillors are elected directly by local councils, labour syndicates and other professional organisations. The next round is scheduled for 2009. The lower house, the Chamber of Representatives, has 325 seats: 295 of these members are elected by constituencies and 30 are elected from 'National Lists' (of suitable candidates) of women. However, the 30 women who were chosen in 2007 are fewer than the 34 elected in 2002.

Morocco's legal system is based on a mixture of Islamic law, and Spanish and French civil systems. Decisions are made by the Supreme Court, and its judges are chosen based on the suggestions of the Supreme Council of the Judiciary. The king is head of this Council.

Generally considered one of the more enlightened political systems in the Maghreb, there are still difficulties involved when the leader of state is an inherited position. Although King Mohamed VI is popular and young, and makes great efforts to appeal to the people, it's difficult to make changes when the monarch is so dominant in politics. Despite the socialist leanings of the country, the monarchy still underlies the political workings. It is not acceptable to wonder about the legitimacy of the country's royals.

There is relatively little censorship in the press. The political thorn in Morocco's side is the issue of the Western Sahara (see page 73) and it would seem that the press is being censored on this issue, since relatively little has been heard from this region lately. Some journalists have been removed from the reporting front after filing their stories. The UN is still deciding under whose jurisdiction the region of Western Sahara falls.

Administratively, Morocco is broken down into 16 regions, which are further divided into prefectures and provinces. The king chooses the Wallis (governors) who will oversee the running of these areas.

ECONOMY

Financially, Morocco is one of the more stable nations in Africa, although not as well off as its neighbours. Lacking the large fossil fuel deposits of Algeria and Libya, it concentrates on its other resources and assets.

Morocco's most prolific physical reserves are phosphate. With an estimated 100 billion tons, the country holds at least three-quarters of the world's known supply. Phosphates are needed to make phosphorus, which in turn is used primarily in fertilisers, but also in a wide variety of products from explosives and fireworks to toothpaste and detergents. This natural resource provides Morocco's largest income and accounts for approximately 75% of its mining output. Other minerals exploited include coal, iron, copper and lead.

Industry and manufacturing play an important role in the economic health of Morocco. In addition to phosphates, other products include cement, paper, timber, metals, plastic and rubber. Services such as food processing, oil refining and vehicle assembly are also increasingly located here, as well as the textile industry, due to cheap labour costs. Recently, semiconductor assemblage has entered into the equation, and in 2003 a new design and development centre was opened in the capital Rabat to keep pace with the demands of new technology. In addition, trade agreements with the EU have allowed favourable export conditions.

Tourism has edged into the number two position for hard-currency income. Since 2001, there's been a 30% increase in the number of visitors. In the 2006 assessment there were over 6.5 million tourist arrivals and over 16 million overnights. The season lasts all year, ranging from lazing about on the beaches at Agadir to hiking in the high mountains. Even the embryonic ski resorts are beginning to draw in the jaded Europeans looking for somewhere new. Morocco's trump tourist card is its culture, exotic yet accessible, strange yet easy to get to, and all relatively safe. The UNESCO-protected cities and locations are heritage sites, and are made particularly visitor friendly. The government is well aware of this golden goose, and is putting serious money into developing visitor potential even further. The Visitor 2010 plan aims to increase hotel beds to 230,000, create 600,000 new jobs and attract foreign currency. The government hopes that the tourism sector will provide 20% of the nation's GDP by 2010.

Once its biggest earner, agriculture remains an important source of funds. Employing almost 50% of the domestic workforce, this labour contributes nearly 20% to the country's income. Wheat and barley production continues, supplying two-thirds of the country's needs. Although in Roman times the grain producing regions were further east, ancient Mauretania still contributed to the area's importance, helping to produce so much exportable wheat and barley that the region became known as 'the breadbasket of Rome'. Export plays a part, with vegetables and fruit (including olives) produced in the north. Maroc oranges are common in the supermarkets of northern Europe. In the south, dates are grown in enormous quantities. The cultivation of new crops is being tried for such commodities as sunflowers, sugar beet and cotton, all of which thrive in warmer climates. Among these cash-rich earners is cannabis, and Morocco is one of the world's largest producers. Shipments are directed mostly to western Europe. It should also be pointed out that the country acts as a transit point for cocaine from South America to the West. This trade is officially condemned by the government, but vigilance is not heavily enforced in some of these areas, and the resultant prosperity is not seriously scrutinised.

With a coastline as long as Morocco's, it's inevitable that fishing plays a part in the country's economy. The Atlantic coast boasts over 240 species, although legislation in 1997 has curtailed exploitation, allowing only ten months' fishing a year. By far the largest part of the catch is sardines, mostly canned for export to the EU; Morocco is probably the largest sardine exporter in the world. A huge new facility opened there in 2003, with the Arabic Economic and Social Development fund of Kuwait contributing 80% of the construction costs. At present, the fishing industry provides 17% of the country's income, and employs around 100,000 people.

Despite the country's efforts, unemployment remains high, up to 20% in the big cities. Economic growth slowed in 2007, due to a drought that affected agricultural production, and forced the import of grain. It is a priority of Morocco to reduce the gap between rich and poor. The National Initiative for Human Development (INDH) introduced in 2005 has incorporated a US$2 billion scheme to eliminate slums in the future. In the meantime, the country is courting foreign investors, offering chances to co-develop some of the country's resources.

PEOPLE

With the latest population estimates hovering around the 34 million mark, Morocco is the most populous of the four countries of the Roman coast of North Africa. With the majority of people between the ages of 15 and 64, the high growth rate of previous decades has slowed down considerably, so that most Moroccans are currently in the workforce. Although potentially earning revenue for the country, it does mean that many workers are out there, searching for jobs.

Life expectancy is lower than in Algeria, Tunisia and Libya, at 74 years for women and 69 for men. The literacy rates still leave a lot to be desired: of the total population over 15, only 52.3% can read and write. This figure is further broken down into 65.7% of the men who are literate, and only 40% of the women (based on the 2004 census). Charities have been set up specifically to help rectify the imbalance (see *Giving something back*, page 88).

Arabic is the official language, with French still used for official functions, such as diplomatic, governmental and business. English is being taught more often due to the demands of both international business and tourism, but is learned more for a practical than official reason. Acceptance of the Berber language is patchy. Its

The numbers of the Berber population are significant, with impossible-to-verify statistics alleging that they make up 40% of Moroccans. Berbers also comprise part of the other Maghreb nations, as 30% of Algerians, 5% of Tunisians and 10% of Libyans. These figures are not etched in stone and vary depending on the source, but they give some idea of how embedded the culture is in daily life. The question of how many ethnic people exist in total also needs to take into account those temporary refugees working in Europe who still consider themselves Berbers. They contribute financially to the well-being of the home community. Face to face with tourists, many locals proudly claim Berber heritage, dressing up in local garb and speaking the language. In normal situations, Berbers can face difficulties with some of the ancient prejudices that apply to many aboriginal cultures, such as being seen as ignorant illiterates still wearing old-fashioned ethnic clothing. There are accusations, for example in Algeria, that Berbers don't speak Arabic, and use French as a second language.

Over time, the Berbers have survived due to their ability to be absorbed into the life of colonists and then revive as a separate culture after that group moved on. Today, the Imazighen are asking for acknowledgment as their own ethnic group, with their languages and their alphabets, and rights. There are several of these tongues, across the breadth of their terrain, not only in Morocco, Algeria and Libya, but also in Mauritania, Mali and Niger. Although several variants are spoken in different areas, there is an effort being made to group all the northern ones together into the standard Tamazight. Attitudes towards establishing an official Berber language as well as general acceptance of the people themselves are different in each of the countries.

dialects are spoken throughout the country and primary schoolchildren are now being taught Tifinagh, the alphabet in which Tamazight, the standardised Berber language, is written.

Most Moroccans live west and north of the Atlas Mountains that run from the southwest to the northeast of the country. The fertile region along the coast of the Mediterranean is the area that the Romans settled, and where many people are still found. Tangier sits prominently at the beginning of the Mediterranean and remains a population centre. Casablanca is the country's biggest city and Africa's sixth largest, with an unofficial population of six million, while the capital Rabat is relatively small with fewer than two million. Both sit on the Atlantic coast. People have also settled in Fes and Meknes, both on the fertile plain that rests just north of the Atlas Mountains and not far from Morocco's most important Roman settlement, Volubilis. Marrakech lies further south, but still nestled against the base of the uplands. It is considered the most Berber of all the North African cities.

CULTURE

Morocco is a short cut to the exotic. The country's flavour is so different from the West, yet so accessible in terms of distance that many visitors return again and again. Crowded markets filled with the scent of spice; narrow passages with small doors that lead to beautiful houses, with huge central courtyards; women wrapped in colourful fabrics, showing only their elaborately henna-tattooed hands: all these things can be found here, and much more besides.

ARCHITECTURE Perhaps it's easiest to start with this most visible aspect of the country. Many of its features are shared with the rest of North Africa, but Morocco has its particular interpretations. The mark of the Moors – graceful arches and elaborate detailing, for example – have found their way into most of the buildings. Whether visiting a private house converted into a small hotel, a museum, palace, mosque or a medieval religious *medersa* (Koranic school) it's possible to see features such as courtyards, often with small fountains, intricate tile work and delicately carved woodwork. Minarets tower over the houses below, beautifully adorned with ceramics or plasterwork. Along the coast and in some of the mountain villages, the houses are painted white for coolness with blue trim to repel mosquitoes. The overall effect is extremely beautiful. In the south, the red desert is used for construction, leading to castles, or *ksours*, literally made of sand. The city of Marrakech is ochre and dark pink, its buildings made from the land that surrounds it. Royal palaces and residences, which seem to be everywhere, are magnificent, often protected by gates made of an extremely complicated mosaic motif. The medinas are made up of a complicated network of passageways surrounded by a thick wall, with entrances that could once be shut at night. The ones in Tetouan, Meknes, Marrakech and Essaouira have been classified as UNESCO World Heritage Sites.

HANDICRAFTS Handicrafts are an essential part of Moroccan culture, and found everywhere. The choice is so vast it's almost impossible to select and buy, although the hawkers, especially in the souks and markets, will certainly try to persuade you otherwise. A brief list includes: mosaics and tile work; ceramics, usually bowls, cups and pottery; carpets, in all sizes; fabrics in a plethora of colours and materials;

HENNA

This green plant, mulched into a paste and used as a temporary dye, is applied mostly to women's hands and sometimes feet. Traditionally, it's laid on in very intricate patterning for the celebration of a special occasion, such as a wedding. The designs can be exquisite, taking ages to put on if done properly, and lasting up to a month. Practitioners of the art have worked out that they can ply their wares to passing women visitors, and will accost every female tourist with offers to decorate their hands and arms. Usually they give a 'free' sample and then expect some financial recognition afterwards. If interested, be selective as to the operator, as some are certainly more talented at application and design than others, and also the henna can be of a poor grade, and not last very long.

woodwork; lanterns and lamps, made of various substances, including dried skins and ironwork; leather goods; jewellery, ranging from antique Berber to exquisitely wrought silver and gold; felt hats and handbags; and even fossils, hewn from the ammonite-trilobyte-rich mountains of the south. There are articles of clothing, worn by the locals but still made with care, such as gowns, djellabas with hoods and kaftans without, the red fez-like caps called *tarbouches* and the slippers, *babouches*, worn by both sexes and sold at colourful market stalls. Remember to have a go at bargaining (see page 69).

PERFORMANCE ART At dusk, the main squares, particularly the Djemaa el Fna in Marrakech, come to life. Storytellers, snake charmers, dancers (some serious, some very light-hearted), musicians and even game players come together to enjoy the cool of the evening. Probably the most visible and special aspect of Moroccan culture, these informal yet spectacular cultural activities should not be missed.

MUSIC The country boasts an incredibly rich heritage of melody and song, and most Moroccans will sing, play an instrument or beat out a drum rhythm. People have been known to string up and play an old petrol can. Melodic sounds are everywhere. More formally, music styles include Andalusian, going back to the 9th century AD; *aissawa,* named after a Sufi brotherhood; Berber music, mixing in African styling with the use of all sort of instruments; *chaabi*, or pop; classical, a complicated and structured discipline dating back to the 15th century; *gnaoua*, a rhythmic form originally from Mali and recently embraced by rock musicians, now the focus of an annual music festival in Essaouira; *griha*, a more casual pop that produces themed songs; *malhum*, a kind of male working-class rap; and *rai*, lively dance music using North African rhythms. There are also other styles, mixes and adaptations that spring from the conventional forms. Typically, many of the more authentic voices are not known outside of the country, but various musical forms can be found on disk as depicted by their performers. Najat Aatabou sings in an Amazigh style, protesting against the restrictions of her family life. Lem Chaheb is among the groups that perform Chaabi. Gnaoua is an extremely popular genre with many exponents, including Gnawa Diffusion and Hassan Hakmoun, and the style has even slipped into pure Western culture, with Robert Plant incorporating it into some of his work. Rai is the best known endemic music in all North Africa, and Morocco's representatives include Cheb Mimoun and Hanino.

CINEMA Although it isn't very well-known, film production in Morocco is so important that studios have been set up in the southern city of Ourzazate. Since before Orson Wells came to Morocco, saw the seaside town of Essaouira and decided it was the perfect location for his *Othello* (1949), the locations and their easy accessibility have made the country an ideal set. So many movies have been made here that Ourzazate is referred to as a Moroccan Hollywood. Some of the better-known productions include *Lawrence of Arabia* (1962, dir. David Lean), *Patton* (1970, dir. Franklin J Schaffner), *The Man Who Would be King* (1975, dir. John Huston), *Monty Python's Life of Brian* (1979, dir. Terry Jones), *Kundun* (1997, dir. Martin Scorsese) and *Gladiator* (2000, dir. Ridley Scott). To honour the importance of the film industry, Marrakech is now the home of an annual international film festival held between November and December.

LITERATURE An important part of the Moroccan cultural scene, many authors write in their languages of Arabic and French. Mohamed Choukri wrote novels, although he's best known for his autobiography, which included encounters with famous ex-pats. Driss Chraibi was also a novelist, whose works had political overtones. Mohamed Zaftaf was notable for his poems and works written in classical Arabic, while Driss El Khouri remains one of the country's best-known writers, with his writing specialising in ordinary life. Some of Morocco's most famous literary sons live abroad, such as the poet Adellatif Laabi, and the writer Tahar Ben Jellooun, both now in France.

The country could well be more famous for the foreign expatriates who wrote here, spending quite a lot of time in the then alternative art community of Tangier, most notably William S Burroughs and Paul Bowles. The latter became best known for his depictions of Morocco, and his most famous book, *The Sheltering Sky*, was used as the basis for a film made years later by the Italian director, Bernardo Bertolucci.

4

Practical Information

SUGGESTED ITINERARIES FOR CRUISE-SHIP PASSENGERS

Cruise ships that include North Africa on their visits stop at few cities in Morocco and spend very little time there. Only Tangier, Casablanca and possibly Agadir are included and then not even for a whole day each. However, it's still possible to get a flavour of the country. The recommendations below are for disembarking passengers who would rather travel about independently.

TANGIER Lying on the Straits of Gibraltar and at the gateway of the Mediterranean, Tangier is the point in Africa closest to Europe. When sailing through the Straits, it's possible to see both continents at the same time. The current port is conveniently located close to the town, and the new passenger one, scheduled for completion by 2013, will sit at the base of the medina, or old town. Most of the sites in Tangier are fairly close to the ship. If you are feeling energetic, begin your day by taking a stroll down the middle of Avenue Mohamed VI (see page 126), which has a palm-lined pedestrian esplanade running through it. From here, you can see all around the bay, with its beautiful beach and the mountains of Spain beyond. Turn back and head towards the medina (see page 126), the white village on the hill. Here was the original Tangier and it remains the heart of the old city. Complicated and fun, the narrow passages lead every which way, passing wedged-in houses and all kinds of shops, both for tourists and everyday. For a break, stop at the Petit Socco Square, full of life as well as cafés. It's just about possible to make your way through here to the Kasbah, an ancient executive residence even more heavily fortified than the already walled city. The Kasbah Museum (see page 128) here is very good, showing examples of Tangier in its prehistoric, Punic, Roman and early Islamic days. It might be easier to exit the medina and go to the Main Square, the Gran Socco, said to be the site of the original Roman forum (see page 127).

From here, follow the outside walls of the medina to get to the top of the hill where there's another more direct entrance to the Kasbah. (Alternatively, continue past the incongruous Anglican church of St Andrews to the building that was once the British consulate and is now the Museum of Contemporary Art. The collection is devoted to Moroccan artists.) From the Kasbah Museum, go through the gap in the outside wall to the north to get to the cliff overlooking the harbour. There's a lovely walk that skirts the blue Mediterranean below, traversing through wonderfully located, but surprisingly dilapidated, residential enclaves. A highlight includes seeing the oblong rectangles dug into the rock that were Phoenician tombs, with a spectacular view east over them to the sea and town. Beyond, the buildings change into magnificent villas, where the rich, both domestic and immigrant, built their houses. Once, Malcolm Forbes, the American millionaire had his North African residence here. It functioned briefly as a museum but has now been taken over by the king, as one of his royal residences. It's possible to view it from the outside. On the way back, stop at the Café Hafa, a hangout since the 1920s for all the artists who pass by.

If time allows, join the tour or jump into a taxi to visit Cap Spartel (see page 128). This charming old lighthouse (closed to the public) is where the wild Atlantic pushes through the narrow Straits of Gibraltar to get to the calmer Mediterranean. Further to the west, now on the open ocean, the drive continues past wide sandy braches to get to the Caves of Hercules. Popular mythology has made these grottos the location of the Pillars of Hercules, but it's said that the true location is further to the east of Tangier. In the meantime, once past the tacky shops and dromedary (a real live one, put here for the purpose of tourist posing), you can see the caves carved into the rock that stone cutters have been enlarging since prehistoric times. To make it worthwhile stretching your legs, a short walk from the car park leads to the remains of the Roman town of Cotta, but there is very little left.

CASABLANCA It's probably worth getting into one of the taxis already waiting at the port and beginning the excursion directly from the dock. Negotiate a rate and the vehicle and driver will be yours for the entire time. The highlight of the city is the enormous Hassan II Mosque (see page 97) that is open to non-Muslims. It's worth paying the relatively high fee to take the one-hour tour. When done, meet the waiting taxi and go to the Quartier Habbous Souk (see page 97). If Casablanca is your only Moroccan stop, then do your gift shopping here. The souks, or markets, sell most items typical of the country, including fabrics, shoes and antiques, as well as pastries and olives. When laden, or at least sated, ask the driver to go to the medina, or the old town. Encompassing a labyrinth of streets and barbers, butchers, ironmongers and grocers, Casablanca's is not the best, but if this is the only opportunity you'll get to see an example of a Moroccan old town it's better than nothing. If you are hungry and want to get away from cruise-ship cuisine, find one of the local restaurants here and try one of the *tagines*. By now, the day in the city is probably close to an end, but if you have a little more time, you might like to stroll along the beach. Inevitably on your way back to the ship you'll see some interesting French colonial architecture, as well as the modern city, which is really far more indicative of the role the metropolis has today, than the old preserved tourist sites.

AGADIR The city's best feature is its broad and beautiful beach. It's great to stroll along the long, flat, wave-caressed sands for at least part of the 8km strand. Unfortunately, closer to the town are all the enormous hotels, shops, bars and kitsch that are present in every seaside tourist town. However, it is nice to stop at a café – fresh orange juice is always recommended – hear the lapping of the waves and maybe even watch the catamarans sailing by. Agadir is relatively characterless due to too much concrete, but running right through the middle of the town is Bird Valley (see page 117), a slightly unkempt garden full of birds, fountains and lush vegetation. It's rather old fashioned but sweet nonetheless, and children love it. You could also grab a taxi and head up to the Kasbah on the hill, one of the few remains of Agadir before the earthquake destroyed it in 1960. Very little is left on the site, but the view overlooking the city and the bay from the top of the hill makes the journey worthwhile. If the city is the only Morocco stop on the tour, and you're keen on picking up some souvenirs, try the souks (markets), especially the Municipal Market. The craft stalls are above the ground floor. If you are looking for character, head to the Suq al Had, where the locals do their shopping. There isn't much else to see. Surprisingly, Agadir is also a major port town and one of largest sardine exporters in the world. The harbour is at the north of town and hardly intrudes upon the activities further south.

UK & Irish Republic 205 Regent St, London WIR 7DE; ☏ 020 7437 0073; ℮ mnto@btconnect.com **Australia & New Zealand** II West St North, Sydney, NSW 2060; ☏ 2 99823752; f 2 99231053; www.tourisme-marocain.com/onmt_EN/Marches/INS/ index.aspx

Canada 2001 Rue Université, No 1460, Montreal PQ, H3A 2A6; ☏ 514 842 8111; f 514 842 5316 **USA** 20 East 46th St, Suite 1201, New York, NY 10017; ☏ 212 557 2520/1/2; f 212 949 8148

IN MOROCCO There are local tourist offices within most of the major cities and resorts. Individual locations are listed at the beginning of each city section.

$ MONEY

If you can't get hold of Moroccan dirhams on the ship, banks will accept major foreign currencies for exchange; US dollars and euros are always welcome, while some will take English pounds as well as Canadian and Australian dollars. Credit cards are fine, although an extra fee will appear on your statement when you get home. Opening hours vary from town to town, but are usually 08.15–12.15 and 14.15–17.15 Monday–Thursday, 08.15–11.15 and 14.30–17.30 Friday, 09.00–13.00 Saturday. Some larger banks may be open all day. ATMs are common in the big cities.

GETTING AROUND

Morocco has excellent domestic transport, including air, train, bus, taxi and road networks. Trains will go to towns that have no airports, and buses will go to villages where the train doesn't run. Taxis help fill further gaps, and renting a car is always the most flexible if not the cheapest option. As a result, journey times are relatively quick, eg: a transfer flight from Casablanca to Rabat takes 30 minutes, plus transfer and scheduling time; 90 minutes if driving; and 70 minutes via the frequent train service. Similar comparisons work for the other major cities. Where the plane has the true advantage is when going much further, for example down to Laayoune in the far southwest of the country. There is no rail network, so going by plane, bus or car is the only way to get there. The first method takes 90 minutes, while the second and third take between 21 and 23 hours.

✈ **BY AIR** Morocco has 16 airports served by commercial aircraft. Most are domestic, with Casablanca being the main international gateway. Flights direct to Tangier and Marrakech are also common. Agadir is predominantly a charter destination. Most domestic requirements are handled by the national carrier, Royal Air Maroc. There are some smaller companies that include air taxi services. When arriving at Mohamed V Airport in Casablanca, an airport train as well as a shuttle bus cover the 30km to the city, although if it's late at night, or you're not sure where you're going, taxis are reasonably priced. You can also pick up a rental car here, and sometimes even drop it off if collected from another location, as long as you arrange it in advance. When arriving at Menara Airport in Marrakech, a bus service transports visitors to the centre of the city, 5km away, and taxis, again inexpensive, and car hire are also available.

🚂 **BY RAIL** Morocco's train network is nationalised, run by ONCF (Office National des Chemins de Fer) (*www.oncf.ma; but only in French*). Although not comprehensive, it services most of the tourist destinations, and certainly the ones along the Roman coast of North Africa. The prices are relatively low; for example, starting at Casablanca Airport, and going to Rabat, an ordinary second-class fare is around MAD65; to Tangier MAD153; and to Marrakech MAD119. Going by rail is surprisingly pleasant, with comfortable seats and big windows. If you are feeling flush, for a very small increase in price, it's possible to upgrade to first class. Facilities switch from padded benches for eight passengers to plush upholstered seats for six. It is safe for women to travel on their own in both classes. However, try to avoid travelling at the end of holidays or weekends when the train is likely to be used by everyone, especially towards the big cities. Often there's only standing room available. Toilets can also suffer from heavy use.

BY BUS Aware of its shortcomings, ONCF has a sister bus company, Supratours, that services the network not covered by train. Supratours is designed to work in parallel with ONCF, so timetables coincide, and it's possible to book the two together via the same website. The buses are very comfortable and efficient, and as reservations are required passengers always get seats (exact position can also be booked, if you get to the office in time). For example, if you want to get from Agadir to the Roman site of Volubilis, take a Supratour bus to Marrakech for MAD90, from there pay MAD143 and jump on the train towards Tangier, stay on for about 5 hours 45 minutes and get off at Sidi Kacem. Although seemingly a small town, it's where the Casablanca to Fes and the Fes to Tangier trains intersect and often requires a line change. By fortunate coincidence, it's also 20 minutes by taxi away from the best Roman site in Morocco, and taxis are available to take you there for around MAD35 (£2.90 or US$4).

BY TAXI Seeming extravagant at first, taxis are actually an excellent way to get around. Petit taxis are small cars that service the cities and prices are so low that even locals take them. They are shared, so that drivers will pull over and collect up to an additional three passengers. Frequent and plentiful, if not exactly luxurious, petit taxis are a good way to get quickly from one place to another and, if your French is reasonable, to have a good natter with the driver. They are also colour-coded per city, so that in Casablanca they're red, in Marrakech yellow, in Rabat blue and in Meknes turquoise. Grand taxis, usually Mercedes, are allowed to travel from town to town. This method of travel is much more expensive than going by bus or train, but it is convenient and works to the passenger's schedule rather than the train or bus company's. Drivers are used to tourists, and will halt at the standard visitor stops, including tea breaks. They will also be willing to wait, or meet you on following days, to show you around, or take you back. You are not obliged to take them up on either unless you've agreed a fee for a return journey, and haven't paid them anything yet for the first half.

BY CAR Driving in Morocco is relatively easy, although with the excellent public transport as well as taxis to deal with the gaps, it's not the best way to get around unless you're in a hurry or going off the beaten track. It's also somewhat expensive. Those that do opt for it should note: Moroccans adhere to their French legacy and navigate on the right; and the speed limits range from 40kmph in the cities, to 60–80kmph on bigger roads and 120kmph on the motorway. An international driving permit is not mandatory; a valid EU (or UK), US, or other document license is acceptable and should be carried at all times. Check with your insurance company at home to make sure you're covered for travelling (remember that Morocco is not an EU country). If not, you can buy local coverage with the larger car rental companies in town. Vehicle registration and rental documents should always be accessible, in case you are stopped by the local police. For rentals, it's advisable to get the collision damage waiver insurance. Be careful about the additional damage costs. Sometimes there is quite a large deductible, but the smaller companies can charge an extortionate amount for this extra.

PUBLIC HOLIDAYS

Fixed annual dates are:

1 January	New Year's Day
11 January	Manifesto of Independence
1 May	Labour Day
30 July	Feast of the Throne
14 August	Fête Oued Eddahab (Oued Eddahab Allegiance Day).
20 August	Révolution du Roi et du Peuple (Anniversary of the King and the People's Revolution)
21 August	King Mohamed's Birthday
6 November	Marche Verte (Anniversary of the Green March)
18 November	Fête de l'Indépendance (Independence Day)

The following holidays are Islamic and vary annually according to the lunar calendar. They are also celebrated on the same dates (variable according to the year) in Algeria, Tunisia and Libya:

9 March	Aïd al-Mawlid (Prophet's Birthday)
21 September	Aïd al-Fitr, or Eid (End of Ramadan)
28 November	Aïd al-Adha (Feast of the Sacrifice)

MEDIA AND COMMUNICATIONS

POST Normal post office hours are 08.30–12.00 and 14.30–18.30 Monday–Friday, 08.30–14.00 Saturday. Don't expect mail to arrive quickly. Airmail to destinations outside Africa takes up to one week and can be unreliable. It's best to post letters at the post office itself or ask the local tour guide which mailboxes are reliable.

NEWSPAPERS Still a popular way of gleaning information, there are several newspapers read on a regular basis. With five national papers, and several additional ones for the towns, catching up on current events is easy. Some publications are politically oriented, such as *Liberation,* affiliated with the socialists; *Al Bayane,* a vehicle for the communists; *Le Matin du Sahara,* a royalist paper; and *L'Opinion,* linked to the opposition party. Newspapers from France are generally available, although allegedly only *Le Figaro* arrives on the day. It's possible to find other foreign newspapers, including English-language ones, at some of the bigger bookshops or tourist-oriented locations. For a full list of papers, check www.newspapers24.com/moroccan-newspapers.

RADIO There are loads of radio stations, but none seem to be national, although information and news are repeated on several sister stations. They're predominantly FM and broadcast in French or Arabic. In Casablanca, there are eight stations, with 2M, Medi 1, Radio Casablanca and Radio Sawa Morocco being the most popular. They play the usual ubiquitous sounds, with some Arabic and North African music, some of which can be very catchy. The other cities also have a selection of stations. In Tangier, it's possible to pick up the British Forces Broadcasting Service from Gibraltar, in English on 93.5 and 97.8FM.

TELEVISION Despite the popularity of satellite dishes and the option of picking up foreign channels, particularly Egyptian ones, Morocco has its own homebred varieties. Radio 2M has a sister television outlet (*www.2m.tv*) and together with

RTM is government run. Most of the larger hotels pick up the standard battery of broadcasts from other countries via satellite.

MOBILE PHONES AND THE INTERNET Mobile phones are everywhere, and have been for some time. As with the rest of the world, Moroccans are glued to their handsets. Reception is very good, even in some places in the desert.

Internet cafés are widespread. The government heavily supports internet use and has even created CyberParc, a green space in Marrakech with card-fuelled phone internet monitors scattered around the grounds.

GIVING SOMETHING BACK

Helping the poor (zakah) is one of the Five Pillars of Islam and should be practised on a regular basis by all good Muslims; it is recommended that at least 5% of their income should be donated to the needy. Theoretically, this assistance ought to minimise the need for aid, but in practice the country is not wealthy enough to support its poor. As a result, the majority of charities appear to be foreign-driven rather than Moroccan.

Amnesty International www.amnesty.org/en/region/middle-east-and-north-africa/north-africa. The human rights organisation's website for all North Africa.
Cross Cultural Solutions www.crossculturalsolutions.org/where_you_can_go/morocco/default.asp. A volunteer programme to help in the local community.
Doctors Without Borders www.doctorswithoutborders.org/news/morocco.cfm. The American version of Médecins Sans Frontières, working in Morocco.
Education for All www.educationforallmorocco.org. A charity set up to educate rural girls.

Handimaroc.org www.handimaroc.org/espace_associatif.php. A website that lists associations for the disabled throughout the country.
Human Rights Watch www.hrw.org/doc/?t=mideast, & for Morocco: www.hrw.org/doc/?t=mideast&c=morocco
Peace Corps www.peacecorps.gov/index.cfm?shell=learn.wherepc.northafr.morocco. The American's volunteer programme's Morocco website.
Save the Children www.savethechildren.net/alliance/where_we_work/AN/map.html. The International organisation works with Moroccan associates.

5

Ports of Entry

TANGIER

Sitting at the head of the Straits of Gibraltar – the 14km-wide gap that separates the continents – Tangier is the closest African city to Europe. For land-based passengers travelling from the north it is the first Moroccan port of entry. This destination is so important to the visitor of the past and the present that it has its own chapter, see page 119.

CASABLANCA *Telephone code 0522*

Morocco's capital – a bustling, modern city with over three million inhabitants – is the sixth largest city in all of Africa. Most people arrive in the country via Mohamed V International Airport, although the manmade port not only welcomes passenger ships, but is also the largest industrial harbour in the Maghreb. Trains go almost everywhere from this central point. The most important visitor attraction is the extremely impressive Hassan II Mosque, the second largest in the world, after Mecca. Non-Muslims are allowed to visit on one of the hour-long tours.

HISTORY If the Phoenicians and Romans passed by here, they didn't leave any trace. Casablanca was a Berber settlement established before AD700. Subsequently set up as the kingdom of Anfa, it was eventually absorbed as part of the Almoravid conquest by 1100. The next invaders, the Merinids, recognised the value of the ocean-side location and developed the port, which became a haven for pirates from 1400. This privateering annoyed the Portuguese, who had been doing their own trading along Morocco's Atlantic coast for at least a hundred years. They destroyed the town of Anfa in 1468, then established their own fortress there in 1515. The settlement that developed alongside became known as 'Casabranca' or 'white house'. Yo-yoing between Spanish and Portuguese rule, the place was left alone by both countries after an earthquake in 1755 wiped out the town. Rebuilt soon after by a local sultan and renamed Dar el Beida (Arabic for 'white house'), the city grew slowly until there were around 10,000 inhabitants in the 1880s. During the French occupation, the city thrived, with the European colonisers further developing the port. Casablanca played a major role during World War II, with an American air base located here. In 1956, along with the rest of Morocco, the city was granted its independence from France.

GETTING THERE AND AROUND

By air Casablanca's Mohamed V Airport (❧ *022 53 90 40; www.onda.org.ma*) services both international and domestic traffic. The arrival point for most European traffic, it's also the departure airport for most of the internal Royal Air Maroc flights, the country's largest carrier. The 45-minute shuttle train to the port and city centre leaves from the arrivals hall and costs around MAD35 (£2.90/US$4)

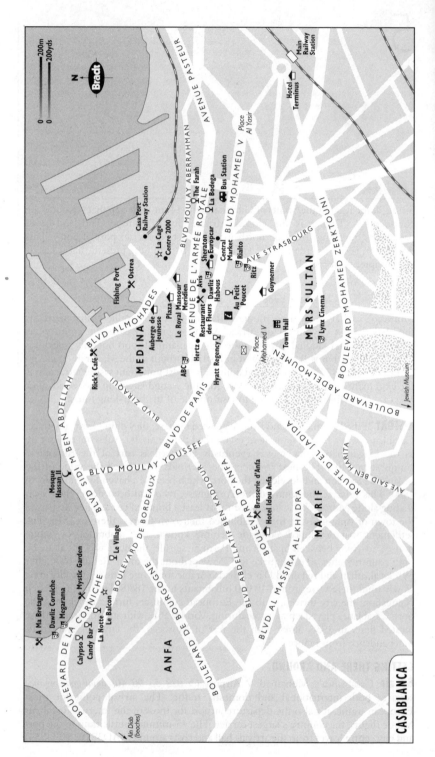

CASABLANCA

200m
200yds
0
0

N
Bradt

Main
Railway
Station

Hotel
Terminus

AVENUE PASTEUR

Place
Al Yasir

BLVD MOULAY ABERRAHMAN

Casa Port
Railway Station

La Cage
Centre 2000

The Farah
La Bodega

BLVD MOHAMED V

AVENUE DE L'ARMÉE ROYALE

Bus Station

Fishing Port

Ostrea

Sheraton
Europcar
Central
Market

AVE STRASBOURG

Plaza

Le Royal Mansour
Méridien

Avis

Dawliz
Habous

Ritz
Rialto

Rick's Café

BLVD ALMOHADES

MEDINA

Auberge de
Jeunesse

Hertz
Restaurant
des Fleurs

Au Petit
Poucet

Guynemer

MERS SULTAN

BLVD ZIRAOUI

ABC

Hyatt Regency

Place
Mohamed V

Town Hall

Lynx Cinema

BOULEVARD ABDELMOUMEN

BOULEVARD MOHAMED ZERKTOUNI

Jewish Museum

Mosque
Hassan II

BLVD SIDI M BEN ABDELLAH

BLVD DE PARIS

BLVD MOULAY YOUSSEF

BLVD DE BORDEAUX

ROUTE D. EL JADIDA

AVE SAID BEN HARITA

A Ma Bretagne
Dawliz Corniche
Megarama
Mystic Garden

Calypso
Candy Bar
La Notte
Le Balcon

Le Village

BOULEVARD DE LA CORNICHE

BOULEVARD DE BOURGOGNE

BOULEVARD ABDELLATIF BEN KADDOUR

BOULEVARD D'ANFA

Brasserie d'Anfa
Hotel Idou Anfa

BLVD AL MASSIRA AL KHADRA

MAARIF

ANFA

Ain Diab
(beaches)

90

while the bus to the central CTM station (*23 Rue Léon l'Africain;* ☏ *0522 54 10 10*) takes about an hour. Taxis are located on the ground floor at arrivals and will get you to your destination much quicker. There is a minimum charge of MAD200 to get to Casablanca. Although this is expensive, the taxi driver knows where you need to go, and is reliable.

By rail Trains from the airport go to two stations in town, the Gare Casa Port (*Bd Houphouet;* ☏ *0522 22 30 11*) and the Gare Casa Voyageur (*Bd Bahmad;* ☏ *090 203 040*). The latter is used more frequently, although the former is convenient for the port. It's possible to get almost anywhere in the country via train, contact ONCF (*www.oncf.ma*) for destinations, times and prices.

By bus For intercity transport, there are various bus companies, but Supratours (via ONCF) is the most organised and reliable and can link up with train timetables. Within the city, the CTM station is the destination for the airport buses. There is also the Gare Routiere (*56 Rue des Oulad Ziane;* ☏ *0522 85 35 45*) from where many of the city buses go. If staying locally and time – and crowds – are not an issue, transport by public bus is an interesting way to travel.

By taxi Petit taxis are the ones that are allowed to travel only within the city and are plentiful. Small and red, they're cheap, mostly because they're also shared – drivers can pick up three passengers *en route*. If you are not happy with hailing one off the street, it's possible to phone ahead via Taxi Radio (☏ *0522 89 24 89*). It's also perfectly acceptable to ask the concierge of the hotel to call for one. However, these cars are much more expensive. It will be much cheaper to walk out the front door and simply flag one down. Grand taxis are the bigger and flashier vehicles that provide private intercity transport. Much pricier than the public alternatives, they're efficient, quick and provide itineraries tailored to the customer. In this case, it is advisable to arrange transport through the hotel, as not only will the driver that arrives be reliable, but he will often be a relative of the person who phones for him. It makes no difference to the passenger, but it does do a favour to the staff. Sometimes these taxis can be shared, to reduce the cost, but it requires a bit of organisation to find other passengers.

Car hire It's not cheap to rent a vehicle, nor is it really necessary, unless you are looking to explore off-the-beaten-track destinations, such as some of the more obscure Roman ruins. Most of the major car hire firms can be found at the airport as well as in town.

🚗 **Avis** 19 Av des FAR; ☏ 0522 31 24 24; www.avis.com

🚗 **Europcar** 144 Av des FAR; ☏ 0522 31 40 69; www.europcar.com

🚗 **Hertz** 25 Rue de Foucault; ☏ 0522 31 22 23; www.hertz.com

TOURIST INFORMATION Casablanca has two tourism bureaux: **L'Office National Marocaine du Tourisme** (*ONMT, 55 Rue Omar Slaoui;* ☏ *0522 27 11 77;* ⊕ *08.30–12.00 & 14.30–18.30 Mon–Thu, 08.30–11.30 & 15.00–18.30 Fri*) and the

5

FAR AND AWAY

Casablanca's Avenue of the Royal Army Forces is known as FAR (Forces Armées Royale) and is one of the many crossroads of the city. It is always referred to as Avenue des FAR, and its name is almost never seen in its full form.

Syndicat d'Initiative (*98 Bd Mohamed V;* ✆ *0522 22 15 24;* ⊕ *08.30–12.00 & 15.00–18.30 Mon–Fri, 08.30–12.00 & 15.00–17.00 Sat, 09.00–12.00 Sun*). There is a movement growing to keep offices open during lunch, so these hours might stretch into entire days soon, The Moroccan National Tourist Office has a slick new website (*www.visitmorocco.org*), which might not be easy to use, but does look flashy.

TOUR OPERATORS Casablanca has many tour operators providing local travel as well as further afield. The website www.travel-in-morocco.com/voyagecasablanca.htm lists what appears to be all of them, but for a starter try the following companies:

Adra Voyages 21 Rue Touki Ahmed; ✆ 0522 22 16 04
Adventure Travel Service 48 Rue Makik Allal; ✆ 0522 25 65 62
Aladin Toursime 47 Rue Allal Ben Abdellah; ✆ 0522 27 63 64
Amorocco 2 Av Saadioune; ✆ 0522 50 10 26

KTI Voyages (Head Office) 3 Rue Isli (rond point Racine); ✆ 0522 39 85 68; www.ktivoyages.com/en/qsn/index.php
Morocco Bound Tour Bd Sidi Abderahmane Hay Hassani; ✆ 0522 89 34 73
Morocco Tours 27 Rue Sidi Belyout; ✆ 0522 27 38 19
Visit Morocco 2 Rue le Golza; ✆ 0522 94 23 37

If you're already on a package and would like something extra, such as additional tours, transport or accommodation, check with your operator's local ground agents. They're the ones employed by your company, are the most interested in keeping you happy, and will do their best to serve you.

 WHERE TO STAY There is a broad range of accommodation options. The following is a condensed selection:

Top end

⌂ **Le Royal Mansour Meridien** (182 rooms) 27 Av de l'Armée Royale; ✆ 0522 31 310 11; www.starwoodhotels.com/lemeridien/property/overview/index.html?propertyID=1816. One of Casablanca's premier hotels, this Starwood property is part of the Le Meridien group. Luxurious & self-indulgent, it has all the usual facilities, including conference rooms, fitness centre & restaurant. The hotel is extremely well located in the centre of the modern city, close to most things worth seeing. $$$$$
⌂ **Sheraton Casablanca Hotel & Towers** (286 rooms) 100 Av des FAR; ✆ 0522 43 94 94;

www.starwoodhotels.com/sheraton/property/dining/index.html?propertyID=307. Another of the hotels under the Starwood umbrella, this Sheraton is extremely modern, offering views of either the city or the port. $$$$$
⌂ **Hotel Idou Anfa** (220 rooms) 85 Bd d'Anfa; ✆ 0522 20 02 35; www.hotel-idouanfa.com. Better than comfortable, this modern 4-star hotel is well located in the new district. The bar on the top floor gives an excellent view over the city, especially towards the Hassan II Mosque. $$$$$–$$$$$

Mid-range

⌂ **Hotel Guynemer** (29 rooms) 2 Rue Mohamed Belloul (ex Pegoud); ✆ 0522 27 76 19; www.geocities.com/guynemerhotel. Request a bigger room & the accommodation can be quite pleasant, with the occasional bit of original Art Deco detailing. Off a side street, but still conveniently situated; there are shops for provisions just around the corner. $$–$$$

⌂ **Hotel Plaza** (*not* the Crowne Plaza) 18 Bd Felix Houphouet Boigny; ✆ 0522 29 76 98. Close to the port & the train station, this old hotel leaves something to be desired, but remains a good bargain. $$

Budget

⌂ **Auberge de Jeunesse** (72 beds) 6 Place El Bidaoui; ✆ 0522 22 05 51. The youth hostel, always

the best bargain accommodation, lies within the medina. There are private rooms available at a higher price, but still great value. This place gets booked up very quickly, especially in the summer. $

⌂ **Hotel Terminus** 184 Bd Ba Hamad; ☏ 0522 24 00 25. The best thing about this cheap hotel is its location close to the main railway station, as well as its basic, but well-maintained facilities. Don't expect too much for the price. $

✗ WHERE TO EAT

Morocco's largest city has some very discerning and sophisticated residents, as well as an affluent business community, so there is an enormous variety of eating establishments. Most hotels that are three-star or more will have their own in-house restaurants, some quite good. After a tiring day, it might not be worth going any further. Throughout the country it's possible to find the same traditional cuisine of couscous and *tagine*, but here might be the opportunity to try something a bit more adventurous. If you are feeling fishy, the active port provides good seafood. Here's a small, but varied, selection of places to eat.

✗ **A Ma Bretagne** Sidi Abderrahman, Bd de la Corniche, Ain Diab; ☏ 0522 36 21 12; ⊙ dinner only. This gourmet venue is 'the best restaurant in Africa', as proclaimed by the proprietors. Primarily a seafood place with some French cuisine thrown in, come here when you want something superb cost be damned. $$$$

✗ **Brasserie d'Anfa** 63 Bd d'Anfa; ☏ 0522 47 42 47; ⊙ lunch & dinner, Mon–Sat. This pricey place presents some excellent cuisine more associated with finer European restaurants than with an African city. $$$$

✗ **Ostrea** Le Port de Pêche (city centre); ☏ 0522 441390; www.ilove-casablanca.com/ostrea; ⊙ 11.00–23.00 daily. This rather smart portside dining experience takes its produce from the sea around it. Specialities include oysters, prawns, lobsters & other shellfish. $$$–$$$$

✗ **Rick's Café** 248 Bd Sour Jdid, Medina; ☏ 0522 27 42 07; www.rickscafe.ma; ⊙ 12.00–15.50 & 18.30–01.30. Yes, there is a Rick's Café in Casablanca, even if it's been recreated decades after *Casablanca*, the 1942 Hollywood film, immortalised the fictional hangout. Run by Americans & complete with a pianist; the cuisine is American, & the location, portside. It's a nice place to go when feeling nostalgic – or homesick. $$$

✗ **Mystic Garden** 33 Bd de la Corniche, Aïn Diab; ☏ 0522 79 88 77; ⊙ 12.00–15.00 & 19.00-02.00. Fusion food is on the menu, but this is more than just a place to eat. With regular entertainment nights, including Latin music on Tue & jam sessions on Fri, you just have to hang around to launch into the disco a little later. It's not as expensive as it could be. $$

✗ **Restaurant des Fleur** 42 Av des FAR. Good for b/fast; the downstairs is fine for something small; upstairs, splash out for more significant Moroccan & French fare. $–$$$

Some remainders of the French occupation are very welcome, such as the plentiful supply of patisseries and *salons de thé* that are generously scattered throughout the city. Virtually any of these inexpensive cafés, whether alongside the sidewalk or hidden inside buildings, are fine for stopping and having a mid-morning snack.

ENTERTAINMENT AND NIGHTLIFE Many of Casablanca's entertainment possibilities consist of going out to nightclubs and bars, although cinema-loving enthusiasts have lots of places to enjoy their passion, with films mostly in French or Arabic. There are also one or two venues offering formal live performance, but these aren't as prolific.

It's to be expected that there are lots of bars and nightclubs in this modern and cosmopolitan city, yet the good ones can be hard to find. Corner cafés and drinking places may be around every corner, but they might also be male preserves. Casablanca has three areas where the best and most tourist-friendly bars and nightclubs are located: downtown offers authentic and slightly seedy options, as well as the odd fine restaurant; five-star hotels offer a range of bars (see page 94) and usually a nightclub, plus the opportunity to drink and dance safely, without

Morocco: Ports of Entry CASABLANCA

5

93

Captain Renault: What in heaven's name brought you to Casablanca?
Rick: My health. I came to Casablanca for the waters.
Captain Renault: The waters? What waters? We're in the desert.
Rick: I was misinformed.

From Casablanca, 1942, director Michael Curtiz

Few cities in the world have been so immortalised, and so incorrectly romanticised. The love story between Humphrey Bogart as Rick, and Ingrid Bergman as Ilsa, was filmed during World War II, before the outcome of the conflict had been decided. Taking place in the demi-monde of the café of exiled American, Rick, the ambience of waiting in an exotic, unoccupied and somewhat disinterested French-colony location just outside the fray, gave Hollywood the opportunity to play with the truth. It's possible that the producers envisaged Casablanca as being mystical and secretive, like Marrakech or Fes, with the extra advantage that it was close to Europe. Lisbon, the place from where so many war refugees really did flee to escape to North America, lay not much further than just across the Straits. It was easy to blend geographical reality with North African strangeness, especially since the entire project was filmed entirely in a studio in Hollywood. The reality was that Casablanca was large, industrial and unattractive, with significant slums and very little to attract tourists. Today, the city is cleaner and somewhat more interesting than it was when the movie was made. It continues to benefit from its Hollywood depiction even if the only things relevant today to the film have been specially created for the seekers.

having to deal with taxis to unknown locations; whilst the Ain Diab section of the city, along the seaside corniche west of the Hassan II Mosque, offers a plentiful number of good bars which stay open until about 01.00 while nightclubs usually start around 23.00 and close around 03.00

Downtown There are many places to drink and party around Place Mohamed V. Some are more colourful than others, but if you are not looking for too much of a local experience, it might be best to seek out the slightly more upmarket ones.

♀ **Au Petit Poucet** 86 Bd Mohamed V; ⊕ 09.00–22.00. Better known as a place to eat, the bar is alleged to be one of the city's best.
♀ **La Bodega** 129 Rue Allal Ben Abdellah, adjacent to the Central Market; ✆ 0522 54 18 42; ⊕ 12.30–15.00 & 19.00–00.00. This tapas & wine bar caters to a somewhat elegant crowd, willing to brave the blaring music & the inner city location.
☆ **La Cage** Centre 2000. Within Casablanca's port-adjacent new shopping centre, this late-night club provides its predominantly younger crowd with live acts. It's quite a popular meeting place.

Hotels Some of the centrally situated five-star hotels come complete with various bars and nightclubs to pass the time into early morning. The more patronised ones are:

♀ **Hyatt Regency Casablanca** Place des Nations Unies; ✆ 0522 43 1234; casablanca.regency.hyatt.com/hyatt/hotels/entertainment/live/index.jsp. There are 2 bars here: the **Living Room** (⊕ 07.00–midnight) in the lobby where you can Wi-Fi friends till late at night, with a drink in hand; & the **SixPM Lounge Bar** (⊕ 18.00–01.00), a venue with easy-listening music & interesting cocktails – it's developing a reputation for the place to go after work. There's also a discotheque, **The Black House** (⊕ midnight–03.00), which is one of the most popular in the city. Modern & trendy, there is an entrance fee, & a minimum age for entry of 18, as well as a smart–casual dress code.

♀ **The Farah** Av de l'Armée Royale 160; ☎ 0522 31 12 12; www.goldentulipfarahcasablanca.com. Part of the Golden Tulip chain, this venue has its own in-house choices. The **Churchill** bar is a nice place in which to lounge, while the **Jazz Bar** does its thing with snacks & cocktails. The **Jet Set** is the Farah's nightclub & provides live performances as a background for a late night meal.

☆ **The Sheraton** 100 Av des FAR; ☎ 0522 43 94 94. The Sheraton's nightlife option is **Caesars** (🕐 21.00–03.00), a very well-attended locale where visitors can dance & nibble at the refreshments till the early hours of the morning. The entrance fee is not cheap.

Ain Diab This stretch along the Corniche is Casablanca's biggest conglomeration of bars and nightclubs, and there are so many that it's hard to choose between them. If money is no object, there's always the pub crawl. Here are some of them:

♀ **Calypso** Bd del la Corniche; ☎ 0522 79 76 29. One among the many bars, this place also acts as a discotheque, & comes complete with a dance floor.

♀ **Candy Bar** Hotel Riad Salam, Bd de la Corniche; ☎ 0522 79 84 40. So cool & trendy that this pink nightclub attracts businessmen away from the capital Rabat, less than 90km north, although its clientele are mostly 20 & 30 somethings.

♀ **La Notte** 31 Bd de la Corniche; ☎ 0522 79 79 70. The name means 'The Night', & the evening visitors who enjoy the discotheque here are distinctly upmarket.

♀ **Le Balcon 33** 33 Bd de la Corniche; ☎ 0522 79 72 05. Its loyal clientele claims that this dance venue is one of the best in Casablanca.

♀ **Le Village** 11 Bd de la Corniche. This venue attracts more of a gay crowd.

SHOPPING Although Casablanca is a big, sophisticated, modern city it's still in Morocco, and the best shopping experiences are to be found in the markets and souks. The original town, the medina, consists of typical labyrinthine passages and is lined with small shops selling all sorts of items. The Quartier Habous, or new medina, holds the craft and kitsch stores that are fine for purchasing souvenirs. Bargaining, of course, is the rule here. These souks are not the finest in Morocco, but good enough to give a flavour of what those extraordinary places in Marrakech and Fes are like. Normal shopping hours are 08.30–12.00 and 14.00–18.30 Monday–Saturday. Hypermarkets like Marjane and Auchan are located in the suburbs with longer hours. During Ramadan, the hours change, as there's very little business during the day, so the shops are generally open briefly in the morning, and after sundown until quite late.

Markets Within the walls of the ancienne medina, bordered on one side by the fishing port and the other by the centre of town at Place Felix Houphouet Boigny, the complex alleyways are stiff with little shops and stores selling mostly day-to-day items. It's really more of an experience than a shopping trip, although if you need some basic ironmongery, or want to extend your breakfast a little, it's a good place to see where the locals go. See page 96 for more information. The Quartier Habous is further into the city, just south of the Mers Sultan district. This much newer area bears more of a resemblance to the legendary Eastern bazaars than the narrow, though more interesting, old medina, and is where local crafts are on display. All kinds of Moroccan artisan work are found here, such as carpets, ceramics, ironwork, lanterns, slippers and wooden boxes, although these examples are probably not the best. Pretty much in the centre of town, off Boulevard Mohamed V and not far from the old medina, is the Central Market. The hours, 06.00–14.00, give you something to do in the morning, and can provide you with edible provisions for the rest of the day. Filled with fresh goods that the locals come and buy, the fruit, fish and flower markets are particularly colourful, and the crowds and energy are exciting to experience. It's worth a visit even if you are not intending to buy anything.

Shops For fixed-price artisan goods, where you don't have to bargain, try:

Artisanat Fenouch 3 Bd Moulay Abdeherrahmane; ➘ 0522 27 72 87. Close to the port & Centre 2000.

Exposition Nationale d'Artisanat 3 Av Hassan II; ➘ 0522 267 064; ⏲ 08.00–12.00 Mon–Sun.

Shopping malls and department stores
Centre 2000 Bd Moulay Abderrahmane, near the port. This glossy new shopping arcade is centrally located & filled with loads of trendy shops – not the place for authentic Moroccan items at cheap prices. There are also similar stores & boutiques scattered around the Place de Nations Unies. **Alpha** 55 Av Mers Sultan; ➘ 0522 22 37 24. The most conveniently located of the department stores.

Specialist shops
Comptoir Marocain de distibution de Disques 25 Av Lallia Yacout; ➘ 0522 36 91 53. The best record shop in the city, this treasure chest is the place to find that obscure Moroccan artist for whom you've been searching. Most other types of music are on sale too. **Thema Maison** 27 Rue Houssine Ben Ali; ➘ 0522 22 03 60. Excellent Moroccan interior design items, such as blankets, cushions & fabrics are on sale at this very classy store. Worth a look even if only to compare with the more standard stuff available at the markets.

Super and hypermarkets **Marjane** is located in the Ain Sebaa, Californie, Hay Hassani and Mers Sultan districts, and **Auchan** has two **Acima** supermarkets located more conveniently at 21 Rue Pierre Parent near Boulevard Mohamed V and Rue Mohamed Smiha, and at Boulevard Rahal el Meskini.

OTHER PRACTICALITIES
Emergency telephone numbers
Police and fire ➘ 19
Ambulance ➘ 15
Highways ➘ 177

All-night chemist Pl Mohamed V
SOS doctor ➘ 0522 44 44 44

Hospitals
✚ **Hospital Ibn Rochd** Anfa; ➘ 0522 26 51 02

✚ **Clinique Badr** 35 Rue El Alloussi Bourgogne; ➘ 0522 49 28 00

Internet cafés Many hotels have internet access, some with Wi-Fi (pronounced 'whiffy'), but often only available in the lobby. Among them are the Farah, the Hyatt Regency and the Sheraton. Otherwise try:

🖥 **Cyber Espace** 32 Rue El Bekri

🖥 **Rick's Café** 248 Bd Sour Jdid. Offers wireless access.

Post The main post office is on Boulevard Mohamed V (enter via Bd de Paris).

Banks Casablanca is the economic centre of the country, so there are banks everywhere. Branches of nearly every Moroccan financial institution are scattered around the Avenue des FAR.

$ **Bank al Maghrib** 115 Bd de Paris; ➘ 0522 22 41 10. There are branches throughout the city.

$ **Banque Populaire** 2 Av Mly Rachid-ex Franklin Roosevelt; ➘ 0522 94 90 80.

ATMs are all over the place, including 117 Rue Felix Houphouet Boigny; 23 & 25 Boulevard Hassan Seghir; 36 Boulevard Lalla Yacout; 48 Boulevard des FAR.

WHAT TO SEE Casablanca is not the most scenic of towns, and for the tourist, there is relatively little to see. However, if you are spending time here, the following sites are certainly worth a look.

Hassan II Mosque (*Bd Sidi Mohamed Ben Abdallah; MAD120; tours run daily (except Friday) at 9.00, 10.00, 11.00 and at 14.00 in winter, and 14.30 in summer.*) Dominating the skyline with its 210m-high minaret (the tallest in the world), this magnificent building is the main visitor attraction in Casablanca. Completed in 1993 and named after King Hassan II, this beautiful religious structure, the second-largest mosque in the world after Mecca, was designed by the French architect Michel Pinsent and is full of superlatives. Standing prominently, in a huge courtyard full of arches and wonderful Islamic detailing, it overlooks the sea. The interior holds 25,000 people, with the capacity for a further 80,000 outside. Its stunning modern version of traditional interior design belies the high-tech innovations, such as a retractable roof that opens to the sky (25,000 people in an enclosed area can create certain problems) and a first-class, but discreetly hidden sound system. As well as the vast and elaborately decorated central hall, a glass-covered gap in the main floor grants a view down to the marble ablutions area underneath. Non-Muslims are allowed in, but only on the one-hour guided tours.

The ancienne medina (*Bounded by the port, Bd Tahar el Alaoui, Av des FAR & Bd Felix Houphouet Boigny*) The old medina, the original town, is a quarter in the centre of town. It's not as interesting as it probably once was, before the earthquake and subsequent desertion of the city in 1755; most of what's here dates from after 1800. The main appeal of the area, enclosed by walls, is its maze-like streets. The secret to finding one's way around any medina is to allow yourself to get lost. Sooner or later you'll find the route out again, or if not, the locals will guide you back to the nearest major landmark. Strewn with shops, there's enough to interest visitors most of the way along.

The Quartier Habous (*Just south of Av Mers Sultan*) The new medina, dating from around AD1900 and created to provide housing for factory workers, the quarter was built in a retro-Moorish style. It's taken over the role of the older medina in providing places for craftsmen and artisans. Tourists and visitors in search of Moroccan souvenirs make their way to this district. Nearby is the 1940 Pasha's Courthouse, now Prefecture, which is sometimes open for perusal of its interior architectural features. One of the king's royal palaces is also a bit further along, and sometimes the exterior – never the inside – can be viewed.

Ain Diab (*On the Corniche, west of the Hassan II Mosque*) Better known for its plethora of nightclubs, the city's beaches are also here. These strands are not Morocco's best, but pleasant for walking, especially along the 3km of the Corniche. Locals dressed in both European and Moroccan attire stroll with their families, on Friday, the holy day, and at weekends. There are also private beach clubs, open to the public for a fee, ice-cream parlours and cafés. If you're already missing the West, there's a McDonald's here, which is one of the world's busiest, serving something like 4,000 meals a day at peak times. Perhaps its because the hamburgers are prepared in accordance with halal, or Islamic, dietary laws.

Museum of Moroccan Judaism of Casablanca (*81 Rue Chasseur Jules Gros, Casablanca-Oasis; ☏ 0522 99 49 40; www.rickgold.home.mindspring.com/ museum_of_moroccan_judaism.htm; ⊕ 10.00–18.00 Mon–Fri, by appointment Sun;*

MAD20, or MAD30 with guide) Located in the Oasis district, about 5km south of the centre of the city, this museum is an ethnographic and historical assembly of items and exhibitions of this religious group who were once prominent residents.

HOW TO GET TO THE ROMAN SITES The Romans didn't really settle this far south, so the closest site is Sala Colonia, in Chellah in Rabat. There is more information about the place and how to get there, in *Chapter 8*, page 152. In the meantime, it's easy enough to head the short distance to Rabat. Trains go every hour, sometimes more frequently, and leave from the Casa Voyageur station, taking about 60 minutes to get there. There are also departures from Casa Port and Ain Sebaa, although these trips last a bit longer. Normal single second-class fares are as little as MAD32. If travelling by car, head north up the coast road, or the A1 Autoroute, to do the 90km to Rabat – it's that simple. Further away, the best Roman ruin in Morocco is Volubilis, and there are more details regarding both the site and how to get there in *Chapter 7*, page 140. Public transport is available and by fortunate coincidence the train to both these cities stops *en route* at a little place called Sidi Kacem. Better known as the spot where you have to change trains to get to Tangier, the place is also the closest town to Volubilis. A taxi will get you to the site in 20 minutes. Journey time from Casablanca to Sidi Kacem by train is about two hours 30 minutes, and the fare is MAD67. By road the quickest way is to take the A1 to Rabat, then switch to the A2 to get to Meknes. Head north on the P2 just past Moulay Idris, and Volubilis should be signposted.

The rest of the Roman remains are close to Tangier. More particulars are to be found in *Chapter 6*, page 128. Going by rail is the cheapest, though not the quickest, way to get there. It's a long journey, taking about five hours 30 minutes direct, and six hours 30 minutes with the stop, although the fare of MAD118 is very reasonable. There are five departures a day. By road the trip is much easier. Take the A1, past Rabat and past Larache, where you might want to stop at the Roman site of Lixus (more information in *Chapter 6*, page 131), and it will lead you straight to Tangier. The journey time is about three hours 30 minutes.

MARRAKECH *Telephone code 0524*

One of the four imperial cities (the others being Meknes, Fes and Rabat) this pink and ochre centre, at the base of the Atlas Mountains, is a favourite with many Morocco-lovers. It's the prime destination of the country with more tourists visiting than ever before, due to an increased number of direct international flights and an explosion of development. The *palmeraie*, a previous palm grove just outside the city that is an enclave of hotels and golf courses, has become the fashionable place for wealthy foreigners to have a second home. The modern city sparkles, but happily the old medina, surrounded by its massive battlements, remains essentially the same as it always was – crowded, bustling, energetic and beautiful.

HISTORY There's no exact date as to the founding of the city, and it's believed that what was originally a Berber encampment became fortified, and a town eventually grew out of it. By AD1100 the Almoravid dynasty had laid out the city and was using it as one of their bases from which to take over the entire country. The leader's son, Ali Ben Yousef, inherited power from his father and made Marrakech his home base. It was under his leadership that the city began to take on some of its glory, with artists brought from Spain to help create the magnificent edifices, and watercourses constructed to make the place livable. During this time, the first stretch of the medina walls was built. The Almohad tribe invaded in 1147. They destroyed most of what they found, but eventually constructed even more beautiful buildings, such as the Koutoubia Mosque, the tall graceful tower that is now Marrakech's landmark. The city began to bear the brunt of internal decline, and although it had a brief moment of revived importance during the Merenid kingdom, from about 1374, its rebirth was brief. Fes then became the capital. From about 1550, power returned to Marrakech when the Saadians, back from conquering the rest of Morocco, chose to reinvest in the city. The remains of the El Badi palace and the ornate Saadian tombs date to this period. The ebb and flow of command and choice of capital continued after the death of the Saadian sultan, when a 60-year-long civil war began. The court moved away to Meknes. By 1700, the Alaouites had emerged as the next controlling dynasty. The current king, Mohamed VI, is of this bloodline. Not much, however, was done to the benefit of Marrakech, even though it remained one of the royal cities. Just before the French arrived to take over the country, the sultans and their courts moved back to Marrakech, marking their short reigns with the construction of a palace or two. After the French left, granting the country independence in 1956, the city grew with the influx of workers coming down from the Atlas Mountains. It also benefited from the new wave of tourists, a trend that continues today.

GETTING THERE AND AROUND

By air Marrakech's Menara International Airport (✆ *0524 44 79 10; www.onda.ma*) is the city's international and domestic airport, and lies about 6km southwest of the centre. Flights usually stop first at Casablanca. Taxis are the easiest way to get into town from the airport, especially if you've just arrived and are not quite sure where you're going. Prices are about MAD50–100. Alternatively, a MAD20 ride on bus 19 takes you to the Djemaa el-Fna, the square at the entrance of the medina and the heart of town.

By rail Marrakech's large, brand-new railway station replaces its charming, but inadequate, predecessor, and is located in the new part of the city, Guéliz, also known as the Ville Nouveau (*Gare des trains ONCF, Av Hassan II and Bd Mohamed VI;* ✆ *0524 44 65 69; www.oncf.ma*). Situated at the end of the train line, the station is the terminal for points north, for services that run on a regular basis. Most trains go to Casablanca and Rabat with stops in between. Lines continue to Meknes and Fes and getting to Tangier usually requires a change (at Sidi Kacem).

By bus To get to other cities, especially those not accessible by train, there are two recommended long-distance bus companies. As with Casablanca, Supratours (via ONCF) is possibly the easier one to deal with, since it links up with the railways, and leaves from Marrakech's train stations. The line is particularly good should you wish to move on to the coast to either Essaouira (page 111) or Agadir (page 111). The other, CTM, has two locations, one in the new town (*12 Bd Zerktouni, Guéliz;* ✆ *0524 44 74 20*) and one at the edge of the medina (*Gare routière, Bab Doukkala;* ✆ *0524 44 83 28*). The local buses are direct, cheap and frequent, but tend to get packed with people. The central bus station is at the northwestern edge of the medina, at the Bab Doukkala, although most transport stops at the Djemaa, at the southwestern edge of the old town. The most useful buses are the number 8 to the train station, the number 10 to the main bus station, and the number 1 from the medina to Guéliz.

By taxi The city's yellow petit taxis are privately owned cars, which usually only take one party, but will drive exactly where and when you want to go. Although a bit more expensive than the shared taxi, they're still reasonable, particularly if you're in a hurry. The ones in front of the hotel are pricier than the ones flagged

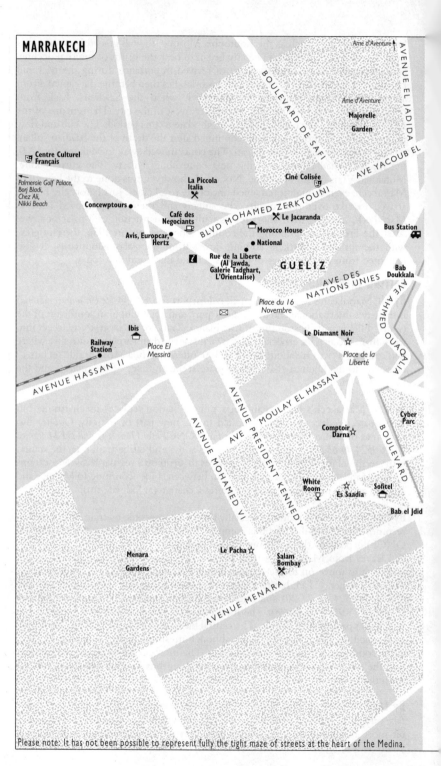

MARRAKECH

Ame d'Aventure

AVENUE EL JADIDA

BOULEVARD DE SAFI

AVE YACOUB EL

Ame d'Aventure

Majorelle

Garden

Centre Culturel
Français

Palmeraie Golf Palace,
Borj Bladi,
Chez Ali,
Nikki Beach

**La Piccola
Italia**

Ciné Colisée

BLVD MOHAMED ZERKTOUNI

Concewptours

**Café des
Negociants**

✕ **Le Jacaranda**

Morocco House

Bus Station

**Avis, Europcar,
Hertz**

● **National**

Rue de la Liberté
**(Al Jawda,
Galerie Tadghart,
L'Orientalise)**

GUELIZ

**Bab
Doukkala**

AVE DES
NATIONS UNIES

AVE AHMED OUAQALIA

Place du 16
Novembre

Le Diamant Noir
☆

Ibis

**Railway
Station**
●

Place El
Messira

Place de la
Liberté

AVENUE HASSAN II

AVENUE MOULAY EL HASSAN

AVE PRESIDENT KENNEDY

AVENUE MOHAMED VI

**Cyber
Parc**

Comptoir☆
Darna

BOULEVARD

**White
Room**
☆
Es Saadia

Sofitel

Bab el Jdid

Menara

Gardens

Le Pacha ☆

**Salam
Bombay**
✕

AVENUE MENARA

Please note: It has not been possible to represent fully the tight maze of streets at the heart of the Medina.

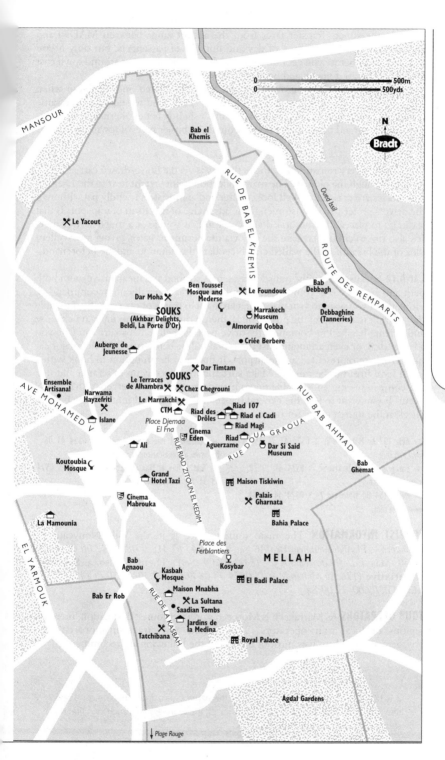

MANSOUR

Bab el
Khemis

0   500m
0   500yds

N

Bradt

RUE DE BAB EL KHEMIS

Oued Issil

ROUTE DES REMPARTS

✕ Le Yacout

Ben Youssef
Mosque and
Mederse

✕ Le Foundouk

Bab
Debbagh

Dar Moha ✕

SOUKS
(Akhbar Delights,
Beldi, La Porte D'Or)

Marrakech
Museum

Debbaghine
(Tanneries)

Almoravid Qobba

Auberge de
Jeunesse

Criée Berbere

✕ Dar Timtam

Ensemble
Artisanal

SOUKS

Le Terraces
de Alhambra ✕ ✕ Chez Chegrouni

AVE MOHAMED V

Narwama
Hayzefriti

Le Marrakchi

RUE BAB AHMAD

Islane

CTM

Riad des
Drôles

Riad 107

Riad el Cadi

Place Djemaa
El Fna

Cinema
Eden

Riad Magi

RUE DOUA GRAOUA

✕ Ali

Riad
Aguerzame

Dar Si Said
Museum

Koutoubia
Mosque

RUE RIAD ZITOUN EL KEDIM

Bab
Ghemat

Grand
Hotel Tazi

Maison Tiskiwin

Cinema
Mabrouka

Palais
✕ Gharnata

La Mamounia

Bahia Palace

EL YARMOUK

Place des
Ferblantiers

MELLAH

Bab
Agnaou

Kosybar

Kasbah
Mosque

El Badi Palace

Maison Mnabha

Bab Er Rob

RUE DE LA KASBAH

✕ La Sultana

Saadian Tombs

Jardins de
la Medina

✕
Tatchibana

Royal Palace

↓ Plage Rouge

Agdal Gardens

down in the street. Transfer fares from the airport range between MAD50 and MAD100, depending on time of day and number of passengers, but only if you agree the price before you get into the cab; whilst, short distances around town cost about MAD5–20 if negotiated beforehand.

Grand taxis – usually big old Mercedes – are the shared ones that stop when flagged down, and collect up to six passengers. They tend to stick with the same routes. They are slower but also cheaper, and a slightly better alternative to taking the bus. The grand taxis usually hover around the busier parts of town, such as the bus stations.

By *caleche* A very romantic way to see the city is via the horse-drawn carriages that wander through the old city. The main collection point is right next to the Djemaa. The horses are reasonably well looked after and appreciate a friendly pat, although the drivers prefer paying customers. The advantage of this form of transport is that it can go to places that motorised vehicles can't, as well as at a much slower pace. It's also fun to circumnavigate the city via the perimeter gates, giving an excellent idea of the breadth of the walled city. Negotiate the duration and fee beforehand.

Car hire Because the public transport system is so good and inexpensive, with both petit and grand taxis at your disposal, renting a car is generally not recommended. However, if you want to visit places that are hard to reach, or on a specific timetable that doesn't match up to the posted ones, then it might be worth the extra expense and driving hassle. Pre-booking a fly-drive package before departure can give you a better deal, or even arranging just the rental online beforehand. All the major car hire firms are represented at the airport. It may also be an option to book with a small local firm but be careful. Make sure the insurance is up to scratch and that the company is big and reliable enough to cope with any emergency that might occur. If you want to join the general melée of the locals and rent a car or bicycle, check at the tourist office for more information.

🚗 **Avis** 137 Av Mohamed V; ✆ 0524 43 25 25; www.avis.com

🚗 **Europcar** 63 Bd Zerktouni; ✆ 0524 43 12 28; www.europcar.com

🚗 **Hertz** 154 Bd Mohamed V; ✆ 0524 44 99 84; www.hertz.com

🚗 **National** 1 Rue de La Liberté; ✆ 0524 43 06 83; www.nationalcar.com

🚗 **Sixt** 9 Rue el Mansour Eddahibi, Guéliz; ✆ 0524 43 31 84; www.sixt.com

TOURIST INFORMATION The main tourist office is in the Ville Nouveau (*Av Mohamed V, Pl Abdelmoumem Ben Ali Sq;* ✆ *0524 43 61 31;* ⊕ *08.30–12.00 & 14.30–18.30 Mon–Fri, 09.00–12.00 & 15.00–18.00 Sat*). There is also a **Syndicat d'Initiative** (*176 Av Mohamed V;* ✆ *0524 43 08 86;* ⊕ *08.30–12.30 & 14.30–18.30 Mon–Fri; 09.00–12.00 Sat*).

TOUR OPERATORS As Marrakech is Morocco's premier tourist destination, there are legions of local tour operators. The website www.travel-in-morocco.com/voyagemarrakech.htm lists most of them, but the following are recommended:

CHURCHTOWN

It is said that Marrakech's new town got the name Guéliz from the French, when they built a Catholic church there. To the locals, the word *eglise* (French for 'church') sounded like Guéliz, and the label stuck.

Ame d'Aventure Case Postale 977-81, Rue Tensift, Semlalia; ☎ 0524 43 90 25; www.ameaventure.ma
Aventure Berbère Immeuble Hamdane No 41, Av Hassan II; ☎ 0524 42 07; www.aventure-berbere.com
Conceptours 220 Av Mohamed V; ☎ 024 43 85 25; www.conceptours.com

Destination Evasion Maroc Villa El Borj, Rue Khalid Ben Oualid; ☎ 0524 44 73 75; www.destination-evasion.com
Partner Aventure 14 Av Allal El Fassi; ☎ 0524 48 41 80/81; www.partneraventure.com/
Uno-Aventure Michel Didriche, Bd Allal el Fassi Imm 12 , Appt. 5, Bureau 4; m 0663 66 44 46; www.uno-aventure.com

WHERE TO STAY There is a huge range of places to stay, from basic and charming to extravagant and exotic. You can opt for inexpensive budget accommodation, a standard but adequate chain hotel, a room in a *riad* or a fine luxury resort. *Riads* tend to be in the medina, while the big luxury chain hotels are in the Ville Nouveau, either in the Hivernage area or the modern downtown (Guéliz). The Palmeraie – the old palm grove to the north of the city that has been converted into a massive tourist area – has both.

Top end

⌂ **La Mamounia** (231 rooms, inc suites) Av Bab Jdid; ☎ 0524 38 86 00; www.mamounia.com. One of the great hotels of the world, this place has been legendary since its opening in 1923. A favourite with celebrities, & indeed Winston Churchill (whose room is still on view), this hotel is *the* place to stay. There's also a very popular piano bar that gets crowded on Sat & Sun nights. Prices are extortionate, but for this class, who thinks about money? $$$$$+

⌂ **Les Jardins de la Medina** (36 rooms) 21 Derb Chtouka, Kasbah; ☎ 0524 38 18 51; www.lesjardinsdelamedina.com. This wonderful hotel is located in the Kasbah district of Marrakech, a little distance from the Djemaa but all the quieter for it.

At its centre is a shady grove of orange trees. The restaurant is top class. $$$$$
⌂ **Palmeraie Golf Palace** (314+ rooms) Circuit de la Palmeraie, BP 1488; ☎ 0524 36 87 04. Although primarily a golf hotel, located in the Palmeraie area north of the city, this Moroccan-style modern luxury hotel is spectacular. There are also eight restaurants on the premises. $$$$$
⌂ **Sofitel Marrakech** (346 rooms) Rue Harroun Errachid Quartier de l'Hivernage; ☎ 0524 42 56 00; www.sofitel.com/sofitel/fichehotel/gb/sof/3569/fiche_hotel.shtml. On the edge of both the medina & the Ville Nouveau, this 1st-class hotel has all the usual Sofitel facilites. Ideal for all the luxuries but nothing too exotic. $$$$$

Mid-range

⌂ **Maison Mnabha** (5 rooms) 32 Derb Mnabha, Kasbah; ☎ 0524 38 13 25; www.maisonmnabha.com. A delightful riad, beautifully detailed & tucked away in the Kasbah district. The proprietors are long-term expats, originally from the UK. $$$$
⌂ **Riad 107** (4 rooms) 107 Derb Jdid Douar Graoua, Medina; m 0661 40 46 63; www.riad107.com. This impeccable riad a 3min walk from the Djemaa has a private hammam, a small relaxation pool in the courtyard & a lovely roof terrace. The family room has a mezzanine sleeping area the kids will love. $$$$
⌂ **Riad Aguerzame** (4 rooms) 66 Derb Jdid Douar Graoua, Medina; ☎ 0524 38 11 84; www.riad-aguerzame.com. There's an orange tree in the courtyard of this characterful & homely riad – the French owner makes breakfast marmalade from its

fruit. Antoine is an enthusiastic & abundantly helpful host. $$$
⌂ **Riad el Cadi** (12 rooms) 86 Derb Moulay Abdelkader, Derb Dabachi, Medina; ☎ 0524 37 86 55; www.riyadelcadi.com. This fabulous riad is more art gallery than guesthouse, run by the daughter of a previous German ambassador to Morocco. $$$
⌂ **Riad Magi** (6 rooms) 79 Derb Moulay Abdelkader, Derb Dabachi, Medina; ☎ 0524 42 66 88; www.riad-magi.com. This charming, unpretentious guesthouse has a delightful central garden & lots of intriguing details. Run by Maggie, a half-London, half-Marrakech resident. $$$
⌂ **Hotel Ibis** (103 rooms) Av Hassan II, Pl de la Gare; ☎ 0524 43 59 29; www.ibishotel.com/ibis/fichehotel/gb/ibi/2034/fiche_hotel.shtml. The basic Ibis hotel with a nice swimming pool. Located next to the train station,

RIADS

Although it's only recently that these traditional courtyarded homes have been converted into guesthouses, their history goes back almost 2,000 years. Based on the Roman villa, with a large interior garden surrounded by high walls to obscure it from the view of passers-by, the principle of the construction was to allow privacy and cooler temperatures inside. Typically, on wandering down narrow passageways with high walls on either side, you will come across a small door wedged into the fortification. Often there is nothing to indicate that this portal is different from any of the others. Having pre-arranged the stay and been told exactly where to go – there is often no other way of finding these guesthouses – you ring the bell, and are admitted. More often than not, inside is a beautiful garden, with four walls around it. Many non-Moroccans have been buying up these old properties with the intention of making them into second homes, and discovered that the extra rooms provide the basis for an excellent small hotel. *Riads* are mostly one-offs, reflecting the taste and wishes of their individual owners. Some of these places, found predominantly in Marrakech and Essaouira, are exquisite – with prices to match. At the last count, there were over 400 in these two cities alone.

this is an excellent place to stay if you're travelling by train & have only a minimum of time in Marrakech. $$–$$$

🏠 **Morocco House** (50+ rooms) 3 Rue Loubnane, Guéliz, Centre-ville; ☎ 0524 42 03 05/06; www.moroccanhousehotels.com. In the centre of the new town, this *maison de charme* offers 3-, 4- & 5-star levels of accommodation. $$–$$$

🏠 **Hotel Islane** (40 rooms) 279 Av Mohamed V; ☎ 0524 44 00 81. Clean & basic, the best thing

Budget

🏠 **CTM** (21 rooms) Djemaa el Fna, Medina; ☎ 0524 44 23 25; hotelctm.com/englais/hebergement.htm. Basic & cheap, this hotel has quite possibly the best view in Marrakech, overlooking the main square. $$

🏠 **Grand Hotel Tazi** Av El Mouahidine & Eue Moulay Rachid; ☎ 0524 44 27 87. The name is somewhat ironic, as this place to sleep & hang out, is pretty rough. Still, it's in a good location & is one of the few locations where it's possible to get cheap beer. There's internet access as well. $+

about this place is its location, across from the Koutoubia & around the corner from the Djemaa. There's also a good Italian restaurant, & Venezia Ice, which serves great ice cream. $$

🏠 **Riad des Drôles** (4 rooms) 23 Derb dabachi Derb Jdid, Medina; ☎ 0524 38 07 25; www.riad-des-droles-marrakech.com. This colourful riad is excellent value given its central location a short walk from the Djemaa. The owner can arrange private hammams at the nearby Riad 107. $$

🏠 **Auberge de Jeunesse** (60 beds) Rue El Jahed Quartier Industriel, nr campsite; ☎ 0524 44 77 13; www.hihostels.com/dba/hostels-Marrakech-039008.en.htm. Located outside the medina, this simple but adequate hostel provides a cheap alternative to staying in the flashier venues in Marrakech. $

🏠 **Hotel Ali** Rue Moulay Ismail, Medina; ☎ 0524 44 49 79. A landmark backpackers' overnight stop. You can find a bureau de change as well as an internet café here. $

✗ **WHERE TO EAT** Marrakech's popularity as a destination for people from all over the world has led to the appearance of a very large number of eating places. Within the medina are small, cheap ones that have been around for ages, especially near the Djemaa el Fna, the main square. In the evening, the Djemaa is filled with numerous open-air 'restaurants', set up in stalls, where you can sit on one of the benches making up a rectangle around the central cooking area. At some, the food that is about to be prepared for your dinner is laid out, and you can choose your dish by pointing at the ingredients. Locals sit knee to knee with tourists. Some places have specialities, such as seafood or soup, but most have the same general selection. There is virtually nothing to choose between them, as they all prepare dishes to your order. Even if you normally prefer more sophisticated dining, the energy of the Djemaa at night is an experience not to be missed. The meal is usually pretty good, and it's a great way to meet Moroccans as well as other tourists. Within the medina (both alongside and beyond the main square) are several restaurants serving both simple and elaborate Moroccan cuisine. A few of these are within beautifully decorated old palaces or *riads*, where the décor is the main feature and the food secondary. Although it's possible to find international dishes in the medina, it's best to go into the Ville Nouveau (Guéliz or the Hivernage) or to the luxury resorts of the Palmeraie, where standards rise, as these areas tend to cater to a more discerning clientele. The top-class hotels located mostly in the Hivernage have superb dining, usually offering Moroccan and broader-based gastronomy. This list is far from comprehensive, and meant only to give a taste of what's on offer. It's also worth doing a bit of websurfing, as Marrakech restaurants have some very creative sites (although the English might still be a bit dodgy).

Medina

✗ **Palais Gharnata** 5 Derb Al Arsa, Riad Zitoun Jdid; ☎ 0524 38 96 15; www.gharnata.com. A stunning evening of traditional food & entertainment inside one of the historic grand residences. $$$$$

✗ **Le Yacout** 79 Sidi Ahmed Soussi; ☎ 0524 38 29 29; ⊕ dinner Tue–Sun. Located within a gorgeous 17th-century Arab residence, this restaurant is arguably one of Marrakech's most exclusive — it's where anyone who's anyone wants to be seen. $$$$$

✗ **Dar Moha** 81 Rue Dar el Bacha; ☎ 0524 38 64 00; www.darmoha.ma. Famous for its new twists on traditional cuisine; the poolside location enriches the ambience. $$$$

✗ **La Sultana** 403 Rue de la Kasbah, Kasbah; ☎ 0524 38 80 08; www.lasultanamarrakech.com; ⊕ dinner daily 19.30–23.30. The restaurant at this luxurious riad-style hotel is top class, offering a menu fusing Moroccan & other Mediterranean dishes. $$$$

✗ **Narwama** 30 Rue Koutoubia; ☎ 0524 44 08 44; ⊕ daily. Hidden almost within the medina walls, this *riad* with a surprisingly large courtyard holds an even bigger secret — it's an excellent Thai restaurant. $$$$

✗ **Le Foundouk** 55 Souk Hal Fassi Kat Bennahid; ☎ 0524 37 81 90; www.foundouk.com;

⊕ 12.00–midnight. It's worth meandering through the souks to find this place, as the usual Moroccan dishes are given a French-Mediterranean twist here. $$$$

✗ **Le Marrakchi** Pl Djemaa el Fna, 52 Rue des Banques; ☎ 0524 44 33 77; www.lemarrakchi.com; ⊕ 12.00-01.00. This venue has views of both the Djemaa & the sunset behind the Koutoubia. It serves well-prepared Moroccan dishes & is a great place for a 1st-night dinner. $$$-$$$$

✗ **Tatchibana** 38 Derb Bab Kisba, Kasbah; ☎ 0524 38 71 71; ⊕ dinner daily except Mon. An intriguing combination — Franco–Japanese gastronomy served in the depths of the Kasbah district of the medina. $$$-$$$$

✗ **Le Terraces de Alhambra** 3 Pl Djemaa el Fna; m 0664 16 79 42; ⊕ 08.30–23.30. Another place on the square, this one has pasta on its menu, for when you've had too many *tagines*. $$-$$$

✗ **Chez Chegrouni** Pl Djemaa el Fna, Rue des Banques ☎ 0524 47 46 15; ⊕ daily. This cheap & cheerful restaurant serving basic Moroccan food has possibly the best view in Marrakech, overlooking the main square of the medina. $$

Guéliz

✗ **La Piccola Italia** 36 Rue Ibn Aïcha; ☎ 0524 42 39 39; www.ilove-marrakesh.com/lapiccolaitalia/index_en.html. A proper Italian restaurant that would look more at home in Italy than Marrakech, the pastas & pizzas offering alternatives to the usual choices on Moroccan menus. $$$

✗ **Le Jacaranda** 32 Bd Zerktouni; ☎ 0524 44 72 15; www.lejacaranda.ma; ⊕ 12.00–15.00 & 18.30–

23.00. This venue has been known for its French cuisine for over half a century, & provides musical entertainment Fri, Sat & Sun nights. $$$$

🍴 **Café des Negociants** Abd El Moumen Ben Ali Sq; ☎ 0524 43 57 82. ⊕ daily. In the heart of the new downtown, here's the place to sip a fresh orange juice or mint tea & watch the modern world go by. $$

Hivernage Virtually all the big hotels located in this area have excellent restaurants attached to them, as well as bars and nightclubs.

✗ **Salam Bombay Restaurant** I Av Mohamed VI (ex Av de France); ☎ 0524 43 70 83. ⏱ daily. Probably the only Indian restaurant in Marrakech; the chef provides a variety of intensities. $$$$

ENTERTAINMENT AND NIGHTLIFE Marrakech's ancient core, the medina, remains essentially Islamic, and is quiet at night. It's possible to sit around drinking a coffee or a mint tea at one of the male-dominated cafés, and most likely end up watching football on the television in the corner, but most of the livelier nightlife is in the new town. The Hivernage has the majority of the bars and nightclubs, usually affiliated with the flashy hotels in the area. If you are staying in the Palmeraie, the hotels and resorts there also host night-time events. Once again, this is a very small selection from a very large number of venues.

☆ **Comptoir Darna** Av Echouada, Hivernage; ☎ 0524 43 77 02; www.comptoirdarna.com; ⏱ 16.00–02.00. A dinner & entertainment show that includes musicians, balancing acts & belly dancers. $$$$$

☆ **Es Saadia** Rue Ibrahim el Mazini, Hivernage; ☎ 0524 44 88 11; www.essaadi.com. This enormous resort is home not only to a hotel & various restaurants but also to late-night bars & a casino. The **Estrade Gourmande** & the **Epicurean** are both restaurants that stay awake daily till 03.00, while the **Egyptian Lounge** & the **Piano Bar** are places to hang out until the late hours. The **Casino de Marrakech** is open 14.00–04.00 Mon–Fri, 14.00–05.00 w/ends. As well as slots, poker, banco & other games there's also the **TheatrO**, a theatre & nightclub.

☆ **Le Diamant Noir** Pl de la Liberté & Av Mohamed V, Hivernage; ☎ 0524 43 43 51; ⏱ 22.00–04.00. One of the city's most popular nightclubs, the venue is a gay hangout during the week, but welcomes everyone on w/ends.

☆ **Le Pacha** Zone Hotelière de l'Aguedal, Bd Mohamed VI; ☎ 0524 38 84 00; www.pachamarrakech.com/club/; ⏱ 20.00–05.00. Billed as 'the biggest club in Africa', this party venue with live entertainment is immensely popular.

☆ **White Room** Royal Mirage Hotel, Rue Paris, Hivernage; ☎ 0524 42 54 00; www.royalmiragehotels.com; ⏱ from 22.00. One of Marrakech's most popular discos; allows women in for free on Wed.

A few venues offer dinner spectaculars, shows that recreate the annual horse-based festival, the Fantasia.

☆ **Borj Bladi** Restaurant Fantasia, 57 Rue Mauritania, Guéliz; ☎ 0524 43 08 90; www.borjbladi.ma. A magnificent evening's entertainment that depicts the horsemanship & regalia of the traditional Fantasia, accompanied by '1,001 tastes' of traditional Moroccan cuisine. $$$$$

☆ **Chez Ali** 7km north of Marrakech on Casablanca road, then turn left & continue for about 3km; ☎ 0524 30 77 30. A chance to see how the Fantasia is re-enacted, with an enormous cast, including an amazing number of skilled equestrians; & dinner. $$$$$

A couple of places outside of town offer a pool-based day – and night – out, that includes entertainment in the evening.

☆ **La Plage Rouge** Route de l'Ourika, Km 10; ☎ 0524 37 80 86; www.ilove-marrakesh.com/laplagerouge/index.html. Swim in the enormous pool in the day, & dance till 01.00 at this out-of-town resort.

☆ **Nikki Beach** Circuit de la Palmeraie; ☎ 0524 36 87 27; www.nikkibeach.com/marrakech. A branch of the international venue, this club has day-time swimming & sunbathing facilities & a night-time trendy party scene.

SHOPPING

Souks Marrakech is a shopper's nirvana. The souks, the Arabic expression for markets, are arguably the most wonderful in the world, full of beautiful crafts, clothing, pastries, spices, fruits and nuts, leather goods, fabrics, ironmongery,

SOUKS

Some of the different souk names in Arabic, French and English are listed below (where there are no French names, they are known by their Arabic ones):

Attarine	–	brassware
Cherratine	tanneurs	tanners
Chouari	ebenistes	cabinetmakers
El Kebir	cuir	leather
Haddadine	fer	iron
Kassabine	epices	spices
Kchacha	–	dried fruit and nuts
Kedima	apothicaire	traditional medicine
Kimakine	des musiciens	musical instruments
Laghzal	laine	wool
Sebbaghine	tenturier	dyers
Serrajine	–	saddlers
Smarine	–	textiles
Smata	babouches	slippers
Zarbia	tapis	carpets

slippers, carpets, meat, fish, vegetables, musical instruments and just about anything else one can stuff into an Aladdin's cave. The souk district in the medina that begins at the main square, the Djemaa el Fna, is so elaborate and complicated, that it's best just to let go of any sense of direction and wander, quite happily accepting the fact you'll get lost. The locals will always point you back to the Djemaa. The souks themselves are actually discrete, each named with its speciality, but only the initiated are aware of this differentiation, as one souk seems to run into another. Occasionally it's possible to see a name on the wall, but the only time it matters is if you're trying to find a stall from a previous day's wander. Sometimes, retracing one's steps seems impossible. It might be best to purchase what you want on the day rather than count on another visit. Remember to bargain in the souks.

Shops Because of the large number of souks and their proximity, Marrakech's shops tend to be specialist or high quality. Moroccan design has become very popular and some of the more upmarket interior houseware stores cater to European clientele. Some places offer superior crafts at fixed prices to those visitors who can't get the hang of bartering. On Rue de la Liberté, Guéliz, it's possible to find several of the nicer shops. Below are a few:

Guéliz

Al Jawda 11 Rue de la Liberté, Guéliz; ☏ 0524 43 38 97; www.al-jawda.com. Some of the best pastries in all of Morocco can be purchased here.

Galerie Tadghart Av Hassan 1 & P de la Liberté, Guéliz; ☏ 0524 43 22 58. Here's where you can go to purchase a carpet, without having to haggle.

L'Orientaliste 11 & 15 Rue de la Liberté; ☏ 0524 43 40 74. This shop sells beautiful Moroccan crafts, including antique furniture & jewellery, as well as domestic table items.

Hivernage

Ensemble Artisanal Bd Mohamed V; ☏ 0524 42 38 35. This little warren of artisans producing their crafts & then selling their wares at fixed prices is charming, & gives a good idea of what such items are actually worth. It's helpful to remember this place when wandering the souks & negotiating.

Medina

Akbar Delights 45 Pl Bab Fteuh; ℡ 0571 66 13 07. A good place to buy *babouches* (slippers).

Beldi 9–11 Rue Mouassine; ℡ 0524 44 10 76. Hidden within the souks, this is the foremost shop at which to buy Moroccan haute couture, patronised by the best & the most famous in both the country & abroad. Goods are not cheap.

La Porte d'Or 115 Souk Semmarine; ℡ 0524 44 54 54. Jewellery, both artisan & antique, as well as ceramics & carpets are on sale.

The **Marjane** hypermarket, in the Menara district, is full of everything that anyone could ever want, from electronics to baguettes. It's handy to have one around for those things you forgot to bring along.

OTHER PRACTICALITIES
Emergency telephone numbers

Police ℡ 19
Fire service & ambulance ℡ 15
All-night chemist Rue Khalid Ben Oualid

Hospital emergency rooms Clinique du Sud; ℡ 0524 44 79 99 (24hrs)

Hospitals

✚ **Hospital Al Antaki** Bab Doukkala, Medina; ℡ 0524 38 04 74

✚ **Hospital El Razi** Guéliz; ℡ 0524 30 21 41
✚ **Hospital IBN Tofail** Guéliz; ℡ 0524 44 80 11

Internet cafés Almost all the larger hotels offer wireless internet, although often it can only be accessed from the lobby. In addition, cyber cafés seem to be springing up on every street corner, although their lives can often be shorter than the time needed to put up the sign. Below are a few reliable sources.

🖥 **Cyber Parc Arsat Moulay Abdeslam** A lovely park just across the street from the Ensemble Artisanal has the added bonus of strategically placed internet-access booths that can be used with phone cards.

🖥 **Cybernet** 4 Av Yacoub Al Mansour, Guéliz; ℡ 0524 43 91 17
🖥 **Hotel Ali** Rue Moulay Ismail, Medina; ℡ 0524 44 49 79

Post The main post office is at Avenue Mohamed V, Guéliz (℡ *0524 43 10 16*). In the medina there is a large sub-branch just to the west of the Djemaa el Fna.

Banks

$ **Bank Al Maghrib** Djemaa el Fna Sq; ℡ 0524 44 20 37
$ **Banque Populaire** Ensemble Artisanal, Bd Mohamed V, Hivernage; ℡ 0524 44 38 76; 69 Av Mohamed V,

Hivernage; ℡ 0524 44 80 30; 79 Pl Djemaa el Fna, Medina; ℡ 0524 44 34 87; Bab Agnaou, Medina; ℡ 0524 44 56 05

There are also branches of BCM, Credit Agricole, Credit du Maroc and others.

WHAT TO SEE Most of the things worth seeing in Marrakech are in the medina, the old part of town totally enclosed by walls and gates, which in themselves are attractions worth looking at. Although there are specific monuments, museums, palaces and sites that warrant a visit, don't forget to wander. One of the best ways to get a sense of the magic of this medieval city is to meander through the warren of alleyways that often end in a cul-de-sac, and will certainly grant a good view of what the place is like. Stop for an orange juice or a coffee at some out-of-the-way café or tiny shop.

Koutoubia (*Just off the Bd Mohamed V*) The tall, graceful 12th-century minaret of the Booksellers' Mosque (named after the booksellers who used to ply their wares at the base) is Marrakech's landmark. Taller than most of the other edifices in the medina, it's not only striking, but also a useful reference point for guidance throughout the city. As it's a mosque, non-Muslims are not allowed in, but the grounds and its rose gardens are open to the public.

Djemaa el Fna The medina's central square must be one of the most exciting folklore-performance spots on the planet. Designated a cultural heritage site for just such a reason, the place functions as a central focal point and residence of orange-juice squeezers and dried fruit and nut vendors during the day. In the late afternoon, snake charmers, monkey owners and strange remedy stalls appear. By the evening, storytellers, and traditional and transvestite dancers emerge, as well as musicians and games players. Food stalls take over a huge part of the square (see *Where to eat*, page 104). Everything seems to end around 23.00, but it's a spectacular, unmissable show till then.

Ben Youssef Mosque and Medersa (*Ali Ben Youssef, Medersa;* ✆ *0524 39 09 11;* ◷ *09.00–18.00 daily, till 19.00 in summer; MAD30, combination entry fee with Almoravid Qobba & Marrakech Museum: MAD50*) Built as a school for the study of the Koran in the 16th century, the simple cells of the students are in complete contrast with the extraordinarily beautiful and ornate details of the common rooms. The mosque is near by.

Almoravid Qobba (*Pl Ben Youssef/Kissaria;* ✆ *0524 39 09 11;* ◷ *09.00–16.00 daily; MAD50 combination entry fee with Ben Youssef Medersa & Marrakech Museum*) The only remaining structure from the occupation of the Almoravid dynasty in the 12th century, this ablutions pool looks basic on the outside, but is quite lovely on the inside.

Le Musée de Marrakech (*Pl Ben Youssef, Medina;* ✆ *0524 39 09 11;* ◷ *09.00-18.30 daily; MAD30, MAD50 combination entry fee with the Medersa Ben Youssef & Almoravid Qobba*) Traditional and contemporary art is displayed within a beautifully decorated former palace.

Dar Bellarj (*9 Rue Taoualat Zaouiat Lahdar, Medina;* ✆ *0524 44 45 55*) This former refuge for wounded storks, a favourite bird in Marrakech, has been converted into the Foundation for Moroccan Culture and stages all sorts of national arts exhibitions.

Debbaghine (*Bab Debbagh*) Nestling within the city walls to the east lies the tanners' district, a vision of barely clothed labourers dipping in and out of different pools in which leather is cured and dyed. Not as spectacular, nor as smelly, as Fes's (see *Chapter 7*, page 139), it's still worth a visit, especially when viewed from above.

Dar Si Said Museum (*Derb El Bahia, Riad Zitoun el-Jedid; Medina;* ✆ *0524 44 24 64;* ◷ *09.00–12.15 &15.00–18.15 daily except Tues; MAD20*) A wonderful 19th-century palace filled with traditional Moroccan wooden works of art.

Maison Tiskiwin – Musée Bert Flint (*8 Rue de la Bahia, nr Riad Zitoun el Jedid, close to the Dar Si Said Museum;* ✆ *0524 38 91 92;* ◷ *09.30–12.30 & 15.30–17.30 daily; MAD15*) The collection of the Dutch art historian Bert Flint is displayed within his own traditionally styled home.

Bahia Palace (*Rue de la Bahia, Riad Zitoun el-Jedid;* ◷ *08.30–12.00 & 14.30–18.00*) Although less than 150 years old, this grand vizir's palace built for his harem is quite beautiful, with a labyrinth of private gardens, courtyards and 160 rooms.

Mellah The ancient Jewish quarter no longer contains the residents it once had, but there are still places of interest to visit, notably Sagha, the still-functioning gold arcade, the spice market and the ancient Lazama synagogue (*Derb Manchoura;* ⊕ *09.00-18.00 daily; donations accepted*)

El Badi (*Toualet Bellarje Le Mellah;* ⊕ *08.45-12.45 & 14.30-18.30 daily; MAD10, with minbar – ancient pulpit – MAD20*) This 16th-century palace was supposed to have been one of the most magnificent buildings in Marrakech and took the 17th-century Moulay Ismail ten years to strip (see page 99). Now it's a huge ruin, dominated by an empty pool, with a surprisingly tranquil atmosphere, punctuated by the occasional stork landing on its balcony nest. If you get the chance, visit the nearby cafés on the upper floors for a closer look.

Kasbah (*Bab Agnaou*) This 12th-century fortified part of the medina, built for the staff of the nearby Almohad royal palace, is the most complete urban kasbah in Morocco. The beautiful mosque dominates, but is open only to Muslims.

Saadian Tombs (*Rue de la Kasbah, Kasbah;* ⊕ *09.00-12.00 & 14.30-18.00 daily; MAD10*) The area of the tombs of the 16th- and 17th-century Saadian dynasty, with its cool gardens and elaborately decorated rooms, must be one of the nicest graveyards in Marrakech, and worth a visit for its beautiful interiors.

Agdal Gardens Located just south of the Kasbah, this huge grove of olive and fruit trees is right next to the royal palace. Within it are two large concrete pools, filled with big fish that get larger every Friday, when the gardens are open to the public and people come to feed them.

City walls The medina is enclosed within 6km of ramparts that have been fixed and patched since their construction in the 12th century. There are breaches, but the continuity of the walls is maintained. Some of the babs, or gates, are impressive, including the Bab Agnaou and the royal palace's Bab Ighlil, as well as the entrance from the Avenue de la Menara. The best way to view the circumference is by *caleche*.

Squares Some of Marrakech's squares are particularly interesting. Besides the **Djemaa** there's the **Criee Berbere**, where carpets are laid out and sold; the **Ferblantiers**, the place for the iron lamp makers; the **Gran Mechouar**, a large space close to the palace that once acted as a waiting room for royal visits; the **Kissaria**, the central point between the Ben Youssef Medersa, the Marrakech Museum and the Almoravid Qobba; and the **Qzadria**, a park with benches and shade that's a good spot in which to get your bearings.

Zaouias As well as being a draw for jetset tourists, the city remains an Islamic pilgrimage destination due to the presence of the final resting places of the Seven Saints. In the 17th century, Moulay Ismail decided to trade on the trend of Sufism and create the Festival of the Seven Saints, in order to encourage visitors to come to Marrakech. He transported to the city the graves of the holy men of Sidi Bel Abbas (1129–1204), Sidi Muhammad al-Jazuli (died 1465), Sidi Abu al-Qasim Al-Suhayli (1114–1185), Cadi Ayyad ben Moussa (1083–1149), Abdelaziz al-Tebaa (died 1499) and Abdallah al-Ghazwani (died 1529). When a tomb becomes the central focus of a mosque, it is known as a *zaouias*. Some of the more notable resting places are of **Sidi Abdel Aziz el Harrar** (*Rue Mouassine*), **Sidi Bel Abbes** (*Rue Taghzout*) and **Sidi Ben Salah** (*Place Ben Salah*).

Within the Ville Nouveau there is relatively little of interest for the tourist, with two exceptions.

Jardin Majorelle (*Av Yacoub el Mansour, Guéliz;* ❧ *0524 30 18 52; www.jardinmajorelle.com;* ☉ *Oct–May 08.00–17.00 daily; Jun–Sep 08.00–18.00*) This extraordinary garden was once the home of the artist Majorelle, which was then bought and restored to its current glory by the fashion designer Yves St Laurent. It houses the Museum of Islamic Art, (*MAD15*) which shows off its collection of religious arts from all over the Muslim world in an amazing dark blue building.

Menara Gardens These gardens to the west of the Hivernage, and very close to the international airport, surround a 12th-century Almohad reservoir. The picturesque pavilion, built in the 19th century by Sultan Moulay Abd el Rahmen, was supposedly a spot where he'd rendezvous with his lover. Although usually not that attractive, it is spectacular in the winter when the snow-covered Atlas Mountains are reflected in the water. The grounds are popular with visitors on Fridays and Saturdays.

HOW TO GET TO THE ROMAN SITES It's possible that the Romans followed the Phoenicians to get to Essaouira, a charming fishing town about 2½ hours' drive to the west on the Atlantic coast. Although nothing remains of any ruins, legend has it that the purple dye for which both cultures were famous came from the Murex shells found at this little Moroccan port (see page 117). To get to Essaouira, take a Supratour bus (costing about MAD65). A grand taxi will take about the same time, not including any stops you'd like to make, and will cost about five times as much. A train to see Sala Colonia in Rabat will take just over four hours and cost MAD112; the journey to Sidi Kacem to see Volubilis near Meknes takes about 4¾ hours and costs MAD143; the journey to see the sites near Tangier costs MAD190 and takes just under 10 hours. Because of the motorways, car journey and grand taxi times are much faster, but also much more expensive.

AGADIR Telephone code 0528

Situated to the far southwest of the country along the Atlantic coast, Agadir's best points are its beach and its climate. Although it boasts one of the largest sardine ports in the world, the tourist's only real interests here are the sun, sea and sand. Hotels, restaurants, bars, clubs and recreational facilities are developed to the same degree as resorts in Europe. Smaller seaside complexes can be found slightly north of Agadir, and further still towards Essaouira where there are beautiful bays with huge empty beaches which have been discovered only by surfers so far. To the south is the desert; Berbers can be found here, including the elusive 'blue men' – the Touareg – who can be visited on an organised day trip. Overall, Agadir is a hedonistic destination, proving particularly attractive to northern Europeans in the winter.

HISTORY Although the Phoenicians have been traced no further south than Essaouira, it's possible that they could have continued sailing the relatively short distance to Agadir. Nothing was documented until 1505, when the Portuguese set up a trading post for both contraband and legal goods. By 1541 the ruling dynasty, the Saadians, threw the Europeans out, building a huge kasbah on a hill overlooking the harbour, the shell of which still exists. Not long after, the Alaouites arrived, taking over from the Saadians and building up Agadir into a thriving port. Trade faltered a bit after independence in 1956, and the government began to recognise the possibilities of tourism, constructing a few hotels. In 1960 all plans were shattered, as well as most of the city, when a 15-second earthquake wiped out Agadir and killed 15,000 people. Rather than desert the city, King Mohamed V used the disaster as a rallying cry, and rebuilding began almost immediately. The new Agadir is very much a product of the 1960s, incorporating much of the town planning of the period, with its broad boulevards and liberal use of concrete. Unfortunately the medina wasn't rebuilt, and somehow the modern city seems to have lost its soul. Still, this absence is more than compensated for by its large hotels and modern shopping areas, in commercial potential, if not in spirit.

GETTING THERE AND AROUND

By air The Aeroport Agadir Al Massira (❱ *0528 83 91 12; www.on~da.ma*) is located 25km from the centre of the city and services both international and domestic carriers. There are no public buses to town so you can either take a grand taxi (starting at around MAD120) or rent a car. Avis, Budget, Europcar, Hertz, National and Sixt have branches at the airport (see *Car hire*, below). Alternatively, if you are in Agadir as part of a pre-arranged package, the tour operators will arrange transport to your hotel.

By bus If you are already in Morocco and getting around the country by public transport, the easiest way to get to Agadir is via the long-distance bus companies. The quickest trips are either from Essaouira to the north, a journey of about three hours 30 minutes costing approximately MAD60, or from Marrakech, which costs MAD90 and takes around four hours 30 minutes. Supratour (*www.oncf.ma*) is the most reliable operator, and the air-conditioned coaches are very comfortable. A reservation is mandatory and guarantees a seat, but the routes can get very busy, so book ahead as far as possible. Other bus companies exist, such as CTM (*1 Rue Yakoub El Mansour Talborjt;* ❱ *0528 82 53 41*) but are not necessarily as consistent, nor as easy to access on the internet. Buses drop passengers in the older part of town, close to the mosque. Yellow petit taxis wait to take arrivals to their hotels, or there are local buses. Ask for directions. The city is fairly small, and the weather should be nice, so it's possible to walk. If you reach the seafront and decide to opt for transport, there's always the local Noddy train that visits most of what there is to see before stopping at all the big hotels. At MAD18, it's cheap enough to use as a conveyance.

Car hire Getting around by car in Agadir is not the best option, as the town isn't very large, and there are several cheaper alternatives. However, if you are planning to explore the area, especially further south, having a vehicle might be a practical way to see the less touristy sites.

🚗 **Avis** ❱ 0528 83 92 44; www.avis.com

🚗 **Sixt** ❱ 0528 83 90 13; www.sixt.com

🚗 **Budget** (airport) ❱ 0528 83 91 01; www.budget.com; (town) Bungalow Hotel Marhaba, Av Mohamed V; ❱ 0528 84 82 22

🚗 **Europcar** (airport) ❱ 0528 84 03 37; (town) Angle Bd Mohamed V & Rue Hubert Giraud; ❱ 0528 84 02 03; www.europcar.com

🚗 **Hertz** (airport) ❱ 0528 83 90 71; (town) Bungalow Hotel Marhaba, Av Mohamed V; ❱ 028 84 09 39; www.hertz.com

🚗 **National** (airport) ❱ 0528 83 91 21; (town) Av Hassan II, Immeuble Sud Bahia; ❱ 0528 8400 26; www.nationalcar.com

TOURIST INFORMATION Agadir has a tourist board (*Av Mohamed V, Immeuble Ignaouan;* ❱ *0528 84 63 77;* ⊕ *08.30–12.00 & 14.30–18.30 Mon–Thu, 08.30–11.00 & 15.00–18.30 Fri*), tourist information (*Av Mohamed V;* ❱ *0528 82 53 04*) and a regional council of tourism (*Av Hassan II;* ❱ *0528 84 26 29*).

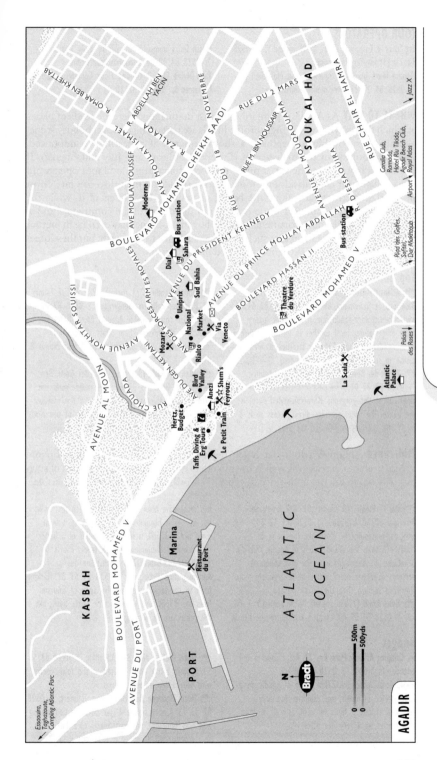

AGADIR

ATLANTIC OCEAN

PORT

KASBAH

SOUK AL HAD

Marina

TOUR OPERATORS

Erg Tours 4 Complexe Anezi, Av Mohamed V; ☎ 0528 84 11 11; www.ergtours.com
Menara Tours Immeuble Iguewane, Bd Mohamed V; ☎ 0528 84 27 32; www.menara-tours.ma

Match Tours Immeuble Oumlil No 6, Av Hassan II; ☎ 0528 84 38 96; www.matchtours.com
Taffs Diving Bloc D, Ground Floor, Complexe Anezi, Bd Mohamed V; ☎ 0528 82 10 27

 WHERE TO STAY As Agadir is primarily a tourist destination, there are loads of places at which to stay. Most of the high-profile hotels are part of the package-holiday scene, although it's possible to negotiate a short-term rate if appearing unannounced, especially outside of the high season (European holidays and July and August). If planning a few days by the sea, it might be worth contacting a local tour operator in one of the bigger cities in advance to see if you can ride on their discount rate. Most of the flashier resorts are along the beach, or within a few streets of it, while the cheaper little places are near the bus station in the centre of the commercial town. There are also villas and apartments that can be rented. Some may even be in prettier villages outside of the main city, such as Taghazoute, just to the north, but these quiet backwaters can become extremely crowded in high season.

Top end

🏠 **Atlantic Palace Agadir** (332 rooms) Secteur Balneaire et Touristique, BP 194; ☎ 0528 82 41 46; www.atlanticpalace-agadir.com. A landmark luxury hotel that features local touches in its architecture & also provides golf, spa & beach facilities, as well as a casino to spend the last of your money. $$$$$
🏠 **Palais des Roses** (405+ rooms) Cite Founty; ☎ 0528 82 82 01; www.palaisdesroses.com. The emphasis of this gorgeous Moroccan-styled hotel is the beach. The hotel provides direct access to it & to all the sporting facilities in the area. $$$$$

🏠 **Sofitel Agadir** (273 rooms) BP 226, Cité Founty P4, Baie des Palmiers, Bensergao; ☎ 0528 82 00 88; www.sofitel.com. Arguably Agadir's nicest hotel, this branch of the luxury chain offers all facilities, including access to a private beach, 2 golf ranges & a spa. $$$$$
🏠 **Riad des Golfs** (8 rooms) Riad des Golfs, Ben Sergao; m 0661 23 71 61; www.riaddesgolfs.com. Within its eucalyptus forest location a few minutes away from the tourist centre, the focus of this *riad* is on golf. Horseriding is also available. $$$$

Mid-range Although a four-star hotel might not sound like a mid-priced option, special deals out of season as well as bargain offers online often reduce the cost of such places down to the medium-price category. It's worth checking out what's available.

🏠 **Dar Maktoub** (10 rooms) BP 727, Inezgane Principal 80350, Inezgane; ☎ 0528 33 62 88; www.dar-maktoub.com. More like the *riads* of Marrakech than the grand hotels of Agadir, this *dar* is located in the woods near the golf course & presents a calmer, more individual & arguably more Moroccan sojourn than the beach resorts. $$$$
🏠 **Hotel Anezi** (250+ rooms) Bd Mohamed V, 5 PB 29; ☎ 0528 84 09 40. Located just above the beach,

this must have been a 4-star hotel when first built, but its age is beginning to show, making it seem more like a 3. Still, it has the facilities of a better resort, with 3 swimming pools & tennis courts. $$$
🏠 **Hotel Sud Bahia** (246 rooms) Rue des Administration Publiques; ☎ 0528 84 63 87. Harking back to the large hotel complex style of tourism from the 1960s, this place can be fairly basic, but the prices are in keeping. $$–$$$

Budget

🛅 **Camping Atlantic Parc** Km 27, Rte Essaouira Imi ouaddar (Aghroud); ☎ 0528 82 08 05; www.atlanticaparc.com. 27km north of Agadir on a wide stretch of beach, this campsite has fully equipped chalets & tents for rent, as well as loads of activities, at a very low price. $

🏠 **Hotel Diaf** Av Allal Ben Abdellah; ☎ 0528 82 58 52. A basic 1-star hotel located in the town centre, with only a few en-suite rooms. $
🏠 **Hôtel Moderne** Rue Mehdi Ben Toumert; ☎ 0528 82 33 73. A very simple 1-star hotel nestled among adjoining buildings, not particularly nice, but cheap, so recommended if money is a serious issue. $

Also try the village of **Taghazoute**, on the coast a bit north of Agadir. There are several companies online, including **Home Holidays** (*www.homelidays.com/EN-Holidays-Rental/ma/taghazoute_r0.asp*) that can give an idea of what sort of flats are available and how much they cost. Depending on the size and time of year, weekly prices can be quite low ($$–$$$).

✗ WHERE TO EAT As Agadir's tourist trade continues to grow, particularly with visitors from Europe and North America, restaurants pop up to cater for it. There are several places to eat, ranging from fine fish venues to quickie hamburger joints. Beachside cafés are very common on the long seafront, and in the tourist areas, while pubs and fast-food outlets can be found on every corner. Some of the best places to eat are at the four- and five-star hotels, of which there are many. Below is a small choice of restaurants provided just to give a head start, but it's worth asking around, as new places are springing up all the time.

✗ La Scala Complexe Tamelalt; ☎ 0528 84 67 3; ⏰ daily for lunch & dinner. A highly regarded restaurant in the area, the feature here is fish, served as fresh as possible. $$$$–$$$$$

✗ Feyrouz Hôtel Al Madina Palace, Bd 20 Août; ☎ 0528 84 53 53; ⏰ daily for b/fast, lunch & dinner. Serves Lebanese food & a range of kids' meals. $$$

✗ Mozart 24 Av des FAR; ☎ 0528 82 45 64; ⏰ daily except Sun for b/fast, lunch & dinner. If you've had enough of Moroccan food & would like to try some Austrian dishes, like wienerschnitzl, this is the place! $$–$$$

✗ Restaurant du Port Yachting Club; ☎ 0528 84 37 08; ⏰ 12.00–15.00 & 19.00–23.00 daily. One of several cheap-&-cheerful fish restaurants close to the port. Has shellfish & serves alcohol. $$–$$$

✗ Restaurant Jazz Bd 20 Août; ☎ 0528 84 02 08; ⏰ daily. A reasonable fast-food & sandwich place. $$

✗ Via Veneto Av Hassan II (opposite Bird Valley); ☎ 0528 84 14 67; ⏰ 11.00–23.00 daily. A good pizza joint, well located between the beach hotels & the centre of town. $$

Beachside snacks Consuming coffee, orange juice or a light meal at lunch or in the evening at any of the cafés strewn along the promenade is fine. The view over the ocean, especially at sunset, makes up for the lack of fine cuisine ($–$$$).

Hotel restaurants If in doubt, all the better hotels have their in-house places to eat, some quite good, if perhaps catering a bit too much to the European palette ($$$$–$$$$$).

ENTERTAINMENT AND NIGHTLIFE The best bars and discotheques are in hotels. They are certainly reputable and reliable, the dress code can be quite strict (elegant) and the costs can add up quickly. Drinking and dancing in the hotels of Agadir is not a cheap option.

Hotel bars Each hotel has its own one(s). Some of the best are:

☆ **Coralia Club** Bd du 20 Août; ☎ 0528 84 01 36
☆ **Ramada** Bd de 20 Août; ☎ 0528 84 02 33
☆ **Royal Atlas** Bd 20 Août

☆ **Sofitel** BP 226, Cité Founty P4, Baie des Palmiers, Bensergao; ☎ 0528 82 00 88

Hotel discotheques Listed below are some of the more popular spots. In some cases, better-off locals who are not necessarily guests at the hotels might come into party.

☆ **Papagayo** (also the **Zanzibar** piano bar) Hôtel Riu Tikida Beach; ☎ 0528 81 54 00
☆ **Actor's** Royal Atlas Agadir; ☎ 0528 29 40 40

☆ **Flamingo** Agadir Beach Club, Av Oued Souss, Secteur Touristique BP310; ☎ 0528 84 43 43

Cabarets and pubs Various cabarets are scattered throughout the tourist areas, often organised by the hotels. There are also several pubs that line the boulevards of the tourist areas. The large national flag on the outside of the building is probably a bit of a giveaway as to what countries are best catered for on the inside.

Casinos Losing your money in an organised fashion, betting on cards, games and wheels is legal in Agadir. Fortunately, the venues in which you liberally give away your dosh are quite nice, and probably almost worth the price.

☆ **Shem's Casino d'Agadir** Hotel Sheraton, Av Mohamed V; ✆ 0528 82 11 11; ⊕ 16.00–06.00 daily. With slots & all the usual facilities, the casino speciality games are Carribean stud poker & punto banco.

☆ **Casino le Mirage** Village Valtur, Parcelle 31, Secteur Touristique et Balnéaire, Sous-Massa-Draa; ✆ 0528 84 87 77; ⊕ 17.00–05.00 daily. Slots, cards & roulette are all here, as well as video terminals.

SHOPPING People do not come to Agadir to shop and there is very little here that even comes close to the magnificent souks of Marrakech or Fes. Still, there is a local populace that needs to buy goods.

The **Municipal Market** on Avenue Prince Sidi Mohamed and Avenue des FAR has fish stalls on the ground floor and artisan goods on the first. Prices for the tourist items can be a bit excessive. The **Suq al Had** on Rue Chair al Hamra Mohamed Ben Brahim, lacking the age of the older Moroccan cities, tries to recreate some of the atmosphere of a traditional market.

Uniprix Bd Hassan II & Rue de Prince Sidi Mohammed. This large department store sells almost everything, including tourist souvenirs, & is virtually a landmark in its own right.

Marjane Quartier Founty, Rte d'Inezgane Bensergaou; ✆ 0528 28 13 40. The big French hypermarket is here too, typically outside of town.

OTHER PRACTICALITIES
Emergency telephone numbers
Police ✆ 19
Fire service and ambulance ✆ 15
All-night chemist Rue de l'Hotel de Ville, off Av du Prince Moulay Abdallah

Doctor Dr Lazarak; m 0661 16 25 67. Speaks English.

Hospitals
✚ **Clinique Argana** Bd Hassan II & Rue d'Oujda; ✆ 0528 84 60 00

✚ **Clinique al-Massira** Av du Prince Moulay Abdallah & Bd Mohamed V

Internet cafés The larger hotels have internet access, by now almost entirely wireless. As with other cities, you might have to take your laptop down to the lobby to pick up the network. Otherwise, cyber cafés come and go. Some haven't even bothered to name themselves and can be found simply by the large 'internet' sign outside. There are more in the town than close to the resort, particularly on and around Boulevard Hassan II. The following places were highly recommended, but there's no guarantee they'll be functioning for long.

🌐 **Cyber Salaam** Rue de Fes & Rue Asfi
🌐 **Futurenet** Av de 29 Fevrier

🌐 **Internet Suisse** Immeuble Oumilil, Av Hassan II & Rue de l'Hotel de Ville. This place is more expensive than the others.

Post The main post office is on Avenue du Prince Moulay Abdallah.

Banks Hotels will exchange money, although not always at the best rate. There are banks and exchange bureaux throughout the town, as well as ATMs. Try the following:

$ **Bank Al Maghrib** Av Mohamed V; ☎ 0528 82 66 30
$ **Banque Populaire** Av du General Kettani (with ATM); ☎ 0528 83 72 65; Bd 20 Août; ☎ 0528 88 67 85

$ **BMCI** Av du Prince Moulay Abdallah & Av Prince Sidi Mohammed; ☎ 0528 84 07 10
$ **Wafa** Av du General Kettani; ☎ 0528 81 76 92

WHAT TO SEE Once past that wide, 9km beautiful sandy beach, there isn't much to see. The commercial fishing port could be interesting, but there's no special facility for showing it off to visitors. The seafood restaurants nearby might be worth a visit, but they're more for eating at than viewing. The markets are not worth seeing for anything other than buying goods.

Bird Valley or Valle des Oiseaux (*MAD15*) This old-fashioned but quaint park runs through the middle of town, from Boulevard 20 Août to Boulevard Hassan II. Full of birds and animals, some free on the ponds and fountains, others in clean cages, this pleasant greenway is actually quite sweet. It's worth the money just to avoid the long, boring, busy roads. Children love the place, and parents frequently bring them here.

Kasbah Dominating the hill to the north of town is a line of a wall that was the old town, before the earthquake of 1960 wiped everything out. Once the original fortified village, there's nothing left, although the view from the top, looking down upon the harbour and the wide sweep of the bay, is excellent. It's an 8km taxi ride to get there.

Le Petit Train Agadir (*leaves from outside Bird Valley and can be joined at any of the hotels at which it stops; MAD18*) Agadir's Noddy train takes visitors on a tour around the city, pointing out the central tourist area, the main town, and the resorts on the southern end of the bay. Agadir doesn't have much to offer in terms of tourist attractions, but the little train does do a good job of showing off what there is.

HOW TO GET TO THE ROMAN SITES If you want to take in the Iles Purpuaires of Essaouira, the legendary islands of the Murex shells that the Phoenicians and Romans used in making their royal purple dye, take a bus or grand taxi for the journey north (see *Getting around, by bus*, page 112). The islands themselves are Sites of Special Scientific Interest and closed to the public, but their silhouette makes a nice backdrop to the lovely fishing town of Essaouira, worth seeing in its own right. For the rest of the sites, it's best to head to Marrakech, either by bus or grand taxi, then take the train to Meknes (for Sidi Kacem), Rabat or Tangier. See the relevant chapters for more information.

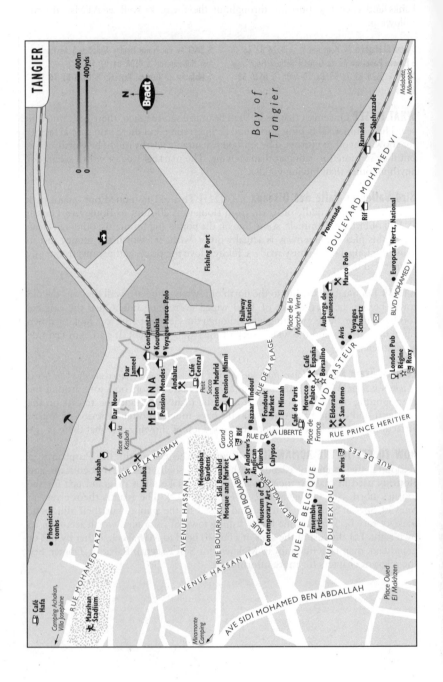

TANGIER

400m
400yds

N

Bract

Bay of
Tangier

Café
Hafa

Camping Achakar,
Villa Josephine

Phoenician
tombs

Marshan
Stadium

Fishing Port

Kasbah

Place de la
Kasbah

Marhaba

RUE DE LA KASBAH

Dar Nour

MEDINA

Dar
Jameel

Continental
Koutoubia
Voyages Marco Polo

Pension Mendes

Andaluz

Café
Central

Petit
Socco

Pension Madrid

Pension Miami

Rif

Grand
Socco

Mendoubia
Gardens

Sidi Bouabid
Mosque and Market

St Andrew's
Anglican
Church

Museum of
Contemporary Art

Calypso

Bazaar Tindouf

Fondouk
Market

RUE DE LA PLAGE

El Minzah

Café de Paris

Place de
France

RUE DE LA LIBERTÉ

Morocco
Palace

Eldorado

San Remo

Café
España

Borsalino

RUE DANGLETERRE

RUE SIDI BOUABID

AVENUE HASSAN I

Ensemble
Artisanal

RUE DE BELGIQUE

RUE DU MEXIQUE

AVENUE HASSAN II

RUE BOUARRAKIA

Railway
Station

Place de la
Marche Verte

Auberge de
Jeunesse

Marco Polo

Avis

Voyages
Schuartz

BLVD PASTEUR

London Pub
Régine
Roxy

Promenade

BOULEVARD MOHAMED VI

Ramada

Shehrazade

Rif

Europcar, Hertz, National

BLVD MOHAMED V

Le Paris

RUE PRINCE HERITIER

RUE DE FES

AVE SIDI MOHAMED BEN ABDALLAH

Place Oued
El Makhzen

Miramonte
Camping

RUE MOHAMED TAZI

Malabata,
Mövenpick

6

Tangier

Telephone code 0539

Tangier, also known as Tanjah, Tanger and Tangiers, is Morocco's most international city. It's also one of the prettiest, resting on Africa's closest point to Europe, overlooking the narrow straits across the Mediterranean Sea towards Spain, a mere 14km away. For centuries the main gateway into Africa, Tangier is a beguiling mix of European and exotic influences. The city and its location have always been a draw for visitors, from the passing Phoenician sailors 3,000 years ago, who saw the potential of the entrance to the Mediterranean, to the artists of the 1920s and later, who simply liked the light. Today, overshadowed by the rise of Marrakech as the country's main tourist destination Tangier remains beautiful and still has a great deal to offer the visitor.

HISTORY

Recognised also as the point of exit of the Mediterranean Sea by the Phoenicians more than 3,000 years ago, it's believed they set up one of their trading posts here, as part of the chain of ports that continued into the Atlantic. By 500BC, Carthaginians wandering west from their capital Carthage decided to create a more permanent settlement. The Greeks were also around, and the narrow straits that separated the continents were given mythic significance, associated with the demi-god, Heracles (the Romans later embraced the name and the spot, giving it the label the Pillars of Hercules). Caves nearby were said to be the place Heracles rested for the night *en route* to fulfilling the eleventh of his Labours, retrieving the golden apple from the Garden of the Hesperides, believed to have been near Lixus (see page 131). In the process, he killed the giant Antaeus, married his widow, and named the town nearby Tingi, after her. Alternative versions of how the city got its name go back to the Amazigh word, *tingis*, meaning marsh, although the Berbers didn't really live on the coast, preferring to spend their time much further south. A third interpretation goes back to a tribute to the Berber goddess Tinjis or Tinga. In any case, the name stuck, and after Carthage was destroyed by the Romans in 146BC, the city came under the jurisdiction of the Roman Empire. After the assassination of Juba II's son Ptolemy in AD40, the province of Mauretania was absorbed and Tingis became the chief city of Mauretania Tingitana, before the Romans moved the capital to Volubilis (see page 140). Part of the Vandal Empire for about a century, from around AD430, the Byzantines followed by taking Tingis back, and the city remained Roman until the Arab invasion just after AD700.

From sometime after 1400, the Portuguese controlled the port as part of their trading empire along the west coast of Africa, and maintained it until 1661, when it was given to Charles II of England, as part of the dowry of his bride, Catherine of Braganza. Continual attacks by Sultan Moulay Ismail at last paid off, and the English finally left in 1684, but not without destroying significant parts of the town and harbour, leaving little for the sultan. Despite his efforts, the city went into decline, continuing to do so until the beginning of the 19th century.

When England, France and Spain were greedily dividing up North Africa for their 'spheres of influence', it was decided in 1923 that Tangier would be made an international zone. During this period, the city boomed, due to its absence of loyalties to one nation, and trade as well as political intrigue flourished. The arts also thrived with creators arriving to take advantage of the light and the zone's neutrality. Painters including Matisse had come to the region decades earlier and inspired others to follow. Writers like Tennessee Williams, William S Burroughs and Paul Bowles were some of the more famous literary residents. Even after World War II, and the return of Tangier to Morocco after the country's independence in 1956, foreigners continued to flock into the city. The American millionaire Malcolm Forbes obtained a palace in 1970, and on the occasion of his 70th birthday party in 1989, gathered a bevy of famous political, cinematic and economic celebrities to celebrate it with him in Tangier.

By now, Tangier traded on its position on the hippy trail, particularly as the Rif Mountain town of Ketama, not far away, was and continues to be, the major producer of kif (hashish) in Morocco. For a while travellers found the delights of an Africa that was such a short distance from Spain attractive, but the excitement began to fade when cheap flights made 'real' Morocco, such as Marrakech, much easier to reach. Hotels began to run down and Tangier gained a reputation as a dangerous city. The tourists who arrive today are predominantly from Spain, popping over the channel to take advantage of cheaper prices. Now, as part of the king's tourism development plan for 2010, renovations and repairs are firmly in place, with the beach having been cleaned up and lined with new cafés and discotheques, and the main boulevard, renamed Mohamed VI, given a well-maintained central pedestrian promenade. A new commercial port is being built a little distance from the centre so that the existing one will revert to being solely for cruise ships. In all, the government is hoping that tourists will make an effort to return to this beautiful city, either en route to some of the delights further south, or coming here as a destination in its own right.

GETTING THERE AND AROUND

BY AIR Ibn Batouta Airport (*Boukhalef;* ✆ *0539 39.37.20; www.onda.ma*) is situated about 11km from the city centre. Royal Air Maroc, British Airways, Iberia and easyJet (to/from Madrid, only) fly here from abroad. The domestic carrier, Royal Air Maroc, handles internal runs, although city-to-city flights aren't popular as they cost quite a bit and don't take much less times than the far cheaper trains. If you're not met by your hotel or tour operator, take a grand taxi, which will set you back around MAD100, depending on where you want to go. Alternatively, walk the 2km to the main road and take a bus, but with luggage it might be easier to pay the taxi, and save your pennies somewhere else.

BY SEA There are eight ferry companies that cross the Straits to land in Tangier, and a variety of disembarkation ports. The website www.cemar.it/dest/ ferries_morocco.htm gives an overall view. The quickest crossing is from Tarifa and the catamaran can do the journey in 35 minutes. Cross-Strait departures are frequent. Prices depend on distance, size of vehicle, time of year and whether the passenger is an adult or child, but start at €31 per adult/€19 per child plus €85 for the car for the shortest voyage, and can cost as much as €525 per person for a deluxe cabin and €365 for a car, on the voyage from Genoa, Italy.

FRS Spain; ☎ 956681830; www.frs.es; Morocco; ☎ 039 94 26 12. Crosses the Straits from Gibraltar in 80 mins.

Comarit Tangier; in town ☎ 0539 32 00 32; at the port; ☎ 039 94 74 02; www.comarit.com. Goes from Tangier & Nador in Morocco to Algeciras & Almeria in Spain, as well as to Sete in France via conventional ferry. The cheapest rate to Spain is €33 per adult/€22 per child + €91 for the car, while the 30hr crossing to France costs €93–239 per passenger, depending on the type of overnight accommodation & from €442 per vehicle.

Euroferrys Spain; ☎ 907658841; www.euroferrys.com. Catamarans do the voyage from Algeciras to Ceuta, a Spanish enclave in Morocco, not far from Tangier, in 35 mins. They also have regular ferries from Algeciras to Tangier.

Ferry Morocco Spain; ☎ 950274800; www.ferrimaroc.com. Daily departures from Almeria to Nador, just south of the Spanish enclave of Melilla.

Transmediterranea Spain; ☎ 902454645; www.trasmediterranea.es. Have a fast ferry that takes 35 mins from Algeciras to Ceuta. They also have regular ferries that take 90 mins, as well as services of 2hrs 30 mins from Algeciras to Tangier, 6hrs from Almeria in Spain to Melilla 7 hours from Malaga to Melilla & 6hrs from Almeria to Nador, in Morocco.

There are also ferry operators that cross from other departure points. The voyage takes much longer, but if you are coming from other parts in Europe, they might be more convenient. It's a makeshift way of taking a Mediterranean cruise while being able to bring the car along.

Comanav Casablanca; ☎ 0522 30 30 12; www.comanav.ma/ferry. Boats sail from Genoa, Italy (a 48hr voyage); & Sete, France (36hrs) to Tangier.

GNV Italy; ☎ 03882390101; www.traghettiweb.it/ferries/grandinaviveloci.htm. Travels from Genoa via Barcelona to Tangier.

SNCM France; ☎ 825 88 80 88; www.sncm.fr. Sails from Sete to Tangier.

BY CAR If coming by car, the sea crossing (see above) is part of the journey. For the quickest route using the shortest sailings from Tarifa, take the N-340 to get to the bottom of Spain, then make your way to the ferry port. For other disembarkation cities, check the maps of Spain, France or Italy to see how best to get to the departure points. Once in Tangier, the port is right in the centre of town. Try to take care of all the formalities on board, although if taking a quick catamaran trip, there might not be enough time. As well as a personal entry/exit form – which should be kept for the return back to Europe – you might have to make some declarations regarding the car, including guarantees that the vehicle will return with you (if leaving the car in Morocco, tax can be extortionate). Make sure you have adequate insurance to cover your stay in Africa and if not, buy some locally. Legal and financial issues can be terrifying, if you're not protected. Bring along a decent map – the tourist boards have some that are good enough to get around with – or pick one up, and then you can begin your journey once on Tangier turf. The roads in Morocco are very good, and the autoroute, although a little pricey, is excellent. The facilities resemble those in France, with high speed limits, and rest areas at regular intervals. The cost prevents many people from travelling, so the roads are reasonably clear. The normal roads are good too and, barring the off-road paths for which an excellent 4x4 vehicle is mandatory, such as along some of the passes in the Atlas Mountains, easy to travel along.

BY RAIL Tangier's flashy railway station, Tanger-Ville (*Route Malabata Charf;* ☎ 090 20 30 40; *www.oncf.ma*) opened in 2003 and moved the departure point from the harbour into the centre of town. More convenient for central Tangier, though less so for arriving sea passengers, it's still a bit of a trek to walk to most of the places you need to go, especially if carrying luggage. Buses don't run from the station to the city centre, so it's easiest to take petit taxis (the small blue ones) to get around. They circulate throughout the entire city, so it's easy to flag one down on the street, and a journey is not likely to cost more than MAD10–25, depending on the distance.

BY BUS AND TAXI As there are quite a few places in the area worth seeing that are not serviced by train, such as the beautiful blue village of Chefchaouen, Larache (for the Roman site of Lixus) and Tetouan (for the wonderful archaeological museum and the ruins of Tamuda), it's worthwhile getting familiar with the two long-distance stations. The grand taxis can take you further afield, at a price, while the petit ones can transport you the smaller distances, usually within the towns.

CTM (*next to the port; ☎ 0539 931 172*) has several departures to routes throughout the country, including Rabat, Casablanca, Fes, Marrakech, Agadir and many other lesser destinations. **Supratours**, (*www.oncf.ma*) the train's offshoot that goes by bus to places not on the rail network, leaves from the station and, like CTM, also goes to Tetouan. Other companies leave from the Gare Routiere (*☎ 0539 94 69 28*). Locally, buses are most useful for visiting attractions out of town, such as number 2, which begins near the medina at the Grand Socco, and heads out almost to the Caves of Hercules (all the way at times on the weekend). Number 16 services both the train and bus stations, bypassing the city centre, but does go east to Cape Malabata for good views back over Tangier. Otherwise, it's easiest walk around or, if necessary, grab a blue petit taxi for the shorter distances, and a beige grand taxi for the longer ones.

CAR HIRE It's no cheaper to rent a car in Tangier than it is anywhere else in Morocco but it's more worthwhile, as there are so many places to see that are not easily accessible. The city itself can be covered on foot or by taxi, but once in pursuit of some of the more obscure Roman sites, having your own transport is a better option. It's possible to pick up a car in one city and drop it off at another.

🚗 **Avis** (airport: Sat/Sun only) ☎ 0539 39 30 33; (town) 54 Bd Pasteur; ☎ 0539 93 46 46; www.avis.com
🚗 **Europcar** (airport) ☎ 0539 94 19 38; (town) 97 Bd Mohammed V; www.europcar.com
🚗 **Hertz** (airport) ☎ 0539 32 22 10; (town) 6 Bd Mohammed V; ☎ 0539 32 21 65; www.hertz.com
🚗 **National** (airport: Sat/Sun only) m 0663 05 34 32; (town) 1 Residence Lina, Bd Mohammed V; ☎ 063 05 34 32; www.nationalcar.com
🚗 **Sixt** 9 Rue Al Jabha Al Watania Hispam; ☎ 0539 93 31 13; www.sixt.com

TOURIST INFORMATION

The main tourist board is at 29 Boulevard Pasteur (*☎ 0539 94 80 50; ⏲ 08.30–12.00 & 14.40–18.30 Mon–Fri*).

TOUR OPERATORS

There are several local tour operators and travel agents who can handle just about anything to do with travel. Many are located close to the ferry port. The better hotels have reliable agents who can arrange day trips or transport. Some of the companies in Tanger are:

Calypso 71 Bis, Rue de la Liberté; ☎ 0539 33 69 86; e info@calypsotangier.com; www.calypsotangier.com
Koutoubia 12 Bis, Av d'Espagne; ☎ 0539 93 46 87
Maghreb Tours Av de la Mediterranee; ☎ 0539 94 10 04
Voyages Marco Polo 72 Av d'Espagne; ☎ 0539 93 77 89
Voyages Schuartz Bd Pasteur; ☎ 0539 93 60 28. American Express's representatives in Tangier.

There are some wonderfully indulgent places to stay, for which you certainly pay for the privilege, as well as historic hotels of varying qualities. It's worth checking online beforehand for availability – particularly in summer – and also obtaining special price deals. It's possible to find much cheaper places, particularly in the medina, but again, don't expect too much – you do get what you pay for.

TOP END

⌂ **El Minzah** (140 rooms) 85 Rue de la Liberté; ☎ 0539 93 58 85; www.elminzah.com. Tangier's most famous & possibly most luxurious hotel has a 75-year history, priding itself on its Hispano-Moorish style, while providing all the benefits of an English gentleman's club. $$$$$

⌂ **Mövenpick Hotel & Casino Malabata** (227 rooms) Rte de Malabata, Baie de Tanger; ☎ 0539 32 93 00; www.moevenpick-hotels.com/en/pub/your_hotels/worldmap/tangier/overview.cfm. This representative of the chain is renowned for its indulgent décor & services, as well as its view over the Bay of Tangier. The Casino Royale provides gambling well into the night. $$$$$

⌂ **Ramada** (138 rooms) 43 Av Mohammed VI; ☎ 0539 94 07 55; www.ramada.com. Another modern hotel with all necessary conveniences & great sea views, but also expensive. $$$$$

⌂ **Rif Hotel & Spa** (127 rooms) 152 Av Mohammed VI; ☎ 0539 34 93 00; www.hotelsatlas.com/rif-spa.htm. This place has some history & it's recently been remodelled in the best modern Moroccan style. It now has full luxury facilities, inc restaurants & spa. Its best feature, however, is its location, overlooking the beach & Spain beyond. $$$$$

⌂ **Villa Josephine** (11 rooms) 231 Rte de la Montagne; ☎ 0539 33 45 35; www.villajosephine-tanger.com. An extravagant bed & breakfast located slightly out of town with great views, this former summer residence was built in the early 20th century by Walter Harris, a famous *Times* journalist. $$$$$

MID-RANGE

⌂ **Dar Jameel** (8 rooms) 6 Rue Mohamed Bergach; ☎ 0539 33 46 80; www.magicmaroc.com. This restored, traditional house is well located close to the old town, providing a welcome alternative to the same old modern hotels. $$$–$$$$

⌂ **Dar Nour** (11 rooms) 20 Rue Gourna, Kasbah; m 0662 11 27 24; www.darnour.com. A pleasant & charming guesthouse conveniently situated in the kasbah of the medina. $$$–$$$$

⌂ **Hotel Continental** (60 rooms) 36 Rue Dar El Baroud; ☎ 0539 93 10 24. The glory of this extraordinary hotel has faded into a 3-star (although currently in the process of a total renovation). This historic venue has fabulous details, plus a list of famous guests, that must, at least, be visited. $$$–$$$$

⌂ **Hotel Shehrazade** Av Mohammed VI; ☎ 0539 34 18 21. Cheap but clean rooms with almost the same views as the Ramada, next door. $$–$$$

BUDGET Most of the one-star and lower places to stay are located close to or within the medina. There's not all that much to choose between them and if you can, try to go in and take a look at which room you'd be willing to stay in. The

---

FILM FAME

In 1990, film director Bernardo Bertolucci made *The Sheltering Sky* based on the 1949 book of long-term Tangier resident, the American author Paul Bowles. Although the story is intriguing with the original novel laden with autobiographical elements, the movie does a better job of showing off how beautiful Morocco and parts of Algeria are. Most of the events take place in the deserts of the south of both countries, but some of the historical aspects are recreated in places that still exist, such as the Hotel Continental in Tangier (see above).

Rue Salah Eddin el Ayoubi has quite a few cheaper, and sometimes historic, pensions and hotels. The area around Ave d'Espagne also has quite a few little places to stay, close to the beach and there's always the youth hostel, also in the same area. Tangier also has a couple of campsites, which offer the cheapest options for accommodation.

🏠 **Pension Madrid** 140 Rue Salah Eddin el Ayoubi; 🕻 0539 93 16 93. $–$$

🏠 **Pension Miami** 126 Rue Salah Eddin el Ayoubi; 🕻 0539 93 29 00. $–$$

🏠 **Auberge de Jeunesse** 8 Rue el Antaki, Av d'Espagne; 🕻 0539 94 61 27. Cheerful &, most importantly, cheap. $

🏠 **Pension Mendes** 80 Av d'Espagne; 🕻 0539 93 31 59. The showers are shared, & cost extra. $

⛺ **Camping Achakhar** Close to Cap Spartel (to the west of the city); 🕻 0539 33 38 40. $

⛺ **Miramonte Camping** On the continuation of Av Allah Ben Abdellah, about 3km west of the centre of town; 🕻 0539 94 75 04. $

✕ WHERE TO EAT

As usual, the better hotels always provide eating options too. Some, such as the **El Minzah**, offer quite good food in their own right. A few of the better guesthouses, such as the Villa Josephine, can supply full board, if you don't feel like braving the big city (**$$$$–$$$$$**). A few of the cheaper pensions in the medina, like Restaurant Mendes (see budget accommodation above), **Hotel Marco Polo** (*Av d'Espagne & Rue el Antaki*) and **Hotel Miramar** (*168 Av d'Espagne*) serve good value food (**$–$$**). Not surprisingly, the least expensive places to eat are in the old town, and there is a huge selection from which to choose, although one small restaurant might seem just like another. Moroccan and fish dishes are the easiest to find, with continental cuisine more often resident in the newer part of town (Ville Nouvelle).

✕ **Café Espana** Rue Jabha Al Watania; 🕻 0539 93 80 19; 🕐 daily. With the country so close, why not try eating at a place that serves Spanish specialities, including 3 different paellas: seafood, vegetarian & Valenciana. $$$

✕ **Restaurant Eldorado** 5 Rue Ahmed Chaouki; 🕻 0539 93 84 51; 🕐 for b/fast, lunch & dinner daily. International cuisine in a somewhat more sophisticated atmosphere, without being too pricey. $$$

✕ **Restaurant Marhaba** 67 Rue de la Kasbah; 🕻 0539 93 79 27. On the edge of the medina, the décor of this old palace is Moroccan, as well as the food. $$$

✕ **Restaurant San Remo** Chez Toni, 15 Rue Ahmed Chouki; 🕻 0539 93 84 51; 🕐 daily. A better Italian joint, serving good pizza & pasta. $$$

✕ **Restaurant Andaluz** 7 Rue de Commerce. In the medina this cheap & cheerful place has the best fish & seafood in the simplest of surroundings. $–$$

CAFÉS There's a delicious faded glory to Tangier that seems to be epitomised in the remnants of its café society. One of the best ways to see how life goes on, as well as meeting some of the regulars who patronise their favourite spots, is to find a café and linger. The Petit Socco in the heart of the medina has a few places to sit and drink a mint tea, espresso or orange juice, while watching the characters. In addition, it's possible to grab a quick snack or, if feeling decadent, a fabulous pastry or two, as good as those found in Paris.

☕ **Café Central** Petit Socco. Offering a great view of the happenings in the little square; grab a ringside seat for a refreshment break, particularly welcome after having lost your way inside the medina.

☕ **Café Hafa** Marshan district, to the west of the medina. This ramshackle little place hidden in a back alley dangling over the sea, was the hangout of many famous writers of the past, including Paul Bowles & his American friends. The location is far better than the décor or the food, but the atmosphere is legendary.

☐ **Café de Paris** Place de France. A blast from the past, when radicals used to gather here; the new town location is still a gathering point for the last foreign residents.

FAST FOOD If the urge to go Western becomes overwhelming, there are a couple of **McDonald's** in the Dawliz complex, Rue de Hollande, close to St Andrew's Church and also on the beachfront, as well as a **Pizza Hut** along the beach.

ENTERTAINMENT AND NIGHTLIFE

Tangier isn't the party town it once was, particularly in the days of its foreign celebrities. Trendy visitors have decamped for Marrakech. There are still a few places to spend the evenings, though, if you have energy to spare.

Activities for tourists seem to revolve mostly around the hotels. The best bars and nightclubs located in the top end include the **El Minzah Hotel** with a wine bar and Caid's Piano Bar, the **Mövenpick** and its casino, the **Ramada**'s discotheque, and the **Rif**'s Churchill Lounge, Rif Bar and Plaza Club nightclub. At the more affordable end, there are hangouts near the cheaper hotels and pensions in the medina, for example on the ground floor of the **Hotel Marco Polo**.

☆ **Borsalino** 30 Av Prince Moulay-Abdellah. One of the better-known discotheques in the city, it tends to get lively after midnight.
♀ **London Pub** 15 Rue Mansour Dahbi; ☏ 0539 94 20 94. There's always a pub, somewhere, & here you can get a drink – of alcohol!
☆ **Morocco Palace** 13 Rue Prince Moulay-Abdelleh. Generally agreed to be the best nightspot in Tangier,

partying goes on till 04.00. Often a show is put on, usually of traditional music or belly dancers.
☆ **Régine** 8 Rue El Mansour Dahbi. A disco where anyone can bop, opens around 22.00.
♀ **Tangier Inn** 1 Rue Magellan. A throwback to the old days, with pictures on the walls of some of the more famous visitors from the period. You can drink till late here.

SHOPPING

There's nothing to write home about regarding the markets and shops in Tangier. Wandering through the medina one can find the usual tacky craft items hanging on the walls and laid out on tables in the narrow streets, but nothing of great value. The items in the shops of the better hotels look gorgeous, but prices are extortionate. The Boulevard Mohamed V in the Ville Nouvelle and its continuation as Boulevard Pasteur are major city thoroughfares that have all the stores you could ever want, from opticians to bookshops and the closer you get to the Place de France, the more packed in they are.

Bazar Marrakech Rue des Siaghines. If you can't get to Marrakech, at least you can pick up some antique jewellery at its namesake.
Bazaar Tindouf 64 Rue de la Liberté. Jewellery, crafts & antiques are on sale here but the only way to get good prices is to bargain for them.
Ensemble Artisanal Rue Belgique. Half art exhibition & half craft-selling venue, here is where you can see & buy some of the best new Moroccan goods, without bargaining.
Fondouk Market Not far from the Grand Socco. You can pick up fruit & veg here.

Marjane Rte de Larache, Km 6.2; ☏ 0539 31 81 94. It's always worth knowing where the local hypermarket is, for all those things you've forgotten to bring along.
Sidi Bouabid Market Sidi Bouabid, just southwest of the Grand Socco. A small complex of shops selling various items, including some interesting food that might be worth a taste.
Uniprix 24 Rue la Fayette; ☏ 0539 94 77 24. A useful store that has most practical items.

OTHER PRACTICALITIES

EMERGENCY TELEPHONE NUMBERS

Police ☏ 19
Fire service and ambulance ☏ 15
Highway ☏ 177

All-night chemist 22 Rue de Fès; ☏ 0539 93 26 19
Doctor Dr Abdelouahid Torres, 62 Rue Moussa Ben
Noussaire; ☏ 0539 93 46 00. Speaks English.

HOSPITALS

✚ Clinique Assalam For emergencies: 10 Av de la
Paix; ☏ 0539 32 25 58

✚ Polyclinique de la Sécurité Sociale Rte de Malabata;
☏ 0539 94 01 99. 24hr casualty department.

INTERNET CAFÉS As with all the other cities in Morocco, these cafés come and go.
The easiest way to find one is to follow the big 'Internet' signs that can be found
all over the place. In the meantime, here are a couple that will hopefully last longer
than their rivals. Also check out the hotels.

🖥 Cyber Espace Pasteur 31 Bd Pasteur

🖥 Hotel Intercontinental Parc Brooks, Bd Mohamed
Ben Abdellah; ☏ 0539 93 01 50. Has internet café.

POST The main post office is at 33 Boulevard Mohamed V.

BANKS Hotels will exchange money, although not always at the best rate. There are
banks and exchange bureaux throughout the town, as well as ATMs. Try:

$ Al Maghrib Bank 78 Av Mohamed V; ☏ 0539 32
23 10
$ Banque Populaire de Tanger 76 Bd Mohamed V;
☏ 0539 93 12 06

$ BMCE Bd Pasteur; ☏ 0539 93 10 44
$ Crédit du Maroc Bd Mohamed V & Bd Moussa Ibn
Moussair BP 276; ☏ 0539 93 19 16
$ SGMB 58 Bd Mohamed V; ☏ 0539 32 20 29

WHAT TO SEE

WITHIN THE CITY

Beach and Avenue Mohamed VI The town beach is a lovely bay of white sand
stretching from the medina in the west to Cape Malabata in the east. Recently
cleaned up, it seems to extend as far as the mountains of Spain, visible on a clear
day. There are a few cafés and discotheques along its edge. Avenue Mohamed VI
has a pedestrian walkway down the middle of it with large palm trees on either side
that create an esplanade leading to the medina. All sorts of people stroll here.
During the day, it's a delightful way to get to the old town and at night both it and
the beach are beautifully lit.

Medina Tangier's old town gleams white in the distance, a haphazard collection of
houses nestled against each other and rising up a hill overlooking the harbour and the
sea. It's a very picturesque northwest end to the tree-lined walkway of Avenue
Mohamed VI. From the sea and the port, pass by the terrace of French colonial
buildings and their street-side cafés, and walk up into the maze. You can opt for
wandering aimlessly in the little passageways that twist and turn, or for orientation you
can follow the signs to the Hotel Continental, gaining a view over the harbour. Try to
stop in and take a look at the hotel itself. Continuing north, it's extremely easy to get
lost and that's much of the fun. If determined to find your way, take the Rue des
Chretiens (or Rue des Almouhidines) and follow it, and its various name changes, till
you reach the kasbah wall. Alternatively, and somewhat less adventurously, follow the
edge of the medina around the Grand Mosque and take Rue de la Marine to get

straight to the little square of the Petit Socco. It's worth noting this spot as a reference point, as well as a place to have a coffee or mint tea, when the meandering gets too much. Continuing west on the main street, you'll get onto Rue es Siaghin, allegedly a Roman road and one of Tangier's main streets of the past.

Grand Socco The route will soon pass through the medina gates, leading out to the main square of the old town. This large place is known as the Grand Socco, but officially – and rarely – called the Place du 19 Avril 1947 (named after the pre-independence date on which Sultan Mohamed V visited the city). Said to be the site of the Roman forum, there's been no archaeological evidence to confirm this. With an impressive and cooling fountain in the centre, and gardens around it, the area is a pleasant environment in which to stroll. Many of the attractions of the town use this spot as a starting point and it lies at the crossing between the medina, just to the east, the kasbah, to the northeast, the coast and the smart residential area of the Marshan to the northwest, and the new city, to the west and southwest. Just past the market, at 50 Socco, lies the incongruous Victorian church of St Andrew's. It looks as if it were transported from some rural English town and dropped on this prominent location. Anglican services are still held *(for times, check www.achurchnearyou.com/venue.php?V=8442)* and the adjoining cemetery is a reminder of those expats who lived here, with gravestones of English names rising out of the Moroccan soil. Facing the new town, the former British Consulate now houses the **Museum of Contemporary Art** *(Rue d'Angleterre BP 426; ☎ 0539 33 84; ⏰ 09.00–12.30 & 15.00–18.00 Wed–Mon; MAD10),* that shows the latest and best of new Moroccan art.

Kasbah To the far northwest of the medina is a walled-off section known as the kasbah, or specially fortified area. Access is easiest from the west of the medina, via the Rue de la Kasbah, going till you reach the bab (gate), although it's just about

A CLIFFSIDE WALK

To the north of the square in front of the Dar el Makhzen, there's a small gap in the kasbah wall. Walk through it and you emerge on the cliff edge, overlooking the beach and the city of Tangier, to the east. On a clear day, the mountains of Spain are so visible they look like they're in the next village. The view alone is worth the few steps, but if you want to see more, follow the narrow path to the west, now outside the kasbah walls. Continue the wander, passing ramshackle residential areas that probably have the most scenic locations in the city. Eventually you'll be led back to the main street, but when you reach Rue Asad ibn Farrat, walk until you see the two large Graeco-Roman columns. Head towards the sea, and you'll come across a series of deep rectangular holes in the rocks of the cliff that are Phoenician tombs. Whatever items were found there have long since been carted away, some to the Kasbah Museum, but the point of the visit is not only to see where the Punic graves were, but also to appreciate the superb sea views. Locals come here to enjoy the vistas, carefully stepping between the gaps. It's worth continuing the walk west along Rue Shakespear (ex Rue Mohammed Tazi), reaching the La Marshan district. Here is where the wealthiest foreign and Moroccan residents had their homes. Just off Rue Tabor is Café Hafa where you can have a coffee break and take in the fabulous view over the Mediterranean, in possibly the same seats that writers like Paul Bowles, Tennessee Williams, Jack Kerouac and Truman Capote once sat. It might be easier to ask someone where the café is, rather than trying to find the way yourself. If you don't fancy the stroll back, a bus can take you to the Grand Socco.

possible to make your way there through the medina. An intriguing area where once many of the celebrities in Tangier's heyday had their homes, today the most important reason to visit is the **Kasbah Museum** (*Palais Dar al Makhzen, Pl de la Kasbah;* ✆ *039 93 20 97;* ⊕ *09.00–16.00; MAD10*). Situated inside the former sultan's palace, this recently modernised museum holds an excellent collection of artefacts celebrating the history of Tangier, from prehistoric times to the 19th century. There are rooms dedicated to Phoenician and Roman eras, as well as later Islamic periods. The highlight of the ground floor's exhibition on trade between Tingis and other Mediterranean cultures is a large mosaic of Venus riding on a ship, taken from the Roman site of Volubilis (see page 140).

AROUND TANGIER
Cape Spartel, the Caves of Hercules and Cotta To the west of Tangier, where the Mediterranean ends and the Atlantic begins, is the dramatic Cape Spartel. The sea below this cliff can get pretty savage, and seafarers, who have been sailing in and out of these waters since Phoenician days, have a lighthouse, built in 1864, to guide them. The atmosphere at this merging of the waters is exhilarating. Further south along the Atlantic, the road passes some broad and deserted beaches, and leads to the Cave of Hercules. A tacky, but naively charming makeshift resort has sprung up here, with souvenir shops and even completely incongruous camels upon whom visitors can pose. Myth has it that these caves were where the Greek Heracles, or the Roman Hercules, spent the night when on his way to performing the 11th of his Labours, finding the golden apple of the Hesperides (supposedly found in Lixus, on the coast further south). On calm days, it's possible to tour the caves during daylight, for a small entrance fee. A short walk from the car park leads to the very few remaining ruins of Cotta, a Roman settlement from just before AD300. Not much is left, although the traces of a *garum* (fish sauce) works, an olive press and vestiges of a courtyard and a temple can be made out amongst the unrestrained vegetation.

Cape Malabata To the eastern side of Tangier is another lighthouse on a cliff, built last century. Again, the location is dramatic, but Cape Malabata is better known as the site of most of Tangier's big resorts. More are being planned. Although perhaps a bit intensively touristy, the region could suit people who want bigger and larger facilities in a less urban location.

THE ROMAN SITES

Ancient Morocco, or Mauretania, was never as fully developed as the purer Carthaginian and later Roman regions to the east. Neighbouring Berber tribes meant trading posts, and later cities, were frequently attacked; centuries (a group of Roman soldiers) were all too aware that they were at the frontier of the empire. Tingis (Tangier) was the capital of the province, before the Mauretanian king Juba II moved it to Volubilis (page 140) although it did regain its position during the Byzantine era. A few other settlements grew into larger towns usually starting off as military bases and if not along the coast, near to navigable rivers. Once the Romans arrived, Mauretania enjoyed a brief period of autonomy, before being absorbed as a fully fledged province. Even then, the natives were always restless and eventually Rome shed most of its enclaves, hanging on to Sala, near Rabat (page 153) and Tingis. Other than the Phoenician tombs on the hillside in Tangier's Marshan, and what's visible in the Kasbah Museum (most coming from Volubilis), whatever remains of Tingis is hidden under 1,600 years of subsequent living. However, in the area, there are two sites of note that still have something, if not a lot, to see, Tamuda and the grander Lixus.

TAMUDA Just on the southwestern outskirts of the city of Tetouan, less than 60km from Tangier, is the unassuming Roman site of Tamuda. Allegedly deriving its name from the Berber *tamda*, another word for swamp or marsh, it was built on a hillside 70m above sea level and lies just outside the town on the road to Chefchaouen. The town sits on the east bank of the River Martil, which in Phoenician and Roman days, was navigable and gave access to the Mediterranean, probably close to today's city of Martil.

History Ruins have been found that indicated the site was settled before 400BC by the Carthaginians. It's been surmised that like Carthage, the city was destroyed in a war, but resettled and converted into a Roman colony afterwards. By AD400 the site was abandoned, most likely with the arrival of the Vandals. It seems there was no interest by the reconquering Byzantines to revive the place, and the town gradually disappeared under a dirt mound. Inspired by mentions by Pliny, excavations began in the 1920s and continued through the 1990s.

Getting there Supratours buses leave from Tangier for Tetouan twice a day, the journey takes an hour and costs MAD20. There are also other bus companies that leave Tangier for Chefchaouen (see below) and stop in Tetouan *en route*. It's a few kilometres out to the site, which can easily be walked, or reached via taxi. To go by car is easy and it's worth renting one if planning on visiting the rest of the attractions in the area. The journey from Tangier to Tetouan takes about 45 minutes.

 **Where to stay** Tetouan (see page 130) has lodgings for visitors, ranging from four-star hotels on the outskirts like the **Hotel Chams** (*Rte Abdelhak Torres;* ☎ *0539 99 09 01;* $$$–$$$$), to one-star establishments in the centre such as the **Hotel Regina** (*8 Rue Sidi Mandri;* ☎ *0539 96 21 13;* $).

What to see The extraordinary thing is that the trace of a Roman Imperial fort has been discovered here, the only example found in today's Morocco. Large, with 80m-long sides and surrounded by a wall enhanced by 20 evenly spaced guard towers, the fortress had a dominant position on the hillside. Little but a ground plan and some low foundations remain of this impressive construction. On the western side, a spacious rectangle has been discovered, most likely the site of the forum. Remnants of the baths remain to the south, and their arches identify them. The boys that play on the spot are most likely to guide visitors here. Although not one of the more significant Roman sites, the location is impressive, with its hillside aspect overlooking both Tetouan and the river valley beyond. In addition, there's still a sense of discovery, as bits emerge from the ground triggering the imagination of the keen explorer as to what might lie below.

AROUND TAMUDA

Chefchaouen Another 60km further south into the Rif Mountains, this charming hilltop village shouldn't be missed. The old town rises up an incline and is coloured blue, to ward off mosquitoes, and white, to keep the houses cool. Over the years, repeated painting has caused the angles to soften, so that the whole town seems to have an organic quality about it.

Where to stay and eat Aware of its tourists, the town has cafés and restaurants and a few hotels and guesthouses, but it's not overrun due to its position off the beaten track. Buses from Tangier, Fes, Meknes and other towns stop here. Stay at the **Parador Chaouen** (*Pl el Makhzen;* ☎ *0539 98 63 24;* $$$) for the best in the town

If you're willing to rent a car, it's possible to combine all the above attractions as well as some extras, in a delightful day. Start early, and begin at Tangier, taking the P28 to Tetouan. Park and wander into the town, visiting the archaeological museum and the medina. Stop for a quick coffee at one of the local cafés, if you require a bit of caffeine, before driving the few kilometres to Tamuda. Wandering around the site, you can see where those figurines in the museum came from. Follow the signs to Chefchaouen, rising into the heavily wooded mountains, then head towards the town centre. Park, probably close to the Parador Chaouen, and take off on foot, meandering through the tiny blue-and-white pedestrian passageways. By now, it's probably time for lunch, and a snack as well as an obligatory mint tea at one of the cafés in the Place Outa el Hammam, would be the thing to do. Afterwards, drive back towards Tetouan, but turn to the right on a secondary, but well-paved road, signposted to Oued Laou. The scenery quickly becomes dramatic. The natural beauty of the Rif Mountains has been acknowledged by the government with the establishment of the Talassemtane National Park. You can drive through or stop to take a hike. Eventually, the hills flatten out and the road heads straight to the coast. The little town of Oued Laou isn't that impressive, even though traces of Phoenician and Roman occupations have been found here. What makes this slow, but enjoyable drive worthwhile is the journey back to Tetouan. The road rises up, with forest on one side, and the Mediterranean-side beaches far below. Development is planned for this area of coast, but not much has been done yet, and the sleepy little fishing villages still exude a relaxed feel. A few little resorts are springing up, and it's possible to spend a bit of time here, unwinding from the exertions of the big city. Eventually, the road heads back to Tetouan, and from there, returns to Tangier. This entire journey can be done in a day, but stretching it out into several days is easy enough to do.

or **Hotel Sevilla** (*Av Zerktouni;* ☏ *0539 98 71 13*) for an overnight lodging that's basic but convenient.

Tetouan This small city is worth a look, while wandering in pursuit of the archaeological museum. There is a Spanish flavour to the architecture, stemming from repeated conquests by Spain. The ancient medina is a UNESCO World Heritage Site and full of character, and not so large as to be overwhelming. Another of the king's royal palaces is here, as well as a kasbah and various mosques. Tetouan has political significance as much of the country's Jewish (Sephardic) population settled here and, more recently, was the home of some of the perpetrators of the 2004 Madrid bombings.

The Archaeological Museum of Tetouan (*2 Rue Ben Hussain;* ☏ *0539 96 73 03;* ⏱ *08.30–16.30; MAD10*). This wonderful little museum, hidden in the back streets of the white Andalusian-style city of Tetouan, is a treasure trove of finds from both Tamuda and Lixus (page 129 and opposite). Items from nearby Tamuda include Punic and Roman ceramic and glass jars, bronze statuettes of Roman deities, fragments of inscriptions and even belt buckles from Roman military uniforms, probably found near the fort. The exhibitions of discoveries from Lixus are even more exciting, comprising mostly mosaics found from the residences and amphitheatre. Some of these tableaux are spectacular, such as Venus and Adonis, and Mars and Rhea Silvia found in the house of the same name. Many of the tessellated pieces of artwork are displayed in the garden, a pleasant place for an impromptu picnic before entering the dusty, but fascinating, museum.

LIXUS Around 85km south of Tangier is the seaside town of Larache, and just on its northeast outskirts is arguably the second most important Roman site – after Volubilis – in Morocco, Lixus. Its position in Phoenician times, close to the coast and next to the navigable Loukkos River, occasioned the need for a permanent settlement.

History Although items have been found here that date back to 800BC, it's likely the site was established at least two centuries earlier. With its Atlantic coast location, on the route between Tingis and Mogador (today's Essaouira), Lixus must have been an important trading post. As part of the Carthaginian domain, the ancient city was taken by the Romans when they defeated Carthage. Like the rest of Mauretania, the empire absorbed Lixus into its influence, and then province. The city was never really abandoned until the Arab conquest around 650AD, when the invaders decided that Larache, with its saltpans and situation directly on the coast, was a better place to settle.

Getting there Lixus is well signposted on the A1 motorway from Tangier, although poorly marked on the surface road. Get onto the P2 until about 2km east of Larache, and turn towards the sea at the sign that says Plage Ras R'Mal. Pull over almost at the intersection, parking just alongside the smaller road. There, behind the green railings, are the ruins.

 Where to stay The nearby town of Larache (see below) is a small seaside resort. The best hotel in town is the **Hotel Riad** (*Pl de la Liberation & Gare Routiere;* ✆ *0539 91 26 26;* $$–$$$) although it's possible to stay much more cheaply at the **Pension Malaga** (*4 Rue de Sale;* ✆ *0539 91 18 68;* $).

What to see A placard tells you that you've arrived, and soon after, a guardian will appear, offering to show you the sights. This man is not a guide, and will do very little more than point at the remains, but he will lead you through and discreetly expect a tip at the end. The town is located in two areas. At the base of the hill are tanks where fish were kept, as well as remains of the *garum,* or fish paste factories. A few arches are intact and easily recognisable. Taking the path up the hill, the ruins become more impressive, with the remains of the amphitheatre, the only one found in Morocco, and nearby baths. Behind are the city walls, and past them, the view stretches down to the city of Larache, and the Atlantic Ocean behind. Soon, the layout of the city becomes apparent, with the bare bones of houses, ordinary and peristyle, public buildings and even a Christian church, later to be a mosque. At the highest point, the acropolis grants a superb view of the Loukka River below, meandering into the distance. The jewel in the archaeological crown is the mosaic of Neptune that is temporarily covered up for protection. A team of Spanish excavators is busily working here at the moment, digging out the remains of the Punic settlement (the stones under ground level are noticeably different from the Roman ones above). Nearby are the remnants of a Phoenician citadel, and the walls of a much later Roman construction. Scrambling down the hill over ancient stones, the way leads back to where the car is parked. Alternatively, walk the few kilometres back to town, and wait for the bus to where you next want to go.

Larache This low-key small fishing village is lying in wait for the 2010 resort development of Lixus Port, construction of which is already in progress. In the meantime, this sleepy little coastal town is pleasant enough, with a seafront promenade that offers great views over the Atlantic at sunset.

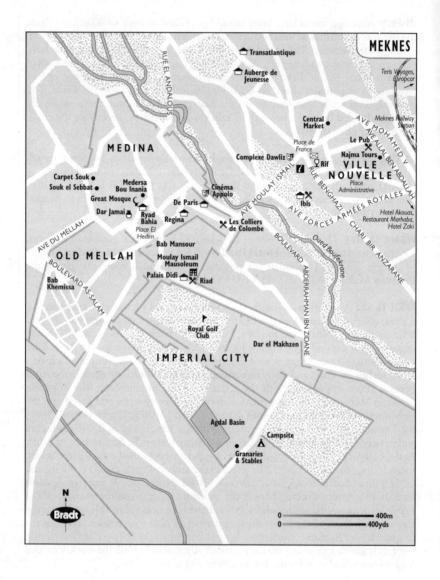

MEKNES

Transatlantique

Auberge de
Jeunesse

Teris Voyages,
Europcar

RUE EL ANDALOUS

MEDINA

Central
Market

Meknes Railway
Station

Place de
France

Le Pub

AVE MOHAMED V
AVE ALLAL BEN ABDALLAH

Complexe Dawliz

Rif

Najma Tours

VILLE
NOUVELLE

Place
Administrative

Carpet Souk
Souk el Sebbat

Medersa
Bou Inania

Cinéma
Appolo

Great Mosque

De Paris

Ibis

AVE MOULAY ISMAIL

RUE BENGHAZI

AVE FORCES ARMÉES ROYALES

Dar Jamai

Ryad
Bahia

Regina

Les Colliers
de Colombe

Hotel Akouas,
Restaurant Marhaba,
Hotel Zaki

CHARI BIR ANZARANE

Place El
Hedim

OLD MELLAH

AVE DU MELLAH

Bab Mansour

Moulay Ismail
Mausoleum

Oued Boufekrane

Palais Didi

Riad

BOULEVARD AS-SALAM

Bab
Khemissa

Royal Golf
Club

Dar el Makhzen

BOULEVARD ABDERRAHMAN IBN ZIDANE

IMPERIAL CITY

Agdal Basin

Campsite

Granaries
& Stables

N

Bradt

0   400m
0   400yds

7

Meknes

Telephone code 0535

Often bypassed in favour of nearby Fes, Meknes is still very much worth a visit. Together with Rabat and Marrakech, these four locations make up the Imperial Cities, each allocated the role of capital at some point in Morocco's history. Meknes does not let its side down and is dominated by the walled Imperial City created by its most important historical figure, the 17th-century AD Alaouite Sultan Moulay Ismail. He left a legacy of extravagant royal remnants, including beautiful city gates, enormous storerooms and impressive stables. His mausoleum (see page 138) is exquisite, although surprisingly small for someone so absorbed with large spaces. Meknes is also an excellent base for exploring some of the sites nearby, particularly Morocco's best Roman ruin, Volubilis (page 140). In addition, the city's altitude of 552m provides a nice climate and a gentle introduction to the middle Atlas Mountains, just to the south.

HISTORY

Historical settlement dates back to Neolithic times, with evidence of habitation found in the area. First the Carthaginians, then the Romans settled there. People continued to live in the city beyond the Arab invasion, leaving only when Moulay Idris, the founder of the Idrisid dynasty around AD800, set up his eponymous town nearby. At approximately the same time, it's believed that the Berbers also built a settlement.

About 200 years later, another Berber tribe arrived and laid the foundations of a more significant city. Things carried on until 1673, when Moulay Ismail, the country's sultan, decided that here was the ideal spot for his capital. Construction began on an enormous scale, when he put into place his dream of an extraordinarily lavish and impressive city, with a series of ramparts, stables, grain warehouses, mosques, residences and even gardens. The sultan's son, followed by his son, Sidi Mohamed ben Abdallah, continued to build according to the original plan and managed to finish Moulay Ismail's mausoleum before the Lisbon earthquake in 1755 destroyed the city. The capital was moved to Marrakech, and Meknes suffered. It wasn't until the French protectorate that things revived, and today the city is on the tourist trail as one of the four Imperial Cities.

GETTING THERE AND AROUND

BY AIR The closest airport is Fes-Saïs Airport (*BP 11, Fes;* ☎ *0535 62 48 00*), 60km from Meknes. Although the intake is international, flights to Fes are expensive and require at least one stop from the UK or North America. It would probably be easier and cheaper to fly to Aeroport Mohamed V in Casablanca, Morocco's main international airport with the best connections, and take a train from there to Meknes.

BY RAIL The main railway station (*Av des FAR; ☎ 0535 52 06 89; www.oncf.ma*) is in the new town to the east of the river, while the smaller gare (*Rue Amir Abdelkader; ☎ 0535 52 27 63*) is close to the centre. Trains arrive from all over the country and go to both stations, but the most convenient method on arrival from Mohamed V Airport is to change at Casa Voyageurs in Casablanca and get onto the train for Meknes for the four hour 30 minute journey. If staying in the old town, get off at El Amir Abdelkader, but if your hotel is in the Ville Nouvelle, stay on board for the extra five minutes to get to the main station. Single fares from Casablanca are MAD120.

BY BUS AND TAXI The CTM station (*Av de FAR; ☎ 0535 52 25 84*) is in the new town. There are other small bus companies that have drops closer to the old town, but these organisations are not as reliable, or as frequent, as CTM. If your accommodation is far from the station, take one of the low-priced green petit taxis. If you'd rather arrange long-distance transport on your own terms, the grand taxis are always at your disposal but at a much higher price. It might well be worth considering hiring a taxi for the day to show you around Meknes, or to take you to some of the sites outside the city.

CAR HIRE If you are planning to visit the nearby sites of Moulay Idris, Volubilis and Fes, and the idea of going by grand taxi doesn't appeal, hiring a car for the day is a reasonable option. The major car rental firms are not represented in Meknes, the closest agents being in Fes. Automobiles can be hired from local tour operators and there may well be other reliable local car rental companies around. Check with the tour operators below or your hotel or the local tourist office for recommendations. Alternatively, if planning a visit to Fes in any case, it might be worth getting there by bus or grand taxi, and renting your car from there.

Companies in **Fes** include:

Avis (airport) ☎ 0535 62 69 69; (town) 50 Bd Chef Chaouani; ☎ 0535 62 69 69; www.avis.com
Europcar (airport) ☎ 0535 62 65 45; (town) 45 Av Hassan II; ☎ 0535 62 65 45; www.europcar.com
Hertz (airport) ☎ 0535 62 28 12; (town) Bd Lalla Meryem; ☎ 0535 62 28 12; www.hertz.com
National Hotel Palais Jamai Bab Guissa; m 0662 14 51 45; www.nationalcar.com
Sixt Hotel Jnan Palace; ☎ 0522 23 23 20; www.sixt.com

TOURIST INFORMATION

The regional tourist office is located at the Place Administrative (*☎ 0535 52 44 26; ⌚ 08.30–12.00 & 14.30–18.30 Mon–Thu, 08.00–11.30 & 15.00–18.30 Fri*).

TOUR OPERATORS

El Menzeh Voyages 9 Passage El Huseini; ☎ 0535 51 75 08
El Yousre Diour Salam, Rte de Sefita; ☎ 0535 55 02 97
La Boussole 14 Rue de Paris; ☎ 0535 52 45 05
Najma Tours 3 Bd Allal Ben Abdellah; ☎ 0535 51 26 44
New Frontier Travel Km 5, Rte d'el Hajeb, BP 293; ☎ 0535 55 00 52
Teris Voyages 10 Av Hassan II; ☎ 0535 52 26 61
Voyages Alla 5 Rue Beyrout; ☎ 0535 52 07 25
Voyages Oualili 21 Av Idris II; ☎ 0535 52 42 14

WHERE TO STAY

TOP END

Hotel Zaki Bd Al Massira, Ville Nouvelle; ☎ 0535 52 07 90. This modern 4-star hotel has all the luxuries, including swimming pool & spa. $$$$

Hotel Transatlantique (120 rooms) Zankat Al Marinyen, Ville Nouvelle; ☎ 0535 52 50 50. The 4-star accommodation is the city's best, providing almost everything tourists could want, barring proximity to the medina. $$$–$$$$

🏠 **Palais Didi** (11 rooms) 7 Dar Lakbira, Medina; ✆ 0535 55 85 90; www.palaisdidi.com. This

MID-RANGE

🏠 **Ryad Bahia** (7 rooms) Tiberbarine, Medina; ✆ 0535 55 45 11; www.ryad-bahia.com. Close to the old city's heart, the Place el Hedim, this lovely guesthouse has been recreated with authentic Moroccan décor. $$$

🏠 **Hotel Akouas**, (50 rooms) 27 Rue Amir, Ville Nouelle; ✆ 0535 51 59 69; www.hotelakouas.com. This modern, clean hotel has some delightful traditional touches & is well located in the new

BUDGET

🏠 **Auberge de Jeunesse** (Youth Hostel) (60 beds) Av Okba Ibn Nafi, Ville Nouvelle; ✆ 0535 52 46 98; www.hihostels.com/dba/hostels-Meknes-039010.en.htm. Up to the usual youth hostel standard, the shared rooms are cheap. $

🏠 **Hotel de Paris** 58 Bd Rouamzine, Medina; no phone. This hotel is so simple that the showers are

guesthouse is situated within one of the few 17th-century buildings still standing after the 1755 earthquake, & has been superbly restored in traditional style. $$$–$$$$

centre, especially handy if arriving by bus. $$–$$$

🏠 **Hotel Ibis Moussafir Meknes** (104 rooms) Av des FAR, Ville Nouvelle; ✆ 0535 40 41 41. In keeping with the usual good standard of the Ibis chain, this hotel offers clean, nice rooms & has a swimming pool, as well as a bar that's open 24/7. $$–$$$

located next door at the hammam (public baths), but the rooms are large & clean. $

🏠 **Hotel Regina** 19 Rue Dar Smen, Medina; ✆ 0535 53 02 80. Basic & perhaps a bit dreary, the rooms have washbasins & the showers are charged extra by the half-hour. $

✖ WHERE TO EAT

In the centre of the Ville Nouvelle, on the main road especially near the station, are loads of cheap little places ($), serving traditional Moroccan food, as well as the chicken you can smell roasting on a spit. It's also possible to find similar low-key venues in the medina. On the high-quality end, most of the good hotels have their own in-house restaurants. Among these better places, **Restaurant Riad** adjoining the Palais Didi serves traditional dishes ($$$–$$$$). The Moroccan speciality food at the **Ryad Bahia** ($$$–$$$$), and the **Ibis** with its French cuisine and liquor licence ($$$–$$$$), are also worth mentioning.

✖ **Le Pub** 20 Bd Allal Ben Abdallah, Ville Nouvelle; ✆ 0535 52 42 47; ⏱ 11.00–midnight. This Italian pizzeria also serves different sorts of French dishes & has a liquor licence & piano bar. $$–$$$

✖ **Les Colliers de Colombe** 67 Rue Driba, Medina; ✆ 0535 55 50 41 ⏱ daily. A classier version of some more familiar dishes is served here. The

pigeon – or other – pie, *pastilla*, is excellent. $$$

✖ **Restaurant Marhaba** 23 Av Mohamed V, Ville Nouvelle; ⏱ 12.00–21.00. This place seems to be everyone's favourite, including the local clientele, & serves good, basic Moroccan dishes. $$–$$$

CAFÉS AND FAST FOOD There are lots of cafés at which to have a mint tea or espresso. In the medina, the venues tend to be more traditional, full of men, and with little or nothing to eat. In the Ville Nouvelle, it's possible to find pastry shops resembling Parisian patisserie. These locations open early – try a breakfast – and remain operational until 21.00–23.00.

If desperate for American fast food, try **Mo Di Niro** (*Rue Zankat, Ville Nouvelle*) a burger joint that the local youth patronise ($$). Failing that, there's always **McDonald's** (*Av Moulay Ismail, Ville Nouveau*; $–$$).

ENTERTAINMENT AND NIGHTLIFE

Meknes doesn't have the nightlife and bar scene that the larger, more resort-like areas have. The Place el Hedim is a smaller version of Marrakech's Djemaa el Fna, and by late afternoon, the storytellers, dancers, hawkers and street entertainers come out. It's not on the larger city's scale, but it's fun anyway. Many of the bars in the new town are pretty much for men only and not really a place for women to feel welcome. If you're looking to have a drink, or discover a nightclub, the better hotels in the Ville Nouvelle are the places to go. The **Hotel Transatlantique** is a good place for a drink, and also has O'Night, a discotheque where you can bop after you eat. You can imbibe at the **Hotel Zaki** after hours. The **Hotel Rif** (*Rue Accra;* ✆ *0535 52 25 91*) has a good scene, and the price of drinks is reasonable. The **Le Pub** restaurant is another venue where you can have dinner and then hang out later over a drink or two.

SHOPPING

Meknes has its share of small souks, and though not as prolific or large as the ones in Marrakech or Fes, they are still good places to buy both tourist items and comestibles. The markets here are less intimidating than those in the larger cities and give a good insight into the variety of Moroccan crafts.

AROUND THE PLACE EL HEDIM Goods from inside the covered area start spilling out onto the square, with tourist items, including *tagine* pots, laid out in the open. To the west, descend down the steps into the crowded dungeon-like market and a whole different world appears. Under the Moorish arches is the **food market** filled with the usual plethora of olives, dates and dried fruits, and spices. There are also more graphic raw materials, such as hanging meat, sometimes together with cows' heads, and live chickens, sold by the flapping kilo. It's quite an experience.

Behind the Dar Jamaï Museum, also on the square, is the **Souk el Sebbat**. Here are more conventional touristy things where you can pick up your souvenirs. Further west from here is the obligatory **carpet market**. The items are good quality, and you'll pay enough for them, although they'll still be cheaper than the ones you find at home.

Central Market Av Hassan II, Rue Tetouan & Rue Omar ibn Aiss. In the Ville Nouvelle is the produce market that also sells fresh flowers.
Label'Vie Av Moulay Youssef & Bd Ibn Khaldoune, Ville Nouvelle. Located within this large complex are shops of different varieties, as well as a supermarket on the lower level.
Marjane ✆ 0535 52 03 85. This reliable hypermarket sits outside of town, indicated on the Meknes–Fes autoroute. A taxi will get you there.

OTHER PRACTICALITIES

EMERGENCY TELEPHONE NUMBERS
Police ✆ 19
Fire service and ambulance ✆ 15
Highway ✆ 177
All-night chemist Hotel de Ville; ✆ 0535 52 26 64

HOSPITALS
✚ **Hospital Mohamed V** Bd Zerktouni; ✆ 0535 52 43 53
✚ **Hospital Moulay Ismail** Av des FAR; ✆ 0535 52 28 05
✚ **Polyclinique Cornette de Saint Cyr Hospital** 22 Esplanade du Dr Giguet; ✆ 0535 52 02 62

INTERNET CAFÉS Internet access can usually be found in the bigger hotels. In addition, there are cyber cafés all over the place. The following places have been around for a while, and hopefully will remain so.

🖂 **Club Leisure Company** Rue de Dakhla
🖂 **Cyber de Paris** Rue Accra

🖂 **Meetnet** Rue Rouamazine
🖂 **Quicknet** 28 Rue Amir Abdelkader

POST The main post office is on Place Administrative, Ville Nouvelle. There are various sub-offices, including one in the medina at Rue Dar Smen and Rue Rouamazine.

BANKS All the usual Moroccan banks are here, situated mostly around the Ville Nouvelle's main square, Place Administrative, as well as a few in the medina, including:

$ **Al Maghrib** 10 Av Mohamed V; ✆ 0535 52 10 12
$ **Banque Populaire Maroc** 17 Av Mohamed V;
✆ 0535 54 00 58

$ **BMCI** Pl el Hedim, Medina; ✆ 0535 58 31 90
$ **Credit du Maroc** 28 Bd Mohamed V; ✆ 0535 52 00 20

WHAT TO SEE

WITHIN THE CITY

City walls and babs (gates) Meknes's surrounding walls are impressive, and even more so are the beautiful gates that guard the entrances. The most spectacular of these portals is the wonderfully elaborate Bab Mansour, facing the main medina square, the Place el Hedim. Some of the columns are Roman, lifted from the nearby site of Volubilis. Bab Khemissa (the Thursday Gate), granting entry through the walls from the west, is also well decorated.

Place el Hedim The local version of Marrakech's Djemaa el Fna, this large square in the medina provides a central point, housing the various souks by day and street entertainment by night. It's worth spending some time here from dusk, especially if this is your only opportunity to catch traditional street performances.

Imperial City This heavily fortified and virtually separate part of the city, wedged against the southern edge of the medina, is the legacy of the Sultan Moulay Ismail. Although only a mere glimpse of his extravagant vision remains, enough is here to leave the visitor awed with the scale. The entire area is too large to see it all on foot, so it might be an idea to join a tour or take a taxi to see the highlights. Otherwise, here are some of the best things to view.

> ### MOULAY ISMAIL
>
> One of Morocco's most colourful rulers, this Alaouite dynasty sultan who ruled from 1672 to 1727, was legendarily a man of extremes. Declared both terribly cruel, yet very wise, amazingly self-indulgent yet incredibly good for the country, stories about this strong character abound. Creating a workforce allegedly captured from raiding parties of the Barbary pirates as well as black Saharans, Moulay Ismail had between 25,000 and 30,000 slaves at his beck and call. They acted as his army, civil enforcement and labour force. The sultan had no qualms about working them to death or using the sword as coercion. At the same time, he was able to unify the territory that extended from Algeria to Mauretania, control most of the Berber tribes, drive the European occupiers off Moroccan soil and rule strongly and convincingly. Personally, he was said to have had between 500 and 2,000 women in his harem, with at least 1,000 children. His stables were believed to have housed more than 12,000 horses. Ultimately, assessed as hard, but fair, historians have decided on balance, that his legacy was more good than bad.

The **Agdal Basin** is a large pool filled with water. In the sultan's time, it provided the supply for all of Meknes while today it fulfils only the needs of the Imperial City. It's quite lovely with the elaborate exterior walls reflected in the surface. On a hot day, it's delightfully cool here. Just past the reservoir, and within a discrete fortified area, are the **granaries and stables**. The former, called the Heri es Souani, is a vast covered area, comprising a series of labyrinthine arcades and doorways. Within this were kept supplies for Moulay Ismail's vast army and also his wives and children. The thick walls keep the area at a comfortable temperature all year long. Just beyond are the stables. Although the historical purpose of providing accommodation for 12,000 horses of 'stunning beauty' is impressive, today the open-air arches within arches create beautiful illusions of perspective. Once covered, the Lisbon earthquake of 1755 badly affected the stables and destroyed the roof, although the disaster barely touched the granaries. Within another set of fortifications, still part of the imperial grounds, is the **Dar El Makhzen**, finished more than a century after the flowering of Moulay Ismail's building programme. Built to be another of the royal residences, today it's the only one that remains. This palace is where the king and his family stay when in Meknes and is not open to the public. Just next door, the garden that was once the domain of the sultan's wives and concubines has been converted into the nine-hole **Royal Golf Club** *(Jnan Al Bahraouia;* ⟍ *0535 53 07 53; www.royalgolfmeknes.com; from MAD200)*. Here's a chance to get in a round fit for a king.

Moulay Ismail Mausoleum *(Bab Moulay Ismail;* ⊕ *09.00–12.00 & 15.00–18.00 Sat–Thu; free)* Surrounded by another series of walls, just outside the northern edge of the royal city, is the mausoleum of the sultan himself. One of only three Islamic sacred locations to which non-Muslims are granted entry (along with Hassan II Mosque in Casablanca, page 97, and the Mohamed V Mausoleum in Rabat, page 151), this one was declared open to the public by King Mohamed V when he renovated the complex in 1959. The open space just outside leads to an ornate gate, through which are located a series of inner courtyards, arriving at a small white-marbled columned square, at the centre of which is a little fountain. The whole room is decorated in extraordinary detail, yet remarkably intimate. From here, it's possible to peek into the next room, closed off to visitors, which contains the tombs of the great sultan and his son and grandson, the following dynastic rulers.

Inside the medina It's almost impossible to tell where the Imperial City ends and the medina begins, but it's easy enough to judge that once back in the Place el Hedim, you're in the old inner city. Just to the northwest of the open square is the **Dar Jamai Museum** *(Pl El Hedim;* ⟍ *0535 53 08 63;* ⊕ *09.00–12.00 & 15.00–18.00; MAD20)*. This collection of traditional Moroccan arts and crafts, including ironwork, carpets and ceramics, is housed within a 19th-century palace. It also has a delightful courtyard garden, filled with plants and trees that attract chattering birds. Just a bit further into the medina, just north of the Grand Mosque, is the **Medersa Bou Inania**. This Koranic school from the mid 14th century is nicely detailed and includes the usual central square. The students' cells are upstairs. Throughout the medina, tiles in green, Islam's sacred colour, give a clue to the many of the buildings' purposes. If passing by a mosque when calls for prayers are heard, try to peek in – discreetly – to catch a glimpse of both the interiors (closed to non-Muslims) and the celebrants.

AROUND MEKNES

Fes/Fez A mere 60km to the east of Meknes lies the UNESCO World Heritage Site of Fes. One of Morocco's most amazing places, time should be allocated for this city, even if only for a quick visit. Established by Moulay Idris II in AD808 and another of the four Imperial Cities, it's the religious and craft heart of the country. A centre of commerce since the caravan days, Fes is a showplace of the best traditional arts and souks as well as the medina location in which they thrive.

Tourist information Tourist board (*Pl de Resistance, Immeuble Bennani;* ☎ *0535 62 34 60;* ⏱ *08.30–12.00 & 14.30–18.30 Mon–Thu, 08.30–11.30 & 15.00–18.30 Fri*), tourist information office (*Pl Mohamed V;* ☎ *0535 62 34 60*) and regional council of tourism (*89 Av Allal Ben Abdellah;* ☎ *0535 94 24 92*).

Where to stay Hotels abound, and accommodation can be found on any level from the **Sofitel Palais Jamai Fes** (*Bab Guissa;* ☎ *0535 63 43 31; www.sofitel.com;* $$$$$+) to the **Auberge de Jeunesse** (*18 Rue Abdeslam Seghrini, Ville Nouvelle;* ☎ *0535 62 40 85; private rooms* $). Restaurants, night entertainment venues, shops, markets and attractions are all available in profusion.

What to see The urban areas are divided into three parts: the section built after World War II, the Ville Nouvelle; the walled areas of Fes el Jdid, the 'new' (13th-century) town; and Fes el Bali, the oldest and automobile-absent area. Crammed into a narrow valley, the city seems to be squeezed out the sides. The hilltop viewpoints on the northern and southern edges of the city provide the best visual introductions. The Borj el Nord fortress and the remains of the Merenid tombs to the northeast are best at sunrise, while Bab Ftouh to the southwest gives a great view at sunset. Inside, negotiation of the crowded, labyrinthine and fascinating medina of Fes el Bali is aided by signs provided by UNESCO, but if wanting to get around efficiently, it's probably best to join a tour or hire a guide. If you have the time, wallow in the pleasure of getting lost. Don't miss the tanneries, the most famous of Morocco's collections of different coloured open-pit leather treating and dyeing works. The mosques, medersas and especially the souks are true pleasures to discover. If funds and suitcase space are not issues, succumb to the temptation of purchasing some wonderful examples of the craftsman's art. Tourism is Fes's main industry, and there are loads of facilities for visitors.

Moulay Idris Around 25km north of Meknes is the holy enclave of Moulay Idris named after the founder and the site of his tomb. For the poor who can't afford the haj to Mecca, one of the Five Pillars of Islam, seven visits to this pilgrimage site fulfils the obligation. Well, so say the Moroccans. In the meantime, this town, picturesquely placed in the hills between two valleys (from which a fresh water spring emerges), is full of Islamic buildings identified by their green tiles. Wandering up through the village, past tightly packed houses and even an occasional communal bakery, the trek to the top is rewarded by a lovely view. Overlooking the town that spills down the hill, the green splashes of the roofs of the holy sites remind the visitor as to why this small place is so important and also provide a visual contrast to the white-and-brown buildings. The **Moulay Idris Shrine** and *zaouia* (when a tomb becomes the central focus of a mosque) are best seen from here. Also notable is the circular minaret of the **Khiber Medersa Koranic School**, the sole example in the country. Tolerating the non-Muslim visitors who stop by – there's even a **tourist office** (*Pl de France;* ☎ *0535 52 44 26*) – the site is primarily a destination for Islamic pilgrims. Cafés and small restaurants, mostly in the main square, welcome non-Muslim visitors but there are no overnight facilities for them in the town.

VOLUBILIS A mere 30km north of Meknes are the remains of the most important Roman city in Morocco and, at one time, the province of Mauretania. The ruins can be spotted about 7km below the hills of Moulay Idris. Even now, in times when the land is less intensively cultivated than in the Roman era, there is evidence of active agricultural use. The area remains fertile, and the springs that once

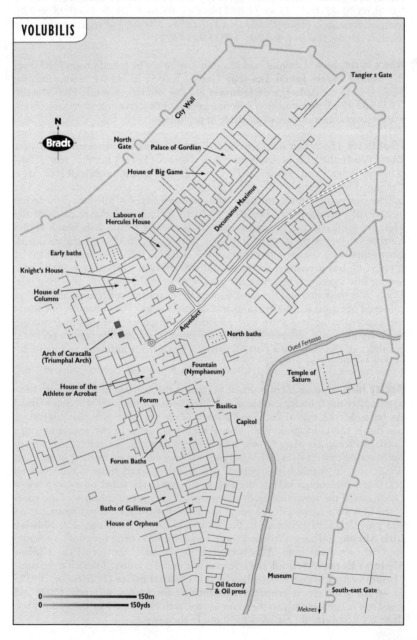

VOLUBILIS

Tangier s Gate

City Wall

N

Bradt

North Gate

Palace of Gordian

House of Big Game

Decumanus Maximus

Labours of Hercules House

Early baths

Knight's House

House of Columns

Aqueduct

North baths

Arch of Caracalla (Triumphal Arch)

Fountain (Nymphaeum)

Oued Fertasso

Temple of Saturn

House of the Athlete or Acrobat

Forum

Basilica

Capitol

Forum Baths

Baths of Gallienus

House of Orpheus

0 ——— 150m
0 ——— 150yds

Oil factory & Oil press

Museum

South-east Gate

Meknes ↓

watered the ancient settlement still flow into Moulay Idris. Located at a slight altitude, the breezes blow and the temperature is pleasant, even in the summer. It's not surprising that King Juba II chose this site for his capital. Today, the ruins are substantial enough for the grandeur of the town to be obvious. The skeletons of important civil buildings stand prominently, and a triumphal arch is still intact. Most amazing is the large number of beautifully preserved mosaics, lying in the living and leisure quarters for which they were originally made. Deserted and stripped of its most valuable materials, such as the marble façades for Moulay Idris, or the columns for cities such as Meknes and even Rabat, the ruins have crumbled, although the good weather and the work of recent archaeologists allow the remains to give an indication of how the royal city must have looked in its heyday.

HISTORY Punic remains have been found that date the site to as early as 300BC, when the lushness of the area as well as the convenient location, encouraged development of a substantial city. Unlike the site at Lixus, almost nothing has been found from this period, as subsequent construction has virtually wiped out pre-Roman traces. Stylistically, it looks as if buildings were influenced by Carthage, but it's believed that Volubilis never really came under Carthaginian control. The land was too valuable, both in its fertility and location, for it to be left alone, and from the days of its Phoenician settlement till just past AD800, it remained inhabited. When Juba II came to the throne in 25BC (see page 11) the capital of the province of Mauretania as well as his residence was in Iol (today's Cherchell, in Algeria). He renamed it Caesarea, in Augustus's honour, but soon began to come up with plans for his own royal city to be located at Volubilis. His ideas were grand, and the existing ruins prove that many of them came to fruition. Iol Caesarea remained the most important administrative centre, but Juba II's own dream city flourished. All was well while the client king remained alive, but after his death, his son Ptolemy couldn't stave off the tribal attacks, let alone the Romans. His assassination by Caligula allowed the empire to abolish the autonomy of Mauretania and absorb it, eventually converting Volubilis into a proper Imperial City.

The Berbers, or those tribal members who never quite got into the Roman swing of things, were always rumbling at the borders of Mauretania. By AD100, sections of the province in today's Algeria were attacked, and eventually the Romans acknowledged the royal status of the Berber leader. Over the years, the imperial forces fortified the cities in the firing line but also attempted to make peace with the foreign rebels. An uneasy truce existed. At its peak, Volubilis had a population of almost 20,000, extremely large for a Roman town. In 285, after the Crisis of the Third Century, the Romans left, and the shrunken province of Tingitana continued to be governed from Tingis. At Volubilis, relatively little changed despite the Romans' departure. After the Arab arrival in 708, Volubilis remained inhabited. The new development of Moulay Idris (see page 139), established in 808 and located a little bit further south and up on the hill, took the last of the population of the once Roman enclave away, leaving the old city empty.

GETTING THERE The easiest way to get to Volubilis is either via taxi from Meknes, or the small train station to the north, Sidi Kacem. It's simple enough to get here by car, taking the P6 from Meknes north to Moulay Idris, then following the signs to the Roman remains. A reasonable alternative is to book a tour from travel agents in Meknes or Fes, and take advantage of the local guides.

 WHERE TO STAY AND EAT At the moment, there are no facilities at the site. A picnic is a nice thing to bring along, but if getting some food in advance isn't possible, cafés are available for snacks and light meals just up the road in Moulay Idris. The hotel *in situ* is under construction but will open in the next year or two. Both Meknes and Fes are located within 35km and have all the facilities anyone could want.

WHAT TO SEE The main entrance to the site (⊕ *08.00–18.30; MAD 20*) is near the car park at the bottom of the hill. For the present, the common areas aren't open, although the Volubilis Hotel is under construction and should be welcoming visitors by the time this book has gone to print. A modern Roman-style walkway creeps up and along the western brow of the hill and snakes around to lead to the first foundation walls. It's easy enough to be attracted to the grand buildings of the centre, but if you have time, and a map, it's worth slowing down and taking in the sights *en route*. If going strictly in order, the first important remains you see is the **olive press**. Here was the 'factory' where the local olives were harvested and milled to produce the multi-purpose oil. In the valleys below, some of the groves are still there, and with their extraordinary longevity, it's possible that some of those trees were the same ones used by the Romans. One of the industrial rooms has been reconstructed to show how the production worked.

One of the next places to see is the **House of Orpheus**, so called due to the fantastic mosaic showing the legend of magical lyre-playing Orpheus who was able to charm even the beasts, many of them depicted in coloured tiles. The artwork is very large and almost complete, and a delight to view. The house was clearly significant, not only because the owner commissioned such a large floor covering, but also due to the size of the villa. The entranceways into the different rooms are still visible. One of these quarters contains an intact depiction of dolphins fancifully heading in their separate directions, within squares of scroll and flower decorations. The **Baths of Gallienus** are next door. It's possible they were a part of the House of Orpheus, or even an extension of the forum baths, not that far away. With their columns, arches and hypocausts, baths are one of the remains that are the easiest to recognise.

By now, you're on the edge of the capitol and a few steps further leads to the platform upon which was placed the **temple to three deities**: the main god, Saturn (in Rome his counterpart is Jupiter), his wife Juno and the goddess of wisdom, Minerva. From this higher viewpoint, it's easy to see the grandeur of one of Volubilis's most distinguished and identifiable structures, the **basilica**. This civil building was used as a law court and administrative office, and it typically faced the forum. Partially restored, the arcades give a hint of how intimidating it must have been to criminals when they were on trial.

The **forum** lies just to the west and is the large open square around which were located the city's official buildings. Right across from here, in an extremely privileged position, the **House of the Athlete**, or Acrobat, shows off the mosaic of a cartoon-like depiction of a man riding a donkey backwards. There are other pieces here too, but not in such good condition. To the east was the site of the nymphaeum or **public fountain**; low trough-like remnants still exist. The fountain was not merely ornamental: the flow provided drinking water for the city, and also helped flush the public latrines located just to the north. You can walk through the public streets, or wander through the foundations of a few more villas, before you get to the **Arch of Caracalla** or Triumphal Arch. The arc is complete, with its keystone in place, but the monument is low and stocky, not one of the more graceful examples of the form. It was constructed by the inhabitants of the city in AD217 to thank Emperor Caracalla, and his mother Julia Domna, for granting the populace Roman citizenship and tax exemption. Looking over the open space towards the right, the **decumanus maximus**, the main east–west street comes into view. There are still porticoes and columns lining the route that give an idea of how important this thoroughfare was.

Stories about the Roman Hercules date back to Greek times when the hero was known as Heracles. He was born out of one of the infidelities of the king of the gods, Zeus, with a Greek woman Alcemene, and his wife Hera was so jealous that she attempted to kill the issue. Being the son of a god, however, the boy was powerful, and grew up to be a very strong man. Throughout his life he was plagued by Hera, and when he was already established as a great warrior and then happily married, the goddess came again, causing Heracles to kill his wife and children in a bout of madness. Emerging, the hero took the insanity personally, begging the god Apollo to give him penance. From this plea came the **12 Labours of Heracles**, a series of myths that became so popular that the Romans embraced the same stories when renaming the protagonist Hercules. Close to the end of these tasks, when reaching number 11, the job was to steal the golden apples from the Garden of the Hesperides. Various stories spring from here, including marrying his wife Tingi (see page 119), battling with Atlas and holding up the world and several other tales. Pertinently, though, it is said that the garden was in Lixus, and that it was here that Heracles/Hercules had his fruity 11th adventure.

Because of the proximity to the centre of the city, as well as the situation adjoining the main boulevard, to have a residence in this area was very prestigious. The **House of the Columns** enhances its interior with a variety of differently carved pillars. Just next door is the **Knight's House**, or House of the Rider, named because of the discovery of a bronze statue of a rider – without his horse – found here, and now in the Rabat Archaeological Museum (see page 150). It's worth viewing due to its mosaic, not of a horseman, but rather of Bacchus coming across Ariadne. Beyond, backing onto the arcades of the decumanus, are a series of houses of the wealthy. Quite a few have mosaic floors still in place. Some of the most charming are found in the **Labours of Hercules** house. Rendered in an almost naive style, the main piece portrays the 12 tasks the hero had to perform (see box above). There is also another mythological subject depicting the kidnapping of Ganymede. A tessellated version of the Four Seasons also resides here. Other villas *en route* are in various states of repair, but the **House of the Big Game**'s claim to fame is its large floor mosaic showing off various wild animals, including a tiger. Volubilis was known for its animals, bred and kept for events in the nearby Roman arenas, and this piece of artwork celebrates the fact. Shops along the decumanus were located on its eastern flank. The villa's next-door neighbour was rumoured to be the emperor, as the very large 4,488m² residence is called the **Palace of Gordian the Third**, but this nomenclature was given not because of its owner, but rather the period in which it was built AD238–44. Just in front, at the eastern end of the decumanus, is the Tingis Gate, named after the next major city in Roman Mauretania.

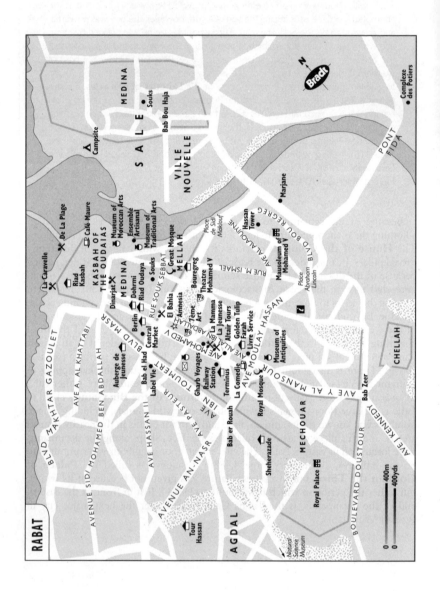

RABAT

N Bracht

Complexe des Potiers

MEDINA
SALE
Souks
Bab Bou Haja

Campsite

VILLE NOUVELLE

PONT FIDA

De La Plage
Café Maure
Museum of Moroccan Arts
Ensemble Artisanal
Museum of Traditional Arts

Marjane

La Caravelle
Riad Kasbah
KASBAH OF THE OUDAIAS
Dinarjat
MEDINA
Dohrmi
Riad Oudaya
Souks
Great Mosque
MELLAH
Bouregreg

Place de Sidi Maklouf
Hassan Tower
Mausoleum of Mohamed V

BLVD MAKHTAR GAZOULET
AVE A. AL KHATTABI
BLVD MASR
Berlin
Central Market
RUE SOUK SEBBAT
El Bahia
Amnesia
7ème Art
Theatre Mohamed V
Fès
AVE M. ISMAEL
AVE AL-ALAOUYINE

Place Abraham Lincoln

AVE HASSAN II
AVE PASTEUR
Auberge de Jeunesse
Bab el Had
Label Vie
BLVD MOHAMED V
AVENUE SIDI MOHAMED BEN ABDALLAH
RUE AL ALAY IBN ABDALLAH
La Mamma
Golden Tulip Farah
La Jeunesse
Altair Tours
Livre Service
AVE MOULAY HASSAN
Museum of Antiquities

CHELLAH

AVE TOUMERT
AVE IBN
Gharb Voyages
Railway Station
Terminus
La Comedie
Royal Mosque
AVE Y AL MANSOUR
Bab Zeer

AVENUE AN-NASR
Bab er Rouah
Sheherazade
MECHOUAR

AVE J KENNEDY

Tour Hassan
Natural Science Museum
AGDAL
Royal Palace

BOULEVARD DOUSTOUR

0 ___ 400m
0 ___ 400yds

8

Rabat

Telephone code 0537

One of Morocco's imperial and most important cities, Rabat has risen above its competition to become the country's modern-day capital – the cultural, political and royal centre. Although the king seems to have residences in every attractive location, the main royal palace is found here, and the surrounding sub-city has schools, stables and even a mosque specifically for the use of royalty. The French built a whole new section during their occupation and made the city their capital in 1912. Thankfully, earlier architecture has not been destroyed in the process; monuments and old sections are still very much in evidence.

Sitting on the western side of the wide and navigable Bouregreg Estuary and looking out over the Atlantic Ocean, Rabat's location is one of its virtues. The river is a makeshift port for fishing boats and construction has begun to create a major marina and recreational complex. On the opposite bank is the town of Salé and to the north are lovely golden sand beaches. Gardens crop up everywhere in the city centre, whether alongside the public memorials or within sheltered spots, such as the depths of the kasbah or inside the ancient fortress of Chellah.

Most of the government is housed here, together with various ministries and international embassies, and the country's largest university. There are also quite a few cultural venues and museums.

HISTORY

It's not surprising that the safety of the Bouregreg Estuary enticed visitors, and the Phoenicians were the first to establish a settlement here. The Carthaginians followed them, and by the 1st century AD, the Romans had built a port in the area now known as Chellah. They named their village Sala Colonia and this working city eventually became the southwesternmost North African outpost of the empire. It finally fell to the local tribes when the imperial inhabitants retreated back to Tingis. The Berbers did well here, their occupation lasting well into the 8th century. By now, Moulay Idris and his Idrissite dynasty over in Fes saw this rival kingdom as a threat, and invaded, setting up their own fortifications, *ribat*, in today's kasbah district. The refugees headed over the river to set up Salé which, even though it still exists, never achieved the importance of their original city. Following the general waves of invasion from subsequent dynasties, the Almohads arrived in the mid-12th century. Their sultan, Abd el Mumene, found the location extremely convenient for his raids on southern Spain, and rebuilt the *ribat*. Two generations later, Yacoub El Mansour refortified the area, building the walls around the kasbah that still exist today, and making this fort his capital, Ribat el Fath (Camp of Victory). El Mansour envisaged an enormous mosque in 1199, but the only part to be built was the minaret known as the Hassan Tower. Work was scheduled to make the tower taller than the 69m-high Koutoubia in Marrakech. Sadly it was stopped short, but nevertheless remains an impressive site.

Fickle with their capitals, the next dynastic family, the Merenids, preferred Fes, and let Rabat fade, although they did construct a burial site next to the original Sala Colonia, which they named Chellah. By now, the only vestige of city life was in the kasbah. Things changed significantly by the 1600s, when the Moors forced Spain to retreat. The local Barbary pirates recognised that the Bouregreg River could be a great base for operations. Living in the kasbah and rebuilding the medina, they established their own republic and continued for the next hundred years, until Moulay Rashid and his brother, the great Sultan Moulay Ismail, took over control. After the overthrow, the name of the kasbah was enhanced, to include 'of the Oudayas', in memory of the tribe whom the sultan enlisted to help fight the privateers. Such lucrative profiteering could not be put down easily and it continued until towns on the Barbary coast, including Rabat, were attacked by the Austrians in 1829 in retaliation for a ship lost during a pirate raid. From then, the once glorious city slipped into obscurity until the French decided that here would be the centre of the country's administration in 1912. With their help, Rabat rose in stature to become the nation's present-day capital.

GETTING THERE AND AROUND

BY AIR The closest international airport is Mohamed V in Casablanca, and the easiest way to get from there to Rabat is via train. Journeys take around two hours and cost about MAD65 (*www.oncf.ma*). Bus companies also do the trip, but they are not as convenient, nor as frequent. There is also a domestic airport, Aéroport de Rabat-Sale (٦ *0537 80 80 90*), that isn't of much use for foreign travellers.

BY RAIL The large train station is well located in the centre of the Ville Nouvelle (*Av Mohamed V;* ٦ *0590 20 30 40*) and, as Rabat is the capital, is the heart of an efficient and busy network. It's possible to get to anywhere in the country from here. Grand taxis will take you from the station to nearby cities including Sale; the petit ones are probably the easiest way to get to your hotel.

BY BUS AND TAXI Three kilometres from the centre is the long-distance CTM bus terminal (*Av Hassan II, Rte de Casablanca;* ٦ *0537 28 14 78*). Take a city bus or jump into a petit taxi to the main town from here. Rabat isn't large, and most of the attractions can be visited on foot. However, local bus routes are useful, especially if visiting Sale or some of the beaches. As with the rest of Morocco, the grand taxis, the bigger and more expensive ones, travel to locations outside the city while the petit, little grey-and-blue ones, can be hopped into for shorter distances.

CAR HIRE It probably doesn't make much sense to hire a car strictly for Rabat, as distances between attractions are relatively short, and taxis are available everywhere. Car hire is not cheap. If you do need to have a vehicle, most of the major companies are represented. The following have branches at both the domestic airport and in the city.

- Avis (airport) ٦ 0537 83 16 77; (town) 7 Rue Abou Faris El Marini; ٦ 0537 72 18 18; www.avis.com
- Europcar (airport) ٦ 0537 72 41 41; (town) 25 Bis, Rue Patrice Lumumba; ٦ 0537 72 23 28; www.europcar.com
- National (airport) ٦ 0537 72 27 31; (town) Angle Rue Du Caire & Rue Gandhi; ٦ 0537 72 27 31; www.nationalcar.com.
- Sixt Hilton Hotel, Quartier Souissi; ٦ 0537 67 02 10; www.sixt.com

TOURIST INFORMATION

The Moroccan National Tourist Office (℡ 0537 67 39 18; ⏲ 08.30–12.00 & 15.00–18.30 Mon–Fri) is on the corner of Zalaqa and Oued al Makhazine-Agdal.

TOUR OPERATORS

Altair Tours International 467 Av Mohamed V; ℡ 0537 72 99 40

Chams Voyages 24 Av de France-Agdal; ℡ 0537 77 28 72

Gharb Voyages 289 Bd Mohamed V; ℡ 0537 70 98 61

Merveilles Tours 2 Rue Tihama; ℡ 0537 76 97 17

Voyage sans Frontiers 1 Bis, Rue Tanta; ℡ 0537 708 215

⌂ WHERE TO STAY

Though not the largest city in Morocco, Rabat is the capital, and it has to accommodate all levels of tourists. There is a high proportion of top-end hotels, but it's possible to find somewhere cheap, and in between, to stay.

TOP END

⌂ **Golden Tulip Farah Rabat** (193 rooms) Pl Sidi Makhlouf, Centre Ville; ℡ 0537 73 47 47; www.goldentulip.com. Part of the luxury chain, the best thing about this modern hotel is its location, overlooking the ocean & river, right next to the Hassan Tower & Mausoleum of Mohamed V. $$$$

⌂ **Riad Oudaya** (4 rooms) 46 Rue Sidi Fateh, Medina. More luxurious – & pricier – than the Riad Kasbah (run by the same people) & is well placed in the old town. $$$$$

⌂ **Tour Hassan** (140 rooms) 26 Rue Chellah, Centre Ville; ℡ 0537 23 90 00. Rabat's top hotel is built in a Moorish style & situated close to government offices & not far from the Museum of Antiquities. $$$$$

⌂ **Riad Kasbah** (6 rooms) 39 Rue Zirara Kasbah des Oudaïas; ℡ 0537 70 23 92. This charming guesthouse is located right in the heart of the kasbah, within its blue & white maze. $$$$

MID-RANGE

⌂ **Hotel Bouregreg** (69 rooms) Av Hassan II & Rue Nador, Centre Ville; ℡ 0537 72 04 14. A modern, friendly 3-star hotel well placed in the newer area of town. $$$

⌂ **Hotel Mercure Sheherazade** (77 rooms) 21 Rue de Tunis, Centre Ville; ℡ 0537 72 22 26; www.mercure.com. This comfortable hotel comes under the French branding of Mercure, & is up to its usual standards. $$$

⌂ **Hotel Terminus** 384 Av Mohamed V, Centre Ville; ℡ 0537 70 52 67. Right across from the train station, here's a convenient place to stay if needing a quick getaway, & comfort isn't a major concern. $$–$$$

BUDGET There are quite a few inexpensive lodgings along the main Boulevard Mohamed V, particularly in the Centre Ville. Here are a couple of the cheaper ones.

⌂ **Auberge de Jeunesse** (Youth Hostel) (52 beds) 43 Rue Marassa, Bab El Had; ℡ 0537 72 57 69. Clean & nice, the medina location & low price are definite pluses for the very budget-conscious traveller. $

⌂ **Hotel Berlin** 261 Av Mohamed V, Centre Ville; ℡ 0537 70 34 35. Small, basic with shared bathrooms & a premium charged for full washing facilities, this place gets full pretty quickly. $

⌂ **Hotel Dorhmi** 313 Av Mohamed V, Centre Ville; ℡ 0537 72 38 98. This inexpensive place to stay provides one of the best values in the medina even if you have to pay more to wallow in the shower. $

✕ WHERE TO EAT

Catering to a wide variety of both official visitors and tourists, the capital's eating establishments can be pretty good. There is quite a large variety for a relatively small city, and venues range from cheap cafés to fancy restaurants.

✗ **Restaurant Dinarjat** 6 Rue Belgnaoui; ℡ 0537 70 42 39; ⏰ daily for b/fast, lunch & dinner. One of those Moroccan eating experiences that takes place in a 17th-century palace & comes with the usual excellent typical food & entertainment – at a price. **$$$$$**

✗ **Restaurant de la Plage** Kasbah des Ouaidas Beach; ℡ 0537 72 31 48; ⏰ 12.00–15.00 & 20.00– midnight. This chic place specialises in fish dishes & is slightly cheaper than its neighbouring restaurants. **$$$$**

✗ **Restaurant la Caravelle** Beneath the northern bastion of the kasbah, overlooking the ocean; ℡ 0537 73 88 44; ⏰ 12.00–15.00 & 19.00– 23.00. Highly recommended both for its sea view & its food; you can sip a pastis here while waiting for your meal. **$$$**

✗ **Café-Restaurant El Bahia** Bd Hassan II; ℡ 0537 73 45 04; ⏰ 06.00–midnight. Situated in a garden & built into the medina walls, this venue serves reasonably priced traditional food. **$$-$$$**

✗ **La Mamma** 6 Rue Tanta; ℡ 0537 70 73 29; ⏰ 12.00–15.00 & 19.30–00.30. This popular restaurant serves both pizza & pasta, although the ambience is more French than Italian. **$$-$$$**

✗ **Restaurant de la Jeunesse** 305 Av Mohamed V. Basic *tagines* & the usual fare, but served in large amounts at small prices. **$$**

⬛ **Café Maure** Next to the gardens in the Kasbah des Oudaias. This little café serves mint tea & traditional sticky cakes in a lovely setting, overlooking the Bouregreg Estuary. **$**

⬛ **Patisserie la Comedie** 5 Av Mohamed V. A good place to get a decent French croissant, fancy pastry or even an ice cream. **$**

ENTERTAINMENT AND NIGHTLIFE

Diplomats let their hair down as well as tourists, and the city has a few places to drink and dance into the night. Many of the bar cafés are for men only, and some of the rest can be pick-up joints for both prostitutes and ships that pass in the night. Some are better than others, though.

☆ **Amnesia** 18 Rue Monastir; ℡ 0537 73 52 03. This popular place to party attracts a variety of people & makes a change from the usual hotel crowd.

There are also bars and discos in districts of the city that are petit taxi rides away, including **Agdal** which has **Le Mombay** (*26 Av de France; ℡ 0537 67 07 39, also a restaurant*); the **Seven Lounge** (*Av Omar Ibnou Khattab*); **Souissi**, which harbours the **Cesar Palace Arena** (*73 Av John Kennedy, Rte Des Zaers; ℡ 0537 75 55 00*); and **Harold's** (*Av Imam Malik*) which has salsa dancing on Tuesday nights.

SHOPPING

Though not one of the seriously touristy souk towns, Rabat is a reasonable place to purchase things. In some ways it's simpler to buy goods here, even if there's not such a variety, as there's not so much pressure. If you don't enjoy bargaining, then the capital is a much easier place to get your souvenirs, as there are several fixed-price shops that sell the same items for which you have to negotiate in other cities.

Central Market Av Hassan II, between Bab el Adhad & Bab el Bouab. Sells the usual produce & flowers, & is open all day & into the evening.

Ensemble Artisanal Bd Tariq al-Marsa, alongside the estuary; ℡ 0537 73 05 07. If you'd rather go into a regular store & not be overwhelmed by the selection or the sales pitch, here's the place to buy your fixed-priced goods.

Kasbah des Oudaïas Although not a shopping district, there are a couple of places worth mentioning. The Nougia Gallery of Art (*Rue Jemaa;* ℡ 0537 71 16 46) regularly shows regional artists, with a special emphasis on photographic exhibitions. Their collection of posters, postcards & books offers good bargains, if the prices of the originals are too high. Also nearby, at the end of the same street, you can watch the women weavers at the **carpet co-operative**.

CARPET QUALITY

The range of styles and prices of these beautiful woven rugs can sometimes be overwhelming, and it's difficult to understand why some are so much more expensive than others. The artisans and government ministries have set up a formal classification in order to distinguish the qualities of carpets. Standards are based on the number of knots per square metre; that is, the more the better, or at least the more work put into fabrication. Here's the scale:

Extra superior 40 x 40, or 160,000 knots per square metre
Superior 30 x 30, or 90,000 knots per square metre
Middle 25 x 25, or 62,000 knots per square metre
Ordinary 20 x 20, or 40,000 knots per square metre

Subjective aesthetics don't come into the assessment, but at the end of the day, if a carpet is exactly to your taste, then perhaps it's worth the price.

Label Vie 4 Av Maghrib el Arabi, nr Bab al Had. This major supermarket sells everything edible, including basic comestibles & good picnic fodder.
Livre Service 6 Av Allal Ben Abdellah; ℡ 0537 72 44 95. A bookshop with helpful staff that offers texts in all languages. A good place to go if you need an additional guidebook.

Marjane The local outlet of this hypermarket chain is situated on the Rabat–Sale road, a petit taxi ride away, but worth it if there's something you need that only a major store can provide.

SOUKS Although not as prolific – or as intimidating – as Marrakech, Rabat does have its share of medina markets, located on the main streets of the medieval city. Sprawling along **Rue Souika** are items for daily local use, the goods themselves are nothing special, but the ambience gives an insight into the market mentality. Further along, at the **Sabbat Souk** things get more interesting, as here are small stores that sell items of more tourist interest, such as leatherware, jewellery and modern and traditional clothing, like slippers (*babouches*) and robes (*jellabahs*). Northeast on the same street, a left turn brings you to **Rue de Consuls**. Until 1912, this was where foreign dignitaries lived and it's now been converted into a major shopping area. Stores sell all sorts of wonderful Moroccan items, including leather goods, hide lamps, traditional clothing, ceramics and even carpets. If you want to bargain for such big rugs on a grand scale on Mondays and Thursdays, in the mornings you can try your hand at bidding at the public auction. Scattered throughout the district are fun little boutiques selling all sorts of strange items. It's worth going inside, having a chat with the proprietors – many of whom speak English – and letting them show you some of their more unusual pieces.

OTHER PRACTICALITIES

EMERGENCY TELEPHONE NUMBERS
Police ℡ 19
Fire service and ambulance ℡ 15

Highway ℡ 177
All-night chemist Rue Moulay Sliman

HOSPITAL
✚ Hospital IBN Sina Rte de Casa, Adal; ℡ 0537 67 44 11

For a list of doctors recommended by the US Embassy, see http://casablanca.usconsulate.gov/rabat.html.

INTERNET CAFÉS Most of the larger hotels include some sort of internet access, often via Wi-Fi in the lobby, or the business centre. As for cyber cafés, they come and go, although there are likely to be more of them in Rabat, due to the presence of the country's largest university. The following have been around for a while, and should probably continue to remain in operation.

🖳 **Acdim** 44 Rue Abou Derr, Agdal; ☎ 0537 67 36 00

🖳 **Cybercafe** 68 Av Fall Ould Oumeir, Agdal; ☎ 0537 68 37 12

🖳 **Webcafe** 7 Zankat Al Maarif, Souissi

POST The main post office is at Avenue Mohamed V and Jean Jaurés.

BANKS The regular banks have branches, particularly around Avenue Mohamed V.

$ **Al Maghrib** Av Mohamed V; ☎ 0537 70 26 26
$ **BMCE** 60 Av Mohamed V; ☎ 0537 72 17 98

$ **Credit du Maroc** 21 Av Allal Ben Abdalla; ☎ 0537 72 19 61

WHAT TO SEE

THE ROYAL PALACE (MECHOUAR) Not necessarily the most interesting place in Rabat, but it's still worth beginning the visit here as this complex is the official residence of the king and his extended family and also the seat of much of the government. Many ministries are situated in this rather bland walled section of the city. The heart of the Ville Nouvelle and lying to the southwest of the medina, the entrance is guarded, but the grounds are open to the public. There is no charge to go in, although be aware that you will no doubt be watched the entire time you are inside. The broad boulevards cross vast empty spaces. The Royal Mosque to the northeast is where the imperial family prays, and a bit further south is the palace. Built alongside the 12th-century Almohad walls, the building dates from around 1850, reconstructed from Sultan Sidi Mohamed Bed Abdellah's 1785 version. This enclosure is not open to unofficial visitors, but the gates reflect those seen in the other royal cities and are manned by red-unformed blue-hatted guards who despite regulations are still happy to pose. Some of the other buildings scattered around in the distance are stables for the horseriders in the family, schools for the employees, and headquarters for various government departments.

THE MUSEUM OF ANTIQUITIES (ARCHAEOLOGICAL MUSEUM) (*23 Rue Brihi, Centre Ville;* ☎ *0537 70 19 19;* ⏲ *09.00–12.00 & 14.00–17.00 Wed–Mon; MAD10*) Morocco's best archaeological museum is located to the east of the Grand Mosque, and very close to the royal palace. Although the collection isn't very large, some of the pieces are superb, with important remains found on the sites of Volubilis and Chellah that were brought here to be displayed. The dates range from prehistoric to Islamic, but the specialities of the assembly are the Roman artefacts, and especially the bronzes (mosaics are absent here, displayed either on site, as in Volubilis, or in other museums in the country, eg: Tangier and Tetouan).

The prime Roman statues and portrait heads are in the annex and the first one on display, and one of the newest discoveries found in nearby Chellah, is a life-size marble of Ptolemy, the ill-fated son and heir of Juba II and Cleopatra Selene (see box, page 11). His confident muscular stance is typical of the Roman style;

probably the only accurate part is his head. It's one of the very few depictions of the last Mauretanian king.

To the left are the bronzes. The most extraordinary portrait is of Juba II, the legendary client king of Mauretania who was raised in Rome and placed on the throne by Caesar Augustus. Initially, the bust fits very much into the usual iconography, with the tousled hair, but this young ruler is looking down, seemingly more concerned with his thoughts, than with looking regal. Juba II was said to be an intellectual, and perhaps the sculptor thought to put this attribute into the portrait. Another famous head is of Cato the younger, far less handsome than the young king, with his big nose, large ears and cropped hair, but also thoughtful, perhaps working out some major philosophical problem. Both of these bronzes were found in Volubilis as were other stunning examples, including an Ephebe (a young man), and a knight or horserider (without the horse) found in the same house; and many other exquisitely rendered pieces. There were also similar works found in Chellah, Lixus and other smaller sites. The Roman archaeology outshines the rest of the collection, but there are displays of other periods that are worth a glance. On the next floor are exhibitions that contain remains from prehistory and later Phoenician and Carthaginian periods.

THE HASSAN II TOWER AND THE MAUSOLEUM OF KING MOHAMED V (*Bd Tour Hassan & Bd du Bouregreg, along the city walls overlooking the estuary; free*) These two monuments occupy the same large open square, overlooking the Bouregreg Estuary. The Hassan II Tower is the only remnant of the Great Mosque that the sultan, El Mansour, envisaged being the largest mosque in the Islamic world. Neither the religious structure nor the tower itself was ever finished, and the 300-plus pillars that are laid out evenly over the large square are the sultan's main legacy. Ten of these columns are said to have been taken from Volubilis while the rest are copies. At the southern edge of the square is the Mausoleum of King Mohamed V, the man who guided Morocco when the country gained its independence from France. As sultan, he and his family were exiled in 1953, but returned in 1955 eventually to become the king of a new nation, two years later. A year after his death in 1961, construction of his mausoleum began, and today the beautifully decorated, green-tile roofed, marble edifice houses his tomb. One of only three Islamic holy sites open to non-Muslims (with the King Hassan II Mosque in Casablanca, and the Mausoleum of Moulay Ismail in Meknes), the public are welcome to come inside. Both the east and west entrances of the gates are protected by two horseback guards, who perform a formal, if somewhat low-key, changing ceremony, at periodic intervals. The entire area is impressive, and quite lovely, with the open space, the graceful structures, the rhythm of the even spacing of the columns, and the view of the river below, especially in the late afternoon.

KASBAH DES OUDAÏAS (*the northeasternmost section of the city, overlooking the Atlantic Ocean & the Bouregreg Estuary*) This protected, 12th-century part of the city is probably the most interesting to tourists and was named for one of the local tribes. Fortified, as are all kasbahs, here is where the original *ribat* (or fort) began under Yacoub el Mansour. The village rises above the town, looking almost like a mirage over the fishing boats in the bay. The walls are formidable, although softened by the lovely green grass and low palm trees of the gardens near to the biggest gate, the Bab Oudaïa. There are four other babs, but the small gate just alongside the grand one is the main entrance to the kasbah. Once inside, the large, orange expanses of the outside world change to narrow pedestrian passageways totally of blue and white. The high walls and sharp turns prevent being able to see more than the length of the route immediately in front, and the junctions with cross paths

come as a surprise. The kasbah is quite small, and even if you don't know exactly where you are, sooner or later you'll discover all the things worth seeing. At the limit of the wall to the northeast is the platform, from where you get an excellent view of the wide beach below, as well as to the medina to the west and the lighthouse beyond, and Sale to the east. Back down into the labyrinth, the pleasure is in the wandering. Spot the *dars* (guesthouses) and art galleries that are beginning to spring up.

Hidden in the southern corner is the **Museum of the Oudaïas** (*1 Bd Al Marsa, Kasbah des Oudayas;* ☏ *0537 73 15 37;* ⊕ *10.00–18.00 Tue–Sun; MAD10*) holding a collection of carpets, jewellery, musical instruments, Qur'ans and other items, located within Moulay Ismail's first palace in Rabat of the 17th century. Just about now might be the perfect time to stop for a mint tea and a sticky pastry, and the **Café Maure** (see page 148) just happens to be located in the ideal place for a break. It lies at the gate of the **Andalusian Gardens**, an oasis that opens out within the next set of walls. Lush and not over-manicured, this traditional garden is full of trees and flowers and the chatter of birds attracted by such greenery.

OTHER MUSEUMS Rabat has other museums that might not be world class, but are quite interesting.

The Postal Museum (Musée National des PTT) Av Mohamed V; ☏ 0537 70 23 74; ⊕ 08.30–12.00 & 14.30–18.30 Mon–Thu, 08.30–11.30 & 15.00–18.30 Fri; free

Natural Science Museum Ministry of Energy & Mining, Centre Ville; ☏ 0537 77 79 42. Featuring the geological history of the earth, the highlight of the museum is the 15m-long skeleton of the Sauropod dinosaur found in the Atlas Mountains to the south.

THE ROMAN SITE

CHELLAH A couple of kilometres to the south of the main conurbation of Rabat, rising up out of an undeveloped plain overlooking the Bouregreg Estuary, is a fortress that resembles a kasbah. Totally enclosed and separate, it looks like someone's private castle. In fact, the walls are Merinid, dating from around AD1300 and were constructed to surround the dynasty's necropolis, or burial place. The fortifications encircle not only the remains of a family member, but also the ruins of a settlement that had existed long before.

History Here was the town of Sala Colonia, the last outpost of the Roman Empire to the west, and a thriving community in its heyday. Even before the Romans came, such an inviting estuary was irresistible to the Phoenician traders, and their traces have been found at Sala. The successors also knew the value of navigable safe havens, and set up a port that by the beginning of Augustus's reign had proven to be a commercial success. Although fishing was certainly one of the activities, the value of the location was as an export harbour, and from here, the goods of North Africa were sent to the rest of the empire. Cereal from Morocco's fertile lands, oil from the thriving olive groves, wine from the prolific vineyards, and even wild animals bred for combat in the amphitheatres, were shipped out from Sala. Strangely enough, for such a busy place, the remains unearthed indicate that the city wasn't particularly rich, even though some exquisite statues and other similar items have been found. There's a marked paucity of mosaics, something present in profusion in Volubilis, the sister city further to the east. The wealthy probably had their villas elsewhere, away from this industrial centre. Also unusual is that remnants of the standard entertainment venues of the working classes, such as amphitheatres or theatres, haven't been found (the only one found in Morocco is at Lixus, quite a distance north). Perhaps the recycling of subsequent empire builders was so successful that many Roman traces are simply buried within later settlements. By around AD250, the Romans left, dragging the last of their remaining Mauretanian province back to Tingis. People stayed on, working the port and living in the city until about 1150.

What to see

Roman Sala (☉ *09.00–17.30; MAD10*) What's left of Sala Colonia just about makes up a Roman ruin. Potentially, the most interesting remnant, the port, has been lost under the ebb and flow of the Bouregreg River. What's believed to be the forum lies above in the city area, east of the later Merenid graveyard, and the decumanus can still be recognised as leading from it. A triumphal arch is visible, but its patron hasn't been found, although the era from which it dates indicates it might have been dedicated to the emperor Trajan. The city rises in levels, taking advantage of its hill position overlooking the estuary. The houses found were basic working-class residences with little or no decoration remaining, in contrast to the lavishly decorated upper middle-class manors found in other sites. Bordering on the walls of the necropolis are the last examples of the baths, with recognisable hypocausts, and a nymphaeum nearby. It was not a coincidence that the Merenids began their construction at this point as they also took advantage of the water supply set up by their predecessors. Columns lie strewn about the place, and a few inscriptions have been found, yet not that much is known about the place other than what was actually found here.

Islamic Chellah The later Merenid necropolis is the most impressive part of Chellah, and in contrast to the unembellished remains of Sala, is quite beautiful. Just after the site was abandoned, the walls that remain today were built by the Almohad dynasty, to construct a fortress as a base for attacks against Spain. No doubt useful for a while, Chellah, along with the rest of Rabat, lost popularity when the capital moved to Fes. Sultan Abou Said decided to use the interior of the defences as a royal graveyard for himself and his successors, hoping they would look similar to the Saadian ones in Marrakech. His son Abou el Hassan built a mosque, decorative ruins of which still exist today, plus a few holy sites for attracting contemplative pilgrims to the complex. Wandering back towards the entrance from the depths of the site, you will find a small pool of dark, mysterious water that allegedly contains eels. Local tradition has it that throwing hard-boiled eggs into the depths, conveniently available for a small fee from the old woman sitting nearby, will help infertile women conceive. There's no explanation offered for the efficacy of this cure, but the practice continues. Finally, at the gate just as you leave, notice the incredible number of cats, at recent count 37, being taken care of by another female attendant. They're quite friendly, especially if being fed, but the pack en masse can be pretty intimidating.

Beyond the Romans

THE BEST THINGS TO SEE SOUTH OF THE ROMAN PROVINCES

Morocco has a great number of attractions for the visitor beyond the realm of the ancient lands of the Roman Empire. The Atlas Mountains' spine runs through North Africa and ends up in the Gulf of Gabes in Tunisia and was the border between Roman and Berber lands. Although there were the occasional army-led exploratory expeditions further into the south, most of the province of ancient Mauretania only existed north of the imaginary line drawn from Rabat on the Atlantic coast, to Volubilis, and then northeast into Algeria and beyond. There is much scenic and cultural beauty outside this region that beckons today's tourist.

Because the focus of this book is on the Roman coast, the list below is necessarily extremely brief, and only meant to be a guide for further enquiry. Essentially, the tourist areas away from the coast can be broken down into three sections.

THE ATLAS MOUNTAINS These peaks are spectacular in themselves, and if you are looking to hike up the summits, the scenery is beautiful. Organised treks go into the mountain Berber towns and villages and casual gîtes are found for overnight accommodation *en route*. It's possible to ascend the 4,167m up to Mount Toubkal, the highest in North Africa and almost always snow-covered. On a more recreational basis, in the winter, Oukaimeden, a 45-minute drive from Marrakech, and Ifrane, very close to Fes, both offer skiing. The facilities and architectural style bear a striking resemblance to European resorts. While in the former, look out for the prehistoric rock carvings. If feeling a bit less energetic, driving across the range is a wonderful experience. The views change dramatically from the rich plains of the coast to the terracotta-coloured villages set in the rock, barely distinguishable from the land around them. The mountain roads vary in difficulty, from easy highways to tricky 4x4 tracks, but all are visually worth the journey. Stop at some of the waterfalls, including Ouzoud, if you have the time. If passing through, try to do so on market days, where locals from all the nearby tiny villages gather to sell and buy wares, including local animals and produce.

SOUTH OF THE ATLAS: ROUTE OF THE KASBAHS Once you are on the other side of the mountains, the Romans disappear completely, and the country is back in the land of the Berbers. Caravans came through here, taking goods from the heart of Africa to the coast, to be transported to Europe and the world. Slowly disappearing, traces of the nomadic lifestyle can still be found. Agriculture exists here for those inhabitants who are more sedentary, but dates replace grain, and the vast palm groves, or palmeraie, are a dark green contrast to the orange soil around them. Here are the valleys such as the Draa and the Ziz, that gather the waters of the rivers for which they're named and use them for cultivation. Along these waterways and in defensible positions are the kasbahs, fortresses constructed from local soil, and the *ksours*, connected villages made from earth. Examples of both abound. Ait ben Haddou, a huge and wonderful village that sprawls up a mountainside, and is famed for being a well-used film set, is one of the most picturesque representatives. Other famous sites are the Glaoui forts in Telouet and in Ourzazate.

EVEN FURTHER SOUTH: INTO THE DESERT Morocco's share of the Sahara isn't that large, but its fringe is an excellent introduction. Passing through the market towns of Errachidia and Erfoud, where the heat and dryness of the approaching desert become increasingly obvious, you eventually come to the Dunes of Merzouga, on the Algerian border. These bright orange and remarkably high hills of sand can be assailed on foot or via camel. It's best to go either at sunrise or sunset. Towns further west include Zagora, with its famous sign that tells you it takes only 52 days to get to Timbuktu. While here, look out for the nomads, especially the Touaregs, the tribe that is covered almost head to toe in blue fabric, although be aware that most of the members you're likely to see today are dressed up for tourists.

Part Three

ALGERIA

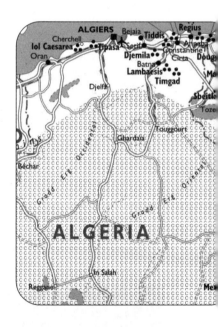

Location North Africa, 28°00'N, 3°00'E. The Mediterranean Sea is to the north. Morocco is to the west, Tunisia to the east.

Size 2,381,740km²; 2nd-largest country in Africa, 11th largest in the world.

Climate Along the coastal region, dry hot summers, wet winters; in the mountains, cold, sometimes with snow; hot, dry summers in the desert region to the south, with occasional sciroccos (hot winds)

Status Republic

Population 33,769,669 (2008 estimate)

Life expectancy 73.77 years: male 72.13 years, female 75.49 (2008 estimate)

Capital Algiers; population 2,900,000

Other main towns Oran, Tlemcen, Constantine, Annaba, Batna, Setif, Hassai Messaoud

Economy 95% of export earnings come from fossil fuels (8th-largest natural gas and 14th-largest oil reserves in the world)

GDP US$6,500 per capita (2007)

Languages Officially Arabic, although Berber (Tamazight) is also spoken throughout the country. French is the language of commerce.

Religion Muslim 99%, Christian and Jewish 1%

Currency Algerian dinar (DA)

Rate of Exchange £1 = DA107, US$1 = DA73, €1 = DA97 (Apr 2009)

National airline/airport Air Algerie; Algiers: Houari Boumediene Airport

International telephone code +213

Time GMT +1 hour

Electricity 220 volts AC, 50Hz; European two-pin plug

Weights and measures Metric

Flag Half green to the left, white to the right. In the centre is the Islamic red crescent moon to the left, facing a red star to its upper right.

National anthem *Kassaman* ('We swear by the lightning that destroys')

Public holidays 1 January, New Year's Day; 10 January, Islamic New Year; 19 January, Ashoura; *9 March, Mouloud, Birth of the Prophet; 1 May, Labour Day; 19 June, Revolutionary Readjustment; 5 July, Independence Day; *21 September, Eid al-Fitr, end of Ramadan; 1 November, Anniversary of the Revolution; *28 November, Eid al-Adha, Feast of the Sacrifice.

(*for 2009: starred dates change according to the Muslim calendar)

10

Background Information

GEOGRAPHY

Situated between the nations of Morocco to the west, Tunisia to the east and Libya to the south/southeast, Algeria takes up a significant part of North Africa. Located at a latitude of 28°00'N and longitude of 3°00'E, it is the largest country in the region, the second-biggest on the continent (after Sudan) and the eleventh largest country in the world. Its coastline is relatively short – 1,200km along the Mediterranean Sea. Nevertheless, the shore is what made the area so valuable to the Phoenicians, Carthaginians, Numidians, Mauretanians (Juba II had his capital here, in Cherchell) and the Romans. Later invaders, including Barbary pirates, found the seaports ideal for hideouts. And even today trade along the Mediterranean remains vibrant and the ports of Oran, Mostaganem, Algiers, Bejaia, Skikda and Annaba provide important cargo terminals for export of Algeria's considerable natural resources and extra income from other countries using these stopovers.

It's easiest to divide the country into four separate geographic regions running laterally. First is the Tell, the small but lush plain that benefits from proximity to the coast. Rainfall is prolific here, rendering this strip the prime agricultural region of the country. Not only is this where most of the northern invaders and colonisers settled, but it's also where the majority of today's population remains. The second geographical classification is the hilly and low mountain region that provides the backdrop and first natural barrier to the coastal plain. Included are the Kabylie Mountains, an intriguing area of hilltop villages with an extraordinary cultural diversity, as well as some beautiful often snow-topped scenery. In the Massif de Djurdjura, south of Bejaia and west of Setif, the elevation reaches 2,308m. The range is broken, allowing easy access to some of the plains further south, such as Batna. The Romans established their southernmost settlement, the headquarters of the Second Augustan Legion at Lambaesis, just outside Batna.

Third is the Hauts Plateaux (High Plateaux), the Algerian Saharan branch of the Atlas Mountains that begin in Morocco, continue east all the way across the country. Reaching 1,900m at their highest point, they're still no match for the Kabylie Mountains. Nevertheless, this range is considered to be the border between the fertile coastal plan and high hills of the Tell, and the encroaching Sahara Desert. Divided into three massifs, the Ksour, the Amour and the Oulad are links in the Saharan Atlas chain that reaches from the western border to just south of where the Romans had their last outpost in today's Algeria. Generally arid, the northern flanks do receive of rain, and green fields and flowers are not unusual in the spring. As the mountains rise, the land becomes more barren, although rainfall and the water table allow for oases, appearing in various points heading northeast along the range, from Bechar, near the Moroccan border, to Biskra close to Batna in the east, with Ain Sefra and Laghouat in between.

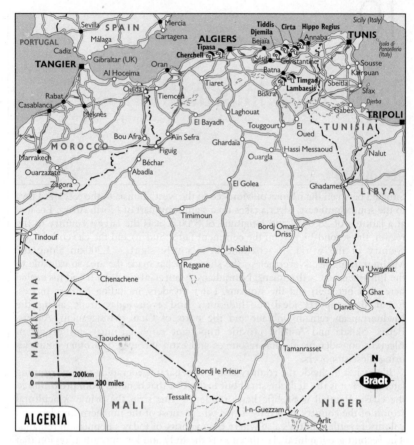

ALGERIA

The descent to the south leads to the the fourth region, the Sahara, a land that excluded the Romans, but today is the home of various tribes (notably the blue-robed Touareg nomads).

NATURAL HISTORY

Although there are large uninhabited regions of the country, some quite beautiful, Algeria is not the best country in the Maghreb for pursuing wildlife. Distances are vast, and infrastructure is poor in these deserted parts. Political issues add to the problems of travelling, with some of the southern Saharan regions as well as the Kabylie Mountains subject to terrorist attacks.

Where the foothills begin, rising into the higher elevations, forests of cedar and cork begin to populate the hillsides. Animals, such as wild boars, gazelles and jackals, live in these areas, as well as barbary apes. Further south, as the mountains slope down into the desert beyond, the geography and its corresponding flora and fauna change. The date palm (see page 73) that can survive on relatively little water replaces the thirsty mountain trees. Reptiles, such as snakes, monitor lizards and other rodents, are at home here.

The country has quite a few more unusual animals that are not often visible. The fennec, the native fox with the large ears, and the jerboa, a jumping mouse-like rodent, are around but rarely seen. Even harder to spot are cheetah, allegedly living in the mountains in the south, and leopards, panthers and servals, an endangered species of wild cat, living somewhere in the north. The Mediterranean Sea plays host to the usual variety of saltwater creatures; of note is the rare endangered monk seal.

In addition, birdlife is prolific, whether spotted as storks nesting on high spots in urban areas, or desert predators, such as falcons, eagles or vultures, hunting in the sparser populated regions. There are said to be 180 species in the country.

POST-ROMAN HISTORY

The Islamic invasion that began in the east and led to Okba founding his holy city in Kairouan, Tunisia, spread through Algeria on its way to Morocco. Sometime

THE SAHARA

The world's largest hot desert covers more than nine million square kilometres and is the barrier between Africa's northern and central/southern areas. Stretching south for 1,500km, the lion's share is held within Algeria, and encompasses 80–90% of the country. The name is said to come from the Arabic word *sahra*, a translation of the Touareg word for desert. Tradition has it that the original meaning was deserts, plural rather than singular, as there are so many different types of terrain within the Sahara. Algeria contains several of them. The most iconic image is of high sand dunes, ideally enhanced with trains of camels plying the caravan route across them. To some degree, this depiction is not only valid, but one that is exploited by tour operators who readily offer dromedary excursions through these sands. However, this aspect is at most 25% of the landscape and only one part of an extraordinarily diverse, though dry, environment. Much of the Sahara consists of *hamadas*, barren areas with more rock than sand and nothing of particular interest. Some of the most fascinating features occur in the country's southeastern (and Libya's southwestern) mountain areas. In Algeria, the Hoggar Massif and the Tassili N'Ajier Highlands (see page 233) (and in Libya, Jbel Acacus and Wadi Methkandoush, see page 376) are mountain regions which once contained rivers that carved the canyons and valleys visible today. Peaks rise as high as 3,000m here. The area is extremely scenic and worth visiting, despite its distance (there are internal flights here from some of the bigger Algerian cities, but make sure to check dates and times beforehand).

Although the landscapes are good reasons to visit in their own right, the main attraction, and why these areas are protected within national parks, is the rock art. Petroglyphs (carvings) and pictograms (paintings) dating back at least 10,000 years are visual documents of what life was like in those early days. The region was far more lush and fertile than today, and the art depicts the diversity of animal life as well as activities of the day. The repositories on both sides of the border have been declared UNESCO World Heritage Sites.

At the end of the last ice age, an increase in rainfall caused grasses, low shrubs and trees to start growing in an area that was once desert. As it gradually became more appealing for habitation, people began to settle in the region. From about 9,000 years ago, the fauna of central Africa spread north, due to increased cooling. Further evidence of life here has been provided by satellite images using ground-penetrating radar, that indicate ancient watercourses, as well as the *wadis*, or dry riverbeds, that today get water only during flash floods. Radiocarbon techniques used on the fossils and artefacts found in the area back up the dates. The area began drying out around 6,000 years ago although vegetation remained for another 2,500 years. It's believed rainfall decreased and a shift in the earth's orbit precipitated exaggerated weather effects.

Ahaggar In the Hoggar Mountains – the Great South
Belezma Near Batna
Chrea Between Blida and Medea
Djebel Aissa High Plateaux
Djurdjura Between Bouira and Tizi Ouzou – Kabylie
El Kala Between the Tunisia border and Annaba
Gouraya Bejaia – Kabylie
Tassili N'Ajjer Near Djanet – the Great South
Taza Between Bejaia and Jijel – Kabylie
Theniet In the Atlas Tell Mountains
Tlemcen Around Tlemcen

after AD650, Abu el Mhair Dina consolidated the invaders' position, particularly by mass conversions to Islam in the area around Tlemcen. The Berbers remained in the majority, but were resistant to the religious beliefs of these new conquerors. It was easy enough to create an Arabic state along the coast, but the heartland stayed firmly local. At the same time, the Arabs thought of the Berbers as primitive, holding fast to the definition of their being barbarians. Dissension was always brewing. In AD746, the leadership changed to the Abbasid, based in Baghdad. The North African Muslim world split into three parts, with the Aghlabids in Kairouan, the Rustamids in Tahart in Algeria and the Idrisids in Fes, in Morocco. Fifteen years later, the Rustamids took over much of Algeria. An adherent of the Kharjites, a sect that believes in total equality for each Muslim, the caliph headed a period in Algeria's history that was known for its scholarship and enlightenment. Unfortunately, reinforcing their position by military force wasn't on the agenda, and the next conquering faction, the Shiite Fatimids, found it easy to take over. The new leaders were welcomed by the Kabylie Berbers, always a troublesome group, and were able to take over from the Aghlabids in Tunisia, before the Fatimids continued their journey into Egypt, eventually settling in the new city of Cairo. Before their departure, however, they left a large part of North Africa that included Algeria, to the Zirids, a Berber tribe, who founded Algiers as the capital of the area's most important local power base. Succumbing to the inevitable, the Zirids converted to the Muslim branch of Sunnism, in contrast to the Fatimid Shiia. However, these squabbles proved relatively unimportant in the face of the subsequent invasion from the tribes of both the Arabian Peninsula and Upper Egypt, when the entire area of North Africa was systematically destroyed. Although a few places remained in Berber hands, most of North Africa was now well and truly Arab.

The Berber dynasties, including some from Morocco such as the Idrisids, and their successors the Almoravids, who founded Marrakech in 1086, began to empire build. Lands were incorporated from as far as Algiers to the east, Senegal to the south, and southern Spain in the north. In 1160, when the Almohads took over, the enormity of government was too great, and the territory and their government were divided into three administrative areas. Ifriquiya, Tunisia and part of Libya, was to be under Hafsid rule, Algeria was to be governed by Banu Abd al-Was from Tlemcen, and Morocco was to be controlled by the Merenid dynasty. These divisions were the first ones that approximated the modern country borders.

By the time Columbus began his travels in 1492, the country that sponsored him, Spain, had become the leading power in North Africa. Having expelled the Muslims, a series of forts were built in the 16th century along the coastline, set up for the purpose of accosting passing trade and demanding payment for allowing trespass. Opposition thrived in the form of more individual piracy, and the Turkish-born privateer Barbarossa, or Red Beard (Khayr al-Din), and his brother El Uruj (Arudj), became legendary. Initially seizing goods off the Spanish coast, the pair diversified into gunrunning to the downtrodden Spanish Muslims, and then ferrying them away across the Straits. The two rose in skill and rank, turning into naval commanders in the battles between Spain and North Africa, some of which threatened Algeria. In 1516, El Uruj moved to Algiers to escalate operations, while his brother remained in command in the east of the region. The local leaders, the sultans, began to fear El Uruj, thinking their own positions were in danger, and allied with the Spanish. The fearless pirate not only defended Algiers, but also eventually deposed the sultan. In 1518, however, the Spanish caught up with El Uruj. A year later, when the Spanish launched another attack against Algiers, Khayr al-Din took over from his sibling. A more practical man, he realised he couldn't fight the might of these combined powers, and sought to ally with the Ottomans in Turkey, by offering his submission, and asking aid to defeat the Christians. Having recently absorbed Egypt into their empire, the mighty Easterners were suddenly interested in the West, and especially the Mediterranean. From here began Khayr al-Din's rapid rise through the ranks, first being offered the regency of Algiers, then troops and a fleet to back up his position of power. By 1533 and already acknowledged as the man in control of central Algeria, he was promoted to admiral of the Ottoman fleet and launched an ultimately successful campaign for absorption of Tunisia into the empire. Although Khayr al-Din retired to Turkey in 1544, battles for control between the Spanish and the Turks continued until late in the century. Now solidly Ottoman, a government was set up that comprised a pasha (governor), a *dey* (administrator) and *jannisaries* (soldiers). For the next 250 years or so, Algeria and its near neighbours remained under Turkish control.

In 1830, the French king Charles X, allegedly under the pretext that his country had been insulted by the Algerian *dey*, attacked Algiers. It's believed that the real motivation was that he felt he needed something to bolster his popularity, and an attack on a nearby nation would do it. In any case, a large number of French troops trampled the city and their desecration, looting, and slaughtering of the locals overwhelmed the *dey*, offering no choice but to surrender. Ironically, the campaign didn't help Charles X, as he was deposed soon after. The government now felt they were firmly involved in Algeria. Four years later, the country lost its sovereignty and became a part of France, now under the government of a French military leader. Opposition to the French gathered in strength

Life in Algeria under the French was fine for the *colons*, or *pieds noirs* (literally black feet, immigrants from France, Italy and Spain, as well as Malta and other countries), but at the sacrifice of the original Algerians. The colonising country, under the guise of 'modernisation', squashed the old way of life of the locals, razing the medieval town centres and replacing them with broad boulevards. Benefits that were extended to the new settlers, such as voting and citizenship rights, were withheld from the North Africans. In an attempt to quieten down some of the angry voices, the French instigated a limited programme to educate some of the better-off Algerians, ironically paving the way to an even more literate rebellion. Just after World War I, soldiers who had fought joined the educated graduates and began to form independence movements. In the 1920s and '30s, the FLN (National Liberation Front) and the National Algerian Movement were set up to get the French out, and by the beginning of World War II, Algerians felt they should fight separately from France. In 1943, Ferhat Abbas, a political leader who later formed the nationalist party and eventually became the country's president after independence, submitted a proposal to the government for Muslim equal rights. Its rejection instigated a demonstration in the town of Setif that was viciously quashed, leading to between 8,000 and 45,000 deaths. Two years later, Muslims were granted French citizenship and allowed to work and live in the mother country.

On 1 November 1954 the War of Independence began, springing from an attack that began near the town of Batna. Bombings, torture, collaborative penalties and indiscriminate killing were used in this guerrilla war for the country's autonomous survival. In 1956, Morocco and Tunisia encouraged Algeria's efforts, having recently gained their own independence and the Egyptian president, Gamal Abdel Nasser, voiced his support. The street-level fighting emerged into the capital, as popularly immortalised in the film, *The Battle of Algiers*. In 1957, the FLN called a national strike, and in 1958 the returning French premier got involved in determining a solution. By 1959, France began to realise its African empire was falling apart as it watched country after country gain sovereignty. A ceasefire was called in 1962 and on 3 July, the French premier gave Algeria its freedom. On 25 September 1962, the date chosen to commemorate the exact day on which the French initially invaded, the Democratic and Popular Republic of Algeria was declared. Over 12% of the population left the country almost immediately. Statistics over the war period are appalling, with unsubstantiated claims of nearly one million Algerian, 18,000 French soldier and 10,000 European settler deaths.

Where before the oppressors were the problem, now the struggle existed to establish a viable state. Ahmed ben Ball became the first elected president, and he promised to set up a 'revolutionary Arab-Islamic state based on the principles of socialism and collective leadership at home and anti-imperialism abroad'. Three years later, however, he was overthrown by a consortium headed by the minister for defence, and the FLN leader Colonel Houari Boumedienne. The latter struggled to bring the country into modern times, with programmes to revolutionise industry and agriculture. His rule was marked by attempts at his overthrow, but he held onto power until his death in 1978. By now, oil and natural gas reserves had been discovered in the Sahara, and hope was rising that these resources might financially bail out the nation. With his successors not much changed, although improvements in the well-being of the nation led to a high birthrate and population bulge together with all the problems that accompanied them. By 1980, a nation that depended on the income generated by natural resources suffered badly when the price of oil dropped, and more Algerians looked towards Islam as a solution to their problems. The single party rule system also caused dissent and by October 1988, all these issues brewed up into violent riots in many of the country's big cities. A year later, the government instigated changes that allowed additional political parties, and the FIS (the Islamic Front) proved more popular than the long-standing – and previously only – other party, the FLN.

On 26 December 1991, the first election in which more than one party was represented led to an overwhelming victory by the FIS. However, the military intervened, abolishing parliament, setting up a Council of State and taking Mohammed Boudiaf out of exile and appointing him president. Further elections were dispensed with and the opposition party leaders were taken to prison. Boudiaf was assassinated six months later in an incident riddled with conspiracy theories, but in any case, he was replaced by an even more conservative leader, Ali Kafi. From here began the Dark Decade, a period of civil war that was essentially between the ruling army, and the Islamic party that had won the elections. Battles and bombings stemmed from both sides, with many civilians caught in the crossfire. In the midst of the struggle, in 1995, Liaimine Zeroual, a previous military general, was elected leader and a year later was voted in with a five-year term, but still couldn't control the conflict. That year, in July, Algerian terrorists broadened their dominion by exploding a bomb on the Paris metro and in December, hijacking an Air France plane from Algiers. Despite the changes in policy and the willingness of the FIS to call a halt to its militant tactics, the GSPC (the Salafist Group for Call and Combat) took their place, and there was still no peace. In 1999, Abdelaziz Bouteflika was elected to power by 74% of the electorate, although without the participation of the opposition parties this majority must have been easy to achieve.

By 2002, the war had simply faded, with militant groups either giving up or accepting the situation. Islamic differences seemed to be resolving, but other issues were unfortunately beginning to rise to the surface. In 2004 Bouteflika became the first popularly elected president, although he couldn't shake off the accusations of vote rigging. In 2005, the GSPC declared they were willing to cease operations, but then not only sided with al-Qaeda, but two years later took on the name and values of the larger organisation. They claim responsibility for the bombings that occurred as recently as June 2008. In 2006, rebel groups in the Kabylie Mountains waged a terror campaign that sporadically continues to this day, successfully keeping visitors and tourists away from certain regions of the country.

POLITICS

Despite its socialist-sounding title of the People's Democratic Republic of Algeria, Algeria is a democratic presidential republic, with an effective, if not official, military bias. After various political struggles, there is now a system which allows opposition parties, but they must be approved by the Ministry of the Interior. The leader of the country is head of state and elected for a five-year term and can be voted in for one additional period. It is his responsibility to appoint the Prime Minister, who is head of government. The latter chooses the Council of Ministers, over which the President presides. It is also within the President's jurisdiction to be the top man in the High Security Council. At present, the Prime Minister is Abdelaziz Belkhadem, appointed in 2006, and the President is Abdelaziz Bouteflika, now in his second term, both from the FLN party. A constitutional referendum may be scheduled, allowing for Bouteflika's third term as there is no new presidential candidate looming on the horizon. However, the current leader's poor health may necessitate the prompt grooming of someone new. In addition, some opposition leaders fear that a third term and a change in the constitution might signal the return to one-party elections.

The running of the country is backed up by parliament, which has two chambers. The People's National Assembly (APN) has 389 seats and participants are elected every five years. The last election, held on 17 May 2007, saw over 12,000 people competing for the positions. Immigrants in other countries, including France, were allowed a say. Hardly more than a third of the voters turned out, the lowest in the country's short independent history, as Islamic party leaders called for a boycott. The al-Qaeda faction called the elections sinful, adding to the number of abstainers. Despite the presence of 24 opposition parties, not surprisingly, the FLN won the majority of seats. The other chamber, the Council of the Nation, consists of 144 representatives, two-thirds of whom are elected by local authorities and the remainder chosen by the President. The terms of these members are six years, but elected alternately, so that every three years there is a change in the membership. Proposal of laws may be brought up by either the President or either of the chambers, but must be put before both branches before being enacted.

Although government is centralised and based in the capital, Algiers, Algeria is divided into 48 *wilayas*, or provinces, with their own semi-autonomous control.

They are governed by *walis*. Each wilaya is further broken down into *dairas,* which are subsequently separated into communes. These administrative districts are run by elected officials.

ECONOMY

Fossil fuels and their exploitation are the driving forces of Algeria's economy. Since their discovery in the 1950s, the production of oil and natural gas has generated the majority of the country's earnings. With the eighth-largest natural gas reserves in the world, closely followed by having the 14th biggest pool of oil, 95% of export earnings come from these sources. Domestically, 60% of budget revenues and 30% of GDP come from the hydrocarbon industry. While many countries are bemoaning the soaring cost of fuel, Algeria relies on it, as being so heavily dependent on oil and gas income they benefit from the record high prices. In the 1980s, when costs dropped, Algeria suffered, while now the administration is using the additional income, hopefully, for the benefit of its citizens.

Realising its vulnerability in having one predominant income stream, the government is attempting to diversify into other sectors. The difficulty in doing so, combined with the easy-to-exploit and lucrative petrochemical industry is leading to relatively little success. There is not much agriculture, and despite occasional attempts to revive viniculture, the little wine that is being produced is shipped to France, and hardly touched domestically in a predominantly Islamic culture. Today, revenues from the agricultural sector make up only about 8% of GDP, employing 14% of the labour force. Citrus fruit is grown and exported, mostly to France, but the comparative lack of investment as well as competition from more organised producers, such as Morocco, defeat attempts to make agriculture a significant income earner.

The government is trying to attract both foreign and domestic investment in other fields such as the massive building programme of over a million new residences that it has promised. Evidence of the future of this new housing is clear in the huge construction sites visible in the urban centres of the country. At present there doesn't seem to be much interest from abroad, and the projects are being funded internally, mostly from petrochemical income. Attempts to restructure international financial institutions, such as the banking system, are still being thwarted by internal problems, and other countries are understandably hesitant to invest in an infrastructure riddled with accusations of corruption and reluctance to change.

Tourism is seen as the golden egg of potential income in all of the Maghreb. The country's neighbours on both its flanks, Morocco and Tunisia, have successfully cultivated the field and are visible proof of the benefits. Algeria has not yet managed to organise its visitor assets and the tourist industry is embryonic. Political difficulties chase away foreigners, and the threat of physical danger will close the door on visitors. Even if such fears can be assuaged, the country perhaps needs to develop a tourism infrastructure. Hotels could be constructed on a much larger scale, especially outside of Algiers and closer to the tourist attractions, and better transport would be required. At present, security guards accompany tourist groups, whether visiting the Roman sites or within the confines of the casbah. Even though these teams provide employment for the local police, the manpower might be better used in servicing the more conventional tourism facilities. If the need for such watchfulness was to be eliminated, chances are more visitors would come.

Small, but noteworthy sources of money come from Algerians who have gone abroad. Expatriots who left the country to work in more affluent nations continue to send money to their families. Many such makeshift methods are necessary in a country that has an overall unemployment rate of over 14% (higher in the big cities) and a population where more than 68% are between the ages of 15 and 64. The situation is particularly bad for women, 44% of whom aren't working.

On a more positive note, Algeria has been successful in reducing the debts incurred by foreign loans, now less than 10% of GDP, after a period of significant borrowing in the 1990s. Negotiations with the European Union have led to increased trade and reduced tariffs for trade goods.

PEOPLE

Although five times as large in area, Algeria's population of almost 34 million barely matches its neighbour, Morocco. With almost 80% desert, it's not surprisingly that the vast majority live in the more hospitable north and over half of these people live in towns and cities. National statistics show that there is a density of 11.7 people per square kilometere, but this number doesn't give a true impression. In the most tightly packed urban areas, the figure can rise up to 1,100.

A full 99% of the people of the nation are officially classified as Arab-Berber, but this attribution is not straightforward. Due to the overwhelming influx of Arabs from around 650, and intermarriage, the races have become somewhat mixed. There are some people who claim pure Berber heritage, and even members who have a smaller amount are banding together to re-establish their individuality. Of the four nations that comprise the scope of the Roman coast of North Africa, the Algerian Berbers are the most insistent in maintaining their identity, although the other countries do acknowledge their rights. There are constant rumblings for the creation of an autonomous state from the Berbers in the Kabylie Mountains, just east of Algiers, sometimes accompanied by violence, but the government is not bowing to pressure. As a concession, they are supporting the creation of schools to teach the language and its unique alphabet, and pass on the distinct culture.

The legacy of the European population is fading, having been at its strongest during the French occupation. The French, as well as the *colons/pieds noirs*, bumped up the non Arab-Berber inhabitants, and although their numbers were plentiful for a while, most left after Algeria was declared independent. There was also a large Jewish population, as with the rest of the Maghreb, but they also left after 1962.

CULTURE

Influenced by the wide range of invaders and settlers that occupied the country, Algeria has a diverse and vibrant contemporary culture.

ARCHITECTURE Although there doesn't seem to be one specific form, the range of influences is what makes the style not only Algerian, but also extremely interesting. From the Roman cities, Spanish fortresses, Ottoman mosques and French colonial flourishes and broad boulevards, to the desert villages of the original settlers, buildings mix the exotic with the familiar, creating a fascinating Berber-Euro-Turkish melange. Examples lay side by side, often with constructions that contrast completely with their neighbours. There are some surprising juxtapositions, like finding a Roman column adorning a mosque.

CINEMA It's possible that it's here where Algerian culture has made its greatest international mark. Home-grown filmmaking is surprisingly prolific for a country not competing with the popular appeal of Egypt's industry, and the smaller nation's emphasis is on quality. The most famous depiction of its struggle for freedom, *The Battle of Algiers* in 1965, was directed by the Italian Gillo Pontecorvo, but funded by the Algerian government. Subsequently, the cinema has thrived. Audiences enthusiastically patronise the movies and some examples have gone on to receive worldwide recognition. *The Ball* (1984), *Dust of Life* (1996) and *Days of Glory* (2007) all received nominations for the Best Foreign Language Oscar. In 1970, the film *Z* by the director Cost Gavras won the prize.

HANDICRAFTS Traditional goods continue to be produced in the country, although perhaps not on the same touristic or commercial scale as in Morocco. Carpets and ceramics, jewellery, especially Berber and Touareg traditional silver items, leather goods, musical instruments and glassware are still made the old-fashioned way. Note that bargaining is not really the way to go, and that the price quoted is usually the amount paid.

LITERATURE Algerians are well read, with bookshops even in the provincial airports stocked with intellectual material. There is a thriving literary culture, with examples stemming from the French occupation as well as today's independent nation. Much of the literature deals with the struggle for freedom, and the plight of today's oppressed. There are several writers of note. The most famous is Albert Camus, 1913–1960, often claimed to be an existentialist, although he refuted the association. This *pied noir* wrote many definitive works, including *The Stranger* and *The Plague*, and became the first African-born author to win the Nobel Prize in literature, in 1957. Another luminary was the Martinique-born psychiatrist and literary figure, Frantz Fanon. He came to the country as a soldier in the French army, transferring from the French West Indies in the 1940s. After a short sojourn back in his birthplace, he studied medicine in France, where he began producing written work. Returning to Algeria, he became concerned with the everyday life of ethnic Algerians. The work of this mixed-race doctor took a political turn during the independence movement and he produced *The Wretched of the Earth*, a book that described some of the appalling treatment of the locals by the French army. Vociferous and radical, he was expelled from Algeria in 1957, but after his death, was returned and buried in Algerian soil. His works continue to have a major effect on political and sociological thinking, especially regarding the morality and practicality of colonial government. Various writers penned books that were concerned with Algeria's struggles for freedom and even now the written arts thrive, with authors continuing to produce controversial works. Assia Djebar, born 1936, is a woman novelist and filmmaker, working under this pseudonym and considered one of the Maghreb's most important authors, having been the first to be elected to the Academie Française in 2005.

MUSIC remains the most accessible form of contemporary culture. The nation's endemic version is extremely popular, especially among expats abroad, who help immortalise the genre. Historically a mix of the legacies left behind by various invaders, today's musicians living in Europe continue to perform the uniquely Algerian blend. At home, Algeria also has its own varieties, such as *kablylia*, Berber folk music that has become somewhat of a banner for the Amazigh in modern Algeria. The controversial Lounes Matab was one of the foremost exponents of this form. Other artists include Ferhat, Ait Menguellet and Idir, although politics have forced some of these singers into exile in France. Female singers are also well known for their local renditions The most popular local listening material in both Algeria and the rest of the Maghreb, is *rai,* a pop-influenced form of folk music that uses strong rhythms as a framework on which to hang political expression. Cheb Mami is well known outside of North Africa, partly because of his collaboration with western rock musicians. Khaled is another popular performer. An annual music festival is held in a specially built arena in Timgad, near Batna, close to the Roman site.

11

Practical Information

SUGGESTED ITINERARIES FOR CRUISE-SHIP PASSENGERS

Unfortunately, the domestic problems of Algeria have scared off much of the cruise-ship trade. Although there are several ferry ports on the Mediterranean, luxury vessels tend to give the country a miss. Until this situation changes, cruises that do stop have a choice of five ports, and those visitors who come by sea might be interested in Oran, Algiers, Bejaia, Skikda and Annaba.

ORAN Coming from the west, Oran is the first substantial port within Algeria, and nearest to the (closed by land) Moroccan border. The country's second-biggest city has a reputation for being fairly open, as well as the home of *rai*, the North African rhythmic and political musical form. Not founded until AD903, there are no Oran ruins that date from before then. The city has a Spanish and French feel to it. Ships dock at the maritime station in the city centre. If there are no organised excursions, or if you'd rather just go by yourself, it's best to start straight off the ship by wandering along the seafront. Most of what is worth seeing can be visited on foot. Head into the town, passing by the 11th-century Bey's Palace, also known as the Chateauneuf, which is open to the public. Just beyond is the Pasha's or Grande Mosque, and from here it's not far to the city's main square, the Place du 1 Novembre, which is a good point from where to orient yourself. There are several impressive buildings around here, but be careful when entering some of the more cramped areas as it's possible they're not the safest places to stroll. Give yourself a bit of time to see the Sacre Coeur, once a cathedral that's now the university library, and if you are not allowed within, at least take a good look at the outside. Also notable is the Church of Santa Cruz and even better the view from the top of Murdjadjo the hill on which it stands. Even if you feel you need to stretch your legs, try to find a taxi, as the area through which you need to walk might again be somewhat dodgy. The overlook grants an excellent prospect of the city. The chapel dates from the end of the French colonial period, and the fortress, although enticing, is used by the military and closed to the public. If the weather is unkind, walking doesn't appeal, or if in pursuit of more intellectual activities, try the Museum Zabana. It's located further into the city, and has material from the Numidian and Roman periods, as well as other collections that stretch into modern times.

ALGIERS One of the highlights of the country, this big, lively city stands white and gleaming on the hillside as the ship sails into port. It's difficult to visit quickly without an organised excursion, or at the very least a taxi available at your beck and call. There is far too much to see for a brief visit, so the following attractions are recommended if time is short. It's probably easiest to begin with museums, and the Bardo Ethnographic Museum, located within an Ottoman palace, has a very broad-ranging collection of items that run the gamut from prehistoric remains, including examples of rock art, to traditional regional garments. Quite close is the National Museum of Antiquities which is even more interesting in that it contains remains from most of the country's best Roman sites. Getting back into the bus or taxi, when heading off into the city centre, it's possible to get glimpses of an enormous hilltop structure in the gaps between the high-rises. Looking like a gigantic tripod, this modern sculpture is the *Monument of the Martyrs*, particularly those fighters who perished in the war for independence. Its site on high is imposing, but if time is tight, even seeing it from a distance is impressive, which is most likely how it's meant to be viewed,

Probably what most tourists want to visit, and the place that is unique to Algiers, is the casbah. It is essential that when coming here, you are accompanied by a guide, not only for steering through the labyrinth, but also security. This district is extremely dangerous which is what makes it all the more intriguing. Police headquarters at the entrance might well require that you register, and it is possible that security guards will accompany visitors. The casbah is seedy and fascinating at the same time, with ramshackle residences crumbling next to beautifully renovated dwellings. The district follows the contours of the hill, with tours starting either from the bottom or the top, granting views of the Mediterranean far below, down the end of the narrow pedestrian streets. The claustrophobic and sometimes slightly paranoid atmosphere is electric, and architectural gems shine out from behind the neglected appearance of the 'village'. Heading down, eventually the streets broaden, past mosques and shops, and lead to the French colonial city centre, although the uneasy juxtaposition of the cultures is fascinating. As long as there is adequate supervision for the entire visit, the casbah should definitely not be missed.

As a treat and to counter the uncontrolled and raw ambience of the casbah, stop for tea at the E Djazair Hotel, a taxi drive up into the hills. Once the French colonial hotel, the St George's, this lovely establishment has gorgeous gardens in which you can sit and sip an afternoon beverage. It's easy to imagine how things were for the privileged during the days of the occupation – for a price that still reflects exclusivity.

For most cruises, and certainly the history-based ones, excursions will be included to the beautiful seaside Roman site of Tipasa, 70km from Algiers, and once the Mauretanian capital. The modern city of Cherchell, about 18km further west, is also on the itinerary. Just before Tipasa, tours stop at the ancient hilltop construction known as the Mauretanian Tomb, supposedly the burial place of Juba II (who died in AD23) and his wife Cleopatra Selene, king and queen of Rome's client kingdom of Mauretania. Back down the slope and about 11km further, Tipasa was an affluent and successful imperial city that thrived for several hundred years, while Cherchell was Juba II's headquarters during the latter part of his reign (see page 215). If you want to visit the locations independently, allow an entire day for the excursions, plus another day to make the arrangements via a local tour operator or reliable taxi driver from Algiers.

BEJAIA Organised cruises that stop at Bejaia do so to visit the marvellous Roman site of Djemila (page 208). At the moment, getting to Bejaia by car is not recommended, as the road passes through the problematic area of the Kabylie Mountains, but arriving there by sea is fine. An excursion to the ruins should be included in the cruise itinerary, but if not, do not miss Djemila, even if it means going into town and finding someone to take you there. Not much further, and equidistant from Skikda, is Tiddis, another well-preserved Roman site (page 215) notable for its hilltop location and red soil, from which the ancient city was constructed. It's worth noting that the Rhumel River below, then called the Ampsaga, was the border between Mauretania and Numidia. As for Bejaia itself, there isn't too much of great interest to see within the city. The prime attraction is its proximity to the Sapphire coast, a region of arguably the most beautiful beaches in the country. This stretch of coast might be a good place to take a break and go for a day at the beach. There are resorts here, and more are coming, so facilities are available.

SKIKDA Despite its Phoenician origins, and importance as the Roman city of Ruiscade, subsequent destruction by the Vandals and reconstruction by the French have left nothing very ancient to see. Today, the city is heavily industrial. In French colonial days, when the city was known as Philippeville, several beautiful buildings were constructed. More modern examples of the period also exist, such as the railway station and town hall both designed by the architect Le Corbusier. The port is near enough for a quick taxi ride, or a long stroll to the centre, so it's easy enough to take a closer look at some of the more interesting architectural examples. As with Bejaia, the best part of Skikda is its proximity to some good beaches and lovely coastline. Sometimes the city of Constantine located about 75km south, with its Roman and later history as well as fascinating scenery, is offered as a tour option.

ANNABA The main touristic reason for stopping here is to visit the nearby ruins of Hippo Regius, the ancient city where St Augustine spent his last years from AD391–430. Overlooking the site is the Basilica of St Augustine, dedicated in 1900 and of a similar date to Paris's Sacre Coeur. If continuing the cruise to Tunisia, you will see a similar construction, the Cathedral of St Louis on Byrsa Hill, overlooking Carthage. Tours will probably be included with the cruise but if not it's possible to find a taxi or tour operator in town who will arrange a trip. Otherwise, Annaba is a big, industrial city. It's not far from the harbour to the city centre, and if you have the time, worth strolling into town to see the predominantly French colonial heritage. The Cours de la Revolution is the green heart of town, and a great place to walk and people-watch. The city's other attractions include the Djamaa El Bey Mosque, and the attractive Rue de Tanger, a blue-and-white street just off the Place des Armes. Beaches around here are also attractive and popular. See if you can get a taxi to go to the Cap de Garde lighthouse and perhaps a bit further, to the lovely Plage Djenanne El Bey strand.

ℹ️ TOURIST INFORMATION

There are no organised tourist offices abroad, and the embassies do not give out tourist material. The websites are the best bet for finding out information before departure. A good introductory website is www.algeria.com; www.algeriantourism.com/index.php (in French).

IN ALGERIA Tourist offices are thin on the ground, although the capital, Algiers, has one. Some of the local tour operators might be able to offer information.

$ MONEY

Algerian dinars are not available abroad, credit cards are not readily accepted (except perhaps at the big hotels in the major towns) and travellers' cheques are hard to change. As a result, you will almost certainly need to deal with a bank or bureau de change. Black market swaps exist, but they're dodgy, and don't really offer significantly better rates than legitimate businesses. Banking hours are usually 09.00–17.00 Sunday–Thursday, although bureaux de change, especially at hotels, will have longer hours.

Travelling independently as a tourist in Algeria right now is not recommended due to the political problems that currently exist in the country. Tourists on their own have been recent targets for kidnappings especially those wandering away from the beaten path. Tour groups and organisers have their methods and security teams are on hand and good at getting around. They also receive constant updates as to what and where things are happening, and will reschedule or reroute destinations accordingly. Hopefully, the situation will change and stabilise soon and allow for safe individual visitors again. Perhaps by then there will be more of a sympathetic travellers' infrastructure as well.

✈ **BY AIR** With distances being vast and roads being relatively poor and subject to frequent security checks, and other forms of transport unreliable, domestic flying is actually a very good way to get around the country. Internal flights leave from terminal 2 of the country's main air hub, Aeroport Houari Boumediene in Algiers (✆ *021 50 60 00*). Air Algerie (✆ *021 74 24 28; www.airalgerie.dz*) flies to several destinations, including the main ones that might be of tourist interest, such as Annaba, Constantine, Setif, Batna and those far to the south, such as Djanet and Tamanrasset. Package tours often incorporate air travel to speed the process. Even so, schedules can change, flights can be delayed for no apparent reason, and information might be hard to come by, especially if you don't speak French.

🚂 **BY TRAIN** There is a train network in Algeria, although it doesn't seem to be used much by tourists. Details are available online via the Société Nationale des Transport Ferroviaires (✆ *021 71 15 10; www.sntf.dz*). Algiers's main station is on Boulevard Mohamed V (✆ *021 71 15 10)*, and trains to Annaba, Setif and Constantine as well as other cities leave from here. Getting from Algiers to Constantine by train should take about six hours.

🚐 **BY BUS** Travelling to other parts of the country by bus is possible if time is less important than money. The network is mostly government run, and SNTV (or TVSE in the south) includes many tourist locations on its routes. Standards vary and departure times can be awkward. Partly because of the low cost, there can be a high demand for relatively few spaces, and getting advance reservations is highly recommended. There are also a few private bus companies, but it's easiest to find out about them when in the departure city. The main bus station in Algiers is the Station Gare Routière El Kharrouba (✆ *021 49 71 51*). It's located a bit out of the way of the city centre. It's possible to take a bus there, but allow lots of time and give yourself an option to walk part of the way.

🚕 **BY TAXI** Sooner or later, the need for taking a taxi is bound to arise. Private taxis are hard to get hold of, and not as common as shared ones, in which drivers stop to pick up passengers on the same route, until the car is full. Slower than individually hired ones, they end up being cheaper. It's possible to phone ahead, although on-call taxis are not necessarily faster or more reliable than ones hailed on the street, and they are more expensive. It might be best to ask the hotel to get hold of someone, even though prices will certainly shoot up. If you come across a friendly driver who's keen to help, keep his number and don't hesitate to get in touch. He might be pleased to cultivate a guaranteed customer and you might get someone who can be relied upon.

🚗 **CAR HIRE** With the security problems, constant roadworks, accident rates due to poor drivers and the high cost, there might be better options than car rental. It might be an idea to hire a local driver with the vehicle, especially if venturing into the desert, or simply opting for an organised tour. If you do require a self-drive, check in the individual cities for reliable companies.

PUBLIC HOLIDAYS

Fixed annual dates are:

1 January	New Year's Day
10 January	Islamic New Year
19 January	Ashouara
1 May	Labour Day
19 June	Revolutionary Readjustment
5 July	Independence Day
1 November	Anniversary of the Revolution

These holidays are Islamic and vary annually according to the lunar calendar. They are also celebrated on the same dates (variable according to the year) in Morocco, Tunisia and Libya:

9 March	Aïd al-Mawlid (Prophet's Birthday)
21 September	Aïd al-Fitr, or Eid (End of Ramadan)
28 November	Aïd al-Adha (Feast of the Sacrifice)

MEDIA AND COMMUNICIATIONS

POST Taking a lead from the French colonists, all the big cities and most of the small towns have post offices. With a reasonable, if not speedy, service, letters and postcards sent from Algeria will arrive, taking up to a week to points in Europe and proportionately more to further destinations. Bureaux are normally open Saturday to Wednesday from 08.00–17.00 and Thursday from 08.00–12.00, although some of the smaller branches might close for lunch from 12.00–14.00. The main office in Algiers is open 24 hours a day.

PRINT For a country that once prided itself on being literate, standards are not what they were, and daily readership is low, despite the large number of newspapers on the stands. Three papers lead the popular pack, with *El Khabar*, printed in Arabic, French and English and *El Watan* and *Liberté* in French. *Algeria Daily* keeps up with what's going on in English. For further information on the plethora of news media around, as well as a taste, check out: www.onlinenewspapers.com/algeria.htm. The bigger international papers and magazines, especially those that are economic or news based, are usually available at the bigger hotels or finer bookshops.

RADIO There are several local radio stations, including the government-run Algeria Radio that broadcasts in Arabic, Berber and French. The others are private and play all sorts of music, particularly *rai* and the usual favourites, although the occasional Western pop tune might sneak in.

TELEVISION Although it's possible to view a wide range of channels via satellite dishes that seem to perch on every house, there is only one national channel, ENTV (Enterprise National de Television). By law, private ownership of television channels is forbidden, so that the local network is government run. Despite the alleged absence of censorship laws, there is a certain amount of material that is simply not broadcast, creating a de facto restriction of news. Recently, ENTV has joined with Khalifa TV, an Algerian network in Paris, to create a second, semi-private channel. BRTV is a Berber channel, also sent from France and picked up via satellite, that caters to the relatively large minority. The usual range of international channels, including CNN and BBC World, are usually available at the better hotels.

MOBILE PHONES AND THE INTERNET Throughout the Maghreb, mobile phones have become the way to talk, and everyone will give you a mobile number through which to get in touch. As with the West, phone companies advertise everywhere and have high-profile shops. The three main operators are Djezzy, Mobilis and Nedjima. The instant you turn on your phone in the country, a text message will appear welcoming you to the network with which your home network is affiliated. Coverage is good, surprisingly so for such a big country.

There are internet cafés all over the place, and big hotels usually offer Wi-Fi. More and more establishments are setting up websites for their businesses.

GIVING SOMETHING BACK

Algeria www.algerialinks.com/dir/algeria-human-rights-liberties. General search engine on this subject.
Algeria-Watch www.algeria-watch.de/index_en.htm. Provides information on the human rights situation in the country.
Algeria Watch international www.pmwatch.org/awi/
Amnesty International www.amnesty.org/en/region/middle-east-and-north-africa/north-africa. The human rights organisation's website for all North Africa.

Human Rights Watch www.hrw.org/doc/?t=mideast. Lists human rights issues for Algeria: www.hrw.org/doc/?t=mideast&c=algeri
Medecins Sans Frontières
www.msf.org/msfinternational/countries/africa/algeria/index.cfm. The French 'Doctors without Borders' website in Algeria.
Relief Web www.reliefweb.int/rw/dbc.nsf/doc103?OpenForm&rc=1#show. Shows disasters & emergencies throughout the world, including North Africa.

12

Ports of Entry

ALGIERS

It's easiest to get into Algeria via its main entry port, Algiers; as a centralised country almost everything goes through here at some point. This big, dramatic and quite beautiful city sits gleaming white above the blue Mediterranean waters, having been alternately welcoming and resistant to settlers, invaders, pirates, colonists and tourists over the centuries. The Romans settled here when it was Icosium, although the Mauretanian capital, Iol Caesarea (today's Cherchell), was about 90km from the capital. Algiers gets its own write-up (*Chapter 13*) as do Setif (*Chapter 14*), Constantine (*Chapter 15*), Batna (*Chapter 16*) and St Augustine's city of Annaba (*Chapter 17*).

ORAN Telephone code 041

The first major city on the Mediterranean coast in the west of the country, Oran is not a frontier town, as the border with Morocco is currently closed. However, if you are coming from the west by sea, here is the first major port of Algeria. The nation's second-biggest urban area attracts many migrants due to its importance as an industrial and educational centre. Subject to the demands of modernity, there is quite a lot of ugly architecture, such as high-rise apartment buildings and mass housing. Between these concessions to the modern age are examples of very attractive buildings from previous eras, some of which were constructed as showpieces or places of reverence.

HISTORY The bay of Mers el-Kebir on which Oran lies, was believed to have been occupied by a Berber tribe more than 100,000 years ago. In Palaeo and Neolithic times, caves in the area functioned as residences. The Phoenicians and the Romans seem to have passed over this region, as no traces of their visits were ever found. The first record of settlement was in AD903 by Islamic sailors coming from Andalusia. As a good stopover between Spain and Morocco, Oran flourished, benefiting by its location on the trade route. Subject to handovers resulting from the change in dynasties, by 1509 the Spanish returned, taking Oran as part of their African empire. Not exempt from the battles for control of Algeria between them and the Turks (see page 163), the city suffered. It was during this period that the Spanish reinforcements were built, leaving some of the most interesting architectural legacies visible today. An enormous earthquake and its subsequent tsunamis in 1790 devastated the city, killing nearly a quarter of its inhabitants and the Spanish finally gave up, leaving Oran in 1792. The next man in control, the bey Mohamed El-Kebir, erected many landmarks during his reign, including the palace, the Pasha's Mosque, and new quarters. Internal struggles left the city weak and when the French invaded in 1831, there was no resistance. As part of France's claim to Algeria, they developed Oran into a sophisticated city worthy of being part of Europe, with appropriate edifices still seen today. The port regained its

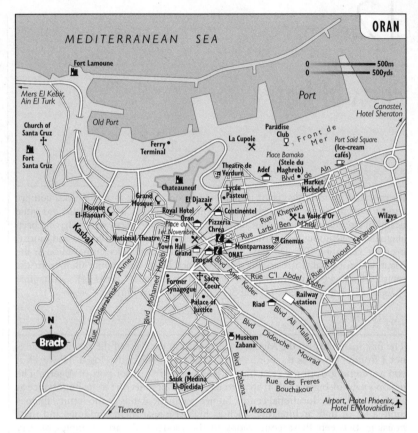

ORAN

MEDITERRANEAN SEA

Fort Lamoune

Mers El Kebir,
Ain El Turk

Old Port

Church of
Santa Cruz

Fort
Santa Cruz

Port

Canastel,
Hotel Sheraton

Paradise
Club

La Cupole

Ferry
Terminal

Place Bamako
(Stele du
Maghreb)

Theatre de
Verdure

Adef

Blvd de Ain

Front de Mer

Port Said Square
(Ice-cream
cafés)

Chateauneuf

Grand
Mosque

Mosque
El-Haouari

Lycée
Pasteur

El Djazair

Royal Hotel
Oran

Place du
1er Novembre

Kasbah

Continentel

Pizzeria
Chrea

Market
Michelet

Rue Khemisti

La Voile d'Or

Rue Larbi Ben M'hidi

Wilaya

National Theatre

Town Hall

Grand

Timgad

Montparnasse

ONAT

Cinemas

Rue C'l Abdel Kader

Rue Molmoud Feraoun

Former
Synagogue

Sacre
Coeur

Palace of
Justice

Riad

Blvd Amir Kader

Railway
station

Blvd Ali Mallah

N

Bradt

Museum
Zabana

Blvd Didouche Mourad

Blvd Tabana

Souk (Medina
El-Djedida)

Rue des Freres
Bouchakour

Tlemcen

Mascara

Airport, Hotel Phoenix,
Hotel El Movahidine

importance, especially during World War II during which it became a strategic
naval base. After the war, Oran had the most *colons*, or *pieds noirs* of the country,
eventually leading to almost 50% of the population. By the time independence was
declared, most had left to return to France, leaving a city with half of its inhabitants
gone. However, the appeal of the big city and its work opportunities drew in
migrants, eventually returning Oran's population to its former level.

GETTING THERE AND AROUND

By air Es Senia Airport (✆ *041 51 11 50*) is located about 20km from central Oran.
There are reasonable numbers of domestic flights that land here from places such
as Algiers, Annaba and Constantine. Internationally, planes come from Alicante
(Spain), Casablanca (Morocco), Jeddah (Saudi Arabia) and the French cities of
Lyon, Marseille, Paris and Toulouse. Taxis that cost on average about DA400 will get
you into town, although it might be better to pre-book one with your hotel and have
the driver waiting for you on your arrival. There is also a bus service operated by the
airport that goes into the centre; much cheaper but not as convenient as a taxi.

By rail The network runs only within the country, but is fairly reliable for some
destinations including Algiers. The exterior of the huge station, looking more like
a mosque than a railway terminus (*Gare SNTF, Bd Mellah-Ali;* ✆ *041 40 15 02*), is
close to the middle of the city and modern and clean. A short walk or an
inexpensive taxi ride will get you there.

By bus and taxi The Gare Routière (*Av Cheikh-AEK & Colonel Lofti*), has several buses going to many places throughout the country, although the organisation leaves something to be desired. Check the day ahead for wheres and whens. Here is also from where many of the collective taxis depart. One will take you where you want, but it might take some time before enough people pile in to make it worthwhile for the driver to leave. Oran is relatively walkable, but if you need transport, it's easiest simply to flag down a taxi. Most of the time there will be another passenger already inside, but with time and patience you will get where you want to go.

By sea The Gare Maritime (☎ *041 39 28 81*) is situated in the city centre, next to the Theatre Verdure and the palace. Regular ferries arrive in Oran from Almeria and Alicante, Spain and Sete and Marseille, France. Journeys take about 12 hours from Alicante, and 26 hours from Marseille.

Car hire If you decide to pick up a rental car from Oran, rather than from Algiers, Hertz has branches at the airport (☎ *041 59 10 06*) and in town (*1 Rue Sissi Hasbi Mediouni;* ☎ *041 58 70 23*). Local rent-a-car companies also have vehicles, but make sure the one you choose comes with good recommendations from reliable sources, such as your hotel. Alternatively, consider hiring a car and driver, again with suggestions from your accommodation.

TOURIST INFORMATION The Office of Tourism (ONAT) is located on 4 Boulevard Khemisti (☎ *041 39 51 30*).

TOUR OPERATORS Being the country's second-biggest city, Oran is not short of companies for people who want to travel or arrange excursions. Try one of the following local agencies:

Maghreb Tours 10 Rue des Aures; ☎ 041 39 44 83
Misserghin Tours 9 Av Sidi Chami; ☎ 041 67 99 97; www.misserghin-tours.com

ONAT 10 Bd Amir Abdel Kader; ☎ 041 39 82 64
Zenata Voyage 24 Rue de Tripoli; ☎ 041 39 12 57; www.zenatavoyages.com

WHERE TO STAY
Top end

🏠 **Royal Hotel Oran** (112 rooms) 1 Bd de la Soummam; ☎ 041 39 17 17; www.royalhoteloran.com. This 5-star hotel is probably the city's best, with period architecture combined with the most modern of facilities. $$$$$+

🏠 **Sheraton** (312 rooms) Rt des Falaises, Av Canastel, Seddikia; ☎ 041 59 01 00; www.starwoodhotels.com. Typical for the Sheraton

chain, this hotel is rated a 5-star hotel & is located outside of town but enhanced with a sea view. $$$$$+

🏠 **Hotel Phoenix** (103 rooms) Airport Roundabout, Es Senia; ☎ 041 49 89 91; www.hotel-oran.com. Located a mere 5 mins away from the airport, this modern if somewhat boring lodging is one of the better places to stay in the area. $$$$–$$$$$

Mid-range

🏠 **Hotel Montparnasse** 9 Rue Bensenouci Hamida; ☎ 041 39 53 38. A decent 3-star lodging in the heart of town. $$–$$$

🏠 **Hotel Timgad** 3 Bd Amir Abdel Kader; ☎ 041 39 47 97. Comfortable & friendly, although a bit unremarkable from the outside, this hotel provides a reasonably priced option. $$–$$$

Budget

🏠 **Hotel Grand** 5 Pl du Maghreb; ☎ 041 39 54 69. Located in the heart of the city, this once

'grand' hotel has seen better days, but is an adequate place to stay. $$–$$$

⌂ **Hotel Riad** 46 Bd Mellah Ali; ✆ 041 40 38 50. Oran's cheapest acceptable overnight accommodation, close to the train station. Some rooms even have showers. $

✗ **WHERE TO EAT** Oran does far better for cafés than for restaurants, even though it is such a large urban area. The better hotels are good for a fancy meal and open to non-residents, as long as the potential diner is dressed properly. The area around the Pecherie, near the entrance to the casbah has some recommended seafood restaurants as well as the Gambetta district, a little east of the city centre.

✗ **Hotel Sheraton** Good seafood dishes & a great view are at **Le Ciel D'Oran** ◷ 19.00–01.00 daily except Sat (**$$$$$**), Spanish/North Africa fusion cuisine at **Andalous** ◷ 19.00–01.00 Tue–Sat (**$$$$$**) & something less formal at the **Canastel Brasserie** ◷ 05.30–22.30 daily. (**$$$$**)

✗ **Restaurant les Ambassadeurs** at the Royal Hotel Oran. The top restaurant located in the best hotel: the price of a meal with wine matches the classification. **$$$$$**

✗ **Grand Café Riche** The hotel restaurant at the Hotel Timgad, much less luxurious, despite its name, serving basic French cuisine & wine, in an unpretentious atmosphere. **$$$**

✗ **La Cupole** On the seafront nr Pl Bamako; ✆ 041 33 43 16. Enjoy a variation from the standard North African cuisine while having a glass of wine. **$$-$$$**

✗ **La Voile d'Or** 62 Rue Mohamed Khemisti. Seafood is served in this basic place a little distant from the centre, but all the more reasonable for it. **$$-$$$**

☕ **Place Port Said** Stop at this little oasis & have an ice cream, along with the regulars. $

ENTERTAINMENT AND NIGHTLIFE

The nicer hotels have good places to spend the evening, such as the **Pacha Bar** in the Hotel Royal and the Sheraton's offerings, **The Pub** and the **l'Atmosphere** discotheque. The **Paradise Club** on Boulevard de l'Aln at the seafront is a trendy venue that gives a taste of what it offers via its website (*www.oranparadiseclub.com/eng.htm*).

Ain-el Turk is a seaside resort, best in high summer when the tourists are in, and has many clubs that feature *rai*, the endemic North African music born in Oran. About 15km to the west of the city centre, the district is easily accessible by taxi. Some of the clubs worth considering spending the night in include **Le Biarritz**, **The Blue Sapphire**, **Le Chalet**, **El Jawahra** and **Sun House**.

In August and September, the annual **Festival of Rai** is held in its birthplace, with live concerts featuring some of the biggest stars of the genre. The open-air Theatre de Verdure in the town centre is one of the main venues. Details are hard to get hold of, but the site www.visitoran.com has some information.

SHOPPING **Rue Larbi ben M'hidi**, where the cinemas are located, and **Mohamed Khemisti** are the primary shopping streets and offer much the same things you'd find in most big cities. The **Medina El Djedida** is a buzzing outdoor market made famous more by its mention in *rai* than the goods it has for sale, and there is another one at **Rue des Aures.** The main supermarket, **Morchid**, is located just outside of the centre in the St Eugene district.

OTHER PRACTICALITIES
Emergency telephone numbers
Police ✆ 17

Ambulance ✆ 041 40 31 32

Hospital
✚ **Civil Hospital** 76 Bd Benzerdjeb; ✆ 041 34 33 11

Internet cafés The bigger hotels will have access either via Wi-Fi, or their business centres. Internet cafés pop up and disappear, spotted by the signs that give no name, other than 'Internet'. The following come recommended:

ⓔ **Cyber Web** Pl du Maghreb, next to the Grand Hotel

ⓔ **El-Menzah Cyber Space** 3 Rue Pomel, close to the Lynx Cinema

Post The main post office is at Rue Mohamed Khemisti.

Banks Most hotels offer foreign exchange at a rate that's probably not as good as the banks'. Within the centre, some institutions have ATMs that might accept bank and credit cards. The situation is getting better, so that if these places don't take foreign ones at the moment, they might by the time you visit. Here are a few of the many branches.

$ **Banque Centrale d'Algerie** 13 Bd de la Soumman
$ **Banque Nationale d'Algerie** 4 Bd de la Soumman
$ **Credit Populaire d'Algerie** Bd de la Soumman, close to the Hotel Royal

$ **Societe Generale** Bd de la Soumman & Rue des Soeurs Benslimane

WHAT TO SEE It's easiest to orient yourself via the Mediterranean, and the seaside promenade is the best place to start your wanderings. The city is full of architectural gems, mostly from the French colonial period with a few Ottoman and older buildings scattered among them. Follow your instincts and stay away from the rougher areas, no matter how picturesque they might seem. For example the casbah may not be safe. Below are some of the highlights.

Chateauneuf (Oasr el-Bey; Bey's Castle) (*Rue Meftah Kouider;* ⊕ *09.00–16.00 Sat–Wed; DA20*) It's hard to miss this large, fortified construction *en route* from the sea to the city centre. Traces of various periods remain, from its dynastic origin to the subsequent additions by the Spanish, Turks and French. Despite its pedigree, there isn't much to see here. Ask the guard to let you in and you can wander through the rather rundown and derelict remains. Plans for its future have stalled.

The Grand Mosque (Pasha's Mosque) (⊕ *to the public when not being used for prayers*). Situated alongside the western side of the Bey's Castle, the mosque was constructed in 1797.

Theatre de Verdure To the east of the palace is this open-air venue best known for hosting the annual *rai* festival held in late August early September. At that time, it's the liveliest place in town.

Place du 1er Novembre The grand square, known as Place d'Armes from its French days, has a huge fountain and monument to Winged Victory (the Greek Goddess Nike) and is the heart of tourist Oran as well as a popular place for the locals to linger. Located within it are two of the city's flagship attractions. The **Town Hall** stems from 1882 (take a peek inside if it's open) and the **National Theatre** built a couple of decades later, sometimes open to the public to take a look outside of performances.

Sacre Coeur This large, domed and elaborately decorated former church looks more Turkish than French. The retro architectural style is distinctive and the deconsecrated building now functions as a university library. If possible, try to get inside but if not, the outside and its detailing still warrant more than a passing glance.

Great Synagogue of Oran Close to the Sacre Coeur is a large imposing structure that served as the city's main synagogue for the once large Jewish population, up until the 1970s. By then, most of the Jews had moved to Europe or Israel and rather than becoming disused, the building was converted into a mosque. Non-Muslims are not allowed to enter.

Santa Cruz It's hard to miss this fortress and church sitting on top of Murdjadjo, the hill rising up over the port. The fort was built by the Spanish in the late 1500s, and was part of a chain of fortifications constructed to protect their interests. The chapel was built more than three centuries later by the French although the church has been around for only about 50 years. The religious structures can be visited, but the main point of the visit is the view. Oran spreads below and the vistas both day and night are spectacular. Despite the temptation to walk, it's best to take a taxi, for both the distance and circuitous route, as well as for safety.

Museum Zabana (*Bd Zabana;* \ *041 40 37 81;* ⊕ *08.30–12.00 & 13.30–17.00 Sat– Thu; DA20*). Oran's museum covers the natural and political history of the city, as well as finds from the eras of its various occupiers, including the Romans.

Beaches Although the strands in the city are not recommended, close by are little village beaches that offer far better swimming and sunbathing opportunities. These strands are not secrets, and the locals not only know about these places but also crowd them out on weekends, especially in the summer. Try **Ain el-Turk**, a resort to the west that also has the best nightlife, as well as **Les Andalouses**, a few kilometres past it. Supposedly the supreme beach in the region is the cove of **Madagh**, just a bit further along. A taxi will get you there, or if you have your own transport take the road along the coast.

HOW TO GET TO THE ROMAN SITES Excursions to the Roman sites are offered from Algiers or other centres closer to the ruins, although local tour operators would be happy to arrange something for you. It might be easier and cheaper to take a flight, train, bus or shared or private taxi to the capital and book a trip from there. If on a tour or cruise, visits to the sites will most likely be included. Two major Roman cities, Tipasa and Cherchell (Iol Caesarea) are located on the northwest coast of the country, but they are better viewed on a day trip from nearby Algiers, than as a fairly long journey from Oran. Despite the fact that this region is one of the safer ones in Algeria, it is not recommended that you travel independently by car.

BEJAIA *Telephone code 034*

The main centre in the Kabylie district, the Berber city of Bejaia has quite a different feel from the other Arabic/Islamic parts of the country. The nearby mountain region is a base for militant ethnic movements, and can be dangerous to travel through. However, Bejaia, with its 150,000 population and its importance as a major port, is quite safe. Despite its position as a Mediterranean harbour, it's known mostly as a resort town due to its proximity to some of the most beautiful beaches in Algeria. Ferries cross from France and cruise ships also stop.

HISTORY The Phoenicians acknowledged the bayside location and set up a small trading post, followed by the Carthaginians. The Romans, following in their footsteps, established the unimportant veteran colony of Saldae, under the auspices of Emperor Vespasian by AD100. No doubt a pleasant beach resort even in those days for retired soldiers, the settlement never made much of a mark until the Vandals arrived around 429. For over 100 years, this was their North African capital, until the Byzantines, or late Romans, destroyed it in their reconquest of 533. Only when the Hammadid dynasty and its head, En Nasser, arrived, did the city's fortune revive, when it was declared the capital and eponymously renamed En Nassria. Subsequently attacked by the Moroccan Almodhads in 1152, then the Hafsids of Tunisia 100 years later, by 1600 the location operated as a haven for the notorious Barbary pirates. The Spanish came and went, as did the Ottoman Turks, and it wasn't until the crushing assault and subsequent takeover by the French, who renamed the city Bougie, in 1833, that the activities of the pirates ceased. It celebrated independence in 1962 along with the rest of the country.

GETTING THERE AND AROUND

By air At the time of writing, the local airport, Abbane Ramdane, was not operational. The closest air terminal is about 100km to the south, at Setif, (*named '8 May 1945';* ✆ *036 93 31 40*).

By bus It's possible to take a bus from Setif Airport, although it's not recommended for safety reasons. By the time security and transfer concessions are allowed for, it might be easier simply to take the four-hour bus journey from Algiers. At present, this land journey is the only regular, secure route.

By sea Algerie Ferries (✆ *+39 010 5731805; www.traghettiweb.it/en/tw_index.php*) Boats cross from Marseille to Bejaia (✆ *034 21 18 07*) in about 22 hours. Some cruise lines stop here.

By taxi Bejaia is small enough to discover on foot, but if wheels are necessary it's simple to hail or phone for taxis from the hotel or flag them down around the main square.

TOURIST INFORMATION

🄾 **The Office of Tourism (ONAT)** 31 Rue Ahmed Ougana; ✆ 034 21 20 22

🄾 **Direction du Tourisme Wilaya** ✆ 034 21 16 30

TOUR OPERATORS

Bejaia Tours Rue Krim Belkacem; ✆ 034 20 66 25

Sarazine Tours Av des Freres Amrane, Port Sarasine; ✆ 034 22 67 69

WHERE TO STAY Most visitors come to Bejaia for the seaside, and it's not surprising that most of the tourist accommodation lies outside the centre. The resort of Tichy, about 15km to the east, is more geared to visitors and has a greater selection of places to stay, and the beach is nice.

Town
Mid-range

🏠 **Hotel Madala** Rue Hassiba ben Bouali; ✆ 034 21 52 92. A decent modern hotel, located in the newer part of town. $$–$$$

🏠 **Hotel Royal** Rte de l' Université; ✆ 034 21 69 40. A reasonable place to stay that's a bit far from the city centre. $$–$$$

Budget

⌂ **Hotel Etoile** Pl du 1er Novembre; ✆ 034 21 18 00. Among the few cheaper hotels that come recommended, this one includes a well-attended café & is centrally situated. $$

Tichy
Mid-range

⌂ **Hôtel Club Alloui** ✆ 034 23 58 62. A buzzing place that's a reasonable hotel. Facilities include a pizzeria, nightclub, games room, swimming pool & a view of the bay. $$$

⌂ **La Grande Terrasse** ✆ 034 23 53 13. Situated where the action is, this trendy hotel has a restaurant & a terrace overlooking the sea. $$$
⌂ **Les Hammadites** ✆ 034 23 57 00. This 3-star complex located on 'the golden sands' has what many tourists want, including a disco. $$$

✗ **WHERE TO EAT** There's not much going on in **Bejaia**, although cafés abound, and its possible to grab something quick at one of the various fast-food places. Some of the bigger city centre hotels might offer meals.

Tichy The tourist complexes usually include a café, cafeteria or even a restaurant. Generally the cuisine is French oriented with lots of seafood. There isn't much to choose between them.

✗ **Green Room** Seafront. This hangout has a somewhat sophisticated ambience that attracts a youthful clientele to its restaurant & bar. $$$

✗ **La Corniche** Baie Sidi Yahia. $$
✗ **Le Diplomate** 13 Rue des Freres Kara. $$
✗ **Petit Bateau** 10 Rue Si El Houes. $$

ENTERTAINMENT AND NIGHTLIFE

As with the restaurants, most of the excitement of the evening is in Tichy. Activities tend to take place in the summer so it's probable that if you're travelling during the week, especially outside the months of June, July and August, not much will be going on. During the season, raucous discos line the coast, with *rai* being the predominant musical style. The hotel resorts also offer things to do in the evening including the **Hôtel Club Alloui**, **La Grande Terrasse** and **Les Hammadites**. The **Green Room** also has a bar.

SHOPPING

Rue Larbi Ben M'hidi Between Pl Gueydon & Pl Medjahed. This automobile-free street has some small, but intriguing stores, as well as a supermarket, where you can buy basic foodstuffs.

OTHER PRACTICALITIES
Emergency telephone numbers

Police ✆ 17

Fire department ✆ 14

Hospitals

✚ **Hospital of Bejaia** ✆ 034 21 01 01

WHAT TO SEE

Place Gueydon This is the square overlooking the port (less commonly known as the Place du 1er Novembre). There are a few notable buildings, including the French colonial-style Bank of Algeria as well as the 16th-century Mosque of Sidi el Mouhoub.

Town hall The impressive 'mairie' is located on a small square at the bottom of the hill where a Roman mosaic is displayed in the main hall.

Fort Sidi Abdel Kader (*military: no entry*) This is the sea fort, one of the fortifications built by the Spanish around 1520, allegedly constructed from materials gathered from numerous Roman and Hammadite ruins. It encloses an underground cistern.

Hammadite city walls Constructed in the reign of Sultan En Nasser (1067–1141), this immense wall was once 5,000m long and flanked by high towers, manned by sentinels. There were originally six gates of which two survive today, the Bab el Bahra (Porte Sarrasin) and the Bab El Bounoude (Porte Fouka).The ancient barrier formed a vast triangle, the long side of which fronted the sea. There are no traces of the walls around the old city limits.

Kasbah In1154, the Almohad dynasty built this governmental citadel that included a mosque. In 1510, the Spanish came and constructed their fortifications on the site. When the French arrived, they continued transforming the building. The casbah is classified an historic monument and not open to the public at present.

Fort Moussa (*Pl du 1er Novembre;* ✆ *034 22 14 81*) Built and maintained by the Spanish in the first part of the 16th century, it was taken over and occupied by the Turks from 1555 to 1833.When the French arrived, it was used as a military prison until 1962. After achieving independence, the liberation army occupied the building until it was abandoned. In 1987 it was converted into the Museum of the History of Bejaia and an art gallery.

Bab el Louz Close to Fort Moussa, this narrow, cramped but picturesque historic area is being restored with UNESCO aid. The tomb of the 12th-century holy man Sidi Touati is here.

Many of Bejaia's best attractions are not in the architecture of the city, but in the scenery just outside.

Cap Carbon Less than 5km from the city centre, this beautiful area in the heights north of the city overlooking the sea is definitely worth a visit. Go through the tunnel to get a great view of Cap Carbon and the water below. This landscape is probably the main draw of Bejaia and the lighthouse is one of the tallest in the Mediterranean.

Gouraya National Park Over 1,000ha are protected in this park that borders the city of Bejaia. There is a tomb of a holy man protected here, and the site has become the destination of pilgrimages. Lots of monkeys, the Barbary apes, come out to visit.

HOW TO GET TO THE ROMAN SITES Despite its status as the Roman veteran colony of Saldae, there is very little left of the empire here. The mosaic in the town hall can be viewed, and if you are particularly astute it's possible to spot physical remnants of ancient Rome embedded in the Hammamide walls. The Bay of Aiguades, a beautiful spot on the coastal path to Cap Carbon, is believed to have been a halt for visitors since Phoenician times. The main Roman site close to Bejaia is Djemila, a very important Roman town in Algeria. The ruins are 87–95km to the southeast, depending on the route taken, and Djemila lies very close to the city of Setif, on the main road. Tiddis, another Roman city that is spectacularly located and built of the terrain's red soil, is not much further east, although it might be better reached from the next major port, Skikda. At the moment, the area between Bejaia and these locations is in the stronghold of the Kabylie, the region where the

Berber freedom movement is based, and it is not advisable to travel through here. It might be best to go to Algiers and use the capital as a base for excursions.

SKIKDA *Telephone code 038*

Despite its position on a scenic section of the Mediterranean coast, Skikda is primarily an industrial city and has little to offer the tourist. The port is very important to the Algerians as a major export outlet for many of the country's assets, particularly its fossil fuels. Cruise ships will sometimes stop here, but more as an access point for visits inland, including the city of Constantine (see page 211). If a free afternoon arises, there are a few things to see that will help pass the time.

HISTORY The Phoenicians found the bay convenient for their activities, and they established the city of Russicada. The Romans who followed renamed it Rusicade and it housed a small settlement, although the town didn't really make much of a mark in the annals of history. The Vandals trashed the place when they marched through in the 5th century and not much was heard of Rusicade again. When the French arrived in the early 19th century, they found the location useful, and built the city of Philippeville. Unfortunately, a little over a century later, the name became immortalised as the site of hostilities during the Algerian struggle for independence. In 1955, locals took up arms, rising against the *pieds noirs* and leaving over 100 fatalities. The French militia responded fiercely, resulting in deaths of between 1,200 and 12,000 depending on which side did the estimation. Soon after, the discovery of natural resources lying deep within the ground helped the city to gain prominence. After independence, Skikda became one of the country's richest cities.

As a tribute to the fertility of the region, the three-day Festival of the Strawberry is held every May to celebrate the profusion of fruit that grows here, complete with folkloric troupes and artisans selling their wares.

GETTING THERE AND AROUND

By air There is no airport in Skikda and if travelling by plane the alternative ports are at Constantine, about 75km to the south, or Annaba, around 90km to the east.

By bus Buses go from Constantine and Annaba. Skikda's bus terminus is in the centre of town.

By rail A station exists, but it is used mostly by industry and almost never by tourists.

By sea Algerie Ferries (+39 010 5731805; www.traghettiweb.it/en/tw_index.php). Crossing from Marseille to Skikda takes about 22 hours. Some cruise lines stop here. The port is located close to the city centre.

By taxi If walking isn't sufficient, it's best to get around by taxi. They are plentiful and relatively inexpensive.

TOURIST INFORMATION
Office of Tourism (ONAT) Rue Rezki-Kahal; 038 75 69 15
Syndicat d'Initiatives 4 Rue Didouche-Mourad; 038 75 61 14

 WHERE TO STAY As the city is small and predominantly industrial, there are few hotels. Many visitors stay at nearby beach resorts, and Collo, some kilometres to the west, is a popular place. Locals can make it very busy in the summer. However, as this village has a history of being one of the havens for terrorists, it's important that you check the current situation before heading there.

Town

🏠 **Hotel Es Salam** (300 beds) Pl du 24 Février; ✆ 038 75 39 90. The best option for tourists, this hotel is situated on a hill, granting good views over the town, & also has an excellent fish restaurant. $$$

🏠 **Hotel Terminus** (32 beds) Pl du Gare. Simple, but well located, this place is adequate for a short stay & has a restaurant. $$

🏠 **Auberge de Jeunesse** Cite Freres Saker; ✆ 038 75 54 18; www.hihostels.com/dba/ hostels-Skikda-001049.en.htm (info only). Opened in 2005, this youth hostel offers clean, extremely basic, but very cheap lodgings. $

Collo

🏠 **Hotel Torche** (72 beds) Teleza; ✆ 038 71 76 66. A beachside hotel located some distance from the centre of Collo, but compensated for by its shuttle buses into town in the summer. $$$$

🏠 **Bougaroun** (150 beds) Rue Rouibah-Tahar, Ain El Doula; ✆ 038 91 55 00. This good-value 3-star accommodation has a swimming pool, restaurant & private beach. $$$

✖ **WHERE TO EAT** There are the usual cafés and local fast-food places, but within the centre of town, there is nowhere recommended. The nearby beach towns have decent food, particularly in high season, and some of the resorts serve cuisine.

ENTERTAINMENT AND NIGHTLIFE The city is not a party town, and outside of sitting at cafés, whatever nightlife there might be is more likely to be located in the beach areas. Some of the resorts have discos.

SHOPPING

Didouche Mourad Skikda's main street is filled with stores, as well as places to take an indoor or outdoor coffee or mint tea break.

OTHER PRACTICALITIES

Emergency telephone numbers

Police ✆ 17

Fire department ✆ 14

Internet cafés Mainly on Didouche Mourad.

WHAT TO SEE

Colonial architecture There are many good examples of the city's incarnation as the French 19th-century Philippeville, including the theatre and the courthouse. It's worth taking a stroll around the centre to examine them. The train station and town hall, designed by Le Corbusier in 1936, warrant a look, especially the Islamic-influenced town hall and the nearby town museum (*free*) which holds a collection of Roman items from the days of Rusicade, including coins and statues, as well as a skeleton of one of the town's ancient inhabitants. There are also various items dating from the French period.

Views Clamber up any of the hills to get good views of the city and scenery beyond.

Stora This fishing village with its lighthouse is located a few kilometres outside Skikda, along the coast just east of the Grand Plage. It's a pleasant walk, with the option of taking a taxi if going both ways is too much.

HOW TO GET TO THE ROMAN SITES Unfortunately, what little traces of the Roman town of Rusicade that are left are buried under modern construction. The theatre that once held 6,000 seats is hidden under a school. Outside Skikda, but virtually invisible, are the last of the ancient cisterns. Nearby Constantine is a city with its own Roman remains and proximity to other sites, such as Tiddis, and there is a regular bus that leaves from the Skikda city centre bus station to go the 75km south to get there. Another location is Annaba, which has the important remains of Hippo Regius, especially those from the period of the city's most famous resident, St Augustine (AD391–430). This site can also be reached via a scheduled bus service from Skikda, a journey of about 90km.

13

Algiers

Telephone code 021

The political and cultural heart of Algeria lies within the capital city of Algiers, also known as Alger and Al Djazair. With around three million people divided unevenly within the limits of the city (the Casbah area has a history of being densely packed, the suburbs are more spacious), almost 10% of the population of the country lives here. The history of the city can be seen in the variety of today's inhabitants, from the darker colours of the people from the south, to the lighter-skinned descendants of the French colonists. Algeria has the largest percentage of Berbers in the Maghreb and the ethnic group is well represented here, most obviously in the fluent use of the language, which differs greatly from Arabic and French. A fairly recent contribution to the racial mix is the Chinese community. These immigrants have been drawn here by the need for labour in a place where construction is being done on a massive scale and being funded by the country's enormous fossil fuel wealth. With such endemic diversity, visitors from virtually any destination fit right in.

Officially a secular country, the influence of Islam, to which 99% of the population adhere, remains strong. Headscarves are not mandatory for women, yet many choose to wear them. Traditional clothing can be seen, but perhaps not as much as in either the provinces or other big cities. Algiers is a modern capital, and fashion for those who choose to follow it is as important here as in many of the centres in France. For the visitor, wearing Western styles is fine, as long as it is done with respect for the Muslim traditions. Miniskirts, shorts, tank tops and other skimpy clothing should be reserved for the poolside or beach resorts.

Algiers is located on the hills above what some consider one of the most beautiful bays on the Mediterranean. The city, known as 'the White' in French, is so labelled due to the colour of many of the buildings. Trims of blue and other shades add to the appeal. Today Algiers is divided into more or less three parts. The lowest area is predominantly French, left over from the colonial period. Here the old Algerian residences were cleared to make way for the 19th-century wide streets and grandiose constructions such as the theatres, cathedrals and educational establishments, which remain today. The upper part is the Casbah, the French name for the medina, or old town. Legendary for its claustrophobic and densely packed atmosphere and its sense of danger, this ancient district is one of the most intriguing in the Maghreb. Immortalised in films, this enclosed city within a city houses a citadel, mosques, ancient palaces and architectural gems hidden among decaying residences. The third area, and probably the part of least interest to the tourist, is the suburbs, where urban sprawl is taking over. The government is engaged in a massive building programme to supply housing, and much of their effort is visible here.

Unfortunately, Algiers is the capital of a country that is still prone to militant attacks, and some of these events occur in the main city. It's important to be constantly on guard, especially in packed areas such as the Casbah. Periodically, foreign embassies advise their nationals not to visit. If planning to come here, be aware of what is going on and check for the latest updates of the situation.

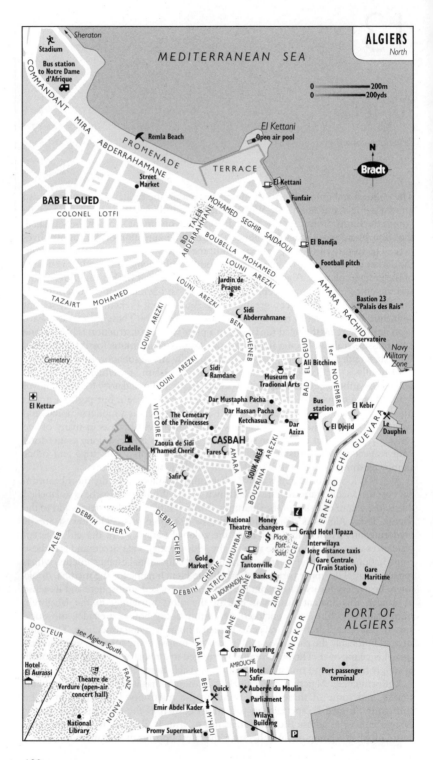

ALGIERS
North

MEDITERRANEAN SEA

Sheraton

Stadium

Bus station
to Notre Dame
d'Afrique

COMMANDANT MIRA ABDERRAHAMANE

PROMENADE

Remla Beach

El Kettani
Open air pool

TERRACE

El Kettani

Funfair

Street
Market

BAB EL OUED

COLONEL LOTFI

MOHAMED SEGHIR SAIDAOUI

BD TALEB ABDERRAHMANE

BOUBELLA MOHAMED

El Bandja

Football pitch

LOUNI AREZKI

LOUNI AREZKI

Jardin de
Prague

AMARA RACHID

Bastion 23
"Palais des Rais"

TAZAIRT MOHAMED

Sidi
Abderrahmane

BEN CHENEB

Conservatoire

Navy
Military
Zone

Cemetery

LOUNI AREZKI

Sidi
Ramdane

Ali Bitchine

BAD EL OUED

1er NOVEMBRE

El Kettar

LOUNI AREZKI

Museum of
Tradional Arts

Dar Mustapha Pacha

Bus
station

El Kebir

VICTOIRE

The Cemetary
of the Princesses

Dar Hassan Pacha

Ketchaoua

Dar
Aziza

El Djejid

Le
Dauphin

Citadelle

Zaouia de Sidi
M'hamed Cherif

Fares

CASBAH

AMARA ALI

SOUK AREA

BOUZRINA AREZKI

ERNESTO CHE GUEVARA

Safir

DEBBIH CHERIF

DEBBIH CHERIF

National
Theatre

Money
changers

Grand Hotel Tipaza

TALEB

Gold
Market

PATRICA LUMUMBA

Café
Tantonville

Place
Port
Said

Interwilaya
long distance taxis

Gare Centrale
(Train Station)

Gare
Maritime

DEBBIH CHERIF

AU BOUMANDJEL

Banks

DOCTEUR

see Algiers South

FRANZ FANNON

ABANE RAMDANE

ZIROUT YOUCEF

ANGKOR

PORT OF
ALGIERS

Hotel
El Aurassi

Theatre de
Verdure (open-air
concert hall)

LARBI

Central Touring

AMROUCHE

Hotel
Safir

Port passenger
terminal

National
Library

BEN M'HIDI

Quick

Emir Abdel Kader

Promy Supermarket

Auberge du Moulin

Parliament

Wilaya
Building

0   200m
0   200yds

N

Bradt

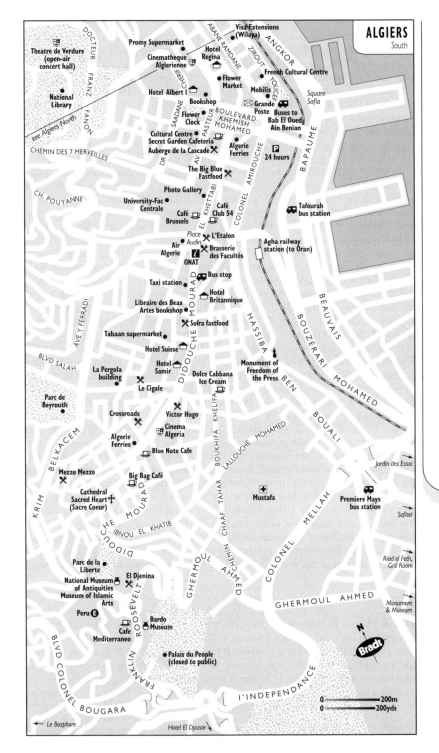

Theatre de Verdure
(open-air
concert hall)

DOCTEUR

FRANZ FANON

National
Library

see Algiers North

CHEMIN DES 7 MERVEILLES

CH. POUYANNE

AVE J FERRADI

BLVD SALAH

Parc de
Beyrouth

BELKACEM

KRIM

Mezzo Mezzo

Cathedral
Sacred Heart
(Sacre Coeur)

Big Bag Café

Parc de la
Liberte

National Museum
of Antiquities
Museum of Islamic
Arts

Peru

Cafe
Mediterraneo

BLVD COLONEL BOUGARA

← Le Bosphore

ABANE RAMDANE

Promy Supermarket

Cinematheque
Algierienne

Hotel Albert I

Flower
Clock

Cultural Centre
Secret Garden Cafeteria
Auberge de la Cascade

DR   AV PASTEUR   SAADANE

Visa Extensions
(Wilaya)

Hotel
Regina

Flower
Market

Bookshop

BOULEVARD
KHEMISH
MOHAMED

The Big Blue
Fastfood

Photo Gallery

University-Fac
Centrale

Café
Brussels

Air
Algerie

Place
Audin

ONAT

Taxi station

Libraire des Beax
Artes bookshop

Tabaan supermarket

Hotel Suisse

Hotel
Samir

La Pergola
building

Le Cigale

Crossroads

Algerie
Ferries

Blue Note Cafe

EL KHETTABI

Café
Club 54

L'Etalon

Brasserie
des Facultés

Bus stop

Hotel
Britannique

Sofra fastfood

DIDOUCHE MOURAD

Dolce Cabbana
Ice Cream

Victor Hugo

Cinema
Algeria

IBNOU EL KHATIB

DIDOUCHE MOURAD

El Djenina

FRANKLIN ROOSEVELT

Cafe
Bardo
Museum

Palais du People
(closed to public)

GHERMOUL AHMED

CHEMIN AHMED

BOUKHIFA KHELIFA

HASSIBA BEN BOUALI

Monument of
Freedom of
the Press

LALLOUCHE MOHAMED

CHAAF TAHAR

Mustafa

COLONEL AMIROUCHE

ZIROUT JOUCEF

ANGKOR

Mobilis

Grande
Poste

24 hours

BAPAUME

French Cultural Centre

Square
Sofia

Buses to
Bab El Oued
Ain Benian

Algerie
Ferries

Tafourah
bus station

Agha railway
station (to Oran)

BOUZERARI MOHAMED

BEAUVAIS

COLONEL MELLAH

Premiere Mays
bus station

Jardin des Essai

Sofitel

Riad el Feth,
Grill Room

GHERMOUL AHMED

Monument
& Museum

N

Bradt

0   200m
0   200yds

l'INDEPENDANCE

Hotel El Djazair

ALGIERS
South

Algeria: Algiers

13

191

A coin has been found that shows a settlement on the site of today's city dating from around 700BC. It was most likely built by the passing Phoenicians as a trading post and later taken over by their heirs into the Carthaginian Empire. The town was given the name Ikosium, and legend has it that the place was set up by 20 friends of Hercules ('eikosi' means 20, in Greek). After the defeat of the Carthaginians in the Third Punic War, Ikosium was absorbed by the Romans as part of the spoils, and renamed Icosium. The city went the way of the rest of the empire, being ravaged by the Vandals by AD450, retaken by the Byzantines and then overwhelmed and acquired by the Arabs around AD650, during their conquest.

In AD950, the founder of the Zirid dynasty, Bologhin Ibin Ziri, changed the name of Icosium to Al Djazair, allegedly coming from 'gzir', the four islets guarding the entrance to the city's bay. Algiers's history then follows the pattern of the country's other coastal cities, with the Berber dynasties battling between themselves over the next 550 years. At the end of this period, Spain began trading with Algeria and by 1516 the Spanish threatened the city to such a degree that the locals called upon Aruj, the first of the Barbarossa pirates, to come and help them defeat the aggressors. Enlisting the assistance of the powerful Ottomans, Algeria became part of their empire for the next century. By the end of the century, the city became independent and the centre of operations for the Barbary pirates. Foreign powers were getting fed up with the attacks and in 1815, the United States navy headed by Captain Stephen Decatur, stormed the city of Al Djazair, demanding and receiving assurances that American ships would never again be attacked by Algerian pirates. The following year, Dutch and British forces followed suit. However, it wasn't until 1830, when the French came and devastated the last of the pirates, that privateering really stopped.

Once situated, the French weren't going to leave, and they remained in control until the country gained its independence in 1962. Al Djazair was renamed Alger. During World War II, still under French auspices, Algiers quartered the Allies in 1942 and a year later Charles de Gaulle set up the centre of Free France activities. By the 1950s, the French yoke became too much for the Algerians to bear, and revolts and cries for independence began to incur serious consequences. The attacks, repercussions and casualties that raged through the country during this time were figure-headed in the capital. Eventually, freedom was won, although many of the city's residents left for other countries immediately after. Renamed Al Djazair, the capital continued to bear the brunt of the nation's difficulties, including the effective civil war of the 1990s. Emerging as a European-style metropolis, Algiers has become very important in the modern world. A major capital, it represents a country that takes part in organisations such as OPEC, due to its oil reserves and production, the Organisation of African Unity and the Arab League. As the focus of Algeria to the rest of the world, it continues to be the location of national disquiet.

GETTING THERE AND AROUND

BY AIR Houari Boudemdiene Airport (↘ 021 50 91 00; www.algiersairport.free.fr) accepts both international and domestic traffic, and is located about 20km from the centre of Algiers. The new international terminal opened in 2006 and is spacious and surprisingly accessible, considering its stylish décor. The domestic branch, which most tourists are likely to see at some point considering the difficulties of travelling via any means other than air, is much more basic. There are bus shuttles between airport and town that run whenever they seem to feel like it, so it might be easier to pay around DA1,000 for a taxi. Alternatively, if travelling with a tour group, transport will have been arranged.

BY SEA The ferry companies that do the 23-hour ferry crossing from Marseille include Algerie Ferries (*www.algerieferries.com*) and SNCM Ferryterranee (+39 010 5731805; *www.traghettiweb.it/en/tw_index.php*). There are other companies that make the crossing, but they go indirectly via other cities, either in Europe or Algeria.

BY CAR Certainly not a wise option, it's theoretically possible to enter Algeria via a car ferry from Europe. The only land border that's open at the moment is from Tunisia and there is a good highway that goes from its capital, Tunis, to the Algerian city of Annaba, just past the frontier. Once within the country, driving is dangerous, with poor drivers causing a phenomenal number of accidents, and repeated security blockades slowing down journeys. There are a few reasonable highways.

Car hire Driving in Algeria in general is not recommended. If you need a private car, especially in Algiers, it might be worth hiring a vehicle with a driver. If a rental car is definitely required, it will probably be easiest to obtain one here in the capital.

🚗 **Djafricar** 98 Bd Colonel Krim Belkacem; 021 72 84 97
🚗 **Olympic Automobiles** 4 Rue Chebout Abdelkrim, Hussein Dey; 021 77 19 41
🚗 **Prestige Car** Lot Med Saidoune, Kouba; 021 28 20 33
🚗 **Rapid Car** Hotel El Aurassi; 021 74 82 52
🚗 **Rapid Location** Cite 1er Novembre 54, Bt 1 & 2, Dar El Beida; 021 50 61 12

BY TRAIN There are no international services. Domestic trains are run by SNTF (*www.sntf.dz/home.php*), with two main train stations in Algiers that make the journeys to other large cities. The Gare Central (*Direction Generale, Bd Mohamed V;* 021 71 15 10) is located close to the port and the terminal for eastbound trains to Bejaia, Setif, Constantine and Annaba. The Gare de l'Agha (*nr Rue Hassiba ben Bouali;* 021 71 15 10) is the station for trains to the west, including Oran.

BY BUS The long-distance bus station, the Gare Routiere (*Hussein Dey;* 021 49 71 51), is located somewhat out of the way along the coast, to the south of town. A local bus, the 134, gets there from Audin, but allow for a bit of a walk as well as extra time, in case it decides to run to its own schedule. From the station, buses run to most of the major cities in the country. Sample times are from six hours to Oran and from nine hours to Annaba.

Locally, the Place 1er Mai is probably the best location from which to take a bus, as there are several routes through the city that can be reached from here. It's also possible to catch a bus at Audin, Bab el Oued, the Place des Martyrs and the Place Grand Poste.. Although walking is often a good alternative, the city is large and if you are travelling independently, going by bus or taxi is inevitable.

BY TAXI It's as difficult to get a taxi here in rush hour as in any other big city. Some taxis are equipped with meters, but it might still be best to ask the driver the cost, to get an idea before starting out. It's possible to phone for a taxi, best from the hotel, but prices are higher and there's no guarantee the car will arrive on time.

🚗 **Radio Taxi** 021 56 56 56
🚗 **Taxi Minute** 021 66 66 66

There are collective taxis here too. The routes and prices are fixed and can be a good deal. Cruising the main streets (Audin is a good place to start), they usually have their final destinations written somewhere on the front of the car. Hail one, and it's bound to pick you up if there's room inside.

TOURIST INFORMATION

The main tourist board, the Office National du Tourisme, is at 2 Rue Ismail Kerrar (☏ *021 71 30 60; www.ont-dz.org*).

TOUR OPERATORS

ONAT www.onat-dz.com. Has several locations: Aéroport Houari Boumédiene; ☏ 021 50 94 80; 2 Rue Didouche Mourad; ☏ 021 63 79 17; 5 Bd Ben Boulaïd; ☏ 021 71 85 71; 25 Rue Khelifa Boukhalfa; ☏ 021 74 33 03; Riadh El Feth; ☏ 021 67 12 50
Club d'Aventures Africaines 7 Rue des Freres Oughlis, El-Mouradia; ☏ 021 69 79 22; www.caa-dz.com. Specialists in desert excursions, they also organise trips to the Roman sites.

L'ile de l'Occident 98 Bois des Cars; ☏ 021 30 01 34; www.liledeloccident.com. Covers all Algeria & offers specialist cultural tours including the ancient Roman cities.
Touring Voyages Algerie Centre Commercial El Hammadia-Bouzareah; ☏ 021 54 13 13; www.touring-algerie.com. A general agency that provides most services, & also gives themed tours, including the Roman Cities of Algeria.

WHERE TO STAY

Algiers has lots of hotels, but the best, and even decent, ones are pricey. The really cheap places are pretty rough and have few facilities. There are no youth hostels within Algiers itself. Relinquish your dinars here for a good place to stay in the city and save them in other parts of the country.

TOP END

⌂ **Hotel Al Djazair** (296 rooms) 24 Av Souidani Boudjamaa; ☏ 021 69 21 21; www.hoteleldjazair.dz. Formerly the St George's, this hotel built in 1889 is overwhelmed with history & charm & undoubtedly the city's old-world best. Don't miss the fabulous gardens, even if coming only for afternoon tea. $$$$$+
⌂ **Sofitel** (331 rooms) 172 Rue Hassiba Ben Bouali; ☏ 021 68 52 10; www.sofitel.com/sofitel/fichehotel/gb/sof/1540/fiche_ho tel.shtml. This beautiful hotel is extremely convenient for the city centre & is particularly useful for business people. $$$$$+

⌂ **Hotel El Aurassi** (455 rooms) 2 Bd Frantz Fanon; ☏ 021 74 82 52; www.el-aurassi.com. A block hotel with gardens & a pool, but the fabulous view is what recommends it most. $$$$$
⌂ **Sheraton Club des Pins Resort and Towers** (419 rooms) Staoueli; ☏ 021 37 77 77; www.starwoodhotels.com/sheraton/property/overview/in dex.html?propertyID=1160. With the distance from the city centre compensated for by its location on the beach, this Sheraton offers all the facilities of a 5-star hotel. $$$$$

MID-RANGE

⌂ **Hotel Albert I** 5 Av Pasteur; ☏ 021 73 65 06. Perhaps a bit basic for the price, this colonial-style hotel is superbly situated, right in the middle of the city. $$-$$$
⌂ **Hotel Regina** 27 Bd Ben Boulaid; ☏ 021 74 00 35. Not far from the port & Algiers's centre, this hotel is good value for money. $$-$$$

⌂ **Hotel Safir** 2 Rue Asselah Hocine; ☏ 021 73 50 40. It's possible to get a sea view for a price supplement from this historic harbourside hotel, that once was one of the best in town — things have changed a little since then. $$-$$$

BUDGET

⌂ **Central Touring Hotel** 9 Rue Abane Ramdane; ☏ 021 73 76 44. This popular & central hotel is one of the better inexpensive options. $

⌂ **Grand Hotel Tipaza** 4 Rue Rachad Kessentini. Very basic backpackers' accommodation, it's noisy & offers only shared showers, but convenient, & cheap. $

✘ WHERE TO EAT

As usual, some of the best places to have a meal are within the hotels. Prices are relatively low, and the atmosphere usually quite international. The in-hotel eating venues are conveniently located, especially if you're staying within the relevant accommodation, and the quality is reliable. Algiers also has its share of good restaurants, and it's well worth getting away from the big places, at least once, to see how the locals eat.

HOTELS

✘ **Al Djazair** The Taous is the hotel's; the Pavillon de Confucius has Chinese specialities; & the Brasserie Les Voutes is less formal. $$$$$

✘ **Hotel Mercure** Near the airport, Rte de l'Université, BP 12, 5 Juillet, Bab Ezzouar; ☎ 021 24 59 70; www.accorhotels.com/accorhotels/fichehotel/gb/mer/3173/fiche_restaurant.shtml. Three restaurants are here: the Mediterranean El Beida; & the two themed places, the El Behdja & the Mu Dan. $$$$$

✘ **Sheraton** There are several places, including La Brasserie, with good European-style eating; La Dorade serving Mediterranean cuisine; La Trattoria, good Italian food; Le Tassili, on the 1st floor; and Le Petit Bleu, offering poolside pizza. $$$

✘ **Sofitel** The Continental, with eponymous cuisine; El Mordjane, with Algerian food; the Difa Coffee Shop. $$$-$$$$

CITY

✘ **Auberge du Moulin** 24 Rue Abane Ramdane, Cheraga; ☎ 021 36 10 73. Allegedly one of the best restaurants in town, although too far from the centre to walk. French & Algerian dishes are presented in this garden environment, enhanced by excellent service. $$$$$

✘ **Grill Room Es Sofra** Bois des Arcades, Riad El Feth; ☎ 021 67 80 41. When the craving for a decent meal whatever the price overwhelms the desire for traditional cuisine, here's the place to come. $$$$$

✘ **L'Etalon** 2 Rue Bitche; ☎ 021 61 76 84. This 3-star venue offers excellent Algerian & European food in an elegant atmosphere. $$$$$

✘ **Le Dauphin** Rampe de la Pecherie; ☎ 021 71 65 57. Expensive but worth it, this is arguably the premiere place for fish, complete with sea views & fine wines. $$$$$

✘ **Le Bosphore** Residence Chabani, Val d'Hydra; ☎ 021 60 03 18. The legacy of the Ottoman

occupation lingers in the first-rate Turkish cuisine of this popular place. $$$$

✘ **Brasserie des Facultés** 1 Rue Didouche Mourad; ☎ 021 63 40 21. This university-side restaurant can get overcrowded with slightly better-off incoming students, but the cuisine is worth the extra price. $$$

✘ **Quick** Pl Amir Abdel Kader; ☎ 021 71 37 52. Also at Rue Sidi Yahia, Hydra. The first major fast-food chain to show up here. $$$

✘ **Café Tantonville** 7 Pl Port Said; ☎ 021 74 86 61. Just next to the National Theatre, this cheap & cheerful restaurant has long had its fans & its self-service annex is equally popular. $$-$$$

☕ **Café Brussels** 2 Rue Didouche Mourad; ☎ 021 63 37 54. Trendy, this place attracts all sorts of young(ish) people, with its selection of excellent pastries & café-style drinks. $-$$

ENTERTAINMENT AND NIGHTLIFE

The fears that linger from the dark decade of the 1990s and the recent terrorist attacks still haunt the locals. Combined with the reticence to drink, in the Muslim tradition, there is not much to do at night in Algiers outside the home. The venues that cater mostly to foreign visitors, ie: the hotels, are the best places to go to find bars and nightclubs. There are other local hangouts, but be careful as many of these are unsuitable for women and are often where the locals go to pick up prostitutes. If your French or Arabic is up to scratch, cinemas and theatres provide entertainment although for such a large city, the number of them is relatively small.

13

HOTELS

☆ **Hilton** Pins Maritimes, El Mohammadia; ☎ 021 21 96 96; www1.hilton.com/en_US/hi/hotel/ALGHIHI-Hilton-Alger-hotel/dining.do;jsessionid= 40896580B56D7A3A19FC30DD1EC8C792.etc34. The Hilton is a bit far from town, but it does have a few places to linger until early morning: the Kantara Bar ⊕ all day until midnight; the Crystal Lounge ⊕ 12.00–midnight; the Havana Lounge, to come to drink & smoke a cigar, ⊕ until midnight.

☆ **Hotel Al Djazair** The Pacha Nightclub & discotheque ⊕ Wed & Thu & the Dey Bar stays active till 01.00.

☆ **Sheraton Club des Pins** A little far from town, the bars here are probably best patronised if you're staying at the hotel: the 1001 Nights Piano Bar plays till 03.00; Le Café keeps people awake until 01.00.

☆ **Sofitel** Has 3 bars: the Casbah, with music, ⊕ 23.00–06.00; the Djamila ⊕ till 23.00; the Oasis, also with music, ⊕ until 23.00.

SHOPPING

The two main shopping streets of the city are **Rue Didouche-Mourad** and **Larbi Ben M'Hidi**. Many international stores are here, mostly from France, and prices are comparable to Europe. Look out for bookshops on Didouche-Mourad.

The medina souks that are so prevalent in other North African countries are missing in the Casbah, which might be fortunate, considering the security problems. There are **markets** near the Mosque Ketchoua (lower Casbah) and the Bab el Oued.

Riad El Feth Macham ech Chaid, El Madania. This large commercial centre has lots of boutiques showing off traditional crafts, as well as bookshops & an art gallery.

Societe Nationale de l'Artisanat Traditionel (SNAT) 2 Bd Mohamed-Khemisti & 1 Bd du Front de Mer, Bab el Oued

OTHER PRACTICALITIES

EMERGENCY TELEPHONE NUMBERS
Police ☎ 17
Ambulance ☎ 021 73 69 69

Medical ☎ 115
Security ☎ 112

HOSPITALS
✚ **Hospital Bab El Oued** Bab El Oued; ☎ 021 57 02 22
✚ **Hospital Hussein Dey** Hussein Day; ☎ 021 59 82 00

✚ **Hospital Mustapha** Pl du 1er Mai; ☎ 021 67 33 33

INTERNET CAFÉS Most hotels have internet access. Internet cafés appear and disappear virtually spontaneously. Here are some that will hopefully stick around.

🄴 **Cyber ADSL** 53 Rue Larbi ben M'hidi
🄴 **Cyber SOLI** 16 Rue Hassiba ben Bouali

🄴 **Orange Net** 1 Rue Hassiba ben Bouali
🄴 **Planet Internet** Rue Didouche Mourad

POST The main post office, grand poste, is located on the place with the same name. Another branch is at 119 Rue Didouche Mourad.

BANKS The better hotels will swap money for Algerian, usually at a worse rate than the banks. In town the following, among others, will assist foreign transactions.

$ **Banque d'Algerie** 8 Bd Zirout Youcef; ☏ 021 73 96 73
$ **Banque Nationale d'Algerie** 8 Bd Ernesto Che Guevara; ☏ 021 71 35 19; www.bank-of-algeria.dz/banque.htm

$ **Credit Populaire d'Algerie** 2 Bd du Colonel Amirouche; ☏ 021 63 57 05; www.cpa-bank.dz
$ **Société Generale** 75 Chemin Cheikh Bachir El Ibrahimi, El Biar; ☏ 021 92 92 00; groupe.socgen.com/bhfm/sga/gb/___algeria_a.htm

WHAT TO SEE

Much of what's worth seeing in Algiers is packed in a relatively small area, especially around the Casbah, but other attractions can seem to be quite far. Because of security issues it's best if sightseeing is done either in groups or accompanied by an official guide. If going it alone, it might be wise to hire a taxi for part or all of the day. That way, knowledge of the locations can be provided, and transport will be waiting for you wherever you want to go.

MONUMENT (MAKKAM ECHCHAHID) On the way from the airport to the centre, it's hard to miss an enormous hilltop concrete sculpture that looks like a tripod. This three-pronged 92m-high construction is the Monument to the Martyrs, built in 1982 to commemorate those people killed in defence of their country, particularly during the War of Independence. The 'legs' evoke the triple pillars of modern Algeria: agriculture, industry and culture. Among the locals the jury is out as to whether this memorial is a piece of artwork, or an eyesore, but there's no argument about the vista. The view from the top is spectacular. Nearby is the Riad El Feth commercial complex with some shops and cafés, as well as the Museum of the Armed Forces and the National Jihad Museum (see below).

THE CASBAH This legendary district and UNESCO World Heritage Site is probably what most tourists want to visit when they come to Algiers. Basically the remains of the ancient medina after having been somewhat ravaged and contained by the French occupiers, the Casbah's reputation, enhanced by its film depictions, is of secrecy, menace and unlawfulness. To some degree, these preconceptions are true, and it remains a somewhat dangerous area. For the present, it's virtually essential that you enter here accompanied by an official escort. If travelling with a group, and the Casbah is on the itinerary, a guide, and probably a security team, will come along. Otherwise, contact your hotel, local tour operator or police to ask for someone to show you around.

The Casbah is divided into the higher and lower sections. Tours usually drive to the top and stop just outside the walls and close to the citadel to let people out to walk down, starting at the higher Casbah. The citadel was built for the pirate Barbarossa, when he sought Ottoman aid in 1515. A royal residence, it also housed later rulers. It is currently closed for renovations. From here, the road narrows into a pedestrian-only route and slopes downwards. Look out for beautiful details such as tiles or elaborate doorways amongst the crumbling buildings. The next site is a small unassuming mosque with a minaret, barely emerging out of the wall. The 11th-century building dedicated to Sidi Ramdane is believed to be the oldest such construction. The views down to the harbour and sea beyond through the gaps on the opposite side of the street are lovely. Continuing through the streets lined with ramshackle residences built so high as to nearly block out the daylight, the route drops down. Here is where the Casbah is at its most atmospheric, with glimpses of locals seemingly disappearing into the doorways, or through archways leading into who knows where. Eventually, a larger street with car traffic is reached and, walking along, it's possible to see long sets of staircases leading back into the maze. A bit further is a building with a series of black domes and inside are some Arabic-style tombstones. Here is where the daughters of Hassan Pacha were buried, and the site is known as the Cemetery of the Princesses. The accompanied gardens are lovely, if a bit neglected, and cats appear to be on guard, allowing you to enter at their discretion. Further inside is a small building where, on Friday, people chant, lost in prayer. Non-Muslims are granted entry, although the atmosphere is deeply devout. If entered, treat the worshippers with silence and respect.

Once outside, the road drops down into the lower Casbah, a broader and busier area, reminiscent of the French period. Although the streets are broader, more modern and less claustrophobic, this area is much busier and livelier than the upper Casbah. Life bustles, with 19th-century multi-storeyed apartments garnished with balconies that drape laundry and satellite dishes. Markets spring up here and the street eventually leads to one of the city's most impressive and historic buildings, the Ketchaoua Mosque. Located on a large square, this construction dates from 1600 and was revamped almost 200 years later by Hassan Pasha, at the time he was setting up his eponymous *dar* or palace just next door (currently undergoing renovations and closed). When the French came in 1830, they converted the place into St Philippe Cathedral, and it functioned as such until Algerian independence. On the day freedom was declared, the church reverted back to being a mosque, and remains one to this day. Take a good look around, as there are traces of the Ottoman heritage sandwiched between the predominant colonial styles. The Museum of Traditional Arts, located within the Dar Khadoudja Palace is also nearby (see *Museums*, below). The Betchnine Mosque is another large religious building from 1622 that changed its religion during the French occupation.

PLACE DES MARTYRS The route down past the mosques leads into this square. The eastern side, towards the port, houses the Djamaa El Djejid. The mosque here dates from 1660 and is known variously as the Mosque of the Fishery or, ironically, the New Mosque. Normally entry to non-Muslims is banned, although tours are sometimes offered in the mornings (not on Fridays). Just past here is another Islamic icon, the Djamaa El Kebir or Great Mosque, possibly the most important in the city. Begun around 1097 and periodically rebuilt, this location is where the events of Ramadan are celebrated by the president.

SEAFRONT The route continues towards the sea and just to the north is the Palais des Rai or the Bastion 23 Museum (see *Museums*, below). It's nice to stroll along the seaside towards the Bab el Oued district. Further north and higher up is Notre Dame D'Afrique (⊕ *11.00–12.30 & 15.00–17.30; free*), a purpose-built church completed in 1872 with an impressive Byzantine-style exterior, where mass is still celebrated every evening in French, and on Friday mornings in English. The elaborate interior includes a statue of the Black Virgin. Look back towards town for good views, including the distant lighthouse that's been here for hundreds of years. To the south, towards the city centre, the seafront passes the old harbour, with fishing boats and seafood restaurants. The way continues to the commercial port.

PLACE PORT SAID This is a nice place to stroll. The interesting colonial building on the western side is the National Theatre, built in 1853 and home to live performances. Just past here is a market. The urban city begins to bustle, and many of the central buildings are located near here, such as the main railway station (just to the east, close to the sea), and the cheaper hotels near it. Further south are lots of government buildings and one of the more interesting is the grand poste, not only the main post office, but also an early 20th-century architectural landmark, done up in an Islamic, rather than a bureaucratic, style. One of the two biggest commercial streets of the city, Rue Larbi Ben M'Hidi, passes alongside the west, and the other, Didouche Morad, is the continuation of El-Khettabi, which intersects the other major thoroughfare here.

SACRE COEUR Continuing up into the hillside of the more affluent area of the city, you'll see that the modern 1962 construction of the Sacre Coeur church bears no resemblance to its famous namesake in Paris, other than its name. One of the newest icons in Algiers, it houses one of the most ancient: a mosaic of Jesus Christ dated to 324 and discovered in the town of Chlef, located about 200km west. Nearby are the Parc de la Liberté and the city's best museums, the Bardo, the Museum of Antiquities and the Museum of Islamic Arts (see *Museums*, below). Also a bit further is the Al Djazair Hotel, the former Victorian St George's, where the Allied forces during World War II had their headquarters. The lush oasis of the gardens is a great place to linger and have a tea break. If going for a drive in the area, take a good look at the beautiful villas, some of them ambassadorial residences.

GARDENS The city is full of green parks. Some of them provide great views of the city below. Ask advice and use your street sense as to which ones are safe to wander in and don't go to any of them at night. The Jardin d'Essai (*180 Rue Belouizdad Med, El Annassers; www.jardinessai.com*) is located next to the sea, close to the commercial port. This very large green space, full of plants, including some large palm groves, is very well maintained.

MUSEUMS
National Museum of Antiquities (*177 Bd Krim Belkacem;* ☎ *021 74 66 86; www.musee-antiquites.art.dz;* ⊕ *09.00–12.00 & 13.00–16.30 Sun–Thu, 13.00–16.30 Sat; DA20*) This museum close to the Parc de la Liberté and the Al Djazair Hotel is surprisingly good, especially for Roman artefacts from all the sites in Algeria. Later Islamic art is also on display.

Bardo Museum (*3 Rue Franklin Roosevelt & top of Didouche Mourad;* ☎ *021 74 76 41; www.musee-bardo.art.dz;* ⊕ *09.00–12.00 & 14.00–17.00 Sun–Thu, 14.00–17.00; DA4, DA100 for recommended guided tours*) Located within an 18th-century Ottoman palace and spectacular in its own right, this ethnographic museum has an excellent assembly of remains from the Stone Age and later periods. Included are examples and displays from the rock art of the south of the country, as well as later-era traditional crafts.

Bastion 23/Palais des Rais (*23 Bd Amara Rachid;* ☎ *021 73 95 70; www.palaisdesrais-bastion23.dz;* ⊕ *10.00–12.00 & 13.00–16.30 Sun–Thu, 13.00–16.30 Sat; DA20*) This assembly of four 16th-century buildings offers an insight into how Ottoman royalty lived, while acting as a contemporary centre of arts and culture.

Museum of Armed Forces and the National Jihad Museum (*Martyr's Monument Plaza;* ☎ *021 66 92 08;* ⊕ *09.00–17.00 daily except Sat/Sun morning; DA20*) Both are located at the Monument of the Martyrs (Makkam Echchaid) and cover the period of the French occupation 1830–1962. The former has a collection of war artefacts including a guillotine, while the latter focuses on items relating to the battle for independence.

National Museum of Fine Arts/Musée des Beaux Arts (*Pl Dar Essalam, El Hamma;* ☎ *021 66 49 16;* ⊕ *09.30–12.00 & 14.30–17.00 Sun–Thu; entry DA20*) Close to the Monument of the Martyrs, this gallery is similar to its equivalents in Western cities, with works from Algerian and European artists, including Renoir.

Museum of Traditional Arts (*9 Rue Akli Malek;* ✆ *021 73 34 14;* ⊕ *09.00–12.00 &* *14.30–17.30 daily except Fri; DA20*) A collection that resides inside a beautiful 16th-century Ottoman palace, the assembly features Algerian traditional crafts, including carpets, ceramics, furniture, jewellery and musical instruments.

THE ROMAN SITES

The entire stretch of coast that borders Algeria was extremely important to the Romans, and to their predecessors. In the heart of the southern shore of the Mediterranean and blessed with many navigable bays, it's not surprising that the Phoenician sailors established several small trading stops along here. Continuous inhabitation and development has virtually wiped out whatever was left of the Roman settlement. The Museum of Antiquities displays some of the local finds. In the region, the best Roman sites are to the west.

TIPASA (*Telephone code 024*) Located about 70km west along the coast from Algiers, this very pleasant seaside town has a reputation for being a bit of a party place, with locals from Algiers coming here to drink and relax. Buses arrive from the capital on a regular basis. The Romans must have recognised how nice the locale is, as this is one of the best-situated ruins in North Africa.

History Although the Phoenicians were here, there are no physical remnants of their habitation. It was during Emperor Claudius's reign (AD41–55) that the town become notable. Set up as one of the veteran colonies, many denizens were ex-Roman soldiers, often enlisted from outside Italy, who had served their country well. After 25 years of service, they were granted citizenship and frequently land in the provinces. Setting up villas and extremely productive fields, Tipasa became the commercial centre of the region and served the needs of the rich citizens and their 'employees' (more often than not, slaves). In addition, the seaside location allowed the harvesting of fish and manufacture of their by-products, particularly *garum*, the fish paste required on every epicurean table in Rome. The vestiges of a large tannery have been found, implying that cattle were kept.

Tipasa was an important Christian site. Much religious activity went on, including the martyrdom of St Salsa, a believer who threw a pagan idol into the sea and was stoned to death by the locals. The remains of her basilica can still be seen. The great basilica is said to be the largest Christian excavation in Algeria. Around AD400 the rebel sect, the Donatists, tried to overtake the city, but the Catholics held firm. The Arian branch succeeded in becoming the main faith, via the Vandal adherents who included Tipasa in their bid to conquer North Africa. Domination of the region alternated briefly between them and the Byzantines, the latter finally hanging on until the Arab invasion around AD647. Damage from repeated earthquakes eventually led to the abandonment of the city, allowing what was left to remain through the centuries.

Getting there Buses that cover the distance to Cherchell stop at Tipasa en route, arriving from the capital on a regular basis Monday to Friday. The stop is on the main road at the eastern entrance to the town (the departure point for the return trip is on the other side of the street). The journey takes about 1½ hours,

🏠 **Where to stay** Tipasa is a mere 70km from Algiers, and if you are planning to visit other sites further south, or prefer somewhere high quality to stay, it might be best to return to the capital. If you'd like to linger a while, join the other city exiles who've come to party, and lodge locally. These places aren't great, despite their beautiful beach locations. Check beforehand for availability, as these resorts can get pretty crowded on weekends and during holidays (especially the Muslim ones)

🏠 **Complex Madares** & the **Hotel del a Baia** Plage Chenoua; ☎ 024 46 18 22

🏠 **Le Corne d'Or** Just east of town on the main road to Algiers; ☎ 024 47 08 15. $$–$$$$

✗ **Where to eat** There are lots of restaurants and cafés especially on the main street and near the harbour, supposedly the site of the original Punic port. They are all similar, although the **Creperie Cleopatra**, the **Restaurant Massinissa** and the **Restaurant Romana** come recommended (**$$–$$$**). Alternatively, the roast chicken sold at fast-food places smells good!

What to see When visiting the Roman ruins (*in the heart of town*; ⊕ *09.00–12.00 & 14.30–18.30; DA20*), it's worth stopping first at the museum (*www.musee-tipasa.art.dz*; ⊕ *09.00–12.00 & 14.00–17.30*) located above the entrance to the remains. Full of artefacts, the best indications of how things were during imperial times are visible in the delightful mosaics, particularly in the depiction of captives receiving justice that came from the civil basilica and the small, beautifully coloured *Pax et Concordia* with Christian symbols. The tombstones also show daily life, via the sculpted portraits.

Through the entrance gates, past the Roman fortifications and crumbling walls of the great baths, the first major remains are of the amphitheatre. Large and well preserved, the venue was used for several purposes, including executions performed in mythological fashion, for example in the style of Hercules. The arena was also the place for ceremonial functions. Sometime after AD300, gladiatorial combat was made illegal, but the performance of killing wild animals was allowed.

Continuing, the ancient main roads of the decumanus (east to west) and the cardo (north to south) come into view, both with columns that once supported porticoes. The cardo is particularly impressive, with pillars leading straight into the sea. Most likely, the road went further in its Roman days, but centuries of crashing waves have eroded the city limits. Today, the sea and the beaches beyond are a lovely backdrop to the ruins. The decumanus runs the length of the site.

Following the coast west, you soon come to the enormous Christian basilica. This religious complex was believed to be the largest in Roman North Africa. There are traces of floor mosaics, as well as the arches of the nave. The official Catholic church was here, and the battle between the sects came to a head, when the Donatists severely damaged the building. Later, earthquakes, a common occurrence in this part of the Mediterranean, seemed to finish the job. Beyond is the western necropolis, with its impressive graves including a circular mausoleum. Both pagan and Christian burial plots were here. On one of the promontories a little further along is a memorial to Albert Camus, the French philosopher, writer and Algerian native. Here was where he looked to the sea for inspiration.

Returning via the inland route, one finds the theatre, an atmospheric and beautifully preserved ellipse. This small performance space is relatively unusual as it is low level, rather than staggered into the brow of a hill, as are most other Roman theatres. The foundations of the stage remain in place, and the semicircular alcoves that fronted it are still there, although no longer decorated. The path to the exit goes back via the amphitheatre.

The Mauretanian Tomb (⊕ *09.00–12.00 & 14.00–17.00 daily; DA20*) *En route* to Tipasa, tours usually stop here, and if travelling independently it's worth heading into the town and taking a taxi back. About 11km before reaching Tipasa from Algiers, the road heads up a hill. On the crest is an enormous sand-colour, squat conical building, constructed of cut blocks of stone. Spaced at even intervals all around the 18.5m circumference are flattened Ionic columns embedded in the walls. Known as the Mauretanian Tomb, this ancient monument was supposedly the burial place of Juba II and his wife Cleopatra Selene, king and queen of Rome's client kingdom of Mauretania. Allegedly based on the tomb of Alexander the Great, this comparison is fanciful, as the appearance of the original was never known. Traces of Cleopatra's Egyptian background show in the false door, but when the real entrance was found and penetrated, no traces of the bodies or their goods were found. If anything had ever really been left in there, grave robbers had probably discovered the booty years before, as the monument's existence was hardly disguised. It's also believed that the building's presence was memorial, rather than actual. It's possible to peek inside through one of the openings, but there isn't much to see. The view from the location is excellent, granting a vista of the sites and sea below.

CHERCHELL (*Telephone code 024*) This city of 42,000 people is located about 90km west of Algiers, and 20km beyond Tipasa. A seaside community with a lovely port and lighthouse, the place is popular and friendly, even if those people seeking a glimpse into its illustrious past will find few traces hidden under the modern conurbation. Cherchell is a thriving town, and has been continuously inhabited since Phoenician times. Because it was never deserted, buildings have been built on buildings, often using the valuable already-cut materials of the previous incarnation. Very little is left of any of the ancient settlements

History Another of the Phoenician pit stops, Cherchell, then known as Iol, came into its own during the reign of King Juba II (25BC–AD23). Although heir by birth to the throne of Numidia, that kingdom had already been absorbed by the Roman Empire. The emperor Caesar Augustus, needing an ally in the client kingdom of nearby Mauretania, granted the position to the Roman-raised but African-born prince. In honour of the appointment Juba II renamed Iol as Iol Caesarea, and made the city his capital. Even though he later moved to his purpose-built city of Volubilis in Morocco (see page 140), Iol Caesarea became increasingly important to the Romans. After the assassination of Juba's son, Ptolemy, Mauretania was relegated from a client kingdom to a province and it was subsequently integrated into the empire of Rome. Like Tipasa, the city became a prominent Christian enclave and was also besieged by Vandals and Byzantines. When the Arabs arrived, they did away with the name of Iol, and relabelled the city, Sharshal. From here, Cherchell's history began to resemble that of Algiers, with Spanish attacks in 1520, aid being sought from the Turks, pirates thriving under Ottoman control and the French arriving, albeit in 1840, ten years later than in the capital.

Getting there Organised day trips usually include both Tipasa and Cherchell on the excursions. Otherwise, buses leave from Algiers. It's also possible to get here via public transport from Tipasa, with the regular Monday to Friday buses that stop on the way.

Where to stay and eat Tourists tend not to spend the night here as the distance from Algiers isn't great and Tipasa is a far nicer place to hang out. To some degree, the same could be said regarding eating in the area, although there are the usual fast-food outlets and rotisseries in the busier parts of town.

What to see Passing by the Place des Martyrs, a plaza in the middle of town that was the site of the Roman forum, it's worth making a first stop at the **museum**

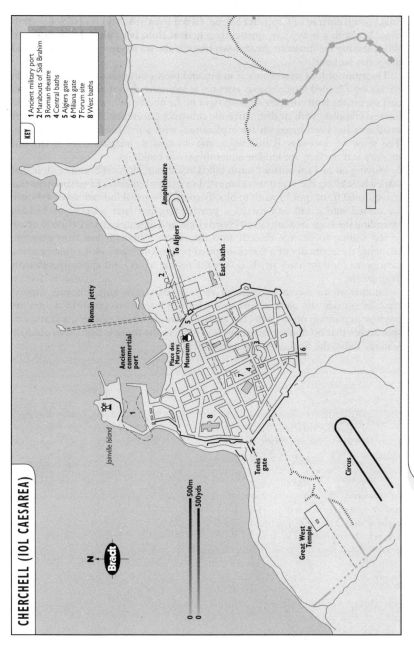

CHERCHELL (IOL CAESAREA)

KEY
1 Ancient military port
2 Marabouts of Sidi Brahim
3 Roman theatre
4 Central baths
5 Algiers gate
6 Miliana gate
7 Forum site
8 West baths

Amphitheatre

To Algiers

East baths

Roman jetty

Ancient commercial port

Place des Martyrs

Museum

Joinville Island

Tenès gate

Circus

Great West Temple

N

500m
500yds

0
0

Bradt

(*central square;* ⏲ *09.00–12.00 & 14.00–17.00 Sun–Fri, except holidays; DA20*). The museum has stunning, wall-size mosaics. The *Three Graces* is lovely and another one of agricultural labourers gives a very good insight into the workings of the country estate. Where this collection has an edge is in the portrait busts. An idealisation of Juba II has a headband indentation denoting royalty, which in ancient times was probably filled with a real strip of gold. Even more rare is the only known portrait of Cleopatra Selene, carved in marble, and realistic enough to show her with a heavy jaw, apparently inherited from her father, Mark Anthony. When leaving the museum, head down towards the sea to view the lighthouse and the pretty harbour.

The ruins of Iol Caesara appear in bits and pieces throughout the town. If you are not on a guided tour, a map is essential as locations are not obvious. One of the first sites is the bath complex situated right in the middle of town and not far from the sea, complete with its distinctive tile construction, arches and even mosaics. A small area has been hived off for exploration, with a few columns still standing. The sense of discovery is infectious, and it's easy to imagine what wonderful mosaics and artefacts are hidden under the newer buildings.

Moving on to a site further south billed as a theatre, it soon becomes clear that somewhere along the way it was converted to an amphitheatre. Entertainment was transformed from spoken word to bloody sport. The usual indications of a theatre are carved into a hill and there's a proscenium, but later adaptations include extending the stage area into an awkward circle, and digging entrances into the base of the seating to emerge directly into the centre. Although less than graceful, changing the aesthetics of a Greek-inspired performance area into a clumsy arena catering to contemporary needs is very interesting to see, and epitomises Roman pragmatism.

Another more recent example of reuse is the (real) amphitheatre, located typically outside the walls of the town. Initially barely recognisable, despite its prominent position on the map, the gradually familiar shape emerges, and you can spot arches that no doubt once supported roofs to the tunnels that led to outdoor seating. Today, the field is used as a football pitch.

14

Setif

Telephone code 036

This city of almost a quarter of a million inhabitants lies within a beautiful and surprising part of the country. In contrast to the stereotypical view of a North African landscape, Setif sits at an altitude of 1,300m in the region of the Little Kabylie Mountains. Located about 300km east of Algiers, and just over 100km south of Bejaia and the Mediterranean coast, the line of mountains that runs through the country passes just to the north. The city has a pleasant climate, although nights get cold in the winter. Setif is situated on the main road between Constantine and Algiers; a motorway between the two bigger urban areas is being constructed, and Setif will be one of the major stops *en route*. At the moment, traffic speeds along on the completed sections, only to crawl when the road returns to its normal state.

Setif is a pleasant if not spectacular place with a large industrial sector to the south, dealing mostly with plastic manufacture. There's not much here for the tourist, except for it being the closest full-service location to the wonderful Roman site of Djemila (see below, page 208). It's also worth lingering in the National Archaeological Museum (see page 208).

HISTORY

Artefacts date from the pre-Acheulean culture in the lower Palaeolithic period (over one million years ago), continuing through the later Stone Age, and include items from one of the first tribes specially named in the area, the Capsians. After a gap, perhaps because the locals moved or maybe just didn't leave anything, archaeological remains return with the Phoenicians who had a settlement here called 'Azdif'. During his brief two-year reign (AD96–98), the emperor Nerva set up a colony here and named it Colonia Nerviana Augusta Martialis Veteranorum Stifensium, or Sitifis. ('dark earth'). Originally military, the city evolved into a civil and commercial settlement, aided by the lush and readily cultivated fields nearby. In AD297 Diocletian annexed the area of eastern Mauretania Caesariensis to create Setifean Mauretania, declaring the Sitifis as its capital. Like the rest of coastal North Africa, this area was prone to earthquakes, and one severely disrupted the colony in AD419. Ten years later the Vandals invaded, adding human destruction to the natural one. In AD539, the illustrious Byzantine general Salana, or Solomon, returned with his forces, reconquering the city for the empire (the remains of a Byzantine citadel have been found in the environs of today's city). Sitifis was swept up in the Arab invasion, becoming an important centre to the Tamazert (Berbers). The region followed the general history of the rest of Algeria, changing allegiances to the various local dynasties. Increasing insecurity from the raiding nomads and a shift in political emphasis to the coastal regions led to the city's eventual abandonment. From then, until the French arrived in 1838, the place disappeared from history.

The French redeveloped Setif, building it back up into a large, colonial town. However, on 8 May 1945, the first organised and violent rebellion against the French colonial forces occurred. Despite assurances by the occupying government that fighting on their Free French side during World War II would gain Algerians independence, the locals soon discovered that these promises would not be peacefully realised. During a march organised to celebrate VE Day, tensions exploded and colonists were attacked, resulting in the death of over 100 *pieds noirs* colonists. The French police struggled for several days to restore order, then set about their reprisals. According to the French, just over 1,000 locals were killed, and to the North Africans, the estimate was 45,000, although outside sources put the numbers at 6,000. In any case it was clear that a war was brewing, even though it took until 1954 for battle to begin in earnest. Today, Setif is thought of as where the independence movement started.

GETTING THERE AND AROUND

BY AIR The airport (☏ 036 93 31 40) is named after Setif's most infamous day in history, 8 May 1945, and is located about 12km from town. Predominantly domestic, especially due to recent land-based security problems, there are some international flights that arrive here from France. If travelling independently and unmet, virtually the only way to get into Setif is via taxi. If on an organised tour, transport will be waiting.

BY RAIL Setif's train station is an easy walk to the east from the centre. Trains from Algiers to Constantine stop here *en route*. The journey takes four hours, quicker than buses, or private cars, which are often held up at security checkpoints. However, speed is at the sacrifice of convenience, as the departure from the capital is at 06.00. The Algiers to Annaba route also includes a halt here. Things change all the time, so check before departure as to exact details.

BY BUS Bus transport to Setif from various points in the country is pretty good, and passengers are let off at the Gare Routiere (*end of Av Said Boukhrissa;* ☏ 036 84 21 40), about a 30-minute walk from the city centre. Journeys should take around six hours from Algiers, two hours from Constantine and 15 hours from Oran. Don't count on these times always being accurate as roadworks and frequent police inspections tend to hold up journeys. As compensation, fares are relatively low, and if time is less important than funds, this form of transport is a good way to go.

BY TAXI Shared taxis are also an option. They usually leave from near the bus station and go to the larger cities. There might be more destinations available, but getting there will be offered on a spontaneous basis. If touring with a small group, travelling by taxi is easy to arrange and if doing it independently, the cost will be a lot higher, but the timetable will be at your convenience.

Locally, Setif is small and its few highlights can be visited on foot. Taxis are around and will transport you to whatever destination you require within the city. If you are not willing to flag one down in the street, ask at the hotel, or call Radio Taxi (☏ 036 91 59 79).

TOUR OPERATORS

Koutama Club Voyage ☏ 036 83 93 23	**Touring Voyages Algerie** 14 Rue Fida; ☏ 036 91 64 16
Oriental Tourisme ☏ 036 93 84 64	**Tropic Tours** ☏ 036 92 30 35

WHERE TO STAY

 El Kenz Hotel (35 rooms) 10 Rue Said Guendouz; 036 84 54 54; www.hotel-elkenz.com. The city's newest hotel is arguably its best, with full facilities & a view over the amusement park. $$$

Hotel El Rabie 4 Pl de l'Indépendance; 036 84 57 95. Located next to the city's most visible attraction, the Ain Fouara fountain, this modern & spacious hotel is one of the better places to stay in town, although more recently built rivals are threatening its position. $$$

Hotel Hidhab Rue de l'Armée National de l'Indépendance (ALN); 036 92 65 65. This good 3-star accommodation is well placed for the sites of the city, including the National Museum just next door. $$$

WHERE TO EAT

Some of the hotels have reasonable and reliable places to eat, for example the **El Kenz** with its French **Restaurant Mosaique** ($$$) and the **Mohktar Hotel** (*39 Av 8 Mai 1945;* 036 84 35 50; $$$), complete with a restaurant that serves decent full meals. Street food and the usual fast-food chicken and pizza typical of most Algerian towns are also here. For something a little more interesting, try **Le Lisboa** (*Cite Hachimi 1er Tranche;* 036 91 35 48; $$$), some distance from town but worth it to try the Portuguese food and **Restaurant W11** (*11 Rue Ahmed Aggoun;* 036 82 09 09; $$$–$$$$), which serves seafood and alcohol.

OTHER PRACTICALITIES

EMERGENCY TELEPHONE NUMBERS
Police 17
Medical 115
Security 112

INTERNET CAFÉS Cyber cafés are scattered throughout the busier areas of town. Surfing is usually very inexpensive.

POST The main post office is on Avenue du 1er Novembre.

BANKS Many banks have a branch along the main boulevard, Avenue 8 Mai 1945. If they, or their ATMs, are reluctant to accept cards or change money, the hotels will usually be willing to exchange foreign currencies.

WHAT TO SEE

There isn't much to see. Most people spend the night here in preparation for a visit to Djemila about 50km away. If time is available and there's nothing else to do, there are a few things to take a look at to pass the time.

PARC D'ATTRACTIONS This large green space in town functions today as an amusement park, complete with some fairground rides in its heart. Close to the centre is an old-fashioned zoo (⊕ *09.00–17.00; DA20*) with lions and tigers. The attractions are best visited in summer when the temperature is pleasant.

BYZANTINE REMAINS Not much remains here to view, but this wall shows that the Byzantines were here. Believed to be part of the citadel built after General Solomon chased off the Vandals, the ruin has more historical than visual interest.

AIN FOUARA The city's most famous landmark sitting in the middle of Avenue 8 Mai 1945 is a fountain, graced by a statue of a naked woman. Strange for an Islamic city, this vestige of *fin de siècle* art left by the French is beloved by the locals.

THE NATIONAL MUSEUM OF ARCHAEOLOGY (*Rue de l'Armée National de l'Indépendance;* ✆ *036 84 35 36; www.setif.com/Musee.html;* ⊕ *Apr–Aug 08.30–12.00 & 14.00–17.30 Sun–Thu, 14.30–17.00 Fri; Sep–Mar 08.00–12.00 & 14.00–17.00 Sun–Thu, 14.30-17.00 Fri; DA20*) To the east of the Byzantine citadel, this excellent museum, built in 1985, features the prehistoric, Numidian, Roman, Byzantine and Islamic periods. There is also a room that holds coins struck with the visages of Roman emperors as well as gold and silver items from later eras. The mosaics have their own display area and were all found in and around Setif (Sitifis). The enormous, intact and stunning *Procession of Bacchus* going to India, accompanied by tigers, lions and his entourage is wonderful. Another mosaic from AD300–400 was found in the baths, and is of Venus, appropriately enough, bathing.

THE ROMAN SITE

DJEMILA About 50km to the northeast of Setif are the remains of the Roman city of Djemila. Known also by its Latin name, Cuicul or Curculum, the place is laid out at 900m altitude, on a hillside, with a view of tree-covered distant hills beyond. The ruins were declared an international heritage site by UNESCO in 1982, for being 'an interesting example of Roman town planning adapted to a mountain location', but this description is faint praise. Djemila is one of the most beautifully situated and intact Roman remains in Algeria.

History Although the prehistoric zone of Ain Lahnece, where artefacts of Stone Age man were found, is very close, there was no settlement here until Cuicul was founded by the emperor Nerva about the same time as Setif. Set up as a garrison, the military bias shifted from active to retired, so that gradually the place was filled with veterans of the legion, rather than those soldiers on active service. Eventually, the purpose of the city became commercial, rather than defensive, reaching a population of 10,000–12,000 at its height, a large metropolis by Roman standards. The dynasty of the African-born Roman emperor Septimius Severus (AD193–235), left many of the site's more impressive constructions, and during the next two centuries expansion continued south. Christianity became the main faith, and relevant religious buildings began to appear. Cuicul did not escape the conflict between the Donatists and the mainstream Catholics, although it seems the situation was eventually resolved. Inscriptions found on location imply that the Romans held sway here at least until AD476, although by AD553 their authority appears to have waned. Despite having been saved from Vandal destruction and the subsequent absorption into the Byzantine Empire, Cuicul disappeared soon after. Historians disagree as to whether this desertion was due to earthquake damage, fires set off by the Donatists or simple pillaging after having been abandoned by its inhabitants. When the French colonists arrived, they became fascinated by the ruins and nearly carted away to Paris one of its most iconic landmarks, the Arch of Caracalla. More comprehensive excavations began at the beginning of the last century and continued until the middle, by which time more contemporary political issues halted the work.

Getting there Tours usually do the visit as a day trip, most commonly from Setif, but also from Constantine, about 90km to the east. Cruise ships offer excursions from Bejaia, subject to security, a four-hour drive each way. It's possible to get to Djemila indirectly with public transport (bus or collective taxi) by going to El-

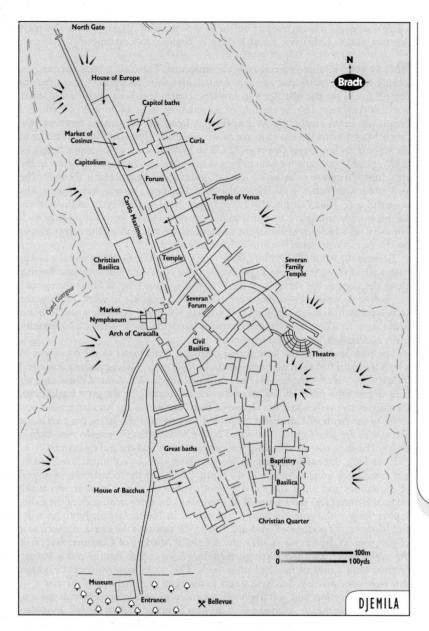

North Gate

House of Europe

Capitol baths

Market of
Cosinus

Curia

Capitolium

Forum

Temple of Venus

Cardo Maximus

Christian
Basilica

Temple

Severan
Family
Temple

Oued Guergour

Market
Nymphaeum

Severan
Forum

Arch of Caracalla

Civil
Basilica

Theatre

Great baths

Baptistry

Basilica

House of Bacchus

Christian Quarter

0   100m
0   100yds

Museum

Entrance   Bellevue

DJEMILA

Eulma and then continuing via taxi to the site. Alternatively, if time is pressing, it's easiest to get here via taxi from Setif. It might be worth negotiating a price for the driver to wait. If continuing to Constantine, it's possible to arrange for a taxi to spend the day, starting in Setif, waiting at Djemila and finishing in Constantine.

Where to stay and eat The **Bellevue** (*outside the gates;* ↘ *036 94 51 10*) is a small hotel, where it's possible to spend the night. Nice, but basic, the main draw of the place is its convenience. Make sure you book ahead, as there are not many rooms. There's also a little restaurant (you can re-enter the site by showing your ticket), which serves good Algerian cuisine. Otherwise, return to Setif, or continue to Constantine.

What to see The first stop is usually the **museum**. There are wonderful mosaics, usually from the villas that are now named after these artworks. On display are objects found on the site, such as bronzes, lamps, jewellery, utensils and other items of daily use. On the outside of the building is an additional collection of fascinating items, including an **impressive head of Septimius Severus**, the Leptis Magna-born Roman emperor, who was clearly a presence in this area far to the west of his home turf (see page 12). With his distinctive twin-tressed beard, he is recognisable not only for who he was as ruler, but also for his deity status in the area. Imperial cult worship was common, and it was understandable for him to be associated with other gods, including Baal Haamon, Saturn and Jupiter. His powerful wife, Julia Domna, also has her stone head on display. In addition, there are memorials and grave markers, indicators of a society keen on making itself immortal, in which, by virtue of the fact visitors are still reading the names almost two thousand years later, it seems to have succeeded.

To enter the ruins (⊕ *09.00–12.00 & 15.00–19.00 daily; DA20*), there is a lovely, long walk of trees, leading to a spot where there is an excellent overview. Resting along the slope is the skeleton of the Roman city, stretching as far as the eye can see, before dropping down into a green valley. It's possible to work out how the archetypal Roman town-planning grid was adapted to the available space. It seems daunting as to where to start, but the usual standards, such as the cardo, forums, baths and basilica, act as reliable guides.

The path leads into the later period Christian quarter and to the baptistery, in which the baths had been later converted to religious use. Hiding under a dome and locked away – ask for the key – is one of the few mosaics left *in situ*. Continuing, it's hard to resist the main attractions of the site and passing by the great **baths**, with their distinctive arches, and the **House of Bacchus**, one of the later large villas, you come to the **Arch of Caracalla** (AD216). Towering over the ruins, the arch is the gateway to the new forum, dominated by the Severan family temple. Also here is the civil basilica, the nymphaeum, one of the markets and the public latrines.

From here, the **cardo maximus**, lined on both sides by columns, is impressive and extends for quite a distance to the north. Passing by the foundations of several of the houses and villas and through another arch, the main road arrives at the original forum. Here is the **capitol** (the temple to the three main gods of the town, Jupiter, king of the gods (or Saturn, commonly in North Africa); Juno, his wife; and Minerva, the goddess of wisdom. Also on the square is the **curia**, the local seat of government. Just to the north is the delightful **Market of Cosinus**. Several of the tables have charming carvings, including lions, other figures and a strange creature with a human face and snake body. The cardo passes vestiges of houses that were once privileged to have access to the main thoroughfare of the city.

If time is fleeting, and you have only the morning or afternoon to visit the site, dash back to the theatre, located east of the new forum and down the hill. In its day, the venue could accommodate up to 3,000 spectators. Either wonderfully intact, or sensitively reconstructed, the well-preserved semicircular arena typically takes advantage of the hillside location, with its seats carved into the incline, and the beautiful view dropping away behind the stage. The acoustics are excellent. If you have more time don't rush, and save the theatre for after the midday break. Here's a chance to eat your pre-packed picnic lunch or head off to the Bellevue Restaurant. On your return, linger a bit longer at each place, absorb the atmosphere and imagine what life was like in the heyday of this large, beautiful, Roman town.

15

Constantine

Telephone code 031

Algeria's third city, after Algiers and Oran, Constantine is an extraordinary place. Straddling the huge gorge created by the Rhumel River (the same one that about 90km to the north, along the coast, defined the border between Numidia and Mauretania), the population of about half a million people lives on both sides. The transport between them is facilitated by a series of bridges. This impressive gash dominates the place. The craggy canyon has been left pretty much to itself, with vegetation happily thriving unimpeded all the way down. The traces of humanity are visible, barely in the case of the now disused bridge at the bottom that has Roman origins, and unfortunately much more so in the tendency for the locals to use the gorge as a rubbish tip. Although the city doesn't have much else to offer in terms of tourist attractions, the scenery, and its proximity to the Roman sites, makes Constantine worth visiting in its own right and also a convenient base.

HISTORY

Algerians claim that Constantine is 'the oldest city of them all'. Within the walls of the gorge, caves have been found that argue the case for prehistoric habitation. From around 300BC, the Phoenician name for city, 'kirtha', was transformed to Cirta, and the place became a major metropolis in Numidia. The Battle of Cirta in 203BC was one of the named victories for the Roman general Scipio Africanus, during the Second Punic War. After Julius Caesar's victory at the Battle of Thapsus in 46BC, Cirta became part of the North African spoils. Designated as the capital of Roman Numidia, the city flourished during the reign of Julius's successor, Augustus. Christianity also took hold here. Not much changed until AD311 when civil war broke out between the emperor Maxentius and the Numidian challenger, Alexander, that led to the destruction of the city. That fight led also to the end of Cirta, and when the emperor Constantine arrived two years later to rebuild it, he named the place after himself. By now well and truly Byzantine, Constantine – the city – resisted the Vandals, but fell to the Arabs, during the invasion.

Constantine's more modern history follows a similar pattern to the rest of Algeria's, with the notable exception that it initially successfully resisted France's attempts at colonisation. Holding them at bay for several years, it finally succumbed to their occupation efforts in 1838. An allied base during World War II, the city joined its fellow rebels in calls for independence.

GETTING THERE AND AROUND

BY AIR Aeroport Mohamed Boudiaf (✆ *031 92 52 88*) is located about 20km to the south of Constantine's centre. Primarily domestic, flights go to most cities served by air transport, including the deep south. The airport is notorious for delays, and it might be worth considering flying instead to nearby Batna or going by road or

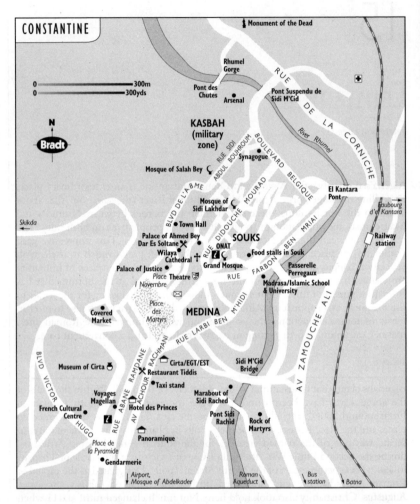

CONSTANTINE

Monument of the Dead

Rhumel Gorge

Pont des Chutes

Arsenal

Pont Suspendu de Sidi M'Cid

RUE DE LA CORNICHE

River Rhumel

0 ——— 300m
0 ——— 300yds

N
Bradt

KASBAH (military zone)

RUE SIDI ABDUL BOUROUM

BOULEVARD MOURAD

BOULEVARD BELGIQUE

Synagogue

Mosque of Salah Bey

El Kantara Pont

Faubourg d'el Kantara

Skikda ←

BLVD DE L'A BME

Mosque of Sidi Lakhdar

RUE DIDOUCHE MOURAD

FARBON BEN MRIAI

Railway station

Town Hall

Palace of Ahmed Bey
Dar Es Soltane

Wilaya

Cathedral

Palace of Justice

Place I Novembre

SOUKS

ONAT

Grand Mosque

Food stalls in Souk

Passerelle Perregaux

RUE

Theatre

Madrasa/Islamic School & University

Place des Martyrs

MEDINA

RUE LARBI BEN M'HIDI

Covered Market

AV ZAMOUCHE ALI

RUE ABANE RAMDANE

AV ACHOUR RACHMANI

Museum of Cirta

Cirta/EGT/EST

Restaurant Tiddis

Sidi M'Cid Bridge

Taxi stand

Voyages Magellan

Marabout of Sidi Rached

BLVD VICTOR HUGO

French Cultural Centre

Hotel des Princes

Pont Sidi Rachid

Rock of Martyrs

Panoramique

Place de la Pyramide

Gendarmerie

Airport, Mosque of Abdelkader

Roman Aqueduct

Bus station

Batna

train. A few flights from France also arrive here. Unless you are being met or are part of a tour, taxi seems to be the only way to get into town. It's not cheap, and prices rise at night, but at least you'll get to your destination on time.

BY RAIL Trains from Algiers and points *en route* stop at the station (✆ *031 64 19 88*) connected to the old city by the Sidi Rached Bridge. The trains for the six-hour journey to Algiers leave very early and very late, while the one to Annaba goes in the afternoon.

BY BUS AND TAXI Two bus stations serve the city, depending on the destination. The main SNTV (*at Boussouf*) is some distance from the centre (take a taxi), and is the terminus for services to Algiers and Setif. The other SNTV (*17 Juin*) goes east to Skikda, Annaba and even to Tunis, in Tunisia, and is much more centrally located. Shared taxis also leave from this latter station, taking off whenever they're full. Be aware that timings are unpredictable, based on security checks as well as how much of the motorway to Algiers has been completed. Locally, most of what there is worth seeing can be viewed by walking and with some of the bridges only for pedestrians the city is more accessible on foot. Otherwise, flag down a taxi or arrange one via your hotel to get around. If planning a visit to some of the nearby Roman sites, and not on a tour, negotiate a rate, as much time will be saved by having your own transport.

TOURIST INFORMATION

Office National de Tourisme 32 Rue Abane Ramdane; ℡ 031 93 26 61; www.ont-dz.org

TOUR OPERATORS

EGT/EST Hotel Cirta, Av Rahmani Achour; ℡ 031 94 18 55
ONAT 6 rue Zaabane; ℡ 031 94 39 54; & 16 Rue Didouche Mourad; ℡ 031 94 14 03; www.onat-dz.com

Touring Voyages Algérie 35 Av Touati Mostefa; ℡ 031 92 67 72
Voyages Magellan 27 Rue Abane Ramdane; ℡ 031 91 27 70

 ## WHERE TO STAY

Hotel Cirta (87 rooms) 1 Av Rahmani Achour; ℡ 031 92 19 80. This extraordinary hotel is a centrally located tourist attraction in its own right, with its palatial lobby & entranceway, which aren't quite matched by its rooms. $$$$
Hotel Panoramic (100 rooms) 59 Av Ouati Mustapha; ℡ 031 92 93 03. As promised by its

name, this place offers good views & rivals the Cirta for quality if not character. $$$$
Hotel des Princes 27 Abane Ramdane; ℡ 031 91 27 70. Reasonably priced & cosy, this family-run residence is well located & has all the basic requirements for a comfortable stay. $$–$$$

 ## WHERE TO EAT

Despite the dearth of restaurants, strange in such a large town, there are lots of little places serving fast food Algerian style. It's almost always possible to find ad hoc meat grilled on a stick (brochettes) or soups (chorba). They're usually freshly prepared, and tummy troubles are rare. On a relatively more formal basis, the following places are suggested.

Hotel Cirta Located in the sprawling & elaborately decorated hall of the hotel, the best food in town is French-Algerian & can be accompanied by wine. $$$$

Dar Es Soltane 23 Rue Hamlaoul; ℡ 031 64 22 56. Reasonably priced & well located. $$$

ENTERTAINMENT AND NIGHTLIFE

There's not much to do at night in Constantine, despite the constant noise that seems to be circulating around the city centre. The hotels will serve drinks, although not very late, and the Hotel Cirta is fun to walk around, although the bar is small and the restaurant somewhat cavernous. Save your energies for the next day, wandering through the town or clambering over the nearby Roman sites.

SHOPPING

The city has its fair share of small specialist shops, as well as some recognisable from the bigger cities in France. The medina offers many things that are typical of North African markets. In general, bargaining isn't as common, nor the choice as wide, as it is in Morocco or Tunisia.

EMERGENCY TELEPHONE NUMBERS

Police ☏ 17
Medical ☏ 115
Security ☏ 112

HOSPITAL

✚ Hospital Ibn Badis ☏ 031 94 49 66

INTERNET CAFÉS Ask for local recommendations. Many phone shops also offer internet access as well now. As Constantine has a university, it's likely that the number of cyber points will increase.

POST The main post office is on Place 1 Novembre, located in the heart of the city.

BANKS Place 1 Novembre has several banks and some ATMs, although there is no certainty the machines will take foreign cards. One or two of the better hotels, eg: the Hotel Cirta, might exchange money, although they will probably accept cash only, and would prefer it if you were a guest at the hotel.

WHAT TO SEE

It's hard to get past the gorge, in both the visual and literal senses, and it certainly dominates the town and the memory.

BRIDGES There are seven bridges here, plus a cable car that was due to open soon after research was being done. From the south, around the bend of the river, they are:

Pont d'Arcole No longer viable, this iron bridge at the southern end of town has been condemned.

Pont du Diable At the entrance of the gorge, this bridge rises 65m above the rock and waterfall below, in an environment some think resembles hell – maybe that's why it's called the Devil's Bridge.

Pont Sidi Rached (and mausoleum) When completed in 1912, this bridge was the highest stone one in the world, and its 27 arches still extend for a length of 450m. The eponymous saint's mausoleum is nearby.

Passarelle Perregaux (Mellah Slimane) A pedestrian-only suspension walkway that wobbles so much it's called 'the moving bridge'. It leads right into the centre and while on it, gives an excellent view of the river deep within the gorge, and the remains of the Roman bridge below.

Pont El Kantara Although its current form dates from 1863, this crossing is one of the oldest, once part of the Roman aqueduct system. Repeatedly destroyed and rebuilt, one of its incarnations used the rubble from the Roman amphitheatre in the bridge's reconstruction.

Pont Suspendu de Sidi M'Cid This suspension bridge, inaugurated in 1912, is bad news for anyone with vertigo, as it sits 175m above the bed of the river. Along its

164m length it gives terrific views of both the town and the fields to the north. It's a breathtaking experience.

Pont des Chutes The last of the city's bridges, to the north; the height isn't impressive, but the location over the waterfalls (chutes) is an impressive finale to the gorge. After having your fill of being dazzled by this natural feature, the city has a few other things worth visiting.

MOSQUES Although mosques are not open to non-Muslims (with the exception of the Emir Abdelkader, see below), it's impossible to miss the minarets of these religious buildings. Even if gaining only a glimpse into the interior – if the doors are open during prayer times – it's worth a look. Some of the city's better examples are the **Grand Mosque** (*Rue Larbi ben M'hidi*), the **Sidi Lakhdar** (*off Rue Didouche Mourad*) and **Salah Bey** (*close to Rue Sidi Abdul Bouhroum*).

Mosque and University of Emir Abdelkader The beautiful modern white twin-towered mosque dominates the view of the new town, and is part of the university of Islamic sciences, built at the beginning of the 1980s. The interior is stunning. Non-Muslims are allowed in, but must be conservatively dressed. Women will be given headscarves and if clothing is too risqué, will also be handed a loose-fitting robe.

PALACE OF AHMED BEY (*Place Si Haoues*) Having been under renovation for the last quarter of a century, there's no saying when the place will be open to the public, but when it is, this early 19th-century residence of the Ottoman bey will be worth viewing. This elaborate residence contains gardens and detailing that should make the place one of the city's major attractions.

MONUMENT OF THE DEAD Over the gorge opposite the town, accessible via the Sidi M'Cid Bridge, is a war memorial, dedicated by the French to those soldiers killed in World War I. The location is its notable feature, perched on a clifftop and offering views that stretch far and away.

ROMAN AQUEDUCT On the southern outskirts of the city are the remains of an aqueduct that brought water into the city from 35km away. Although broken up, the arches that remain give an idea of what the system was like when it extended into the town, possibly even including the original Pont El Kantara.

MUSEUM OF CIRTA (*Coudiat Aty;* ✆ *031 92 38 95;* ⊕ *08.00–12.00 & 14.00–17.00 Sun–Thu; DA20*) Built in a contemporary version of a Graeco-Roman villa, the assembly ranges from prehistoric fossil animal heads, to French bronzes from the last century. Included are remnants of funerary stones with inscriptions in both Punic and Latin. There are also mosaics as well as a few excellent pieces of Roman glassware. The best of the artefacts from the nearby Roman site of Tiddis are on display here.

THE ROMAN SITE

TIDDIS Northwest of Constantine, about 28km, are the beautifully located remains of the Roman town of Tiddis, known in its day as Castellum Tiditanorum. Overlooking areas of hills and valleys, standing alone in a landscape that's been minimally developed, the atmosphere is of a place that's been sleeping for a long time. The adjacent canyon, the distant ribbon of river winding away and the red earth make the scenery spectacular.

History Evidence exists of this site having been inhabited in Neolithic times, and Punic remains have been found, but the remnants visible today are what are left of the Roman town. Originally constructed as a *castellum*, or fort, in Augustus's time, the military settlement eventually grew into a civil one, spilling down the hill. The standard urban planning grid has been adapted to fit the space, and it's possible to make out its elements. The necessity for the location of the original army fort isn't hard to figure out – below is the Rhumel River, the Ampsaga in ancient times, which was the border between Mauretania in the west, and Numidia in the east. The picturesque river below, in plain sight of the fort with incredible visibility and an excellent defensive position, marked the frontier. Nestled against the steep incline, there are definite reminders of some of the contemporary hill towns on the other side of the Mediterranean.

Getting there Tours usually include this site, but if travelling independently, the only way to get here is by taxi. Outside of organised excursions, the place is poorly visited, so make sure you make an arrangement with the driver, either to wait or to return.

 Where to stay and eat Part of the beauty of this site is its isolation, but for the same reason, there is nowhere to stay or eat in the area. It's possible to spend a half day here, but then it's best to return to Constantine or continue to your next destination.

What to see Climbing up the hill, past some initial ruins, the entrance to the city (⊕ 08.30–16.00 daily; DA20) is by the north gate, with its stocky arch dedicated to or by O Memmius Rogatus. Soon after, a small side chamber holds an intriguing red block with a rough inscription dating from about AD300. Here is the Sanctuary of Mithras, a god important to Roman soldiers, and particularly the officer class (see page 23). Along what was probably the cardo is a Christian chapel most likely contemporary and co-existing with the pagan (Mithraic) temple across the road. Nearby is an inscription, lauding Tiddis's most famous son, especially to the Brits, Quintus Lollius Urbicus (see box).

Further along is the forum. Traces of kilns provide evidence of the pottery trade, clearly a thriving and important business particularly for creating vessels for the exportation of agricultural products (olive oil, grain). Below, accessible either directly from Rogatus's gate, or via steep paths from the cardo, are the last vestiges of an urban settlement including the occasional villa. Sandwiched within were the main baths, with tiles and hypocausts made from the local red that are still visible. At the bottom of the hill are the remains of ramparts that pre-date the Romans.

16

Batna

Telephone code 033

About 120km southwest of Constantine and further up into the mountains, the city of Batna sits at an altitude of 1,040m. This modern city of over a quarter of a million inhabitants has cold winters and hot summers and sits at the end of the Atlas climate zone. In just over another 100km south, the Sahara begins. Pleasant enough, if not spectacular, the city is a good central point from which to explore the attractions of the area, including the scenery of the region and, not least, the Roman sites.

HISTORY

Batna is barely 160 years old, but its location has been significant for centuries. The frontier between desert and mountain, and the coast beyond, the area has long been a crossroads for people travelling between the Sahara and the Mediterranean. The city's name, Batna, means 'bivouac', or where one camps for the night. Although people didn't seem to stop, they certainly passed through. In AD75, the Romans moved the headquarters of the Third August Legion, the main fighting force of North Africa, from Ammaedara, in present-day Tunisia, to Lambaesis, just 11km south of Batna. Resting against the mountains to the south, this position is a natural border.

The French, too, recognised the advantages of the situation, and they set up a military outpost here in 1846. Located midway between Algiers and Tunis, the benefits of having a base here occasioned the founding of the city a couple of years later. The people of Batna were vociferous in crying out against their French oppressors, and were very active in the early independence movement in the 1950s. Within a decade of having achieved their freedom, the Algerians started investing heavily in the welfare of both the city and the country, with the establishment of an industrial zone as well as a university.

GETTING THERE AND AROUND

BY AIR The pleasant Aeroport Ben Boulaid (☏ *033 86 85 43*) has flights to Algiers, as well as to various destinations in France. Air services here might not be as frequent as to Constantine, but the airport is said to be more reliable. Unfortunately, it is a bit of a distance from the city centre, and can only be reached by taxi (or tour bus, if part of an organised excursion).

BY BUS AND TAXI Buses to other parts of the country are frequent: to the north usually via Constantine two hours away; and to the south, via Biskra, about an hour. They leave from the gare routière on the outskirts of town. Shared taxis also depart from here and go directly to the larger cities. The town is small enough to discover by walking. If you need a taxi or want to visit the Roman sites independently, private ones can be flagged down, or arranged through the hotel.

TOURIST INFORMATION

🛈 **Direction de la Tourisme de la Willaya de Batna**
Cite Administrative 05000; ☏ 033 86 82 02

TOUR OPERATORS

ONAT 14 Allee Benboulaid; ☏ 033 80 43 45

Timgad Voyages 1 Pl de la Liberté; ☏ 033 80 70 30; www.timgad-voyages.com

WHERE TO STAY

🏠 **Hotel Chelia** (71 rooms) 2 Allee Benboulaid; ☏ 033 86 53 34; www.chelia.8m.com. This 4-star accommodation is one of the best places to stay in town, especially if you like the facilities of a large hotel. $$$

🏠 **Hotel & Restaurant Hazem** 1 Rue Ben Badis; ☏ 033 85 24 23; http://membres.lycos.fr/

hotelhazem/. This delightful family-run hotel offers full facilities including Wi-Fi, TV & refrigerator in some rooms with just enough quirkiness to make it charming – its appeal means it's often fully occupied. $$$

🏠 **Hotel Karim** 10 Rue de la Republique; ☏ 033 80 51 81. One of the cheaper hotels in town. $

✖ WHERE TO EAT

The area around **Allee Ben Boulaid** and further along on **Rue Mohamed Salah Benabbes** holds lots of the Algerian version of fast-food places. Here is your best bet for getting a good, quick and cheap meal, or perhaps a light lunch or late snack ($–$$). On a more formal basis, the **Hotel Chelia** ($$$–$$$$) has a menu with an international flavour, and the **Hotel Hazem** ($$$–$$$$) offers excellent Algerian food – and lots of it! Otherwise, try **Mango Pulp** (*75 Allee Ben Boulaid*) for a pizza or sandwich ($$$).

WHAT TO SEE

Clean and spacious, the city has very few attractions of note, acting instead as a centre for the sites around it. The architecture is more modern in parts than other cities, and there is the occasional example of something delightfully idiosyncratic in some of the domestic buildings, such as small makeshift turrets on the roofs. The Grand Mosque, with its two minarets reminiscent of the Emir Abdelkader in Constantine, is notable, but not impressive.

THE ROMAN SITES

TIMGAD A mere 35km southeast of Batna is one of the most impressive Roman sites in North Africa. Officially named Colonia Marciana Trajana Thamugas, it became more commonly known as Thamugadi in its ancient days. Not only are there substantial remains of this city that once was home to more than 15,000 people, but also its town planning is so archetypal that it can be used as an example of the perfect Roman grid (see *A typical Roman town* in *Chapter 1*, page 25). Located on a relatively flat piece of ground, and developed with a final number of inhabitants in mind, there were no aberrations that had to be incorporated. Today, on the flat, the streets stretch out in straight Roman fashion, and the sections of the city are divided into even quadrants. From the air, the layout is so exemplary that it almost looks like a map. The two main boulevards divide the town, the cardo maximus heading north–south, and the decumanus maximus going east–west. Complete with all the

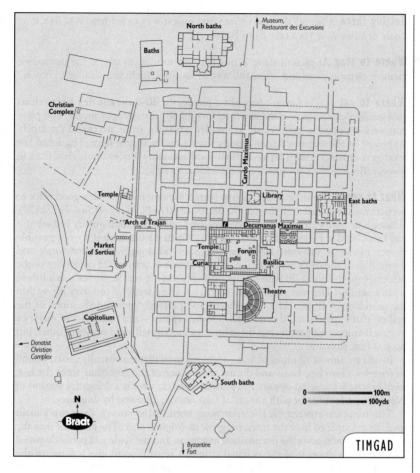

Museum,
Restaurant des Excursions

North baths

Baths

Christian
Complex

Cardo Maximus

Temple

Library

East baths

Arch of Trajan

Decumanus Maximus

Market
of Sertius

Temple

Forum

grafiti

Curia

Basilica

Theatre

Capitolium

Donatist
Christian
Complex

South baths

N

Brad†

0 ———— 100m
0 ———— 100yds

Byzantine
Fort

TIMGAD

elements of a large Roman town – forum, capitolium, curia, basilica, baths, markets, theatre, triumphal arch, nymphaeum, Christian complex and Byzantine fort – there's even an extra, the library, something found in very few Roman cities throughout the empire. The only thing that has not yet been found is the amphitheatre, but there's no doubt that there was one, somewhere.

History Set up in the year AD100 by the emperor Trajan, this fortified city was constructed as a civil settlement, primarily for army veterans. Prosperous due to the harvest of the fertile fields in the area, the city seems to have escaped many of the traumas that plagued others. Not until the Donatists attacked the mainstream Catholic Church, realised here by the destruction of some of the city's buildings, did any major discord make its way into the city's history. After the Vandals came and went, destroying much of the city in the process, Solomon, the noted general, claimed it back for the Byzantines in AD535. Despite Berber incursions, the city remained staunchly Christian until the Arab invasion trampled the entire region. From here on, Timgad disappeared, until the 18th-century intrepid explorers and ruin seekers found its remains. Never resettled, the site has been explored by archaeologists, and in 1982 was declared a UNESCO World Heritage Site, for 'its excellent example of Roman town planning'.

219

Getting there A bit off the main route, the easiest way to get here is with a tour, easily organised, or via a taxi, from Batna.

Where to stay At present there is nowhere for tourists to stay in the immediate vicinity. Batna is close and offers full tourist facilities, including a range of hotels.

Where to eat If you haven't brought a picnic, the **Restaurant des Excursions** (*just outside the main gates of the site;* ✆ *033 81 12 86*) does proper meals. The place gets very crowded in high season at midday when the ruins are closed for lunch, and most of the organised tour groups have a reserved spot here. The usual fast food gets enhanced with an occasional local speciality. Prices are higher than in town, reflecting the convenience of the location (**$$$**).

What to see The museum located just within the entrance gates is a good place to prepare for the grandeur of the site (⊕ *08.30–12.00 & 13.30–17.00 Sun–Fri; DA20*), although its hours are erratic. If necessary, find one of the local guards and ask if it can be opened (easier if with a tour group). Worth a look, even if it's not possible to get inside, is the outside of the buildings lined with the tombstones and memorials of the city's residents. Note the flat stones with raised depictions of the offerings (to the gods), in which were probably put the real items, such as a fish in a place setting. The naive style gives the items a real sense of ordinary life within the grandeur of Rome. The magnificent and perfectly carved dedications of the arches, marketplaces and theatres recount the exploits – and finances – of major or even self-important people, but these little memorials tell vivid stories of other, but no less real, Romans.

Inside are almost all mosaics, but enormous ones that are virtually intact. Found in temples, churches, baths and dining rooms, one of the best came from the last, with precisely rendered oysters and prawns. Also on view is a delightful version of Neptune on his chariot with a team of four horses, followed by dolphins.

The ruins are entered via the enormous north baths outside the town's main grid, an example of how the town outgrew its original plan. The entrance into the heart of the town is via the decumanus maximus, and the wide and perfectly paved boulevard has enough of the original columns remaining to give a sense of the importance of the town. On the way to the forum are the remains of one of the very few libraries still visible in North Africa. Once in the main square, look out for some Roman graffiti scratched into the paving: 'Venare, Lavare, Ludere, Rioere, Occest Vivere', ie: 'Hunting, Washing, Playing, Smiling – this is Life'. In the southeastern corner is also something akin to a sundial. Here are the curia, civil basilica and a temple. The site is vast and full of things to see, but from here, it's hard to resist the enormous Arch of Trajan to the west. Strolling down the wonderfully pillared cardo to get there, it's extremely easy to imagine the walkway covered with porticoes to protect from the sun in the summer and from the bad weather in the winter. Deep indentations from cart tracks are clearly visible, proving the popularity of this route for wheeled transport. The arch is notable, with an inscription that showed a good example of *damnatio memoriae* (see box, *Chapter 1, page 13*). Its most impressive feature is how it stands above the grid of the city. From any viewpoint, this memorial rises above the urban sprawl, not only providing a reference point but also reminding the inhabitants of the glory of Trajan.

The arch marks the western border of the original city, although there are a few buildings on the outside. Just to the north is another temple, and to the south the vestiges of the Markets of Sertius. Following the line due south, you come to the capitolium, the temple mound to the three main deities, here on a slight hill and visible throughout the city. Further to the west, and far from the central grid, is the Christian complex, populated by the large number of Donatists (see *Chapter 1*, page 24) who resided here.

Returning along the southern edge, passing the south baths, and heading slightly north from here, is the theatre. The complex is cut into the hill and wonderfully preserved. Scrambling up to the 'cheap seats' gives an idea of how intact the tiers are as well as an excellent view of the entire city. Other than by airplane or helicopter, here is the best way to see the city's grid. The acoustics are also good.

LAMBAESIS *En route* to Timgad, in the town of Tazoult-Lambese about 11km southeast of Batna, a large, impressive, square, arcaded and roofless building is visible alongside the road. Soon after, a lone but striking arch can be seen in a field. These monuments belong to the site of Lambaesis, definitely worth a visit.

History Lambaesis was the location of the headquarters of the 3rd August Legion, the main army presence in North Africa. Originally set up by Augustus Caesar, the base had been moved here in AD75 from its previous situation in Tunisia, by Trajan, or possibly slightly later by Hadrian. Resting on the northern edge of the Aures Mountains, the legion was stationed here to patrol this section of the southern perimeter of the Roman provinces of North Africa. Beyond and into the Sahara, were the Berber tribes who made periodic attempts to seize back some of their traditional lands. The Roman army was here not only to keep the peace, but also to take on civil duties, such as engineering feats, like road and aqueduct building, and fiscal responsibilities such as financially monitoring the caravan routes. The camp followers set up their own residences a bit further from the barracks and soon, a second city grew up composed of non-military settlers. Working on the arguable theory used by archaeologists that the size of a Roman metropolis was three times the number of people that could be accommodated in the amphitheatre, the conurbation of Lambaesis had up to 36,000 people. However, this figure can be somewhat distorted, to allow for visitors who were sometimes invited to the games. Inscriptions remain that show the city stayed inhabited until the Vandals arrived, although with the periodic disbanding and re-establishment of the 3rd August Legion, it's hard to tell whether its military purpose continued. Nothing of Christian relevance has – so far – been found. Afterwards, Lambaesis seems to have disappeared until the early archaeologists rediscovered it. In 1852 the French built a prison in the nearby city of Tazoult, a maximum-security version of one that still exists today. As far as ancient Lambaesis is concerned, archaeological excavation continues even if the dig is in a relatively unknown, though extremely interesting, Roman site.

Getting there There are buses that go from Batna to Tazoult, but visiting the two areas of the site, which are quite far apart, as well as the museum in the local town, might be easiest done by taxi. It's probably best to hire one for at least half a day.

Algeria: Batna **THE ROMAN SITES**

16

Where to stay and eat There aren't really places to stay or eat in Lambaesis or Tazoult, although it's possible to find some small snack bar or fast-food place in the town. Take a picnic, or wait until your return to Batna.

What to see The most obvious indication of evidence of a Roman city is visible from quite a distance. In what looks like the middle of a field, a large construction rises up above the grass. Approaching, a 23m by 30m two-storey rectangle of a roofless building composed of four solid walls punctured by arches comes into view. The crossing hall, as the edifice is known, is an impressive site especially as, initially, there seems to be nothing else there. Find a security guard to open up a small, obscure gate into the grounds, and go inside. It soon becomes apparent that the remains of Lambaesis lay beneath you, half excavated and under the level visible from the road. Emerging from the vegetation are clearings and stumps of columns in even intervals. These rows are what had once been barracks. The cardo leads straight to the crossing hall. Closer to the columns near this grand building are half-covered inscription stones. It seems that the last archaeologists at the site put them here, but it was so long ago that they too became buried. Inside the building, nothing is left. Further to the south are the remains of the baths. These wash houses are extremely easy to spot, not only because of the unmistakable tile arches, the standard mark of such places throughout the empire, but also because of the hypocausts, either still standing, or well reconstructed. With thick floors still balanced on top of a few of them, these examples are some of the best in Algeria.

Although the crossing hall is unique among the ruins found in North Africa, the Commodus arch is often the image used in pictures of Lambaesis. Located a bit further south, towards the amphitheatre, the arch itself isn't that impressive, but its location is. It stands alone, but looking back it frames the crossing hall and the mountains beyond. Somehow, the triumphal arch gives a sense of what this military outpost must have been like, standing at the edge of the civilised world.

Continuing south across the grass, the explorer comes across an enormous amphitheatre, half buried in the earth. Although it's easier to see the arena approaching it from the southern or eastern entranceway, especially as the latter has two small but intact arches, there's more of a sense of discovery to come across it from the field to the north. The central games area has been excavated. Spend a few minutes envisaging the kinds of bloodthirsty and no-holds-barred games that soldiers played, with the roughest of the gladiators and the wildest of animals, watched by an audience of up to 15,000 people. This section of the ruins ends, and there's a car park just beyond. Tours will meet their members at this spot, or you can arrange for a rendezvous with your taxi driver here.

Further south, past bits and pieces that definitely look Roman, there seems to be a second site. This section is the civil area of Lambaesis and it's probable that the city extended here, rather than being a separate entity. There doesn't seem to be much here, but the more one looks, the more one sees and the city seems to get larger the closer you get to its attractions. Most impressive is the capitolium, with the columns that announce the triumvirate of temples. Also visible is another temple, presently attributed to Aescalapius, the god of medicine. Despite the major discoveries, there's still a great deal underground waiting to be found.

The museum (⊕ *09.00–12.00 & 13.30–16.30 Sun–Fri; DA20*) explains the history, but it's located back in the town of Tazoult, a few kilometres back up the road toward Batna. The garden is filled with inscriptions, memorial tablets, tombstones and other engraved traces that bring the inhabitants of the town to life. Some of the grave markers are carved with figures of the people once buried beneath them. Inside, there's a small collection of some beautiful mosaics as well as a statue of the city's probable founder, the emperor Hadrian.

Text on some of the tombstones has famous names, such as the emperor Pertinax, or the god Mithras, and puts things in historical and religious perspective. It's worth spending a bit of time here and even if you can't understand Latin, some of the words and personages should seem familiar. Note that dates on many of the tombstones are described in days and months, as well as years. This notation was apparently a common occurrence in ancient Rome, as such information was required by astrologers in their capacity as analysts and omen readers to the superstitious Romans. In addition, the reason for some of the complicated names is not only to indicate family connections, but also as a nomenclature tribute, an obligation of being left money from a donating individual.

MEDRACEN On the road between Constantine and Batna, about 35km before the latter, a conical structure can be made out on the hill to the east. Turning off the road directly towards it, after about 5km you reach the building. Bearing a striking resemblance to the Mauretanian Tomb, this mausoleum is known as the Numidan Tomb. Standing 18.5m high and 59m in diameter, it's not surprising it's visible from so far away. Once believed to be the burial place of King Micapsa in 119BC, recent tests estimate it was built much earlier and is up to 200 years older than its twin near Tipasa (see page 201). For the moment neither who was interned there nor who commissioned construction is known. At the time of research, it wasn't possible to enter as the site was under repair, but it's estimated the restoration should be completed sometime in 2009.

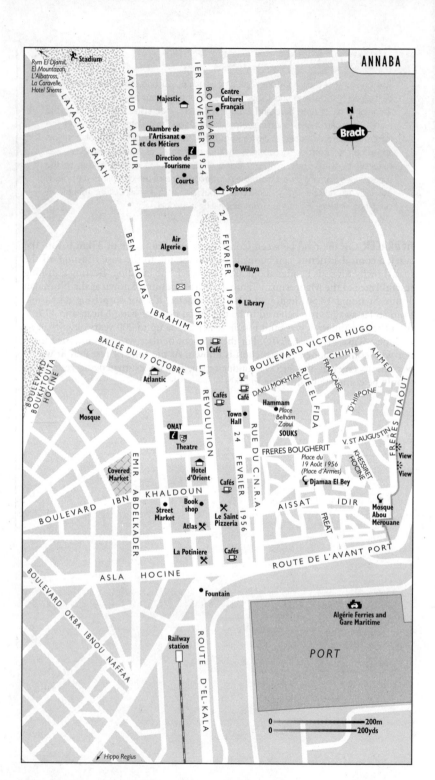

ANNABA

Rym El Djamil,
El Mountazah,
L'Albatross,
La Caravelle,
Hotel Shems

Stadium

LAYACHI SALAH

SAYOUD ACHOUR

BOULEVARD 1ER NOVEMBER 1954

Majestic

Centre Culturel Français

Chambre de l'Artisanat et des Métiers

Direction de Tourisme

Courts

Seybouse

BEN HOUAS IBRAHIM

Air Algerie

24 FEVRIER 1956

Wilaya

Library

COURS DE LA REVOLUTION

BALLÉE DU 17 OCTOBRE

Café

BOULEVARD VICTOR HUGO

BOULEVARD BOUKHTOUTA HOCINE

Atlantic

Mosque

Cafés

Café

DAKLI MOKHTAR

CHIHIB

RUE EL FIDA

FRANCAISE

AHMED

D'HIPPONE

Hammam

Place Belham Zaoui

SOUKS

ONAT

Theatre

Town Hall

24 FEVRIER 1956

RUE DU C.N.R.A.

FRERES BOUGHERIT

Place du 19 Août 1956 (Place d'Armes)

V. ST AUGUSTIN HOCINE

KHESSIRET HOCINE

FRERES DIAOUT

View

View

EMIR ABDELKADER

Covered Market

Hotel d'Orient

Djamaa El Bey

BOULEVARD IBN

KHALDOUN

Book shop

Cafés

Mosque Abou Merouane

Street Market

Atlas

Le Saint Pizzeria

AISSAT IDIR

FREAT

La Potiniere

Cafés

ROUTE DE L'AVANT PORT

ASLA HOCINE

Fountain

BOULEVARD OKBA IBNOU NAFFAA

Railway station

ROUTE D'EL-KALA

Algérie Ferries and Gare Maritime

PORT

0 — 200m
0 — 200yds

Hippo Regius

Bradt

N

224

17

Annaba

Telephone code 038

Situated on a large Mediterranean bay in the northeast corner of the country, Annaba is one of Algeria's largest cities and, despite the 400,000+ population, one of its most pleasant. The place has a more relaxed ambience than some of the other heavily populated centres, and draws residents and tourists to its easy-going ways and lovely beaches. It's primarily French in feel, and many people from France and the north have settled here, giving the impression that Annaba is more European than African.

At the same time, much of this laid-back attitude is deceptive. Not only is the city's port one of the biggest in Algeria, but industry also thrives. Manufacturing includes chemical and aluminium works, and the country's natural resources of iron, phosphate, zinc and other minerals, are exported from here. Agricultural goods are also produced, and grain, a source of income since Roman days, continues to bring money into the country.

HISTORY

The first inhabitants date back to nearly 1100BC. Hundreds of years later, the Phoenicians used the safe haven as one of their port stops. As it grew into a city, the Numidians took over from their predecessors, and after the defeat of the rebel Jugurtha (see page 9), the city was annexed into the Roman Empire. The city became known as Hippo Regius; the latter half of the name is Latin for 'royal' and was bestowed in honour of the previous kings. The city was one of the most important in Roman Emperor Julius Caesar's North African province, benefiting from its proximity to Carthage, just over 200km to the east. Hippo's most illustrious resident was St Augustine, the Catholic philosopher and theologian (see box below).

ST AUGUSTINE OF HIPPO

A native of North Africa, Augustine was born in the town of Thagaste (Algeria) in AD354. Originally a non-religious sort, complete with concubine and child, he was first an academic in Carthage, then in Rome. While employed as a professor of rhetoric in Milan, he was struck by an epiphany one day in August AD386, and converted to a Christian life. Choosing a celibate lifestyle in the Church, he found himself pressed into service as a local priest in Hippo Regius, back in his home province. Becoming bishop in AD395, he envisaged his role as being one of the foremost advocates against Donatism. His written work, particularly his remarkably candid *Confessions* and his most important work, *City of God*, gained him a great deal of notoriety. In AD430 the Vandals invaded Hippo and it was during this attack that Augustine was killed. He was later canonised.

The Vandals invaded in AD429, taking Hippo by siege a year later. King Gaiseric made the city his capital, and it remained so until the Byzantine takeover in AD533. The Arab conquest arrived in AD697 and the city was renamed Bled El Anned. At some point, the location was moved to higher ground, most likely to avoid the sea rushing in, and the old city disappeared. Like the rest of the settlements on the Barbary coast, Annaba had a legacy of piracy and Ottoman collusion lasting until the French arrived in 1832. Renamed Bone, the city developed quite a European flavour with the government encouraging *pied noir* settlement as well as financial and industrial growth. During World War II, Bone played an important part in the theatre of war, having been taken over by the Allies and used as a military base. After Algerian independence in 1962, the city's name was changed to Annaba.

GETTING THERE AND AROUND

Security is problematic in certain areas of Algeria, and travelling in the northeast can be tricky due to the activities of the Berber independence movement, focused around the Kabylie Mountains. It might be easier, or at least safer, to fly or take a ferry, in and out of Annaba, and some of the other cities in the area. Keep informed as to what the latest situation is via the Foreign Office website (see page 388).

BY AIR The Rabah Bitat Airport (\ *038 52 01 31; www.egsa-constantine.dz/ annaba/presentation.php*) is located about 12km from the centre of the city. If you're not travelling with a group with pre-arranged transport, the easiest way to get into town is by taxi, either private or shared. Fares are around DA300 for a private one, much less for shared. There is also an airport bus that takes you into the centre for about DA30. Plans for a new terminal are in the works, so it's possible the whole area will be much more modern by the time you arrive.

BY SEA Algerie Ferries (\ *+39 010 5731805; www.cemar.it/dest/ferries_algeria.htm*) offers a weekly 19-hour crossing from Marseille.

BY RAIL Annaba's station (*Place de la Gare, Av ALN;* \ *038 86 33 02; www.sntf.dz/home.php*) sits close to the main street of the town as well as the port. Trains go to various points in the west and north of the country, including Constantine, Setif, Algiers and Oran. There is also an overnight service to Algiers that gives you enough time to sleep. There is no rail transport to Tunisia, even though it's so close, but it might be possible to find a shared taxi heading that way.

BY BUS AND TAXI Considering the time it takes and the difficulties that might be encountered on the way, going by road is not the best way to get to this part of the country. There is a J station not too far from the centre (*Gare Routière, Carrefour Sidi Brahim*) with coaches travelling to Guelma, Constantine, Setif and Algiers, and some smaller places in between. Shared taxis also leave from here, going to many of the same destinations as the buses, and for the moment are the only way to get to Tunisia on land-based public transport. Generally, it's much easier to jump into one of the many waiting taxis than to try to figure out the bus system.

BY CAR It's not advisable to try to drive to Annaba from other cities in Algeria, as the route from westward points goes through some potentially dangerous areas. Ferries to Annaba from France will get you into the country from Europe (see above). If coming from Tunisia, the border crossing at El Kala is open.

TOURIST INFORMATION

Direction du Tourism de la Wilaya d'Annaba 9 Rue du 1er Novembre 1954; ☏ 038 86 30 13

TOUR OPERATORS

Medina Tours 2 Rue des Frères Bouattit; ☏ 038 86 73 26
ONAT 1 Rue Tarik ibn Ziad; ☏ 038 86 58 86

Tourisme Voyages Algerie 1 Rue Zighout Youcef; ☏ 038 86 29 17

 WHERE TO STAY

Hotel Seybouse (288 rooms) 7 Rue Ali Biskri; ☏ 038 86 24 26. The city's top hotel is in a centrally located modern building that offers a full service including a restaurant & bar, although it caters more to the business visitor than the tourist looking for local appeal. $$$$–$$$$$
Hotel Majestic (91 rooms) 11 Bd du 1er Novembre 1954; ☏ 038 86 54 54; www.hotel-lemajestic.com. This new hotel is located just off the city's main boulevard & comes with all

the luxuries that you expect from its 4-star rating. $$$$
Hotel d'Orient Cours de la Revolution; ☏ 038 86 03 64. This historic hotel is a throwback to its glory in French colonial days, although both it & its facilities have aged somewhat. $$–$$$
Hotel Atlantic Rue Bouzebid Ahmed; ☏ 038 86 57 59. This basic & adequate hotel for visitors with low funds has the advantage of being situated in the heart of town. $

It's also worth mentioning a couple of hotels that are located outside the city but are great places to relax and enjoy the views.

Hotel Rym El Djamil (72 rooms) Rte du Cap Garde, Belvedere; ☏ 038 88 21 43; www.Rym-el-djamil.com. Situated above Belvedere Beach, one of the nicest strands in the area, this lovely hotel seems more like a luxury resort than accommodation that's a mere 10mins west of the city centre. $$$–$$$$

Hotel El Mountazah (102 rooms) Seraidi, about 12km west of Annaba along the W16 road & up into the hills; ☏ 038 57 42 18. The spectacular white-domed architecture of this hilltop hotel is matched by its views over the sea, & the staff members are accustomed to non-residents coming up to see the place. $$$

WHERE TO EAT

In keeping with the French café tradition, the area around the city's main street, the Cours de la Revolution, has several places to stop for a break. The lemon ice is a local speciality. There are also plenty of snack outlets, usually featuring rotisserie chicken or pizzas. Both the **Hotel Majestic** and the **Hotel Seybouse** have their in-hotel restaurants, although the food, and the costs, are more Western than Algerian. For more substantial local fare, try the following.

Restaurant Atlas 2 Zenine Larbi; ☏ 038 80 25 70. It's possible to get a more typical Algerian meal here at a reasonable price & even enjoy an alcoholic drink alongside. $$$
La Potiniere 1 Cours de la Revolution; ☏ 038 86 61 41. A classic place that's been around for a

while, the cuisine is French, the location central & the prices higher than the cafés on the street. $$–$$$
Le Saint Pizzeria 9 Cours de la Revolution; ☏ 038 32 77 15. One of the better pizza joints is a favourite with locals & situated just off the Cours. $$

Many of Annaba's best restaurants are located on the seafront a bit further out of town. If looking for a good place to eat, especially for seafood, it's certainly worth taking a taxi for a few kilometres and dining by the Mediterranean.

✕ L'Albatros Plage Rizi Amor; ☎ 038 88 36 61. The views from the 1st floor as well as the excellent fish make this place one of the best known, & arguably the best, in Annaba. **$$$$**

✕ La Caravelle Rte de la Corniche; ☎ 038 86 89 31. Another restaurant highly recommended for its fish dishes, it's located a little further out on the Corniche, but worth the journey. **$$$$**

ENTERTAINMENT AND NIGHTLIFE

Café life in Annaba is a pleasure, and it's fun to amble around the Cours de la Revolution, stopping for a coffee and to people-watch. The seafront is where the Algerian tourists go, and there's a café scene here, too. Closer to the resorts on the beaches are clubs and karaoke bars. *En route* to Cap de Garde are more hotels with bars and discos.

☆ Hotel Shems Complexe Touristique, Shems-les-Bains, Rte du Cap de Garde, Ras El-Hamra; ☎ 038 88 21 55. An older place, it's said to have one of the most notorious evening shows in the city.

SHOPPING

The **Cours de la Revolution** seems to be the area with the most going on, in terms of shopping. Somewhere among these little stores you can find most of what you need. Included are bookshops, souvenir stands and travel basics. Just to the west is the **covered market**.

OTHER PRACTICALITIES

EMERGENCY TELEPHONE NUMBERS
Police ☎ 17
Medical ☎ 115
Security ☎ 112

INTERNET CAFÉS Cyber.net (*23 Rue Emir Abdelkader;* ☎ *038 80 53 25*) seems to have greater sticking power than many of the other places that come and go.

POST The main post office is situated at 1 Avenue Zighout Youcef.

BANKS Many banks have a branch along the Cours de la Revolution. Some have ATMs, although whether they take foreign cards is constantly changing. The bigger hotels will change, and in some cases, accept other currencies. It's probably best to take euros along.

WHAT TO SEE

COURS DE LA REVOLUTION The city's central street is a reminder of French colonial days, when the city was full of Gallic charm and many foreigners. Here is where the best buildings, cafés and city life are located.

DJAMAA EL BEY (*Pl 19 Août 1956*) Situated in the old town, this mosque was built during the latter period of the Ottoman occupation, and was renovated by the French when they took over in 1832.

MOSQUE OF ABOU MEROUANE Close to the Djamaa is this much older mosque, dating back over a thousand years and constructed partly from material liberated from the nearby site of Hippo Regius. Its purpose in life changed when the French arrived and converted it to a military building, but it's now been returned to religious use.

THE SEAFRONT Perhaps the most attractive feature of Annaba is what lies just west of it, the Corniche with its beautiful beaches. Retreating towards the promontory of Cap Garde are Saint-Cloud, Rizi-Amor, La Caroube, Toche, Belvedere and Ain Achir. Not yet overdeveloped, the area can still get extremely busy with locals, especially during the summer

THE ROMAN SITE

HIPPO REGIUS Also known as Hippone, the Roman site is the predecessor to today's Annaba and is located southwest of the modern city centre.

History Originally by the sea that has since receded, there are traces of the area's use as a settlement that pre-dates the Phoenicians. The Roman remains are the most visible, even though they were hidden until French archaeologists started digging early last century. Tales of Hippo were prolific in writings, especially since the city was the home of St Augustine, the Christian theologian and philosopher (see box, page 225). Today, the site sits in an undeveloped area and the much newer Basilica of St Augustine, dominant on top of an ancient temple site, gives a view of greenery and the sea beyond.

Getting there Located about 3km from the centre of Annaba along the N16 in the direction of Guelma and Constantine; taxis will take you if you don't want to walk.

What to see The site (⏱ 09.00–12.00 & 14.00–17.00 daily; DA20) sits between two hills: on top of the first was a penitentiary from French times, which has since been converted to the museum; on the second is the Basilica of St Augustine. The area of this once extremely important city is large, over 148 acres, but there is still a great deal to be excavated. The layout is somewhat odd, adapting the Roman grid to allow for the variations in elevation, as well as the pre-existing settlement. Entry to the ancient ruins is from the sea side, not far from where tour buses and taxis let out passengers. Near here, benefiting from the breezes that then came off the water, were the villas of the wealthier citizens of the town. The Villas of the Labyrinth and the Villa of the Procurator as well as some of the smaller ones, can still be visited.

Past the southern baths, the route goes to the Christian quarter, arguably the most notable part of the site, due to its St Augustine associations. Lines of the perimeter of the grand basilica have been drawn on the ground, showing the extent of the building, and the unusual north facing of the central apse. There is no definitive argument that this church was St Augustine's, other than the fact that the dates match. With all his writings it's surprising he didn't mention it. Eventually the route leads to the forum, the vast open space around which were located not only the central administrative offices and religious structures, but also the heart of the city. So far, the largest found in Roman North Africa at a size of 76m by 43m, the square is paved, and there are still vestiges of its grandeur to be seen, with a few of the columns still in their original locations.

Beyond are the large baths, and the ones of Septimius Severus just a bit further. Water was piped in via an aqueduct from the nearby hills of Seraidi (about 12km northwest) and stored in cisterns.

It's worth heading up the little hill where the museum is located, to get a bit of background as well as an idea of what the city was once like. Inside are three

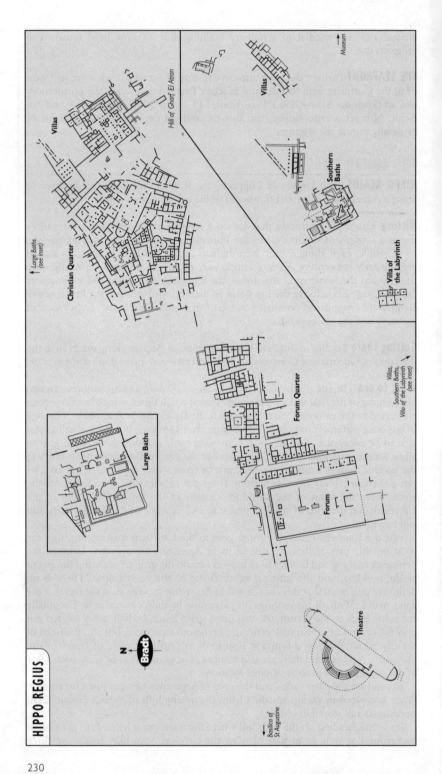

HIPPO REGIUS

N

Bradt

Basilica of St Augustine

Theatre

Large Baths

Forum Quarter

Forum

Villas, Southern Baths, Villa of the Labyrinth (see inset)

Large Baths (see inset)

Christian Quarter

Villas

Hill of Gharf El Atran

Villas

Southern Baths

Villa of the Labyrinth

Museum

exhibition halls, two showing mosaics and one displaying sculpture, mostly from the forum.

The entire site is in the shadow of the hilltop Basilica of St Augustine of Hippo. In pre-Roman times, a temple to the chief god, Baal Hammon, was put here. Steles from the Phoenician period that were found during the basilica's construction are now in the museum. The Romans, embracing the belief and adapting it into their own, replaced the temple with one to Saturn. This church, constructed in a Byzantine style similar to its contemporary, Sacre Coeur in Paris, was built in 1881 and consecrated 18 years after its completion. The apse of the basilica holds a funerary monument that represents St Augustine on his deathbed and within it, one of his real elbows is clearly visible, placed anatomically appropriately in the right arm of the lying figure. This relic is the goal of many pilgrimages, and a new officially sanctioned tourist route visiting Christian sites is being planned, highlighting St Augustine and his haunts. Views from this hillside are lovely, especially looking over the Roman site of Hippo as well as Annaba and the sea.

18

Beyond the Romans

THE BEST THINGS TO SEE SOUTH OF THE ROMAN PROVINCES

The region that is possibly the most spectacular and the one that consistently defeated the Romans is the desert. Left to the Berbers, primarily nomads, the northern occupiers might have monitored the comings and goings of travellers, particularly those traders on the caravan routes, but they never made major incursions into the area.

Almost 80% of Algeria consists of these arid lands, mostly in the Sahara. The environment is one of the main tourist draws of the region, despite its extremes. Aided by the construction and gradual improvement of the Trans Sahara Highway, running from Algiers to Lagos, Nigeria, this rough and ready highway is the basis for adventure tours into Algeria's southern desert areas. Security concerns remain a real issue and effectively prevent independent travel, but reliable tour operators know the safe areas, and offer trips to the most accessible highlights.

The Algerian Sahara is vast, and there is much to see, even if it takes a lot of effort to get there. By necessity, the descriptions below are superficial and presented only to give an idea of the natural beauties that the Romans completely missed. Once past the mountain barrier, the terrain changes at the Grand Erg Occidental, a great sand region, slightly west. Now in the area of the northern Sahara, the oasis towns begin. Ghardia, 625km down the road from Algiers, is a convenient tourist stop, particularly as the base for exploring the UNESCO World Heritage Site of the M'Zab Oasis. Designated worthy of international recognition in 1982, the M'Zab is 'A traditional human habitat, created in the 10th century by the Ibadites around their five ksour [fortified cities], [that] has been preserved intact in the M'Zab valley. Simple, functional and perfectly adapted to the environment, the architecture of M'Zab was designed for community living, while respecting the structure of the family. It is a source of inspiration for today's urban planners.'

The road continues south, and the next destination on the long journey west into the Grand Erg Occidental is to Timimoun, an oasis town that's as red as the sand around it. A favourite with visitors, there's everything one looks for in the desert, from dunes to ruins to dramatic views. To short-cut the trip, there is an airport that takes flights from Algiers and Oran. Beni Abbes, further west and also accessible via Tlemcen and Ain Sefra, is another oasis town, with a palmeraie (palm grove) and more dunes.

It's about a 1,300km drive, or a flight, to the next significant region of attractions around Tamranrasset. There is a great deal of interest to see here and to the east towards the mountains that border Libya, particularly the extraordinary scenery and the prehistoric rock art (see page 4) situated in the Ahaggar (Hoggar) National Park. Some of the highlights are the views from Assekrem, just north of Tamanrasset and the dramatic sculpted landscapes of the Tassili de Hoggar, to the east, on the route to Djanet. There's a weekly flight to the town. People come here to see some of the most important sights in Algeria, encompassed by the country's only natural UNESCO World Heritage Site, the Tassili N'Ajjer National Park. It's officially described thus: 'Located in a strange lunar landscape of great geological interest, this site has one of the most important groupings of prehistoric cave art in the world. More than 15,000 drawings and engravings record the climatic changes, the animal migrations and the evolution of human life on the edge of the Sahara from 6000BC to the first centuries of the present era. The geological formations are of outstanding scenic interest, with eroded sandstones forming "forests of rock".'

Part Four

TUNISIA

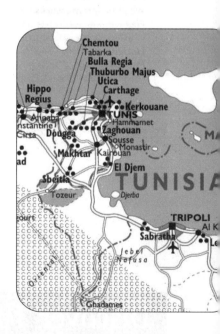

Location North Africa, 34°00'N, 9°00'E. To the north is the Mediterranean Sea.

Neighbouring countries The country is sandwiched between Algeria to the west and Libya to the east

Size 163,610km²; 32nd-largest country in Africa, 93rd largest in the world.

Climate Temperate Mediterranean on the coast with rainy winters, hot and dry in the desert to the south

Status Republic

Population 10,383,577 (July 2008 estimate)

Life Expectancy 75.56 years: male 73.79 years, female 77.46 (2008)

Capital Tunis, population over 2.3 million (2007)

Other main towns Bizerte, Beja, Nabeul, Le Kef, Sousse, Hammamet, Monastir, Sfax, Kairouan, Medenine, Tozeur Jerba

Economy Agriculture provides the main source of income, with industry (including mineral exploitation) and tourism also important

GDP US$7,500 per capita (2007)

Languages Arab is the official language while French is used for business

Religion Muslim 98%, Christian 1%, Jewish and other 1%

Currency Tunisian dinar (TND)

Exchange rate £1 = TND2, US$1 = TND1.4, €1 = TND1.8 (Apr 2009)

National airline/airport Tunisair; Tunis: Tunis-Carthage Airport

International telephone code +216

Time GMT+1, increases one hour in the summer (Daylight Saving Time)

Electrical voltage 220 volts AC, 50Hz; European two-pin plug

Weights and measures Metric

Flag Red with solid white sphere in the centre, in which are a red crescent moon to the left, and a red star to its upper right (the symbol of Islam)

National anthem *Himat Al Hima* (Defenders of the Fatherland)

Public holidays 1 January, New Year's Day; 10 January, Hegire, Islamic New Year; *9 March, Mouled, Prophet's Anniversary; 20 March, Independence Day; 21 March, Youth Day; 9 April, Martyrs' Day; 1 May, Labour Day; 25 July, Republic Day; 13 August, Women's Day; *21 September, Eid al-Fitr, End of Ramadan; 7 November, New Era Day; *28 November, Eid al-Idha, Feast of the Sacrifice. (for 2009: starred dates change according to the Muslim calendar)

19

Background Information

GEOGRAPHY

The little country of Tunisia, ranked 32nd in size among its 46 African neighbours, sits between two giants. At 163,610km², it's 14.5 times smaller than Algeria, and less than one-tenth the size of Libya. Sitting at exactly 34°00'N and 9°00'E, it hugs the Mediterranean Sea with a coastline on both its northern and much longer eastern edges extending in total to almost 1,300km. Although the land area is small, its proportion of navigable shoreline is high, and the bays safe havens, and accessible harbours are probably why the region was so important to the ancients. Even today, the port of Tunis, the capital city, remains a major shipping centre. Tunisia is a mere 160km away from Sicily, making the country the closest African nation to Italy and in a strong position to oversee the narrow channel between the western and eastern Mediterranean.

Because of its size and location, most of the land is fertile, and the Tunisians exploit this benefit. The northern coastal region has good soil and combined with generous rainfall continues to yield agricultural products, including the grain for which it was famous in Roman times. Further south, the temperature can get cold, as the Grand Dorsal, part of the Atlas chain, passes through here, ending in the Cape Bon peninsula that extends east into the sea. Not as impressive as they get in Morocco and Algeria, the mountains still rise up to 1,544m.

As the mountains are not high, their tapering off to the south is also not as dramatic, but the land beyond remains fertile. Fields of grass turn lush and green in the rainy season and this area is the northern end of the grape-growing and wine-producing, region. Further south, the land is dry and heats up. Here, olives and their products, especially oil, are grown in groves that extend as far as the eye

NORTH AFRICA IN CALIFORNIA

In 1942, when it was decided that America would send military aid to North Africa to help the Allies, it was necessary to train the troops for desert combat. For this reason, the Desert Training Center, California-Arizona Maneuver Area (DTC-CAMA) was established. This part of southern California was chosen to be the base of US operations, because the terrain closely resembled what was believed to be that of North Africa. General George S Patton Jr was the first commander.

Despite the initial failure of the US army against the Germans, the Allies defeated the Axis powers in 1943. Perhaps the exercises practised at this remote and arid site helped. By 1944, after the Germans quit North Africa and the region was safely in the hands of the Allies, the California centre was closed. Today, there's a museum that commemorates the war effort, as well as subsequent events (**General Patton Memorial Museum** 65–510 Chiriaco Rd, Chiriaco Summit, 30 miles east of Indio on Interstate 10; www.generalpattonmuseum.com; ⏰ 09.30–16.30 daily; US$4)

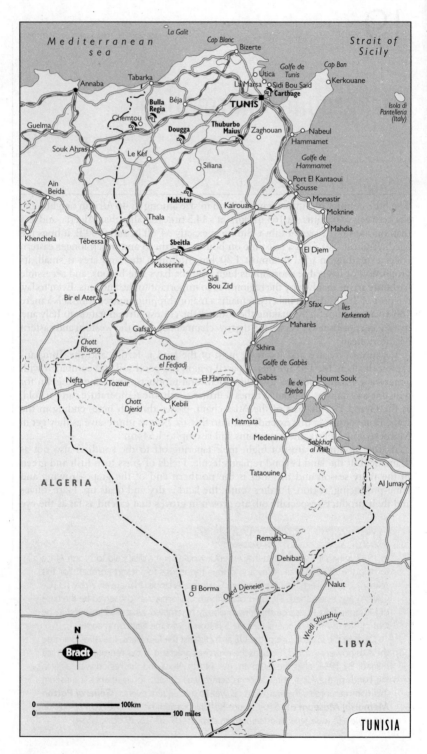

BOU-HEDMA East of the city of Gafsa, this large acacia forest includes the gumtree among its 300 varieties of plants and is home to animals such as the antelope, gazelle, mouflon and what's left of the ostrich population.

BOUKORNINE Consists of a forest just south of Tunis, and houses boars and porcupines and the Persian cyclamen.

CHAAMBI Some 6,723ha of Aleppo pine forests with 100 plant, 24 mammal and 16 reptile and frog and toad species. The site sits near Kasserine.

FEIJA In the northwest of the country is this cork and oak forest that features over 500 types of orchids and ferns as well as wild boar, jackals and local deer plus various reptiles.

ICHKEUL A 12,000ha site that contains 600 plant and 180 different wintering bird species. Located close to Bizerte in the north, not far from Tunis, this site is listed as the country's only UNESCO natural site. The park has been set aside due to its importance as a major halt on the migration route for ducks, flamingos, geese and storks. The park is the sole vestige of a series of lakes that once stretched across the entire north of the continent.

JEBIL Tunisia's only park located completely in the Sahara, about 80km south of Douz, protecting a true desert environment.

ORBATA West of Gafsa, a prime location for the mouflon which thrives in this 3,000ha refuge of dry, mountainous terrain.

SIDI TOUI Sits at the northern rim of the Sahara, close to the town of Medenine, and preserves features of a desert environment and its animals.

ZAGOUAN The mountain refuge from where the Romans piped water to Carthage, and a high-altitude location which is home to the golden eagle, one of the few such places in the Mediterranean.

ZEMBRA AND ZEMBRETTA These islands just off the coast of Cap Bon, in the Gulf of Tunis, were the first to be declared a national park, and protect 266 plant species and the native wild rabbit.

Tunisia: Background Information **GEOGRAPHY**

19

can see. As the land gets hotter, dates are cultivated in the massive almeraie, the dark green oases that stand out against the yellows, oranges and reds of the sand. Harvesting still employs the largest percentage of the population and contributes a portion of the country's wealth, although not the biggest.

About halfway down the length of the country, the desert begins, the border virtually marked by the salt flat depression of Chott El Djerid to the east. The town of Douz, situated halfway between the mountains that border Algeria and the Mediterranean Gulf of Gabes, is known as the Gateway of the Sahara. Further south, into the wedge that gets more and more narrow until it ends with Algeria and Libya bordering each other, is true desert. A few little towns are here for those visitors who want a true Sahara experience, but there is very little development. The few tracks that exist are 4x4 only. There are some Berber and Touareg (blue men, ie: travellers wrapped totally in blue) nomads, who traverse the landscape, but both Algeria and Libya have higher numbers.

NATURAL HISTORY

Despite the country's small size, there is a wide diversity of environments, many of which are protected, or at least on the itinerary to become so. Consisting of only a small slice of land that doesn't include much desert, most of the country is conducive to a variety of plants and animals, and easy to access. The density of population thriving on this cultivatable land causes problems and the public and UNESCO are aware of these issues.

In recognition of the differing landscapes and their vulnerability the government has stepped in and set aside ten national parks, 16 natural reserves and 14 priority natural sites and areas.

POST-ROMAN HISTORY

After AD701, Tunisia was firmly under Arab control, ruled by the Ummayad dynasty. As prone to the changes in rulers as the rest of North Africa, the country's royal family was deposed, replaced by the next wave, the Aghlabids, in AD746. With Islamic North Africa then divided into three parts, the Aghlabids, under the leadership of Ibrahim ibn-Al Aghlab, controlled Tunisia and points east, based in the capital Kairouan. Managing to stay put for over a century, some of the country's most important constructions dated from this period, including the Great Mosque and the huge eponymous water basins, both in Kairouan. The Aghlabids were not immune to takeover, and the Fatimids, Shiities on their way from Algeria to Cairo, took over the country *en route*. They established their local capital in Mahdia. While the Fatimids were off in Egypt, the Zirid dynasty, a Berber tribe also in Algeria, began to make their presence felt and although initially in collusion with the Fatimids, they switched religious alliance to the Sunni branch of Islam in 1045. The subsequent religious war was escalated into systematic destruction, especially when tribes from Upper Egypt as well as Arabia came into the fray. For the subsequent 100 years, the lands of North Africa were left in ruins.

The next wave of government came from the west, with the Moroccan Almohads incorporating Tunisia in their conquering wave, swallowing Mahdia as they passed. However, the empire was too vast for them, and separating North Africa into three regions once again, the country, as part of Ifriquiya that also included Libya, fell under Hafsid rule. The borders created then are more or less the ones that still remain.

In the world to the north, the Crusades had begun. Tunisia's proximity to the Holy Land was noted when the Eighth Crusade thought to use it as a base for incursions, first into Egypt, and then into the Middle East. The devout king Louis IX, later St Louis, took his role as a good Christian to heart, and led the assault, but died in Tunis in 1270. The king's legacy remains with his eponymous huge 19th-century church dominating the site of Carthage on top of Byrsa Hill.

By 1500, Tunisia shared the fate of Algeria, with the Barbarossa pirate brothers, El Uruj and Khayr-al-Din, setting up their base on the island of Djerba. Soon after the Spanish captured El Uruj in 1518, the remaining half of the privateers asked for aid from Turkey. Generously granted, especially to Khayr-al-Din, the Ottomans gained control with Barbarossa as their general. Tunis's nationality was the focus for battles between the nations, but the city finally became decidedly Turkish in 1574. Local squabbles over influence continued until the 1700s, when Hussein

Ben Ali established his line, providing beys (governors) who remained in power, until the country's transition to a republic in 1957.

As with the rest of the Barbary coast, ships from northern Europe as well as the United States sailed into Tunisia and demanded the cessation of pirate activities in 1816. Together with the abolition of slavery 30 years later, the termination of two of the country's most lucrative activities created a situation of bankruptcy. Financial organisation had to be turned over to an international organisation, further demoralising a country that had once been rich and independent. A fortunate by-product is that because of the agreements to stop such activities, the French didn't have the same reason to enter Tunisia as they had with Algeria. However, they used the excuse of monitoring Tunisian marauders who crossed into the French-controlled nation to the west as a justification in 1881 for stationing troops. Tunisia officially became a French protectorate in the same year. Britain colluded by trading acknowledgement of the French position for allowing the UK's control of Cyprus.

Tunisia followed the lead of its 'protectors' during World War II, changing loyalty to the Vichy and Axis governments after France fell to the Germans. Now foes of the Allies, Tunisia was absorbed into enemy territory. Although most of the fighting occurred on the Libyan–Egyptian border (see pages 330–1), Tunisia became involved during Operation Torch, launched in November 1942. In February 1943, the Allied and Axis armies crossed near Kasserine, not far from the Algerian border. It was the first time the forces of the United States and Germany met on the field. The Americans were seriously outclassed and suffered significant losses. Losing the battle but not the war, the US army broke through enemy lines in March 1943. They met up with the British army coming from Libya by May and forced the capitulation of the Axis army in Tunis on 13 May 1943. North Africa was now firmly in Allied hands.

There were rumblings for independence before World War II and the movement grew in earnest once the conflict was over. Habib Bourgiba had already founded a breakaway political party but was repeatedly forced to escape to neighbouring lands, when the French hardened their attitude. With the changing political climate, France was willing to discuss terms, and on 20 March 1956, Tunisia became its own nation, with Bourgiba elected as the country's first prime minister. Named as a constitutional monarchy, with the representative of the lingering bey system Muhammad VIII al-Amin declared king, the next year Bourgiba rid the country of any of the vestiges of the old monarchical system. However, in 1975, Prime Minister Bourgiba was granted the post of president, for the rest of his life.

With the rise in Islam as a political force, and the government's willingness to use the military to repress it, dissidence increased. Although freer elections were called, Bourgiba still remained, and some of the party faithful were beginning to question his capacity to govern. Finally, at the age of 83, he was declared unfit, and replaced by his prime minister Zine el Abidine ben Ali on 7 November 1987. Despite the relatively heavy-handed attempts to control opposition parties and issues, Tunisia has a reputation of being one of the more liberal Maghreb nations.

POLITICS

The country that virtually everyone knows as simply Tunisia is officially named Al Jumhuriyah at Tunisiyah. A republic with an elected president, the people of the nation seem to prefer devils they know to those they don't, and tend to re-elect repeatedly the same heads of state. A democratically elected government since France granted it independence in 1956, there have so far been only two leaders, each chosen by the electorate for five-year terms. The previous president, Habib Bourgiba, who came to power on Independence Day, 20 March 1956, was actually elected president for life, but was eventually deposed when declared too old for the post. The current president, Zine el Abidine ben Ali was then voted in and since 1987 has been the man in power. The last election in 2004 guarantees he'll remain until at least 2009. His official title is chief of state. Although multi-party elections have been allowed since 1981, the president received 94.5% of the vote. The head of government is Prime Minister Mohamed Ghannouchi who's been around since 1999. The Cabinet of Ministers is appointed by the president.

The law-making branch of government consists of two chambers. The first is the Chamber of Deputies, which has 189 positions. The members are elected by popular vote, and they each serve five-year terms. The Chamber of Advisers has 126 seats, 85 of whom are elected by local dignitaries, such as councillors, deputies, mayors and trade unions, while the last 41 are also selected by the president. The advisers serve for a six-year period.

The judicial system is overseen by the Court de Cassation, a high court that has a status similar to that of the Supreme Court in the United States. It's also the court of last resort, and what they decide is the final decision, regardless of the previous jurisdiction.

The capital of the country is Tunis and there are 24 areas in the country, each overseen by a governor.

ECONOMY

Alongside tourism and phosphate mining – the most important sources of income – agriculture, additional mineral exploitation and manufacturing also play a role in the financial well-being of the country. Services, catering heavily to foreign and domestic visitors, account for over 62% of the GDP, while industry plays a 25.7% part, and agriculture nearly completes the pie at 11.6%. The distribution of employment is completely different, with agriculture taking up 55% of the labour force, industry 23% and services, the relative jewel of the economy, only needing 22%.

Tunisia does have some oil and natural gas reserves, but they are only a small percentage compared to Libya and Algeria, and domestic consumption outstrips supply. As a result, fuel has become an expense, rather than a source of income.

The agriculture of the country is diverse. In the liberally rainwatered north, the harvesting of grain continues in the tradition established in Roman times, while both dairy and beef cattle are bred for domestic and export consumption. The somewhat drier regions south of the Dorsale Mountains are excellent for citrus and olive farms. Even the desert areas are cultivated where water appears, and the magnificent date palms that huddle together in the oases produce excellent fruit. In areas where the pollution is high, such as near the industrial city of Sfax along the coast, and the fruit produced is not up to export standards, so used instead as animal fodder.

Tourism is a significant money earner for Tunisia. With less scenery and less 'ethnic' tourism than its main Maghreb rival, Morocco, the country has concentrated on luxury facilities. Spa and golf holidays are big business, and there are a very large number of beautiful hotels and resorts. Financial investment in the tourism sector has been significant. Emphasising a more European feel, the appeal of the country is for beachside holidays, with perhaps a little culture or adventure thrown in. Based on its revenue figures, the strategy seems to have worked.

Tunisia is thriving, and its growth rate of 6.3% in 2007, as well as its GDP per capita income of US$7,500 (second only to oil-rich Libya in the Maghreb) indicates good financial health. The World Economic Forum in 2007 gave Tunisia glowing reports on the international stage, by rating it the most competitive economy in Africa as well as the Arab world, and considering it as the 29th-ranked economy on the planet. However, its unemployment rate is still 14.1% and with 69.7% of the population between the ages of 15 and 64, jobs need to be found. The increased output of university graduates will exacerbate the problem, especially as the well-educated will not settle for agricultural or menial jobs. The government is turning its attention to these issues. By easing control and inviting more privatisation, while at the same time managing debt more efficiently, actions are in place to encourage investment and a better financial state.

PEOPLE

A small country with a small population, Tunisia's ten million people fit into an area of just over 163,600km², with a density of around 62 people/km², and a large number work in agriculture. Nearly 75% of Tunisians live in the fertile strip near the coast, with the capital city, Tunis, the largest in North Africa except for Cairo, estimated as having almost a fifth of the country's inhabitants.

At 98%, virtually the entire population is Arab, with almost no Berber mix. Europeans and Jews evenly make up the balance. Once, these smaller ethnicities existed in larger numbers, but they left after independence was declared. Arabic is considered the official language, but both it and French are used in business transactions.

After a population bulge some years ago, growth has slowed to 0.99%, and now issues of a high unemployment rate and the need and cost of education are coming to prominence. Differential between the sexes in literacy still occurs, with 83.4% of men able to read, while only 65.3% of women can, but this number will perhaps eventually be evened out.

CULTURE

Culture is so much a part of Tunisian life that the government, together with rich organisations and individuals, formalise its existence with the establishment of institutions and subsidies to events. Not only are museums encouraged and supported, but also art galleries, libraries, theatres and performance venues. The large number of art-based festivals are a source of pride for the state, with participants joining in from all over the world. The important role that film, fine art, music and theatre play in everyday life is acknowledged in annual celebrations.

ARCHITECTURE As soon as you arrive in Tunisia, the most obvious cultural element becomes apparent. Influenced by the different civilisations that passed through North Africa, the country's buildings have an arabesque flavour that is often mixed with Roman, Spanish, Turkish and French styles. The archetypal town generally comprises three standards: a main mosque, a market and a public bath (*hammam*). UNESCO have declared three cities' medinas as World Heritage Sites: **Tunis**, because it was 'considered one of the greatest and wealthiest cities in the Islamic world'; **Kairouan**, with 'its rich architectural heritage'; and **Sousse** for being 'a typical example of a town dating from the first centuries of Islam'.

Many of Tunisia's buildings are painted white with a blue trim. These colours perform a cooling function in the heat and are extremely appealing. Often doors in these white-and-blue towns are painted contrasting hues, such as red or yellow. Sidi Bou Said, just outside the capital Tunis, is a village of such decoration and one of the country's most attractive. Modern architects are often inspired by these styles, building some wonderful examples, usually hotels and resorts that suit the climate.

There are also the troglodyte houses, or cave dwellings, particularly in Matmata. At the northern edge of the desert, up in the hills, temperatures in the winter can get very low at night and in the summer very high in the day. For hundreds of years locals have dealt with this variation by burrowing their homes into the earth, essentially living underground. Dug into a hill, but usually clearing a central courtyard open to the sky, they are entered via a doorway carved into the earth, emerging into a large clearing, before re-entering the earth to get to the individual rooms. Reused and rebuilt in the same way for generations, these dwellings have enabled living here to continue in the traditional manner. Notably, some of these residences were used as sets in the film *Star Wars*, as their living style appears weird enough to be from another planet.

HANDICRAFTS As in Morocco, handmade items are readily produced in the country, with some superb examples around, as well as tacky versions usually sold in the tourist towns. Common among the souvenir stalls are ceramics, ironwork lamps, hookahs, three-dimensional representations of typical doors in various forms including mirrors, fridge magnets and mosaics. The last of these crafts is no doubt a legacy from the Romans, who seem to have left the best examples still remaining from the ancient world in Tunisia. Some of the ones produced today, even on the outdoor stands, can be quite beautiful. Painting, too, is alive and well, encouraged not only by private individuals who run galleries, at present about 50 of them, but also by the cultural institutes set up by the government.

THEATRE The actor and director Ali Ben Ayed (1930–72) brought both domestic and international recognition for Tunisian theatre and with the assistance of one of his fans, President Bourgiba, established the art form here. In later years, the Ministry of Culture formalised government assistance by founding the National Theatre (the Palace of Kheireddine), the Regional Drama Centre at El Kef and Gafsa, and the National Puppet Centre.

MUSIC An integral part of all the Maghreb, Tunisia has its own forms of music. The most notable is *malouf* ('customary'), an Andalusian derivative dating from the 15th-century Spanish period. There's some Berber influence and even though it tends to be performed only at traditional events, the government and keen individuals have contributed to its continuation. Other forms common with the rest of the Maghreb are also performed. Modern artists have penetrated the international markets: the jazz musician Anouar Brahem has become popular in the West.

CINEMA Despite the fact that most of the films playing in the bigger houses tend to come from the mega-production output of Egypt, Tunisia does have its own burgeoning cinema industry. Some endemic productions have received awards and commendations outside the country. More visible is the scenery, used as locations in high-profile films, such as *Monty Python's Life of Brian*, *Star Wars*, *Raiders of the Lost Ark* and *The English Patient*.

LITERATURE Some of Tunisia's most revered writers have been poets, with Abou al-kacen Echebbi (1909–34) one of the most famous. Despite dying far too young, he's immortalised for having written the last two verses in the Tunisian national anthem and his work is taught in every school. New writers have emerged, with a large number of authors producing work even though many of them do so from bases abroad. Often written in French, many books have been translated into English.

FESTIVALS The country has a very large number of formal festivals, celebrating the arts. Government sponsored and often with international participation, these events are very well attended. Among them are the following.

12 July	Yasmine Hammamet Festival	Hammamet
23–25 June	Falconry Festival	Haouaria
5–8 July	Thoroughbred Horse Festival	Meknassy (Sidi Bouzid)
12 July–23 August	International Festival of Carthage	Tunis
13 July–22 August	International Festival of Hammamet	Hammamet
14 July–18 August	International Festival of Sousse	Sousse
17–25 July	Ulysse Festival	Djerba
17–31 July	International Festival of Testour (Malouf)	Testour (Béja)
14 July–17 August	International Festival of Bizerta	Bizerta
22 July–6 August	Plastic Art Festival	Mahrès (Sfax)
15 July–5 August	International Festival of Dougga	Dougga
14 July–11 August	International Festival of Symphonic Music	El Jem (Mahdia)
15 July–15 September	Carthage-Byrsa Festival (exhibition)	Carthage
13 July–18 August	Nights of El Marsa	La Marsa
1 August–15 September	Shopping	Tunis
8–11 November	Sahara Douz Festival	Douz
3–6 November	Oasis Festival	Tozeur
12 November	Tourism Saharan Day	Sud
Ramadan	Medina Festival	Tunis

20

Practical Information

SUGGESTED ITINERARIES FOR CRUISE-SHIP PASSENGERS

Tunisia is a very popular port of call for cruise-ship passengers, usually on trips that tour the eastern Mediterranean. There are several itineraries that include Libya and Egypt on the route, either ending or beginning in Europe, although there are virtually none that ply the entire Maghreb. Cruises to Tunisia that are part of a grander scheme stop at Tunis and perhaps one other destination such as Sousse or Sfax. Trips that specialise either in the country or the ancient sites might also include Tabarka

TABARKA Generally visited only coming from Annaba, Algeria or specialist cruises, Tabarka (see page 253 for main entry) is a small city close to the Algerian border. Known primarily for its landscapes, especially water-related ones, the resort aspect is featured, with a modern yacht harbour and the best scuba diving in the country. The city is the closest seaport for the spectacular Roman site of Bulla Regia. A short drive south into the hills, this ancient city is unique in that so many of its wonderful villas are actually underground, some with mosaics still *in situ*. No conclusions have been agreed as to why. Just a bit further west is the site of Chemtou, where the Romans quarried their red-and-yellow marble, and built a small settlement on top of a previously existing Numidian one. If no tours have been organised, it's easy enough to arrange a taxi to visit both sites, as neither is very far from port. Alternatively, Tabarka is a good place to get off the ship and do a bit of snorkelling.

TUNIS Ships sail into the port of La Goulette, located closer to the suburb of Carthage than the centre of Tunis. A charming little seaside port area in its own right, with excellent fish restaurants, the prime sight nearby is Carthage itself. The ancient city was so enormous, and has been so heavily built upon, that the attractions are few and literally far between. It's easiest to start with Byrsa Hill, legendarily Queen Dido's site (see box, page 6). Overlooking what's left of the ancient harbour below, and itself overlooked by the huge 19th-century Cathedral of St Louis on the incline behind, here was the original city. The museum is worth a look. Also on the tour, either the excursion that will be arranged, or the hired taxi-driver's one, will be the archaeological area by the sea, the highlight of which is the Antonine baths. Scattered among the neighbourhoods are glimpses of the ancients, including the Carthaginian *tophet*, or cemetery, the theatre (usually closed to visitors, but viewable from the road), and columns that spring up out of nowhere, or can be found as part of the local houses. The ancient cistern has recently been excavated, and if on a more extensive tour, some groups go into the outskirts towards the south to see the remains of the aqueduct.

One of the very best things to see in Tunis is the Bardo Museum. Housing the world's best collection of North African Roman mosaics, this extensive assembly is dazzling. You also shouldn't miss the medina, the ancient heart of the city of Tunis and a UNESCO World Heritage Site. Here's also the best chance to do your souvenir shopping.

SOUSSE South of Tunis is the next port of call. The city of Sousse is a tourist destination, with another UNESCO World Heritage Site medina, a fine museum, good shopping and an ancient *ribat* (a fort built during the initial year of the Arab invasion). The excursions usually on offer from here are two of the most impressive and important in the country. Kairouan is the holy city of Islam, the fourth most important after Mecca, Medina and Jerusalem, and the site of Okba's first foothold in North Africa in 670 when he first spearheaded the Arab invasion. In addition, it's a delightful place full of winding alleys, great shopping and lots of beautiful detailing. Conventionally, the other tour is to El Djem, the magnificent Roman amphitheatre that is in excellent repair. The third largest of the ancient world, and arguably the best preserved, it's almost possible to hear the roars of the crowd. The museum is excellent, and the House of Africa on the grounds is an actual Roman villa, with its mosaics still in place. Neither of these trips should be missed.

SFAX The country's second-biggest city is basically industrial and not really a tourist destination. The large harbour is a good place to dock and some companies offer tours to both Kairouan and El Djem.

i TOURIST INFORMATION

UK & Irish Republic 77A Wigmore St, London W1H 9LJ; ↘ 020 7224 5598
USA 1515 Massachusetts Av, Washington, DC 2000; ↘ 202 466 2546; www.tunisiaguide.com

Canada 1253 McGill College Bureau, No 655 Montreal, Quebec H3 B2 Y5; ↘ 514 397 1182

A good introductory website is www.tourismtunisia.com/?agent=wx927.

IN TUNISIA The country has a very good tourist infrastructure, with offices in almost every bigger town and resort. Check the individual city listings.

$ MONEY

The Tunisian unit of currency, the dinar, is soft, which means it cannot be obtained outside of the country, nor can it be exported. Inevitably, this means that at some point you will most likely have to come across a bank, or a currency exchange. Banks will be happy to swap US dollars and euros and, to a slightly less enthusiastic degree, English pounds and Canadian and Australian dollars. Usual opening hours are 08.00–16.00 Monday to Friday in the winter, and the same days, but different hours, 07.30–13.00, in the summer. ATMs are becoming more common all the time. Theoretically, you are supposed to exchange any dinar that are left over into hard currency (money that can be purchased abroad), but rates to change back are poor. It's best not to buy more dinar than are probably going to be necessary. Remember that many tourist shops accept credit cards.

GETTING AROUND

Although the country is probably the safest of the Maghreb nations, be careful when getting close to the Algerian border in the south. Recently tourists were kidnapped there, more to do with Islamic issues than national ones. Despite the

Algeria

Tunisia

Tunisia: Roman ruins

left   Sbeitla's superb capitolium is dedicated to the Roman god Jupiter, his wife Juno and daughter Minerva page 314

below   Better preserved than Rome's own version, the colosseum at El Djem is a must-see page 317

bottom   Perfectly preserved mosaics decorate the floor of Bulla Regia's colosseum page 301

Libya

right   Traditional dancers at Tripoli's port

below   One of the best ways to explore Tripoli is via horse and carriage

bottom   Libya's south boasts some exquisite rock paintings; these ones can be found at Jamahirya Mus page 333

Libya: Roman ruins

temptations to visit some of the less explored regions of the country, it might be best to stick to more populated areas, where there may be other tourists. Otherwise, it's easy to get around the country There are seven airports that offer domestic service; a reasonable train network that can be accessed on the internet; an excellent internal bus system; automobile, motorbike and bicycle hire; decent roads on which to drive; and, when needed, *louages* (collective taxis) to fill the gaps.

✈ **BY AIR** Tunisia's main international airport is Tunis-Carthage and many of the planes from out of the country land here. Servicing the capital, this port is the hub for many domestic flights. Tunisair (*www.tunisair.com*) and Tuninter (*www.tuninter.com*) are the carriers. There are five to six departures every day that go to Djerba, five per week to Tozeur and four per week to Sfax. There are others that go from Djerba to Monastir twice a week, Djerba to Tozeur three times week, and Monastir to Tozeur once a week. Other combinations ply routes to and from the other airports at Tabarka and Gabes. Check OACA (*Office de l'Aviation Civile et des Aeroports; www.oaca.nat.tn*) for comprehensive information.

🚆 **BY RAIL** SNCFT (*Société Nationale des Chemins de Fer Tunisien, www.sncft.com.tn*) monitors and provides information for trains. Some places, like Kairouan or Djerba are not accessible by rail, but others, like El Djem (for the Roman amphitheatre) or Jendouba (close to the Roman site of Bulla Regia), are on the line. Going by this method is probably best for heading off to further distances that are either directly accessible, or close enough to the station for local buses or *louages* to get there. Prices are reasonable with a return journey from Tunis to Hammamet costing around TND7. For shorter distances, it might be quicker and cheaper to take the bus.

🚌 **BY BUS** Priced at around TND0.03 per kilometre, going by national bus is an inexpensive way to get to where you want to go. The company SNTRI (*Society Nationale de Transport Interurbain, www.sntri.com.tn*) has 178 buses per day heading all over the country, and it's possible to get almost anywhere within Tunisia. For example, setting off from Tunis for Djerba, an island that isn't accessible by train, although it is by plane, will take nine hours and cost around TND26. The buses tend to be air conditioned and to some southern destinations during the summer, the journeys take place at night. There are other regional buses that do similar trips possibly even cheaper, but they might not be as efficient or comfortable as the national ones. You need to check locally for their departure times.

🚕 **BY TAXI** Tunisia has one of the best systems of *louages*, or collective taxis, in all the Maghreb. Leaving when they get full, with between four and eight passengers, the destinations and prices are fixed, although the times are dependent on when capacity is reached. The *louages* are usually found near the bus stations, providing a handy service to finish the journey. Going by *louage* is the easiest way to travel by land into Libya, for example (although you need to get a visa first). It's also possible to hire a long-distance taxi privately, although it's more expensive – figure on at least four to eight times the price of a collective one.

Local taxis are also available in all the bigger towns. It's best to negotiate a price before departure and if you feel the driver is asking too much, find another one that will go for less (if unsure how much to pay, ask at the hotel, tourist office or tour desk for the going rate). If the service is excellent, ask for a card and consider using the same taxi again. This method is not only good for getting future service, but often the driver can act as a makeshift tour guide showing you things you never would've known about.

🚗 **CAR HIRE** It's easy and relatively safe to drive in Tunisia, once you accept the fact that the locals don't believe in separate lanes. Roads are broad and well marked, so that if you go with the flow you'll be fine. If you are travelling independently, and especially if on a timetable, touring by car is one of the best ways to get to some of the harder-to-reach Roman sites. All the major car rental companies have branches in Tunisia, usually with offices at both the arrival airport and within the towns. If you haven't pre-booked, hotels might also be able to get you a better deal. If you don't anticipate doing much travelling and are just looking for the occasional day out it might be worth hiring a car with driver.

PUBLIC HOLIDAYS

Fixed annual dates are:

1 January	New Year's Day
10 January	Hegire (Islamic New Year)
20 March	Independence Day
21 May	Youth Day
9 April	Martyrs' Day
1 May	Labour Day
25 July	Republic Day
13 August	Women's Day
15 October	Evacuation Day
7 November	New Era Day (Commemorating President Zine Ben Ali's coming to power)

These holidays are Islamic and vary annually according to the lunar calendar. They are also celebrated on the same dates (variable according to the year) in Morocco, Algeria and Libya:

9 March	Aïd al-Mawlid (Prophet's Birthday)
21 September	Aïd al-Fitr, or Eid (End of Ramadan)
28 November	Aïd al-Adha (Feast of the Sacrifice)

✆ MEDIA AND COMMUNICATIONS

POST There are post offices in most of places that are worth visiting, and their winter hours are generally 08.00–12.00 & 15.00–17.00 Monday to Thursday, and 08.00–12.30 on Friday and Saturday. In the summer, hours are 07.30–13.00. Post is fairly slow, but if you drop a postcard in the box it will arrive within a week or two, depending on the destination. There is also a Rapide Service, which will guarantee your letter or package's arrival much more quickly, but there is a price supplement.

PRINT There are dozens of national newspapers, most of which are government controlled. *La Presse*, *La Temps* and *Le Renouveau* are the most popular French-language ones, and *Tunisia Daily* is published in English. Dailies from other countries are available on the news-stands in the better bookshops of the cities, and more generally in the tourist resorts, although usually at least a day late.

RADIO There are four national radio stations under government auspices: Radio Tunis, RCTI Live, Radio-Jeunes and Radio Culture (www.radiotunis.com). There are also a couple of new private Franco-Arab stations, Radio Mosaique FM and

Jawhara, which are on the pop side. For religious edification, there's Ezzitouna Radio, a religious network broadcast from Carthage.

TELEVISION There are two national television channels, Canal 7 and Canal 21, run by the government. There's also whatever can be picked up by satellite. It's most likely the hotels will also show the more popular foreign channels, such as France 2, Rai Uno (Italy), BBC World and CNN.

MOBILE PHONES AND THE INTERNET There's one private mobile network, Tunisiana, that seems to dominate the airwaves. You can't miss it, either on your phone or via the plethora of advertising throughout the country. Service is reasonable. Internet access is available everywhere, through Wi-Fi in the hotels and in the multitude of cyber cafés. Be aware that censorship is exercised by the government and that when surfing, quite a few sites will be out of bounds, even some of the apparently innocuous ones.

GIVING SOMETHING BACK

Amnesty International www.amnesty.org/en/region/middle-east-and-north-africa/north-africa. The human rights organisation's website for all North Africa.
Human Rights Watch hrw.org/doc/?t=mideast. Lists human rights issues; Tunisia: www.hrw.org/en/middle-east/n-africa

SOS Children's Villages www.soschildrensvillages.org.uk/sponsor-a-child/africa-child-sponsorship/tunisia.htm. This charity for orphans has villages in three towns in the country.

21

Ports of Entry

Tunisia has definitely got its act together and offers direct international entry to almost every one of its tourist areas. Six airports – Tabarka, Tunis-Carthage, Monastir H Bourgiba, Sfax-Thyna, Tozeur-Nefta and Jerba-Zarzis – accept flights from other countries so it's easy to get directly to a specific location. In addition, there are sea ports that welcome cruise ships at Tabarka, Tunis, Sousse and Sfax. It's even possible to cross the border by bus or car, with entry points on the coast with Algeria, leading to Tabarka, and Libya, with Zarzis being the closest big town.

TUNIS

If you are planning to tour the country, rather than spend two weeks sitting in the sun at an all-inclusive resort, it's best to begin the trip flying into the capital's airport. The second-biggest metropolitan area in North Africa (after Cairo) has an illustrious history. Carthage, capital of both Carthaginian and Roman Africa, is now a suburb. Thriving even today, Tunis rightfully deserves its own section (see *Chapter 22*, page 278).

TABARKA *Telephone code 078*

This small, seaside town is being groomed for serious development, offering some of the best diving and sailing in the country. With clear waters, a large yacht marina and excellent purpose-built tourist facilities, it is hoped that Tabarka will join the list of contributors to the tourism coffers. The annual jazz festival in July draws in many visitors. There's an international airport, a harbour that welcomes cruise ships and an open border with Algeria, taking traffic from Annaba.

HISTORY One of the links in the chain of Phoenician trading posts, Thabraca (Tabarka's old name), became a Carthaginian possession. After Carthage's defeat in the Third Punic War in BC146, the Roman victors readily absorbed this seaside base into the empire. Thabraca was particularly useful in acting as a port from which the yellow-and-red marble quarried in nearby Simmithu (today's Chemtou) could be exported. Reaching its Roman heights from about AD200 it gained fame by exporting wild animals, particularly cats, for games held throughout the empire. Thabraca was not immune to the interchange between Romans, Vandals and Byzantines. From AD300, the stronghold of Christianity in St Augustine's city of Hippo Regius, and the traffic between there and Carthage, made Thabraca a convenient stopping-off point. Even during the Vandal period the city remained important as one of their bases in nearby Bulla Regia. General Belisarius took back the land for the Byzantines, but the Arab invasion soon after trampled any Christian gains. Thabraca was prone to the different Berber dynasties that wrested power from each other. By 1500 various European powers were arguing over the port and the Genoese even built a fort, remains of which still exist today. Tabarka became part of the notorious pirate-controlled Barbary coast, adding coral from its reefs as one of its assets. When the French entered, today's borders were already established and the city became part of the protectorate. Considered unimportant, the town was isolated enough that when Habib Bourgiba was making a fuss regarding independence in 1952, the French 'banished' him here. There's a statue in the town in memory of his sojourn.

GETTING THERE AND AROUND

By air The Aeroport du 7 Novembre (☎ *078 680 005; www.oaca.nat.tn*) is situated about 10km from the centre of town. As of the last check, the place was operational for only three months of the year, but there are efforts to extend the opening period. The terminal is quiet enough that no bus service has been organised, but taxis transport people to the town from TND10.

By bus The national bus company SNTRI (*www.sntri.com*) has a good network to Tabarka, including a five times daily service from Tunis that takes about three hours 15 minutes. Buses arrive at the station (*Rue de Peuple;* ☎ *078 670 404*). The SRN (*Société Regionale de Transport General de Jendouba, 84 Av Habib Bourgiba;* ☎ *078 670 087*) provides a more local service that can also get you to Tunis.

By taxi Going by collective taxi, or *louage*, is one of the best ways to get around. It's possible to find one near the end of Avenue Habib Bourgiba. The more desirable the final destination, the more frequently the taxis run. It is also theoretically possible to get here from Annaba in Algeria, if enough people also want to make the trip, as the border is open. Locally, you'll probably take a taxi at least for airport transport, also to ferry you around town.

By car It's easy enough to drive to Tabarka from various points in the country. Having a car at your disposal is convenient for visiting some of the more out-of-the-way Roman sites.

Car hire There are various car rental companies including **Europcar** (*airport:* ☎ *078 45 42 04; town: at Porto Corallo:* ☎ *078 45 42 04*) and **Hertz** (*airport:* ☎ *078 64 00 05; town: at Porto Corallo:* ☎ *078 67 06 70*).

TOURIST INFORMATION The **Commisariat Regional du Tourisme de Tabarka** is at 65 Boulevard de 7 Novembre (☎ *078 67 14 91*).

TOUR OPERATORS
Tabarka Voyages Av Ennasr 13, Route d'Ain Draham 8110; ☎ 078 64 37 40

 WHERE TO STAY Tabarka is very seasonal, and prices shoot up in the summer months. Away from these times, a real bargain may be had, but it can be cold and rainy on the Mediterranean coast in late autumn, winter and even into the early spring. Price estimates below are for high season.

Top end
🏠 **Hotel Dar Ismail** (200 rooms) Zone Touristique; ☎ 078 67 01 88; www.hoteldarismail.com. Located in the tourist area just east of the harbour, this luxury hotel, arguably the nicest hotel in the region, seems to be more of a resort, complete with its own stretch of beach. $$$–$$$$

Hotel Mehari (57 rooms) Rte Touristique; ☎ 078 67 00 01. The hotel has swimming pools, a private strand, a fitness centre, tennis courts & even a spa. $$ $$

Mid-range

Hotel de France (38 beds) Av Habib Bourguiba; ☎ 078 67 07 52. 3-star rated, this place has corresponding facilities (inc TV) & is convenient for people-watching at the café just below. $$$

Les Aiguilles (19 rooms) 18 Av Habib Bourguiba; ☎ 078 67 37 89. Located in a historic hotel a bit more authentic than most, the hotel also has excellent views of the sea & the Genoese fort. $$–$$$

Budget

La Plage (14 beds) 11 Av 7 Novembre; ☎ 078 67 00 39. This 1-star accommodation is clean though somewhat small. $

Mamia (18 rooms) 3 Rue de Tunis; ☎ 078 67 10 58. The cheapest decent place to stay in town is basic but adequate. $

WHERE TO EAT Tabarka's contribution to good eating is seafood, and it's possible to buy some from the day's catch and take it to a local restaurant for preparation.

There are lots of basic places in town around the Rue de Peuple, including **Les Etoiles**, a simple eaterie that will almost certainly cook your purchase, or prepare one of their own for you. (**$$**)

Around the marina are the finer and more expensive restaurants, still offering mostly fish specialities. Among them is **Le Pescadou** (*Pl de Frejus;* ☎ *078 67 15 80*) with a sea-based menu that includes bouillabaisse.

Some of the hotels also have decent places to eat, often with a reasonably fixed-price three-course meal (*prix-fixe*) at **Les Aiguilles**, for example.

ENTERTAINMENT AND NIGHTLIFE Some of the more resort-like complexes, for example the Hotel Dar Ismail, organise activities such as folklore evenings, but it seems the thing to do in Tabarka is to hang out at the cafés. Try the Café de France (*Av Hedi Chaker*) that has a history and is a good place to linger. Around the Avenue Bourgiba, or the marina, are various pizza joints and yet more places to sit around drinking and chatting.

Tabarka is well known for its festivals. Music features highly, but there are also other pursuits that are celebrated:

May	Spring Festival
June	Rai North African Music Festival
July–August	International Festival of Jazz
August	World Music Festival
September	Latin Music Festival; Coralis Diving Festival

The **Amphitheatre of the Sea** is a brand-new outdoor, seaside venue at which most of these events are, or will be, held. For further information on all the music festivals, check out www.tabarkajazz.com/.

SPORTS Tourism is being developed in Tabarka mostly on the lines of activities. There are lots of sports offered, mostly to do with water.

Diving This part of the Mediterranean is supposed to be the best in the country for scuba diving, and is being exploited as a speciality here. The Centre de Loisirs de Tabarka (*Port de Plaisance;* ☎ *078 67 06 64; www.loisirsdetabarka.com*) does diving courses as well as trips out. The Mehari Hotel also has its own diving facility, Le Merou (*www.meharidivingcenter.com*).

Golf Tunisia is building up its golf appeal, and here too is an 18-hole course, at the Tabarka Golf Club, part of the Golden Yasmin Hotel group (*Zone Touristique;* ↘ *078 67 10 31; www.tabarkagolf.com*).

Horse- and camel-riding Riding is usually done along the beach. Treks can be arranged at places near the Golf Beach Hotel (*Zone Touristique;* ↘ *078 67 30 02*) and the Royal Rihana (*Ain Draham;* ↘ *078 65 53 91*).

SHOPPING It's possible to find the usual range of tourist souvenirs in the hotel shops, as well as some stalls in town. You can buy fruit and veg at the **Central Market** (*Rue Ali Chaswani*). The **Monoprix** supermarket is located at Avenue 7 Novembre 1987. The newly redeveloped port will soon be fitted with a modern shopping area. If possible, though, save your tourist shopping requirements for the medinas of the larger cities, as they're not only much better stocked, but also significantly more interesting.

OTHER PRACTICALITIES
Emergency telephone numbers
Police Rue de Peuple; ↘ 078 67 00 21

Secours Routières (roadside assistance)
↘ 078 67 00 21

Hospitals
✚ **Polyclinique Sidi Moussa** 5 Av Habib Bourgiba;
↘ 078 67 12 00

Internet cafés
🖥 **Cybernet** Rue des Etats-Unis

🖥 **Publinet le Corail Tarbarka** Residence Le Corail

Post The main post office is at Rue Hedi Chaker at the corner of Avenue Habib Bourgiba.

Banks The better hotels can offer exchange although they will probably only be interested in currency. There are some banks in the centre, along Avenue Habib Bourgiba, where it will be easier to obtain local currency using bank or credit cards.

WHAT TO SEE Most museums and sites charge an additional fee to take photographs, usually around TND1.

Marina Newly redeveloped, this yacht harbour and port seem to be the centre of town activities, with restaurants, cafés and shops. There's a European feel here and the place resembles some of the more charming French Mediterranean boating resorts.

Genoese fort This well-preserved fortress is a reminder of when the Genoese briefly held Tabarka and is now administered by the military. It sits on a peninsula that can be reached by a long walk, or a quick car ride, although only the outside can be viewed.

Les Aiguilles Walkway A small craggy rock formation rises straight out of the sea and sits right next to a jetty, and can be reached by an easy walk from the marina. These pillars are one of Tabarka's most famous landmarks.

Museum (*Rue de la Basilique;* ⊕ *Apr–mid-Sep 09.00–13.00 & 16.00–19.00; mid-Sep–Mar 09.30-16.30 Tue–Sun; TND1*) has displays on archaeological evidence found in the area, including artefacts from the Roman occupation.

Basilica (*nr the Hotel de France*) Today a decommissioned church used for summer exhibitions, this building was once a Roman cistern dating from AD200–300.

Beaches All along the coast, in either direction, are lovely beaches. If you have your own transport explore those strands that are out of town, and the crowds and rubbish lessen the further you go.

HOW TO GET TO THE ROMAN SITES Although Tabarka is the closest tourist city to Bulla Regia and Chemtou, most people who go to these Roman remains leave from Tunis, and it's at the end of *Chapter 22, Tunis* (see page 290) that these ancient sites are described. If you're in Tabarka, it's easy enough to visit these ruins. Join an organised tour that can be arranged via local tour operators, get a taxi (or a bus to Jendouba, then a taxi from there), or rent a car. Bulla Regia is straight down the GP17 for 60km and just east off the GP59, right before Jendouba. To get to Chemtou, follow the same route, only turn west when you reach the GP59, driving 11km on a paved road, then another 5km on a decent gravel track. Both places are signposted.

MONASTIR *Telephone code 073*

Lying alongside Tunisia's east coast on the Gulf of Hammamet, about 170km south of Tunis, Monastir is one of the country's biggest tourist destinations. Because of its beautiful protected beaches and extensive facilities, not to mention an international airport that accepts traffic from all over Europe, many sun seekers think that there is nothing else to see in the country. In the city there are a few outstanding sites, including the *ribat* (Islamic fortress) and mausoleum of the first president and native of Monastir, Habib Bourgiba.

HISTORY The foundations of today's Monastir were laid by the Phoenicians on their travels and they named this little village Rouss Pena. Swallowed up by the Romans as part of their spoils after the Third Punic War, Ruspina, the Romanisation of the Punic name, came to brief prominence when Julius Caesar arrived. Here was his base of operations in the civil war against Pompey, who was based at Hadremetum (today's Sousse). Their violent encounter led to the Battle of Thapsus, close to today's town of Mahdia, about 45km south of Monastir, in which Pompey lost. In fact, this defeat paved the way to the end of the republic and while Julius became dictator, his successors, beginning with his nephew Augustus, became emperors of the Roman Empire. After such an illustrious moment, Ruspina sank into obscurity, until around AD700, when members of the Abbasid dynasty decided to build their first Tunisian *ribat* here. When the Fatimid dynasty made nearby Mahdia their capital sometime after AD947, Monastir became a major religious city, taking over from the declining Kairouan, located about 70km inland. It's possible that today's name stems from this period, referring to the monasteries of that time. During the Turkish occupation, the city was aided by its extensive fortress, but soon after its prominence began to fade and it dropped into obscurity. Habib Bourgiba, the independence provocateur born in 1903 would revive the city's fortunes after he was elected the country's first president in 1956. Retiring here after having been stripped of his title 'President for Life', one of the major attractions in Monastir is his elaborate mausoleum.

GETTING THERE AND AROUND

By air The Aeroport International de Skanes-Monastir (↳ *073 46 03 00; www.habibbourguibaairport.com*) is about 9km from Monastir on the road to Sousse.

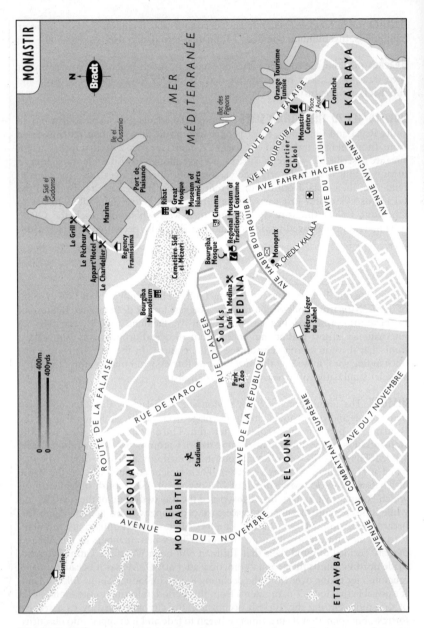

The Light Rail goes from the airport depot, close to the terminal, to anywhere on the Monastir–Mahdia–Sousse route. The Monastir exit is at the main station. Taxis are more expensive, from about TND5, and prices double after 21.00.

By rail Monastir is on the network and SNCFT (Société Nationale des Chemins de Fer Tunisien, *www.sncft.com.tn*) runs trains that get into the Gare Habib Bourgiba train station (*Rue Salem B'Chir;* 📞 *073 46 07 55*). The line goes via Sousse, north to Tunis or south to Sfax, also stopping at El Djem, convenient if wanting to visit the Roman amphitheatre by public transport. There's only one mainline train a day to Sousse and Tunis. If you can find your way to Sousse by other means, eg: via the Light Rail or bus, then the possibilities for travelling by rail are increased.

By bus The bus station is at Avenue de la Republique (↘ *073 46 10 59*). Services to Sousse and then to Tunis go every half-hour while services to Kairouan and Hammamet leave once a day.

By taxi (*louage*) The *louage* gathering point is right next to the bus station and most shared taxis go to Sousse, although it's possible to pick one up that goes to Mahdia. Monastir is a fairly large place, especially if you're staying in the Zone Touristique and want to get into town, so it's useful to get accustomed to the idea of using the local taxis. They can be flagged down, or arranged through the hotel.

By car The RN1 is the country's main thoroughfare and goes from Tunis to the Libyan border. The A1 motorway from Tunis to Sousse cuts quite a bit off the total time of the journey and once you've reached the end, switch over to the RN1 to continue to Monastir. There are places to see in the general area, such as Mahdia, and Kairouan, that can be awkward to reach by public transport, so having a car may be useful. Roads are fine, especially to the main tourist destinations, and usually well signposted.

Car hire The big rental companies are represented at the airport, including Avis (↘ *073 52 10 31*), Hertz (↘ *073 52 13 00*) and National (↘ *073 46 03 00*).

TOURIST INFORMATION

🛈 **Commissariat Regional du Tourisme** Zone Touristique de Skane; ↘ 073 52 02 05. There's also an office at the airport.

🛈 **Syndicat d'Initiative** Rue de l'Indépendance; ↘ 073 46 19 60

TOUR OPERATORS
Monastir has its share of local operators and the bigger hotels usually sell package tours directly from their concierge desk. You can also go to one of these companies independently and join an existing tour, if there are enough people already booked, or arrange something for yourself.

Orange Tourisme Tunisie Complexe Monastir Centre; ↘ 073 44 83 08

Ribat Tours Rue 18 Janvier 1952; ↘ 073 46 51 45
Voyages Plus Av de la Republic; ↘ 073 44 90 04

 WHERE TO STAY Being a popular destination for both foreign and domestic tourists, Monastir has lots of places to stay. Here is a small cross section. Please note that as the resort is seasonal, prices in the summer, as listed below, are much higher than at other times, sometimes more than twice as much. If dates aren't a problem, avoiding July and August will save a lot of money.

Top end

🏠 **Regency Framissima** (187 rooms) Cap Marina; ↘ 073 46 00 33. Owned by the French group FRAM & arguably Monastir's best hotel, this 4-star has everything for a resort stay, from swimming pool & private beach to a spa centre. $$$$–$$$$$
🏠 **Appart'Hotel** (59 rooms) Cap Monastir; ↘ 073

46 23 05; www.marinamonastir.com. These fully equipped flats, available for short term as well as long, are situated in the marina village, handy for sailing, eating & chilling out & *much* cheaper in low season. $$$$

Mid-range

🏠 **Hotel Monastir Centre** (175 rooms) Av Habib Bourgiba; ☎ 073 46 24 03. What you'd expect from a 3-star hotel located in the middle of town, with the addition of a swimming pool flanked by palms & flowers. $$

Budget

🏠 **Hotel Corniche** Just off Pl 3 Août; ☎ 073 46 14 51. This little family-run place is located right in the centre, close to the beach & the café life; genial but the rooms are small. $

🏠 **Hotel Yasmine** Rte de la Falaise; ☎ 073 50 15 46. Though not centrally located this 1-star basic but clean place is a nice, friendly contrast to the big flashy hotels along the beach. $

✗ **WHERE TO EAT** Cafés and places to have a quick snack are easy to find and inevitably fish and local specialities are on the menu. Most places are fine. The better restaurants are close to the yacht harbour.

✗ **Le Grill** Cap Marina; ☎ 073 46 21 36. Possibly the best restaurant in Monastir, with prices to match. Makes superb dishes of both shell & sea fish. $$$$–$$$$$

✗ **Le Chandelier** Cap Marina; ☎ 073 46 22 32. This very pleasant place has a menu of seafood & Tunisian specialities, with good views of the port & sea beyond. $$$$

✗ **Le Pecheur** Cap Marina; ☎ 073 48 61 36. Cheaper & quieter than most, the menu of primarily fish dishes is reasonably varied. $$$

✗ **Café la Medina** Pl du 3 Septembre 1934. A good, central place to hang out while having anything from a quick drink to a larger meal. $$

ENTERTAINMENT AND NIGHTLIFE

Monastir is not party central, and most bars and discotheques are attached to hotels. Some of the more central and less exclusive places to stay will allow outside visitors while the flashy ones, eg: the Regency, will probably not allow any non-residents, or if they do, charge an entrance fee. There is one independent nightclub, **Luna Mare** (*Rte de l'Aeroport-Skanes;* ☎ *073 52 08 03*), that bears the brunt of the non-hotel clubbers.

SHOPPING

Homt Chraqua is the place to go to shop for souvenirs, located deep in the medina, the oldest part of town. All the usual Tunisian handicrafts can be bargained for here, such as leather goods and ceramics. The **National Office of the Artisan** is located right across from the Bourgiba Mosque, where the same items are offered at a non-negotiable price. Jewellery can be found at **Houmt-Trabelsa**, and is probably hand crafted. For something less artistic but more immediately satisfying, dried fruits and nuts are for sale on **Rue du 2 Mars**. There's a **weekly market** on Saturday, but for day-to-day items there's the supermarket **Monoprix**, on Avenue Habib Bourgiba, close to the medina gates.

OTHER PRACTICALITIES
Emergency telephone numbers

Police Rue de Libye; ☎ 073 46 14 31

Internet cafés There are several internet access points. Check out the list online at www.yatounes.com/2m/publinet/mo.html. Here are some of the more convenient ones.

🖳 **Monastir Web Centre** Rte de Kairouan, Bd de l'Environnement; ☎ 073 50 41 03

🖳 **Publinet El Omrane** Bd de l'Environnement; ☎ 073 50 45 21

Post The main post office is on Avenue Habib Bourguiba.

Banks There are branches of several banks in the airport as well as around the Place du 3 Septembre in town. STB and the Banque of Tunisia, also located here, have ATMs. Check with other banks regarding their machines, as well as their willingness to accept foreign cards inside.

WHAT TO SEE Please note that most museums and sites charge an additional fee to take photographs, usually around TND1.

Ribat (⊕ *May–mid–Sept 09.00–20.00; mid-Sep–Mar 08.30–17.30; Apr 09.00–19.00; TND4*) The most important attraction in Monastir is the *ribat*. Defined as a military fortress, dating from the early days of Islamic North Africa, the one here is believed to be the best-preserved example in the country. Situated just off the harbour and dominating the skyline, this series of walls, turrets and interior alleyways looks like the perfect Arabian fantasy complex. The original structure, built by Governor Harthama in AD796, has been significantly enlarged over the centuries. Today's version is a surprisingly harmonious blend of the periods. The *nador* (tower) is one of the oldest features, and it's possible to ascend it to get a great view of the entire *ribat* as well as sea views beyond. Various films have been made here, including *Jesus of Nazareth* (1977, director Franco Zeffirelli) and *Monty Python's Life of Brian* (1979, Terry Jones). Also within the enclosure is the **Museum of Islamic Arts** (see *Museums*, on page 262).

Great Mosque Resting on the side of the *ribat*, this religious structure dates back to the Aghlabids and has been repeatedly enlarged, particularly by the later Zirids. Notable are the columns, recycled from Roman Ruspina.

Habib Bourguiba sites The first president of independent Tunisia was born in Monastir and he returned after having been declared unfit for his role as president in 1987, at the age of 83. The town never forgot his importance and there are various places of note in his honor worth visiting.

Bourgiba Mosque The main prayer hall in the city was built in 1963 and based on the Hammouda Pacha Mosque in Tunis. The architecture and decoration represent a revived interest in religious and traditional Islamic art, mixing magnificent materials, such as rose marble and onyx columns and gold mosaics. Unfortunately, non-Muslims are not allowed in, although it's hard to miss the 41m-high octagonal minaret.

Bourgiba Mausoleum (*to the north of the Bourgiba Mosque;* ⊕ *14.00–16.30 Mon–Thu & 09.00–16.30 Fri/Sat; free*) Just next door, at the north end of the city's cemetery, is the burial place of Bourguiba and his family, a place of reverence to which the public is granted entry. Also built in 1963, anticipating the man's death by 37 years, this twin-towered monument with a central gold dome flanked by two green ones is extremely impressive, especially when approached from the front courtyard. This elaborate and lavish mausoleum is definitely worth a visit.

Medina The ancient heart of the city retains its surrounding walls and its battements are now a tourist attraction. There are a dozen gates, or *babs*. Inside are the usual souks.

Museums

Museum of Islamic Arts (*in the* ribat; ⊕ *as for the* ribat; *TND3*) Situated in the old chapel, this assembly has a wide collection of items, including illuminated manuscripts, glassware from the dynastic periods, pottery and ceramics, astrolabes, and ancient tomb steles.

Regional Museum of Traditional Costume (*in the same building as the tourist office, Syndicat d'Initiative, Rue de l'Indépendance;* ⊕ *09.00–13.00 & 15.00–19.00 Tue–Sun; TND1.10*) Shows off the types of apparel worn in different parts of the country, from past to present.

HOW TO GET TO THE ROMAN SITES If you're not already on an organised tour, but would like to join one, local travel companies, as well as the hotel conciergerie, will be happy to book you on an excursion to the nearby Roman sites. If you prefer to visit independently, a local Monastir taxi driver would be delighted to take you especially if you hire him for the day. Another way is to rent a car. The magnificent Roman amphitheatre of El Djem and its superb museum are about 70km to the southwest. An excellent day out is to head first to Sousse, then south on the RN1 to the Roman site, cut northwest to Kairouan (see *Chapter 23*, page 311) on an unclassified but paved and well-signposted road, and then return to Monastir. If travelling with your own transport and planning a longer trip, using Monastir as a starting point, then it's possible to go further to other archaeological destinations. See the Roman sites in the *Kairouan* chapter (page 311) for more information. For public transport, it is almost always necessary to go first to Sousse, as the larger city is a better hub. From Monastir, trains go once a day, buses go frequently, and *louages* head north on demand. See Sousse's entry below for how to get to the Roman sites.

SOUSSE *Telephone code 073*

With close to 175,000 residents, Tunisia's third-biggest city (after Tunis and Sfax) is a buzzing place known as 'the pearl of the Sahel (this region of the coast)'. Sitting in an admirable position on the Mediterranean, with a strategic and commercially exploited harbour, Sousse lies about 140km south of Tunis. The economic standard of living is high, due its light industry, such as processing food and textiles, and olive oil production, with raw material gathered from the massive groves nearby.

For such a large urban centre, it's a surprise that Sousse is also such a popular tourism destination. The prime draw is the beach, with soft sand strands bordering the gorgeous turquoise sea. Hotels, cafés and restaurants have sprung up along the edge. The large, purpose-built marina and adjoining tourist complex of Port El Kantaoui, about 10km north, provides a world in itself, although it doesn't resemble Tunisia very much. As for Sousse, there are some attractions that warrant straying from the beach, including a medina that has earned UNESCO heritage status, mosques and minarets, a couple of museums – one of which is the excellent archaeological museum with its wonderful mosaics – and even catacombs.

HISTORY The Phoenicians set up a halt at the southern end of this enticing bay sometime around 800BC, calling their settlement Hadrumete. A few hundred years later, when the Carthaginians became strong enough to name their territory after themselves, this port town shifted its allegiance to them. Famous in the Second Punic War as being a stronghold, Hannibal took advantage of its defensive position. Taking Rome's side in the Third Punic War to avoid being razed to the ground as

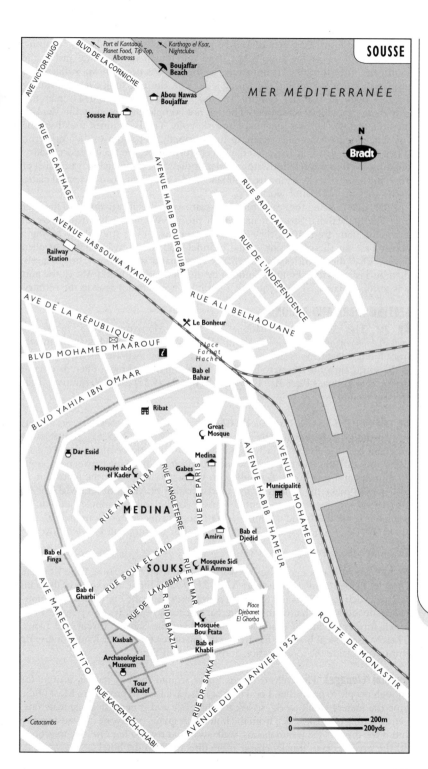

SOUSSE

MER MÉDITERRANÉE

Port el Kantaoui,
Planet Food, Tip Top,
Albatross

Karthago el Ksar,
Nightclubs

Boujaffar Beach

Abou Nawas Boujaffar

Sousse Azur

BLVD DE LA CORNICHE

AVE VICTOR HUGO

RUE DE CARTHAGE

AVENUE HABIB BOURGUIBA

RUE SADI-CAMOT

RUE DE L'INDÉPENDENCE

N

Bradt

AVENUE HASSOUNA AYACHI

Railway Station

AVE DE LA RÉPUBLIQUE

RUE ALI BELHAOUANE

Le Bonheur

BLVD MOHAMED MAAROUF

Place Farhat Hached

Bab el Bahar

BLVD YAHIA IBN OMAAR

Ribat

Great Mosque

Dar Essid

Medina

Mosquée abd el Kader

Gabes

AVENUE HABIB THAMEUR

AVENUE MOHAMED V

Municipalité

RUE AL AGHALBA

RUE D'ANGLETERRE

RUE DE PARIS

MEDINA

Amira

Bab el Djedid

Bab el Finga

RUE SOUK EL CAID

SOUKS

RUE EL MAR

Mosquée Sidi Ali Ammar

AVE MARECHAL TITO

Bab el Gharbi

RUE DE LA KASBAH

R. SIDI BAAZIZ

Place Djebanet El Ghorba

Kasbah

Mosquée Bou Ftata

Bab el Khabli

Archaeological Museum

Tour Khalef

AVENUE DU 18 JANVIER 1952

RUE DR. SAKKA

ROUTE DE MONASTIR

Catacombs

0 ———— 200m
0 ———— 200yds

Tunisia: Ports of Entry SOUSSE

21

Carthage had been, they later backed Pompey in the Roman civil wars. Thapsus, the battlefield where the famous last stand was fought in 46BC, was just to the south, and unfortunately, Hadremetum, as the city was now known, suffered the repercussions of supporting the wrong side. The Romans took over and during Trajan's reign in the 2nd century AD, the empire encouraged Hadremetum's growth as a provincial settlement. Though not completely spared by the Vandals, the little that was left was renamed Hunerikopolis. The Byzantines, took back the city, changing its name once again, to Justinianoplis, in honour of their emperor. When the Arab invasion arrived in the 7th century, Okba, the man immortalised as building the first mosque in Kairouan, siezed the settlement, giving it the label of Susa, the name of a city dating from 3000BC, and a word that exists in several places in the ancient and Islamic world.

Partly due to being the seaport for Kairouan, as well as its proximity to the later holy city of Mahdia, Susa remained high profile. When the Normans were in charge of Sicily from 1091, they decided to reinforce their strength by having a power base on the other side of the channel, and for 11 years they controlled Sousse. Over the centuries, the city changed nationality several times, first Spanish, then Turkish and then French. Bombed by the Germans in World War II, the port was seriously damaged. Subsequently rebuilt it's now a major asset to the country.

GETTING THERE AND AROUND

By air The Aeroport International de Skanes-Monastir (↘ 073 46 03 00; www.habibbourguibaairport.com) is about 15km from Sousse. Flights arrive mostly from foreign destinations and unless you are taking the once-a-week trip to Tozeur in the south, the only reason to be here is if coming from abroad. There is a metro that goes to Sousse's Place Bab El Djedid (↘ 073 22 49 55) every 30 minutes. Taxis are also around.

By rail SNCFT (*Société Nationale des Chemins de Fer Tunisien; www.sncft.com.tn*) gets you to the Gare Ferroviare (*Bd Hassouna Ayachi;* ↘ 073 22 49 55). Sousse is an excellent hub for almost anywhere the train runs, mostly because of its 11 daily departures to Tunis (starting at 03.30 and ending at 20.20, taking between one hour 30 minutes and two hours, depending on when it leaves). Take the metro for an easy way to make the rounds of the tourist resorts of Monastir and Mahdia. An alternative way to get from central Sousse to the tourist complex of Port el Kantaoui is via the Noddy Train, leaving from Avenue Habib Bourgiba. It costs about TND3.50 one-way and TND5 return, but it's fun, and kids will love the ride.

By bus There is also a good bus network, leaving from the station, Gare Routière Grandes Lignes (*Souk du Dimanche;* ↘ 073 23 79 72). Duplicating some of the train services, such as to Tunis and Sfax both eight times daily, the bus continues to non-rail destinations, like Kairouan and Djerba, twice a day each. It's also possible to go much further afield, for example to the edge of the Sahara, Tozeur and Douz. There's also a local bus that has frequent departures for Port el Kantaoui leaving from just outside the tourist office, at the Place Sidi Yahia.

By taxi (*louage*) The collective taxis linger around the bus station, waiting for enough people to go further. Local taxis are also available in profusion. Most of the time the meters 'don't work', so ask for the price and if necessary, negotiate one, before setting off. Ask advice from the hotel, tour guide, or anyone else trustworthy and if the driver's fee is outrageous, walk away and try another one. Try to get one off the street, as taxis usually charge more directly from the hotel.

By car The A1 motorway from Tunis to Sousse is a toll road, but worth it if you're in a hurry. Otherwise, the RN1 goes the same way, but is subject to traffic. Sousse is a great location from which to explore by car, as many of Tunisia's attractions are easily accessible from here. Monastir and Mahdia are just along the coast, El Djem is straight down the RN1, Kairouan is a short drive, and the Roman sites are just beyond, eg: Sbeita heading south, and Makhtar heading north. Going by car isn't necessary, but it does make touring much easier.

Car hire The big car hire firms are represented by **Avis** (*Bd de la Corniche;* ℡ *073 22 59 01*) and **Hertz** (*17 Av Habib Bourgiba;* ℡ *073 22 54 28*). There are other companies who offer short-term rentals, but confirm the reliability of these outfits from other sources, such as a tour operator or hotel concierge.

TOURIST INFORMATION The **Commissariat Régional du Tourisme** is at Avenue Habib Bourgiba (℡ *073 22 51 57*) and the **Syndicat d'Initiative** is at Place Farhat Hached (℡ *073 22 04 31*).

TOUR OPERATORS There are legions of tour operators in Sousse, spilling into Monastir and Mahdia. Hotels have their own local companies, while the Syndicat (see above) can provide official guides. For organised tours, especially to Kairouan and the Roman sites, try the following:

Belami Travel Services 3 Rue de Bizerte-La Corniche; ℡ 073 22 32 07

Eden Tours 12 Bis, Bd Khezama; ℡ 073 27 07 12

Marhaba Tours Bd 7 Novembre; ℡ 073 27 21 67

Sahel Voyages 6 Rue de Palestine; ℡ 073 22 05 31; www.sahelvoyages.com

Tunivers Voyages 6 Bd 7 Novembre, Karthago Centre; ℡ 073 27 68 00; www.tuniversvoyages.com

 WHERE TO STAY The purpose-built tourist complex and marina at Port el Kantaoui, about 10km north, has many places to stay, from large full service resorts, to holiday villages and apartments. Sousse itself has many tourist rooms available. If travelling independently, here is a very small selection from across the range with the emphasis on central location.

Top end

🏠 **Hotel Abou Nawas Boujaffar** (234 rooms) 4 Av Habib Bourgiba; ℡ 073 22 17 22; www.abounawas.com.tn. With the full-service luxury you'd expect to find at the resorts, this conveniently situated giant complex on the beach offers everything, from spa to sport facilities to restaurants. $$$$

🏠 **Karthago el Ksar** (380 rooms) Bd du 7 Septembre; ℡ 073 24 04 60. This beautiful 4-star accommodation has a private beach, 3 swimming pools & a spa, & every room faces the sea. $$$

Mid-range

🏠 **Hotel Restaurant Medina** 1 Rue Othmen-Osmen; ℡ 073 22 17 22. The proximity of the medina allows for some good views from the terrace & the accommodation is roomy & decent. $$

🏠 **Hotel Sousse Azur** 5 Rue Amilcar; ℡ 073 22 77 60; www.sousse-azur.com. Not far from the sea & the flashy hotels, the rooms of this place are basic, but adequate. $$

Budget

🏠 **Hotel Amira** 52 Rue de France; ℡ 073 22 63 25. Right in the medina, this charming & bargain-priced place has lovely detailing – & clean rooms. $

🏠 **Hotel Gabes** 12 Rue de Paris; ℡ 073 22 69 77. Simple rooms with shared baths are the rule for private quarters although the rooftop sleeping options are great for watching the stars – & hearing the first pre-dawn call to prayer. $

WHERE TO EAT There are loads of cheap-and-cheerful little places wedged into corners in the medina and they're pretty much all fine for snacks and basics. Here's a good place to hang around if you're saving pennies, or trying to avoid somewhere flashy. It's tempting to find a spot to eat around the beach, but you'll pay more for the privilege. For a better meal, the luxury hotels offer finer restaurants, for example the Abou Nawas Boujaffar has **Le Golfe**, which specialises in fish (and a great seaview) (**$$$$**), while almost all of the larger residences in Port el Kantaoui offer varying forms and qualities of food service.

✗ **Albatross** Bd de la Corniche; ⟋ 073 22 84 30. Located on this well-trodden stretch, the food here is fine but nothing extraordinary, although some efforts have been made to make the ambience a bit smart. **$$$**

✗ **Le Bonheur** Pl Farhat-Hached; ⟋ 073 22 57 42. This popular place offers a decent & well-priced *prix fixe* menu that remains reliably good, if unchanging. **$$**

✗ **Planet Food** Bd de la Corniche. Despite the fact this venue tries to be American, the majority of the patrons are locals in this trendy-priced hamburger joint that also serves chicken & pizzas. **$$$**

✗ **Restaurant Tip Top** 73 Bd de la Corniche; ⟋ 073 22 61 58. Recently redecorated, this restaurant is one of the types that are standard in every Tunisian tourist city, although the menu, featuring seafood, is a bit better & pricier than most. **$$$**

ENTERTAINMENT AND NIGHTLIFE It's always an option to hang out at your favourite café and sip tea or coffee until the place closes. The finer restaurants serve alcohol, and it's possible to linger till almost midnight over a bottle of wine. On a more expensive level, bars and disco are located in the big hotels in the Zone Touristique. Below are some of the better ones.

☆ **King** Hotel Samara, Rte de la Corniche; ⟋ 073 22 66 99 A hot spot that holds up to 1,000 people, there are also a piano bar & a rather impressive sound system. There's also the **Caraibes Casino** that has slots, roulette, Baccarat & other games, in case you find Tunisian prices too low, & need to get rid of your money somehow.

☆ **Le Bora Bora** Karthago el Ksar Hotel. This open-air venue has a nice, youthful atmosphere.

☆ **Maracana Disco** Tej Marhaba Hotel, Bd Taieb M Hiri; ⟋ 073 22 98 00. This place can be easy-going despite its 1,000-person capacity.

☆ **Disco night** Port el Kantaoui. Happening every evening in Jul & Aug & takes place at the various discos located at the beach.

FESTIVALS Sousse becomes lively during its annual festivals. In mid-March, the **Festival of Regional Folk Art** is a spring celebration of traditional music and dance. In July and August, there are the **Festival of Bab Aoussou**, a carnival and folklore event that pays homage to the sea (originating from ancient rites to the Roman god, Neptune), and the International **Fair & Festival**. Check with the tourist office for exact dates for all these events.

SHOPPING Sousse's medina is an authentic old town centre and houses souks that are great places to shop. Here the crafts of North Africa are on offer, with goods that are not only locally made, but also brought in from neighbouring countries (watch out for those imported from further afield, like China or Thailand). Spilling out from the sides of covered passageways, the colours and textures of traditional handicrafts are dazzling. It's hard to make a choice from the enormous array that after a while begins to look the same from stall to stall. Vendors will call you in, inviting you to 'just take a look'. As bargaining in these places is conventional, another common catchphrase is 'I will make you a good price' (see the section on *Bargaining*, page 69). Salesmen are multi-lingual and will shout to you in different languages until they hear you speak. If shopping and interacting with the locals in this manner is part of the experience, then here is a great place to spend some time and acquire some souvenirs in the process. If haggling is a chore and an imposition, Sousse has also quite a few fixed-price sales outlets. The largest is the four-storey **Soula Shopping Centre** (*Pl des Martyrs*) at the northeast corner of the medina and handy if you come in by cruise ship. Enclosed and grand, shops line each floor offering similar goods to the souks, although with less variety. It's much less of a hassle to shop here, but also a lot less fun.

There is a weekly market on Sunday that takes place outside the centre near the gare routière (bus station) that is known as the Souk du Dimanche. This event is a gathering for the locals, although tourists are catered for. These goods are more practical than the brightly coloured things on sale in the souks. Come here for the atmosphere and seeing locals that might have come in from countryside.

OTHER PRACTICALITIES
Emergency telephone numbers
Police Rue Pasteur; ☎ 073 22 55 66

Hospital
✚ **Farhat Hached University Hospital** Av Ibn el Jazzar; ☎ 073 22 14 11

Internet cafés There are several internet access points. Check out the list online at www.yatounes.com/2m/publinet/so.html. Here are some of the more convenient ones.

🌐 **Cybernet** Av Remada; ☎ 073 21 44 31
🌐 **Publinet** Bd Mohamed Mahrouf; ☎ 073 21 27 80

🌐 **Publinet Essokri** 20 Av Tahar Sfar; ☎ 073 21 33 33

Post The main post office is at Avenue Mohamed Mahrouf.

Banks With so many tourists, finding banks as well as ATMs is no problem. Most of them are well represented in the centre, particularly along Avenue Habib Bourgiba and Boulevard de la Corniche.

WHAT TO SEE Please note that most museums and sites charge an additional fee to take photographs, usually around TND1.

Great Mosque (⊕ 08.00–14.00 Sat–Thu, 08.00–13.00 Fri; TND3) Taking pride of place in a prominent position within the medina this mosque was built in AD850, during the period of the Aghlabid dynasty, with the dome added two centuries later. The interior is unadorned, with almost no decorative features, unusual for a mosque but typical for the Aghlabites. Perhaps it's due to the simplicity that the place is surprisingly peaceful. Even stranger is the absence of the minaret, raising the question as to how the muezzin was able to rise above the medina walls and call the faithful to prayer. Here's an example of ancient Islamic recycling: the mosque was located so close to the *ribat* that it was able to use the previous construction's tower, or *nador*, as its own minaret. Before entering, make sure you're properly dressed, or you can rent proper covering at the entrance. Non-Muslims are allowed only in the courtyard. It's possible to peek into the prayer hall, even if you can't step foot into it.

Ribat (⊕ Apr–mid-Sep 08.00–19.00 daily; mid-Sep–Mar 08.00–17.30; TND4) Sousse's magnificent fort might not be quite as large as the one in Monastir, but it's still a significant and impressive sight. Constructed at the end of AD799 as one of the chain of 'fortress-monasteries', built to defend the North African coast while offering spiritual sanctuary, this complex is one of the best-preserved examples still in existence. The order for which the *ribat* was built bore a similarity to the Knights of St John, or the Knights Hospitaller, of Malta, except that the residents were part of a religious and military order committed to defending both North African territory and Islamic beliefs. The Byzantine style of the architecture reflects Christian predecessors, and some of the remains of Hadremetum have been recycled into the main entranceway. Once inside, the central courtyard is flanked on three sides by the soldier-monks' cells, while on the fourth is the prayer hall, believed to be one of the oldest Islamic examples in North Africa. The *nador*, or watchtower, added in 821 rises up above the medina walls, offering a superb view not only of the *ribat* and the city, but also of invaders coming from the sea.

Kasbah and ramparts Sousse's other fortress lies in the diagonally opposite corner of the medina from the *ribat* and dates from around AD850. Its most obvious feature is the 30m tower, the **Tour Khalef el Fata,** at present closed for renovation. The most interesting attraction of the complex is the **archaeological museum** (see listing opposite). The medieval walls, the ramparts, are still visible, following the Byzantine layout. Three of the gates, or *babs*, were built with the original construction, and were later joined by three additional ones made by the French when they arrived.

Catacombs (*Rue du 25 Juillet 1957, close to the louage station;* ⊕ *Apr–mid-Sep 09.00– 19.00 daily except Sun; mid-Sep–Mar 09.00–17.00; TND3*) With the overwhelming Islamic domination that came with the Arabs, it's easy to forget the previous importance of Christian Tunisia. Site of one of the earliest mass conversions to the religion, adherents had their share of persecutions by the pagan Romans. The Sousse catacombs are indicative of the numbers of the faithful. With over 15,000 graves that extend for more than 5km, and spaces for covert gatherings, this underground cemetery and makeshift church are part of one of the largest catacomb systems in the Christian world. Not as flashy as the one in Rome, although in better condition, only about 100m are open to public wandering. The end of the section is closed by a gate, and it's possible to see beyond into the tunnel that continues. Two of the graves are open, showing the skeletons of its permanent inhabitants behind glass.

Boujaffar Beach Lining the length of the city is this beautiful sandy beach with its Mediterranean turquoise water. Right along the main road, most of the stretch is open to the public (a few small sections are roped off for hotel 'private beaches'). Locals and visitors fill the place in the summer, and there is usually someone who can rent out umbrellas or offer whatever sports equipment you might need to enjoy the water still further. The promenade is a lovely place to stroll in the late afternoon or evening, before the night's other activities.

Port el Kantaoui (*10km north of Sousse on the coast; www.portelkantaoui.co.uk*) It's worth briefly mentioning this vacation village that was specially built in 1979. The Tunisian way seems to be to develop huge complexes that include everything holiday visitors could want, from large hotels and restaurants, to marinas and golf courses. Although intimidating and relatively characterless, these places have full facilities and do allow the preservation of some of the older cities' traditional centres by diverting less cultural requirements into these tourist ghettos. Port el Kantaoui appears to be one of the more successful attempts and it does have a style, even if it looks more Euro-Spanish than Afro-Tunisian.

Museums

Archaeological museum (*inside the Kasbah;* ✆ *073 23 36 95; closed for renovation at time of research; otherwise* ⊕ *Apr–mid-Sep 09.00–19.00 daily except Mon; mid-Sep–Mar 09.00–18.00; TND4*) Tunisia's second most important museum, after the Bardo in Tunis, is an essential to visit, mostly for its collection of superb Roman mosaics. Gathered from the extensive villa network in the area, there are some wonderful examples, including the Triumph of Bacchus, the Triumph of Neptune, the Abduction of Ganymede, Venus adorning herself, and other subjects that are repeated throughout the Roman world, but no less charming for that. There are also steles from the Punic tombs that were found in the casbah and other items discovered in the catacombs, as well as the stuff of daily life of the ancient Romans.

Dar Essid (*65 Rue des Remparts;* ✆ *073 22 05 29;* ⊕ *Apr–mid-Sep 10.00–19.00 Tue–Sun; mid-Sep–Mar 10.00–18.00 Tue–Sun; TND2*) Hiding in a corner of the medina, this privately owned museum shows how an affluent 19th-century local official lived together with his family, including two wives and all their close relatives. The house itself dates from after 900, and is possibly the oldest one remaining in the casbah. There are lots of nice details and if all this decorative stuff gets to be too much, there's a café, reached by a spiral staircase.

HOW TO GET TO THE ROMAN SITES Sousse is an excellent place to begin exploring the Roman sites of Tunisia. There are several within close range that can be visited either on day trips or short journeys. Local tour operators can arrange excursions to any or all of these places, depending on time, number of passengers and money. Be aware that it's probably easier to sort out a trip from the tourist resorts than from Tunis. Although the relevant sections in *Chapter 23* (Kairouan, page 311) and *Chapter 22* (Tunis, page 290) go into more details about the places themselves, here are a few suggestions as to how to visit the vestiges of ancient Rome from the resorts of the seaside.

El Djem Seeing this city is a must, mostly because of its superb Roman amphitheatre, but also for its excellent museum. Travelling by train is a good option, and long-distance buses also go there. If you have your own car, zip down the RN1 till you see the huge arena (you can't miss it). The same route applies if you're going by taxi, but the driver will know the way.

Kairouan Not a Roman site, but an extremely important early Islamic one (the first in Tunisia), this city is also an excellent point for getting to sites further inland. Buses and *louages* go there and it's less than a 60km drive from Sousse, along the RN12.

Sbeitla The ancient site of Sufetula is essential for Roman Empire seekers and is a wonderful and evocative place. It's possible to get a *louage* from Sousse although if leaving from Kairouan there's also the option of going via a twice-daily bus service. If travelling by private car, simply follow the RN12 and continue along the same route when it changes name to the RN3, then RN3a2 (despite the different labels, it's pretty much a straight road). There should be signs to guide you the whole way.

Makhtar This extraordinary site, with its large public baths (significantly enhanced by the Byzantines), unique school for youths and Vandal church, among other important vestiges, is another must to visit. There is a *louage* that goes directly from Sousse, although again it's easier to go from Kairouan. To go by car, stay on the RN12, the same one that goes from Sousse to Kairouan.

Located on the coast to the south of the country, virtually on the Libyan border, Djerba's 514km² make up the largest island in the North African Mediterranean. Reached by a short ferry crossing across a shallow, narrow strait, or via a causeway with Roman, and possibly earlier, origins, there's also an international airport. Despite the ease of getting there, the separateness has allowed a slightly different culture to evolve. Many of the inhabitants still speak a Berber dialect. Religion has been allowed to take its own course, with the local Ibadite (also known as 'Kharjite', 'separate') sect of Islam differing from the more common Malkite practised by the rest of the country. A series of small but architecturally interesting mosques pepper the landscape. There was once a large group of practising Jews in Djerba and although many have now left (there was a mass departure after independence and later, to Israel), there are still two Jewish towns.

These features are not why most visitors come to Djerba. Quieter than the big resorts, with a gentle and consistent climate, the main draw for tourists is the beaches. The Zone Touristique sits astride the Plage de Sidi Mahres, with its family-friendly sandy strands, lined with a score of resorts. The eastern side of the island is almost totally dedicated to servicing holidaymakers. Much of the rest of Djerba remains traditional, with crafts, fishing and simply getting on with life. The main town, Houmt-Souk, is a shopper's paradise, as indicated by 'Souk' (market). There is no better location in the entire country for shopping. There are other villages and enclaves that are worth a look, but they are not necessarily major attractions.

HISTORY The Phoenicians came through here by 800BC and laid claim to what they called the Island of Menix. Within these waters in the Gulf of Gabes were found *murex*, shells which when ground up produced the purple dye for which the Phoenicians were famous. About a hundred years later, the location had its first brush with fame. The Greek epic poet, Homer, alleged that here was the location of the land of the Lotus Eaters that his Greek hero of the Trojan War, Odysseus, came upon during his decade-long post-war wanderings.

Inherited by the Carthaginians and then seized by the Romans as part of their Punic War spoils, the island proved useful to the empire. A gathering point for African goods, including slaves, the first causeway was built from the mainland to allow for easier passage. Four cities were established and it was from one of them, Girba, that the island got its present name. The island did not establish its importance enough to escape destruction by the Vandals, and in the familiar story of reconquest by the later Roman Byzantines, the Arab invasion and the ravages of subsequent Berber dynasties, Djerba suffered, falling into eventual obscurity. Its fortunes revived from around 1100 when rivals for control of the Mediterranean realised the strategic location. The Normans arrived, sitting for 20 years before the Almohad dynasty seized the island. The Spanish took over from them, to be ousted less than half a century later. By the later 1400s, piracy was beginning and Djerba became the Barbarossa brothers' base. Later on, their associate Dragut continued the privateer cause with the sponsorship of the Ottoman Turks. Successfully fighting off the Spanish around 1550, his legacy of 'free enterprise' was maintained, until foreign naval powers banded together to stop it. By 1881, the French took over from the Turks, leading to the protectorate. Djerba was part of the free nation of Tunisia when independence was granted in 1956.

GETTING THERE AND AROUND
By air The Aeroport International de Djerba-Milita (✆ *075 65 02 33*) is about 10km west of Houmt-Souk. Both international and domestic flights land here.

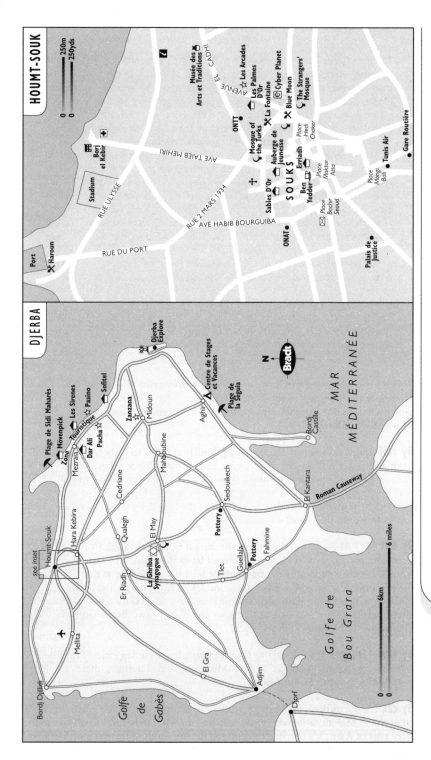

HOUMT-SOUK

0   250m
0   250yds

Port
✕ Haroun

RUE DU PORT

Stadium
RUE ULYSSE

Borj
el Kebir
✚

RUE 2 MARS 1934

AVE TAIEB MEHIRI

AVE HABIB BOURGUIBA

EL CADHI

AVENUE

ℹ

Musée des
Arts et Traditions ✖

✕ Les Arcades
☆ Les Palmes
D'Or
✖ La Fontaine
🅔 Cyber Planet
✖ Blue Moon

ONTT ●

Mosque of
the Turks ℭ

Auberge de
Jeunesse

✚

Sables D'Or

SOUKS

Ben
Yedder

Erriadh

Place
Bechir
Seoud

ONAT ●

Place
Hedi
Chaker

ℭ The Strangers'
Mosque

Place
Moktar
Atta

Place
Mongi
Bali

● Tunis Air

● Gare Routière

Palais de
Justice ●

DJERBA

Plage de Sidi Maharès
Zone
Mövenpick
Les Sirenes
Touristique ☆ Pasino
Mezraia Dar Ali
Pacha ☆

Sofitel
Djerba
Explore

Zantana
☆
Midoun

Centre de Stages
et Vacances ✕

Plage de
la Seguia →

Aghir

N
Bradt

Hara Kebira

Cedriane

Qualegh

Mahbhubine

Sedouikech

MAR

MÉDITERRANÉE

see inset
Houmt-Souk

Er Riadh

El May

La Ghriba
Synagogue ☼

Tlet

Guellala

Fahmine

Pottery ●

Pottery

Bordj
Castille ○

El Kantara

Roman Causeway

✈
Mellita

El Gra

Adjim

Djorf

Golfe
de
Gabès

Golfe de
Bou Grara

Bordj Djillidi

0   6km
0   6 miles

The great Greek poet Homer follows up the *Illiad,* his account of the Trojan War, a legendary event dated from between 1194 and 1184BC, with the *Odyssey.* The story of how the triumphant Greek general ended up touring the eastern Mediterranean and meeting its strange occupants for ten years because he couldn't get the sea to co-operate to get him home is one of the world's great literary works. Djerba was alleged to be the Land of the Lotus Eater, with fruit so delicious, and so magical, that it made those who ate it forget about anything else.

There's no magic lotus of forgetfulness to be found today but the interesting thing is that this place, believed to be Djerba, is mentioned at all. With it being under Phoenician influence, rather than Greek or Spartan, and even then not settled until several hundred years after the war, Homer used his poetic licence to describe an exotic location. Word of the island's delightful appeal must have reached Greece by Homer's time. Djerba is far off the relatively short sailing route between Troy and Odysseus's Greek island home of Ithaca and proves the point that the gods were annoyed enough to keep the general sailing further and further away. If the legend is true perhaps someone told the blind author about the location, and Homer projected his story onto this convenient island. In any case, this quiet place, with its gentle breezes, soft sand beaches, nice people and away-from-it-all feeling could still be said to have a lotus-eater quality about it.

The legend is celebrated by the locals in July, at the annual Ulysses Festival, in which the landing of Odysseus, in his Romanised guise as Ulysses, is re-enacted, accompanied by some more recent folklore events.

There is no organised public transport other than taxis, which can take you to Houmt-Souk, or hotels in the Zone Touristique. Many of the tourist resorts have their own transport from the airport, and if you are on a tour the operator will have arranged something.

By rail Trains don't cross the causeway, but they do go to Gabes, a town on the mainland not far from the island, and then a bus service takes over to get to Houmt-Souk. It's possible to buy a through ticket. There is an overnight service that originates in Tunis and stops at Sousse *en route* to Djerba. If the time is not convenient, it might be worth going by one of the four daily services to Gabes, then continuing onto the island via bus or *louage*.

By bus SNTRI buses run directly to the station in Houmt-Souk (` 075 65 04 75; www.sntri.com.tn`), located close to Avenue Habib Bourgiba. The daily bus service from Tunis takes as long as the train, but at least it's in the day, so that you can see the countryside as you pass. Fares are around TND21. There's also a daily journey in daylight direct from Kairouan. Two services leave from Gabes, both arriving late afternoon. Locally, there's a bus that goes about every two hours from the Zone Touristique to Houmt-Souk and back.

By taxi (*louage*) It's possible to find transport from the big cities. From nearby mainland locations, such as Gabes, Medinine and Tatouine, there are more possibilities to get to Houmt-Souk.

By car It's not difficult to get to Djerba by car. If coming from the north, the RN1 takes you to Mareth, from where you switch to the MC116 heading east to get to the ferry port of Ajim. It's possible to continue further south to the town of Medinine (somewhat more interesting) and then head north on the MC108 to the same embarkation point. From the west, follow the MC104 to Medinine. The ferry runs frequently, 24 hours a day, takes 15 minutes and costs 800 millimes for the car (passengers go free). If coming from the south, for example the Libyan border or the town of Zarzis, then there is a land route via the causeway (MC117). However, if you are not in the area, it's not worth going the 77km out of your way simply to drive where the ancients did, as it's far off the main path and nothing of its past is visible.

Car hire

🚗 **Avis** (Mellita Airport) 📞 075 65 02 33; (Houmt-Souk) Rte Touristique; 📞 075 65 01 51
🚗 **Europcar** (Mellita Airport) 📞 075 65 02 33; (Houmt-Souk) Av Abdelhamid Cadhi; 📞 075 65 10 45

🚗 **Hertz** (Mellita Airport) 📞 075 65 02 33; (Houmt-Souk) Av Habib Bourgiba; 📞 075 65 01 96

TOURIST INFORMATION The **Commissariat Regional du Tourisme** is at Boulevard de l'Environnement (📞 *075 65 00 16*). The **Syndicat d'Initiative** is on the Place des Martyrs (📞 *075 65 09 15*).

TOUR OPERATORS There is no shortage of companies willing to show you the beauty of the country. Many also include desert treks, with camels, 4x4s and overnight bivouacs. Most are located in Houmt-Souk while a few are in the island's second city, Midoun. Among them are the following:

Dream Travel Toute de l'Aeroport, Km4; 📞 075 67 34 51; www.dreamtravel-tunisie.com
Magic Tours Rue Habib Thameur; 📞 075 65 56 93; www.magictourstunisia.com

Pro Travel 56 Bd de l'Environnement; 📞 075 62 16 63; www.protraveltunisia.com

WHERE TO STAY

Houmt-Souk Although the main place for accommodation is on the beaches to the east, the following are listed in case you'd prefer to stay in town. The selection is smaller and the accommodation is simpler and cheaper than in the Zone Touristique, but more authentic.

Mid-range

🏠 **Hotel Les Palmes D'Or** (32 beds) Av Abdelhamid; 📞 075 65 33 69. This small hotel has comfortable

rooms with AC as well as a restaurant & ice cream parlour. $$

Budget

🏠 **Auberge de Jeunesse** (Youth Hostel) (90 beds) 11 Rue Moncef Bey; Houmt Souk; 📞 075 65 06 19; www.hihostels.com/dba/hostels-Djerba-058009.fr.htm?himap=Y. $
🏠 **Hotel Erriadh** (58 beds) Rue Mohammed Ferjani; 📞 075 65 07 56. A modern-day inexpensive place to stay located in an old *foundouk*, a merchant's inn,

where participants once stayed when travelling on the caravan. This example with its flower-laden courtyard is one of the better ones. $
🏠 **Hotel Sables D'Or** Rue Mohammed Ferjani; 📞 075 65 04 23. Situated among the tiny alleys of the main town, this simple place is clean & charming, although washing facilities are only semi-private. $

Zone Touristique As with many of the other resorts, prices soar in the summer. Hotels that seem pricey in July and August can be excellent value at other times of the year. Djerba is the furthest south of Tunisia's big beach resorts and has a much longer fine-weather season. If you're looking for good value, consider coming before mid-June or after mid-September and make sure to avoid the Christmas period. Price approximations below are for high season.

Top end Many of the smarter hotels seem the same, and as they generally have similar views, and their own sections of the identical beach, there's not much to choose between them, except for whether you want a three-, four- or five-star. Below is a sample selection.

⌂ **Mövenpick Ulysse Palace Resort & Thalasso Djerba** (259 rooms) Plage de Sidi Mehrez, BP 239 4128; ☎ 075 75 87 77; www.moevenpick-hotels.com/en/ pub/your_hotels/worldmap/djerba/overview.cfm. This stunning 5-star resort sits on the beach, & the pool overlooking it is enormous & gorgeous, not to mention all the other extravagances such as thalassotherapy & fine cuisine. $$$$$+

⌂ **Sofitel Palm Beach** (261 rooms) North Shore; ☎ 075 75 77 77; www.sofitel.com/sofitel/fichehotel/ gb/sof/2788/fiche_hotel.shtml. This member of the French luxury hotel chain is a beautiful local architecture-styled hotel situated right on the beach, equipped with facilities that cater for over-indulgence, such as swimming pools, restaurants & a spa. $$$$$+

⌂ **Complexe Les Sirenes** www.djerbasirenes.com. Has 2 hotels, the 3-star **Les Sirenes Beach** (138 rooms) ☎ 075 75 72 66 ($$$) & the 4-star **Les Sirenes Thalasso and Spa** (165 rooms); ☎ 075 758 133 ($$$$). Both are less intimidating places to stay than the enormous blocks nearby, with facilities in accord with their ratings & spa facilities available for all residents.

Mid-range

⌂ **Residence Dar Ali** (15 rooms) Sidi Mehrez; ☎ 075 75 86 71. An aberration in this land of flashy big resorts, this little place is low key, but still nice with its swimming pool & hangout atmosphere, especially for the visiting kite surfers. $$$

Budget

⚑ **Centre de Stages et Vacances** Rue Oasis; ☎ 075 27 02 71. Campsite in a good location not far from the sea. $

✗ WHERE TO EAT

Houmt-Souk Even if you're not staying here, it might be a nice change to get away from the Euro-style Zone Touristique and come into town and eat locally. Here is a small list of eating places compiled from the many restaurants in the city.

✗ **Blue Moon** Off the Pl Hedi Chaker; ☎ 075 65 05 59. Hidden in one of the tiny streets, the totally blue interior is home to some of the best food around, served in this quiet location. $$$– $$$$

✗ **La Fontaine** Rue 2 Mars; ☎ 075 25 42 05. There are several different styles here, both in the décor, & on the menu, but basics, such as pizzas, crepes & sandwiches, are good, & a fixed price menu is available later in the day. $$

✗ **Restaurant Haroun** Le Port; ☎ 075 65 04 88. Save your pennies somewhere else & come to the smartest restaurant in Houmt-Souk, situated by the new yacht harbour, & enjoy some of the best fish dishes in the area. $$$–$$$$

Knowing where there are recommended **cafés** is always good, not only for a decent coffee, but also for entertainment and seeing how the locals live. The **Café Les Arcades** (*Rue Abdel Hamid el Kadi*) goes on for 24 hours a day, while the **Café Ben Yedder** (*Pl Farhat Hached*) provides pastries to go with your brew.

Zone Touristique As virtually every visitor in this area is staying at one of the big resorts, most of the eateries seem to be located within the hotels. Prices and quality are relative to the calibre of the accommodation, although most places have a variety of levels, from poolside snack bars to fine cuisine restaurants. All of them welcome non-residents.

ENTERTAINMENT AND NIGHTLIFE Café life is fun if non-alcoholic and hanging around in Houmt-Souk nursing coffees or mint teas is a good way to spend the evening. Most of the bars and discotheques in party Djerba are attached to the hotels in the Zone Touristique. Occasionally non-residents are charged an entrance fee. Some of the bar/discos are:

☆ **Les Arcades** Sofitel Palm Beach; ☎ 075 75 77 77
☆ **Le Pacha** Hotel Rui Royal Garden, Rte Touristique; ☎ 075 74 57 77

☆ **Zanzana** Hotel Mariqueen, Zone Touristique, Midoun; ☎ 075 73 04 18

There's also a casino, **Pasino** (*Zone Touristique;* ☎ *075 75 75 37; www.casinocity.com/tn/djerba/tunpas/*). Open 24 hours, the options to lose your money include slots, gaming machines, and table and poker games.

FESTIVALS Every July, the legendary arrival of Ulysses and his Trojan army-weary crew who found perhaps too much peace in the Land of the Lotus Eaters is re-enacted in the **Ulysses Festival** in Houmt-Souk. The event is also the occasion for an accompanying folklore show. More details are available from the tourist office.

In Midoun, on Tuesdays (17.00 in summer, 15.00 in winter), a **Fantasia** is performed, re-enacting a traditional wedding ceremony. With a dromedary, but without a bride, this weekly event is a fun celebration of folklore, even if it is laid on a bit thick for the tourists.

SHOPPING It's hard to imagine a better place to shop for handicrafts and souvenirs than in the town of Houmt-Souk. Spilling out onto the streets, wedged into alleyways, under cover and in the open, there are so many items that it seems they burst out from the already overcrowded stores. With the area punctuated by open-air cafés, it's a delight to buy here. If the choice gets too much, just sit down, sip a fresh orange juice and enjoy how other tourists deal with the same dilemma. Particularly good are the ceramics, but typical Tunisian items such as mosaics and leather goods, especially slippers, are also on display.

There is a fish market and the daily late morning auctions are fun to see if you're passing. Fruit and vegetables are also sold. Both are at the Marche Central. Note that it's hard to find places that sell alcohol. There are a few shops in Houmt-Souk and a supermarket close to the Hotel Al Jazira but be aware that prices can be very high. It might be better just to enjoy a drink at one of the hotels.

In addition throughout the island, there are weekly markets at **Houmt-Souk** (Mon & Thu), **Sedouikech** (Tue), **Guellala** (Wed), **Midoun**, **Mellita** (Fri) and **Ajim, Mellita, Riadh** (Sun).

OTHER PRACTICALITIES
Emergency telephone numbers
Police ☎ 075 65 04 44

Late-night chemist 166 Av Habib Bourgiba, Houmt-Souk; ☎ 075 65 07 05

Hospital
✚ **Hospital Sadom Mokadem** Midoun Rd; ☎ 075 65 00 18

Internet cafés Almost all the hotels have internet access and the better ones will most likely be using Wi-Fi that should be available to guests. More cyber cafés spring up every day, but here are a few that seem to have lasted longer than many.

Cybernet Close to the tourist office & next to the louage station, Houmt-Souk
Cyber Planet Pl Sidi Brahim, Houmt-Souk

Publinet Centre of town on the road to Houmt-Souk, Midoun

Post The main post office is on Avenue Habib Bourgiba (✆ 075 65 00 97).

Banks Most of the major Tunisian banks are represented in the centre of Houmt-Souk as well as Midoun and are equipped with ATMs. At a pinch, hotels will change money for an extra commission.

WHAT TO SEE Please note that most museums and sites charge an additional fee to take photographs, usually around TND1.

Borj el Kebir (*Rue Ulysse, at the harbour, Houmt-Souk;* ⊕ *Apr–mid-Sep 08.00–19.00 Sat–Thu; mid-Sep–Mar 09.30–16.30 Sat–Thu; TND3*) A magnificent, if somewhat heavily restored fortress that had its golden age when Dragut, the infamous 16th-century pirate, rebuilt the fortification for his own use.

Architecture Although Djerba isn't far from the mainland, those little stretches of water, the flat landscape, and the island's strategic and defensive position caused the evolution of a unique building style. Low level, sometimes even squat, the domestic forts were built in thick mud and stone, for insulation against the heat, and painted white, for additional cooling. Domes, arches and splashes of colour, usually blue or green, provided decorative relief. Inside, the central courtyard helped the air circulation. Look out for examples of local architecture. In addition, the needs of non-mainstream religious believers, such as the Ibadite (Kharjite) Muslims and the Jews, helped create some very distinctive constructions. They are scattered throughout Djerba, but look out for the following.

In Houmt-Souk The Strangers' Mosque (*Av Abdelhamid el Kadhi*) with its decorated square minaret; Zaouia of Sidi Brahim (*across from the Strangers' Mosque*), a holy man's tomb dating from 1674; Mosque of the Turks (*Pl d'Algerie*), the city's most distinctive mosque, with a round minaret and seven domes.

In Mahboubine (*about 3km from Midoun*) The El Kateb Mosque. Although barely a century old, it's still an impressive copy of the Haghia Sophia in Istanbul, a reference to the country's own Turkish past.

El May (*in the centre of the island*) Famous for its 16th-century mosque, this small but beautiful solid white iconic building is the most photographed landmark in Djerba.

La Griba (*Erriadh, 7km south of Houmt-Souk*) More impressive for its past than its exterior, this extremely important Jewish synagogue has been in existence in its current form only since the 1920s. However, its history could date back as far as the Jews' arrival in 586BC, when they came here after their expulsion from Babylon. An alternate version has them landing on the shore after Jerusalem was sacked by the Romans in AD71. It remains a pilgrimage site for Jews all over the world. Visitors are allowed to enter to view the religious artefacts, as long as shoes are removed and heads are covered (with a skullcap or shawl).

Guellala In the south of the island, this little town is famous for its pottery production. The mosque is another example of typical Djerban architecture. There is another potters' village at **Sedouikech,** about 6km east, which has a market on Tuesday.

Djerba Explore (*La Phare de Taguermess, Rte Touristique de Midoun;* ☎ *075 74 52 77;* *www.djerbaexplore.com;* ⊕ *summer 09.00–02.00; winter 09.00–20.00; TND7.30*) This large leisure centre close to the Zone Touristique and the Taguermess Lighthouse is built around one of Tunisia's most unusual attractions, its Nile crocodile farm. Also within the complex are cafés, restaurants, boutiques and the **Lalla Hadria Museum** which displays 1,000 pieces of Arab-Islamic art straddling 13 centuries.

MUSEUMS

Museum of Popular Arts and Traditions (*Av Abdelhamid el Kadhi, Houm-Souk;* ☎ *075 65 05 40; closed for renovation at time of research; otherwise* ⊕ *Apr–mid-Sep 09.00–18.00 daily except Fri; mid-Sep–Mar 09.30–16.30; TND4*) Situated within the Zaouia of Sidi Zitouni, the building is as interesting as the traditional crafts, including jewellery and woodwork, and clothing collections.

Musée Guellala (*Musée du Patrimoine;* ☎ *075 76 11 14;* ⊕ *Aug 08.00–23.00 Sun–Thu; Sep–Jul 08.00–18.00 Sat–Thu; TND5*) The traditional life of Djerba's past is depicted in various tableaux, peopled by life-size dummies.

HOW TO GET TO THE ROMAN SITES From Djerba it's quite a distance north to get back to the best Roman remains. It's probably easiest to head towards the city of Sfax, then to El Djem, via bus, bus/train combination, *louage* or car. From here, you can continue to Kairouan and follow the routes to the sites from there. It's also possible to go on to Sousse, and use this point to start the Roman-ruin excursions.

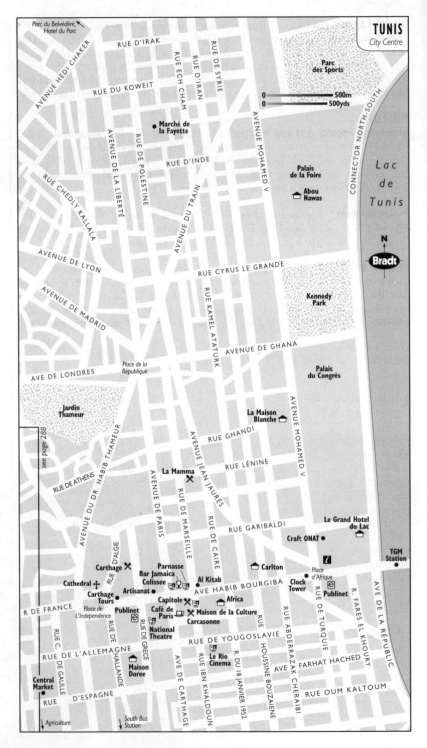

TUNIS
City Centre

Parc du Belvédère,
Hotel du Parc

RUE D'IRAK

AVENUE HEDI CHAKER

RUE DU KOWEIT

RUE ECH CHAM

RUE D'IRAN

RUE DE SYRIE

Parc
des Sports

0   500m
0   500yds

AVENUE DE LA LIBERTÉ

RUE DE POLESTINE

Marché de
la Fayette

AVENUE MOHAMED V

RUE CHEDLY KALLALA

RUE D'INDE

AVENUE DU TRAIN

Palais
de la Foire

CONNECTOR NORTH-SOUTH

*Lac
de
Tunis*

Abou
Nawas

AVENUE DE LYON

RUE CYRUS LE GRANDE

N

Bradt

AVENUE DE MADRID

RUE KAMEL ATATURK

Kennedy
Park

AVE DE LONDRES

AVENUE DE GHANA

Place de la
République

Palais
du Congrès

Jardin
Thameur

La Maison
Blanche

AVENUE MOHAMED V

see page 288

RUE DE ATHENS

AVENUE DU DR. HABIB THAMEUR

AVENUE JEAN JAURÈS

RUE GHANDI

RUE LÉNINE

La Mamma

AVENUE DE PARIS

RUE DE MARSEILLE

RUE DE CAIRE

RUE GARIBALDI

Le Grand Hotel
du Lac

Craft ONAT

TGM
Station

Carlton

Carthage

Parnasse
Colissee

Bar Jamaica

Al Kitab

Place
d'Afrique

Cathedral

Artisanat

Capitole

Africa

AVE HABIB BOURGIBA

Clock
Tower

Publinet

RUE D'ALGIE

Carthage
Tours

Publinet

Café de
Paris

Maison de la Culture

Carcasonne

RUE DE TURQUIE

R DE FRANCE

Place de
L'Independence

National
Theatre

RUE DE YOUGOSLAVIE

RUE ABDERRAZAK CHERAIBI

AVE DE LA RÉPUBLIC

RUE DE C.

RUE DE L'ALLEMAGNE

Le Rio
Cinema

R. DU 18 JANVIER 1952

HOUSSINE BOUZAIENE

AVE FARHAT HACHED

R. FARES EL KHOURY

DE GAULLE

Maison
Doree

RUE DE GRECE

AVE DE CARTHAGE

RUE IBN KHALDOUN

Central
Market

D'ESPAGNE

RUE

RUE OUM KALTOUM

Agriculture

South Bus
Station

22

Tunis

Telephone code 071

Tunis, capital of Tunisia, is one of the most important cities in the Maghreb. Second only to Cairo in the whole of North Africa, its development, sophistication and number of inhabitants make this Tunisian metropolis a thriving, modern conurbation. A population of over two million in the centre alone means that 20% of the entire nation resides in this northern city.

Situated between two salt lakes, close to the sea but not actually on it, a canal connects the capital with the port of La Goulette, where the cruise ships berth. A long causeway to the sea straddles the eastern lake for car traffic and a new bridge will soon join the northern part of the nation with the port, bypassing central Tunis. Examples of further international co-operation are evident in the large building programmes funded by the Far and Middle East. The city's future is almost as exciting as its past.

Tunis has its French colonial legacy, the Ville Nouveau, with a delightful collection of period buildings, including an Art Nouveau theatre on the main boulevard of the new town. The old heart of the city, the medina, is fascinating and a living reminder of its medieval past when it was 'one of the greatest and wealthiest cities in the Islamic world [with its] ... 700 monuments', according to UNESCO's designation of Tunis as a World Heritage Site.

It's in the environs where the greatest historical events occurred, particularly Carthage. Described more fully in both the *History* (page 5) and *Carthage* (page 290) sections, the settlement became the greatest city in Roman North Africa from its pre-Phoenician days until the Arab invaders decided to develop the more defensible enclave of Tunis. Today the ruins are not as impressive as one would think. The urban development that has continued on the spot without a pause has caused many of the remains to be absorbed into the next generations. There are a few sites left, and it's worth looking at some of the details on the rather nice houses in this affluent area, as some of those Roman columns might be not reproductions.

Although some of the other suburbs don't have the same illustrious past, today they're delightful areas. Some, such as La Marsa and Gammarth, are predominantly seaside resorts, the former containing upmarket summer residences, the latter big hotels. The charming hilltop village of Sidi Bou Said is a short tram ride from the centre of Tunis, yet feels a world away, with its beautiful white Andalusian-style architecture and distinctive blue trim. Even the port has its appeal with excellent seafood restaurants. Located on the other side of town, the Bardo has not much going for it, except one of the finest museums in the world. Here is unarguably the greatest collection of North African mosaics in existence, located in the palace of one of the city's old Turkish rulers, or beys.

HISTORY

Despite it's ancient history being overshadowed by Carthage, Tunis pre-dated its more famous neighbour by quite some time. It is believed to have been initially inhabited by Berbers and named Tunes as long ago as 2000BC, then the Numidians moved in. When the wandering Phoenicians founded Carthage in 814BC, they took in the little adjoining town as part of their territory. For a while from around 300BC, battles raged between the Berbers, the Greeks attacking from Sicily, and the Carthaginians, but eventually both Tunis and Carthage settled into being good Punic cities. Siding with its greater neighbour throughout the Punic Wars, Tunis unfortunately suffered the same fate as Carthage during the third and last one, being totally destroyed and sprinkled with salt. However the Romans, recognising the strategic importance of the area, reconstructed Carthage, and Tunis as well, although the latter never achieved the heights of the former.

Tunis came into its own when Carthage was again destroyed, but this time by the Arabs in AD698. Recognising the need for a more defensible city, yet appreciative of the salt lake access to the nearby sea harbour, the conquering dynasty decided to make Tunis the new capital. Although replaced by Kairouan, by AD900 the Aghlabids returned to the city in the north. Its capital status would not again be challenged and the city grew both in population and prominence, eventually becoming one of the most important in the Islamic world.

The Western world was also aware of the city's location, particularly as a stop for the Crusaders on their way to the Holy Land. In the late 13th century the French arrived, led by their king, Louis IX, who died there in 1270. A large, Victorian Byzantine cathedral was erected in his honour by the French six centuries later, and although no longer a church, it still dominates the landscape from its site atop Carthage's Byrsa Hill.

Part of the shore that became known as the Barbary coast, Tunis shared the situation with that of its neighbours, and became pirate territory. As the haven for the Barbarossa brothers and then the privateer Dragut, the city continued to flourish, assisted and then taken over by the Turkish who helped defeat any Western enemies, such as the Spanish. Now under Turkish control, the region became semi-autonomous. Ottoman rule continued until the French arrived, initially to make sure that pirates from Tunisia didn't cross into their territory of Algeria but eventually as 'protectors' of the province.

The nation of France happily incorporated Tunisia into their dominion and made Tunis a major capital, redeveloping and adorning it with huge boulevards and impressive buildings. They also populated it, inviting other communities, like the Italians, to settle. The French certainly made their mark, creating the whole Ville Nouvelle (new city), but still leaving some of the ancient medina. During World War II, Tunis was a city controlled by the Axis powers, acting as their headquarters from November 1942 until North Africa fell to the Allies in May 1943.

After the country was granted independence in 1956, Tunis rose in position second only to Cairo. From 1979 till 1990, the Arab League moved from the Egyptian to the Tunisian capital. Tunis's importance remains and when the Palestine Liberation Organisation was forced to quit Lebanon during the Israeli incursion, they temporarily moved to Tunisia's main city. Today, the city's fortunes are better than ever, with its politic appearance somewhat softened by the country's importance as a tourist destination. Although not visited by holidaymakers as frequently as the resorts down south, Tunis remains a fascinating city that should be included in everyone's visit, even if only as a too-short day trip.

GETTING THERE AND AROUND

BY AIR Tunis-Carthage International Airport (\ 071 75 70 00; www.oaca.nat.tn) lies about 8km northwest of the city centre. Clean and modern, with a prompt immigration service, this terminal is a good entry point for the country, although heading further south it might be better to fly to Monastir. Domestic flights also come here, if you're in a hurry to get from point to point. The bus gets you into town for around TND0.6, while taxis cost between TND4–7.

BY SEA Ferries depart from various cities in Italy as well as Marseille, France. The shortest crossing is from Palermo in Sicily, taking about ten hours. Check www.cemar.it/dest/ferries_tunisia.htm for more information. Boats land at the port of La Goulette, a short taxi drive into the centre. Cruise ships also arrive here, and shore excursions will include transport to the sights in and around Tunis.

BY RAIL The central station is Tunis-Ville (*Pl du Barcelone;* ✆ *071 25 44 40; www.sncft.com.tn*) and trains connect to all the stations on the SNCFT (Société des Chemin de Fer Tunisiens) network.

BY BUS SNTRI (*www.sntri.com.tn*) oversees two stations in Tunis for departures further afield. The one for destinations heading north is the Gare Routière Tunis-Nord (*Bab Saâdoun;* ✆ *071 56 25 32*), for example to destinations such as Tabarka, Tebersouk (for the Roman site of Dougga) and Jendouba (for the sites of Bulla Regia and Chemtou). For the rest of the country, heading south, go to the Gare Routière Tunis-Sud (*Bab El Falla;* ✆ *071 39 93 91*).

Yellow local city buses traverse the city and cost around TND0.5 (500 millime). It's easier, more fun and even slightly cheaper at TND0.41 (410 millime) to take the tram, or Metro Leger: there are five lines across town. However, it's probably best to walk around the central city – there's no alternative in the medina. The Metro Leger line 4 is good for getting out to the Bardo Museum.

For the eastern suburbs, the TGM, departing from the Tunis Marine terminus, is the best way to visit La Goulette, Carthage, Sidi Bou Said and La Marsa. The little train is quick and efficient, if occasionally a little crowded, and gets you to the attractions.

BY TAXI (*LOUAGE*) Collective taxis leave from close to both bus stations, going to places in the same direction as the buses. There is a *louage* terminus at Place Sidi Bou Mendil in the medina from where it's possible to cross to Algeria in the north, and Libya to the south.

BY CAR North: the Route National (RN) 1 heads to Mateur, where it connects with the RN11 to Bizerte and to the RN7, where it goes to Tabarka and the Algerian border. South: the RN1 follows the coast all the way to the Libyan border. An autoroute, the A1, short cuts to Sousse.

Car hire There is no shortage of car hire firms. It might well be worth considering doing the Tunis leg of the trip on foot and/or public transport and then renting a car for a few days to see the sights outside the capital, particularly the Roman ruins.

🚗 **Avis** (airport) ✆ 071 75 02 99; (town) Hotel Sheraton, Av De La Ligue Arabe; ✆ 071 78 71 67; Zone Industrielle Charguia; ✆ 071 80 72 52; www.avis.com

🚗 **Europcar** (airport) ✆ 071 23 34 11; (town) 81 Av de la Liberté; ✆ 071 79 44 32; 1 Rue H Nouira & Av Habib Bourgiba; ✆ 071 34 03 03; Zone Industrielle Charguia (behind sorting office); ✆ 071 94 01 00; www.europcar-africa.com

🚗 **Hertz** (airport) ✆ 071 75 40 00; (town) Charguia, Rue des Entrepreneurs, near the Zone Industrielle; ✆ 071 838 098; www.hertz.com

🚗 **Sixt** (airport) ✆ 024 53 96 13; (town) Ghana St; ✆ 051 071 33 40 64; Charguia 2; ✆ 071 94 25 07; www.sixt.com

TOURIST INFORMATION

ONTT (Office National du Tourisme Tunisien) 1 Av Mohamed V; ☎ 071 34 10 77; www.tourismtunisia.com

Commissariat Regional du Tourisme 31 Rue Hasdrubal; ☎ 071 84 56 18

TOUR OPERATORS

The Tunisian Tourist Office lists over 120 tour operators and travel agencies operating out of Tunis. The following have websites:

Batouta Voyages 97 Rue de Palestine; ☎ 071 80 28 81; www.batouta.com

Carthage Tours 59 Av Habib Bourgibba; ☎ 071 35 18 33; www.carthage-tours.com

Millesima Travel 9 Rue Jerusalem, Apt 9; ☎ 071 28 23 24; www.millesimatravel.com

Travel Academy 11 Av Habib Thameur; ☎ 071 42 82 04; www.travel-academy.com

Tunisian Travel Agency 67 Av Alain Savery; ☎ 071 84 10 30; www.tunisiantravelagency.com

Tunisian Travel Team 8 Rue d'Arabie Saoudite; ☎ 071 80 07 18; www.tunisiantravel.com

Tunisie Voyages Rue 8612 Imp No 4, Charguia, Zone Industrielle; ☎ 071 20 55 00 www.tunisie-voyages.com

WHERE TO STAY

There are many, many places to stay in this important capital city. The nicer hotels are either in the Ville Nouvelle or the suburbs, while the medina has more basic, if somewhat quainter ones.

Unless business or shopping calls, it's nice to stay in the suburbs, especially in the delightful village of Sidi Bou Said, when you can see how tranquil the place is when the tourists leave, or the beach resorts of La Marsa or Gammarth. The TGM provides easy, fast and cheap transport to the metropolitan area.

CITY CENTRE
Top end

Hotel Africa (212 rooms) 50 Av Habib Bourgiba; ☎ 071 34 74 77. In the Ville Nouvelle, here is one of the top business places to stay with décor that eschews the classic in favour of glitz, glamour & all manner of room facilities including minibar, cable TV & internet. $$$$+

Mid-range

Du Parc (51 rooms) Av de l'Arabie Saoudite; ☎ 071 84 30 22; www.hotelduparc.com.tn. Better than its 3-star rating, this full-service hotel sits in the nicer section of the city, close to Belvedere Park. $$$

Carlton (78 rooms) 31 Av Habib Bourgiba; ☎ 071 33 06 44. This bijoux colonial hotel has satellite TV & sits on the main thoroughfare of the Ville Nouvelle. $$$

Budget

Maison Doree (93 beds) 6 Bis, Rue de Hollande; ☎ 071 24 06 32. A well-established & comfortable family-run establishment that straddles the budget to

La Maison Blanche (40 rooms) 45 Av Mohammed V; ☎ 071 84 98 49. Another business hotel but with an older charm that the other top-class hotels seem to lack, including a period bar. $$$$$

Le Grand Hotel du Lac (180 rooms) 2 Rue Sindbad; ☎ 071 24 83 22. This listing isn't necessarily a recommendation, but merely a mention of this upside-down triangle that is not only a business hotel but was also, allegedly, the inspiration for the enormous slave transport vehicle in *Star Wars*. $$$

mid-range categories, depending on whether you are willing to share a bathroom, or want one of your own. $–$$

🏠 **Agriculture** (57 beds) 25 Rue Charles de Gaulle; ✆ 071 32 63 94. Basic but friendly, this place is close to the station. $

🏠 **Hotel El Medina** 1 Rue des Glaciers, Pl de la Victoire; ✆ 071 32 74 97. In the medina, this hotel has private showers, but shared bathrooms. $

🏠 **Auberge de Jeunesse** (54 beds) 25 Rue Saida Ajoula; ✆ 071 57 48 84; www.hihostels.com/dba/hostel058008.en.htm. Accommodation doesn't get cheaper than this & backpackers can stay in this 18th-century palace. <$

EASTERN CITY SUBURBS
La Goulette

🏠 **La Jetee** (65 rooms) 2 Av de la Republique; ✆ 071 73 60 00; http://lajetee-hotel.com. One of the few decent places to stay here, some of these 3-star rooms have a sea view. $$$

🏠 **Le Lido** Rue Ali Bach Hamba; ✆ 071 73 83 33. A decent, if somewhat typical 3-star hotel, close to the sea, with some rooms that overlook it. $$–$$$

Carthage

🏠 **Villa Didon** (10 rooms) Rue Mendes France; ✆ 071 77 28 98; www.villadidon.com. Combining the most elegant modernity with one of the most ancient settings on Byrsa Hill in the ruins of Carthage, this boutique hotel mixes style & comfort. $$$$$++

🏠 **Amilcar** (238 rooms) Plage Amilcar; ✆ 071 74 07 88; www.hotel-amilcar.com. Situated in Carthage, this large modern 3-star hotel looks out at the beach. $$–$$$

Sidi Bou Said

🏠 **Residence de Charme Dar Said** (24 rooms) Rue Toumi; ✆ 071 74 05 91. This beautiful & exclusive boutique hotel has positioned itself in an old villa in the heart of the village, & the swimming pool sits in front of one of Tunisia's most beautiful views, overlooking the bay & Cape Bon. $$$$$

🏠 **Hotel Sidi Bou Said** Sidi Dhrif; ✆ 071 74 04 11.Halfway between Sidi Bou Said & La Marsa, this modern, comfortable hotel has all modern conveniences & very helpful personnel. $$$

🏠 **Hotel Sidi Bou Fares** (8 rooms) 15 Rue Sidi Bou Fares; ✆ 071 74 00 91. Located in a quiet pedestrian street just off the village centre, the rooms are basic, but the staff very friendly. $$

La Marsa and Gammarth

🏠 **The Residence** (170 rooms) Rte Touristique Raoud, Chott Errich; ✆ 071 91 01 01. This spa refuge is a modern-day Arab Andalusian palace & one of the leading hotels in the world. $$$$$+

🏠 **Golden Tulip** (264 rooms) Av de la Promenade; ✆ 071 91 01 07; www.goldentulip.com. On Gammarth Hill overlooking La Marsa & the sea, this beautiful 5-star resort hotel with a fabulous

swimming pool is a town in itself, & includes an 8-lane bowling alley. $$$$$

🏠 **Tour Blanche** Les Cotes de Carthage, Av Taieb Mehirir; ✆ 071 77 47 88. Cheap & cheerful with a young clientele. The little swimming pool offers a place to socialise for those travellers more concerned with budget than décor. $

✕ WHERE TO EAT

MEDINA Finding a decent place to eat in the medina isn't difficult, as there are several small restaurants throughout the medieval heart, some that cater specifically to the souk shoppers and open only during the day. Cafés abound, too, and just about every one will provide good espresso (cappucinos are much harder to find) and mint tea.

✕ **Dar El Jeld** Rue Dar El Jeld; ✆ 071 56 09 16; www.dareljeld.tourism.tn; ⏱ lunch & dinner Mon–Sat excluding Aug. An excellent restaurant serving the

best of Tunisian fine cuisine, located in a 17th-century Ottoman building. $$$$$

✖ Dar Hamouda Pacha 56 Rue Sidi Ben Arous; ☏ 071 56 65 84; ⏱ café: 08.00–20.30, dinner: 20.00–22.30, Mon–Sat. Entering through a narrow door in the ancient wall, diners emerge into this beautiful 18th-century former palace, with adequate traditional food, but a wonderful ambience. $$$
✖ M'Rabet Souk el Trouk; ☏ 071 56 36 81; ⏱ 12.00–15.30 & 19.30–22.00 Mon–Sat. By day,

downstairs is a legendary place to have a coffee; by night, the upstairs formal restaurant is a Turkish extravaganza with entertainment (inc belly dancing). $$$
✖ Mahadaoui 2 Rue Jemaa Zitouna; ⏱ 12.00–15.30 Mon–Sat. Close to the Zitouna Mosque, this place is great for lunchtime basics, such as couscous & the usual meat dishes. $$

VILLE NOUVELLE The Ville Nouvelle is an interesting mix of colonial France and modern North Africa, reflected in the restaurants as well as architecture and atmosphere.

✖ Capitole 60 Av Habib Bourgiba; ☏ 071 25 66 01; ⏱ daily. On the main street of the modern town here's a place to try well-cooked local dishes without spending very much. $$–$$$
✖ Carthage 10 Rue Ali Bach Hamba; ☏ 071 25 56 14; ⏱ 12.00–15.00 & 19.00–23.00 Mon–Sat. It's best to overlook the tacky décor that proposes to represent Carthage in ancient Roman days & concentrate instead on the good national food, including seafood dishes. $$$

✖ La Mamma 11 Bis, Rue de Marseille; ☏ 071 33 23 88; closed in summer. When you've reached the point where you've had enough couscous, come here for some good Italian cuisine, in a nice location. $$$
✖ Carcassonne 8 Av de Carthage; ☏ 071 24 07 02; ⏱ 12.00–22.00. This popular little place is fine for a good basic meal, at an equally reasonable price. $$

EASTERN CITY SUBURBS La Goulette is well known for its fish restaurants and any number of them situated around the harbour offer tasty seafood fare. Here are two examples from both ends of the price spectrum.

✖ Café Vert 68 Av Franklin Roosevelt; ☏ 071 73 61 56; ⏱ 12.30–15.00 & 19.30–23.30 Tue–Sun. Expensive, but worth it for its finely prepared freshly caught fish, this place has remained an institution over the years. $$$$

✖ El Stambali Av Franklin Roosevelt; ☏ 071 73 85 06. ⏱ daily. Probably the least pretentious – & cheapest – restaurant in the district. $$–$$$

While Carthage is primarily a residential area and doesn't really have good places to eat, the trendy little village of **Sidi Bou Said** has a few that cater specifically to tourists. If looking for something small to hold you over until eating a large meal, head to the makeshift bakery, just past the main square, that sells a fried doughnut-type large pretzel-shaped pastry dipped in sugar, that's delicious and cheap.

✖ Restaurant Dar Zarrouk Rue Hedi Zarrouk; ☏ 071 74 05 91; ⏱ 12.30–14.30 & 19.30–22.30 Tue–Sun. This elegant restaurant affiliated with the Residence de Charmes Dar Said, offers a spectacular view over the sea towards Cap Bon, serving fine Mediterranean cuisine. $$$$

✖ Le Chargui Rue Hedi Zarrouk; ☏ 071 74 09 87; ⏱ Apr–Oct 12.00–23.00 daily; Nov–Mar 12.00–20.00. Go for the location, in the town square, particularly for people-watching. $$–$$$

In **La Marsa** and **Gammarth**, the better hotels have restaurants, but if looking for something more local, try these places:

✖ Restaurant La Falaise Rue Sidi Dhrif, La Corniche, La Marsa; ☏ 071 74 78 06. Close to the Hotel Sidi Bou Said, on the road to La Marsa, this restaurant

specialises in superb seafood that holds 2nd place to the wonderful vista over the Mediterranean. $$$$$

✕ Restaurant Les Ombrelles 107 Av Taïeb Méhiri, Gammarth; ✆ 071 74 29 64. Located at the water's edge, the restaurant has a very good reputation for both its food & its sea view. **$$$$**

ENTERTAINMENT AND NIGHTLIFE

DINNER SHOWS A few of the restaurants offer accompanying evening entertainment on the traditional side, such as **M'Rabet**, **Le Malouf** and the restaurant at the **Hotel Abou Nawas** (*Av Mohammed V;* ✆ *071 350 355*). Some of the restored historic palaces also provide programmes, but these presentations are usually done up for visitors, and will probably be part of a tour.

DRINKING Tunis is a Muslim city, with few alcoholic-drink establishments. For example:

♀ Bar Jamaica 10th Floor, Hotel El-Hana, 49 Av Habib Bourgiba, Ville Nouvelle; ✆ 071 33 11 44

As usual for Islamic countries, cafés replace bars, including:

☕ Café de Paris Av Habib Bourgiba, Ville Nouvelle   **☕ Café Ezzitouna** Jemaa Zitouna Medina

Most of the nightlife bars and discos in the **eastern suburbs** are in the big hotels, particularly in La Marsa and Gammarth.

Cinemas and theatres The **International Festival of Carthage** (*Av du 7 Novembre, Carthage;* ✆ *071 73 13 32; www.festival-carthage.com.tn*) takes place annually in July and August and puts on dance, music and theatre performances, as well as movie screenings, from around the globe.

SHOPPING

SOUKS The best places to go shopping in Tunis are the souks in the medina. Acknowledged by UNESCO as a World Heritage Site, the selection is dazzling to the eye and the choice so enormous that it's sometimes difficult to shop. If you're looking for something and find what you like, brave the friendly cries of the salesman and ask what the price is. You'll inevitably have to bargain (see *Cultural etiquette* in *Chapter 2*, page 67). The **Rue Jemaa Zitouna**, named after the medina's main Zitouna Mosque, is the main 'street'. Most of the souks lead off from it. The entire area is a labyrinth, so it's easier to ask someone what item you're looking for, rather than searching out the name of a particular corridor. Just wander, willingly getting lost. The locals are always happy to offer directions back to the mosque. With time, patience and enjoyment of the ambience, you're almost certain to hit the enclave of your desired speciality. Here are some of the better-known named markets.

- **Souk el-Attarine** Traditionally the perfume market, now it's predominantly souvenirs.
- **Souk des Etoffes** The fabrics' market still sells cloth and material.
- **Souk el-Trouk** Finer clothes are available here, many tailored. A few antique shops can be found in the doorways.
- **Souk des Chechias** *Chechias* are the Tunisian version of the circular red felt hat most people in the west think of as a fez. The colourful market here sells them literally in stacks.

- The **Souk de la Laine** sells silver items, while the **Souk des Orfevres** features gold. In between are several smaller stalls selling items that don't quite fall into a specific category.

If bargaining really isn't for you, then there are some fixed-price shops. The **Société de Commercialisation des Produits de l'Artisanat** (*La Palmarium, Av Habib Bourgiba*) is an official store operating under government administration that sells crafts at both a higher quality and price, not subject to negotiation. Check out what the people in charge think is the true value of these goods, and it's worth keeping these figures in mind when let loose in the souks.

A similar concept for fine items produced by women can be found in the **Mains des Femmes** (*47 Av Habib Bourgiba*), particularly with the carpets.

Hanout (*52 Jemaa Zitouna*) sells distinctive quality crafts at higher fixed prices located right in the heart of the souks.

There are a number of shops in Tunis that sell books, mostly in Arabic and French, but occasionally in English. **Al Kitab** (*43 Av Habib Bourgiba, Le Coliséee;* ✆ *071 35 32 91*) is one of the better-known ones. It's possible to find guidebooks here.

There is a daily food market at the **Central Market** (Rue Charles de Gaulle) and a weekly one on Fridays at the **Souk Ejemaa-Ariana**.

In the eastern suburbs, at Sidi Daoud, between La Marsa and Tunis city, is a gigantic **Carrefour** shopping centre that includes the hypermarket, where you can find practically anything, and several other stores.

OTHER PRACTICALITIES

EMERGENCY TELEPHONE NUMBERS

Police ✆ 197

Ambulance ✆ 190 or 071 34 12 50

Medical ✆ 071 34 12 50

Doctor ✆ 071 78 00 00

There are several **night chemists**, including some on the Avenue Habib Bourgiba.

HOSPITALS

✚ **Hospital Charles Nicolle** Bd du 9 Avril 1938; ✆ 071 57 83 46

INTERNET CAFÉS Besides the big hotel, there are several Publinets. Check out www.yatounes.com/2m/publinet/tunis.html for the full list, but in the meantime, here are some useful ones.

In the centre

🖥 **Publinet Barcelone** 14 Rue de Grece; ✆ 071 33 76 26

🖥 **Publinet des ingenieurs** 28 Av Habib Bourgiba; ✆ 071 34 53 11

Bardo These are close to the museum, handy for emailing friends right after you've seen the spectacular mosaics.

🖥 **Publinet Khaznadar** 21 Av de l'Indépendance, Khaznadar; ✆ 071 51 77 84

🖥 **Space net** 71 Av Habib Bougatfa; ✆ 071 51 18 59

Eastern suburbs

🖥 **Publinet de Sidi Daoud** 11 Av de Carthage, Rte de Carthage, Sidi Daoued; ✆ 071 77 97 79

🖥 **Le net club** 4 Rue Cheikh Zarrouk, Av Habib Bourgiba, La Marsa; ✆ 071 72 71 28

POST The main post office (grand poste) is located on Rue Charles de Gaulle, close to Place Barcelone.

BANKS The main street in the Ville Nouvelle has representation from almost all the Tunisian banks including the following:

$ **Banque de l'Habitat** 44 Av Habib Bourgiba
$ **UBCI** 23 Av Habib Bourgiba
$ **UIB** 29 Av Habib Bourgiba
$ **BIAT** 1 Rue Jamel Abdelnasser

There are ATMs all over the place, including the airport.

WHAT TO SEE

It's easiest to divide the city into four main sections. The medina, the Ville Nouvelle and the Bardo are described below, while the pleasant eastern suburbs are briefly mentioned above, in the introduction. Carthage has its own entry (page 290). Most places with entry fees charge an additional TN1 for allowing photography.

THE MEDINA The heart of the old city is surrounded by a wall broken by entrance gates, or *babs*. Entering this intricate and complicated series of pedestrian alleyways can seem pretty intimidating, but relax and enjoy the atmosphere and the sites, knowing that the friendly locals can always guide you to a known landmark. It's always a pleasant surprise to lose yourself completely in wandering and then suddenly come across a wide-open space or somewhere familiar. One of the best places to start the walkthrough is at the **Bab el Bhar** (Gate to the Sea) at the Place de la Victoire, on the eastern side, and also the entrance closest to the Ville Nouvelle. Tours usually start on the western side, at the large Place de la Kasbah and the Place du Gouvernement. Whichever way you decide to breach the inner city, here are some of the highlights worth viewing.

Mosques Although non-Muslims are not usually allowed inside, the exteriors are dramatic and often interesting to look at. The religious halls are often wedged among small shops and occasionally, right before and after the five-times-daily prayer times, doors are open and it's possible to look into the central courtyard. Take a moment to look back down the narrow streets where sometimes the high minarets become visible in the distance. It's also a common feature of some of the shops and bazaars to offer rooftop prospects, where there's a better viewpoint of how these buildings fit into the context of the old city.

Zitouna Mosque (⏰ 08.00–14.30 Thu–Tue; TND2) Everything in the medina leads to or from here, and this enormous complex, especially its high minaret, is an excellent central point. Get your bearings via this place, as it's the most obvious reference from which to navigate. This religious institution is an important historical landmark dating from within a hundred years of the initial Arab invasion. The current building was constructed not long after. From ground level, visitors from other faiths are allowed inside for a small fee to view, but not enter, the courtyard. Take advantage of the rooftops of the shops nearby, to which a payment of a small tip is customary, to see how impressive the mosque really is. Some of the other mosques that warrant a longer look at their exteriors include the following.

Mosque Sidi Youssef (*Rue Sidi Ben Ziad*) This dates from 1616 and was built in appropriate style during the Ottoman occupation.

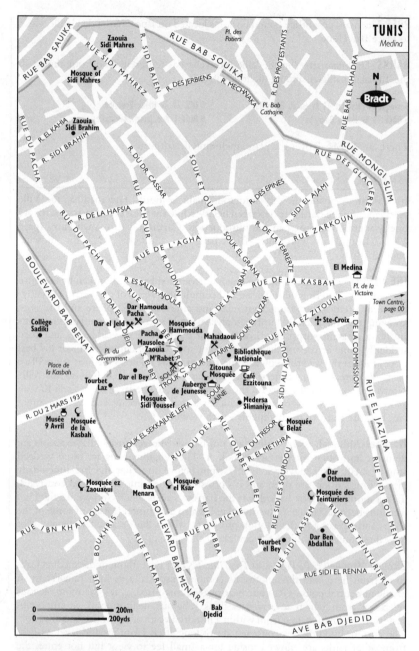

Mosque Hamouda Pacha (*Rue Sidi Ben Arous*) This one dates from the same period, in a Turkish style.

Kasbah Mosque (*Pl de la Kasbah*) Just outside the medina walls and once within the kasbah that no longer exists, the 13th-century building is from the time when the Hafsids had connections with the Moroccan Almohads.

Mosque of Sidi Mahres (*Rue Sidi Mahres*) Built in 1675, on the Turkish model, this mosque is the only one in Tunis with domes. Named after the city's patron saint, his *zaouia* (tomb) sits right in front.

Mosque des Tenturiers, or the Dyers Mosque Jemaa el Djedid (*Rue des Tenturiers*) Situated in the southern end of the medina, this early 18th-century mosque built by Hussein ben Ali, the first bey in the Husseinite line, is distinctive for its octagonal minaret.

Medersas Koranic schools, common throughout the Islamic world were, and still are, housed in buildings often as old, impressive and beautiful as the mosques to which they were usually affiliated. Four of these institutions still exist, although only the first one here remains in its original capacity. All were built in the 100 years between the 1650 and 1750 and are located close to the Zitouna Mosque: **Medersa Palmier** (*11 Rue des Librairies*), **Medersa Ali Pacha** (*19 Rue des Librairies*), **Medersa Mouradia** (*37 Souk Etouffes*), **Medersa Slimanya** (*Rue des Librairies & Souk el Karachine*).

Other buildings of note With over 700 monuments cited by UNESCO, there are a huge number of things to see. Some of the better-known edifices include the following.

Tourbet El Bey (*62 Rue Tourbet*) This large domed construction built sometime after 1750 housed the graves of most of the royals from the Husseinites, including the last one buried in 1957.

Dar Othman (*16 Bis, Rue El M'Bazaa*) This elaborate palace built by wealthy privateer and government official around 1600, is mostly offices, but the courtyard is open to the public.

Dar el Bey (*Pl du Gouvernement*) Constructed about 1800, yet another former palace sits prominently on the square, although this one houses the headquarters of the prime minister and is closed to the public.

There are lots of other things that merit a glance, whether delightful little makeshift details, for example the red-and-green columns of an entrance to a *hammam* (bathhouse) or further magnificent reminders of the city's glorious past, such as royal residences. Some of the latter now house museums (see below).

THE VILLE NOUVELLE The majority of interesting things to see in the new town lie along the main street, Avenue Habib Bourgiba. It has recently been revamped, and the broad boulevard, lined with ficus trees and adorned with elaborate streetlights, is a popular place to promenade. With the TGM station, the marine terminus of the suburban tram railway that heads to the eastern suburbs, at its eastern end the road passes the enormous landmark clock tower, built in 2001. Strolling along the grand corridor, you will find that much of the colonial influence of the French is visible, including various official buildings and hotels. Predominant among the attractions is the National Theatre, with an Art Nouveau frontage dating from 1902, and the enormous and imposing Cathedral of St Vincent de Paul, 20 years older than the theatre and looking rather Byzantine. Just alongside is the Place de l'Indépendance and soon after, the Place de la Victoire and the walls of the medina.

THE BARDO

Le Musée National du Bardo *(4 Pl du Chateau;* ☏ *071 51 36 50; www.informatique-tunisie.com/museebardo* ⊕ *May–Sep 09.00–17.00 daily; Nov–Apr 09.30–16.30 daily, Tue–Sun; TND7)* This museum is not only the best of Tunis's museums, but also one of the finest in the world, with the largest collection of North African Roman mosaics in existence. Spectacular and unique, the density of display of such beautifully preserved relics on how the Roman Empire saw itself gives an almost contemporary sense of provincial life. From courthouses and temples that relay tales of the gods, to dining-room floors that show the bounty of the sea, the variety of what is depicted is magnificent. Housed within an exquisite 19th-century palace of the ruling beys, even the venue is worthy of exhibition. There are also displays on pre-Roman remains, as well as Islamic items.

Organised tours consider themselves generous in allowing a few hours here, but that amount is far too little. Here is a list of must-sees, plus a few extras in case you have a bit more than the minimum, or can return another time.

Ground floor In the Baal Hammon room is a stele from Carthage dating from the 3rd century BC, showing a priest holding a child. In the Bulla Regia Room are statues from the site, including one of Apollo, who, according to mythology, was quite beautiful, as is this supposedly accurate depiction.

First floor Here is where the best mosaics are. Rooms, named after where the pieces were found, are Carthage; Oudna; Dougga from where the famous one of Ulysses and the Sirens came; El Djem including the Triumph of Bacchus, and the Nine Muses; and Althiburos, in the elaborate quarter that was once the bey's music room that shows ancient sailing ships surrounded by fish. Also here are mosaics from other part of Roman Tunisia. In the little section just beyond is a wall-mounted mosaic showing the only known portrait of the poet Virgil. As it's his epic poem, the *Aeneid*, that popularised the apocryphal story of the founding of Carthage, his place is well earned. Also on the floor are items from ancient Greece brought up from the deep from the *Mahdia* shipwreck of the 1st century BC.

Second floor The Acholla Room houses mosaics that come from the site of the same name (now Ras Bou Tria, about 40km north of Sfax) and are some of the oldest ones found in the country. One of the best is the Triumph of Dionysus.

The Islamic museum at Reqqada, near Kairouan, is being expanded, and the relevant items at the Bardo are slowly being diverted there. In the Bardo, there are still a few objects of interest remaining, particularly on the ground floor. Also on that level are prehistoric and Punic pieces that are worth a look. Take a glance at the rooms themselves, as they are pretty fantastic, but anything that isn't a mosaic, or at least something Graeco-Roman, will inevitably take second place.

THE ROMAN SITES

Most of the sites listed below are some distance away from Tunis, but they are included in this section because they can all be visited as day trips from the capital. Although it would be best to view them in a circuit, accommodation can be pretty sparse along the way. If centrally based, it might be easiest to take a few different excursions out to the remains, perhaps even grouping a couple of places together for a full day's adventure. Most sites charge an extra TN1 for the privilege of taking photos.

CARTHAGE Today relegated to being one of Tunis's suburbs, and easily accessible via a short tram journey from the city centre, this peaceful and affluent residential area was once the most important city in North Africa. The area of Punic and Roman Carthage is massive, but today it's difficult to see much of the ancient remains, as most of the city has been continuously inhabited and redeveloped. Not only is over-building an issue, but the already-cut stones of the ruins were recycled as construction material for new dwellings.

History Although the Roman section (*Chapter 1*, page 3) goes into much more detail, here is an extremely brief precis of Carthage's past. The Phoenicians settled and developed their great centre and population estimates of the city at its height were up to 700,000. Centuries later, the Carthaginians battled, and lost to, the Romans in the Punic Wars. Augustus Caesar rebuilt the city in his empire's style, creating an international centre of learning and culture. It's believed Roman Carthage had as many as 400,000 inhabitants indicating one of the largest cities in the empire. The Christians made themselves at home here and until the Vandals, and the corresponding decline of the Roman Empire, Carthage continued to be the province's centrepiece. When the Romans returned, in their reincarnated guise as the Byzantines, the city was a prize to be retaken. It was only when the Arabs arrived, conquering all in their path, that the metropolis lost its prominence. The Fatimids on their way to the east, established their new religious capital in Cairo, Egypt, while the local Arabs preferred the protected position of Tunis. Carthage fell into ruin and the site slipped into obscurity with only the legends sustaining its memory. The area's proximity to growing Tunis as well as its lovely seaside location made it a desirable neighbourhood, particularly for businessmen, diplomats and even the president. In 1857, archaeological digs began in earnest, and the Carthage of myth began to be confirmed in reality. Since then, more and more of this massive city has been uncovered, with excavations discovering new old things almost daily.

Getting there The TGM tram departs from the Tunis Marine terminus, costs about TND.650 per journey, and is the best way to visit the various Carthage stops.

Where to stay and eat See *Eastern suburbs*, pages 283 and 284.

What to see To visit the various sites scattered across the area, a ticket is available on a daily basis that allows entry to all of the ones that charge an entry fee. All the remains that can be visited with this single payment are open daily and have the same hours (⊕ *May–mid-Sep 08.00–19.00; April 08.30–18.00; mid-Sep–Mar 08.30–17.00; TND8*).

Byrsa Hill and the Carthage Museum To get an overview, it's best to begin the day's tour at Byrsa Hill. Take the TGM to Carthage-Dermech and walk up the steep incline to arrive at the legendary original site of the city (see box, *The Legend of Queen Dido* in *Chapter 1*, page 6). The view here is breathtaking, particularly looking over the few remains still left, as well as towards the sea and Cape Bon peninsula. The immediate area is laid out in a grid pattern, showing traces of the Punic settlement and its remarkably modern conveniences, such as drainage and tiled floors. The Romans later built the forum and the capitol in this area. Remains of massive supports dating from this period have been found. Don't miss the small museum. Although it suffers in comparison with the Bardo, it's worth seeing some of the objects found on site while here. The items on display straddle the age of the settlement, from Phoenician and Punic pottery and steles through Roman mosaics and massive sculpture to Islamic ceramics.

The huge Byzantine structure behind is the L'Acropolium, or the Cathedral of St Louis. Built around 1890 to immortalise the memory of the Crusader King

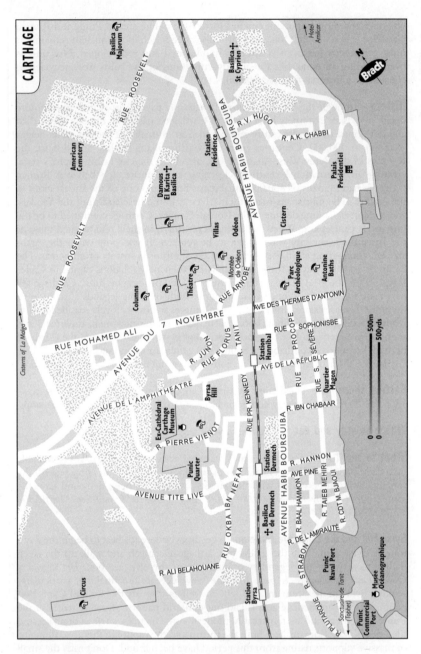

Louis IX (see page 240), this former religious site has been converted into an exhibition centre.

While up on the hill, take a look down and imagine how the city looked when fully populated. Take special note of the port. Although not impressive today, this barely discernible ramshackle circular harbour surrounding a small island was not only the premier one in ancient North Africa, but also the reason why Carthage became so prominent. If you'd like a seaside walk, the little lagoon can be visited, but the only acknowledgement of its former glory is the few souvenir stalls on its banks. There's a small oceanographic museum nearby, open afternoons.

The Antonine Baths The next site that is definitely worth viewing is the baths, located within the gated archaeological park. If going there directly from Tunis, take the TGM to Carthage-Hannibal, and walk down to the Avenue des Termes d'Antonin. The stroll from the entrance towards the sea shows some of the remains of the ancient settlement, enhanced by a rather lovely garden. It's not long before you come to the enormous and very impressive baths. One of the largest bathing complexes in the Eempire, reflecting both the size and importance of Carthage, these give a good idea of how the system was laid out, from the three temperatures of pool – the frigidarium (cold), tepidarium (luke warm) and caldarium (hot) – to the adjoining leisure and sports facilities. Parts of the underground heating passages have been preserved, as well as bits of the mosaic flooring above. Try to visualise here some of those fabulous mosaics of the type seen at the Bardo, such as the Cyclops at the forge of Vulcan from the baths at Dougga. No doubt, the tiled artworks in such an important bathhouse were spectacular.

The vestiges of ancient Carthage are scattered across a wide area. As they are generally not very visible, it requires a bit of imagination to fill in the gaps of the foundations. Tours will drive visitors from site to site, up to a point when bored non-specialists want to move on to something more interesting, and individuals travelling by foot will find the distances too great. Of the things still to see, here are some of the more interesting.

Damous el Karita Basilica The foundations of this once great Christian church lie to the northeast of the so-far-excavated remains of the city. Based on its line, the dimensions were 45m by 65m and had nine aisles.

Cisterns of La Malga These rows of ancient semicircular water storage tanks to the north of the city were the end of the extraordinary aqueduct network that came from Zaghouan (see below).

Tophet The Punic sanctuary to Baal Hammon, the head god figure that translated into the Roman Jupiter, and in North Africa, Saturn, is located to the west, down the hill from the TGM Carthage-Salambo station. This place is a cemetery, with many thousands of urns filled with ash, allegedly of children, having been found here ('tophet' means place of burning, in Hebrew). Steles and carbon dating place the period of the greatest deposits as being between 300 and 100BC.

Theatre Except during the Carthage International Festival in July and August, access to this reconstructed theatre is usually locked. It's possible to catch a glimpse of the site through the gates. Accusations fly that the venue was inaccurately rebuilt, with its tiers being lower than during its original era, but as the place is still being used, it remains useful, if not strictly Roman.

Don't forget to keep your eyes open for remains wherever you go. Columns and bits appear, seemingly out of nowhere, that often indicate villas or housing. Traces of the amphitheatre and circus are on the outskirts to the north and west, but don't merit special visits, unless you're particularly interested.

ZAGHOUAN About 40km due south of Tunis, is the National Park of Zaghouan located at the base of the 1,300m-high Jebel Zaghouan. This distinctive mountain can be seen when looking towards the sea in its direction at the viewpoints around Tunis.

History Lush, green and with plenty of water, it's because of these features that the Emperor Hadrian chose this spot to be the source of the 144km-long aqueduct, built between AD120 and 131, that piped the precious liquid to Carthage. Although the actual distance between the places was not even a third of the total, the clever use of a gradual incline, to make sure the flow continued, necessitated the length.

Getting there Buses from Tunis, Sousse and Hammamet stop here, as well as *louages*.

Where to stay and eat There are very few facilities in the area and it's probably best to stop off at the major tourist resort of Hammamet, less than an hour's drive east, for sleeping, or just return to Tunis. At the site is a delightful little **café**, open daily 07.00–21.00, that serves the usual coffees and mint tea, but also makes smoothies from the fresh fruit sitting on the counter.

What to see It's possible to view some extremely well-preserved parts of the aqueducts *en route*, on the road from El-Fahs to Tunis. At the source, Hadrian built a large nymphaeum, known locally as the Temple des Eaux, or Temple of the Waters. During its time, the fountain was treated as a shrine, with statues adorning the complex. The remains have now been reconstructed into an archaeological park that is free and open to the public.

UTICA The Site Archaeologique d'Utique sits about halfway between Tunis, 35km to the south, and Bizerte, a coastal city on the northern tip of the country. Slightly inland, Utica was once by the sea at the mouth of the Oued (river) Medjerda, but silting up over the years has resulted in this former port town now lying 15km away from the Mediterranean.

History Utica was far more important than the remains visible today indicate. It's one of the oldest cities in North Africa; the Phoenicians came here to settle in 1101BC, almost 300 years before Carthage was founded. Both places grew to large urban areas from 300BC and throughout the following years they were alternately allies or enemies. During the last Punic War, Utica surrendered before Carthage, helping Rome fight and ultimately destroy its ancient rival. Having willingly capitulated, the Romans gave their new friends the title of 'Free City' as well as the status of capital of the new province of Africa. Taking the 'wrong' side in the civil wars of 46BC, Utica sided with Pompey, losing its most famous personage, Cato the Younger (also known as Cato of Utica), when he killed himself, rather than give in to Julius Caesar. This self-destruction did not prevent the conquering general from entering. Remaining an important centre and still acting as capital of the province, Augustus granted residents citizenship of Rome. Although the rebuilding of Carthage in 29BC took away Utica's role, it still became a colonia under Hadrian. The city soon reached its golden age, thriving particularly during the administration of Septimius Severus (AD193–211). Continuing for more than 400 years, picking up some Christians along the way, Utica seems to have survived the Vandals and the Byzantines, falling only to abandonment, when the Arabs came through. With no subsequent development, the site disappeared into the ground, and it was only in modern times that a team of archaeologists began the excavations, led by historical descriptions and the odd bit of artefact.

Getting there There's a public bus that goes from Tunis to Bizerte that will stop on the road close by on request and from there it's a short walk to the site. By car, take the RN8 north to Bizerte, then turn off at the sign to the ruins near the town, either off the MC50 or the MC69.

Where to stay and eat Not much goes on here or in the town regarding places to stay or eat. There are plenty of facilities in Bizerte, if you don't want to return to Tunis. The **Café Bonjour**, on the main road from the capital, does good sandwiches and coffee and is surprisingly good value for such an obvious place to stop.

What to see For a bit of grounding and explanation of the site, it's best to start at the excellent modern **museum**. Just in front of the entrance in the lovely garden are some mosaics found at the site, including the impressive Oceanus, one of the gods of the sea. Inside, the museum is divided into its Punic and Roman rooms. In the former are remnants of Phoenician items, such as masks, steles, lamps, etc, and in the latter are inscriptions and sculpture, as well as terracotta pots and glassware.

The site itself (⊕ *Apr–mid-Sep 08.00–19.00; mid-Sep–Mar 08.30–17.30 Tue–Sun; TND4*) is a short walk to the northeast (the same ticket for the museum is good for entry here). The ruins are quite overgrown. Wandering past the traces of things that obviously existed but haven't been excavated, such as one of the two amphitheatres and the circus, the heart of the visible remains is the 'Insula' or residential area. Here, the **House of the Waterfall** is the most interesting, with a few mosaics still in place. There's also a beautiful patterned floor composed of different marbles: white from Cararra, Italy; yellow and red from Chemtou, Tunisia; green from Greece; and black from Zaghouan, Tunisia. Other villas that can be seen are the **House of the Hunt** and the **House of Historic Capitals**, which contain temples, believed to be to Minerva and Apollo. Throughout this area are 'bathtubs', dating from the Punic era, as it seems the Phoenicians preferred bathing privately, as compared with the event being a social occasion enjoyed by the Romans. The Punic and Roman mosaic styles are quite different, easily discerned when lined up next to each other. Nearby are the **Punic tombs**, and its possible to view the intact skeleton of a young girl from the period, protected under cover. Beyond is the mound of the second **amphitheatre** (the population of up to 60,000 could support two arenas), and a flat area that was the forum. There are steps along the north side that probably led to the capitolium.

THUBURBO MAJUS These extensive and very well-preserved ruins form one of the loveliest Roman sites in Tunisia. Located on a fertile plain just 60km southwest of Tunis, and about 30km from the aqueduct source of Zaghouan, this enclave was not very important yet it seems that very wealthy veterans settled here. The population probably never exceeded 10,000, large by Roman standards, but not so when compared with the big cities of Carthage or Utica. The vestiges show affluence, and the large number of mosaics taken from the site, now in the Bardo Museum in Tunis, prove that conspicuous consumption was important here. Situated in a field filled with rampant wild flowers in the spring, and rolling hills in view, this area must have been desirable to the Roman soldiers who had served their tour of duty, and were now entitled to a comfortable retirement.

History Thuburbo Majus's origins are not well documented. It's only from recent archaeological evidence that traces of a Punic settlement have been found, dating from the several hundred years before the destruction of Carthage. Knowledge of the early days of its Roman transformation is vague, and it's only during the reign of Hadrian that definite references are made. Encouraged by the promotion of the settlement to a city, renamed Municipium Aelium Hadrianum Augustum, the new status spurred on development. Some years later but still in the same century, the emperor Commodus declared the place to be a colonia, now given the even more impressive title of Colonia Aurelia Commoda Thuburbo Majus. This elevated rank caused further expansion and many great constructions, including the capitolium stem from AD168. Following the downs and ups in the well-being of the empire, the city let its buildings slide into ruin, than renewed them with additions. Going through a good phase, the inhabitants renamed their location Res Publica Felix Thuburbo Majus, or a Successful Place under Public Domain. Although a couple of bishops have been mentioned, Thuburbo Majus wasn't a Christian city and the Vandals didn't make much of an impact. Desertions began by AD400, and 300 years later almost everyone had left. No Islamic remains have ever been found.

Getting there As Thuburbo Majus is close to the town of El Fahs, buses that go from Tunis to Kairouan can stop on the main road, leaving a reasonable walk of about 3km to the site. In the summer, this trek can be quite hot. Alternatively, take a taxi to go the remaining distance from El Fahs. If travelling by car from Tunis along route RN3, turn off at the little brown sign. Apparently, the translation of the Arabic is not the name of the site, but rather 'The Land of the Columns', indicating that the site's presence as a ruin has been known for a very long time.

Where to stay and eat There are no facilities at the site. It's best to return northeast to Tunis, head south to Kairouan or go east to Hammamet for hotels and restaurants. Bring a picnic if you want to eat or drink anything, as nothing much is available at the nearby towns.

What to see Dominating the landscape of the site (⊕ *Apr–mid-Sep 08.00–19.00; mid-Sep–Mar 08.30–17.30 Tue–Sun; TND4*) even from a distance is the capitol, the temple dedicated to the triumvirate of Saturn, Juno and Minerva. Some of the more important villas of the town sit at its base to the north. At the temple complex, the steps lead up to a colonnade south of which lies the forum. Columns remain on the main square and around it are some of the most important civil buildings in the town: the curia (the local government offices) and the temples of Peace and Mercury. Down the path and the small hill is the market and, beyond, the Baths of the Labyrinth (named after the mosaic of Theseus and the Minotaur found there, now in the Bardo Museum in Tunis). To the west, situated within a residential section, is the House of Neptune, so called due to the mosaic of its fountain, now also in the Bardo. Just to the south and part of the elaborate summer

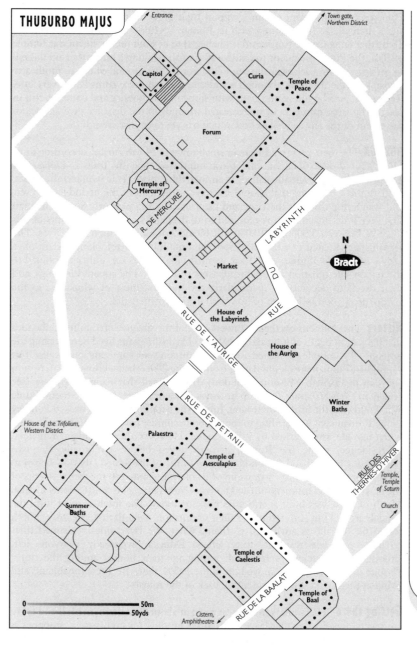

THUBURBO MAJUS

Entrance

Town gate,
Northern District

Capitol

Curia

Temple of
Peace

Forum

Temple of
Mercury

R. DE MERCURE

LABYRINTH

N

Bradt

DU

Market

RUE

House of
the Labyrinth

RUE DE L'AURIGE

House of
the Auriga

RUE DES PETRNII

Winter
Baths

House of the Trifolium,
Western District

Palaestra

Temple of
Aesculapius

RUE DES
THERMES-D'HIVER

Temple,
Temple
of Saturn

Church

Summer
Baths

Temple of
Caelestis

Temple of
Baal

RUE DE LA BAALAT

0 _____ 50m
0 _____ 50yds

Cistern,
Amphitheatre

baths complex, is the second most dramatic ruin of the site, the Palaestra of the Petronii, the gymnasium or exercise yard, With many of its columns still supporting a framework. The summer baths themselves still have some of their mosaics in place.

Continuing southeast, nearby, is a row of columns, believed to be the remains of a church. As if to reaffirm the religious nature of the location, the Temple of

Caelestis (the equivalent of Juno, wife of Jupiter), with steps rising to a platform and a dramatic arch remaining with its Roman keystone, is situated right behind. To further enhance the pantheism it's believed to be built on the site of the Temple of Baal, the Punic precursor to Saturn. It's worth strolling a bit further up the hill to get a viewpoint back over the site to the north. The mound of the amphitheatre is visible in the distance, although wandering around these ruins is not very safe. Returning, pass by the winter bath with some of the mosaics and columns still in place. The large numbers of unexcavated mounds in the distance give an idea of the extent of the site as well as how much has yet to be discovered.

DOUGGA The 'best preserved Roman small town in North Africa', according to its UNESCO designation, and the most impressive one in Tunisia, Dougga or Thugga as it was originally called, is an incredible place. It is wonderfully intact, with almost everything that should exist in a settlement of the period easy to see, and wandering through the large and extensive site is a pleasure. So much is left that very little imagination is required to understand how the inhabitants of this town of between 5,000 and 10,000 inhabitants got on with their daily lives. The remains are situated in a beautiful spot, up on a hilltop overlooking distant olive groves and fields of grain. The local wealthy villa owners certainly contributed to the region's designation as 'the breadbasket of Rome'. The superb buildings, and their excellent decorations (particularly the mosaics, most of which are in the Bardo) are a good indication of how well the landowners did.

History The dolmens on the northwest edge of the site give credibility to the idea that habitation began as long ago as 2000BC. The Numidians lived here, leaving the remains of a temple dedicated to Baal Hammon and some ancient walls. The Numidian/Punic mausoleum dating from before 200BC had a bilingual inscription (now in the British Museum, London). It's believed that King Massinissa (see *History* in *Chapter 1* page 7) set up his royal residence here after the Second Punic War. Following the lead of their king, Juba I, the people of Dougga backed Pompey in the Roman civil war leading to the region becoming part of the Roman Empire, when his side was defeated by Julius Caesar. However, the Numidians remained in residence, while the Roman settlers stayed below. Eventually, the two populations merged and the building programme of the joined city now began in earnest. In around 200AD, citizenship of Rome was granted to the free residents of the newly declared municipium and 60 years later Thugga became Colonia Licinia. Much of what was built at the time remains today. The town thrived until the Vandals arrived but suffered under their occupation, even though the only church found on the site is attributed to them. When the Byzantines reclaimed their territory, very few residents were left in Dougga. Eventually, everyone left, although a few stragglers returned, setting up their homes among the ruins. Despite most having been moved on in the 1950s, there are a few inhabitants still living in their makeshift homes at the back of the ruins.

Getting there Tebersouk is the closest town at about 8km down the hill and there are several buses a day that leave from Tunis heading for points west, stopping at the town *en route*. The trip from the capital takes about one hour 45 minutes. *Louages* also get here. Once in Tebersouk, a taxi or another *louage* should be able to drive you to the Roman site as it's a popular destination. If going by private transport, take the RN5 to the town, then follow the signs to the site.

Where to stay and eat The two-star Hotel Thugga (*RN5, Rte d'El Kef, 9040 Tébersouk;* \ *078 46 66 470*) offers the only reasonable accommodation nearby, and

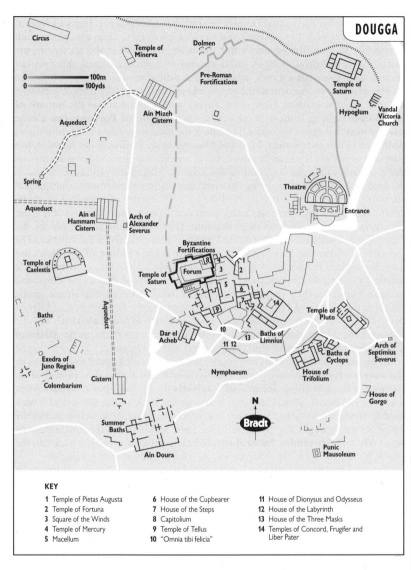

DOUGGA

Circus

Temple of Minerva

Dolmen

Pre-Roman Fortifications

Temple of Saturn

Hypoglum

Vandal Victoria Church

Ain Mizeh Cistern

Aqueduct

Spring

Aqueduct

Ain el Hammam Cistern

Arch of Alexander Severus

Theatre

Entrance

Byzantine Fortifications

Temple of Caelestis

Temple of Saturn

Forum

8
3
1
2
5
6
9
7
14

Baths

Aqueduct

Temple of Pluto

Baths of Limnius

Arch of Septimius Severus

Exedra of Juno Regina

Dar el Acheb

10
11 12
13

Baths of Cyclops

Colombarium

Cistern

Nymphaeum

House of Trifolium

House of Gorgo

N

Bradt

Summer Baths

Ain Doura

Punic Mausoleum

KEY

1 Temple of Pietas Augusta
2 Temple of Fortuna
3 Square of the Winds
4 Temple of Mercury
5 Macellum

6 House of the Cupbearer
7 House of the Steps
8 Capitolium
9 Temple of Tellus
10 "Omnia tibi felicia"

11 House of Dionysus and Odysseus
12 House of the Labyrinth
13 House of the Three Masks
14 Temples of Concord, Frugifer and Liber Pater

is a good base for touring some of the other Roman sites in the area. As the region is famous for its wild boars, the accommodation also caters for hunters, and the big animal head in the dining room doesn't let you forget it. The restaurant is OK and for what it's worth, the best in town. There is also a small café on the site, but it was closed at the time of research.

What to see There are two entrances to the site (⊕ *Apr–mid-Sep 08.30–19.00 daily; mid-Sep–Mar 08.30–17.30; TND4*), via the southwest from Le Kef and the southeast from Tebersouk, but most visitors arrive from the latter, and the highlights listed below use this one as a starting point. Although the path goes to the south and west, the first stop should be at the obvious one, the theatre, just to the right. This enormous entertainment venue in excellent condition is still used as the location for the annual Dougga Festival that takes place in July and August. With its three tiers of 19 rows each, and an elevation of up to 15m, the construction is typically Roman, carved into a hill and using the view of the scenery in the distance as a backdrop. Built by the donations of a wealthy citizen, this open-air performance space has a terrific atmosphere as well as acoustics.

The dramatic monument to the west beckons, and, especially if you are pressed for time, head towards it. Here is the forum, with a fountain and the **Square of the Winds** right in front of it, as well as the **Temple of Fortuna**, but it's the **capitolium** that draws attention. This site is the most impressive of all the temples dedicated to the gods Saturn, Juno and Minerva in all Tunisia, if not North Africa (the one in Sbeitla is just as beautiful, but it actually has three separate shrines on the spot, rather than the one combined as is here). Magnificent and large, although wedged into a confined space by the enclosing walls, its enormous columns still support the framework that once held the roof. Two series of steps lead up to the centre. The nooks and crannies today seem a bit labyrinthine, but probably these alleyways led to a walled-off inner sanctum. Directly behind the capitol are the heavy-handed remains of a Byzantine fortress constructed from the cut blocks of the earlier Roman site. Heading south, past a market, the **House of the Steps** and a small temple, a few wealthy villas appear. No doubt important as proven by their location close to the forum, they have been immortalised due to the decorative mosaics found on their premises, now in the Bardo. Among the artistic jewels found in the **House of Dionysus and Odysseus** was the famous view of Ulysses being taunted by the Sirens. Also here are the **House of the Labyrinth** and the House of the Three Masks. Just to the south are the Lician Baths, or the **Baths of Caracalla**, a large complex with columns and mosaics in place.

To the west are the remains of a residential district with a paved road leading to the summer baths. Heading north, into the woods and fields, then further off to the west is the intriguing **Temple of Caelestis** dating from before AD250. Steps lead to a colonnade which arcs into a semicircle. Back to the grass, and a walk further north, shows where the water was kept in the cisterns as well as part of the aqueduct that brought it to the spot. To the right, and back towards the centre, the squat **Arch of Alexander Severus** stands intact, acting as a gateway back into the city. It frames the back of the forum and its solid Byzantine fortress nicely.

The site is extensive with much still left to be excavated. There are things to be discovered further north, such as the site of the circus, the remains of the **Temple of Minerva**, the pre-Roman walls and their contemporary dolmens, but the walk is a bit of a ramble, and there is more to see in the area already excavated. Return through Alexander Severus's gate and behind the forum, taking a good look at how the Byzantines reused old material. Climb up the back of the theatre to get a glance at the view, and continue in the same direction, eventually reaching the **Temple of Saturn**. Although not much of the construction remains, the site is superb, and it's easy to imagine the shrine when it was dominating the hilltop. Dropping back to the south, the remains of the **Vandal Victoria Christian Church** are visible, also a product of recycling. Following the path, it eventually leads back to the theatre.

It might be time for a break, and the little café with its seating area under the trees, granting a good view of the fields below, serves basics. At the time of research, it was closed, but that could be due to season or renovation. There are more sights to see to the south. Take the trail past the **Baths of the Cyclops**, with its named mosaics in the Bardo, and its tri-temperature bathing system. Also on show are the dozen communal latrines, and the drains running through them, acting as a kind of flush toilet system. It adjoins the trifolium house, so called due to the shape of one of its rooms. The reason for trekking such a distance downhill, however, is the **Numidan/Punic Mausoleum**, rising up 21m in three storeys. One of only two

The Latin term for a building technique typical for North Africa, literally, 'African work', the expression *opus africanum* referred to the way certain walls were built. Distinctive for the way that rubble was piled into even sections divided by equally wide manufactured squared-off slabs, or orthostats, many of the Roman sites in the province used this system. The method long pre-dated the empire and it tends to be found in locations that had once been Punic. One of the strengths of the Romans was their ability to adapt and embrace specialities of wherever they were and they incorporated *opus africanum* into their own North African colonial constructions. Dougga has some particularly good examples. The style remained popular and was used by the Byzantines and the Arabs. Some of the walls at the Great Mosques in both Tunis and Kairouan, as well as the *ribats* of Monastir of Sousse provide instances of where the method seemed to be appropriate and durable.

such tombs found in the entire province of North Africa (the other is in Sabratha in Libya, see page 352), this one is for Ateban, a royal who lived about the same time as Massinissa. The carved inscription on it is in Numidian and Punic and is a key to the Tifnagh language, a derivation of which is still spoken in the Berber areas of the north. The carving's acquisition and subsequent placement in the British Museum led to the mausoleum's destruction, but the monument was rebuilt by the French in 1910. Go by the same path back to the entrance to complete the tour.

BULLA REGIA One of the most unusual Roman sites in all of North Africa lies in the midst of an extremely fertile region where, nevertheless, the heat bakes and the wind blows. At a distance of about 160km from Tunis, 30 from the northern coastal resort of Tabarka, and seven from the nearest town of Jendouba, the remains of this ancient city continue to intrigue, especially with each new discovery found in the ongoing excavations. What makes this site different, and possibly unique, are the underground houses. Although mostly resembling catacombs, Bulla Regia's dwellings below the surface were meant for the living. To prove it, some delightful mosaics remain *in situ*. Built this way to protect from the heat and the wind, rather than for defence, they're curious, as even though similar climatic conditions exist in other parts of the Roman province, no other contemporary examples have been found.

History Interestingly enough, it's underground where the origins of the site are found, via the dolmens that prove the area was inhabited as long ago as 1000BC. Later activity dates from the artefacts found on the site, notably Greek pottery from 300BC, implying that trade with the eastern Mediterranean was common. Bulla Regia sits close to the Medjerda River, the only one that was ever navigable in the country. Today, it's a bit of a trickle, but in ancient days it was a viable waterway. The city was positioned on the best route from Tunis to Hippo in Algeria in a gap in the mountains. Perhaps that's why goods from further afield have been found on this crossroads of various trade routes. By 200BC, it's clear the area came under Carthaginian influence. Urns have been found that indicate Punic burial rituals, as well as remains from a temple to Tanit (the equivalent deity to Juno). Swallowed up in Scipio's Punic War defeat in 203BC, the city became part of the client kingdom of Numidia, headed by Massinissa. As Bulla Regia had not sided with the defeated faction during the civil wars of 49–46BC, Julius Caesar declared it a 'Free City' in appreciation. Romanisation continued and a century later Hadrian granted the city colonial status, renaming it Colonia Aelia Hadriana August Bulla Regia.

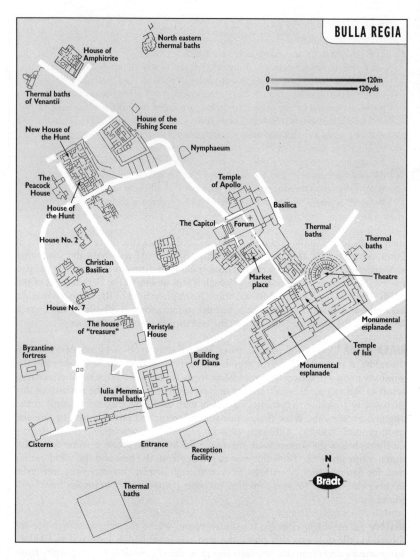

North eastern thermal baths

House of Amphitrite

Thermal baths of Venantii

House of the Fishing Scene

New House of the Hunt

Nymphaeum

The Peacock House

Temple of Apollo

Basilica

House of the Hunt

The Capitol

Forum

Thermal baths

House No. 2

Market place

Thermal baths

Christian Basilica

Theatre

House No. 7

The house of "treasure"

Peristyle House

Monumental esplanade

Byzantine fortress

Building of Diana

Temple of Isis

Monumental esplanade

Iulia Memmia termal baths

Cisterns

Entrance

Reception facility

N

Bradt

Thermal baths

0 ━━━━━ 120m
0 ━━━━━ 120yds

Bulla Regia was clearly an important centre according to the magnificence of the public buildings and elaborateness of the private ones, as seen in the remains. Apparently the city also had a reputation for moral laxity. St Augustine, who had spent some time here on his journeys back and forth between Hippo and Carthage, criticised the theatre as being a focal point for encouraging bad behaviour. An excellently preserved bathtub found in the House of Amphitrite has a beautiful mosaic inscription 'Venanti Orvam Baiae' referring to Baiae, a city in Italy, known for the dubious pleasure-seeking activities that occurred there. Relatively little is known of the Vandal period although their king, Gelimer, chose this city as his headquarters, and it was in AD533 that he heard about the Byzantines taking back Carthage. When he sped off to meet them to refuse surrender terms, it was already too late. Eventually, the Byzantines made their way here, leaving two basilicas as well as various fortifications, including the theatre.

It was never actually abandoned, but Bulla Regia's inhabitants began to leave when the Arabs arrived, although the trickle continued until sometime around 1100, when no-one was left. Excavation of the ruins began around 1850.

Getting there There is a good public transport service to Jendouba from Tunis and from there, frequent buses to the site. There are also taxis available from the local town and if travelling this way it might be best to tell the driver when to return to collect you. By car, take the RN5 from Tunis to Beja, switch to the RN11 for a short distance till you reach the RN6, which takes you to Jendouba. Go north on the RN17 for about 4km and then east off the RN59 for about another 3km.

 Where to stay and to eat The **Hotel Thugga** in Terbersouk, close to Dougga (see page 298), is a good base for touring the sites around here, but if you want to stay even nearer, there are a couple of basic places in Jendouba. The **Hotel Atlas** (*Rue 1 Juin 1955;* ✆ *078 60 32 17;* $) and the **Hotel Simmithu** (*Bd 9 Avril 1938;* ✆ *078 60 40 43;* $) may not represent comfort or value for money, but they are convenient. The usual cafés and stands are around in the town, as well as a Monoprix supermarket. At Bulla Regia, the little visitor centre, with its coffee bar that also sells ice cream, has possibly the nicest public toilets in all of Tunisia.

What to see The first attraction to view, located as soon as you enter the site (⊕ *Apr–mid-Sep 08.00–19.00 daily; mid-Sep–Mar 08.30-17.30; TND4*), is the **Baths of Julia Memmia**. Named after the mother of Alexander and niece of Julia Domna, Septimius Severus's second wife, this large complex has all the elements of a true Roman bathhouse, such as the three different-temperature pools, changing rooms, etc. Preservation has been significantly aided by Byzantine reinforcement, although the mosaics that still lie in place give an idea of what the place looked like in its earlier days. Following the circuit counter-clockwise, the next site is the first of the private villas, the **House of the Treasure**. Named after the Byzantine silver discovered inside (not on view), there are mosaics both on ground level and below. It's possible to go down the steps and taken a closer look.

Next are the remains of the two Christian basilicas left by the Byzantines, with some columns, a mosaic of a cup and a baptismal font. Things keep on getting better and the next villa, the **House of the Hunt**, is the first house with a basement. Above, the courtyard with its column standing is still clearly visible and below is an entire underground residence, with intact decorative mosaics. The open-air central atrium is the main source of natural light, although there are windows high up in the rooms, at ground level outside. To the north is the **New House of the Hunt**. Named after its excellent mosaic of a hunting scene, most of its other artworks are on ground level. At the edge of the current excavations is probably the highlight of the entire site, the **House of Amphitrite**. This villa is intact, with its underground area roofed. Depicting Amphitrite (a former Nereid, then sea goddess and wife of the sea god Neptune), the mosaic flooring of this villa is a delight. The rooms, with their little windows and columned dividers seem habitable, even today. To the east, the **House of the Fishing Scene** is next, another villa with a mosaic and well-preserved lower floor, divided into separate rooms.

Heading south through the seemingly empty fields, passing the nymphaeum, the vast space of the forum is next. There's not much to see, other than some paving and a few steps to show the perimeter and the location of the capitol. A few remains of the location of the Temple of Apollo can be seen, although the statue of the god that was found here now stands in the Bardo. Past the marketplace is the theatre, a semicircular open-air entertainment venue that bore the brunt of St Augustine's rant against easy virtue. Today, the site, hewn into an existing hill, has its lower tier of seats preserved. Just in front of the large stage is a mosaic of a not very scary bear. The acoustics are still good. To complete the circle, pass by the the Temple of Isis to the west of the theatre, revisit the Julia Memmia Baths and then leave by the same place as you entered. The even older dolmens are located some distance south of the main road.

CHEMTOU Approaching the Algerian border, this very different site known in its ancient day as Simmithus, is often missed off the tourist itinerary, but it really shouldn't be. Here was the most prolific and probably biggest quarry in all of North Africa. The yellow-pink marble mined here was prized throughout the empire and regularly shipped to Rome. The place existed in Numidian times and the remnants of an important Roman town have been found. Despite the site's importance, today it's a bit out of the way and surprising to find such an excellent museum here, generously funded primarily by the Germans who have done much archaeological exploration here.

History Chemtou can be dated back at least as far as the Numidians from 200BC. They used the marble for their own constructions and left their mark in the monuments that remain on the site. When King Juba I of Numidia fell on his sword after supporting Pompey, the loser in the Roman civil wars, the valuable marble quarries came under the jurisdiction of Rome in 46BC. It was stone from this quarry that was used in the memorial column erected in Rome after Julius Caesar's assassination. The combination of the mining of this valuable material, together with the settlement's position on the important cross-province route from Carthage to Hippo Regius, made the emperor Augustus declare the city a colonia, with the name Colonia Julia August Numidica Simmithensium. The bridge crossing the Medjerda River, an essential part of the transport link, was repaired three times: first under Tiberius, then under Trajan and once again, around AD300, so that one could go from Simmithus to the headquarters of the 3rd Augustan Legion, first in Ammaedara, then Lambaesis.

Until the reign of Hadrian, going via the Medjerda River was the easiest, cheapest and quickest way to transport the marble from Chemtou. Because of the problems with the silting up of the harbour at Utica, in AD126 the transport of marble was changed to taking it by road over the Khroumirie Mountains, then shipping it out from the harbour at Thrabraca (Tabarka). Despite the distance to Italy, the stone was popular enough that it was exported and illustriously used, not only for Caesar's column, but also for Augustus's and Trajan's forums, as well as Hadrian's villa at Tivoli. Worked through the Byzantine area, the mines and town were left after the Arab conquest. Chemtou's proximity to the border was exploited when the Algerian Liberation Army had a base here during the country's war of independence. Today, the marble is still being quarried, but at another site.

Getting here To get to Chemtou, find your way to Jendouba, then take a taxi. By car, go north on the RN17 and then turn west when you reach the RN59 (Bulla Regia is 3km to the east on the same road), driving 11km on a paved road, then another 5km on a decent gravel track. The site is signposted.

Where to stay and eat The closest place to sleep is at Jendouba (see Bulla Regia, above). A **café** on the site next to the museum offers coffee and ice cream but you need to go to Jendouba to get a meal.

What to see Before the entrance to the Roman town (⊕ *May–mid-Sep 08.00–19.00 daily; mid-Sep–Apr 08.30–17.30; TND4*), the remains of the ancient quarry provide some eerie and colourful rock formations. At the top are the remains of the sanctuary, the Numidian temple dedicated to Baal Hammon, artefacts from which are displayed in the local museum. The Romans commandeered it for their own use as a temple of Saturn. The Christians then built a church there. The rest of the site is large, although much of it is undeveloped. It might be best to start at the museum, which has a great deal of information regarding the history of both the Roman and pre-Roman eras, together with artefacts and several information panels (in Arabic, French and German). As much of the information is in diagrams and maps, it's discernible in any language. There are both ancient mosaics, found *in situ*, as well as modern ones, which show the variety of marbles of the area. Particularly interesting is a copy of a plate commemorating the god Baal-Saturn. It's been rendered in beautiful yellow stone with streaks of pink running through it, and gives a good indication of why the local marble was so valued.

There is much to see emerging out of the soil, but the following gives some of the highlights. Once outside, it's possible to see the much repaired Roman bridge over the Medjerda River in the distance, but it's fallen into ruin yet again, perhaps waiting for the next generation of emperors. Almost immediately in front of the museum is the forum, with its vast partially paved open space flanked by the stumps of a few columns. Just beyond is an enormous and solid ruin, looking like a basilica, but labelled as the nymphaeum. Opposite, is a strange circular construction lying slightly below ground level and just to the side of the forum. This is a Numidian funerary monument, recently restored, that has its origins in pre-Roman days. Down the hill and up again, the road leads to the remains of the amphitheatre. Only half emerging from the soil, the underground tunnels have been dug out and its possible to see that this arena was very large. With enough here to recognise, but not so much as to be over-reconstructed, it's a fun place to let your imagination take over. Return to the exit the same way you came. Still under excavation, there is much yet to be uncovered but the layout of the city is pretty well known and well visualised in the depiction in the museum.

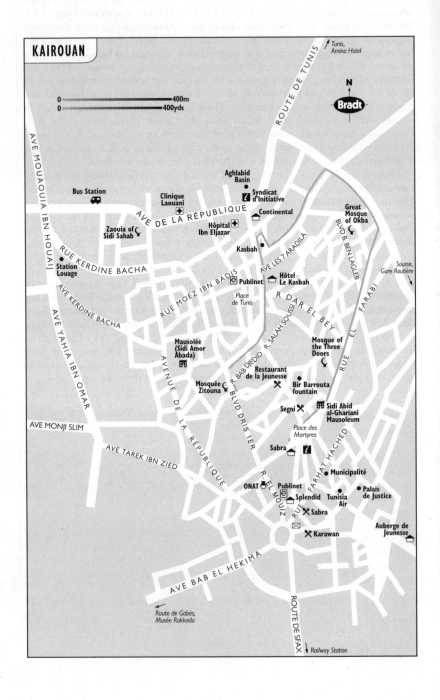

KAIROUAN

↗ Tunis, Amina Hotel

ROUTE DE TUNIS

N

Bradt

0 ————— 400m
0 ————— 400yds

AVE MOUAOUIA IBN HOUAI

Bus Station

Clinique
Laouani

Aghlabid
Basin

Syndicat
d'Initiative

Continental

Great
Mosque
of Okba

AVE DE LA RÉPUBLIQUE

Zaouia of
Sidi Sahab

Hôpital
Ibn Eljazar

RUE KERDINE BACHA

Station
Louage

AVE KERDINE BACHA

Kasbah

AVE LES 7 ARADILA

BLVD B. BEN LAGLEB

RUE MOEZ IBN BADIS

Publinet

Hôtel
Le Kasbah

Place
de Tunis

R DAR EL BEY

RUE EL FARABI

Sousse,
Gare Routière

AVE YAHIA IBN OMAR

AVE MONJI SLIM

Mausolée
(Sidi Amor
Abada)

AVENUE DE LA RÉPUBLIQUE

R. SALAH SOUSSI

Mosque of
the Three
Doors

R. BAB DJEDID

Mosquée
Zitouna

Restaurant
de la Jeunesse

Bir Barrouta
fountain

BLVD DRIS 1ER

AVE TAREK IBN ZIED

Segni

Sidi Abid
al-Ghariani
Mausoleum

Place des
Martyres

FARHAT HACHED

Sabra

ONAT

RUE EL MOUZ

Publinet

Splendid

Municipalité

Tunisia
Air

Palais
de Justice

Sabra

RUE FARHAT HACHED

Auberge de
Jeunesse

Karawan

AVE BAB EL HEKIMA

Route de Gabès,
Musée Rakkada

ROUTE DE SFAX

↗ Railway Station

23

Kairouan

Telephone code 077

This beautiful and historic place lies about an hour's drive inland from Sousse. Designated the fourth holiest in Islam, after Mecca, Medina and Jerusalem, the oldest Muslim city in North Africa has over 220 religious monuments. Established during the Arab invasion, the mosque dates back to AD670 when Okba set up the first mosque. The city still has a pilgrimage feel and it is said, like Moulay Ismail in Morocco, that seven visits here equal one to Mecca. Not only are its ancient religious roots still a living part of its daily life, with the many mosques, *zaouias* and medersas scattered throughout the medina, but also the commercial ones. The bazaar-like feel in the souks is vibrant, particularly with the carpets, the speciality for which Kairouan is famous, decorating shop walls and laid out on the public pavements. The splash of the reds, yellows and other colours of the woven work stand out wonderfully against the white buildings with their blue and green trim. Although the old inner city is a bit maze-like, the streets are clean and fairly wide, with broad courtyards and architectural gems appearing almost out of nowhere. These attributes must have been some of the reasons why Stephen Spielberg used this city to fill in for Cairo, when he filmed *Raiders of the Lost Ark*.

HISTORY

Unlike many of the settlements in North Africa, Kairouan has a precise beginning. Founded by the Arab general Okba ibn Nafi after his successful conquest of the region, the location was chosen to be both a religious and secular capital. Legend has it that when he passed here, a spring appeared miraculously in the middle of the desert and that a golden cup, lost years before in Mecca, floated up out of it. The position was practical, too, in that it was one day's walk from the mountains to the west, and one day's walk to the sea. Okba chose to build his magnificent mosque here as, lying in a flat plain, the enclave was easy to protect and the minaret acted not only as a watchtower, but also an indicator of the mosque's location, visible from a distance. Despite its potential civilian value, Kairouan was initially set up as a military outpost, and its name comes from the Arabic *kairuwan*, camp or place of arms.

Only a few years after the sacred construction, Berbers invaded, destroyed the building and temporarily claimed their territory back from the Arabs. The Byzantines too had a last-gasp attempt at hanging on but, by AD800, the Arabs took hold, not to let go again. When the Aghlabhid dynasty took power, they invested their renewed Arab city with magnificent construction and considerable importance. They rebuilt the mosque, using it to house a university. By the following century, Kairouan had become a major centre of Islamic culture, drawing in the best brains from the Arab world for scientific as well as religious learning. Some of the architecture that attracts visitors today dates from this period. Fame was fleeting, even among the intellectuals, and when the next dynasty, the Fatimids, came through, they deserted Kairouan, preferring the coastal town of Mahdia, lying almost due east. They continued in that direction, eventually founding the city of Cairo. The Zirid dynasty caretakers were left to administer Kairouan. However, when the tenants turned against their landlords, rejecting Egyptian Shi'ite Islam in favour of Sunni practice, the Fatimids sent pillaging hordes to teach them a lesson and, in 1057, Kairouan was razed almost to the ground.

As with other parts of the Maghreb, many areas fell into ruin and disrepair over a long period but, by 1200, things began to improve. By 1800, the Husainid dynasty helped raise Kairouan back into prominence. When the French assumed the protectorate, non-Muslims were finally allowed into the city. Kairouan has been declared the Capital of Islamic Culture for the year 2009.

GETTING THERE AND AROUND

BY BUS SNTRI (*www.sntri.con.tn*) has several buses a day that do the two hour 30 minute journey from Tunis, arriving at the gare routiére (*Av Farhat Hached;* ☎ 077 30 00 11). Other bus companies provide transport from Sousse, which might be more convenient if you are landing at Monastir Airport (50km east). They can also be booked at the terminal, although not at the same office.

BY TAXI (*LOUAGE*) Collective taxis (*Sidi Saheb;* ☎ 077 30 29 99) cover the same routes as the buses, at more convenient times, and include transport to the resort of Hammamet. There are also regular runs to the towns and ruins at Makhtar and Sbeitla.

BY CAR The RN3 goes directly from Tunis to Kairouan, but it's quicker to take the A1 motorway to Sousse, and then change to the RN12. The route from Monastir Airport is the same from Sousse.

Car hire It might be more sensible to pick up a car at a bigger city, as it requires road transport of some sort to get here. There are no branches of the larger car hire firms in Kairouan, although there are at Monastir (see *Chapter 21*, page 259), Sousse (*Chapter 21*, page 265) and Tunis (*Chapter 22*, page 281). Locally, ask at the hotel or tourist office for a reliable agency.

TOURIST INFORMATION

☑ **Regional Tourism Bureau** Pl des Martyrs; ☎ 077 23 18 97

☑ **Syndicat d'Initative** Aghlabid Basins, Av Ibn el Jazzar & Ibn el Aghlab

TOUR OPERATORS

Most companies operate from nearby Tunis or Sousse, but a couple are based in Kairouan.

Hend Voyage 17 Av Dr Hamda Aouani; ☎ 077 22 84 49

Options Voyage Place de la Victoire; ☎ 077 22 61 02

 WHERE TO STAY

TOP END

🏠 **Hotel le Kasbah** (97 rooms) Av Ibn el Jazzar; ☎ 077 23 73 01; www.goldenyasmin.com/la-kasbah/en/. This beautiful 5-star hotel sits within the northern medina wall & offers every comfort, but caters predominantly to upmarket tour groups. $$$$

MID-RANGE

⌂ **Amina** (103 rooms) Rte de Tunis GP2; ☎ 077 22 65 55. A decent place to stay where the inconvenience of the location, outside of town on the way to Sousse, is made up for by nice rooms & swimming pool. $$

⌂ **Continental** (150 rooms) Av Ibn el Aghlab; ☎ 077 23 11 35. Another 3-star hotel that might lack a bit of charm, but does have reasonable-sized rooms. It sits just across from the Aghlabid Basin to the north of the medina. $$

⌂ **Splendid** (80 beds) Rue 9 Avril; ☎ 077 23 00 41. Comfortable & convenient, & only a 5-min walk to the medina, this well-situated hotel merits its 3-star rating – by Tunisian standards. $$

BUDGET

⌂ **Sabra** Pl des Martyrs; ☎ 077 23 02 63. Cheapness is the motivation for staying at this slightly better alternative, a youth hostel, although the rooftop offers great views & a place to sleep in the summer. $

✖ WHERE TO EAT

Nowhere, other than the Hotel Kasbah, offers great cuisine, but the usual range of cheap and cheerful glorified cafés is around, generally just south of the medina towards the Ville Nouvelle. Couscous is available just about everywhere. Below are listed a few places that are perhaps slightly better than the rest. Also worth mentioning is *makhroud*, a sticky, solid pastry cut into squares of various shapes, usually filled with dates. It's a local speciality that's best when you're desperately seeking something sweet and filling to eat, or looking for souvenirs.

✖ **Segni** Av 7 Novembre. The best-known & most attractive place to buy *makhroud*, pre-packed in handy souvenir sizes & available by the kilogramme. $-$$$

✖ **Restaurant de la Jeunesse** Av 7 Novembre. Good-value couscous in the centre of the old city – great if you need a break from sightseeing or shopping but don't want to leave the medina. $$

✖ **Restaurant Karawan** Rue Soukina ibn el Hussein. A fine little family-run place close to the Hotel Splendid, here's a good place to try some Tunisian specialities, including *brik*, the delicious fried savoury pastry. $$

✖ **Restaurant Sabra** Av de la Republique; ☎ 077 23 50 95. Recommended in the good-value category, the food here is cheaper if ordered à la carte. $$

ENTERTAINMENT AND NIGHTLIFE

As Kairouan is the fourth most holy city in Islam, there's not much of a nightlife scene. The café life partly makes up for it, and it's fun to linger over a coffee, mint tea or even a *sheesha* (hookah) while people-watching. If really in need of some alcohol, the **Hotel le Kasbah** is the best place to go, although the prices are also five-star.

SHOPPING

Kairouan is the carpet centre of Tunisia, and if you're looking for a rug or floor covering, this is definitely the place to go. Literally strewn about the streets of the medina are all sorts of knotted or woven tapestries, although you can buy one from inside the shop rather than a sample that's been trodden on. The choice is enormous and here is probably the best place in the country to try out your bargaining skills. If the prospect of negotiating for your carpet is just too overwhelming, the **Centre des Traditions et des Métiers d'Art de Kairouan**, in the medina, close to the Bir Barouta fountain, is run under the auspices of the tourist board and is fixed price. Showing off the methods of handicraft production, carpet making is featured, buying is encouraged. There's a carpet auction on

Saturday mornings in the Souk el Blaghija, but it's recommended only for watching, as the action can be pretty hectic. Most other traditional crafts are also on sale here, including ceramics, copper, leatherware, clothing and the usual range of items typically made by hand. There is a weekly market on Mondays.

OTHER PRACTICALITIES

EMERGENCY TELEPHONE NUMBERS
Police ⤏ 077 23 05 77

HOSPITAL
✚ Hopital Ibn Jazzar Close to the Aghlabid Basin & Hotel Kasbah; ⤏ 077 230 036

INTERNET CAFÉS Publinet is close to the Agil Gaz petrol station, near Rue Zouagha (⤏ *077 23 10 41*) and there's also one at Rue du Juge abou Zomaa El Balaoui (⤏ *077 23 10 41*). There are others scattered throughout the town that come and go.

POST The main post office (grand poste) is located on Place du 7 Novembre and Farhat Hached.

BANKS Most of the local banks are represented close to the Place des Martyrs, and there are ATMs on Avenue Hamda Laaouani.

WHAT TO SEE

The UNESCO World Heritage Site, the Medina of Kairouan, is a pleasure to walk through, with its mix of historic and traditional attractions. The white of the buildings is contrasted with splashes of bright colour on the doors and windows, generally blue or green, and the detailing, particularly on the frames and balconies, is delightful. Narrow streets open out into broader courtyards and then contract again. Although it seems easy to get lost here, the medina is fairly small and well signposted. Eventually, you'll get to where you want to go. There are sights, including the Islamic monuments, that must not be missed. The tourist board is aware that most visitors will want to see most, if not all, of the attractions listed below, and has come up with a multi-entry ticket good for one day, costing TN7. It can be obtained at the visitor centre at the Aghlabid Basin, the Great Mosque and the Mausoleum of Sidi Sahab.

GREAT MOSQUE OF OKBA (*in the northeast of the medina;* ⊕ *Apr–mid-Sept 07.30–14.00 daily; mid-Sep–Mar 08.00–14.00; TND7*) This mosque is the most important attraction in Kairouan – and Islamic Tunisia. Dating predominantly from around

AD800, with later additions, it lies on the site of the first one built by the Arabian general and conqueror Okba. The central courtyard is enormous, but the decoration everywhere is surprisingly simple. The dramatic series of arches is unadorned and the basic tiles that make up the construction are visible. Only the occasional Corinthian pillar provides a splash of flourish. Non-Muslims are not allowed into the prayer area, but are permitted to look inside from behind the barricades.

SIDI ABID AL-GHARIANI MAUSOLEUM (*Rue Sidi el Ghariani, Medina;* ⊕ *08.30–13.00 & 15.00–18.00 daily*) The room into which the tomb of the eponymous holy man was placed in 1386 is enhanced with elaborate Islamic decorations. The beautiful arched open-air courtyard remains the most memorable aspect of this mausoleum.

BIR BARROUTA (*close to Av Ali Belhouane, Medina* ⊕ *daily*). The spring that legendarily caused Okba to choose the site of Kairouan as his capital rises here in a tiny room, constructed in 1676. What makes the site unmissable is the ornately adorned camel that turns the wheel that draws the water, in this very cramped space. For all its tacky quality, there's something reverential in the atmosphere, perhaps due to the believers who truly venerate the site.

AGHLABID BASIN (*Av Ibn el Aghlab;* ⊕ *Apr–mid-Sep 07.30–18.00 daily; mid-Sep–Mar 08.00–17.45*) Even though the city was founded on a trickle of water, the semi-desert area barely had enough to supply its thirsty population. The Aghlabids built this reservoir to corral the resource piped in via aqueduct from 36km away. Still holding water, the not terribly impressive site is best viewed from the top floor of an adjoining building, which also holds a comprehensive visitor centre, good bookshop and decent little café.

ZAOUIA OF SIDI SAHAB (ABOU ZAMAA AL-BALAWI MAUSOLEUM) (*Av Zama el Belaoui;* ⊕ *Apr–mid-Sep 07.30–18.00 daily; mid-Sep–Mar 08.00–17.45*) The occupant of this mausoleum is also known as the Barber, due to his carrying around three hairs from the beard of his friend, the Prophet Mohammed. The complex is made up of three sections: the mausoleum, the guest quarters and the religious buildings. The monument welcomes visitors to its consummate examples of Islamic decoration – the arcaded courtyard and ceramic tiles are particularly lovely – yet still functions as a mosque and medersa (Koranic school).

Also included in the one-day pass is entry to the **Raqqada National Museum of Islamic Art** (*in the town of Raqqada, 7km south of Kairouan;* ⊕ *Jul/Aug 08.00–14.00 Tue–Sun; Sep–Jun 09.00–16.00 Tue–Sun*). Located within a former presidential palace from the 1960s, this centre features architecture, ceramics, coins, objects of glass and bronze, and the Koran and its calligraphy, all relating to Islam in Tunisia.

Not included in the day pass, but still worth exterior viewing is the **Mosque of the Three Doors** (*Rue de la Mosquee des Trois Portes*). One of the oldest original buildings in the city, dating from 866, its decoration is detailed, and the three doorways topped with period Kufic script (a delicate and artistic form of calligraphy dating from the period).

THE ROMAN SITES

Kairouan sits halfway along the hypotenuse of a triangle, the points of which are three of the most impressive Roman sites in North Africa: Makhtar, Sbeitla and El Djem.

MAKHTAR This large Roman site sits to the northwest of Kairouan, just over 100km away and at an elevation of 900m. Spread over a large terrain, some of the monuments spill out beyond the designated perimeter and into the modern urban area. Much of this large Roman town remains unexcavated, and there are vast spaces of nothing but grass and suspiciously intriguing mounds. The monuments that have been dug out and preserved are extremely interesting, including at least three buildings that are very unusual, the school for youths, the tax office and the Vandal church.

History Evidence of human habitation in prehistoric times exists in the area, and even among the ruins today dolmens show that people lived here around 1000BC. The native Numidians came under the influence of the conquering Carthaginians from 400 to 200BC and eventually converted totally to their way of life. In 153BC Numidia regained control, under the auspices of King Massinissa, and the region remained indigenous until 46BC, when the king, Juba, killed himself (see page 9). A Punic inscription was found dating from this time that named the town M'ktrm. The Romans, once in control, adapted the name to Mactaris. The town remained free until Trajan arrived and late in his reign the forum was built, as well as the magnificent triumphal arch. From then on, Romanisation began on a grand scale, with Mactaris being converted into a true provincial city of Rome, with its wealthier inhabitants granted the status of citizens. When Marcus Aurelius came to power in AD161, he declared the city a colonia, with all its rights and privileges. The capitolium was constructed during the last year of his reign. Things remained peaceful, including the early years after the adoption of Christianity, and Mactaris took its place at the Council of AD256, with its own episcopal representative. By AD411, it seems its bishop was now a member of the Donatists. However, 28 years later the Vandals arrived, and remained *in situ* till AD533, leaving very little except for an excellently preserved Arian church, one of the few that still exist. When the Byzantines came to the Roman rescue, they invested heavily in the city's fortifications, and the reinforced baths complex is one of their best examples of defensive strengthening. It was late, however, and the decline of both the empire and the city was already beginning. The Arabs marched through during their conquest even though nothing of Islamic origin has yet been found in Makhtar. Archaeologists maintain that the city was inhabited until around 1000.

Getting there Via the non-SNTRI buses from Kairouan to Le Kef, with the journey taking one hour 45 minutes to get to the town of Makhtar on the way, it's possible to do a day trip to the site. SNTRI buses take three hours from Tunis, and *louages* cover the same routes. By car it's much faster, with the RN12 going directly from Kairouan to Makhtar.

 Where to stay and eat The local accommodation isn't worth considering but there are the usual cafés in the town

What to see Situated in the mountains, the site (⊕ *Apr–mid-Sep 08.00–19.00, mid-Sep–Mar 08.00–17.30; entry TND4*) is graced by cool breezes in the summer, but can get snow in the winter. Be prepared, as there is very little shelter once in the open. A large Roman arch sits in front of a modern fountain just outside the site entrance, and it's worth a quick look at the small museum, before venturing out onto the enormous site. Believed to have once had up to 10,000 residents, a big city by Roman standards, the attractions visible today are fairly far between. Passing the small and unmemorable amphitheatre, paved roads lead to the ancient heart of the city, the forum. This vast paved space has nothing left of its capitolium or market, but is totally dominated by the impressive **Arch of Trajan** at the southern end. Things get much more interesting from here, with stumps of some of the

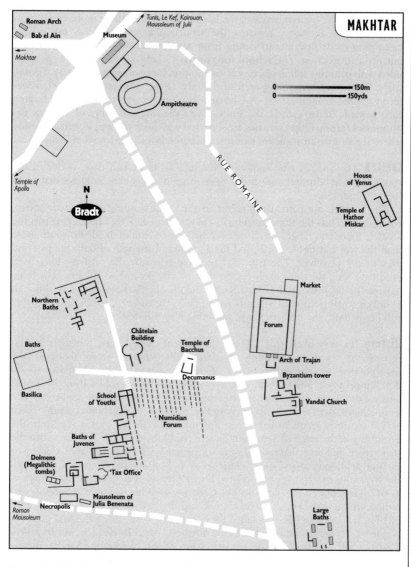

Roman Arch
Bab el Ain
Makhtar
Museum

Tunis, Le Kef, Kairouan,
Mausoleum of Julii

Ampitheatre

0 ——————— 150m
0 ——————— 150yds

RUE ROMAINE

Temple of
Apollo

N

Bradt

House
of Venus

Temple of
Hathor
Miskar

Northern
Baths

Châtelain
Building

Market

Forum

Baths

Temple of
Bacchus

Arch of Trajan

Decumanus

Byzantium tower

Basilica

School
of Youths

Numidian
Forum

Vandal Church

Baths of
Juvenes

Dolmens
(Megalithic
tombs)

'Tax Office'

Mausoleum of
Julia Benenata

Roman
Mausoleum

Necropolis

Large
Baths

Byzantine fortifications and earlier Roman villas. Soon in view are the remains of the **Vandal Arian church**, with its columns as well as baptistery still visible. Continuing to the large remains looming over the southern end of the site, one of the best-preserved large **bath complexes** in Tunisia appears. What's left is mostly the Byzantine modification. Once a location for leisure and pleasure, the structure has been converted into a fort. With its exterior solidly done in typical style, within are tall graceful arches running through the length, with mosaics still *in situ* below. Unusually for a defensive construction, there is a sense of gracefulness here, and perhaps the original aesthetic of the bathing area remains, despite its later purpose.

Heading west, skirting the perimeter walls, are the dolmens, traces of the pre-**Roman Numidian funerary monuments**. A pile of flat stones sits on top of half-submerged tomb sites dug into the earth with whatever has been found inside now in either the local museum or the Bardo. Across from them is one of the most intriguing and distinctive remains, the semicircular arches of the 'tax office' (according to its inscription) dating from AD300–400. To the north is another unusual construction. The **school for youths** (Schola des Juvenes), a large space filled with columns still in place, was the location for a sort of paramilitary training corps for the wealthy young men of the city. Originating around AD100, it was reconstructed around AD300. A Christian basilica sits just to the west. Heading back towards Trajan's Arch, the route passes the original centre of the city, the Numidian forum. Other remains are scattered widely on the site, as well as outside (there is a Roman mausoleum that resembles the Punic one found at Dougga).

SBEITLA The ancient city, known as Sufetula in its Roman days, is one of the country's most beautiful, mostly due to its magnificent golden buildings that are in superb condition.

The remains are particularly scenic in the early morning and late afternoon, when the sun hits the stone, turning its colour into a dark rose hue. Lying past the Dorsale mountain range, the climate on this side resembles the desert south more than the wet and fertile north, and the agricultural strength of both the past and present lies in olives. The fruit and more importantly the oil have long been produced here, the most likely reason that the city became so affluent. The long, narrow site sits between the Oued Sbeitla and the Sbeitla–Kasserine road, although as only a small portion of Sufetula has so far been explored, much of it probably still lies beneath the modern town, adjoining it to the west.

History It's very likely that a Berber settlement existed here, but there are no records or traces of anything pre-dating the Romans from about AD100. Incorporated into the empire when taken over as part of the Numidian spoils, development was due to its olive groves. The history resembles those of similar larger cities, with the contemporary emperor's acknowledgment of the city as a municipium, then as a colonia, turning the qualified residents into citizens. From AD300 onwards seems to have been Sufetula's golden age, and it was from the beginning of the reign of Septimius Severus until the end of Diocletian's, that the majority of buildings that remain were constructed. Christianity played a large part in later development and many churches were built, dating from its arrival until the Byzantine exarch Gregory declared himself leader of an independent empire in AD647. He replaced the old capital of Carthage with his new one at Sufetula and temporarily resisted both Constantinople and the Arabs. The latter got the better of him, however, and he was killed later that same year during the first push for conquest. Struggles continued with the northern-based Byzantines, but by AD698 Carthage fell, and the late Romans left North Africa. Neither the Vandals during their brief stay, nor the Arabs, damaged the city, but the new invaders abandoned it. They set up their city of Sbeitla on the outskirts, using the materials of the old to construct the new. The ruins first came to Western notice with the extension of the Grand Tour in the late 18th century, and in 1907 the French began excavations.

Getting there The 100km from Kairouan are covered in one hour 30 minutes by a daily late afternoon bus from Kairouan. The return is at 05.00, so it might be better to opt for a *louage*. There are also eight buses daily from Tunis, taking four hours 30 minutes. *Louages* do both routes more frequently.

Where to stay and eat If planning to spend the night, the **Hotel Sufetula** (✆ 077 46 53 11; $$$) is a very nice three-star place located just to the north and within view of the ruins, with good rooms, a lovely pool and reasonable food. For those

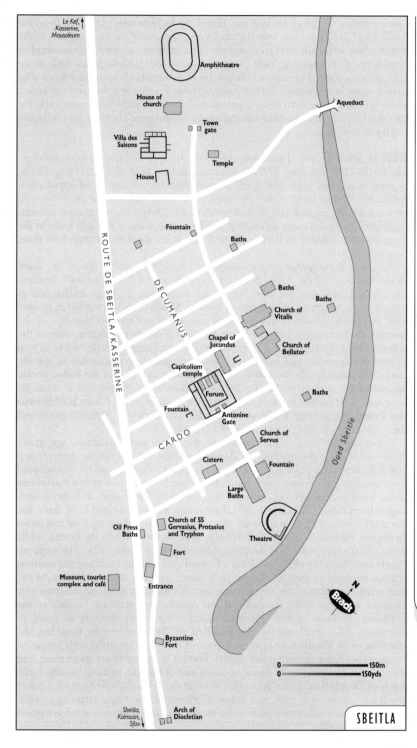

Le Kef,
Kasserine,
Mausoleum

Amphitheatre

House of
church

Town
gate

Villa des
Saisons

Temple

House

Aqueduct

Fountain

Baths

Baths

Baths

Church of
Vitalis

Chapel of
Jucundus

Church of
Bellator

Capitolium
temple

Forum

Baths

Fountain

Antonine
Gate

Church of
Servus

Cistern

Fountain

Large
Baths

Church of SS
Gervasius, Protasius
and Tryphon

Oil Press
Baths

Fort

Theatre

Museum, tourist
complex and café

Entrance

Byzantine
Fort

Sbeitla,
Kairouan,
Sfax

Arch of
Diocletian

ROUTE DE SBEITLA/KASSERINE

DECUMANUS

CARDO

Oued Sbeitla

N

Bradt

0   150m
0   150yds

SBEITLA

visitors with a far lower budget, the **Hotel de la Jeunesse** (*Av Habib Bourgiba;* ℡ *077 46 65 28;* $) is a fine low-cost alternative and one of the best bargains in the country. Just across the road from the site entrance is an excellent tourist complex, consisting of a museum, **café**, souvenir store and bookshop, as well as an information centre. The central courtyard is an extremely pleasant place to sit after having spent hours wandering the ruins, sipping a coffee or cold drink, or eating an ice cream. The modern town is geared up for visitors and has a leisure park, the Parc des Loisirs, with a **restaurant** and a grass central area. There are also cafés and small places to eat.

What to see The area of the ancient city (⊕ *Apr–mid-Sep 07.00–19.00; mid-Sep–Mar 08.00-17.30 Tue–Sun; TND4*), estimated to have held up to 10,000 residents, is very large, and even the small section that has already been explored is substantial. Unlike some of the other sites, particularly Makhtar, the excavations on view are densely packed, and there is much to see. Only some of the most obvious highlights are listed below, although if you have time, wander through some of the more obscure remains, as they might well give you a good insight into how these people lived.

Almost at the entrance are the vestiges of an oil press, with a few of the heavy stones that crushed the olives. It sits right next to a solid Byzantine wall. Towards the northeast is one of the more spectacular attractions, the **large baths**. Not as impressive in height or architecture as those in Makhtar, these are good at ground level and below. Nowhere else has such comprehensive mosaics that line all the rooms with a geometric pattern. There are a few columns that define some of the different areas. The distinctive Rome tile wall composition is clearly visible, as well as the *opus africanum*, and even better are the hypocausts, with many of the tile stacks still standing. To the east is the theatre built as a part of the baths. Poorly reconstructed, with tiers that are far too shallow, the acoustics still seem to be adequate. A bit further towards the centre, the remains of the **Church of Servus the Priest** can be seen. It's believed that this sanctuary was originally pagan and then rebuilt as a cathedral, but possibly a Donatist one.

Following the road, almost certainly the decumanus maximus, the grand boulevard leads to the magnificent **Antonine Gate**. An inscription shows that it was dedicated to Emperor Antonius Pius, Hadrian's successor, and his two adopted sons, one being the future ruler, Marcus Aurelius. The gate works as a marvellous frame to what lies beyond, the vast open space of the forum, and the superb **capitolium** behind. While normally there is one temple dedicated to all three, the assembly here is extremely unusual: this platform houses three separate and intact structures, each dedicated to its particular deity. Jupiter's sits in the centre, while those of his wife, Juno, and daughter, Minerva, sit on either side. The steps up clearly give the sense of approaching a revered spot and the buildings themselves, soaring upwards in their distinctive pink stone, are commanding. It's one of the best temple collections of any Roman site. It's difficult to move on from this fabulous spot, but there are more, if less ostentatious, remains. Slightly to the northeast are some of the Christian churches that mark the city as being so important. The small one of the **Basilica of Bellator**, comes first, but the **Basilica of St Vitalis** houses some baptismal fonts that are lined with preserved mosaics (one has a charming fish motif). Further to the north are more ruins, but they are not in a good state. At the opposite end of the site, to the far south, is the **Arch of Diocletian** or the Triumphal Arch of the Tetrarchy (the four joint rulers when the empire was split, just before Constantine the Great came to power). Sitting alone in a rather nice garden, the monument probably once acted as a grand entrance to the city.

Vindicating the argument that might makes right, Gaius Julius Verus Maximinus (1) was an emperor who rose to power on the shoulders of the army. Deposing and eventually killing Severus Alexander, the last of the dynasty beginning with Septimius Severus, he and his supporters seized the throne in AD235. The wars that raged in Europe, north of the Danube, continued and landowners began to resent having their resources seized and redeployed to support the campaigns. In AD238, when the wealthy chose one of their own, Gordian I (2) and his son, Gordian II (3), to take his place, the Senate in Rome sided with the new men. However, Maximinus returned to crush the rebellion. The senators were unhappy with the victor, having declared him a public enemy during his successor's reign and quickly elected two of their own, Clodius Pupienus Maximus (4) and D. Caelius Calvinus Balbinus (5) as their handpicked successors. Still not popular, they enlisted the support of the Equestrian Guard and appeased them saying that the emperor after them would be the son of Gordian I's daughter, or the future Gordian III. At the same time, Maximinus's war strategies were failing, and his soldiers had enough, eventually killing both him and his son, and sending their heads back to Rome. While Pupienus paid off the troops to temporarily buy loyalty, Balbinus had been away from Rome when a major riot took place that destroyed nearly half the city. Both co-emperors were on shaky ground, when they began to squabble among themselves. Meanwhile, the Praetorian Guard, annoyed that the Senate had decided who would be the next emperor, staged at coup d'etat, during which they dragged the arguing co-emperors back to camp and assasinated them there. Gordian III (6) became the next militarily appointed man on the throne in July 238. His reign lasted six years.

EL DJEM Dominating the flat surrounding landscape, the enormous amphitheatre of El Djem is one of the most magnificent sites in Roman Africa and an absolute must-see. This honey-coloured stone, ancient entertainment complex rivals in size and beauty the Colosseum of Rome, and surpasses it in preservation. It proves that the influence of the motherland thrived even in its far-flung corners. The highlight of this modern-day sleepy market town, there is currently little other evidence of the importance of Thysdrus, once an affluent town and important crossroads on the Afro–Romano trade route. Olives were another reason for its location, as this region was one of the most oil-productive in the entire empire. Arriving from either east or west, the construction is visible from a long way off, making the approach fairly simple. The remarkably intact ruin lies in the middle of town and is clearly the centre of most of the town's present-day activities.

History The town existed long before its famous landmark, with a Punic village dating from before 200BC. When Julius Caesar landed at Ruspina (Monastir), he looked towards the interior on the trade route and saw the value of setting up a town in the midst of this territory of excellent agricultural potential. Thysdrus became the centre of olive growing and the retirement home of many veteran soldiers. By Hadrian's reign, the quality and quantity of the multi-purpose oil was legendary. The wealth generated by this city of up to 30,000 helped Rome and much of the profit poured into Thysdrus's building programme.

Construction of the amphitheatre began in AD230 and was completed eight years later. The project was commissioned by Gordian, Rome's proconsul in Africa, and one of the community's wealthiest landowners who was not hesitant to use the best. The stone came from seaside quarries to the east, over 30km distant from the town, while water for the workers travelled via aqueduct from hills to the

Tunisia: Kairouan **THE ROMAN SITES**

23

west nearly 15km away. Before the complex was properly completed, however, Rome decided to re-levy a tax on olive oil, which instigated a countrywide rebellion. The wealthy villa owners rose up, assisted by the *juvenes*, the young upper-class paramilitary elite (see their school building in Makhtar, above). Following the lead of the Roman army in determining who would be the next emperor by choosing someone sympathetic to their cause, the combined forces made the 80-year-old Gordian and his son their rulers. The rebellion was suppressed and in the process, much of the town was damaged. Legend has is that the amphitheatre's patron and would-be emperor killed himself within his greatest achievement.

With Sufetula now taking over as the region's major city, Thysdrus slipped into provincial obscurity. The amphitheatre still had a couple of important historical roles to play. In AD699, the Berber queen Kahena used the arena as a stronghold for her Berber forces in her battle against Arab aggressors (which she eventually lost). Almost a thousand years later, the amphitheatre was again deployed as a refuge, and this time seriously damaged when Mohamed Bey blew up its side, to chase out followers of his rival, Ali Bey. Never repaired, the gap still exists. Today, about half of the arena has been renovated to allow for spectators during the summer El Djem International Symphonic Music Festival (*www.festivaleljem.com*), while the opposite side remains in its original condition.

Getting there From Kairouan, it's easiest to get a *louage* to Sousse, then continue to El Djem either via bus (seven SNTRI departures from Tunis do the daily Sousse–El Djem run on their way to other destinations; two originate from Sousse) or *louage*. The train from Sousse goes to El Djem four times a day *en route* to Sfax, although only the 08.00 and 12.30 ones are at tourist hours. The 12.00 and 19.15 return journeys from the Roman site make a day trip a possibility. By car, the trip is simple and direct, and only 70km, via the well-signposted MC87.

Where to stay and eat The only reasonable place to stay in the area is the three-star **Ksar el Jem** (*RN1 Rte de Tunis;* ☏ *073 63 28 00; www.hotelksareljem.com;* $$– $$$), located 4km north of the amphitheatre. Comfortable, and nicer when there's water in the swimming pool, the portions of decent, traditional food in the restaurant are enormous. In the town, there are many little cafés and small restaurants, especially close to the entrance of the amphitheatre, serving the usual dishes. Nearby are also several souvenir stands, selling, it seems, a lot of toy camels.

What to see Nearly everything going on in this small market town has to do with the **amphitheatre** (⊕ *Apr–mid-Sep 07.00–19.00; mid-Sep–Mar 08.00–17.30 Tue–Sun; TND7*) situated at its heart. The fourth largest in the Roman Empire, after Rome, Capua (in poor condition) and Carthage (of which almost nothing exists), it is arguably the best preserved. Its length of 149m is only 39m less than Rome's, while its width of 122m falls short of the Colosseum by only 34m. In addition, it rises to a height of 40m and today, with half of it enclosing seats and the other showing the skeleton of the construction, the building seems even more imposing. Some historians argue that the venue could hold up to 60,000, possibly on the strength that El Djem lay on trade routes and could attract wealthy travellers. Once entering the arena, it's easiest to tour the site on three levels. The first, the ground floor, onto which you enter from the exterior courtyard, leads through the series of impressive arches, to the field where the events took place. Imagine the games that took place right in front: in the morning, wild animals, for which North Africa was famous, would be hunted; at midday, the performance would consist of ceremonial or actual killing of criminals (including, briefly, Christians); in the afternoon, the most popular event of gladiatorial combat would commence. The screen over the gap running through the middle of the arena looks down into the tunnels below. It's possible to go down there, level two, and see where the participants in the games, whether humans or other animals, were kept right before their debut. The third level, the tiers, rises up into the heights, and it's always fun to clamber over the ruins of the ancient seating. Eventually, at the top, there are stunning views not only over the amphitheatre, but also of the town and beyond.

A small number of other ruins are scattered throughout the area, but are not significant. A visit to the **museum** (*about 1km south on the Sfax road,* ☉ *Apr–mid-Sep 08.00–19.00; mid-Sep–Mar 08.00–17.00; entry included with admission to the amphitheatre*) should definitely be included. As well as a superb collection of mosaics found in **Thysdrus**, there is also the **House of Africa** archaeological park. Within the grounds, past the exhibition, is a reconstruction of one of the more lavish Roman residences that were typical of the area. Just beyond, is the actual villa upon which the restoration is based. The floor plan is still visible, as well as the traces of the courtyards and separate rooms, most with decorative mosaic detailing still in place. Take another look at the reconstruction as you leave and judge how accurate the visualisation is. On second glance at the beautiful wall mosaics as you pass, think about them sitting on the floors of some of the larger rooms of the villa that you just visited.

24

Beyond the Romans

THE BEST THINGS TO SEE SOUTH OF THE ROMAN PROVINCES

There is very little in Tunisia that the Romans didn't see, and the *limes*, or lines that marked the limit of the Roman Empire, lie far to the south of the country, within the desert regions. There are virtually no traces of their presence close to their ancient limits, but many other attractions and scenic spots of geographical or later origin sit within these ancient borders and are worth a look. Even if the Romans didn't leave their mark, it's likely they did share the view.

It's easiest to describe the best of the rest of Tunisia via an itinerary. From Sbeitla, (see *Chapter 23*, page 314), head southeast, past the city of Kasserine, the site of the Roman settlement of Cillium and a critical World War II battle, to Tozeur. This desert town famous for its green oasis of date palms numbering in the hundreds of thousands, has a unique brick architectural styling, particularly evident in its small, uncommercial medina. Parts of the town centre were used as a film set for *The English Patient*. To the west, in the mountains bordering Algeria, are some spectacular canyons and waterfalls, close to the villages of Mides, Tamerza and Chebika. To the southeast is the town of Nefta, a little dry and dusty despite the huge palm grove running deep through its centre, but better known for its proximity to the desert, and the site of the town of Tatouine in *Star Wars*, not to be confused with the real town of Tataouine, located far to the southeast. The ruins of the film set that lie close to Ong Jemal ('the camel's neck', a landmark in the sand) have become tourist attractions in their own right. Heading east, the road passes Chott El Djerid, the largest saltpan in the Sahara, offering the occasional mirage.

Emerging from this weird landscape, the next attraction is the town of Douz. Known as the Gateway of the Sahara, a festival takes place here every December (*www.festivaldouz.org.tn*). More popularly, here is the place to take a camel ride, whether for two hours or several weeks, and tourist facilities for travelling on these 'ships of the desert' are well organised. Due east, the scenery becomes more dramatic as the road rises into the mountains, passing the charming little Berber town of Tamrezet. Soon after, the road comes to Matmata, the hilly location for the unique troglodyte houses (see page 244) and yet another *Star Wars* film location. To the south, the architectural features are the extraordinary *ksars*, or Berber granaries. Built in levels, these ancient earthen multi-tiered storehouses are now being converted into hotels. Ksar Hadada is one of the more developed. Further south, and sitting on top of a hill, the white Berber hilltop village of Chenini is very scenic. Turning north, Medinine has a large craft centre, and from here, the road heads east to Djerba (see *Chapter 21*, page 270) either via the causeway from Zarzis, or the ferry from El Marsa. The RN1 runs through town, heading north through Sfax, El Djem, Sousse and Tunis, or south, into Libya.

Location North Africa, 25°00'N, 17°00'E. The country's northern border is the Mediterranean Sea.

Neighbouring countries Tunisia lies to the west and Egypt to the east

Size 1,759,540km², 4th-largest country in Africa, 17th largest in the world

Climate Temperate Mediterranean on the coastal strip, extremely hot and dry in the desert in the south

Status Theoretically governed by the people through local councils in a body called the Jamahiriya (State of the Masses); in practice, functions as an authoritarian state.

Population 6,173,579 (July 2008 estimate)

Life expectancy 77.00 years: male 74.81, female 79.44

Capital Tripoli, population approximately 1.7 million

Other main towns Zuwarah, Al Khoms, Misratha, Surt, Ras Lanuf, Al Burayqah, Benghazi, Al Bayda, Tobruk, Ghadames, Sabha, Al Jawf

Economy Income is derived almost entirely from oil

GDP US$12,300 per capita (2007)

Languages Arabic, Italian and English; Berber (Tamazight) is also spoken in the south.

Religion Muslim (Sunni) 97%, other 3%

Currency Libyan dinar (LYD)

Exchange rate £1 = LYD1.9, US$1 = LYD1.2, €1 = LYD1.7 (Apr 2009)

National airline/airport Libyan Arab Airlines; Tripoli International Airport

International telephone code +218

Time GMT+2

Electrical voltage 220 volts AC, 50Hz; European two-pin plug

Weights and measures Metric

Flag Solid green

National anthem *Allahu Akbar* (God is the Greatest)

Public holidays *7 January, Ashoura; 2 March, Jamahiriya Day; *9 March, Mouloud, Prophet's Birthday; 28 March, British Evacuation Day; 11 June, Evacuation Day; *20 July, Ascension of the Prophet; 23 July, Revolution Day; 1 September, National Day; *21 September, Eid al-Fitr, End of Ramadan; 7 October, Italian Evacuation Day; *28 November, Eid al-Adha, Feast of the Sacrifice.
(for 2009: starred dates change according to the Muslim calendar)

Part Five

LIBYA

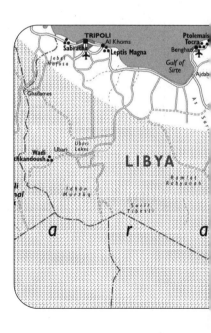

Medenine
TUNISIA
Zuwara **TRIPOLI**
Nalut
Sabratha
Al-Khoms
Leptis Magna
Misrata
Mediterranean sea
Apollonia
Ptolemais Derna
Tocra
Cyrene
Al-Marj
Benghazi
Tobruk
As Sallum
Jebel Nafusa
Gharyan
Gulf of Sirte
Sirte
Ghadames
Al Qaryah ash Sharqiyah
As Sidran
Ajdabiyya
Al Jaghbub
Siwah
Waddan
Zillah
Jalu
Libyan Desert
EGYPT
Adiri
Birak
Ubari
Germa
Sebha
Awiss
Marzuq
Waw al Kabir
Tazirbu
Ghat
Jebel Acacus
Wadi Tashwinat
Al Qatrun
Waw al Namus
Ramlat Rabianeh
Al Jawf
Fezzan
ALGERIA
Sahara Desert
N
Bradt
NIGER
Ma'tan as Sarah
Al 'Uwaynat
Aozou
Bardai
0 ———— 200km
0 ———— 200 miles
CHAD
SUDAN

LIBYA

25

Background Information

GEOGRAPHY

Looking out over its 1,770km-long Mediterranean coastline, Libya is the fourth-largest country in Africa (after Sudan, Algeria and the Democratic Republic of Congo) and the 17th largest in the world. Despite its size, it holds a population of barely six million, as only 1% of its total area can support agriculture. Over 90% of the country is desert, part of the Sahara that forms the border between north and central Africa. The dry and hot region that defines most of Libya is shared with its neighbours, Tunisia to the northwest, Algeria to the west, Niger to the southwest, Chad to the south, Sudan to the southeast and Egypt to the east. The first two nations and the last also border the Mediterranean. Libya sits at 25°00'N and 170°00'E.

The country is divided into three geographic and administrative sectors, originally separately governed regions. Eventually, they came together under one flag after Libya achieved independence in 1951. The first, **Tripolitania**, is a narrow strip of only 16% of the country that includes the capital city, Tripoli, and the fertile western coastal region. It begins at the border with Tunisia and heads east till about two-thirds along the Gulf of Sirte. Benefiting from its proximity to the sea, the long stretch includes lagoons sandwiched between its habitable enclaves. To the south, the flat landscape extends only a relatively short distance, ending along the edges of a plateau that rises up 1,000m.

The second, **Cyrenaica**, comprises 51% of Libya and goes from the Mediterranean Sea all the way to the southern borders with Chad and Sudan and the eastern border with Egypt. There is a lowland grassy plain between Benghazi and Derna that reaches into the interior for 50km at the most. Behind is a small forest region with elevations up to 900m, but beyond, the Sahara takes over. On the border with Chad is the massif where the country's highest elevations of 2,200m are located.

The third region, the **Fezzan**, takes up a full third of the land, and lies to the south of Tripolitania within the Sahara. It consists almost entirely of desert. This place is one of the planet's driest, and dozens of years can go by without any precipitation. The highest air temperature ever experienced was recorded here, at just under 60°C. This desert has a few areas of some very interesting features. Comprising *hamadas* (rocks sculpted into shapes by the wind), *idehan* (sand seas and dunes) and *sahir* (depressions left by salt evaporated from the rare flash floods) this area can be quite beautiful. The aridness is relieved by rare oases, such as at the extraordinary Ubari Lakes. To the southwest is the rock art that dates from as long ago as 12,000 years. By the types of animals depicted on the walls, the creators indicated that this region was once much more fertile.

Today, the lines that separate Libya from its neighbours remain vague, with no landmarks or geographical features that mark the passing from one country to the next. At both the west with Tunisia and the east with Egypt, unofficial crossings are a common occurrence, and only the vast void of the desert to the south prevents people from regularly entering here.

NATURAL HISTORY

The thin strip of land along the coast has the usual range of flora and fauna, with bougainvillea and oleander, as well as cultivated plants, such as citrus and olive. Grain is still being produced, although not on the scale it was during Roman times. Many species of animal typical of this environment live or pass by here, although the Mediterranean monk seal has been declared critically endangered in Libya, as well as the rest of sea-side North Africa.

The narrow buffer zone of the grassy plains remains an important agricultural region. This area ends in the Green Mountains, rising up to about 800m. A small amount of rain falls, and more persistent trees, such as junipers and mastics, live in this environment, and some hardier agricultural products, such as figs and olives, are grown here.

Dropping down into the south the Sahara takes over. On the western side, in the Fezzan, the only cultivation comes from the date palms and fig trees located in oases, watered by natural springs and manmade wells. The desert areas of Cyrenaica are also dependent on its few oases for habitation and cultivation.

The rock art of the far southwest, in the Jbel Acacus region of the Fezzan (and the Tassili N'Ajjer of Algeria, just across the border), shows that a wide variety of animals more associated with central and southern Africa once lived here. Pictures of elephants, giraffe, rhinoceros and other creatures appear on the walls, providing evidence that the region was far more fertile and fauna-populated during the last ice age than now. As the ice further north retreated and the land in the south warmed up, many of the different species migrated, leaving relatively few behind in the increasing heat. Through Roman times, the North African elephant (immortalised by Hannibal's use of them to cross the Alps on his attack on Rome), the Barbary lion and even bears still existed in the climate belt, and the Romans often captured these wild beasts for entertainment in the arena. Today, the very few mammals remaining include the fennec fox, gazelle, gerbil and jackal. The cheetah, which once lived here, is now believed to be extinct. More common are the reptiles and rodents, with varieties of lizard, scorpions and snakes found among the sand. In the Ubari Lakes, one of the oases in the depths of the Fezzan, is a red shrimp used by the human inhabitants to make an edible paste.

Libya is on the migration route for several species of bird making their way between southern Africa and Europe. Most of these visitors are best seen along the coast; for example, the greater flamingo and the Kentish plover setting up temporary quarters in the Benghazi reserve close to the city. About 150km northeast is the Kouf National Park, where beaches and lagoons welcome breeding communities of the lesser kestrel, the Houbara bustard and the European white

THE NATIONAL PARKS OF LIBYA

Libya has seven national parks and five major nature reserves. The national parks are: **Abughilan**; **El Kauf** and **Kouf** along the coast in the northeast; **Karabolli** and **Naggaza** along the coast in the northwest; **Rajma**, slightly inland in the northwest; and **Siman**.

The nature reserves are: **Benghazi**, **Bier Ayyad**, **New Hiesha Natural Reserve**, **Tripoli** and **Zellaf**.

There are also 24 protected sites.

stork. There are lots of other birds that make their permanent residence in the country. In the oases, desert larks, desert sparrows, spotted sandgrouse, and various others have been noted.

CONSERVATION Libya abides by various worldwide agreements that aim to protect areas of biodiversity and wetlands. It also adheres to treaties dealing with climate change and desertification. As far as any active programmes are concerned, the only one currently in the works, besides the Great Manmade River (see page 332) is the Green Mountain Conservation and Development Authority. It aims to protect over 5,000km^2 of the Green Mountain Area, including 217km of coastline and the ancient Graeco-Roman site of Cyrene. A pet project of Colonel Gaddafi's eldest son, Saif, the plan also includes developing green tourism to include environmentally friendly hotels and spas.

POST-ROMAN HISTORY

The Vandals took advantage of the issues and disputes of a declining Roman Empire, and invaded. By AD431 they captured Libya, 24 years before their sacking of Rome. A hundred years later, with Byzantium on the rise, General Belisarius took back the land for his emperor, Justinian. Difficulties with the Berbers made the country impossible to administer in its entirety, and control was limited to the coastal region. Another century, and the Arabs on their march to make all of North Africa Islamic, initially came to Egypt, then into Libya in AD642. Cyrenaica was the first to turn to Islam, and a year later Tripoli fell. In the Fezzan, Okba eventually conquered the region on his way to found the city of Kairouan, in Tunisia. Although Queen Kahena drove the Arabs back to their Cyrenaica stronghold in AD695, she was eventually overwhelmed.

By AD712, all of North Africa, and parts of western Spain as well as the eastern Mediterranean, was within the caliphate of the leader of the Umayad dynasty. As with its neighbours, the Abbasids ousted their predecessors and in AD800 the Aghlabids followed, appointing a new leader who managed to get things back in order. The ancient ideals and efficiency of the Romans briefly flowered. It only took another century before the Shiite Isamilis attacked the Sunni Aghlabids. The Zirids, a Berber tribe, reverted to the Sunni branch of Islam and the Fatimids, in revenge, destroyed the capital cities of Cyrene in Cyrenaica and Tripoli in Tripolitania, along with much of the rest of North Africa. As a result of the Berbers and their culture being systematically hunted down and squashed, the original inhabitants of the region were widely dispersed, and the invaders had free reign to continue their Arabisation. For a brief period, the Normans seized their chance in the midst of this chaos and attacked from Sicily taking charge of passing trade. This control didn't last, and in 1158 the familiar pattern of a new invading dynasty taking over from the old continued with the Almohads arriving from Morocco. Half a century later, the Hafsids came to power. This time, the tribe stayed for almost 300 years, and the stability led to an era of culture, prosperity and substantial trade with Europe.

Lax and pragmatic authority led to the bays and safe ports being ideal for piracy. Established in other parts of North Africa, the Spanish took over Tripoli in 1510 but due to the hassles of maintaining it, gave the city to the Maltese Knights of St John in 1528. By now, the pirate Khayr al-Din (Barbarossa) had already started conquering his territory to the west, and in 1538, drove the knights out from Tripolitania's capital. Unchecked, the shore from here all the way to the Atlantic became known as the Barbary coast and legendary for its privateers. Barbarossa, aware that he did not have the power to fight the Spanish alone, invited the

Ottoman Turks in exchange for allowing his pirate activities to continue, which they happily did for the next two centuries. In 1711, the Karamanlis, a dynasty springing from both Turkish and Libyan blood, rose to power and remained there for the next 124 years. In 1801, Yusuf Karamanli, the pasha and a descendant of the original officer who founded the line, decided to up the bribe that the Americans had been giving for the last five years to ensure they were safe from the Barbary pirates. The United States refused to pay and a war between the two countries began, when the Americans blockaded the port of Tripoli and, four years later, defeated the pasha.

With the Ottomans finally winning out against the Berbers in the Fezzan in the 1840s, things stabilised for a while. In 1843, a new religious and political order was founded in Cyrenaica by the Grand Senussi. At first fighting Turkish rule, for which he gained Berber support, the movement continued, advocating resistance against French incursions into North Africa beginning in 1902. As the new century progressed, the Ottoman Turks were weakening, and the Italians saw their chance to control land on the other side of the Mediterranean. Claiming they were freeing Tripoli from the yoke of Ottoman oppression, they seized the city for themselves in 1911 and formally took over Tripolitania and Cyrenaica as sanctioned by the Treaty of Lausanne. Fezzan remained troublesome, and the response of the Europeans was to import 150,000 Italians into the country, more than the French had placed in Algeria. In 1920, the Italians accepted the dynastic leadership of the Grand Senussi's grandson, the Sheikh Sidi Idris. Rebellion continued, and in an effort to stop militant anti-Italian sentiment, concentration camps were created. Eventually the rebels acquiesced. By 1934, the Fezzan had been tamed.

During World War II, from 1940–43, Italians and Germans, under General Erwin Rommel, fought against the Allies for land between Benghazi and El

On 21 December 1988, a Pan American scheduled flight from London Heathrow to JFK Airport in New York, exploded over the town of Lockerbie, Scotland. Two hundred and seventy people from 21 countries died in a blast caused by the detonation of a bomb. This was considered to be a terrorist incident, and two Libyan suspects were ultimately indicted. Gaddafi's refusal to hand over the accused led to UN and EU embargoes (a US one had been in place since 1982). However, when the neutral location of The Hague, in the Netherlands, was chosen to be the place of trial, the suspects were extradited, and the foreign embargoes were eased and eventually lifted. Only one of the terrorists was sentenced (the other released), and although he still claims he's innocent, he's currently sitting out his term in a Scottish prison.

Alamein, Egypt, although much of the fighting took place around Tobruk. In October 1942, Montgomery's force broke through German defences at El Alamein and by November, retook Cyrenaica. In January 1943, the British took Tripoli, and by February the last of the Axis Power soldiers were gone. Once the enemy fell and left Libya, the British took control of Tripolitania and Cyrenaica, while the French occupied the Fezzan. The far west of the country was attached to French-occupied Algeria. By the end of the war, an estimated 11 million unexploded land mines remained on Libyan soil.

The Four Powers Commission consisting of France, the United Kingdom, the United States and the USSR gathered to decide what was to become of Libya and in 1949, with assistance from the United Nations, the country's independence was approved. On the day before Christmas, in 1951, Libya formally became the Independent United Kingdom of Libya. Sheikh Sidi Idris was declared King Idris I by the National Assembly. Two years later, Libya joined the Arab League. In 1955, the new country received membership of the UN. Four years later everything changed, when oil was discovered. Now, as a much richer country, new legislation was put into effect, including officially joining the three parts of the nation into one, and allowing women to vote.

On 1 September 1969, King Idris was ousted by a coup d'état, staged by the military. A young colonel, Muammar al-Gaddafi, took the role as leader, setting up the Libyan Arab Republic. He published his political ideas in the *Green Book* in 1976, and a year later the country was renamed the Libyan Arab Jamahiria (State of the Masses).

Recent events have occurred in Libya's history that remain vivid in people's memories. After a mob attacked the American Embassy in Tripoli, violently showing their approval for Iranian militants who were holding Americans prisoners, the US requested the removal of the Libyan Embassy in Washington, and enacted an embargo on the country in 1982. A decade later, the UN joined in, after the republic refused to send back suspects in the Lockerbie bombing, although these restrictions were lessened when the accused appeared in court in the Netherlands. By 2003, the UN lifted their ban, and a year later, American and Europe did the same. Today, the US Embassy is back in Tripoli.

POLITICS

Libya is officially known as the Great Socialist People's Libyan Arab Jamahiriya (Al Jamahiriyah al Arabiyah al Libiyah ash Shabiyah al Ishtirakiyah al Uzma in Arabic). When Colonel Gadaffi and his supporters overthrew the monarchy, the idea of 'a

With many thanks to John Swanson of the American University in Cairo

Egypt had been a British Protectorate from 1882–1922 and was reoccupied at the beginning of World War II to protect Suez. The rest of North Africa was controlled by the Axis powers: Libya, by Italy; Tunisia, Algeria and Morocco by France (later to become Vichy France). The border between Egypt and Libya, effectively between Britain and Italy, was the battle line. The following is a timeline of events:

May 1940 Germany invades France and much of the country and its protectorates become administered by the pro-German Vichy government.

10 June The Italians declare war.

September The Libyan–Egyptian border was at Sidi Barrani. Italians marched east to Egypt, with the intent of taking over Alexandria and the Suez Canal: 150,000 Italians faced the 30,000–40,000 members of Britain's 8th Army, under the command of General Wavell.

November Italians stopped to winter.

December Wavell attacked the Italians at Sidi Barrani, with the intent of driving them back to the border.

December 1941 The Italians were forced further back, to Agheila, Libya.

March–April The German general Rommel forces the Allies back to Egypt, but Tobruk held. The British still control the Mediterranean. The only way to get arms and resupplies is by sea, but the routes remain staunchly under UK control. Rommel is told by German command to be on the defensive, as the majority of troops will be needed on the Russian Front, but he refuses to take this advice. In the meantime, the Allies break the German

state of the masses' (Jamahiriya) was to have government by the people administered through local councils, headed by a Revolutionary Command Council. In theory, a democratic system, in practice, the wheels of government turn under the authority of Colonel Gaddafi, operating under his own definition of democracy.

Although Colonel Gaddafi's role has no precedent, nor an official title, the man is effectively the acting chief of state. The head of government, Baghdadi Mahmudi, is also the Secretary of the General People's Committee (equivalent to a prime minister). The cabinet consists of the General People's Committee, which was set up by the General People's Congress. There are elections, but they are indirect, with individuals having to go through several layers of committees, members of which cast the votes. Voting is open to everyone aged 18 and over and is compulsory. There are 2,700 members in this single political house, and they make the laws of the land. The last elections were in March 2006.

The legal system is loosely based on French, Italian and Islamic practice. For religious issues, there are separate courts. There is a Supreme Court, but it is not allowed to review Committee-made laws. Libya has not bowed to the compulsory rulings of the International Court of Justice in those cases in which the courts' decision is legally binding (contentious issues to which both parties have previously agreed to abide by the ICJ's verdict). This attitude caused serious problems in the Lockerbie case, although the issue was eventually resolved by holding the trial on neutral ground.

Tripoli is the capital city, known by its local name of Tarabulus (not to be confused with Tripoli in Lebanon). The nation is divided into 25 municipalities, or *shabiyat*, with these subdivisions referring to the different cities of the country. The code and know their plans. Rommel strikes against the Allied position with a lightning campaign that drives the Allies back to the Libyan border, taking Benghazi, Derna and Cyrene, but he fails to overtake Tobruk – the British–Australian garrison holds firm.

November–December The Allied forces, under the command of General Auchinleck, drive the Axis military back. Rommel finds himself where he started, having ignored the advice of his superior officers not to go.

January–February 1942 The Allies are pushed back to Gazala (just outside Derna).

May Rommel drives the Allies back to El Alamein, 140 km west of Alexandria.

July The Allied lines hold at the Qattara Depression. The confrontation is the First Battle of Alamein. After a month-long battle, both sides are exhausted and stop for reinforcement. Although considered a stalemate, it successfully stops the Axis advance.

30 August–5 September Second Battle of Alamein: the British have five times as many men as the Germans; resupplies for the latter have been sunk at sea by the Allies. The defeat is devastating for Rommel, and he retreats, awaiting reinforcements.

23 October–5 November Third Battle of Alamein: the Allied general Montgomery wages a battle of attrition, knowing the Italian-German army will lose due to poor supply lines as well as their fewer numbers.

2–3 November The line begins to break and Rommel retreats.

4 November The Axis powers retreat to Libya.

December The Allies chase Rommel back to Tripoli. In the meantime, the United States, with General Patton, land in Morocco and Algeria with the Allied forces.

Christmas The Axis powers are still in Tunisia and western Libya, but the combined army of the British, Australian, South African and New Zealand forces come in from the east.

13 May 1943 Some 140,000 Germans and Italians surrender in Tunis.

administrative sectors are constantly being changed, with the *shabiyat* in the 1990s replacing the previous *baladiyat* (also municipalities), which in turn replaced the *muhafazat* (governate) in the 1960s. According to the CIA World Factbook, these divisions might have changed yet again, with the 25 municipalities being replaced by 13 regions, but this reassessment has not been confirmed.

ECONOMY

With both the international and domestic markets relying on its massive oil reserves, Libya has the ninth-largest oil pool in the world. Currently assessed to hold as many as 2,000bbl (billion barrels), with another 1,000 possibly in reserve, these numbers make sense when applied to the 30bbl used annually by the entire planet. The world's usage is increasing, particularly China's, and with the cost having reached US$147 per barrel in July 2008, Libya's coffers are beginning to overflow. A full 95% of Libya's export earnings come from this source. Domestically, 83% comes from industry (including petrochemical-related jobs), services 14.9% and the 1% of arable land provides 2.1% of agriculturally generated income. Libya's efforts are not going into diversification of sources, but rather into changing its economic system. For example, in 2003, long-term sanctions were finally lifted, and the world became more interested in Libya's assets after it had agreed to cease its 'weapons of mass destruction' development programme. Subsequently, the Jamahariya government became more amenable to privatisation and foreign investment. The colonel and his cohorts now invite outside assistance and financing, and are looking into adapting the socialist-biased economy to a market-driven one. Their recent application for membership in the World Trade

Organisation is an indication of their intent. With a per capita income of US$12,300, the fifth highest in Africa, this amount looks to rise rapidly.

Libya's great wealth has encouraged Colonel Gaddafi to invest in an extremely contentious and unique project, the Great Manmade River. Although most of the country is desert, deep below the sands in the south of the country, the Nubian sandstone aquifer system contains vast quantities of fossil water. Left over from when the region was lush and fertile during the last ice age, there is a large supply in the water table. The reservoir was discovered during exploration for oil. The plan is to transport this resource via a huge network of pipes to the areas where it's most needed. At the moment, the thirstiest regions are the cities, although there are hopes that there will be overspill, to enable the development of an agricultural sector. The project was proposed in the 1960s, and by 1984 construction had started. The estimated cost when it was first introduced was US$25 billion, which the country can easily afford, with inflation being matched by increased oil income. Although the desert is so vast that such a transport system won't affect the climate, accusations fly in that the water is a fossil source, and therefore not renewable. There might be serious environmental effects if this biological lifeline is taken away from such a sensitive area. If the pipelines are successful, the question arises as to what happens when the water runs out. Colonel Gaddafi's answer is that by the time that happens, an estimated 100 years after completion (scheduled for sometime around 2030) alternative methods of water extraction will have been found. To hedge his bets, desalination is also being developed. The Great Man Made River is the biggest pipeline system in existence, and not only has the colonel claimed it as the 'Eighth Wonder of the World', but the *Guinness Book of Records* acknowledges it as the largest irrigation project on the planet.

There are small contributions by other sectors of the economy, such as iron and steel production, food processing and handicrafts, and the traditional agricultural products of the region, like grain, dates and citrus. Nothing comes near the money generated by petrochemicals, though. Tourism has barely started. The lovely and long coastline has great potential, and Saif Gaddafi, the eldest son of the colonel, is planning an environmental resort near the ruins of Cyrene. However, at present, there is virtually nothing by the seaside for foreigners. The country's visitor attractions are the mountain rock art, the Greek, Roman and Berber ruins and the desert landscape. The difficulty for non-business Americans to obtain visas puts a serious damper on developing tourism as a going concern, and the infrastructure has barely started. For the moment, the country is wealthy enough to coast on its laurels and not worry about developing new income streams.

PEOPLE

With one of the largest areas in Africa, Libya's population of 6,173,579 (July 2008) is surprisingly small. This paucity is due to the sparse amount of habitable area, as the country is mostly desert. The majority of people live in the relatively temperate area near the coast. Virtually all the larger cities are in the narrow strip bordering the Mediterranean Sea. As this oil-rich nation is one of the world's wealthiest, the per capita income of US$13,100 provides the potential for a good lifestyle, and the socialist government filters quite a bit of its profit back into its people. This dissemination is evident in the literacy rate, assessed at 82.6% (92.4% for men, 72% for women). Life expectancy averages at 77 years, with men typically living until 74.81 and women, 79.44.

The Italian colonisation never really changed the racial nature of the country and 97% of the inhabitants are of Arab or Berber origin (or a mix of the two).

There are five heritage sites, three of which are Graeco-Roman: **Cyrene** (1982), **Leptis Magna** (1982) and **Sabratha** (1982).
In addition, the old town of **Ghadames** in the west, and the rock art of **Jbel Acacus** in the southwest, sharing the general region with Tassili n'Ajer in Algeria, are listed.

Cyrenaica in the east, the first area in North Africa to be assailed in the Arab invasion (after Egypt), is said to be the most true to its invaders' roots with the most amount of Arab blood in the region. Arabic is the first language of Libya, with much of its business conducted in it, although some Italian, and increasingly, English, is also used for commerce. The local version of Berber speech (Tamazight) is spoken in the ethnic enclaves, mostly in the south.

CULTURE

Libyan architecture is a blend of the various cultures that passed through here, rather than a unique style. Inhabiting the region when there were no national borders, the original settlers built constructions here that are similar to their Tunisian neighbours. Although only a small percentage of the people in Libya are considered Berber, the buildings left behind are striking and distinctive. The *qsar* is a multi-storey granary, often perched on a hilltop, and some 12th-century examples are still standing. There are also underground houses similar to the ones at Matmata, Tunisia, but now generally uninhabited. In the Sahara a style applied mostly in the Fezzan uses bricks made from the local mud as a building material. The Ottoman legacy is evident in mosques, with their narrow, circular and distinctive octagonal minarets. This architectural form is the same in most of the North African region once controlled by the Turks. Not the big builders that their French counterparts were, the Italians' colonial style is felt mostly in Tripoli with its somewhat Mediterranean flavour.

As regard the national literature, Libya's writers have always put politics in front, using their literary skills for fighting oppression and documenting social change. The emphasis shifted after the 1969 revolution from resistance to acceptance, supporting the ideals and goals of the government, rather than trying to change it. Because of the specific nature of the works, few have been translated, although some authors are well known throughout the Arabic-speaking world. The most famous is Ibrahim Al-Koni, a prolific award-winning writer who is still producing stories. His writing seems to have more of an international interest, and it's possible to find translations of a few of his books, *Anubis: A Desert Novel* among others. The literature scene is alive and vibrant, and new practitioners are emerging, with women beginning to contribute to this erstwhile male-dominated art form.

As with the rest of North Africa, music is an essential part of Libyan culture, and while some of its forms are common to its neighbours, others are uniquely national. Among them are *mereskawi,* a form springing from the Murzuq region, usually played on the accordion and common at weddings, particularly popular in Benghazi; and *malouf,* music with an Andalusian origin that's blended with local styles, including Berber (see page 81). Although the modern Arabic music scene is dominated by practitioners from Egypt, there are other performers that come from Algeria, Morocco and Tunisia, and even Libya has contributed a few of its own, particularly the *rai* pop singer, Ahmed Fakroun. Seen at weddings or music festivals, traditional dance is alive and well, practised on a grassroots level rather than performed by professional companies. Among these movements is the *kaska*, a group effort with ancient historical origins.

There is a small fine arts scene, with local artists producing work, but it is rarely seen outside the country. The ancient rock paintings and carvings of the south seem to dominate foreigners' concepts of Libyan art, and influence modern creators.

26

Practical Information

SUGGESTED ITINERARIES FOR CRUISE-SHIP PASSENGERS

Libya is a popular destination for people who choose to travel by ship in the eastern Mediterranean. Cruises often stop by, not only because it's a convenient location sandwiched between the major tourist attractions of Egypt and Tunisia, but also because many of the country's sites are located close to the sea. Due to political restrictions, tours are organised by the cruise company.

TRIPOLI There is much to see in the capital. Most operators offer a half-day tour that takes in the excellent Jamahiriya Museum (with artefacts from the Greek and Roman sites among others) located in the medieval citadel, the Arch of Marcus Aurelius and the medina. The city is also a base for other excursions, including the following.

Sabratha Usually offered as a half-day tour, or from the nearby port of Zuwarah on the border with Tunisia, this Roman site is one of the best in North Africa. The highlight is the superb multi-tiered theatre, although the temples and the baths, particularly the seaward one with mosaics overlooking the water, are also spectacular.

Ghadames Some companies offer flights to this desert oasis 630km southwest from Tripoli on the Tunisian–Algerian border. With its fascinating old town, now in ruins, the site offers glimpses into a once traditional way of life. The Romans passed through here as part of their campaign to subjugate the locals, naming it Cydemus.

Nafusa Another desert trip goes by coach to the Nafusa Mountains, where the features are remnants of the Berber culture, particularly the Qsar al-Haj, the ancient multi-storey granary and the underground house at Gharyan.

AL KHOMS The town itself has nothing to offer, but the port is the usual stopping-off point for arguably the best Roman site in North Africa.

Leptis Magna Adjoining the modern city, the standard full-day tour is hardly enough to explore this vast, fascinating and remarkably preserved Roman town. From its extraordinary Arch of Septimius Severus standing at the crossroads of the city's two major boulevards, to its beautifully situated theatre, this site is one of the most incredible remnants of the period. Do not miss this place. Some companies do excursions to this magnificent site from the capital, while others that spend a bit more time in the country will often start the trip here, and pick visitors up at Al Khoms (see above).

BENGHAZI Libya's second city is the port for visits to the Pentapolis, the five cities: Cyrene, Apollonia, Ptolemais (Tomeita), Teuchira (Tocra) and Eusperides/

Berenice/Barca (Benghazi) of the ancient Greeks. They are in various states of repair. Tours to the first four start from here or Derna (see below).

Cyrene This is by far the most spectacular site, not least because of its hilltop vantage point looking down over the sea. This massive site holds the impressive Temple of Zeus, but also has a subdivision, the Sanctuary of Apollo. This part of the city was the first to be settled by Greek refugees from the island of Thera (Santorini). Its superb Greek and Roman remains and the atmosphere are wonderful. The German general, Erwin Rommel, situated his private headquarters overlooking the site during World War II.

Apollonia Nearby, this ancient attraction is usually included in the tour. Despite its Greek origins, the best remains – mostly Christian churches and the amphitheatre – come from around AD300.

Ptolemais Situated slightly to the west of the above site and although not quite as impressive, it's still worth a visit. Most of the usual hallmarks of a Roman town are here, but some Greek features also remain. There is also a good museum.

Teuchira (Tocra) Not the best example from the Pentapolis, but tours do go here. Some columns still stand, and the museum provides a guide as to where most sites in the city were once located.

Eusperides There is virtually nothing left of this site as it sits under modern Benghazi.

DERNA This small city has no offerings for the tourist in its own right, but it is a port that welcomes visitors. Many of the cruise lines stop here, particularly those that don't include Benghazi. Geographically, it allows a straighter route from Tunisia to Egypt. Visits to Cyrene and Apollonia are often arranged from here.

TOBRUK Although there is a large town and a major seaport here, most tourist ships don't stop. Those that do come to visit the battles sites of World War II (see page 345).

ℹ TOURIST INFORMATION

At the moment, Libya has no tourist offices either internationally or domestically. These and other websites are the best source of knowledge before travelling: www.libyan-tourism.org/Index.aspx?ID=2 and http://libya.embassyhomepage.com/. Tour operators and locals can provide more information.

$ MONEY

As with other 'soft currency' countries, Libyan dinars cannot be obtained abroad, nor taken out of the country. It's most likely the local tour operator or guide can cover financial requirements, including small exchanges. However, if the need to change larger amounts arises it's best to do so in a bank. Black market money markets exist but the rates they give are not generally better than the legal institutions. The most readily accepted currency remains the US dollar and it might be best to carry American money for conversion into dinars. Banks are normally open 08.00–13.00 Saturday to Thursday, and also on Saturday and Wednesday afternoons from 15.30–17.00. ATMs are also beginning to appear in the bigger cities.

To some degree, the information below is somewhat irrelevant as, for the moment, all tourist travel to Libya must be done either as part of a tour group, or with a private guide. At the time of research, entry for American tourists is almost impossible, as the Libyan government is extremely reluctant to grant them visas. This reticence is not due to personal animosity or politics, but mostly because US officials are reluctant to grant visas to Libyans and diplomatic reciprocity must be maintained. The American embassy staff in Tripoli say that this hesitation is due merely to the fact that the temporary consulate is located within the Corinthia Hotel and there are no facilities to interview Libyans who request a visa to visit the United States. The information below is general, and currently not of much use to people who want to visit independently.

✈ **BY AIR** Most visitors fly into Tripoli International Airport (☎ 022 60 50 26) situated about 25km south of the city, in the town of Ben Ghasir. There are also international services to Benghazi Benina International Airport (m 061 90 97 147). Services run between the two and are often used by tour operators to get direct to the areas of interest, bypassing the bits of the country where there is nothing to see. Visitors to the Roman coast of North Africa need only be concerned with these two. If heading south, the airport at Sebha is currently used by the tour companies to get to the sights of the Ubari Lakes and Germa. Libyan Arab Airlines is the national carrier and Buraq Air a new locally based private interloper. They both fly outside and within the country.

🚐 **BY BUS** There are two major bus companies and a few smaller ones that travel the distance between the cities. The main route is between Tripoli and Benghazi, although there are services that go to most of the larger destinations within the country. Transport to the far southwest is more difficult to find. The two major cities have bus stations, while smaller places have only stops (ask where they are once in town). Reliability is variable, although many are allegedly air conditioned.

🚗 **BY TAXI** Shared taxis can get you into the country from Tunisia and Egypt, and around it. Depots are usually situated close to the bus stops. They are most often estate cars that leave as soon as they are packed full. Prices are low enough that it's an idea to buy up some of the empty spaces to speed up departure time as well as allow some breathing room. Note that these services ply only the main routes where the shared taxis know they will get full occupancy, so that if you want to get to some of the more obscure sites, you might have to continue the journey with a private one.

Private taxis exist in the big cities and are easy to flag down. If you do find yourself with extra time, are allowed to travel independently and wish to travel further afield, it might be best to arrange transport with the hotel or a local tour guide. Prices will be higher, but more reliable.

🚗 **BY CAR** It's possible, although difficult, to travel with your own car. Crossing the border legally entails lots of documents and paperwork, and once on Libyan soil you will be required to collect a guide from a recognised tour operator, who will accompany you throughout your entire national visit. In common with many of the North African countries, there are also constant checkpoints making sure you are who you say you are, that your papers are in order, and that you stay away from the more problematic areas. An upside of travelling by private transport is that fuel costs are extremely low, not surprising in a country where oil is almost cheaper than water.

PUBLIC HOLIDAYS

Fixed annual dates are:

2 March	Jamahiriya Day
28 March	British Evacuation Day
11 June	Evacuation Day
23 July	Revolution Day
1 September	National Day
7 October	Italian Evacuation Day

These holidays are Islamic and vary annually according to the lunar calendar:

7 January	Ashoura
9 March	Aïd al-Mawlid (Prophet's Birthday)
20 July	Ascension of the Prophet
21 September	Aïd al-Fitr, or Eid (End of Ramadan)
28 November	Aïd al-Adha (Feast of the Sacrifice)

MEDIA AND COMMUNICATIONS

POST Post offices exist throughout the country, but the service is inconsistent. There's no guarantee that items sent by ordinary post will arrive, or that they won't be opened and suppressed by the authorities if containing anti-government sentiments. (Courier companies such as DHL or Fedex provide a more secure and reliable service.) If the mail does get through, it may take up to two weeks to arrive. Hours are Saturday to Thursday, 07.00–14.00 in summer and 08.00–15.00 in winter.

PRINT There about a dozen national newspapers, although they are all government owned and controlled. They are also predominantly in Arabic, with the possible exception of the *Tripoli Post* (*www.tripolipost.com*), in English.

RADIO Also run under official auspices, the eight LJB (Libya Jamahiriya Broadcasting) FM stations are city based, with Tripoli having half of them. There is also the shortwave Voice of Africa. All are in Arabic.

TELEVISION The 12 television stations of the country are firmly in the grip of the government. However, control of information is being undermined by the channels received on satellite dishes that are becoming increasingly common. Most popular are the Egyptian stations.

MOBILE PHONES AND THE INTERNET Mobiles are glued to people's ears here as in most of the developing world. The biggest networks are Al Madar and Libyana. Coverage is usually fine along the Roman coast, but in the desert service disappears. If you are travelling into the deep south, satellite phones can be rented in the tourist centres, and are highly recommended in case of emergency (but not for overpriced chats). Libyans are enthusiastic about the web: many companies advertise by internet, and there are lots of local cafés and venues throughout the country with access.

GIVING SOMETHING BACK

Gadaffi International Charity and Development Foundation www.gdf.org.ly/index.php?lang=ar&Page=101&lang=en. Set up by Saif Al Islam Al

Gaddafi, the president's son, to promote community development, human rights & volunteer services.

27

Ports of Entry

Most visitors who come to Libya do so by air, flying into the country via its two big cities. Each is important enough to merit a chapter, so for the capital, Tripoli, see *Chapter 28* and for the secondary flight-disembarkation point, Benghazi, see *Chapter 29*.

There are land crossings from both Tunisia and Egypt, but the closest border towns are small with nothing of note, other than formalities. The other ports of entry are literally that: seaports that cater to commercial and cruise passenger traffic. Of these harbours, three – Al Khoms, Derna and Tobruk – have facilities for tourists and reasons for them to land.

AL KHOMS (AL KHUMS) *Telephone code 031*

The only reason why tourists come through here is to visit the magnificent Roman ruins at Leptis Magna, located about 3km away. As many visitors include this ancient city as part of their Tripoli sojourn, details of the site will be listed as part of *Chapter 28* (page 356). The commercial port is also active. Despite a deceptively large population of over 100,000, there isn't much else of tourist interest, but for travellers passing through, the information below may be of help.

HISTORY Al Khoms's history goes back only as far as the Ottoman Empire. The single building of any note is the Mosque of Ali Pasha dating from this time. By 1870 the city came into its own for the exportation of esparto grass, a plant used in the making of fibre-based paper, lightweight shoes and rope and string. Today it remains industrially based with activities including tuna processing, soap making and agricultural distribution of the dates and olive oil produced in the nearby areas. The port continues to be the city's most important financial asset.

GETTING THERE AND AROUND If you are arriving by ship, and the tour buses aren't immediately waiting to whisk you away to Leptis Magna, you can stroll into the town centre directly in front. Independently, the Roman town is about 3km away, and if you don't feel like walking, shared taxis ply the route, well aware that visiting the city's famous nearby attraction is why most non-residents are here. Similar vehicles also go to the next larger cities, including Tripoli, 120km or about one hour 30 minutes to the west. They follow the standard route used by most vehicles along the coast.

 WHERE TO STAY It's likely that most visitors would be commuting from Tripoli, residing on the cruise ship or staying in accommodation arranged by the tour operator. However, if the need does arise, the following places offer rooms to spend the night.

🏠 **Severus Hotel** (16 rooms) Al-Fatah Street; 📞 031 262 5086. Newly built, this hotel is situated around 4km from Leptis Magna & has full facilities inc AC, satellite TV, Wi-Fi, restaurant $. $$$

🏠 **Al Madinah** ✆ 031 62 07 99. Not in the luxury class, but still equipped with the basics, & more, this place is one of the best in the city, although that is a relative assessment. $

🏠 **Leptes Hotel (Funduq Lebda)** Sharia al Khoms; ✆ 031 62 12 52. Outside of Al Khoms, but within 1km of the entrance gates of Leptis Magna, this

hotel has been highly rated by its guests, mostly due to its friendly & helpful staff. $

🏠 **Youth Hostel** Alkhums Sport Centre SW; ✆ 091 21 07 861. For the seriously budget conscious, this adequate & popular cheap place to stay is situated a short walk from the town centre. $

✖ **WHERE TO EAT** The centre has some little places along the main boulevard that sell the usual fast-food items, such as sandwiches and pizzas, which are fine for a quick snack. Cafés are also easy to find. The **Funduq al Andalus** (*on the main highway;* ✆ *031 62 66 67*) has a restaurant, as well as somewhere to stay. The best place to eat lunch in the area is **Mat'am Addiyafa** (✆ *031 62 12 10; $$$*), actually inside Leptis Magna.

OTHER PRACTICALITIES

Internet cafés Internet cafés are scattered along the main street, Sharia al Khoms.

Post The post office is located on Sharia al Jamahiriya, next to the city's most distinctive landmark, the Mosque of Ali Pasha.

WHAT TO SEE Basically not much. The Mosque of Ali Pasha is a reminder of the city's Turkish origins, and sits in the heart of town. Otherwise, Al Khoms is a typical small city relying on light industry and its port for its main sources of income, although tourism – those visitors passing by on their way to Leptis Magna – is also becoming a revenue stream. There are some nice beaches in the area, including one in the city, which is open to the public.

HOW TO GET TO THE ROMAN SITES Leptis Magna, arguably the best North African Roman site of all, is only 3km to the east. Shared taxis go there on a regular basis from the centre of town, although it's also an easy walk. Count on spending the whole day there and if you have the time, even more. For more information on Leptis Magna, see *Chapter 28*, page 356.

DERNA (DARNAH) *Telephone code 081*

Situated in the eastern province of Cyrenaica, Derna is an attractive town of about 80,000 inhabitants. Many visitors find themselves here only when their cruiseship docks. The ruins of the Pentapolis, the five ('penta') ancient Greek cities ('polis'), lie between here and Benghazi to the west. Both the sites, as well as Libya's second city, are described in Chapter 29 (see pages 365 and 364). This port is the closest to the two most spectacular of the five, Cyrene and Apollonia, and it's mostly for this reason that foreign tourists come here. Derna's old town contains a souk and the town square is a nice place to spend some time while lingering at one the cafés that sit around it. There are small banana plantations in the area while the beaches nearby are some of Libya's best. Saif, the eldest son of the chief of state, Colonel Gaddafi, has chosen this region as the site of his planned Environmental Green resort.

HISTORY Derna has a good historical pedigree, with its original founding as Darnis occurring when the ancient Greeks landed. Although dominated by Cyrene, 75km to the east, the ancient city still had a role to play along the seagoing trade route. By around AD300, Christians established a foothold by setting up a bishopric here. The city's fortunes followed those of its country, and after having been one of the first enclaves in North Africa to be conquered by the Arabs, fell into decline and eventual desertion. From about 1400 the seaside position and welcoming bay made it desirable and it was rebuilt on its old foundations and renamed Derna. It soon became an important port on the Barbary coast and, in 1805, was the location of the Battle of Derna between the United States and the pirates during the first Barbary war. The ruins of a fort built at the time still remain. After a peace treaty was negotiated, Derna was returned to the Turks and became a port for the slave trade. The buying and selling of human beings in Libya increased when slavery was abolished in the nearby nations of Algeria and Tunisia in 1847, but finally ceased in North Africa in the 1890s. Derna belonged to the Axis powers during World War II, and became part of the battle zone that stretched from Benghazi in the east to Tobruk in the west. With the Allies finally defeating Rommel in 1942, the British took control of the city. When Libya gained its independence so did Derna.

GETTING THERE AND AROUND Buses come here from both Benghazi to the west and Tobruk to the east but as they load up at their origins are often full. Shared taxis do the same routes, and may be a better bet. Their station is about 2km from the centre.

WHERE TO STAY Visitors stay on the ship or at a pre-arranged location, but if the need to find a local place arises, it's generally agreed there's only one place to stay.

Funduq al Fedous To the west, at the end of the Corniche, about 1km south; `\` 081 63 35 70. Despite this place being basic, it has a reputation for being one of the most visitor amenable hostelries in the country. $

WHERE TO EAT Cafés and cheap little restaurants work for snacks, and it's possible to pick up some fresh fruit and vegetables at the market, but for something more substantial try **Mat'am Salsabil** (*Sharia al Corniche;* `\` *081 62 48 63;* $$$) generally agreed to be the best place in town, offering set menus as well as grilled à la cartes.

WHAT TO SEE As far as international tourists on a short tour are concerned, the most important things to see are the Graeco-Roman sites of Apollonia, about 50km to the southwest, and Cyrene, about 75km to the west. Locally, the city is worth a brief exploration, with highlights that include the old town, with the modern Masjed as Sahab Mosque and a covered souk. There's also a museum that displays traditional houses and décor. The old fort built by the Americans during the first war against the Barbary pirates still stands and is a popular attraction. Outside the city, the Wadi Derna is a dry riverbed that still manages to keep some greenery, as well as grow bananas. The beaches between the cliffs are a major visitor draw, while the caves within them are also intriguing, said to have been the refuge for fleeing Christians. An unusual site for Libya, with its 90% desert environment, is a small waterfall, located about 8km to the south, springing from water originating further up the valley.

HOW TO GET TO THE ROMAN SITES To get to the extraordinary site of Cyrene and the lovely seaside remains at Apollonia, it's probably best to join a tour. The cruise ships that stop here do so only to make these visits. For Cyrene, shared taxis go to Al Bayda, and from there, a regular service goes back and forth to Shahat, the small town where the site is located. To Apollonia, taxis do the route from Shahat/Cyrene to Susa, the village by the Mediterranean where the site lies.

The last large population centre in the east of Libya before reaching the Egyptian border, Tobruk lies in an area of relatively little interest. Yet it remains legendary and on the tourist route, due to its role in many of the defining battles during the North African campaigns of World War II. Close to the prize of the Suez Canal, eastern Libya was the edge of Axis-controlled North Africa. Just beyond was Egypt, still British controlled and in the hands of the Allies. For more than three years, from 10 June 1940 until 13 May 1943, North Africa was at war, and many of the confrontations focused in this area. Most foreigners who come here do so to visit the various national cemeteries of the soldiers who lost their lives here, or to see the last physical reminders of World War II, in the shape of the concrete trenches or the rusty barbed wire, still marking the warfare sites. For more information on the history of Libya's role in World War II, see *Post-Roman history* in *Chapter 25*, page 327 and the box on *The war in Africa*, pages 330–1.

HISTORY Tobruk's navigable bay was spotted by the ancient Greeks, and travellers came over from Greece and settled here, naming their colony Antipyrgos ('from Pyrgos', a city on the island of Crete). Despite the port's potential, it seems that agriculture was the main impetus for establishing an enclave. The Romans took over, recognising the military importance of the border location, something that was to be repeated 2,000 years later. After the Arab invasion, the location was a pit stop for travellers plying their wares along the routes of the caravan, heading from both central and southern Africa to the coast, and the east and west of the continent. The city became Italian in 1911, when Italy took over 'the protection' of Libya. It was for its part in World War II, however, that Tobruk became immortalised.

GETTING THERE AND AROUND Cruise ships may stop here, and shore excursions include visits to the sites. Land-based tours fly to Benghazi and continue the distance by coach or car. The coast road is pretty, and passes near the ancient sights of Cyrene and Apollonia *en route*. The much faster route across the desert is dead straight, speeding along the 375km to Ajdabiya, south of Benghazi, with nowhere of interest other than the future route of the Great Man Made River. However, it's a quick way to get to the next major port of call. Buses and shared taxis do the routes and it's feasible to cross into Egypt from here. The reverse is trickier, as visas for Libya are not issued at the border. There might also be flight arrivals in the future, but at the moment, the airport is closed. To get around town, and the cemeteries, private taxis are the way to go. Ask for help from your accommodation or tour guide.

WHERE TO STAY

Al Masera Hotel (153 rooms) Albahr St; ☎ 087 62 57 72. The biggest & priciest hotel in Tobruk, the accommodation is looking a bit long in the tooth, but still has all the tourist facilities, including fairly good bedrooms. $$$

Qartage Hotel Al Da'airy; ☎ 087 62 04 41; www.qartagehotel.com. A couple of kilometres outside the town on the main road, this place has a 3-star rating, which includes reasonable rooms, as well as a restaurant. $$

WHERE TO EAT As usual, there's always the option of eating and drinking in the cheap cafés and restaurants scattered about the town, such as:

Mat'am al Khalij Shariya al Jamahiriya; m 0925 785344; ⊙ daily for lunch & dinner. Fish, grilled meat, pizzas plus other favourites are on offer at

this harbourside venue, generally agreed to be the preferred option in town. $$$

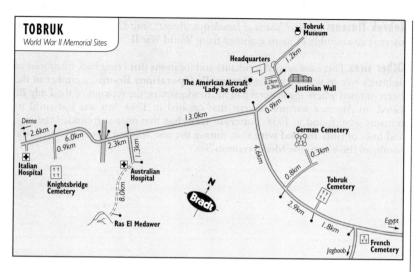

TOBRUK
World War II Memorial Sites

Tobruk Museum

Headquarters · 1.2km

The American Aircraft
'Lady be Good' · 0.2km 0.3km · Justinian Wall

0.9km

13.0km

Derna
2.6km

6.0km
0.9km

2.3km

1.3km

German Cemetery

0.3km

Italian
Hospital

Knightsbridge
Cemetery

8.0km

Australian
Hospital

4.6km

0.8km

Tobruk
Cemetery

N

Bradt

2.9km

Ras El Medawer

1.8km

Egypt

Jagboob

French
Cemetery

WHAT TO SEE Not the cheeriest of places, what the majority of visitors come to see are the war graves. Most people search out someone in particular, and the different cemeteries are named and classified by the predominant nationality buried within them. Unless especially keen, or you know a lot of soldiers from different countries who fought and died in the area, it's not necessary to visit all of them.

Knightsbridge (Acroma) Cemetery *(about 25km west of the city)* Containing 3,649 graves, 986 of unknown soldiers, this is one of the largest of the burial sites. Most of the occupants are British, although there are up to 12 other nationalities laid to rest here, all of whom fought for the Allies. This memorial is located where the battle took place.

Australian (Fig Tree) Hospital On the way back to Tobruk, the hospital lies 12km east of the Knightsbridge Cemetery, and then 1.7km south at the sign. Named after the fig tree that covered a cave in the area, this spot was a short distance from the field of war, and the wounded were carried to this medical facility for treatment.

Tobruk (Commonwealth) Cemetery *(about 7km south of the city)* There are 2,479 burial plots containing mostly Australians, but also others from the Commonwealth nations, as well as Poles.

German Cemetery *(around 3km south of the city, off the border road)* The remains of around 7,000 German soldiers taken from the battlefields extending from Tripoli in the west to Salum, Egypt, in the east, are placed in this castle-like two-storey construction. Their names are written inside on the walls in mosaic.

French Cemetery *(about 10km south towards Jagboob)* French as well as Algerian and Moroccan soldiers are buried here, most of them killed in the Battle of Bir Hakim, which took place around 80km to the southeast.

Greek Cemetery *(outside the city on the Ajdabiya desert road)* This small burial site contains 36 Greek soldiers who were killed by fire from German aircraft. There are also others of the same nationality interred in Tobruk Cemetery.

Tobruk Museum (*north of Sharia al Jamahiriya, about 0.5km; LYD3*) Not often open, there is an assembly of items gathered from World War II.

Other sites There are several remnants and locations that bring back memories of Tobruk's role in war, including **Rommel's Operations Rooms**, a bunker in the heart of town where the general had his headquarters; the remains of the ***Lady Be Good***, an America wartime aircraft that crashed in 1943, but was lost until its remains were found in 1958; **concrete trenches** that once surrounded the city; and lines of rusty **barbed wire** that, during the war, reached from Jagboob in the south, all the way to the Mediterranean Sea.

28

Tripoli

Telephone code 021

Libya's pretty and relatively small capital is an amiable place, situated on the Mediterranean Sea in the greener and wetter part of the country. With a population of around a million and three-quarters, nearly 25% of the country lives within this urban area. The city lies in the far northwest of the country, not far from the Tunisian border. Resting on a large bay that encouraged the development of a large modern harbour, Tripoli takes in all sorts of cargo, as well as cruise ships. Traditionally a convenient stop on the trading routes for all points of the compass, the city benefited by its position. Today, as one of the main depots for a country predominantly dependent on foreign export, the centre remains an important commercial focus.

Known locally by its Arabic name of Tarabulus, mostly to distinguish it from Tripoli in Lebanon, the city enjoys a Mediterranean climate. There's a seaside feel about the place, enhanced by the architectural traces of the different civilisations that have passed through, including the Italians, the penultimate colonists (the British held the place briefly after World War II and before independence). The new city has an open feel, as compared with the old, particularly in the medina. Between the two is a large open space, the Green Square, also known as Marytr's Square, created after the 1969 revolution, a good interface to stroll around, people-watch and catch the feel of the city. Also nearby is the Jamahiriya Museum, an excellent and modern museum exhibiting Libya's distant and more recent past, with a particularly good collection of items gathered from the best of the country's Roman sites.

For the moment, Tripoli retains the sense of being just slightly behind the times, with tourism not very evident, and people amazingly friendly. The buildings are still a little bit rundown, and there are no chain enterprises, either in fast-food joints or major shopping outlets. Evidence of the country's incredible wealth is beginning to show, with the framework of future high-rise buildings popping up everywhere. Parts of the city look like a construction site. As money flows into the capital things will no doubt change very drastically. For the moment, Tripoli feels like a delightful secret, aided by the sense of privilege if you're lucky enough to get a visa to enter. Try to visit before affluence transforms it.

HISTORY

Tripoli was founded by the Phoenicians sometime around 600BC and given the name Oea. Virtually on the front line of the empire-building struggles between the Greeks in the east and the Carthaginians in the northwest, the city's loyalties switched from one to the other, finally settling into becoming a Punic city. As part of the Carthaginian Empire, Oea was claimed by the Romans after the Punic Wars, and was renamed Regio Syrtica, or the region of the Syrticans (Berbers). As the city thrived through the centuries, two neighbouring cities

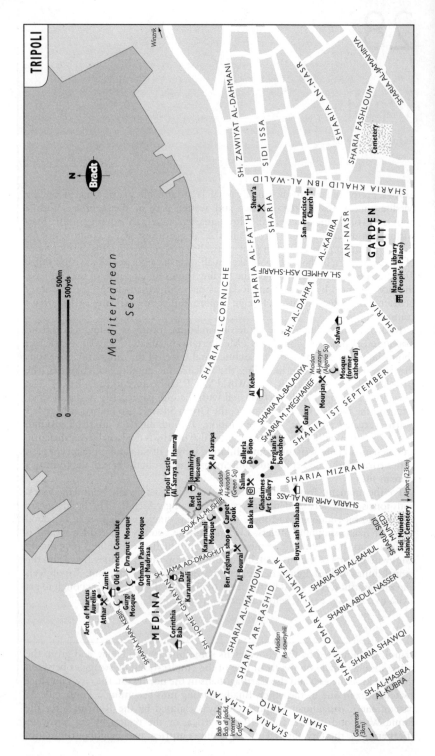

TRIPOLI

Mediterranean
Sea

Winzrik

0   500m
0   500yds

N

SHARIA AL-CORNICHE

MEDINA

Arch of Marcus
Aurelius
Athar ✕ Zumit
        Old French Consulate
Gurgi Draqnut Mosque
Mosque
Othman Pasha Mosque
and Madrasa

Corinthia Dar
Bab Karamanli

SH. JAMA AD-DRAGHUT

SHARIA HARA KEBIR

SHARIA HARA GHARYAN

SH. HOMET GHARYAN

Karamanli
Mosque

SOUK AL-MUSHIR

Carpet
Souk

Tripoli Castle
(Al Saraya al Hamra)

Red
Castle

Jamahiriya
Museum

✕ Al Saraya

As-sadah
Al-kradroh
(Green Sq)

Salim
Bakka Net ⓔ ✕

Ghadames
Art Gallery

Galleria
De Bono

Fergiani's
bookshop ●

✕

Al Kebir

SHARIA AL-BALADIYA

SHARIA M. MEGHARIEF
Maidan
Al-Jezayir
(Algeria Sq)
Mourjan ✕

Galaxy

SHARIA IST SEPTEMBER

Mosque
(former
cathedral)

Safwa

SH. ZAWIYAT AL-DAHMANI

SH. AHMED ASH-SHARIF

SHARIA AL-FAT'H

SHARIA

SIDI ISSA

Shera'a ✕

San Francisco ✝
Church

AL-KABIRA

AN-NASR

SHARIA KHALID IBN AL-WALID

SHARIA AN-NASR

SHARIA FASHLOUM

SHARIA AL-JAMAHIRIYA

Cemetery

**GARDEN
CITY**

National Library
(People's Palace) ⊞

SH. AL-DAHRA

SHARIA

Ben Zegiana shop ●
Al Bourai ✕

SHARIA AL-MA'MOUN

SHARIA AR-RASHID

Maidan
As-sawceyhili

SHARIA TARIQ

SHARIA AL-MA'AN

Bab al Bahr,
Bab al Jadid,
Internet
Cafés

Gargeresh
(3km)

SHARIA OMAR AL-MUKHTAR

Buyut ash Shabaab

SHARIA AMR IBN AL-ASS

SHARIA MIZRAN

Sidi Munedir
Islamic Cemetery

Airport (23km)

SHARIA SIDI AL-BAHUL

SHARIA SIDI
AL-MUNEDI

SHARIA ABDUL NASSER

SHARIA SHAWQI

SH. AL-MASIRA
AL-KUBRA

Bradt

appeared, Sabratha and Leptis Magna, and by AD200, the province became known as Regio Tripolitania (region of the 'Three Cities') with the 'Regio' later dropping out of common usage. Although all three cities fell prey to earthquakes and invasions, Oea was the only one to remain continuously inhabited throughout the centuries. Good for the city but bad for the archaeologists, very little in the way of buildings and artefacts can be found of Tripoli's previous incarnations as compared with the almost perfectly preserved remains of the other two ancient sites.

After the Arab invasion in AD669, the city's fortunes followed those of the region after which it was named, Tripolitania: ruled by the Fatimids then other dynasties, the Spanish taking over in about 1500. Finding the locals and burgeoning piracy traffic too difficult to handle, they passed it over to the Knights of St John in Malta in 1523. The new owners hung on to their prize for just under 30 years, but during this time left a lasting souvenir, in the construction of their defences. The Red Castle, Al Saraya al Hamra, still stands in the centre of Tripoli and houses the Jamahiriya Museum. The Barbary pirates, in league with their new allies, the Ottomans from Turkey, forced the knights out and oversaw their profitable trade for about the next 150 years. In 1711 a new regime started when Ahmd Karamanli, an officer descended from the Turks, killed the sitting governor and took on the role of head of government. Creating a semi-autonomous region, he also established the next dynasty, which lasted until 1835. During this period, the Barbary wars were fought (see page 327). The Ottomans returned to power afterwards and remained until the Italians declared war on them in 1911, finally ceding governmental, if not religious, control. Italy kept the colony until 1943, when the Axis powers lost their position in North Africa during World War II, after which the British took over. The UK held on until Libya achieved its independence in 1951. After various international incidents sanctions were finally lifted. As relations with the rest of the world normalise, and money as well as international commerce and industry flood into the country, Tripoli will benefit enormously.

GETTING THERE AND AROUND

BY AIR TIP, Tripoli International Airport (*about 30km south of the city;* ☎ *022 65 05 026*) has one terminal that handles both foreign and domestic traffic. As transportation for non-Libyan visitors must be pre-arranged, it's almost certain that you won't need to take advantage of the waiting taxis.

BY BUS There are good bus services from the capital to the larger cities of the country. They leave from either the Tunis Garage at the southwestern edge of the medina, or the Dahra Station to the east of the city. Distances can be long and it might be easier to fly.

BY TAXI Shared taxis also do journeys to the big cities. Long-distance taxis leave from the Tunis Garage. Local taxis can be found on most of the streets, distinguished by the patchy black and white motif and the international yellow sign on the roof. Their cost is reasonable, around LYD2, and if you are staying on a ship, it's definitely worth using them to get from the centre to the port.

BY CAR Although not a large place, Tripoli does have a rather complex one-way system that must be respected. Accept that sometimes you might have to drive past your destination to return to where you want to go. Much of the medina is pedestrian only, and you'll need to leave the car at the edge to explore within.

Car hire

🚗 **Avis** (airport) ☎ 021 3362072; (town) Tajura Rd, Ainzara Furnag; ☎ 021 3362072; El Fateh Building 40, Ground Floor, Al Fatah Tower; ☎ 021 336 2072

🚗 **Europcar** (airport) ☎ 091 3753488; (town) Mogama Shati No 37, Ground Floor, Hay Al-Andalus; ☎ 021 4780906

TOURIST INFORMATION

There is no official tourist board within Libya or in other countries. As tourists must already have their itineraries organised via a recognised tour operator, the government seems to believe there isn't much demand for a separate agency. In the tourist bureau's absence, local tour companies are willing to fill the gap. They also act as travel agencies, and can arrange flights, internally and abroad.

TOUR OPERATORS

There are lots of travel agencies around, especially in Tripoli, but the following are recommended.

Alawy Tours PO Box 8271; ☎ 021 3343440; www.alawytours.com
Arkno Tours 38 Abd al-Rahman al-Kawakabi St, Garden City; ☎ 021 4444044; e info@arkno.com; www.arkno.com. They also have offices in England & Canada.

Fezzan Tours I-Kuwait St, Al-Fonoon Wa Alsanaiaa Bldg No 17; ☎ 021 3339815; www.fezzantours.com
Libtra Tours PO Box 972; ☎ 021 4770469; www.libtratours.com
Winzrik 32–37 7th November St & 52 Al Shatt St; ☎ 021 3611123; www.winzrik.com

WHERE TO STAY

Tripoli's accommodation profile is changing rapidly. With money and businessmen pouring in, new buildings are literally on the rise. More hotels are required and at least eight new ones under the auspices of private firms are already under construction. The older ones still exist and are getting a bit faded despite their former luxury status. The Intercontinental, Marriott, Meridien and Radisson should be opening late 2009.

TOP END

🏠 **Corinithia Bab Hotel** (334 rooms) Souk Al Thulatha, Al Gadim; ☎ 021 3351990; www.corinthiahotels.com/hotel.asp?h=6&l=1. The best hotel in town, owned by a private company & the one where top businessmen & diplomats stay (the American Embassy is located here), this new hotel competes with both the quality, & price, of luxury 5-star complexes around the world, but has almost total occupancy most of the time. $$$$$+
🏠 **Plasma Hotel** (30 rooms) Omar al-Mukhtar St No 428; ☎ 021 333 1172; www.plasmahotel.net. This

new non-smoking hotel is a short walk from Green Square & has all modern facilities, inc satellite TV & Wi-Fi. $$$$
🏠 **Zumit** (14 rooms) Marcos Orioles Arc Sq; ☎ 021 3342915; www.zumithotel.com. A full service hotel located within a lovely courtyarded Ottoman building, this 4-star accommodation is not only charming, but is situated in the medina, right next to Tripoli's best Roman ruin, the Arch of Marcus Aurelius. $$$$

MID-RANGE

🏠 **Al-Okhowa** (72 rooms) Al-Rifa'i St, off Omar al-Mokhtar St; ☎ 021 3332191; www.okhowahotel.com. Another full-service modern hotel located close to the centre, complete with coffee shop & restaurant.

$$$. Its sister hotel, **Addeyar** (Jamil St; ☎ 021 3343021), is around the corner, has similar facilities & is slightly cheaper.

🛏 **Bab al Bahr** Sharia al Corniche; ☎ 021 3350676. Trying to be a bit of a resort, this hotel is not only situated next to the sea, but also has a swimming pool & 3 restaurants. It's a popular place for tour groups, but not up to the standards of the better hotels. It's scheduled to be replaced by a German-built hotel complex in 2012. $$$

🛏 **Safwa** (23 suites) Baladiya St, opposite the UN Mission HQ; ☎ 021 3334422; www.safwahotel.com. Friendly & very comfortable, this 4-star hotel is a little off the tourist track, but not far from the business district. $$$

BUDGET

🛏 **Bab al Jadid** Sharia al Corniche; ☎ 021 3350731. To the west of the medina, & along the seaside, this cheaper option fills up quickly, but the less-than-great upkeep explains its low price. $

🛏 **Buyut ash Shabaab** (HI youth hostel) (68 beds) 69 Amru Ben Al-aas St; ☎ 021 4445171. Basic, but OK, these rooms are the cheapest in the city, although they might be nicer if you're not travelling solo (especially for women). $

✖ WHERE TO EAT

More and more restaurants are popping up, as higher income means the locals can afford to eat out more often, and the number of visiting foreigners is increasing. Hanging around Green Square people-watching is the thing to do, whether eating a proper meal or simply having a quick snack or coffee, and there are lots of little places to linger. Hidden within the medina are some more traditional places, while the big hotels, particularly the Corinith Bab, is where the best and priciest meals are served.

✖ **Corinithia Bab Hotel** www.wyndham.com/hotels/TIPBA/dining/main.wnt. There are 5 places to eat here. The **Fes** restaurant serves Moroccan(!) à la carte dishes & has great views from the 26th floor. ⏱ daily for dinner ($$$$$). The **Venezia** pays tribute to the city's Italian heritage in a very upmarket way, with both à la carte & buffet meals. ⏱ daily for lunch & dinner ($$$$). The **Orient Asian** features Indian à la carte dishes ⏱ daily for dinner ($$$$). **La Valette** serves 3 buffet meals a day. ⏱ daily ($$$–$$$$), while the **Tripoli Café** is good for snacks & late afternoon tea almost anytime ($$–$$$).

✖ **Al Saraya** Green Sq; ☎ 021 3334433; ⏱ 12.00–01.00 daily. Upstairs, the place serves expensive meals, featuring Lebanese (ie: from the *other* Tripoli!) food, & is popular with the more affluent locals. Downstairs, snacks & pastries are available & nice to have in the garden. $$–$$$$

✖ **Athar** Next to the Arch of Marcus Aurelius, Medina; ☎ 021 4447001; www.ghazalagroup.com/athatrindex.htm. This place is not only a very good restaurant, serving traditional fish & meat dishes, but also sits adjacent to the city's prime Roman site. The location is particularly nice on a balmy night, when the arch is lit. Part of the Ghazala Group. $$$

✖ **Shera'a** Alshat Alkadim Rd; ☎ 021 7122534; www.ghazalagroup.com/sheraindex.htm. Under the same auspices as the Athar. The wide-ranging choices include the usual Libyan dishes, from fish to meat, but also pasta; not suprising, perhaps, as it's located next to the Italian Embassy. $$$

✖ **Mourjan** Meydan al Jazayir; ☎ 021 3336307. Fish dishes in this popular locale are presented on both the buffet & set menus. $$$

✖ **Al Bourai** Sharia Jama ad Draghut; ☎ 021 4443556; ⏱ lunch Sat–Thu. Just inside the southern edge of the medina walls, the local specialities here are particularly good, & the atmosphere is fun, too, although the venue is open only for the midday meal. $$–$$$

✖ **Galaxy** Sharia 1st September; ☎ 021 4448764. Another one of the better, highly recommended spots, the food served upstairs is well presented, while downstairs, quicker cuisine is on offer. $$–$$$

✖ **Salim** Green Sq; ☎ 021 3333024. This upstairs restaurant–downstairs café is one of the best of the cheaper places around the central square, serving the usual snacks below & basics above. $–$$$

ENTERTAINMENT AND NIGHTLIFE

As alcohol is forbidden in Libya (even foreign cruise ships have to lock up their liquor cabinets while in port), the drinking scene consists of sipping tea or coffee. It's especially nice to do so in the cafés around the Green Square. There are also teahouses and gardens throughout the city, where you can also indulge in smoking a *nargileh* (a water pipe filled with fruit-flavoured tobacco, similar to a sheesha or hookah). There are a few cinemas in the city but they tend to play the usual Arabic favourites, most emanating from Egypt. The performing arts scene is not very developed. In other words, there's not very much public nightlife happening in Tripoli.

SHOPPING

Libya does not have the shopping appeal, culture or variety of Morocco and Tunisia. Yet there are souks, especially in the medina, and they remain the best places to shop, both for the assortment of goods and the atmosphere. It's fun to wander through the narrow streets that are laden with the huge collection of items, sometimes with no obvious discernment. The usual North African goods are here, ranging from copper, silver and gold items, to pottery and carpets. A bit of an eye opener are the skins from animals, such as leopard or cheetah, but these furs are more likely to be imported from other parts of Africa, as these creatures are now extinct within Libya. It's hard to find anything unique to the country, as so many goods come from abroad. There seem to be a lot of things to do with camel motifs, whether woven into tapestries, or carved in little effigies. If you want to buy a carpet or some other bit of handicraft, but don't want to brave the onslaught of the vendors, try **Carpet Bazaar – Ben Zeglam Shop** (*Souk al Attara*). Many typical goods are on sale here, such as the eponymous carpets, but also Berber and Touareg traditional pieces, including jewellery and pottery. There might also be a bit more authenticity in the antiques and old curios that appear scattered amongst some of the stalls in the medina and also in the **shops off Green Square**. For something more two-dimensional, the **Ghadames Art Gallery** (*Sharia 1st September*) close to Green Square has visual depictions of both old and new Tripoli on sale, ranging from sketches to photographs, and a few paintings as well. Close by are the **Dar Fergiani Bookshop** (*Sharia 1 September;* ⟍ *021 4444873*) and **Fergiani 2 Bookshop** (*Sharia Mizran*), which carry examples of travel writing from both the distant and more recent past as well as general books on Libya, also in English.

OTHER PRACTICALITIES

EMERGENCY TELEPHONE NUMBERS

Medical ⟍ 021 4445581. It's possible that they won't understand English. As tourists are almost inevitably going to be with a guide, it's best to contact him or her first.

Ambulance ⟍ 021 191

HOSPITALS

✚ Emergency Hospital Second Ring Rd; ⟍ 021 4442555

INTERNET CAFÉS
Libya businesses have more websites than anywhere else in North Africa. Try the following cafés:

🖃 **A–LOL Café** Hay al Andalus, Main St; ☎ 021
4781632
🖃 **Al Khayam** Hay al Andalus; ☎ 021 4774316

🖃 **Bakka Net** Sharia Mizran & Sharia Haity
🖃 **Dakar** Upper Mohammed Magerif St, in front of
the Wahda Bank

POST The main post office is at Maydan al Jezayir.

BANKS Banks and ATMs are at the airport, as well as around Green Square and
Maydan al Jezayir. It's easiest to find a branch of the Masraf al Umma and Masraf
al Jamahiriya banks although there are others. Don't rely too heavily on credit
cards, especially in the souks and markets, and take along cash in US dollars or
euros to facilitate exchange. Only small amounts of Libyan dinar can be taken in or
out of the country. There is a small black market trade, with rates no better than
the banks, but 'open' outside banking hours, if you want to take your chances with
getting a fair exchange.

WHAT TO SEE

AL SARAYA AL HAMRA (RED CASTLE) Housing the impressive Jamahiriya Museum
(see below), the current form of the Red Castle dates back to when the fortification
was constructed by the Knights of St John of Malta. The new owners only lasted a
decade, but the castle still stands. Archaeologists have discovered that the
foundations were built on a Roman construction, and after that an Arab fortress
dating from after the Arab invasion of AD669. The large pool of water in front of
the castle, within the balustrade, is cooling in the summer and offers some lovely
reflections of the buildings behind.

MEDINA Although not very large, this compact old heart of town retains many
features that earmark it as a medina. Completely walled with entrance gates and
narrow, winding streets, and a delightful derelict quality, this labyrinth is just as
much fun to wander around as other North African counterparts. The size makes
it easy to get around. Filled with souks, mosques, older houses and intricate
doorways, about 3,500 people still reside with these ancient barriers, but around
65,000 come to work here. Hidden within its depths, just off the Roman Columns
Crossroad, so called because of the columns recycled into the corners of the
adjacent buildings, is **Dar Karamanli** (see *Museums*, below). Also worth stopping
to take a look at are the mosques. As at the others, non-Muslims are not allowed
in, but you are permitted to take a glance. Found throughout the medina, the more
prominent examples are the Karamanli, the Gurgi, the Ottoman Pasha and
Madrasa, and the Draghut (see map for their locations).

ARCH OF MARCUS AURELIUS Still in the medina and situated at what was the
crossroads of the decumanus and the cardo in the Roman city of Oea, this arch
looks rather weather-beaten and a bit squat from a distance. Named after the
emperor Marcus Aurelius, in power at the time of its construction in AD163-4, it
stands in the centre of a square that's recessed into the ground around it. Oea lay
at this lower level, and over the years continuous habitation caused the city to grow
literally upwards, leaving what was left of the ancient city beneath. This arc is the
only monument of Oea left standing in Tripoli. Just a bit further south down the
street is the **Old French Consulate** (⊕ *09.00–17.00 Sat–Thu; LYD2*). Beautifully
renovated to match its original condition when it was built in 1630, this
courtyarded building full of details was the official residence of the French
consular staff for over three centuries.

GREEN SQUARE This large space acts as a handy landmark separating old and new Tripoli. Significantly larger than its pre-1969 size by virtue of seaside reclamation, the area was renamed Green (the holy colour of Islam), or Martyrs' Square after the revolution. At the beginning of its new guise, it was used as a meeting place for large crowds to gather in support of the new regime. Today it's a very useful reference point, and a popular place to stroll (it's common to see women or families walking here) and the cafés and restaurants that fringe its edges are good places to linger and watch the locals.

THE NEW CITY 'New' is relative and applies mostly to the Italian colonial era. In the area to the east of Green Square, from the harbour to the interior of the city, are several examples of Italian-influenced architecture. Most notable residuals of the period include the **Galleria de Bono** (*Sharia 1st September*), the **former Catholic cathedral** and now the Masjed Jamal Abdel Nasser Mosque (*Maydan al Jezair*), the **National Library** (*Sharia Mohammed Megharief*) and **San Francisco Church**, where mass is still celebrated, primarily for foreigners (*Sharia Khalid ibn al Walid*).

MUSEUMS

Jamahiriya (National) Museum (*Green Sq;* ☎ *021 3330292;* ⊕ *09.00–13.00 & 14.00–17.00 Tue–Sun; LYD3*) The nation's finest museum holds a superb collection of items, displays and artefacts in its 47 galleries. Dealing with all eras of Libyan history, it stretches from the earliest prehistoric period, with samples of rock art, to current-day descriptions of the Great Man Made River. Constructed with UNESCO aid in the 1960s, the layout on four floors and beautiful Islamic architectural detailing throughout make the assembly seem even newer. The collections are extensive and some of the highlights include Greek pieces found in Cyrenaica (rooms 7 & 8); Roman items gathered from Leptis Magna (room 9); and a fascinating collection of images describing Colonel Gadaffi in both his early and later days. You can't miss his green Volkswagen in room 1, in which he drove around, spreading his message to the people.

Dar Karamanli (*Sharia Houmet Gharyan;* ⊕ *09.00–17.00 Sat–Thu; LYD2*) The home of the head of the Karamanli dynasty is in keeping with the typical lavish courtyarded houses of the era's upper class. Now a museum, the rooms have been kept intact and are filled with collections of musical instruments, arms and other items of the time. Displays, including clothing and marriage preparations, show how the tiny proportion of wealthy people lived.

THE ROMAN SITES

Sites charge an entry fee of LYD6, which includes a camera permit.

The three best Roman sites in Libya are not only superb, but might also be the finest in North Africa. Sabratha is the closest to Tripoli, about 65km to the west, and usually the first of the triad viewed by tourists. Leptis Magna is further east, and Cyrene is in Cyrenaica, and their visits come up later in the standard itinerary. All three have been designated World Heritage Sites by UNESCO.

SABRATHA As it hugs the shore, the Mediterranean situation adds to Sabratha's appeal, especially on sunny days when the turquoise of the sea contrasts beautifully with the pink stone of the buildings. The city goes straight up to the water's edge, and probably beyond, as the combination of sea and time have worn away much of the site. There doesn't seem to be a port, and as the proximity to the coast must have been the reason for the settlement's location, the harbour is

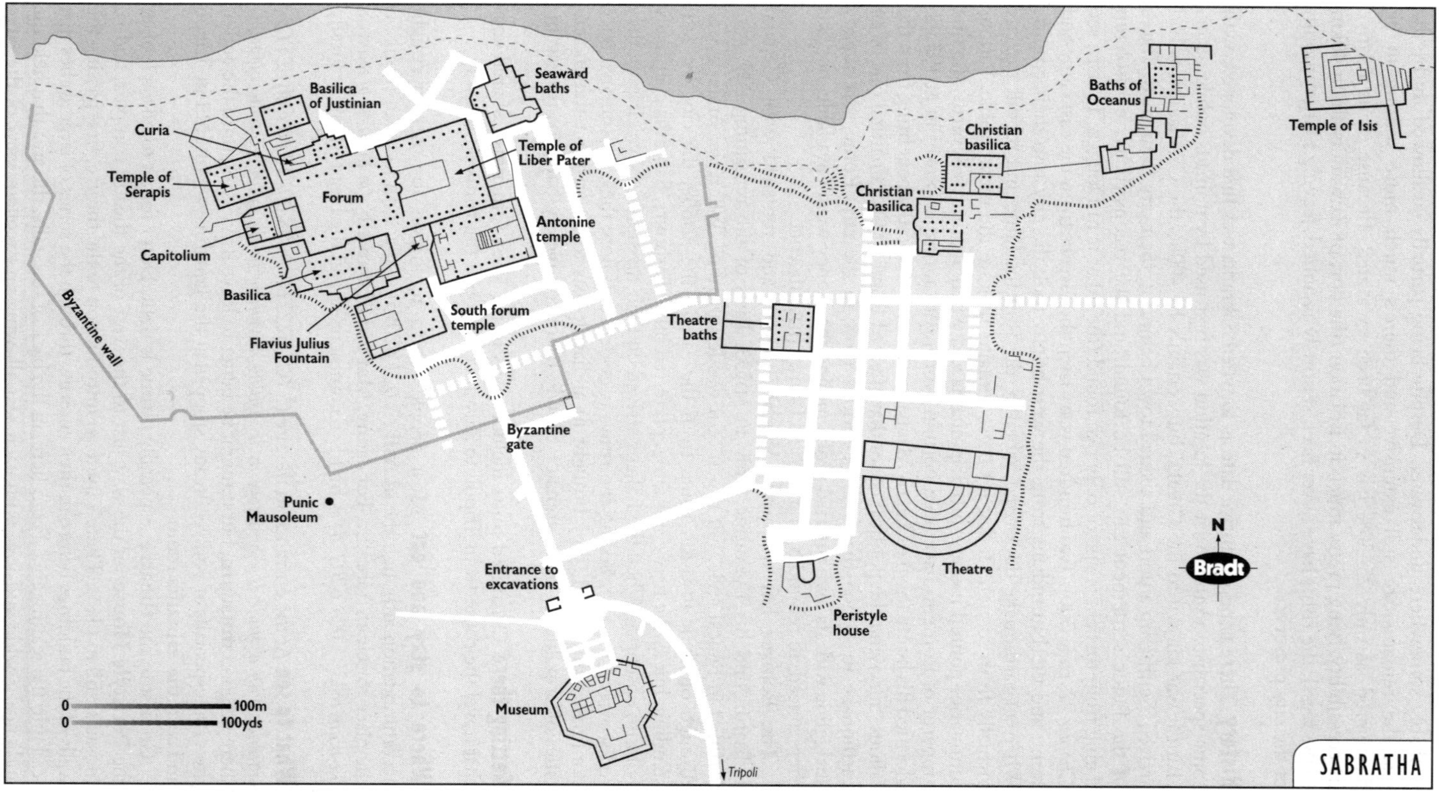

SABRATHA

- Temple of Isis
- Baths of Oceanus
- Christian basilica
- Christian basilica
- Theatre
- Peristyle house
- Theatre baths
- Seaward baths
- Temple of Liber Pater
- Antonine temple
- Basilica of Justinian
- Forum
- South forum temple
- Byzantine gate
- Entrance to excavations
- Curia
- Temple of Serapis
- Capitolium
- Basilica
- Flavius Julius Fountain
- Punic Mausoleum
- Byzantine wall
- Museum
- → Tripoli

N

Bradt

100m
100yds

Libya: Tripoli THE ROMAN SITES

28

353

probably somewhere underwater. Despite being partially swallowed up by the sea, the remains are still extensive and there's much more waiting to be discovered, as only 25–50% has so far been excavated. Because of its relative inaccessibility, lying pretty much in isolation (the port of Zuwara is about 40km to the west), the ruins have never been seriously assaulted, leaving a large amount of the city preserved.

History There is no definitive date as to when Sabratha was first developed, with some specialists arguing that the location was first used by nomads, while others claim it was known to the Greeks, but certainly by 400BC the Carthaginians had arrived. Setting up a port and a small town behind it, their city flourished. Traces of the Punic settlement can still be found, and the reconstructed mausoleum dating from this era is one of only two found (the other is in Dougga, Tunisia; see *Chapter 22*, page 300). Two hundred years later, the Greeks from the east came and went, and the Numidians from the west briefly took the city into their empire. When an earthquake devastated Sabratha, the Romans came and rebuilt the city virtually from scratch. Today, it's these remains that are the most visible. Various luminaries poured money into Tripolitania and when Septimius Severus, the first emperor of Rome to have been born in North Africa, rose to power in AD193, he glorified his home town of Leptis Magna, with nearby Sabratha benefiting from the fallout. Surviving the political crises that affected Rome, it was a natural one of an earthquake in AD365 that dealt a serious blow to the city. Rome was already struggling with its own internal problems and the money wasn't available, nor was there a need, to rebuild Sabratha to its former magnificence.

The Romans left when the Vandals arrived, and returned with General Belisarius and his Byzantine army in AD533. Parts of the remaining city were fortified in typical style, but much of it was left in ruins. When the Arabs passed through on their invasion route from the east in the AD669, the city was still standing, but as the new conquerors preferred other harbours, Sabratha eventually fell into obscurity. When the Italians arrived on their mission to 'save' Tripoli, they rediscovered the site. Seeing the ruins as evidence of how they, as Romans, once dominated the world, they brought in archaeologists to reconstruct the ancient cities of Tripolitania and Cyrenaica. Slowly, if not completely, Sabratha rose again.

Getting there Organised tours include visits to the sites. Otherwise, shared taxis that travel the route from Tripoli to Zuwara can stop at the ruins on the way.

Where to stay and eat Most people return to Tripoli for their overnight accommodation although the **al Asil** (⟍ *021 620959;* $$), with its clean rooms, is the place to stay in Sabratha. For eating, **Mat'am al Bawady** (*to the west of town on the main road;* ⟍ *021 620224*) is highly recommended and the best restaurant locally.

What to see At the entrance to the site (⟍ *021 622214;* ⊕ *08.00–18.00 daily; LYD6; entrance with a guide is mandatory as is visiting anywhere in the country at the moment*) there's a good **museum**, but it might be better to leave its viewing until the end of the visit, especially if you've already stopped at the Jamahiriya Museum in Tripoli and seen the Sabratha room.

Go first to the **theatre**, especially if time is tight. Don't forget to take a look at the **Peristyle House** on the way, just to the west of the theatre complex, and its mosaics, still in place. There's quite an introduction to the theatre, first passing the walls of the buildings before it, then entering through the series of large arches that lead into the seating area. From here, in the back of the stalls, the area that held the audience is wide and low, with each seat allowing an excellent view of the large stage and its enormous backdrop. Rising up in three full storeys, each with a row of complete Corinthian columns, there's a gap in each floor that allows views of the sea behind. There might be more solid theatres in other parts of the Roman Empire, but none is more graceful, or more evocative. At the base of the stage are niches with their complete carvings still in place, something rarely found. The friezes show mythological figures including Hercules and Mercury, characters portrayed on the stage. There are also depictions of the Judgement of Paris and other theatrical scenes. The theatre has been reconstructed to hold 1,500 people, but it's believed that it once could contain up to 5,000. It's extremely difficult to leave such a wonderful place, but there is a great deal more to see in Sabratha, and it makes sense to see how the arena fitted into the context of the city.

Heading towards the sea, the paved road goes in a straight line between the foundations of the houses and passes by the **Temple of Hercules**. Across the way are the theatre baths, with black-and-white patterned mosaics literally on the bathroom floor. At the seafront is a Christian **basilica**, and to the east, the **Baths of Oceanus**. Just a bit further, and certainly worth the trek, is the evocative **Temple of Isis** with its assembly of tall graceful columns prominent against the waves of the sea directly behind. The Egyptian goddess had no Latin equivalent and was worshipped as a deity in her own right. On the other side of the city is the **Temple to Serapis**, another Egypto–Hellenistic god venerated by Ptolemy and his followers. Continuing west, follow the coast and visualise how the city once extended into where the sea is today. The next attraction is the seaward baths, one of the few places where the mosaics, in both black-and-white and coloured patterns, lie at the edge of the water. Take a look at the **communal latrines** with their telltale holes faced in marble. There were statues of the gods positioned alongside; for example, a statue of Venus was found here, to protect the sitters when they were at their most vulnerable point.

The **forum** is on the western side of the site, and the usual assembly of central buildings surround it, including the curia and capitolium. Also here, to the northwest facing the sea, is the impressive **Basilica of Justinian**, built after AD533, during the second, less glorious life of the city. A slender arch still rises among the stumps of the columns. On the east side of the forum are a few pillars left standing from the Temple of Liber Pater (equivalent to Bacchus or Dionysys), a hallowed site never rebuilt after its destruction in the earthquake of AD365. Just to the south, still in the general vicinity of the forum is the **'Antonine' Temple**, dedicated to the emperor Antoninus Pius, or possibly his successor, Marcus Aurelius. Just outside is the **Flavius Julius fountain**, overlooked by the donor's headless statue. Further in the same direction the Byzantine wall comes into view, characteristically distinguished by its solid blocks and entrance gate. The barrier surrounds the smaller city that Belisarius built for protection, and is contemporary with Justinian's basilica. To the west outside the wall, and in one of the residential districts, the tall rocket ship-like structure of the Punic mausoleum rises. There's no indication of who rested inside, but the African god Bes and the Graeco-Roman hero Hercules decorate the outside.

Before departing, leave yourself some time to take a longer look at the **museum**. Not all the best things have been taken away to the National Museum in Tripoli (see page 352), and there are many good items from the site that have travelled as far as this building. The courtyard shows statues found *in situ*, including a headless soldier dressed in full military armour. The largest room features a mosaic that came from Justinian's basilica and takes up the entire floor of this enormous space, while others from the same site are on the walls. Other mosaics from various buildings of the city as well as statues of both mythological and real people fill the rest of the rooms of the museum.

LEPTIS MAGNA (LEBDA, LEPCIS OR LEPKIS) The ruins of this UNESCO World Heritage Site comprise probably the best Roman city remains in North Africa. Only about a third has been retrieved from the earth, but much of that portion is either in excellent condition or has been beautifully revived.

The site is magnificent, managing more than any other Roman location to show how a royal city looked in its prime. With grand boulevards, triumphal arches, a large theatre that looks out to the sea, the remains of a port, a huge circular amphitheatre and even the clearly marked path of a circus, ancient Rome seems to come alive here. Leptis's Punic heritage prevents the idealised grid layout but even so, virtually all the elements that mark a grand settlement of the empire are here. Arguably more than at any other site, it's possible to imagine how Romans got on with their lives, whether entering through the city gates, shopping at the market, hearing the words of the playwright Plautus (c254–184BC) on the stage, or cheering the gladiators in the arena. The seaside location and nearby beaches enhance the pleasure of meandering. Allow yourself at least a long day here.

History The dates of the founding of the original settlement vary. It's most likely that the Phoenicians were sniffing about the location from the beginning of their Mediterranean trading days, perhaps as early as 1100BC. In 1961 diggers from the University of Pennsylvania, dated the city's origins from 500BC, a few hundred years after Carthage was established. There's also debate as to how important the subsequent enclave was, but no doubt commerce thrived here, especially as the Punic capital could be easily reached by sea. Carthaginian until the Romans took over after the Third Punic War in 146BC, the small city remained relatively independent. When the province of Africa was set up, Leptis became a city of the empire and its role as a major trading port began in earnest. Although its position on the edge of Berber lands was potentially dangerous, the city grew in stability, becoming one of Rome's leading North African trade and civil centres. The emperor Hadrian, known for building something in almost every city within his domain, gave Leptis its magnificent baths, which today are perhaps the site's best-preserved and most lavish remains.

When Septimius Severus (see *Chapter 1*, page 12), a local boy, rose to the rank of general in the army and, even grander, was appointed emperor by the might of his military supporters, the city became the focus of importance and funding. Despite its provincial location, Leptis Magna was now the birthplace of the emperor, and the current leader felt compelled to give the place the grandeur it deserved. Enhancing and building, Septimius poured effort into his home town, notably creating the new (Severan) forum and civil basilica, the great arch that greets visitors even today, and many other physical reminders of his reign. The collapse of the Severan dynasty and the Crisis of the Third Century saw the waning of Leptis's prominence. As the city had been boosted artificially during Septimius's reign, it lost its status as subsequent emperors took their place. Although it became the capital of Tripolitania, people were already leaving, and when the earthquake of AD365 hit, the desertion increased. The little remaining was significantly damaged by the Vandals and not long after, the local Berbers saw their chance to invade in the confusion. They raided the city, adding more destruction to the rubble. General Belisarius took back Leptis for the Byzantines, building defensive walls and eventually routing the Vandals, but couldn't bring the city back off its knees. When the Arabs arrived in AD669, they found little resistance in the dwindling vestige of the Roman army that was left. The new invaders stayed around for a few hundred years, but earthquakes and the establishment of more important centres elsewhere eventually led them away, leaving the site to recede into the encroaching desert. By the time the Italian archaeologists arrived in the 1920s, they had to dig the city out to discover its secrets.

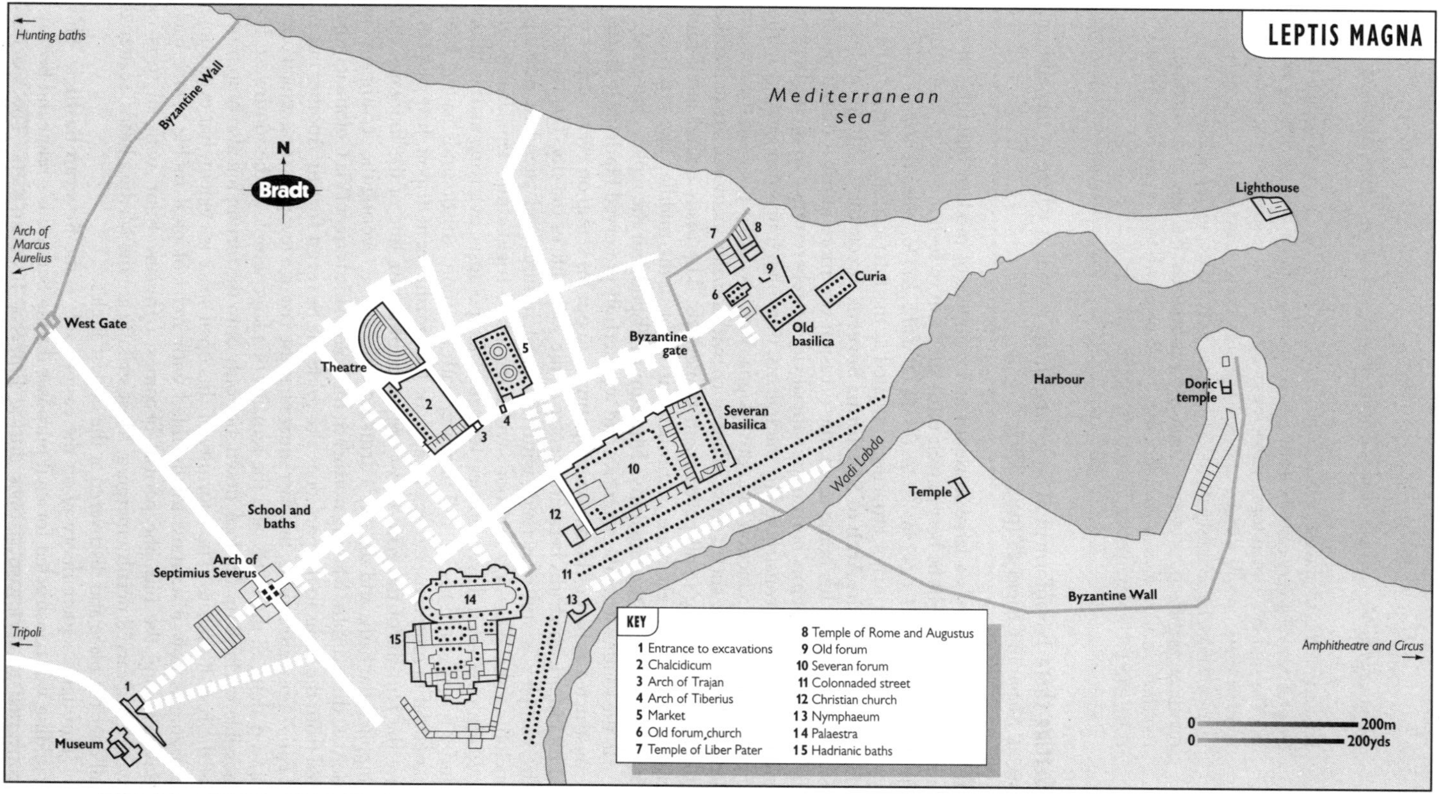

LEPTIS MAGNA

Mediterranean sea

Lighthouse

Harbour

Doric temple

Byzantine Wall

Temple

Wadi Lebda

Curia

Old basilica

Byzantine gate

Severan basilica

N

Brad

Theatre

Market

School and baths

Arch of Septimius Severus

Museum

West Gate

Byzantine Wall

← Arch of Marcus Aurelius

← Hunting baths

Tripoli ↓

Amphitheatre and Circus ↑

0 — 200m
0 — 200yds

KEY

1 Entrance to excavations
2 Chalcidicum
3 Arch of Trajan
4 Arch of Tiberius
5 Market
6 Old forum church
7 Temple of Liber Pater
8 Temple of Rome and Augustus
9 Old forum
10 Severan forum
11 Colonnaded street
12 Christian church
13 Nymphaeum
14 Palaestra
15 Hadrianic baths

Getting there For information on getting there, as well as where to stay and eat, see *Al Khoms* in *Chapter 27* (page 339).

What to see There's a large museum and complex of modern buildings at the entrance, but it might be best to wait until after you've seen the site to visit. Once in the ruins ($\searrow$ *021 624256;* $\oplus$ *08.00–18.00 daily; LYD6; entrance with a guide is mandatory*), the first major attraction, situated at the intersection of the cardo and the decumanus, is the **Arch of Septimius Severus**. Erected in AD203 to celebrate Septimius's visit to his home town, the occasion was more unusual than it might first appear, as emperors born in provincial cities rarely returned to their places of origin. Although reconstructed by the Italians, this solid, four-sided gateway to the city is a superb introduction to Leptis Magna. Very few other places in the ancient Roman Empire give such a sense of entrance, with a major memorial situated at the junction of the city's still paved main boulevards. The roads extend in all four directions and this elaborate monument sits right in the middle. The real friezes from its side are in the Jamahiriya Museum in Tripoli, but the replicas are good.

To the southeast are the extensive and wonderfully preserved **Hadrianic Baths**. Constructed as part of Hadrian's programme to put his stamp on every major city in his empire, the baths became a centre of the social life of the city. The layout of the complex is still preserved, with the usual features and attendant pursuits, including the palaestra, outdoor swimming pool, frigidarium, tepidarium and caldarium rooms and even latrines. Remains of hypocausts, overlying marble floors and a few inscriptions are still in place, with the more artistic finds having been carted off to museums, either in Leptis or the Jamahiriya in Tripoli. Just past here are the remains of the giant two-storey **nymphaeum**, one of the fountains that supplied the baths and the city's drinking water while revering the accompanying deities, the nymphs. Moving northeast, the colonnaded street (Via Colonnata) that led from the baths to the port, goes alongside the **Severan forum**. Another one of Leptis's great attractions, this vast square has the last of a few porticoes, which once spread along all the edges, and the remains of a large temple to the southwest. It's possible to climb up and look down, not only onto the forum, but also onto much of the rest of the site. The enormity of this open space is evident, but even more amazing is how it's almost totally filled with archaeological rubble. Once back down among the bits, the perusal becomes a treasure hunt, with all sorts of wonderful carved details emerging. Most striking are the Medusa heads, scattered all over the place and discovered at the oddest angles.

Through a square doorway on the eastern side is the **Severan basilica**. This building was constructed for civil purposes during Septimius's reign and became converted to ecclesiastical ones during Emperor Justinian's era. The spacious walled and columned ruins that were originally roofed still inspire awe, whether for the might of law or the Church. It's possible to continue northeast along the Via Colonnata to the harbour. Not much is left here, besides a few stones of the lighthouse, as well as some warehouses and a **Temple of Jupiter** on the other side of the *wadi* (dry river bed). The harbour's natural silting-up process increased after Septimius's renovations and gradually the port became unusable, although the layout is still visible. Returning towards the centre, the next series of buildings surround the original forum. Dating from its Punic days, some traces of that era in the form of houses are still being excavated. There are columns strewn about, lying on their sides or reduced to stumps. Surrounding the open space, gradually abandoned after the more fashionable Severan forum was constructed, lay the old original governmental and religious buildings: the curia, the basilica, the Temple of Liber Pater and the Temple of Rome and Augustus. Now, in the midst of what must have been the most intensely occupied part of the city is the extraordinary **market**. The remains of a circular columned structure form the heart, while alongside are the benches of the vendors who once sold their wares. Columns in various states of repair, from bases to partial pillars, lie about in no particular order. Perhaps reflecting the fluid and chaotic nature of a marketplace, there seems to be a jumble of architectural bits and pieces, but the square, complete with yellow/red marble floor tile (perhaps imported from Chemtou in Tunisia; see *Chapter 22*, page 304) is filled with interesting detail. The carvings of two ships, on either side of one of the arches, show one of the methods by which the goods arrived. Just to the east and southeast are the **arches of Tiberius and Trajan**.

From the chalcidium, directly west of the market, the way leads into the **theatre**. Of the stone examples still left from the Roman world, Leptis's is among the largest and oldest, from about AD1, still in existence. It is also one of the best, rising into the hill and sweeping along in a preserved semicircle, looking towards the partially columned stage, with vistas of the Mediterranean Sea stretching out behind. Underneath is a **Punic burial ground**. Leaving the theatre from the seat side, and heading back to Septimius's arch, the school and more baths are to the west. Northwest past the Byzantine wall that later fortified the city, are a couple more sites: the **Arch of Marcus Aurelius**, and much further, the **hunting baths** with their mosaics. The latter can be closed, due to the delicacy of the artwork and the attraction's relative inaccessibility, so make sure they're open before heading out there.

The enormity of the city, believed to have once held as many as 80,000, is evident when searching out some of the further remains. To the east of the port are the **amphitheatre and circus**. This entertainment complex was conventionally outside the city centre, but not as far as it seems today, so that probably the empty space between the venues and the forum had some sort of settlement. It's a long distance to walk and the tours that visit put clients back on the bus to get here. The impressive amphitheatre (⊕ *08.00–18.00; LYD6*) is dug into the earth and well conserved, with its low seats in a wide circle surrounding the central arena. It sits very close to the sea. Even nearer, lying just along the shore, is the track of the circus, still visible in its entirety. It's easy to imagine chariots racing along the 1,100m circumference.

When the visit to the actual ruins is complete, you might want to return to the **museum** (⊕ *08.00–18.00 Tue–Sun*) where there's still a lot of see. The variety and order of the collection bears a resemblance to its larger colleague, the Jamahiriya in Tripoli. Following a specific route, the way on the ground floor runs counter clockwise, while the floor above goes in the other direction. Beginning with the Phoenicians, the route reaches the Romans in room 4 and finally leaves them with the Byzantines in room 21. There's more on Colonel Gaddafi and his achievements in room 25.

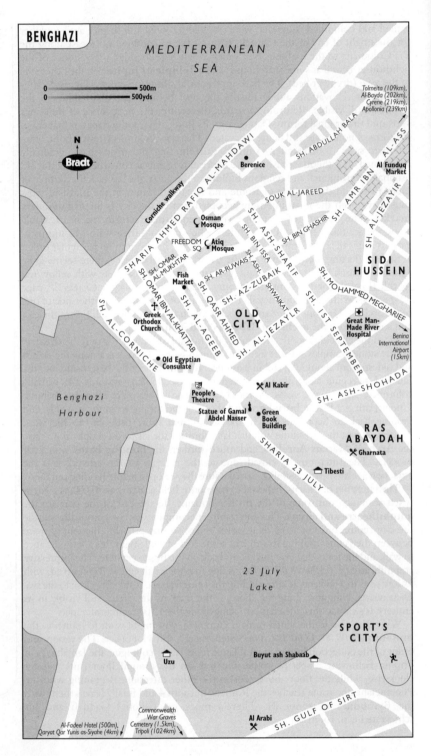

BENGHAZI

MEDITERRANEAN SEA

0 ——— 500m
0 ——— 500yds

N
Bradt

Corniche walkway

Tolmeita (109km),
Al-Bayda (202km),
Cyrene (219km),
Apollonia (239km)

● Berenice

SH. ABDULLAH BALA

Al Funduq
Market

SOUK AL-JAREED

SHARIA AHMED RAFIQ AL-MAHDAWI

☾ Osman
Mosque

SH. AMR IBN

SH. AL-ASS

SH. AL-JEZAYIR

FREEDOM
SQ

✠ Atiq
Mosque

SH. ASH-SHARIF

SH. BIN ISSA

SH. BIN GHASHIR

**SIDI
HUSSEIN**

SH. OMAR
AL-MUKHTAR

Fish
Market ■

SH. AR-RUWAIS

SH. ASH-

SH. AZ-ZUBAIK

SHWAIKAT

SH. MOHAMMED MEGHARIEF

✝ Greek
Orthodox
Church

SH. OMAR IBN ALKHATTAB

SH. QASR AHMED

**OLD
CITY**

SH. AL-JEZAYLR

SH. 1ST SEPTEMBER

✚ Great Man-
Made River
Hospital

Benina
International
Airport
(15km)

SH. AL-CORNICHE

SH. AL-AGEEB

● Old Egyptian
Consulate

SH. ASH-SHOHADA

*Benghazi
Harbour*

🎭 People's
Theatre

✗ Al Kabir

**RAS
ABAYDAH**

Statue of Gamal ⚑
Abdel Nasser

● Green
Book
Building

✗ Gharnata

SHARIA 23 JULY

🏠 Tibesti

*23 July
Lake*

**SPORT'S
CITY**

🏠 Uzu

Buyut ash Shabaab 🏠

🏃

Commonwealth
War Graves
Cemetery (1.5km),
Tripoli (1024km)

Al-Fadeel Hotel (500m),
Qaryat Qar Yunis as-Siyahe (4km)

Al Arabi
✗

SH. GULF OF SIRT

360

29

Benghazi

Telephone code 061

With a population of over 660,000 in the metropolis, and close to a million in the greater area, this city is the country's second largest, situated 650km to the east of the number one, Tripoli. Like its bigger rival, Benghazi sits on the Mediterranean, as well as on the thin strip of fertile soil that receives plenty of rainfall. Tourists arrive here today mostly to see the nearby ruins of Ptolemais, Cyrene and Apollonia, using Benghazi as a base for excursions. There is very little left of the remaining two cities of Teuchira (Tocra), 70km away, and Berenice, which disappeared beneath modern Benghazi.

The modern city itself doesn't have much to offer in the way of visitor attractions. Large and lively, this economic and administrative capital of eastern Libya exists primarily to service the modern needs of its population. The port is one of the country's largest, and industry plays an important part in the well-being of the inhabitants. Convenience rather than beauty is the reason why travellers have an interest in Benghazi.

HISTORY

The city's past is more interesting. By 500BC, the Greeks had already founded Cyrene, moved west and established a new enclave. The settlers named the place Eusperides, possibly as a reference to Hesperides, mythological nymphs who guarded a paradisical garden, supposedly located somewhere in North Africa (see page 143). Eventually abandoned some 300 years later, its position was discovered by the Egyptians and a phoenix rose from the ashes, with the creation of the city of Berenice, or Berenike. Named after the wife of pharaoh Ptolemy III, the next inhabitants remained essentially Greek, as the forces of Alexander the Great had invaded and conquered Egypt almost a century before. Surviving the arrival of the Romans, Berenice rose to prominence, surpassing its other Pentapolis neighbours to become the prime city of Cyrenaica. Thriving during the entire period of the empire's occupation, Barneek, or Barca as it was now known, fell prey around AD429 to the same Vandal forces that had ravaged most of North Africa. By the time the Arabs arrived 150 years later, the unimportant remains of a once great centre were easy enough to take over.

Becoming a trading port once again from around 1400 the place was renamed Bani Ghazi after a local religious figure, Ibn Ghazi. Invaded by the powers of the Ottoman Empire a century later, Bani Ghazi became a stronghold of the Turks. The Karamanli dynasty came and went, leaving the early 19th-century city to be ignored by Istanbul, the authority that was now supposed to be administering it. Due to neglect, the area became one of the most poverty stricken under Ottoman rule, and suffered major outbreaks of the bubonic plague in 1858 and 1874. In 1911, along with the rest of Libya, the occupying Italians arrived and designated Cyrenaica as one of their colonies. The more the Italians suppressed national feeling, the more rebellion grew, and this area of the 'protectorate' turned into a stronghold for the Libyan resistance movement. Omar Mukhtar, (see box on page 328), was one of the leaders. With the setting up of concentration camps for militants, and heavy-handed tactics, the occupiers eventually squashed the rebels. During World War II, due to its location close to the shifting border between the Axis powers in Libya and the Allies in Egypt, Italian-controlled Benghazi bore the brunt of the struggle, with repeated bombing attacks that ravaged the city. Benefiting from subsequent developments, such as becoming part of a united Libya and the discovery of oil, Benghazi's fortunes improved. However, in April 1986 the United States bombed the city in retaliation for terrorist attacks that they believed were instigated by Libyans, including one in West Berlin that killed two American servicemen. Subsequently, things have calmed down with the US, and today peace of some sort has been established.

GETTING THERE AND AROUND

BY AIR Benghazi-Benina Airport (*c20km from city centre;* ✆ *061 9097147*) has a steady stream of both international and domestic arrivals and departures. It's possible to fly to any inland destination that is currently taking tourist traffic, but probably only the one to Tripoli will be of interest to visitors to the Roman coast of North Africa. Transport will be laid on by the tour operator but if it isn't, taxis go into town.

BY BUS There are frequent services to various places throughout the country. They leave from the station, not far from Al Funduq Market.

BY TAXI Shared taxis go along pretty much the same routes and depart from close to the bus station. Consider buying up the empty seats if you're in a hurry. To see some of the ancient sites, taxis from Benghazi will stop at Al Bayda, on the way to Tobruk, and from there, you can pick up a ride to Shahat, for Cyrene. Another taxi continues to Susa, where Apollonia is located.

BY CAR It's most likely that the tour group or private guide will have arranged transport, but if not, it's best to leave the car at the hotel and take advantage of local taxis. For journeys beyond the city, the coast road starts at the border with Tunisia to the west and continues east to Egypt, and includes Tripoli, Al Khoms, Benghazi, Derna and Tobruk *en route*, as well as the sites of Ptolemais, Cyrene and Apollonia. If you are in a hurry to get to Tobruk or Egypt, the desert road that begins at Ajdabaya, about 150km south of Benghazi, speeds across a flat, but fast road.

TOURIST INFORMATION

Libya does not have a national tourist bureau, but travel agencies and tour operators take on the role themselves, offering information and arrangements. For the moment, most organising has already been done by the time of your arrival in Libya and hopefully the company with whom you're travelling can provide details. Before departure, check the internet as there is a great deal of information online.

TOUR OPERATORS

Al Muheet/Ocean Tours PO Box 9225; ✆ 061 9082085; www.almuheettours.net

Libo Tours Sharia Abdul Nasser, Libya Iltaemin Bldg, Eighth Floor, Flat 1; ✆ 061 9094955; www.libotours.com

WHERE TO STAY

There are quite a few places to stay in Benghazi, as one would expect in a big city. Below are a few of the better city hotels.

TOP END

Tibesti Hotel (151 rooms) Sharia Jamal Abdul Nasser; 061 9097177. An excellent full-service hotel situated north of the port, some of the rooms face the lake. $$$

Uzu Hotel (262 rooms) Sharia al Jezayir; 061 9095160. Generally agreed to be one of the city's best hotels, this place located to the south of town offers luxuries & views. $$$

MID-RANGE

Al Fadeel Sharia al Shatt; 061 9099790. Surprisingly good value for this very nice hotel that includes a restaurant, private beach, swimming pool & even some rooms with internet access. $$

BUDGET

Buyut ash Shabaab (HI Youth Hostel) Sport City SW; 061 2234101. Minimal, but clean & well looked after, this youth hostel is a good, very cheap alternative to classier, but more expensive accommodation. $

It's also possible to try some of the family resorts on the beach out of town, such as the **Garunis** (*185 rooms; behind the university;* 061 9095355; $$) that has a range of rooms available, although less so in the summer, when the place is very popular.

WHERE TO EAT

The city has a name for eating well, and there is a large range of small cafés for both having a quick snack and a leisurely tea or coffee. The big hotels, particularly the Uzu and Tibesti, have some fine restaurants with prices to match. In between, for a decent meal, try the following.

Al Kabir Sharia Abdul Nasser; 061 9081692. Turkish cuisine is the speciality in this well-liked & well-attended venue close to the old city centre. $$$
Gharnata Sharia Abdul Nasser; 061 9093509. Another Ottoman-style restaurant that caters a bit better for vegetarians, & has a reasonable set-price option. $$$

Al Arabi Sharia Gulf of Sirt; 061 9094468. With a reputation for being the city's best, this lakesider has seafood on its menu, which is also available at a set price. There's a lower-priced café downstairs & both are open for dinner every day, & lunch except Fri. $$-$$$

SHOPPING

The best place to shop in Benghazi is at the covered market of Souk al Jareed. This large bazaar extends for at least 1km through the centre of the city, from Freedom Square to the Al Funduq Market. The markets here are worth a visit, especially if you're in Benghazi anyway. Featuring traditional crafts, such as weaving, precious metalsmithing, leather working, basket making and pottery moulding, both the craftsmen and their wares are on show here. In addition, there are areas of less touristy items, set out primarily for the inhabitants who shop for daily requirements, and the usual array of clothes, watches and, no doubt, mobile phones are strewn about. It's always fun to wander through markets, and the al Jareed is no exception. Fridays are the busiest days. For more conventional shopping, try Dubai Street, where stores carry goods that are available in most countries. Prices here are high, so it might be better just to window shop.

OTHER PRACTICALITIES

HOSPITALS Allianz Worldwide Care recommends the following hospitals:

✚ **Al Marwah Hospital** Al Fatah St; ☏ 061 2232661;   ✚ **Assafwa Hospital** ☏ 061 2240441
www.almarwahospital.com

INTERNET CAFÉS It's not necessary to list the places where there are internet access venues as they seem to be everywhere. Look for the icons, which you'll soon learn to recognise, or follow the 'Internet' signs that are usually in English. Most of the hotels will also offer internet, some with Wi-Fi.

POST The main post office is on Sharia Omar al Mukhtar, just a bit north of the port.

BANK There's no shortage of places to change money, and most local banks have branches in the centre of town. The Hotel Tibesti has an ATM machine for Visa cards. There's also a black market operating close to the souks that offers exchanges but these rates are probably not much different from the banks, although they do have better opening hours.

WHAT TO SEE

BRITISH COMMONWEALTH CEMETERY (*c5km from the centre in Al Fuwayhat area, across from the children's hospital*) Gathered from the various World War II North African battlegrounds at which they fell, the bodies of 1,700 Allied soldiers of many nationalities are buried here.

BERENICE A few vestiges of the Graeco-Roman city that was part of the Pentapolis and is now mostly buried beneath the modern city still remain. Situated to the north of the city centre alongside the sea, next to the old lighthouse, there are a few bits of rubble that give a hint as to what might still lie below. Indications of two temples, a church, some houses and the city wall have so far been found. Nearby, the still operating lighthouse sits on a nicely paved stretch along the sea.

OTHER SITES There isn't much of a spectacular nature to see in Benghazi, but there are some interesting buildings that can be viewed on a stroll through the city centre. Around Freedom Square, the now empty old town hall shows its Italian origins, with arches and a white façade. It once served as the venue from where the German general Rommel spoke to his army during World War II, and later, the short-reigned King Idris addressed his followers. There are mosques, with the nearby Atiq and Osman being two examples. Some of the other sites of interest include the Old Egyptian Consulate, a period building eroding away nicely, close to Sharia Abdul Nasser, and the domes of a mosque that started off as the city cathedral during the Italian occupation.

THE ROMAN SITES

THE PENTAPOLIS Cyrenaica, the eastern part of Libya, gained its name from its main city Cyrene. Founded by the Greeks in 631BC, gradually other cities rose in the area, each having an economic or strategic reason for its development. The five most important became known by the Greek name of the Pentapolis. There is

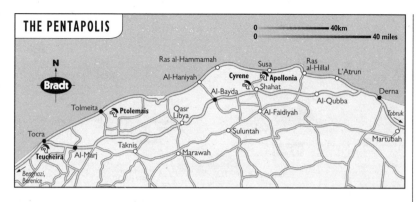

THE PENTAPOLIS

0 ——————— 40km
0 ——————— 40 miles

N

Ras al-Hammamah · Susa · Ras al-Hillal · L'Atrun
Al-Haniyah · Cyrene · Apollonia · Shahat · Derna
Al-Bayda · Al-Qubba
Tolmeita · Ptolemais · Qasr Libya · Al-Faidiyah · Tobruk
Tocra · Suluntah · Martubah
Teucheira · Al-Marj · Taknis · Marawah
Benghazi, Berenice

some confusion as to exactly which ones they were, but Cyrene was first, Apollonia was its port, and Arsinoe, Eusperides and Barca followed. Subsequently names changed, so that Arsinoe became Teucheira and Eusperides became Berenice. Barca's fortunes declined, and the city of Ptolemais took its place. Today, the Pentapolis is considered to be Cyrene, Apollonia (Susa), Ptolemais (Tolemeita), Teucheira (Tocra) and Berenice (Benghazi). The order in which they're listed is based on the importance and quality of the remains that are visible today, with the spectacular site of Cyrene one of the best in the Graeco-Roman world, while the few that remain of Berenice are hidden under the modern city of Benghazi. With the exception of Berenice, already mentioned above (*History*, page 363), they are described below in the same sequence. NB The entry fee of LYD6 includes a camera permit.

Cyrene One of Libya's most magnificent historical monuments, and a UNESCO World Heritage Site, the vestiges of the city that was once capital of the region are not only superb in themselves, but also wonderfully located. High on a hill, slightly inland, the green fields below lead the eye to the blue of the Mediterranean beyond. The layout is a little confusing. The former metropolis exists in layers: historically, from the Greek and Roman eras, and geographically, from the fact it follows contours on the plateau and down the hill. Although walls encompass the whole area, there seem to be three parts: the northeast, where the impressive Temple of Zeus lies; the south, where the centre of the city was; and the Sanctuary of Apollo down the hill past the necropolis where the original Greek city was founded.

History The story of Cyrene's creation in 631BC is legendary, with the Greek who discovered the location, Batthus, nearly as famous as Romulus and Remus, the founders of Rome. Hailing from the island of Thera (today's Santorini), Batthus was told by the Oracle of Delphi to leave his overcrowded home in pursuit of more habitable land across the sea. Stories of how the locals took the arrival of these new colonists are numerous, but eventually Batthus and his refugees found a spring 'where the sky leaks' – or weeps (versions vary), emerging from a cave. Declaring this water source to be Apollo's fountain, the place became the location of the god's sanctuary. Named after one of his nymphs, the new settlement took on the title of Cyrene. The fertility of the soil and the availability of water helped the city grow and it expanded into one of the most important in the Greek world. Its agriculture, which included grain, fruit and silphium (see box below), as well as animal husbandry, meant the large population could be supported.

Batthus's royal dynasty continued for almost two centuries until believers in the Greek concept of democracy overthrew it, replacing the monarchy with a council of

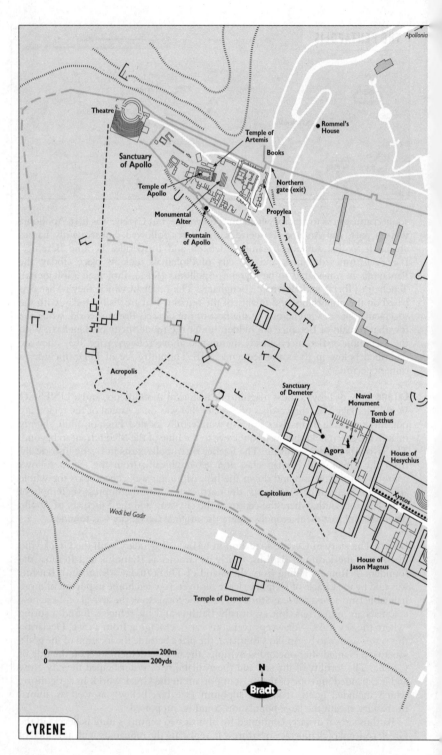

Apollonia

Theatre

Sanctuary
of Apollo

Temple of Artemis

Books

Rommel's
House

Temple of
Apollo

Northern
gate (exit)

Monumental
Alter

Propylea

Fountain
of Apollo

Sacred Way

Acropolis

Sanctuary
of Demeter

Naval
Monument

Tomb of
Batthus

Agora

House
of Hesychius

Capitolium

Xystos

Wadi bel Gadir

House of
Jason Magnus

Temple of Demeter

0   200m
0   200yds

N

Bradt

CYRENE

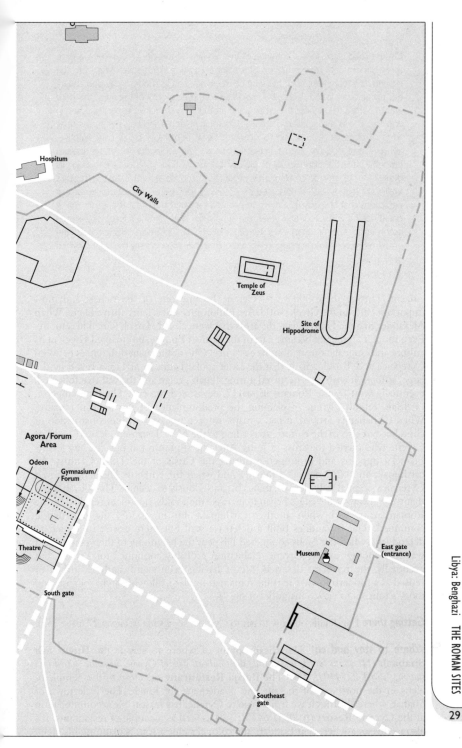

Hospitum

City Walls

Temple of
Zeus

Site of
Hippodrome

Agora/Forum
Area

Odeon

Gymnasium/
Forum

Theatre

Museum

East gate
(entrance)

South gate

Southeast
gate

On the road close to the entrance of the remains of the city of Cyrene is a large three-dimensional representation of silphium. Looking like a stalk rising from the ground, this fennel-like plant has long been extinct, and its modern-day descendant has never been found. Incredibly important to the economy of the area, this herb was exported throughout the empire and attributed with many properties. Used in cooking, it was also applied medicinally, combating and alleviating symptoms of all sorts of diseases. It was said to offer additional benefits, such as contraceptive, abortive and possibly even narcotic functions. The attribution of these qualities probably gave the plant sexual or pleasurable associations, no doubt enhancing its desirability. In any case, silphium's production was so essential to the region's livelihood that it was immortalised on a coin of the realm (one of the few actual depictions that still exists). Grown in profusion around the area, it appears that it could not be cultivated, and when the supply ran out, Cyrene's fortunes suffered accordingly. The historian Pliny alleged that the last example was given to the emperor Nero in the first century AD, although other accounts say the plant survived until 300.

citizens. During these 300 years, Cyrene became one of the richest and most important cities in the Greek world. Art, philosophy and science thrived here. When Alexander marched into Egypt, the areas that were already Greek joined his empire. Even though Cyrenaica became part of the Roman Empire, it remained Greek in its culture and language throughout its existence. One of the main differences between Cyrenaica and Tripolitania is that the latter spoke Latin. In AD115, a revolt by the large, affluent Jewish class occurred during Trajan's reign and the war that followed, eventually won by the Romans in AD117, devastated the city. The next emperor, Hadrian, rebuilt Cyrene, explaining the predominance of the Roman remains. When Christianity arrived, it had a major impact, not only in the construction of churches but also in the culture. According to the New Testament, it was Simon of Cyrene who carried the cross of Jesus. After the silphium ran out, the city lost its financial impetus and prominence during the Crisis of the Third Century. An earthquake in AD262 damaged the city, and when the emperor Diocletian moved Cyrenaica's capital to Ptolemais, things began seriously to decline. The Libyan tribes that were always at the edges began to increase their raids, no longer repelled by the Roman army, and when another earthquake hit in AD365, the destruction continued. The Byzantines built a defensive wall but there wasn't much left to defend, and when the Arabs conquered Egypt at the beginning of their conquest, it was easy enough to take Cyrene. Habitation probably continued for a while, but eventually, the residents deserted. Never having been significantly disturbed or reused as a modern town, the ruins remained in place, allowing archaeologists and today's tourists to view a magnificent site.

Getting there For details on how to get to Cyrene, see *Derna* (Chapter 27, page 343).

Where to stay and eat The cheap option of where to stay is the **Buyut ash Shabaab** (*HI youth hostel, just outside the southeast gate of Cyrene, near the shared taxi station;* \ *061 2234101;* <$). The **Barqa Restaurant** sits close to the Temple of Zeus in the northeast of the site and is adequate for lunch. The little town of Shahat, where shuttles leave from to go to Cyrene, has reasonable accommodation at the **Cyrene Resort** (m *0851 64391;* $$) as well as a couple of restaurants. It's also in this area where Saif Gaddafi, the colonel's eldest son, is planning his green carbon-neutral eco-friendly tourist resort. However, it's likely to be some time before his complex welcomes visitors.

What to see The area of Cyrene's excavations covers more than 1km² and includes a change in elevation (⊕ *May–Sep 07.30–18.00 daily; Oct–Apr 08.00–17.00; LYD6; a guide is required*). Tour transport tends to drop participants at the southeast end and meet them again at the northern gate down the hill. Taxis take a similar route. The description below follows the same direction.

Normally, museums are recommended after the visit, but as this one, the **Cyrene Sculpture Museum**, sits at the eastern entrance, it's worth making a quick stop here first. Not too large to handle, especially if you're anxious to visit the attractions outdoors, the displays show off some very good examples of the range of eras, from Kouros statues dating from the early Greek era to mosaics from the height of the Roman. There's a beautiful statue of the Three Graces that rivals anything the Victorians could produce, as well as portraits of various deities and personages from both periods. Intriguing, and somewhat different, are the idealised statue of Alexander the Great and an enormous marble toe from the eponymous figure that once stood within the Temple of Zeus.

Next, the gigantic **Temple of Zeus** dominates the view just to the north of the museum. Originally constructed c500BC, larger than the Parthenon in Athens, but rebuilt soon after its desecration after the Jewish Revolt, this sacred site has most of its columns still in place. Zeus's toe in the museum makes it easy to imagine how big the central effigy was. Nearby was the site of the hippodrome.

From here, the main centre of the upper town is to the west. The **gymnasium/forum**, was used as the first by the Greeks, and converted to the second by the Romans. Tall columns lining the square are still in place next to solid walls, giving the place a somewhat intimidating and closed-off feeling. The *xystos*, or (no longer) covered walkway used by the athletes, is just alongside. On the outside of the complex is the *skyrota*, the **main street**, flanked with square pillars adorned with figures. Within the forum, a little to the north, and initially a bit hard to spot due to it being inset, is the **odeon**. Differentiated from a theatre by its smaller size and lack of roof, this open-air little venue is one of the best of its type in the Mediterranean. Just next to it is the **House of Heschyus**, with Byzantine traces. To the south of the forum, past the *xystos*, is one of the jewels of Cyrene, the **House of Jason Magnus**. The home of an important high priest and a very wealthy man, the remains of this villa are significant, not only due to the size and position next to the forum but also for the fantastic mosaics, still *in situ*. Scattered throughout this very large complex are floors constructed of tiled geometric patterns. Best of all is the representational Four Seasons, enclosed and protected by a roof. Although off-limits, its surrounding walls have large open windows through which it's possible to get a great view of the masterpiece. The path continues west to the *agora*, the Greek version of the forum and centre of the city. The square is lined with important buildings on three sides. To the east are the **Tomb of Batthus** (the city's founder) and a rather dramatic naval monument topped by the goddess of victory, minus her wings and head, but with her base held up by dolphins. To the west is the **Sanctuary of Demeter**, the goddess of the all-important grain, and her daughter Kore. The temple has an interesting circular construction, within which are figures both seated and standing that depict the deities and their followers. To the south is the capitolium.

The **Sacred Way** follows the contours of the terrain downwards, passing the acropolis (hill) to the south, and the necropolis, with its tombs cut into the hill, to the north, leading to the **Sanctuary of Apollo**. The views are wonderful here, looking down upon the original Greek development. On arrival, this section feels like a different city, quite separate from the agora and forum. Outside the sanctuary walls and within the hill is the natural spring, or **Fountain of Apollo**. It's believed that it was because of this natural source that the city was established. After the barrenness of the Greek islands, the presence of a reserve of water so large as to be flowing to this day, must have been tempting. Once on the other side, through the *propylea* (gateway) from around 200BC, the dominant site is the **Temple of Apollo**. What's on show now is the 2nd-century AD post-rebellion reconstruction of the 4th-century BC version of the original sacred building of the 6th century BC. Note the stone figures, including the less than intimidating lion that greets visitors as they approach. The monumental altar is to the east of the temple, and just behind is the **Temple of Artemis**, built in the same style as the one to Apollo. Headless statues and stumps of columns are scattered about, perhaps lying in readiness for archaeological reconstruction.

Before heading east to the exit, stroll along the lovely and somewhat landscaped path to the west and the theatre. Not in the best condition, the shape of this Greek semicircular entertainment venue that was later Romanised, adheres to the basics, ie: with the seating area carved into the hill, and the backdrop of the stage using the landscape behind as part of the scene. The view is lovely and has probably hardly changed since performances were staged here. Returning along the same path, east of the Greek temples are the extensive **Roman baths**. It's possible to see mosaics on both the floor and inset, showing the previous level of construction, as well as arches and columns that still stand. A rather dramatic palm tree has sprung out of one the rooms, giving the site an African flavour. The northern gate is in this direction, and anticipating exiting tourists are a few small stalls, a bookshop and waiting transport. One last site, a bit more modern than the rest, is the white house on the hill, standing above some of the **necropolis tombs**. This building was one of the residences of Erwin Rommel, the German general who led the Axis troops during World War II. He clearly liked the place, partly for the tranquillity of the location but also, no doubt, for its excellent view of whatever might be approaching.

Apollonia Originally set up to act as the harbour and Mediterranean access point for Cyrene, these seaside ruins are located about 17km east of the great metropolis on the hill. Resting on a coast that has been eroding the city for more than 2,500 years, the crumbling remains of a settlement that once had glory days are beautifully situated. With an undeveloped shoreline, there's a sense of going back in time. In fact, today, the region is far less exploited than it was during Greek and Roman times. The Byzantine city built here overwhelmed the majority of the previous ruins and the few attractions that remain are striking, yet puzzling. So little is left, yet what little there is seems dramatic, indicating that something much more important was once here. While pondering, here is a great place to enjoy the views and the sea breezes.

History The Greeks began to construct a port here a mere few years after Cyrene was founded, from around 600BC. Acting as the older city's outlet to the sea, Apollonia was named after the same deity as Cyrene's patron, Apollo. Sometime after Alexander the Great's death and the absorption of Cyrenaica into the Egyptian kingdom, Apollonia separated from Cyrene and became an independent city. It was probably during this time that the walls that defended the port were built. Archaeologists have managed to find evidence of some of the city's early phases and discovered that from around AD80, Apollonia was significantly enhanced, probably due to a period of increased affluence. In AD359, the city's name changed to Sozusa. A century later, when the capital moved here from Ptolemais, another building transformation took place. Because of this new prominence the city was again enlarged and augmented. A significant governor's palace was built, one of the few buildings that stayed in used into the era of the Arab conquest, and remains of it can still be seen today. Most of Apollonia that can be seen today comprises Christian buildings. Labelled the 'city of churches' these features must have been what made an impression on contemporary visitors, and they continue to do so today. Despite the strength of the fortifications that the Byzantines were so conscientious in constructing they could not withstand the Arab invasion. The city went the way of many of the Roman sites, containing a few Muslim communities before eventual desertion.

Getting there To get to Apollonia, see *Derna* (*Chapter 27*, page 342).

Where to stay and eat The best place is the **El Manara Hotel** (*Susa, at the entrance to the site of Apollonia;* m *084 553001;* $$$). Surprisingly elegant for such an out of the way location, this very good hotel has fine rooms, friendly staff and a first-class, if not quite gourmet, restaurant. If you can't stay, at least have a meal here.

What to see The entrance to Apollonia (⊕ *May–Sep 07.30–19.00 daily; Oct–Apr 08.00–17.00; LYD6; a guide is necessary*) sits virtually in the car park of the El Manara Hotel in Susa. After passing through the gate, the first place of note is the **western church**. Clearly Byzantine, look at the building materials as later contractors certainly reused the previous ones, in this case Roman and Greek columns. A bit further along, and far more impressive, is the central church. With its marble pillars still standing, the layout is clearly visible and some of the details, such as the crosses, are quite striking. It's also interesting to spot a menorah, a Jewish candelabra, naively scratched into one of the bricks, evidence of the community that caused such a fuss, just up the road during the Jewish revolt in Cyrene in AD115. Directly to the east are the **Roman baths**, with columns in place. To the south is the large, sprawling complex of the **governor's palace**. The residence of the leading citizen of the capital of Cyrenaica, the house reflected the man's importance and the layout and foundations show an extended residence that accommodated several people, including both domestic and military attendants. A series of arches still intact stand dramatically. Outside and to the east, are the remains of some Byzantine houses and, just behind, the **eastern church**. It's larger than the central church, although not as attractive; look out for architectural details, such as marble and granite façades, imported from other locations, and a few mosaics still in place.

Give yourself enough time to trek past the miscellaneous remnants in the east, such as the stones that once made up the port and the dockside cisterns and fish tanks, to the **Greek theatre**. Located outside the Byzantine city walls, although possibly it was inside the Graeco-Roman ones, the seats are cut into the base of the **acropolis**, and the stage literally backs onto the beach. There are 28 tiers of low-level seats arranged into three-quarters of a circle, with the small arc of the stage at the apex. The venue is constructed from the pinkish soil and stands out against the blue of the Mediterranean onto which it backs. Climb above it to see how deep the seating is carved, as well as to see the theatre in geographical context. Just to the east is one of the necropolises.

Ptolemais (Tolmeita) Located about 100km northeast of Benghazi along the coast, Ptolemais is the third city in distance heading east from the big city (after Berenice and Tocra, and before Cyrene and Apollonia). Despite its illustrious history, this site doesn't have the attractions of Cyrene or Apollonia. Chances are that somewhere under the ground are remains that might rival the two grander cities of the Pentapolis, but Ptolemais hasn't been thoroughly excavated. Its seaside location has significant appeal, and the nearby beach is a good place to cool down after traipsing around the ruins.

Ptolemais was founded in the early days of the Pentapolis, mostly to be a port for the more important city of Barca, located slightly inland. Although the union of the Pentapolis city-states was dissolved when Alexander the Great absorbed Cyrenaica into his kingdom, in 331BC, Ptolemais was granted city status separate from its larger neighbour. Eventually, Barca waned and its port city took precedence, soon becoming one of the most important of the five-city group. When the Romans arrived, they renamed the city Tolmeita. After the earthquake of AD262 ravaged Cyrene, the capital of the province was relocated to Tolmeita, at which time a massive building programme took place. It was later supplanted by Apollonia, which took over the role less than a century later. After the earthquake of AD365 that wreaked havoc on all the settlements of the coast, Tolmeita held up better than most, and it regained the role of capital. Serving as the administrative centre until the Vandals came, the Byzantines later chased them out. During the emperor Justinian's reign, portions of the city were reconstructed, but Tolmeita never rose to the same heights. The Arabs trampled the weakened enclave on their route west, and the city was eventually deserted, to be covered by sand. It was only at the beginning of the 21st century that excavations began in earnest.

Getting there There is no regular bus service although shared taxi services follow the route to Al Bayda in the east to Al Marj in the west. Transport can also be arranged via a tour or private taxi.

 Where to stay and eat There's really nowhere nearby to eat or stay overnight. Try Al Bayda for the usual selection of small cafés, and somewhere to sleep. Worth trying is the **Al-Tilal Hotel** (*20 rooms;* m *091 3825795;* $$), behind Imarat Arrayat Al-Khodoraa, or the luxury **Marhaba**, which is part of the same group as the El Manara near Apollonia, and due to open soon.

What to see At the entrance to the site (⊕ *07.30–17.00 daily; LYD6; if you're not here on a tour, guides are available at the gate*) is a good museum, but it might be best to leave it till later, when you've had enough of the site. Past the ticket office, follow the line up the cardo (one of two), to get to the first major crossroads. The intersection with the decumanus has traces of three Roman arches, and indicated where the city centre was located. Beyond is a Byzantine church with some well-preserved elements. Just to the southwest is the **Villa of the Four Seasons**, so named for its mosaic, today sitting in the museum. Due east is the odeon which held a relatively small number of seats, usual for this type of entertainment venue. Directly south is the **agora**, translated into the forum when the Romans took over. The stumps of some of the pillars of the **capitolium** still stand. It's underneath the incline where quite possibly the most intriguing aspect of Tolemita lies. Below the ground are the **cisterns**, storing water that arrived via the aqueduct that began nearly 25km to the east. It's possible to enter the tanks via stairs. Heading back northeast is the site's second most interesting attraction, the **columned palace**. Containing a large hall with columns and a peristyle in the centre, it's possible to see the original Greek layout, with subsequent Roman alterations. This grand structure might have been the residence of the governor when Tolmeita went through its phases as the capital of Cyrenaica. On the other side of the palace is the other cardo; follow it north past some future excavation to get to the second major intersection with the decumanus. Again, there are remains of pillars, indicating the way. Follow the route to return to the **museum**. Inside, the best items in the collection are the mosaics, with the Four Seasons (from its villa) taking pride of place. Also on show is a Medusa from the columned palace.

Qasr Libya (☉ 07.30–17.00; LYD6) If you're seeing Ptolemais on a tour, visits here will almost certainly be on the itinerary. Otherwise, make a point of including it in your own schedule. Located slightly inland, 45km west on the road from the closest big town of Al Bayda, Qasr Libya means Libyan castle (note the similarity of the word qasr to ksar or kasbah from the countries further west). The small ancient city of Olbia, the location held two Christian churches, the western and the eastern, dating from around 450. Within them are some of the best jewels of period Byzantine art ever unearthed, consisting of a huge collection of mosaics. Known about only since 1957, 50 of them were discovered within the eastern church and now sit in the museum. Charming and somewhat stylised, the subjects range from a view of the lighthouse of Alexandria to animals and plants and mythological subjects, with some Christian imagery in between. Exquisitely preserved, it's possible to visit the holes in the ground from the floors of the church itself, to see where the mosaic gems were once situated. The western church still has its artwork in place.

Tocra (Teucheira) With the exception of the traces of Berenice that sit underneath the modern city of Benghazi, this site has the least impressive remains of the cities of the Pentapolis. It is situated about 70km northeast of Benghazi on the coast and most tourists don't bother to visit. Never as magnificent as the former capitals, this place was a more modest town and archaeologists haven't put in the same amount of effort into exploring the middle and lower classes as they did discovering how the wealthy lived. If you're really interested, make a quick stop here to find out a bit more about the ordinary classes. It's probably best to go via the few organised trips that do the excursion, or by private car or taxi.

History Founded in the early days of the Pentapolis, the site was renamed Arsinoe in honour of Ptolemy II's wife. The port location gave the site some value, but it was always in the shadow of Ptolemais, about 30km east. Their history was similar, barring the brief moment of glory enjoyed by the bigger city. Renamed Teucheira by the Romans, the primarily sandstone construction couldn't hold up to the rumbles of the repeated earthquakes, and the place literally sunk into the soil. It remains mostly there to this day.

What to see The site (☉ May–Sep 07.30–19.30 daily; Oct–Apr 07.30–17.00; LYD6) includes some Roman tombs carved into a wall, a small fort dating from the Ottoman and later Italian eras, and traces of a basilica and older gymnasium. Beyond are remnants of other indications of daily life, such as the baths and city wall, and death, such as the necropolis. There is also a small museum that gives some explanations of the site, illustrated with artefacts found nearby, including a mosaic.

30

Beyond the Romans

THE BEST THINGS TO SEE SOUTH OF THE ROMAN PROVINCES

With nearly 95% of Libya consisting of desert, it's not surprising that it's into the sands where the most interesting non-Roman attractions lie. The colonists of the empire were not able to make incursions into the desert lands, partly due to the harsh conditions and partly on account of the fierce Berbers who were no friends to these invaders. Nor did the Romans want to enter these inhospitable areas. The coast and the thin fertile strip along it were good enough, as these parts of the country gave them access to the trading routes as well as a small amount of agricultural production. Occasional exploration into the interior by the army yielded no real profit.

Today's tourists will find the desert region beautiful and fascinating. Tour operators have made friends with the locals and the tough environment is softened with the help of 4x4s and air conditioning. The terrain is different enough from the Roman north to feel like a totally different country. If you have the time, and vast, arid wilderness with some spectacular, if somewhat stark environments appeals, don't miss what else Libya has to offer.

It's easiest to break the region down into the western and eastern deserts.

WESTERN DESERT This area, which borders Tunisia in the north and Algeria to the west, has the most to offer in the way of scenery, history and culture, and is also where tourism is better served. The attractions are listed in order of north to south.

Qasr al-Haj The best of the Berber granaries, this 114-room multi-storey structure is constructed from local soil, and dates back to sometime around AD1100. Built in a circle, it encloses a central courtyard. The storehouse is still used and is one of the finest examples of local architecture.

Jebel Nafusa This area to the southwest of Tripoli is an easy drive into the western mountains. The first retreat of the Berbers when they were under invasion, the region still retains their traditions, mostly evident in the architecture. With more of the granaries, as above, Kabau and Nalut represent some of the best of local culture.

Ghadames Further southwest, virtually on the Tunisian–Algerian border, is this wonderful oasis town. Still holding the mystique of a caravan stop, the refuge in the desert with its ancient buildings and refreshing gardens is now deserted of residents, but open to visitors.

From here, distances are too great and unrewarding to drive. It's best to return to Tripoli and fly down to the desert city and exploration portal of Sebha from where many of the local attractions are within local transport range.

Ubari sand, sea and lakes The highlights of this part of the desert are the incredible sand dunes, rising and falling in changing patterns, and the sudden and surprising discovery of blue lakes within them, surrounded by palms. Touareg salesmen hang around here, offering some of the most authentic wares available in the country. The modern town in the area is **Germa**, a convenient base but more interestingly, an important archaeological location. Here was once Garama, the home of the Garamantes, the Berber tribe who were constantly at the heels of the Romans. A museum explains the history.

Ghat Another historic oasis town, this one has a Touareg population and is built in the old way, with walls constructed from local soil made thick to protect against the desert heat. Another of the cities inhabited by the Garamantes, the location also served as a major stop on the caravan routes across Africa. There's an annual New Year's festival celebrating traditional arts, including singing, dancing, handicrafts – and camel racing.

Jebel Acacus This area on the Algerian border has some of Libya's most spectacular scenery, comprising weird wind-blown rock formations amidst the dunes, but even more importantly, ancient rock art. Carvings and paintings of animals that existed at a time when the region was wet and lush, believed to be around 10,000 years ago, are found on the cliffs and in the caves. Particularly good areas are Awiss, for both scenery and artwork, and the Wadi Tashwinat.

EASTERN DESERT This region has far less to see, and is also more difficult to visit due to the permits required and the absence of mainstream tourism. If you want to visit, it's essential to go through a local tour operator, such as Ocean Travel & Tours (*PO Box 9225, Benghazi;* ❧ *061 9082085; www.almuheettours.net*).

Awjila Almost due south from Benghazi, this is an oasis town that once catered to the caravans that crossed the continent from the southeast. Still known for its Berber culture, parts of the old city have recently been restored.

Ramlat Rabianeh Way into the heart of the Libyan desert (that straddles the border with Egypt), this part of the country is known for its high dunes that consist of remarkably fine sand. There is a lake here that may not compete with the beauty of the Ubari, but the water in the area is part of the source of the Great Man Made River.

Waw al Namus Deep in the south, situated between the western and eastern deserts, approaching the border with Chad, this extinct volcano is one of the most out-of-the way locations on the planet. Astonishing, not least because of its inaccessibility, the crater contains different-hued lakes, with a bit of vegetation thrown in. It's hard to get here, visits requiring permits (obtained by the tour operator) and an extra few days just for the trip, not to mention that Waw al Namus means 'Wow – the mosquito!' However, if you manage the journey, you'll have gone somewhere that very, very few people have ever seen.

Appendix I

LANGUAGE

Arabic is the main language of the Maghreb, shared with the rest of the Arab world. The written version is uniform and varies from the spoken, legible to anyone able to read the complicated, but beautiful script. The spoken word is an entirely different matter. With several different groups across the Middle East and Africa, speakers usually can't understand people who are using the same language but come from another country. Egyptian is considered the purest form and is the type usually taught abroad. The corresponding popularity of Egypt's media, particularly its films, has caused most Arabs to understand Egyptian, but it's not what they speak at home. Even though the Maghreb has its own group, the variety within it means that there is a wide differentiation in the Arabic spoken in the four countries. It's difficult for a Moroccan to understand a Libyan if they're both speaking their own form of the language. A few words might seem similar in the list below, but they're not enough to allow flowing communication. In addition, accents and local use might further widen the gap.

In Morocco, Algeria and Tunisia, French is the second language, a legacy from colonial days. In contrast to Arabic, it's less regional and easily understood. In fact, because it's also a foreign language for the locals, it's easier than the Parisian version for less fluent non-French visitors to understand. It makes far more sense to bone up on this tongue, rather than attempt to learn four varieties of Arabic, as almost anyone will be able to communicate with you. The Berbers have their own language that is beginning to be taught in the schools.

In Libya, the language of the colonial fathers, Italian, doesn't seem to have taken as much hold as in the French protectorates, and English is more widely spoken. This language is slowly becoming more common across the Maghreb, although it's not as widespread as one would expect. The younger generation is starting to learn it with the media, especially the internet, promoting its use. If French isn't an option, then English would be the next means of communication.

In instances where the forms vary, the list below refers to greeting a single male.

	French	Moroccan Arabic	Algerian Arabic	Tunisian Arabic	Libyan Arabic
THE BASICS					
Good morning	*Bonjour*	*Sbah lkheer*	*Sbah el khir*	*Sbah el khir*	*Sbah el khayr*
Hello	*Salut*	*Labas*	*Saha*	*Aslaama*	*Ahlan*
Good evening	*Bonsoir*	*Msa el khir*	*Mess el khir*	*Messi koum*	*Masa llkhayr*
Goodbye	*Au revoir*	*Maa el salaama*	*Ebkaw ala khir*	*Bes'slama*	*Ma'salaama*
yes	*oui*	*waha*	*ih*	*ay*	*aywaI*
no	*non*	*lalal*	*lala*	*la*	*la*
Thank you	*Merci*	*Shukran*	*Saha*	*Shukran*	*Barkalla oo feek*
Excuse me	*Excusez moi*	*Smeh leeya*	*Esmahli*	*Samah ni*	*Saamahnee*
Sorry	*Pardon*	*Afwan*	*Esmahli*	*Mitaasif*	*Mitaasif*

	French	Moroccan Arabic	Algerian Arabic	Tunisian Arabic	Libyan Arabic
What's your name?	Comment tu t'appelles?	Asmeetek?	Wasmek?	Shnuwwa ismek inti?	Shismek?
Nice to meet you	Enchanté	Metsarfin	Metcharfin	Nitsharrafoo	Nitsharrafoo
How are you?	Comment vas-tu?	Ash h'barak?	Wash rak?	Schnuwwa hawaalek?	Shinee haalek?
fine/bad	bien/pas bien	bikhir/[?]	labes/shwia	la baas[?]	ilhamdu lillah
Help!	Au secours!	Teqnee!	Aanouni!	Awenni i'eychk!	Saa'adnee!
Do you speak English?	Vous parlez anglais?	Wash kat'ref negleezeeya?	Tahdar l'anglais?	Titkalim ingleeziyya?	Inta bititkalem inglizi?
What?	Quoi?	Ashno?	Washnou?	Shnuwwa?	Shinee?
Who?	Qui?	Shkoon?	Shkoun?	Shkoon?	Shkloon?
Where?	Où?	Ahima?	Win?	Wine?	Waine?
When?	Quand?	Mata?	Wektesh?	Waqtaash?	Wagtaash?
I don't understand	Je n'ai pas compris	Ma f'hemshi	Ma fhamtsh	Ma nifhimsh	Ma nifhimsh

DIRECTIONS

Where is...?	Où se trouve...?	Feen kayn...?	Win Djay...?	Ween...?	Waine...?
To the left	A gauche	Alachimal	Ala l'yessra	Lisar	Al lisaar
To the right	A droite	Alaimine	Ala l'yemna	Limine	Al limeen
Straight ahead	Tout droit	neeshan	Direct	Tool	Tool
here	ici	hna	h'na	mene hna	hinaa
there	là-bas	hunak	l'hik	ghadi	ghaadee
near	près	eeqareb	k'rib	qreeb	greeb
far	loin	yagoog	b'aid	ba'eed	ba'eed

SHOPPING

How much do you want?	Combien voulez-vous?	Kam?	Sh'hal habbit?	Qeddach hada?	Bi gaddaash haadha?

FOOD AND DRINK

water	eau	ma	m'aa	el ma	moyya
tea	thé	atay	latay	tay	shay
coffee	café	qhwa	kahwa	el qahwa	khawa

NUMBERS

1	un	wahad	wahed	wahed	waahid
2	deux	juge	zoudj	tnine	ithneen
3	trois	tleta	t'lata	tlata	thalaatha
4	quatre	arba	rabaaa	arb'a	arb'a
5	cinq	khamsa	khamsa	khamsa	khamsa
6	six	setta	setta	setta	sitta
7	sept	sebta	sebaaa	sab'a	sab'a
8	huit	tmenya	t'mania	tmanya	thamaanya
9	neuf	tse'ud	tessaaa	tes'a	tis'a
10	dix	achra	aashra	achra	ashra
11	onze	hdash	h'desh	hdach	hadaasher
12	douze	tnaash	t'nash	atnach	ithnaasher
13	treize	teltaash	teltashe	tlattach	thlataasher

14	quatorze	rba'taash	r'baatashe	arba'tach	arba'taasher
15	quinze	khamtaash	kh'mastashe	khmastach	khamataasher
16	seize	settash	settashe	sattach	sitaasher
17	dix-sept	sbe'taash	s'baatashe	sba'tach	saba'taasher
18	dix-huit	tmentaash	t'mentashe	tmantach	thamantash
19	dix-neuf	tse'taash	t'saatashe	tsa'tach	tisa'tash
20	vingt	ashreen	aashrine	echrinre	ashreen
30	trente	tlateen	t'latine	tlatine	thalatheen
40	quarante	reb'een	rabaine	arb'ine	arba'een
50	cinquante	khamseen	khamsine	khemsine	khamseen
60	soixante	setteen	settine	settine	sitteen
70	soixante-dix	seb'een	sebaine	seb'ine	sab'een
80	quatre-vingt	tmaneen	t'manyine	tmanine	thamaneen
90	quatre-vingt dix	tes'een	tesaine	tes'ine	tis'een
100	cent	mya	m'ya	mya	meeya
200	deux cent	myatayn	mitine	mitine	meeyatayn
1,000	mille	alf	alf	alf	alf

DAYS AND TIMES

today	aujourd'hui	al yom	elyoum	el youm	il yowm
tomorrow	demain	hedda	ghoudwa	ghoudwa	ghudwa
yesterday	hier	ibareh	elbareh	ibaarah	ilbaarah
Monday	Lundi	Et tnine	Etnine	Inhar il ihtneen	Yowm il ithayn
Tuesday	Mardi	Et tleta	Etlata	Inhar ith thlaatha	Youm ith thalaatha
Wednesday	Mercredi	El arba	Larebaa	Inhar il arba	Youm il arba
Thursday	Jeudi	El khemis	Lekhmiss	Inhar il khamees	Yowm il khamees
Friday	Vendredi	El jamai	Eldjemaa	Inhar il juma	Yowm il juma
Saturday	Samedi	Es sebt	Essabt	Inhar is sibt	Yowm is sibt
Sunday	Dimanche	El had	Elhad	Inharil ahadd	Youm al ahadd
What time is it?	Quelle heure est-il?	Shal fess'a?	Ch'hal essaaa?	Qaddach el weqt?	Gaddaash il wagt?

Appendix 2

ROMAN EMPERORS AND OTHER LEADERS DURING ANCIENT ROME'S OCCUPATION OF NORTH AFRICA

This is not a complete list: there were many other emperors, kings and tribal leaders who took control for varying periods, some for extremely short times. However, the people below had a significant effect on North Africa, usually stayed for a while and often were very colourful characters.

NB Dates for emperors and kings refer to the duration of their reigns. *Italics are for non-Romans*

BC

639–599	*Battus*	*Greek*	*Founder of Cyrene*
247–183	*Hannibal Barca*	*Carthaginian*	*General*
236–183	Scipio Africanus	Roman	General
201–148	*Massinissa*	*Numidian*	*King*
185–129	Scipio Aemilianus	Roman	General
118–105	*Jugurtha*	*Numidian*	*King*
62–46	*Juba I*	*Numidian*	*King*
49–44	Julius Caesar	Roman	last Republican
31–14(AD)	Augustus	Roman	1st Emperor
25–23(AD)	*Juba II*	*Mauretanian*	*King*

AD

14–37	Tiberius	Roman	Emperor
23–42	*Ptolemy*	*Mauretanian*	*the last King*
37–41	(Gaius) Caligula	Roman	Emperor
41–54	Claudius	Roman	Emperor
54–68	Nero	Roman	Emperor
68–69	Galba	Roman	Emperor
69	Otho	Roman	Emperor
69	Vitellius	Roman	Emperor
69–79	Vespasian	Roman	Emperor
79–81	Titus	Roman	Emperor
81–96	Domitian	Roman	Emperor
96–98	Nerva	Roman	Emperor
98–117	Trajan	Roman	Emperor
117–138	Hadrian	Roman	Emperor
138–161	Antoninus Pius	Roman	Emperor
161–180	Marcus Aurelius	Roman	Emperor
180–192	Commodus	Roman	Emperor
192–193	Pertinax	Roman	Emperor

193	Didius Julianus	Roman	Emperor
193–211	Septimius Severus	Roman	Emperor
211–217	(Antoninus) Caracalla	Roman	Emperor
211	Geta	Roman	Emperor
217–218	Macrinus	Roman	Emperor
218–22	Elagabalus	Roman	Emperor
222–235	Severus Alexander	Roman	Emperor
235–284	*The era of 50 recorded emperors including:*		
235–238	Maximinus Thrax	Roman	Emperor
238	Gordian I and Gordion II	Roman	Emperor
238–244	Gordian III	Roman	Emperor
284–305	Diocletian	Roman	Emperor of east
284–305	Maximian	Roman	Emperor of west
306–337	Constantine I	Roman	Emperor
337–340	Constantine II	Roman	Emperor
337–350	Constans I	Roman	Emperor
337–361	Constantius II	Roman	Emperor
361–363	Julian	Roman	Emperor
364–375	Valentinian I	Roman	Emperor
372?–375?	Firmus	Roman	Emperor
365–366	Procopius	Roman	Emperor
367–383	Gratian	Roman	Emperor
375–392	Valentinian II	Roman	Emperor
378–395	Theodosius I the Great	Roman	Emperor
393–423	Honorius	Roman	Emperor
425–455	Valentinian III	Roman	Emperor

Vandals in control of the northwestern part of Africa

429–477	*Gaiseric (or Genseric)*	*Vandal*	*King*
477–484	*Hunseric*	*Vandal*	*King*
484–523	*Gunthamund*	*Vandal*	*shared Kingdom*
484–496	*Thrasmund*	*Vandal*	*shared Kingdom*
523–530	*Hilderic*	*Vandal*	*King*
530–34	*Gelimer*	*Vandal*	*King*

Byzantine or late Roman emperors

527–565	Justinian I	Roman	Emperor
565–578	Justin II	Roman	Emperor
578–582	Tiberius II (I) Constantine	Roman	Emperor
582–602	Maurice	Roman	Emperor
602–610	Phocas	Roman	Emperor
610–641	Heraclius	Roman	Emperor
641–668	Constans II	Roman	Emperor
668–685	Constantine IV	Roman	Emperor
685–695	Justinian II (banished)	Roman	Emperor
695–698	Leontius	Roman	Emperor
	Justinian II (restored)	Roman	Emperor

Appendix 3

GLOSSARY OF ROMAN ARCHITECTURAL TERMS

acropolis (Greek)
A naturally occurring steep hill that is the geographic and cultural centre of a city

amphitheatre
From the Greek words 'amphi', on both sides, + 'theatron', the ancient Roman building type used for gladiatorial contests and other entertainments. El Djem in Tunisia is an excellent example, although many of the sites have amphitheatres.

apodyteria
Changing rooms

aqueduct
An engineering structure designed to bring huge quantities of pure water into the city. The U-shaped stone channel that carries the water is at the top of the arcuated structure that is used to span valleys between the source and the city.

arch/
triumphal arch
The ancient Roman commemorative monument in the shape of an arch

architrave
The horizontal element spanning the interval between two columns

atrium
In an ancient Roman house, the central courtyard

axial co-ordinates
The system of the ancient Romans for the placement of buildings and roads that uses parallel and perpendicular lines in an even spacing. Also called a grid pattern.

basilica
In ancient Roman architecture, a large meeting hall most often used for the law courts. The basilica could also contain the stock exchange, business and administrative offices, and therefore was a physical link between law and business.
There are two very different formal expressions of the basilica, illustrated by the earlier Basilica Ulpia or Trajan's basilica, and the later basilica of Maxentius and Constantine.
The roof of the trabeated structural system in Trajan's basilica is supported by many interior columns thus breaking the large space (182' x c450') into smaller sections.
The basilica of Constantine had an enormous arcuated system (200' x 300') of barrel and groin vaults. It carried the thrust of the vaults on piers, and relied on massive buttressing.
Also a rectangular building with an ambulatory or else a central nave and lateral aisles and lit by a clerestory, the row of windows above the inner colonnades.

baths, hypocaust
A system of heating, comprising stacks of tiles that held up the floor, so that heated air channelled in from the nearby furnace could circulate underneath and heat the rooms above.

baths, unctuarium
Where the bath-goer would have olive oil rubbed into his skin by one of the slaves owned by the baths

baths, public	In ancient Roman architecture, this structure combined public baths, gymnasia, exercise yards, stadia, shops, libraries and meeting rooms. Natural light entered through clerestory windows in the ends of the barrel-vaulted roofs. It was a masterpiece of engineering providing and disposing of clean water of various temperatures for up to 1,600 bathers on a daily basis.
baths, public, caldarium	In Roman baths, the room which contained hot water for bathing
baths, public frigidarium	In Roman baths, the room which contained cold water for bathing
baths, public tepidarium	In Roman baths, the room which contained luke warm (tepid) water for bathing
capitol/capitolium	Temples which were built on hills and other prominent areas in many cities in Italy and the provinces, that honoured the gods, Jupiter, Juno and Minerva
cardo or **cardus maximus**	The primary north–south road that was the usual main street
castrum	The imperial Roman military camp, an extremely rigid and orderly square, divided into four quadrants by the primary roads and oriented to the cardinal directions. This form, which was originally used for the temporary camps of the soldiers in new colonies, became the built form of those cities.
cavea	Spectator seating of a theatre or amphitheatre, usually divided by *baltei* into sections which were assigned to different social classes; these sectors were further divided into wedge-shaped *cunei* by vertical stairs (*scalaria*) which come down from the entrances (*vomitoria*) to the seating area. Also: the subterranean cells in which wild animals were confined before the combats in the Roman arena or amphitheatre.
cella	A *cella* (from Latin for small chamber) or naos (from the Greek for temple), is the inner chamber of a temple in classical architecture, or a shop facing the street in domestic Roman architecture (*see* **domus**)
centuriation	The division of land in which a road, track or path forms a division between plots (often into 100 regular squares or rectangles)
chalcidicum	The vestibule or portico of a public building opening onto the forum
circus	In ancient Roman architecture, the structure built for the running and viewing of chariot races. The one surviving example in North Africa is at Leptis Magna, in Libya.
clivus	A Roman street running up an incline. The distinction from a level *vicus* was strongly felt and a street name sometimes changed when, after running level, it began to ascend a slope.
colonia	Originally a Roman outpost established in conquered territory to secure it. Eventually, however, the term came to denote the highest status of Roman city.
column, commemorative column	The freestanding column in ancient Roman architecture has a commemorative function
compluvium	Unroofed area over a courtyard designed to allow water to fall into the cistern

curia	Any building where local government held office, ie: judicial proceedings, government meetings, bureaucracy, etc. Later, the Senate House.
decumanus	An east–west-oriented road in a Roman city, **castrum** (military camp) or **colonia**
dolmen (Neolithic)	A type of single-chamber megalithic tomb, dating from the early Neolithic period (4000BC to 3000BC)
domus	The ancient Roman word for house. Examples from Pompeii or Ercolano indicate a single-storey house with a central atrium or courtyard which was a garden. The larger of these houses may also be referred to as villas.
ex(c)edra	A semicircular or rectangular recess open on one side to a lobby or court
forica	Latrine
forum	The open-air urban space(s) in ancient Roman cities, generally rectangular in shape, defined by the porticoes and civic buildings at its perimeter, and used for marketplace and public interaction, particularly 'civic discussion'. The temple stood prominently at one end of the forum. The centre of the city.
gymnasium	An educational and/or sporting institution in ancient Greece
hippodrome	An ancient Roman course especially for horse and chariot racing
insula	A city block
laconi(c)a	Sauna in a bathhouse
lapidarium	Toilet room
macellum	A Roman meat or produce market in a covered hall
marabout	The tomb of a personal spiritual leader (also called a marabout) in the Islamic faith as practised in west Africa, and still to a limited extent in the Maghreb
market/marketplace	In ancient Roman cities, the public market was located on or adjacent to the forum and varied somewhat in shape
mausoleum	An external free-standing building constructed as a monument enclosing the interment space or burial chamber of a deceased person or persons. A mausoleum may be considered a type of tomb or the tomb may be considered to be within the mausoleum. A Christian mausoleum sometimes includes a chapel.
municipium	A city with Latin rights or Roman citizenship
natatio	A swimming pool usually found in the **palaestra** of a large bathhouse
necropolis	A large cemetery or burial place (from the Greek *nekropolis* 'city of the dead')
nymphaeum	A monumental fountain consecrated to the nymphs, especially those of springs. Originally natural grottoes they were later artificially constructed, and sometimes arranged to furnish a supply of fresh water.
odeon	A small theatre
oppidum	A town
opus africanum	A building technique, typical for North Africa, in which walls were constructed out of rubble, reinforced at even distances by large, manufactured squared-off slabs and stone uprights, known as **orthostats**, Although there was no specific height or width to these walls, generally, the orthostats were as wide as the rubble sections.

opus tesselatum	A typical Punic touch, this method consists of the placing of small stones or fragments of a contrasting colour into flooring, to make it more decorative
palace	The domestic building for Roman emperors, at the scale of a small city
palestra or palaestra	A yard or hall where a Roman could work up a sweat lifting weights, playing ball games, boxing or wrestling; in Greek areas (eg: Cyrene), there was the ancient Greek wrestling school where events that did not require a lot of space, such as boxing and wrestling, were practised. The palaestra functioned both independently and as a part of public gymnasium. A palaestra could exist without a gymnasium, but no gymnasium could exist without a palaestra.
peristyle	A colonnade surrounding a building
pharos	Lighthouse
plinth	A pedestal supporting a column
portico	A roofed porch or walkway supported by columns
postern	A secondary door or gate, especially in a fortification such as a city wall or castle curtain wall
propylaea (Greek)	Any monumental gateway based on the original gate ('propylaea') at the entrance to the Acropolis in Athens
spina	he divider down the middle of a circus, finished with *metae* at either end
temple	In imperial Rome, the structure used for religious ritual of the priests, and either rectangular or round in plan. The earlier rectangular-plan temples have bearing walls. The round Pantheon employs an arcuated system for enclosing the space. Both forms stood on podiums and were meant to be approached only from the front.
theatre	The ancient Roman building type used for dramatic performance or entertainment. Unlike the Greek theatre, the building is free standing, the wall behind the stage is much higher and the seating area may be covered. Sabratha in Libya is one of the best examples in North Africa, if not the Roman Empire.
tophet	A high place designated for the sacrifice of children to pagan gods. Child sacrifice, mostly in time of national or communal crisis, was an integral element of western Semitic paganism and *tophets* were created not only in Israel and Lebanon, but even in Phoenician colonies such as Carthage, where child sacrifice was well documented.
velatium	The awning stretched above an amphitheatre to protect spectators from the sun
vicus	A street of ordinary width with a relatively flat course
villa	A country house for the ancient Romans, usually one storey with a central atrium or courtyard

Appendix 4

FURTHER INFORMATION
BOOKS

General There are a lot of books around on ancient Rome, but relatively few on Roman North Africa. Try the following:

Breem, Wallace *The Legate's Daughter* Orion 2005. A bit-of-nonsense historical novel that does a good job of depicting ancient Mauretania and King Juba II's court.

Manton, E Lennox *Roman North Africa* Seaby 1988. The author presents a reasonable summary of ancient Rome's role in the Dark Continent.

Raven, Susan *Rome in Africa* Routledge 1993. This excellent book surveys the Roman African territories as a whole, giving an insight into the politics, economy and daily life of the colonial settlements, beginning with the Phoenicians and ending with the Arab invasion.

Rogerson, Barnaby *A Traveller's History of North Africa* Windrush Press 1998. Starting with the Neanderthal, this work describes North Africa virtually up to the date of its publication.

Roller, Duane W *The World of Juba II and Kleopatra Selene* Routledge 2003. The lives of this little-known glamour couple of Mauretania are described in detail in this monograph.

If looking for something a bit more substantial, it's always worth reading the works of the Roman historians themselves, as detailed in box, page 17.

Morocco Many writers have passed through the country and almost as many have jotted down their impressions within fiction. Fortunately, several of their works are in English. Here are a few.

Bowles, Paul *The Sheltering Sky* Libary of America (among others) 2002. Arguably the definitive work of the expat group of American writers who settled in Tangier, this evocative and haunting book was also the basis for a film by Bernardo Bertolucci.

Burroughs, William S *Naked Lunch* Harper Perennial 2005. The classic drug novel of 1959 was written while the author was hanging out in Morocco.

Canetti, Elias *The Voices of Marrakech* Marion Boyars 2002. The Nobel Prize-winning author described his experiences in this exotic city when it was still relatively undiscovered.

Freud, Esther *Hideous Kinky* Penguin 1992. A novel of the author's barely disguised autobiographical experiences of her childhood in Morocco, which was also made into a film.

Algeria The country's most famous writer on the international stage was Albert Camus. His novel *The Plague* takes place in the city of Oran. Most of Algeria's present-day writers have only a national appeal and their books are not available in languages other than French or Arabic. Aziz Chouaki's book is the exception:

Chouaki, Aziz *The Star of Algiers* Serpent's Tail 2006. This novel, first published in France in 2002, takes place in the capital during the country's Dark Decade, and mixes music and the desire for stardom, with the broader political and religious issues of the period.

Palin, Michael *Sahara* Weidenfeld & Nicolson 2002. The jolly traveller traipses through the desert, visiting all the countries covered in this guide. This book is a tie-in with his well-liked television series.

Porch, Douglas *Conquest of the Sahara* Knopf 1984. An analysis of why the French wanted to invade the North African desert, and a good read at that; this non-fiction book reads like a real-life Beau Geste.

Tunisia Despite its accessibility and appeal, the country doesn't seem to have fired up too many foreign writers' imaginations.

Douglas, Norman *Fountains in the Sand* Free ebook: www.gutenberg.org/etext/8185. The author chronicles his journey through Tunisia in 1912.

Highsmith, Patricia *The Tremor of Forgery* Bloomsbury 2006. A writer is sent to Tunisia to work on a film script, but unable to begin, he starts on a novel, but, inevitably, dark things begin to happen.

Libya

Al Koni, Ibrahim *Anubis: A Desert Novel* American University in Cairo Press 2005. A work from one of the new Libyan writers, this mystical novel uses Touareg mythology to garnish a tale about a man searching for his father in the desert.

Bey, Ahmed Hassanein *The Lost Oases* American University in Cairo Press (new edition) 2006. A classic work, this book describes the journey of an Egyptian diplomat who discovered some of the extraordinary oases in the south of the country in 1923.

Matar, Hisham *In the Country of Men* Viking 2006. A novel about a child's view of Colonel Gaddafi's Libya in 1979. It was shortlisted for the Booker Prize in the year of its publication.

Newby, Eric *On the Shores of the Mediterranean* Picador 1985. This travel writer's journey around the Mediterranean includes a visit to the country (as well as Morocco and Tunisia).

HEALTH

Wilson-Howarth, Dr Jane, and Ellis, Dr Matthew *Your Child Abroad: A Travel Health Guide* Bradt Travel Guides, 2005

Wilson-Howarth, Dr Jane, *Bugs, Bites & Bowels* Cadogan, 2006

MAPS There are various maps produced, particularly of Morocco and Tunisia, although ones of Algeria and Libya are harder to find. For the first two, the national tourist boards do an excellent job of providing various free handouts, including quite good road maps.

Algeria Road map, Map for Businessmen & Tourists (1:2,5000,000) GiziMap. Includes all of Morocco (except Western Sahara) Tunisia and northern Libya including Tripoli. The best map readily available of most of the region today.

WEBSITES There are hundreds of good websites for each of the countries. The list below is by necessity a very small selection.

Roman North Africa

www.metmuseum.org/toah/ht/05/afw/ht05afw.htm A brief summary of the period AD1–500 with links, as seen by the Metropolitan Museum of Art, New York.

www.roman-emperors.org A site dedicated solely to the emperors of Rome.

www.roman-empire.net A site dedicated solely to the Roman Empire.

www.romanarmy.com/cms A site dedicated solely to the Roman army.

www.sunsite.ubc.ca/LatinDictionary/HyperText/latin-dict-full.html#V A list of just about every Latin word you can think of (and more); useful for making out inscriptions.

www.unrv.com A chatty, accessible site that covers all aspects of the ancient Roman Empire.

Morocco

www.morocco.com

www.maroc.net

moroccotravelpages.com

www.tourism-in-morocco.com/english/

www.tourisme-marocain.com/onmt_en/General.aspx?id_table=89 This is the official site of the Moroccan Tourist Board.

Algeria

www.algeria.com The best general Algeria site.

www.algerie-monde.com/tourisme-algerie Although in French, it's possible to make out the most important information.

www.ont-dz.org The national tourist office's website is still in French, but the English version is being developed.

www.algeriatouring.dz/articles/index.php?id=92 Broader based than the general tourist ones, this site gives good information, but only in French.

www.onat-dz.com The face of the Organisation Nationale de l'Artisanat Tunisien (ONAT) to the web world, but only in French.

Tunisia

www.tunisiaonline.com The best general Tunisian site has links to the most important organisations, including:

www.tourismtunisia.com The Tunisian National Tourism Office.

www.sites-tunisie.org.tn/EN The portal to the country's best archaeological sites.

www.tunisia.com

tunisia-way.com/index.php

Libya

www.libyaconnected.com A general site with good information.

libya.embassyhomepage.com Another helpful resource, but many of the links don't work.

www.libyaonline.com Abroad-based page with all sorts of information.

General travel information

www.fco.gov.uk UK government website with latest safety information for all countries.

www.smartraveller.gov.au Australian travel advisory site.

www.voyage.gc.ca Canadian travel advisory site.

www.travel.state.gov American travel warnings site.

WIN £100 CASH!
READER QUESTIONNAIRE

**Send in your completed questionnaire for the chance to win
£100 cash in our regular draw**

All respondents may order a Bradt guide at half the UK retail price – please
complete the order form overleaf.

(Entries may be posted or faxed to us, or scanned and emailed.)

We are interested in getting feedback from our readers to help us plan future Bradt
guides. Please answer ALL the questions below and return the form to us in order
to qualify for an entry in our regular draw.

Have you used any other Bradt guides? If so, which titles? . . . .
. . . .

What other publishers' travel guides do you use regularly? . . . .

. . . .

Where did you buy this guidebook? . . . .

What was the main purpose of your trip to North Africa (or for what other reason
did you read our guide)? eg: holiday/business/charity etc. . . . .

. . . .

What other destinations would you like to see covered by a Bradt guide?

. . . .

Would you like to receive our catalogue/newsletters?

YES / NO (If yes, please complete details on reverse)

If yes – by post or email? . . . .

Age (circle relevant category) 16–25   26–45   46–60   60+

Male/Female (delete as appropriate)

Home country. . . . .

Please send us any comments about our guide to North Africa: The Roman Coast
or other Bradt Travel Guides. . . . .

. . . .

. . . .

. . . .

Bradt Travel Guides
23 High Street, Chalfont St Peter, Bucks SL9 9QE, UK
✆ +44 (0)1753 893444 **f** +44 (0)1753 892333
e info@bradtguides.com
www.bradtguides.com

CLAIM YOUR HALF-PRICE BRADT GUIDE!

Order Form

To order your half-price copy of a Bradt guide, and to enter our prize draw to win £100 (see overleaf), please fill in the order form below, complete the questionnaire overleaf, and send it to Bradt Travel Guides by post, fax or email.

Please send me one copy of the following guide at half the UK retail price

Title	Retail price	Half price
...	....	....

Please send the following additional guides at full UK retail price

No	Title	Retail price	Total
...	....	....	....
...	....	....	....
...	....	....	....

Sub total ....
Post & packing ....
(£2 per book UK; £4 per book Europe; £6 per book rest of world)
Total ....

Name ....

Address..

Tel .... Email ....

☐ I enclose a cheque for £ .... made payable to Bradt Travel Guides Ltd

☐ I would like to pay by credit card. Number: ....

Expiry date: ... / ... 3-digit security code (on reverse of card) .....

Issue no (debit cards only) .....

☐ Please add my name to your catalogue mailing list.

☐ I would be happy for you to use my name and comments in Bradt marketing material.

Send your order on this form, with the completed questionnaire, to:

Bradt Travel Guides ROM1
23 High Street, Chalfont St Peter, Bucks SL9 9QE
☏ +44 (0)1753 893444   f +44 (0)1753 892333
e info@bradtguides.com   www.bradtguides.com

Bradt Travel Guides

www.bradtguides.com

Africa

Africa Overland	£15.99
Algeria	£15.99
Benin	£14.99
Botswana: Okavango, Chobe, Northern Kalahari	£15.99
Burkina Faso	£14.99
Cameroon	£15.99
Cape Verde Islands	£14.99
Congo	£15.99
Eritrea	£15.99
Ethiopia	£15.99
Gambia, The	£13.99
Ghana	£15.99
Johannesburg	£6.99
Madagascar	£15.99
Malawi	£13.99
Mali	£13.95
Mauritius, Rodrigues & Réunion	£13.99
Mozambique	£13.99
Namibia	£15.99
Niger	£14.99
Nigeria	£17.99
North Africa: Roman Coast	£15.99
Rwanda	£14.99
São Tomé & Principe	£14.99
Seychelles	£14.99
Sierra Leone	£16.99
Sudan	£13.95
Tanzania, Northern	£13.99
Tanzania	£16.99
Uganda	£15.99
Zambia	£17.99
Zanzibar	£14.99

Britain and Europe

Albania	£15.99
Armenia, Nagorno Karabagh	£14.99
Azores	£13.99
Baltic Cities	£14.99
Belarus	£14.99
Belgrade	£6.99
Bosnia & Herzegovina	£13.99
Bratislava	£9.99
Budapest	£9.99
Bulgaria	£13.99
Cork	£6.99
Croatia	£13.99
Cyprus see North Cyprus	
Czech Republic	£13.99
Dresden	£7.99
Dubrovnik	£6.99
Estonia	£13.99
Faroe Islands	£15.99
Georgia	£14.99
Helsinki	£7.99
Hungary	£14.99
Iceland	£14.99
Kosovo	£14.99
Lapland	£13.99
Latvia	£13.99
Lille	£6.99
Lithuania	£14.99
Ljubljana	£7.99
Luxembourg	£13.99
Macedonia	£14.99
Montenegro	£14.99
North Cyprus	£12.99
Paris, Lille & Brussels	£11.95
Riga	£6.99
Serbia	£14.99
Slovakia	£14.99
Slovenia	£13.99
Spitsbergen	£14.99
Switzerland Without a Car	£14.99
Tallinn	£6.99
Transylvania	£14.99
Ukraine	£14.99
Vilnius	£6.99
Zagreb	£6.99

Middle East, Asia and Australasia

China: Yunnan Province	£13.99
Great Wall of China	£13.99
Iran	£14.99
Iraq: Then & Now	£15.99
Israel	£15.99
Kazakhstan	£15.99
Kyrgyzstan	£15.99
Maldives	£15.99
Mongolia	£16.99
North Korea	£14.99
Oman	£13.99
Shangri-La: A Travel Guide to the Himalayan Dream	£14.99
Sri Lanka	£15.99
Syria	£14.99
Tibet	£13.99
Turkmenistan	£14.99
Yemen	£14.99

The Americas and the Caribbean

Amazon, The	£14.99
Argentina	£15.99
Bolivia	£14.99
Cayman Islands	£14.99
Chile	£16.95
Colombia	£16.99
Costa Rica	£13.99
Dominica	£14.99
Falkland Islands	£13.95
Grenada, Carriacou & Petite Martinique	£14.99
Guyana	£14.99
Panama	£13.95
Peru & Bolivia: The Bradt Trekking Guide	£12.95
St Helena	£14.99
Turks & Caicos Islands	£14.99
USA by Rail	£14.99

Wildlife

100 Animals to See Before They Die	£16.99
Antarctica: Guide to the Wildlife	£15.99
Arctic: Guide to the Wildlife	£15.99
Central & Eastern European Wildlife	£15.99
Chinese Wildlife	£16.99
East African Wildlife	£19.99
Galápagos Wildlife	£15.99
Madagascar Wildlife	£16.99
New Zealand Wildlife	£14.99
North Atlantic Wildlife	£16.99
Peruvian Wildlife	£15.99
Southern African Wildlife	£18.95
Sri Lankan Wildlife	£15.99
Wildlife and Conservation Volunteering: The Complete Guide	£13.99

Eccentric Guides

Eccentric Australia	£12.99
Eccentric Britain	£13.99
Eccentric California	£13.99
Eccentric Cambridge	£6.99
Eccentric Edinburgh	£5.95
Eccentric France	£12.95
Eccentric London	£13.99

Others

Your Child Abroad: A Travel Health Guide	£10.95
Something Different for the Weekend	£9.99
Britain from the Rails	£17.99

Index

Bold indicates main entries, *italics* indicate map entries.
Bracketed abbreviations: (Alg) = Algeria; (Lib) = Libya; (Mor) = Morocco; (Tun) = Tunisia.

397